Modern Canadian Plays

volume one

fourth edition

MODERN CANADIAN PLAYS

volume one

fourth edition

edited by Jerry Wasserman

TALONBOOKS
2000

Talonbooks
P.O. Box 2076
Vancouver, British Columbia, Canada V6B 3S3
Tel.: (604) 444-4889; Fax: (604) 444-4119; Internet: www.talonbooks.com

Typeset in Optima and printed and bound in Canada by Hignell Book Printing.

Fourth Edition, First Printing: December 2000

Talonbooks are distributed in Canada by General Distribution Services, 325 Humber College Blvd., Toronto, Ontario, Canada M9W 7C3; Tel.:(416) 213-1919; Fax:(416) 213-1917.
Talonbooks are distributed in the U.S.A. by General Distribution Services Inc., 4500 Witmer Industrial Estates, Niagara Falls, New York, U.S.A. 14305-1386; Tel.:1-800-805-1083; Fax:1-800-481-6207.

Canadian Cataloguing in Publication Data

Main entry under title:

Modern Canadian plays

Includes bibliographical references.
ISBN 0-88922-436-6 (vol. 1) — ISBN 0-88922-437-4 (vol. 2)

1. Canadian drama (English)--20th century.* I. Wasserman, Jerry, 1945-
PS8315.M63 2000   C812'.5408   C00-910760-6
PR9196.6.M63 2000

The publisher gratefully acknowledges the financial support of the Canada Council for the Arts; the Government of Canada through the Book Publishing Industry Development Program; and the Province of British Columbia through the British Columbia Arts Council for our publishing activities.

CONTENTS

INTRODUCTION

Fifteen years after the original publication of *Modern Canadian Plays* the title no longer seems to me quite as uncomplicated as it once did. "Modern" paradoxically sounds a little old-fashioned today—as maybe it should, given that some of the plays in this volume are now more than thirty years old. It smacks of the historical and ideological specifics of moder*nism* and lacks the cachet of the *post*modern, a category (itself rather slippery) into which many of the plays, especially in Volume Two, actually do fall. "Canadian" is even more problematic. Not only does it elide the distinction between anglophone and francophone, but it presumes what some would consider an essentialist national identity subordinating the realities of regionalism and multiculturalism, the existence of First Nations, and a variety of other political and cultural contingencies. "Plays" is only slightly less contentious. The term implies a literary text, logocentric, scripted and therefore exclusive of theatrical forms such as ritual, dance theatre or performance art which are not so easily documented. It appears to privilege drama over theatre, publication over performance.

The term "plays" probably needs the least clarification. All twenty-four of the theatrical pieces in this edition are recognizable as stage plays, despite the tendency of recent critical discourse and some plays themselves to blur or deny generic distinctions. All have been produced by professional theatre companies. Even those originally performed by their own authors or co-creators (*1837*, *Billy Bishop Goes to War*, *Fronteras Americanas*) have subsequently been performed by other actors. All have previously been published. They exist as autonomous literary documents *and* as (re)producible scripts or production blueprints (or in some cases performance records). Because I come to this material as both an actor and an academic, I have chosen plays that I think work effectively on the stage, on the page and in the classroom; that play well, read well and teach well. I have chosen plays that excite me. But admittedly, I have limited the scope of "plays" to those works that make sense as texts in a book.

That the rubric "Canadian" should need clarification is especially ironic given that one of my original intentions in putting together an anthology was to help define the field, to answer the question posed by Brian Parker's 1977 essay, "Is There a Canadian Drama?" (see Bibliography). It may be hard to remember or even to believe today, but as I discuss later in this introduction, even as late as 1969 some artistic directors of theatres in Canada were challenging the validity of the terms "Canadian play" and "Canadian playwright." Yes, I asserted, there definitely is an identifiable Canadian drama, a body of work by Canadian playwrights written for performance in professional theatres, dating from 1948 in francophone Quebec and 1967 in English Canada. Although the originary dates may be debatable, the existence of Canadian drama is now utterly self-evident.

The problem lies in the terms "Canadian" and "English-Canadian." For the purposes of this anthology, "Canadian play" means a play written by a citizen or resident of Canada and, at some point, produced in English for an English-speaking audience. Canadian plays have been written and performed in Hindi, Italian and Cantonese, but these fall outside my scope. Theatre in French-speaking Canada has its own distinct history which I touch on only peripherally and which, for the most part, has had little impact on modern Canadian theatre in English. But plays by Michel Tremblay, Robert Lepage and Michel Marc Bouchard are included in this anthology. Though written originally in French, they have had wide exposure in translation in English-speaking Canada unlike most francophone plays from Quebec. I realize that "English Canada" and "English-speaking Canada" may be misnomers, since many Canadians even outside Quebec no longer have English as a mother tongue, much less England as a mother country. Nevertheless, to avoid awkward terminology I use "Canadian" with qualifications as noted and assume that most readers will understand what is meant. I also subsume under "Canadian" the various (implied) hyphenations related to such matters as region, race, ethnicity and sexual persuasion: e.g., gay-Canadian, Albertan-Canadian, Native-Canadian, African-Canadian, et al.

As for "modern," I stick with the word in part out of fond familiarity. I'm proud of this book and have been since its inception. The new edition is intended to expand and update, not to fundamentally change the collection that a generation of readers knows as *Modern Canadian Plays*. In the interest of accuracy I guess I could re-title it *Late Twentieth Century Canadian Plays* but that doesn't have quite the same ring. And besides, the next edition will no doubt include plays from the early twenty-first. I have defined "modern" in the context of Canadian theatre history as post-1967, and rather than wrestle with what "contemporary" might mean I retain the term "modern" to include even plays written in the past few years. "Modern" is not intended to delimit style, theme or subject. As the range of material in these two volumes makes clear, modern Canadian plays take in an awful lot of territory in many different forms.

I have also retained in this edition most of my introductory material tracing the history of the Canadian theatre. In his own valuable chronology posted on the Playwrights Union of Canada website, Ric Knowles ponders where to begin. "The history of Canadian theatre is full of originary moments, beginnings, new beginnings, and resurgences," he observes. And when it comes to the high points, he wonders: "*Whose* high points?"[1] I admit that 1967 has always been one of my personal high points, as it has been for many people whose consciousnesses were forged in the crucible of the Sixties. Precisely because 1967 and 1968 have been celebrated *ad nauseam*, they have also generated a backlash. Who could not be cynical in the face of a title like Pierre Berton's *1967, The Last Good Year* (1997). (Berton, born in 1920, doesn't even have the excuse of being a Baby Boomer.) Yet the fact remains that an extraordinary conjunction of historical forces, theatrical developments and demographic trends marks the end of that decade as a very special time for theatre in Canada. My revised sketch of Canadian theatre history reasserts 1967 as the watershed year dividing the pre-modern from the modern era.

At the same time I take a slightly different view than in earlier editions of the events leading up to 1967. Since about 1990, a revisionist school of Canadian theatre historians led by Alan Filewod and Denis Salter has relentlessly deconstructed both the nationalist assumptions and evolutionary perspective built into most models of Canadian theatre history since the nineteenth century, including my own.[2] Some of their conclusions seem dubious—the claim, for example, that the anglophilia and elitist cultural nationalism of some of its prime movers gave rise to a politically toothless and largely unrepresentative modern Canadian stage. Nevertheless, I have modified my views to incorporate a more complex, less naive idea of Canadian theatrical nationalism and its British imperial origins. With that proviso I believe that my original sketch remains historically accurate and worth retaining as background to the plays anthologized here and the period they represent.

The issue of canonization also has to be addressed. Since the publication in the mid-1980s of *Modern Canadian Plays* and two other anthologies (*Major Plays of the Canadian Theatre, 1934–1984*, ed. Richard Perkyns, and *The Penguin Book of Modern Canadian Drama*, ed. Richard Plant), a great deal of discussion has ensued over how such collections may limit, select, privilege, circumscribe and otherwise influence the kinds of plays and theatrical values that come to be understood as comprising the field of Canadian drama. Some critics argue that to anthologize is to canonize, and to canonize is to practice an insidious and reactionary form of powermongering. Others counter that so many disparate forces are involved in shaping the tastes and decisions of writers, producers, actors, audiences, teachers, students and other creators and consumers of theatre that no single individual, work or institution has the power to dictate canonical policy. I have argued that the very term "canon" tends to skew the argument, but that yes, anthologies do help mold preferences and ideas about what is and is not important, and so must be put together with as much care and transparency as possible.[3]

Insofar as this edition of *Modern Canadian Plays* defines a canon circa 1967–97, it is an eclectic one reflecting, first of all, my own tastes. But these are also plays that have all had major impacts, critical and popular, on audiences and other theatre-makers, plays that range widely in style and theme, and reflect a diverse, sophisticated Canadian theatre. All these playwrights have something significant to say. I have tried to retain continuity from previous editions while at the same time offering a fresh, expanded table of contents that indicates the growth of the enterprise and some of the significant new directions it has taken. Of the twenty-four titles in these two volumes (up from twenty in the third edition and twelve in the first), fourteen remain from the third edition, seven from the first. Seven playwrights and ten plays are entirely new to the book.

The plays in Volume One cover the first twenty years of what I'm calling the modern period and include some of the acknowledged classics of Canadian drama's first wave: George Ryga's *The Ecstasy of Rita Joe*, John Herbert's *Fortune and Men's Eyes*, Michel Tremblay's *Les Belles-Soeurs* and David French's *Leaving Home*. Complementing the stylized social realism of those plays are the historical pastiche of Rick Salutin and Theatre Passe Muraille's *1837: The Farmers' Revolt*, the theatrical poetry of James Reaney's second Donnelly play, *The St Nicholas Hotel*, and the cartoon *sturm und drang* of George F. Walker's *Zastrozzi*. John Gray's tour de force musical *Billy Bishop Goes to War* and David Fennario's bilingual, tragicomic *Balconville* round out the 1970s. The family drama and Native-white confrontation plays of the late Sixties/early Seventies are reprised Eighties-style in the complex memory structures of Sharon Pollock's *Doc* and Wendy Lill's *The Occupation of Heather Rose*, while transgressive social and sexual behaviour gets wild, celebratory, metatheatrical treatment in Sky Gilbert's *Drag Queens on Trial*.

The twelve plays in Volume Two date from 1987–97. Nine are new to this anthology. Altogether they make up about as exciting a collection of Canadian plays as I can imagine. Incorporating a decade's worth of extraordinary comic and dramatic flair, they represent the vivid and varied theatrical intelligence of modern Canadian playwrights at the end of the millennium.

I.

Taking into account the ritual activities of the future nation's aboriginal inhabitants, the long and fascinating theatrical history of Canada reaches back beyond the previous millennium. But even Canadian plays by European settlers date from as early as 1606 when Marc Lescarbot wrote *Le Théâtre de Neptune en la Nouvelle-France* and staged it in Indian war canoes to honour the arrival of French dignitaries at Port Royal. Playwriting in Canada in English dates back to the eighteenth century, and in the nineteenth century Canadian playhouses sprang up in substantial numbers, though mainly to accommodate American and British touring companies. The first half of the twentieth century saw the development of a thriving amateur theatre movement and the best radio drama on the continent, as well as the emergence of a handful of noteworthy playwrights.[4] But as late as 1945 there were no Canadian professional theatre companies. As late as 1959 the foremost theatre critic in the country could write, "there is not in Canada a single person who earns a living as a playwright, or who has any practical hope of doing so."[5] Even as late as 1965 a report on "Trends in Canadian Theatre" could omit any mention of the role of Canadian plays or playwrights.[6]

The remarkable fact is that Canadian theatre as an indigenous professional institution dates only as far back as the end of World War II. And English-Canadian *drama*, in the sense of a body of dramatic work by Canadian playwrights written for performance in professional theatres, is a more recent development still. Modern drama in Quebec had its inception with Gratien Gélinas' *Tit-Coq* in 1948. For English Canada the key date was 1967: Centennial Year, the year of Expo and of the first (and last) all-Canadian Dominion Drama Festival. Over the course of that year amateur companies presented sixty-two Canadian plays in French and English in the Dominion Drama Festival competitions, twenty-nine of which were performed for the first time. (Not surprisingly, a play from the already more mature Quebec theatre, Robert Gurik's *Le Pendu*, took home all the major awards.)[7] More important was the success of the new plays given professional productions literally from coast to coast as part of the Centennial celebrations: Gélinas' *Yesterday the Children Were Dancing* in English translation at the Charlottetown Festival, Reaney's *Colours in the Dark* at Stratford, Ann Henry's *Lulu Street* in Winnipeg, John Coulter's *The Trial of Louis Riel* in Regina, George Ryga's *The Ecstasy of Rita Joe* in Vancouver. Right across the country audiences and critics, buoyed by a new national self-consciousness and pride, were taking note of this latest cultural phenomenon—plays written by Canadian playwrights, performed by Canadian actors in Canadian theatres. And in New York, Toronto's John Herbert had a major hit with *Fortune and Men's Eyes*.

These events and the subsequent explosion of Canadian drama over the next decade seem in retrospect products of a particular historical moment, like the new European theatre that appeared in the 1870s, the new American theatre of the 1920s and the British theatrical renaissance of the mid-1950s. Yet all these movements were culminations of social and cultural forces that had been gathering momentum for many years. In the case of Canadian theatre the revolution of 1967 was rooted in an evolutionary process that began to take shape clearly around the time of the First World War.[8]

II.

The Canadian stage at the turn of the century was, in Alan Filewod's words, "a branch-plant extension of the novel American discovery that if theatre was business, then it could be big business ... By 1910 almost every playhouse in Canada was owned directly [by] or contractually locked into the American theatrical syndicates ... "[9] Those syndicates offered Canadian playgoers a predictable commercial product delivered by imported talent—American plays with American players. As an alternative, and an antidote to the Americanism with which many Canadians still attached to the British Empire felt uncomfortable, Canada's theatrical pioneers turned to trans-Atlantic models. In the first decade of the century Toronto's Arts and Letters Club Players devoted themselves to performing contemporary works from the world repertoire. They were inspired by the vogue of European art theatres, especially the Irish Abbey Theatre which would be cited time and again as a positive model for Canadians. Others, like industrialist and future cultural mandarin Vincent Massey, looked to the British model of high art infused with the ideal of a National Theatre. One thing that became clear in the midst of these first stirrings was that a genuine Canadian theatre would need its own dramatists. "There are no signs as yet upon our literary horizon of the arrival of our dramatist," a writer for *The Canadian Magazine* concluded poignantly in 1914, "but we are waiting expectantly, for we feel that he should soon come now."[10] At about the same time Vincent Massey wrote that "if we are to have a Canadian drama we must have a Canadian theatre in which to produce it."[11]

Under Massey's auspices both these ideals began to take form with the founding of Hart House Theatre in 1919. This was a well-equipped building as well as a company of the most talented actors, designers and directors in Toronto, dedicated to doing plays which would otherwise have gone unproduced in that city, including plays written by Canadians. Encouraged by this policy dramatists did arrive, enough to fill two modest volumes of *Canadian Plays from Hart House Theatre* by 1927. The most interesting was Merrill Denison. His Hart House successes, especially the satirical comedy "Brothers in Arms," and his 1923 published collection, *The Unheroic North*, established him as Canada's first playwright of note. Unable to make a living writing for the stage in Canada, Denison eventually moved to the United States in 1931 to write for American radio. Also included in Massey's collection was a play by Carroll Aikins, who would take over the running of Hart House Theatre in the late 1920s. Aikins' own experimental Home Theatre, set up in the middle of an apple orchard in B.C.'s Okanagan Valley, lasted from 1920–22.

Throughout the 1920s and into the '30s amateur theatre flourished under the umbrella of the Little Theatre movement, a burgeoning of homegrown playmaking in large and small communities on both sides of the Canada-U.S. border. Those obsessed with the idea of a National Theatre found new hope even in such humble companies, "because they build the foundation for more mature creative theatres and develop an audience for the Ultimate National Canadian theatre."[12] That imperial goal seemed to move a large step closer to realization with the establishment in 1932 of the Dominion Drama Festival, a nationwide competition organized by the new Governor General, Lord Bessborough, and chaired by Vincent Massey. The Festival was to consist of an annual series of regional playoffs climaxing in a final (held in a different city each year) at which various awards would be given for production and performance. Community theatres, school and university drama groups and such established amateur companies as Hart House would all be eligible, and adjudicators would provide helpful comments as well as determining the winners. The aim of the Festival was to showcase theatre in Canada and at the same time upgrade the quality of Canada's theatrical arts and crafts through competition and cross-fertilization.

During the years of its existence (1933–70, with a hiatus from 1940–46 due to the war) the, DDF helped institutionalize amateur theatre in Canada. Whether it accomplished much more than that has been a matter of some debate. It certainly provided a proving ground for Canadian talent which often went on to New York, London, Hollywood, or by the 1950s to Stratford or other areas of the nascent Canadian professional theatre. Through special trophies and cash prizes the DDF also encouraged the writing and production of Canadian plays, an encouragement which proved at least statistically impressive. In 1934 the Festival organizers could come up with just nine Canadian titles for inclusion on its list of suggested plays sent out to participating groups; by 1966 the list contained 240 Canadian titles in English alone. But the quality and adventurousness of the work the Festival inspired were often questionable. Even as late as 1967, the DDF would refuse to allow Michel Tremblay's contentious *Les Belles-Soeurs* to be produced as part of its all-Canadian celebrations.

An earlier indictment of the limitations of the DDF was its inability to contend with the multi-media expressionism of Herman Voaden's plays, which consistently failed to advance beyond regional competitions in the 1930s because the adjudicators did not know what to make of them.[13] Voaden was an ardent nationalist and theatrical innovator who desired a Canadian dramatic art as distinctive as the paintings of the Group of Seven. To that end he sponsored a playwriting competition in Toronto in 1929 which required that each play be set in the Canadian North and suggested that the play's subject or mood be based on the writer's favourite Canadian painting. Voaden himself combined an obsession with the Canadian landscape and such disparate theatrical influences as modern dance, Wagnerian opera and symbolist drama to create a synaesthetic form he called "symphonic expressionism" in plays with titles like *Rocks*, *Earth Song* and *Hill-Land*. The Play Workshop he ran from 1934 to 1936 with the aim of encouraging Canadian playwriting and an indigenous theatrical style resulted in the production of twenty-five new works as well as continued experiments in total theatre. For all his eccentric and often striking work as playwright, producer, director and educator, Voaden probably made his greatest impact on the development of Canadian drama as a persistent lobbyist for increased government support for the theatre, leading to his election as the first president of the new Canadian Arts Council in 1945.

The Play Workshop and Hart House were not the only centres of Canadian playwriting activity. A group of women journalists organized the Playwrights' Studio Group in Toronto in 1932 and by the end of the decade they had produced more than fifty new plays, mainly society comedies. At the other end of the spectrum were the Progressive Arts Clubs in Toronto, Montreal, Winnipeg and Vancouver, leftist workers' theatre groups that created and performed agitprop and social protest plays throughout the Depression years. In Alberta the Banff School of the Theatre was founded in 1933, later evolving into the Banff School of Fine Arts which is still an important centre for theatre training and workshop production. Associated with Banff from the beginning was Gwen Pharis Ringwood, whose stark prairie tragedies "Still Stands the House" and *Dark Harvest* were among the strongest Canadian plays of the 1930s and '40s. (Later she would teach playwriting at Banff to George Ryga among others.) Ringwood remained a prolific and popular dramatist (in amateur circles) until her death in 1984, but her residence in northern B.C. left her out of the mainstream of the new Canadian professional theatre that grew up during the last thirty years of her life.

Probably the most significant development for Canadian drama in the 1930s and '40s was the rise of radio. The CBC had been established in 1932, and in 1936 it began broadcasting radio plays for which it actually paid writers, producers, directors, actors, musicians and technicians. What came to be known as "The Golden Age" of Canadian radio began when Andrew Allan became Supervisor of Drama for CBC and producer of its weekly *Stage* series. Under Allan from 1944 to 1955 *Stage* and *Wednesday Night* created consistently bold and imaginative drama that maintained high standards of excellence while proving broadly popular—at one time only *Hockey Night in Canada* drew more listeners than *Stage*. The stable of writers and actors that Allan assembled was "far and away the most exciting repertory group that can be heard," *The New York Times* proclaimed in 1946,[14] and it became Canada's equivalent of a national professional theatre. Hundreds of original scripts by Allan's house writers such as Lister Sinclair and Len Peterson were produced for broadcast. Even though radio's golden age faded with the coming of television in the 1950s, and CBC has been slowly eviscerated by budget cuts since the 1980s, radio drama still pays some of the bills for Canadian playwrights who might not otherwise be able to afford the luxury of writing for the chronically impecunious live stage.

In spite of the varied successes of the DDF and the CBC, neither amateur theatricals nor radio drama could satisfy the need for a vibrant, professional domestic stage culture. John Coulter, who quickly became an award-winning DDF playwright and one of the most frequently produced CBC dramatists after emigrating to Canada from Ireland in 1936, was a vocal critic of the Canadian theatre scene. In "Canadian Theatre and the Irish Exemplar," an article published in 1938, he passionately held up Dublin's Abbey Theatre as a model for Canadians, a theatre "showing the Irish to themselves … Irish mugs in Irish mirrors." Canadians too, he argued, could find dramatic subject matter in indigenous situations: "in prairie droughts and crop-failure, in mining disasters, in the poverty of the slum dwellers of city streets or country shacks," although he warned against what he saw as the Canadian propensity for excessive gloom, depression and disillusion.[15] After a series of plays set in Ireland, Coulter took his own advice and turned to Canadian history (about which he had already written for radio), achieving his greatest success with a trilogy of stage plays about Louis Riel. First produced in 1950, *Riel* would serve as a paradigm for the history plays of James Reaney and the Theatre Passe Muraille dramatists of the 1970s: revisionist Canadian history with the rebel or underdog as hero, presented as a synthesis of documentary and myth.

Coulter was fortunate that by the time *Riel* was ready for production there was a professional company to do it: the New Play Society, founded by Dora Mavor Moore in 1946. From 1950 it also included a drama school, one of whose students would be John Herbert (who later went on to act, design and stage manage for the company). Though the New Play Society remained active until 1971, its prime years were 1946–50 when its full seasons of plays in the Royal Ontario Museum Theatre proved to many skeptics the viability of a professional Canadian stage. Its most substantial success was *Spring Thaw*, a musical revue satirizing all things topical in the Great White North, first staged in 1948 and remounted with increased popularity annually for the next twenty years.

In 1954 Toronto found itself with a second homegrown professional theatre, the Crest, which soon superceded the New Play Society in importance, presenting quality work in continuous repertory for thirteen seasons until its demise in 1966. The major Canadian playwright associated with the Crest was Robertson Davies, whose *A Jig for the Gypsy* and *Hunting Stuart* premiered there in 1954–55. Davies had already become English Canada's foremost playwright on the amateur circuit with "Eros at Breakfast," "Overlaid" and *Fortune, My Foe* in 1948–49, satires of Canadian philistinism and what he considered the national disease, "emotional understimulation." Like the Crest itself, Davies remained a significant force in Canadian theatre until the mid-60s when his playwriting career gave way to his work as a novelist.

Aside from his playwriting, Davies' journalism made a strong contribution to the developing Canadian theatre in the 1940s and '50s. Both in his own name and under the pseudonym of Samuel Marchbanks, he raised his voice in protest like Voaden and Coulter against the conditions under which would-be Canadian theatre professionals had to labour—what he called in 1952 "the seedy amateurism which has afflicted the arts here for so long."[16] With fond reminiscences of his experience as a young actor in England, Davies reacted with enthusiasm to the idea of a world-class Shakespearean festival theatre in Stratford, Ontario. Along with Dora Mavor Moore and Festival organizer Tom Patterson, he was instrumental in arranging for the innovative British producer-director Tyrone Guthrie to head the venture, which held its first season of two plays under a tent in the summer of 1953. Guthrie imported British stars Alec Guinness and Irene Worth to play the leads and fleshed out the rest of the company with Canadian actors, a policy that by and large remained standard for Stratford well into the 1980s. Reviewing that first season, Davies concluded that it had given Canadians "a new vision of the theatre":

> This cannot help but have its effect on work everywhere in the country. For one thing, many of our best Canadian actors are working at Stratford ... Are these actors, who have tasted the wine of true theatre, ever again to be satisfied with the sour slops of under-rehearsed, under-dressed, under-mounted, under-paid, and frequently ill-considered and ill-financed theatre projects? ... The Stratford Festival is an artistic bombshell, exploded just at the time when Canadian theatre is most ready for a break with the dead past and a leap into the future.[17]

There is no doubt that the Stratford Festival did have an enormous impact on theatre and the *idea* of theatre in Canada. It became an event of international importance and influence (its new non-proscenium thrust stage designed by Guthrie and Tanya Moisiewitsch made waves in theatres worldwide). Thus it raised the profile of theatre in Canada as nothing else had been able to do and served as a focus of national cultural pride. Stratford also became a training ground for many of the best actors who emerged in Canada over the next three decades, making stars of Christopher Plummer, Frances Hyland and others. Moreover, it was argued,

> Stratford created a model for indigenous Canadian theatre: a non-profit organization, unconcerned with the values of New York, unashamedly using imported personnel where Canadian expertise was lacking, equally unashamedly welcoming subsidy support in return for placing its destiny—at a policy-making level—in the hands of a volunteer citizen Board of Governors, and representatives of the community in which it found itself.[18]

But Stratford did little to effect or support the development of Canadian playwriting. Writers like Herbert and Reaney would receive workshop and small-scale public performances of their plays there in the late 1960s. In 1971 a Third Stage was added, in part to produce Canadian work. But by that time Stratford was no longer an adequate model. With its huge financial operation it became in many eyes a cultural dinosaur, devouring large subsidies at the expense of the smaller theatres whose productions of Canadian plays, often on shoestring budgets, were perceived as being more central to an emerging national drama than was a theatre devoted to Shakespeare. Ironically, while Stratford feasted, Canadian drama came of age in the early 1970s as a kind of poor theatre nourished on just those "sour slops" that Davies had complained of in 1953. A half-century after its creation the Stratford Festival continues to thrive. And even with a fully Canadian contingent of lead actors, directors and designers, and a Canadian artistic director, it continues to occupy a controversial place in the Canadian theatrical pantheon.

In any case by 1956 there was good reason for the feeling that "the Canadian theatre ... like the stock market, is bullish these days ... "[19] The success of Stratford and the other new professional theatres was being augmented by CBC television, which from its inception in 1952 gave starts to a number of important dramatists who would later go on to write for the stage, including George Ryga, David French and Michel Tremblay. On the horizon as well was the Canada Council, whose founding in 1957 would change the nature of theatre in Canada more than any other single development, providing a sudden massive influx of government funding for buildings, companies and individuals engaged in the arts.

The Canada Council was the most concrete manifestation of the Royal Commission on National Development in the Arts, Letters and Sciences appointed by Prime Minister St. Laurent in 1949 with Vincent Massey as chairman. Its mandate was to examine how government could contribute to the development of those areas of endeavour "which express national feeling, promote common understanding and add to the variety and richness of Canadian life."[20] Even if, as Filewod, Salter and others have argued, the Massey Commission proceeded from certain British-imported, elitist cultural biases, its 1951 *Report* proved a tremendously valuable national consciousness-raiser. It found that Canadian culture was being stifled by the omnipresence of American influences and the lack of support and facilities for artists in Canada. Its major recommendation was the formation of the Canada Council for the Encouragement of the Arts, Letters, Humanities and Social Sciences to support Canadian culture at home and abroad. From an initial outlay of $2.6 million in arts grants in 1957, the Council's investment in individuals and groups totalled more than $60 million by 1970, a quantum leap in the funds available to fuel the engine of Canadian cultural nationalism.

Money wasn't the only catalyst for change, though. In 1958 in Winnipeg, with virtually no capital but their missionary commitment to convert a whole province to the ideal of a regional professional theatre, Tom Hendry and John Hirsch merged their amateur Theatre 77 with the Winnipeg Little Theatre to create the Manitoba Theatre Centre, with Hirsch as its first artistic director. From the start the MTC "was meant to be more than a theatre, something that could in fact become a focus for all theatrical energy and resources in one community."[21] Combining mainstage productions in Winnipeg with a touring company, children's theatre, and a school, the MTC succeeded so well in galvanizing the support and resources of its constituency that it became the basis for a new concept: a Canadian national theatre that would be decentralized and regional—a professional theatre version of the ostensible Canadian mosaic. With support and encouragement from the Canada Council a network of regional theatres spread across the country: Vancouver's Playhouse and Halifax's Neptune in 1963, Edmonton's Citadel in 1965 and Regina's Globe in 1966. By 1970 Montreal, Calgary, Fredericton and Toronto also had theatres catering in principle to regional communities.

Canada, it seemed, had indeed become bullish on theatre. The building boom didn't stop with the regionals, either. To train and supply actors for the new national theatre network, the National Theatre School was opened in Montreal in 1960 with separate French and English programs. At Niagara-on-the-Lake the Shaw Festival began operation in 1962, and P.E.I.'s Charlottetown Festival was inaugurated in 1964 specializing in Canadian musical theatre. St. John's got its Arts and Culture Centre in 1967. Finally, in 1969–70 the completion of three major Centennial construction projects—Ottawa's National Arts Centre, Toronto's St. Lawrence Centre, and a new building for the MTC—rounded out a decade of extraordinary growth for the Canadian theatre.

III.

With the superstructure finally intact the question now was, where were the plays that might crystallize the new drama in English Canada, implanting it at the heart of the nation's cultural life the way John Osborne's *Look Back in Anger* had done in Britain and Gélinas' *Tit-Coq* in Quebec (and the way Tremblay's *Les Belles-Soeurs* would do again in Quebec, in a different way, in 1968). Those plays had had in common vernacular speech, anti-establishment anger, and characters, settings and situations that were definitively of their own time and place. So too had the play that finally touched the nerve of English Canada. *The Ecstasy of Rita Joe* premiered at the Vancouver Playhouse on November 23, 1967, in a landmark production that was remounted for the opening of the National Arts Centre in 1969. That year the play was also broadcast on CBC-TV and produced in a French translation by Gratien Gélinas in Montreal, as *Rita Joe* reverberated through the nation's collective consciousness. In a review of a later production, Jamie Portman recalled that "*Rita Joe* happened during Centennial year when Canadians were anxious to look at themselves. But the look that this play provided was an unsettling one. It punctured the euphoria and the smug complacency of Canada's birthday celebrations and declared unequivocally that all was not well with this country and its institutions." Its implications for Canadian playwriting were equally dramatic:

> This was an indigenous Canadian drama that surfaced and succeeded at a time when indigenous Canadian drama was generally considered to be an aberration. It was a play of merit, worthy of production in any Canadian theatre. It prompted an awareness of the existence of other plays potentially worthy of production. It provided resounding evidence that it was not necessary for any Canadian theatre to rely solely on imported fare. With the arrival of *The Ecstasy of Rita Joe*, Canadian plays ceased to be a rarity in English-speaking Canada. Companies dedicated to the production of new Canadian drama sprang up, and in so doing nurtured the further growth of playwriting activity. Canada's regional theatres— some of them grudgingly—found themselves forced to take the Canadian playwright seriously for the first time.[22]

Yet the battle for credibility was not quite so easily won. Just how grudgingly the theatre establishment came to accept the Canadian playwright was vividly registered by a 1971 study that found that in the previous year, the seven major regional theatres had produced the work of a total of two Canadian dramatists, and paid them less than $5000 out of combined budgets of more than $2 million.[23] Consider the case of the once pioneering Manitoba Theatre Centre. Despite its success with Winnipeg writer Ann Henry's *Lulu Street*, more than a decade would pass before the MTC presented another new play by a local playwright. The flurry of Canadian play production in 1967 had obviously been in some respects no more than Centennial Year tokenism.

The stage history of John Herbert's *Fortune and Men's Eyes* is especially revealing of the difficulties faced by Canadian playwrights. *Fortune* had been workshopped at Stratford in 1965. But denied a full production there or anywhere else in Canada, the play opened in New York in 1967 and ran for a year off-Broadway. By the end of 1968 it had had a long run in London and become a full-scale international hit. By 1969 it was already being revived in New York. The play's impact on other Canadian dramatists was immediate and inspirational: "the ice-breaker in the channel," George Ryga called it.[24] But for all that, professional productions of *Fortune and Men's Eyes* in Canada to 1970 consisted of a week at the Vancouver Playhouse's "experimental" Stage 2 and a brief run in the MTC's Studio Theatre. There was not a mainstage production to be seen. Herbert's hometown of Toronto would have to wait until 1975 to see the play at all.

What had gone wrong? The expectations and struggles of a half-century had resulted in a Canadian theatre that by the late 1960s had already become entrenched and conservative. Rather than living up to the original promise of the regionals to create new models adapted to the distinctive needs of their communities, which surely should have meant presenting plays written about those communities from within them, the large subsidized theatres mostly tried to emulate Broadway and London's West End. When artistic directors were asked about Canadian plays and playwrights, their responses were often remarkably similar:

> I don't see how a play can be Canadian.

> I don't think there are any plays that you could call strictly Canadian.

> But if you start to define what is a Canadian and what is a Canadian playwright, what do you end up with?

> What does the phrase mean?[25]

With few exceptions the regionals served up homogenized theatre: safe, commercial seasons of British and American hits plus a smattering of world classics. Moreover, it was theatre as Cultural Event, like the opera or the symphony, the kind of thing you got dressed up for.

But in the late '60s, the Age of Aquarius and the Generation Gap, many theatre artists and much of the potential audience were evolving in a different direction. The Canadian Centennial just happened to coincide with the most radical cultural upheaval of the century in the Western world. There was a sexual revolution, a musical revolution, a drug revolution; long hair, peace marches and a Summer of Love. By 1968 in Chicago, Paris and Prague the revolution would spill over into the streets. Canada wasn't immune to these forces nor could its theatre be, no matter how stubbornly it tried to remain middle-aged and middle-class.

That the most significant Canadian plays of the decade should have appeared in 1967–68 was not coincidental. *The Ecstasy of Rita Joe, Fortune and Men's Eyes* and *Les Belles-Soeurs* are plays very much of their age, marked by strong social consciousness and critical, anti-establishment perspectives. The playwrights too, by virtue of their alienation from the mainstream, were in sync with the temper of the times. Herbert and Tremblay were gay men. Ryga and Herbert were outspoken and uncompromising in their social, artistic and political views. It was characteristic of their outsider status that neither was initially allowed entry into the United States to see his own play in production; characteristic that Herbert refused the DDF's Massey Award (and its $1000 cash prize) for Best Play for *Fortune* in 1968; characteristic that the politics of Ryga's 1970 play *Captives of the Faceless Drummer* would so upset the Board of the Vancouver Playhouse, which had commissioned it, that they would refuse it production. It was ironic but perhaps also inevitable that the two writers whose plays brought modern English-Canadian drama into existence would eventually find themselves virtually unproduced by the major Canadian theatres.

Modern Canadian drama was born out of an amalgam of the new consciousness of the age—social, political and aesthetic—with the new Canadian self-consciousness. Since the larger theatres were generally unsympathetic and unaccommodating to both these forces, an even newer Canadian theatre had to be invented, an alternate theatre. One of its prime movers in Toronto was Martin Kinch, who describes those first heady days as having little to do with nationalism:

> The real influences were Fritz Perls and Timothy Leary, Peter Brook and Jerzy Grotowski, Tom O'Horgan, Café La Mama, Julian Beck, Judith Malina, and the ensemble of the Living Theatre; in short, a host of European and American artists, most of them primarily dedicated to the ethic and the aesthetic of "doing your own thing" … It was an exciting time, a time of experiment and exploration … expressionism, hallucination, confrontation, and audience participation flourished. Perhaps most important, however, there existed a definite bond between the theatres and their audience; an audience that was characterized by long hair, beards, bells, and babies in the front rows of the most outrageous plays. Its concerns were the concerns of "the sixties": the breaking of sexual taboo, the problems of individual freedom, and the yearning for community.[26]

In 1969 Kinch became a co-director of Toronto's Theatre Passe Muraille founded the previous year by Jim Garrard. As its name suggests, Passe Muraille was to be a theatre without walls: neither the traditional fourth wall between actors and audience nor necessarily even the walls of a theatre building. Garrard envisioned "a guerrilla theatre": "Theatre in the subways, get a truck and do theatre in small towns, real circuses, grab people in the streets … I'd like to make theatre as popular as bowling."[27] A milestone for the new alternate theatre movement was Passe Muraille's production of Rochelle Owen's *Futz* in February 1969. An American play about a man in love with a pig (!), in both style and content it established the parameters of the alternate theatre's self-conscious anti-conventionality. The sex, obscenity and nudity it featured would become almost obligatory. When the show was closed by the morality squad, and the company charged and subsequently acquitted, the new movement had its red badge of courage.

By the summer of 1970 alternate theatre in Toronto had developed to the point where it could celebrate itself with a Festival of Underground Theatre. When the smoke from the festival cleared, the emphasis of the alternates could be seen to have undergone something of a shift from sensationalism to nationalism. Central to the new emphasis were Ken Gass and his Factory Theatre Lab, and the new artistic director of Theatre Passe Muraille, Paul Thompson.

Gass, who had been helping run John Herbert's tiny Garret Theatre, set out to prove that there was no lack of Canadian playwrights; they were just waiting to be discovered and encouraged. His theatre would be both a factory and a laboratory, presenting polished new works as well as works-in-progress, fragments, staged ideas. Most importantly it would be "The Home of the Canadian Playwright." His concept paid off almost immediately with a string of notable new plays: David Freeman's *Creeps*, Herschel Hardin's *Esker Mike and His Wife, Agiluk* and George Walker's *Prince of Naples* all in 1971; most of Walker's other plays over the next dozen years; and exciting (though not necessarily enduring) work by Hrant Alianak, Larry Fineberg, Bryan Wade and Gass himself. Gass remained artistic director of the Factory until 1979, then returned to the post again in 1996 to save the company from what seemed like imminent demise.

Paul Thompson came to Passe Muraille after working in France with Roger Planchon, whose process-oriented, political brand of theatre was in direct contrast with Thompson's experiences during a brief apprenticeship at Stratford. Rejecting the Stratford model, Thompson steered his company towards a focus on local subject matter and collective creation, involving his actors in first-hand research, improvisation and continual revision, and utilizing their particular skills as key elements in the play wherever possible. When Thompson took over Passe Muraille there was already a precedent for this kind of theatre in Toronto. George Luscombe had been involved with Joan Littlewood's Theatre Workshops in England in the mid-1950s and had put together Toronto Workshop Productions in 1959 based on Littlewood's political and stylistic principles: left-wing politics and an eclectic style that integrated improvs, documentary, *commedia* and often collective scripting. In the late 1960s and early '70s TWP was creating potent socio-political theatre with agit-prop pieces like *Mister Bones* and *Chicago '70* on race and politics in America, and its bittersweet evocation of the Canadian Depression, *Ten Lost Years*. The partnership of Luscombe and Toronto Workshop Productions lasted for thirty years, finally collapsing in 1989 with the company's folding and its building passing on to Sky Gilbert's Buddies in Bad Times Theatre.

But it was Passe Muraille under Paul Thompson's stewardship that became the most important theatre in Canada in the early 1970s. Creations like *Doukhobors*, *The Farm Show* (first performed in a Clinton, Ontario barn), *Under the Greywacke* and *The Adventures of an Immigrant* (performed in Toronto streetcars among other venues) made often stirring theatrical poetry out of material that was sometimes mundane and always local. Docudrama with a high degree of theatricality became the Passe Muraille trademark: a small company of actors using little but their own bodies and voices to create ingenious stage metaphors. They inspired countless imitators across the country, though in less talented hands the deceptively rigorous demands of collective scripting and Passe Muraille's presentational style sometimes had unfortunate results. Among the best of their offshoots was Twenty-Fifth Street House Theatre in Saskatoon, whose *Paper Wheat* was in the finest Passe Muraille tradition, and Newfoundland's CODCO. In addition the company specialized in resurrecting, popularizing, dramatizing and often mythicizing Canadian history in collective scripts or in conjunction with a writer. *Buffalo Jump* with Carol Bolt, *1837: The Farmers' Revolt* with Rick Salutin, *Them Donnellys* with Frank MacEnany and *Far as the Eye Can See* with Rudy Wiebe were some of the best of the collaborations. Later in the decade two Passe Muraille alumni would create *Billy Bishop Goes to War*, and Linda Griffiths (with Paul Thompson) would let loose *Maggie & Pierre* upon the country. Perhaps the most exciting Canadian playwright to emerge in the 1980s, Judith Thompson, also came out of Passe Muraille with her extraordinary first play, *The Crackwalker*. Passe Muraille remains to the present day one of the primary loci of Canadian theatrical production and development.

Not everything was happening in Toronto. In Vancouver, where Sidney Risk had pioneered post-war professional touring with his Everyman Theatre (1946–53), and where John Juliani's experimental Savage God project had been operating since 1966, John Gray, Larry Lillo and a group of other UBC graduates formed Tamahnous Theatre in 1971, a collective that would remain Vancouver's most original and progressive company for the next ten years. Its most enduring legacy may prove to be the special brand of small-cast musical best represented by Gray's *Billy Bishop* and Morris Panych's "post-nuclear cabaret," *Last Call!* Meanwhile the New Play Centre had come into being in 1970 dedicated to developing new scripts by local writers with production as only a secondary priority. Under the direction of Pamela Hawthorn from 1972 until 1989, the New Play Centre had a hand in most of the drama to come out of B.C., including the work of Margaret Hollingsworth, Tom Walmsley, Ted Galay, John Lazarus, Sheldon Rosen, Betty Lambert, Eric Nicol and Sherman Snukal. In the late 1990s the NPC metamorphosed into Playwrights Theatre Centre, which continues its predecessor's work.

Seeded by government grants from Local Initiatives Programs (LIP) and Opportunities for Youth (OFY), new companies doing indigenous theatre sprouted everywhere in 1971–72: Edmonton's Theatre 3, Calgary's Alberta Theatre Projects, Pier One in Halifax, the Mummers Troupe in St. John's. Lennoxville, Quebec even provided a kind of "alternate" festival theatre. Festival Lennoxville presented all-Canadian summer seasons of plays by the likes of Michael Cook, Herschel Hardin and Sharon Pollock from 1972 until its demise in 1982, a victim of poor demographics and Parti Québécois cultural policy.

Toronto, though, was where most of the action was, and nothing did more to cement its position at the centre of the new movement than Tarragon Theatre. Founded in 1971 by Bill Glassco, who had directed *Creeps* at the Factory Lab earlier in the year, Tarragon opened with a revised version of *Creeps* that proved even more successful than the original. The first Tarragon season ended with a new work which was to become probably the single most influential Canadian play of the 1970s, David French's *Leaving Home*. Its story of generational conflict and a singularly Canadian form of immigrant alienation (ex-Newfoundlanders spiritually adrift in Toronto) elicited strong audience identification, and its straightforward, accessible style had a broad appeal. *Leaving Home* created a vogue for domestic realism that some have argued was a debilitating counterforce to the more adventurous directions that Canadian drama seemed to be taking at the time. Tarragon soon became identified with that particular style, especially in light of Glassco's productions of subsequent plays by Freeman and French that were stylistically tame. But it wasn't really a fair reputation. Tarragon also introduced English Canada to the plays of Michel Tremblay with Glassco as director and co-translator—plays that are domestic in setting but hardly realistic in style. Moreover, from 1973–75 Tarragon produced James Reaney's Donnelly trilogy, which is about as far removed from stylistic realism or naturalism as plays can get. Unlike the great majority of companies devoted to Canadian works Tarragon managed both to combine artistic and commercial success and to sustain it over a number of years. More than any other theatre it succeeded in bringing Canadian drama into the mainstream. Since Glassco left Tarragon in 1985, its status has been maintained under the artistic directorship of former theatre critic Urjo Kareda. The many playwrights in Volume Two of *Modern Canadian Plays* whose work is associated with Tarragon testify to the continued influence, importance and adventurousness of the company.

The great wave of new alternate theatres in Toronto crested in 1972 with the founding Toronto Free Theatre by Tom Hendry, Martin Kinch and John Palmer. Subsidized by LIP grants performances were literally free until 1974 when the impossible economics of that policy led to gradually increasing admissions. But Toronto Free's cultivation of an excellent ensemble of actors and a distinctive taste for the psychologically bizarre in plays and production remained constant until (and even after) its merger with Centrestage in 1988 to create the Canadian Stage Company. Many of its early successes were plays by its in-house triumvirate—especially Hendry and Palmer—along with Carol Bolt. George F. Walker and Erika Ritter were among the most noteworthy later additions to Toronto Free's playwriting corps.

Notwithstanding the dynamism of the alternate theatres, drama in Canada in the early 1970s was in danger of falling victim to an insidious form of ghettoization. Canadian plays were relegated to small, low-budget theatres that lacked the financial and technical resources available to the heavily subsidized festivals and regionals. While non-Canadian works had access to lush productions, large casts and relatively highly paid actors, Canadian plays were doomed to what George Ryga called "beggars theatre."[28] Concurrently, of course, Canadian playwrights were denied the financial opportunities that might allow them to make a living by practicing their craft. In an attempt to remedy this situation a group of playwrights met in the summer of 1971 to consider "The Dilemma of the Playwright in Canada." What ensued was a series of strongly worded recommendations, the most contentious of which called for a 50% Canadian content quota for all theatres receiving government funding. Most artistic directors and editorialists were predictably outraged. ("If it ever happened, then critics should also get Canada Council grants for sitting through the plays," was one wit's response.[29]) Though no formal quota system was ever adopted, the controversy led to a full public airing of the situation and, more importantly, to an informal policy decision by the Canada Council to "appeal" to its client theatres to do more Canadian plays. The results were startling. By the 1972–73 season nearly 50% of the plays produced by subsidized theatres in both English and French were in fact Canadian.

Among the most tangible consequences of this new policy was a return to one of the original precepts of the "regional" ideal, the commissioning of new plays by regional theatres from playwrights with local roots and interests. These arrangements proved mutually fruitful for playwrights and theatres alike, especially Sharon Pollock's work for the Vancouver Playhouse and Theatre Calgary, John Murrell and W.O. Mitchell also at Theatre Calgary, Ken Mitchell and especially Rex Deverell with Regina's Globe, and David Fennario with the Centaur in Montreal. The Blyth and Kawartha Summer Festivals, in their cultivation of Anne Chislett, proved the value of a homegrown product even in the traditionally more commercial milieu of summer theatre. In each of these cases plays written with very specific associations for local audiences made their way into theatres across the country with no lack of success. Maybe Canadian writers and producers had finally learned what John Coulter had called, back in 1938, "the paradoxical truth that the most effective way to keep an eye on Broadway is to keep on looking attentively at the life passing under your own nose in your own home town."[30]

Another way "to keep an eye on Broadway" and the West End was to continue to strengthen and in a sense nationalize the organizational infrastructure of Canadian theatre. 1976 saw the formation of both the Professional Association of Canadian Theatres (PACT) and the Association for Canadian Theatre History, a national academic organization. That same year Canadian Actors' Equity Association declared its independence from U.S. Actors' Equity. Yet a certain amount of retrenchment was also inevitable given the tremendous expansion Canadian theatre had undergone since 1967. Tougher economic times and a general trend towards conservatism put additional strains on an endeavour that is economically marginal even under the best conditions. Theatres as widely divergent as Stratford and Twenty-Fifth Street House had to weather financial and artistic crises that threatened their survival. Some went under: Vancouver's Westcoast Actors, Edmonton's Theatre 3, Montreal's Saidye Bronfman. Facing new audience expectations and a changing ideological climate, the major "alternate" theatres (a term no longer really accurate) in Toronto and Vancouver all underwent structural reorganization and found new artistic directors.

But by the mid-1980s—the point to which this volume takes us—near the end of its second decade, modern Canadian theatre clearly stood on firm footing and still had some major momentum. Passe Muraille, Tarragon, Factory Theatre (minus the "Lab"), Toronto Free and Tamahnous remained in operation (though Toronto Free would soon disappear in a merger and Tamahnous was no longer the force it had been). Those companies along with the resurgent regionals and successful middle-of-the-road theatres like Vancouver's Arts Club continued to provide a springboard for Canadian plays. Across the country a new generation of neo-alternates arose to take the place of those that fell by the wayside or moved into the mainstream. These included Prairie Theatre Exchange in Winnipeg, Rising Tide Theatre in St. John's, and Nova Scotia's Mulgrave Road Co-op and Ship's Company. Nakai Theatre Ensemble in Whitehorse and Tunooniq in the Arctic ensured the exposure of lively theatrical voices in the Canadian North. In Vancouver

Touchstone joined the scene along with Green Thumb, which set the pattern for hard-hitting young people's theatre.

Per capita, probably the most activity was taking place in Edmonton, rapidly becoming Canada's most important centre for English-language theatre after Toronto. Theatre Network, Northern Light, Catalyst, Workshop West and Phoenix Theatre all came on stream before 1982, the year the Edmonton Fringe Festival was born. Modelled on the Edinburgh Fringe, Edmonton's festival has become a hugely successful affair with annual attendance in the quarter-million range, and a prototype for the many other Canadian Fringes which have sprung up in its wake. Meanwhile, Toronto continued its theatrical expansion to the point where it could soon lay claim to being second only to New York as a mecca for theatre in North America. Among its most innovative and important new companies were Necessary Angel, Nightwood (which became Canada's foremost feminist theatre), Buddies in Bad Times (soon the country's most important gay company as well as a key centre for new play development with its spinoff Rhubarb! Festival), Theatre Columbus (clown-based theatre), Cahoots (multicultural), and Native Earth Performing Arts, which led the renaissance of Native theatre in Canada. The Toronto International Theatre Festival in 1981, and its later successor, the Harbourfront, showcased Canadian plays and productions alongside some of the best theatre companies in the world.

Canadian theatre's growing cultural prominence was also signified by the establishment of a series of new awards. Joining the prestigious Chalmers, given by the Toronto Drama Bench since 1972 for best Canadian play produced each year in Toronto, were the Canadian Authors' Association Award for Drama (est. 1975) and, in 1981, the Governor General's Award in Drama honouring the best new Canadian play in publication in French and the best in English. All offer substantial cash prizes. The Doras in Toronto (after Dora Mavor Moore), the Jessies in Vancouver (after Jessie Richardson), the Sterlings in Edmonton (after Elizabeth Sterling Haynes) and most recently, the Bettys in Calgary (after Betty Mitchell) celebrate the best work done on those cities' stages in the name of a local theatrical pioneer. Also commemorating an important early modern figure was the Nathan Cohen Award for excellence in theatre criticism.

In 1985 the old Elgin Theatre/Winter Garden complex in downtown Toronto was restored to its former glories to accommodate a long run of Andrew Lloyd Webber's *Cats*, kicking off a frenzy for megamusicals which would last a decade and which threatened for a while to overwhelm the smaller non-profit theatres where most Canadian plays are born and performed. But Canadian theatre would survive that attempt at re-colonization (a story to be told in Volume Two). And its long-term survival seemed reinforced by the 1984–85 publication of the three Canadian drama anthologies, including the first version of this one. Canadian plays became more accessible to high school and post-secondary classes, more entrenched in curricula, more academically respectable.

By the mid-1980s some things had notably changed. The nationalism that had largely inspired and in some ways kick-started the new Canadian theatre had pretty much gone out of vogue. Free trade and globalism were soon to become the new keywords. Even the old keywords had new meanings. As Alan Filewod points out, "in 1974 the terms 'native' and 'indigenous' meant 'Canadian' as opposed to British or American; by 1984 they had acquired a much more specific value (pertaining to aboriginal peoples) which challenged the very meaning of 'Canadian' as it was understood only a decade earlier."[31] At the same time the theatre itself spoke of how little certain things had really altered. Whatever the terminology—native or indigenous, Indian or aboriginal—the two plays that open and close this volume, nearly twenty years apart, speak of the same terrible gap between Canada's "white" middle-class mainstream and the people of its First Nations.

And yet, also challenging the very meaning of "Canadian" as it had been understood a decade or two earlier is a play like Sky Gilbert's, with three drag queens singing, "Forget your troubles come on get happy," and meaning it. How unmonolithic can a play collection be? As unmonolithic as the Canada—the Canadas, more accurately—reflected and constructed by Canadian playwrights from the late 1960s to the mid-1980s. It's a sad/funny, weird/normal, happy-go-unlucky place. For the moment anyway, don't try to find patterns here or figure out paper topics. Forget your troubles, come on, get reading.

I would once more like to acknowledge everyone who has made *Modern Canadian Plays* possible including my students and colleagues at the University of British Columbia, my fellow scholars and lovers of Canadian drama in the Association for Canadian Theatre Research, the writers themselves and the theatre people who keep the work alive. Thanks to George Belliveau for his research assistance with this edition, and to George Walker, John Gray, Sharon Pollock, Sky Gilbert and Wendy Lill for stimulating talk and helpful information. Special thanks to Karl and Christy Siegler, who keep the flame burning, and the rest of the Talonbooks staff. To Sue for her good editorial advice. To Sue, Kelsey and Brodie for their patience and love. And to my father, Irv Wasserman (1921–1999), to whom this volume is dedicated.

NOTES

1. Ric Knowles, "Just the High Points? A Canadian Theatre Chronology" [1998]. *www.puc.ca/union/ chronology.html.*

2. Denis Salter, "The Idea of a National Theatre" in *Canadian Canons: Essays in Literary Value,* ed. Robert Lecker (Toronto: Univ. of Toronto Press, 1991), 71-90; and Alan Filewod, "Between Empires: Post-Imperialism and Canadian Theatre," *Essays in Theatre* 11 (November 1992): 3-15.

3. For a good cross-section of the debate see, on the anti-canonical side, Robert Wallace, "Constructing a Canon: A Review Essay," *Theatre History in Canada* 10.2 (1989): 218-22; Richard Paul Knowles, "Voices (off): Deconstructing the Modern English-Canadian Dramatic Canon" in *Canadian Canons,* ed. Robert Lecker, 91-111; and Susan Bennett, "New Stages: Questions for Canadian Dramatic Criticism," *Studies in Canadian Literature* 20.2 (1995): 1-9. The three anthologists respond in Richard Perkyns, "A Reader's Response to Two Recent Reviews," *Theatre History in Canada* 11.2 (1990): 219-22; Richard Plant, "An Alternative Scholarship: Canadian Theatre Study, 1970–91," *Theatre Research International* 17 (1992): 190-202; and Jerry Wasserman, "Confessions of a Vile Canonist: Anthologising Canadian Drama," *Australasian Drama Studies* 29 (October 1996): 197-205. For a balanced overview of the issue see Chris Johnson, "'Wisdome under a Ragged Coate': Canonicity and Canadian Drama" in *Contemporary Issues in Canadian Drama,* ed. Per Brask, (Winnipeg: Blizzard, 1995), 26-49.

4. The story of the pre-modern period of Canadian theatre has been told in bits and pieces in a variety of books and articles. For a general overview see Eugene Benson and L.W. Conolly, *English-Canadian Theatre* (Toronto: Oxford Univ. Press, 1987). Unfortunately out of print, Anton Wagner, ed., *Canada's Lost Plays* (Toronto: Canadian Theatre Review, 1978–81) is an excellent anthology in four volumes (Richard Plant co-edits Volume One) presenting plays from the nineteenth through the mid-twentieth century with extensive historical introductions.

5. Nathan Cohen, "Theatre Today: English Canada," *Tamarack Review* 13 (Autumn 1959): 28.

6. Thomas B. Hendry, "Trends in Canadian Theatre," *Tulane Drama Review* 10 (Fall 1965): 62-70. That same year Michael Tait concluded his survey of "the grey wastes of Canadian drama" from 1920–60 by noting "perhaps the most depressing feature of theatre in Canada: the lack of any vital and continuing relationship between theatrical activity and the work of the Canadian playwright." See "Drama and Theatre," *Literary History of Canada,* ed. Carl F. Klinck, 2nd ed. (Toronto: Univ. of Toronto Press, 1976), Vol. II, 159, 167.

7. Betty Lee, *Love and Whisky: The Story of the Dominion Drama Festival* (Toronto: McClelland and Stewart, 1973), 296.

8. For a useful collection of articles documenting twentieth century Canadian theatre, see Don Rubin, ed., *Canadian Theatre History: Selected Readings* (Toronto: Copp Clark, 1996).

9. Alan Filewod, "National Theatre/National Obsession," *Canadian Theatre Review* 62 (Spring 1990): 6.

10. Fred Jacobs, "Waiting for a Dramatist," *The Canadian Magazine* 43 (June 1914): 146. On the relationship between Canada's theatre critics and Canadian theatrical development from the nineteenth century to the

present, see Anton Wagner, ed., *Establishing Our Boundaries: English-Canadian Theatre Criticism* (Toronto: Univ. of Toronto Press, 1999).

11. Vincent Massey, "The Prospects of a Canadian Drama," *Queen's Quarterly* 30 (October 1922): 200.

12. Rupert Caplan, "The Ultimate National Theatre," *Canadian Forum* 9 (January 1929): 143-44.

13. See Anton Wagner, "The Developing Mosaic: English Canadian Drama to Mid-Century," in *Canada's Lost Plays, Volume Three*, ed. Anton Wagner (Toronto: CTR Productions, 1980), 19-21.

14. Jack Gould, "Canada Shows Us How," *New York Times* 1 Sept. 1946, Sec. II: 7.

15. John Coulter, "The Canadian Theatre and the Irish Exemplar," in Rubin, ed., *Canadian Theatre History: Selected Readings*, 125.

16. Robertson Davies, *The Well-Tempered Critic: One Man's View of Theatre and Letters in Canada*, ed. Judith Skelton Grant (Toronto: McClelland and Stewart, 1981), 66.

17. Davies, 74.

18. Hendry, "Trends in Canadian Theatre," 64-65.

19. Mavor Moore, "A Theatre for Canada," *University of Toronto Quarterly* 26 (October 1956): 2.

20. *Report of the Royal Commission on National Development in the Arts, Letters and Sciences* (Ottawa: Edmond Cloutier, 1951), xi. Quoted in Don Rubin, "Creeping Toward a Culture: The Theatre in English Canada Since 1945," *Canadian Theatre Review* 1 (Winter 1974): 8.

21. Tom Hendry, "MTC: A View from the Beginning," *Canadian Theatre Review* 4 (Fall 1974): 16.

22. Jamie Portman, "Ecstasy of Rita Joe Still Manages to Shock and Scourge," *Vancouver Province* 12 April 1976, 10. Cf. Neil Carson, "Towards a Popular Theatre in English Canada," *Canadian Literature* 85 (Summer 1980): 64-65.

23. David Gustafson, "Let's Really Hear It for Canadian Theatre," *Maclean's* 84 (October 1971): 84.

24. George Ryga, "Contemporary Theatre and Its Language," *Canadian Theatre Review* 14 (Spring 1977): 8.

25. Quoted verbatim from a series of interviews with artistic directors of regional theatres in *The Stage in Canada*: Edward Gilbert (MTC), 3 (May 1967), 14; Robert Glenn (Citadel), 3 (June 1967), 7; Joy Coghill Playhouse), 3 (Sept. 1967), 10; Kurt Reis (MTC), 5 (Nov. 1969), 13.

26. Martin Kinch, "The Canadian Theatre: In for the Long Haul," *This Magazine* 10 (Nov.-Dec. 1976): 4-5.

27. Quoted in Robert Wallace, "Growing Pains: Toronto Theatre in the 1970s," *Canadian Literature* 85 (Summer 1980): 77.

28. George Ryga, "Theatre in Canada: A Viewpoint on Its Development and Future," *Canadian Theatre Review* 1 (Winter 1974): 30.

29. Bill Thomas in the *Victoria Colonist*, quoted in "Playwrights," *The Stage in Canada* 6 (January 1972): 17.

30. Coulter, 125.

31. Filewod, "Between Empires," 11.

GEORGE RYGA
(1932-1987)

"Playwright George Ryga Thursday night peeled a cicatrice off Canadian society and showed the bleeding flesh beneath." Jack Richards, reviewing the first performance of *The Ecstasy of Rita Joe* for the *Vancouver Sun* in 1967, identified an essential quality of Ryga's work that proved to be one of his major strengths and most serious difficulties. With stubborn integrity and singlemindedness Ryga made a career of tearing at sensitive wounds, stirring up controversy and often making himself unpopular in the process. Outspoken, abrasive and always fiercely committed to social justice and the defense of human dignity, he created an impressive body of dramatic work that is less well known than it should be in Canada.

Ryga gave warning of his uncompromising political views soon after leaving the Ukrainian community in northern Alberta where he had grown up. At the Banff School of Fine Arts in 1950 he was barred from future scholarships for writing a poem critical of the Korean War. Three years later he lost his job at an Edmonton radio station because of his public protests against the Rosenberg trial. When in 1962 after a decade of poetry and fiction Ryga turned his hand to drama, the imprint of his convictions was immediately clear.

His first play, *Indian*, written for television, is an austere, powerful work that announced a remarkable dramatic talent. The nameless Indian of the title is initially seen as a stereotype but gradually reveals a desperate humanity in whose light his white employer and the complacent government agent (a recurrent character type in Ryga's work) seem bloodless ciphers. The abrupt plunges into memory that punctuate the naturalism of *Indian* look forward to the more sophisticated stylization of Ryga's stage plays, just as the tone of combined anger and sadness would mark the best of Ryga's work to come.

In 1963 Ryga settled permanently in Summerland, B.C. After publishing two novels about the harshness of prairie life, *Hungry Hills* (1963) and *Ballad of a Stonepicker* (1966), he was commissioned to write a Centennial play for the Vancouver Playhouse. *The Ecstasy of Rita Joe* was the result. He followed it with a huge box office hit, *Grass and Wild Strawberries* (1969), a multi-media exploration of the conflict between '60s youth culture and the adult establishment. When his third commission from the Playhouse coincided with the October Crisis in 1970, Ryga reshaped his work-in-progress into a confrontation between a government mandarin and the terrorist holding him hostage. Upset by the script, the theatre's board refused to produce it, scheduling instead a Neil Simon play and firing artistic director David Gardner. Months of bitter public controversy ensued and for a short time *Captives of the Faceless Drummer* became a *cause célèbre*. But long after the play was forgotten the bitterness lingered and Ryga became increasingly alienated from the mainstream of Canadian theatre.

Ryga's subsequent plays were produced in the relative obscurity of Banff (*Sunrise on Sarah* and *Portrait of Angelica*), Edmonton's Theatre Network (*Seven Hours to Sundown*), Western Canada Theatre Company in Kamloops (*Ploughmen of the Glacier*), Kam Theatre Lab of North Bay, Ontario (the excellent *Letter to My Son*), and Vancouver's Firehall Theatre (*One More for the Road*). Few of the larger theatres have ever done any of his work except *Rita Joe*. One of his most interesting and ambitious plays, *Paracelsus*, first published in 1974, didn't receive a professional production until 1986. Ryga wrote two more novels, *Night Desk* (1976) and *In the Shadow of the Vulture* (1985), and a book about his trip to China, *Beyond the Crimson Morning* (1979). Two volumes of his uncollected writings were published after his death in 1987. *The Athabasca Ryga* (1990) and *Summerland* (1992) include stories, essays, TV and radio plays, and his last poem.

For much of his career Ryga's work was more popular on European radio and stage than in Canada. This may have been in part a reflection of the European sensibility in his writing, especially *The Ecstasy of Rita Joe*. The quality of Rita's suffering, her passivity and sense of spiritual homelessness are evocative of Dostoevsky (whom Ryga claimed to have read in full). The nightmarishness of Rita's experience, her feelings of entrapment and unaccountable guilt have roots that go back through Kafka to early expressionist drama—to Büchner's *Woyzeck* and O'Neill's *The Hairy Ape*. Rita takes her place in that tradition: the outsider perceived as a freak, struggling to preserve her integrity in the face of a system socially and politically designed to frustrate her every attempt to make sense of her life; struggling to avoid internalizing the guilt imposed by a world that grows increasingly monstrous until it completes its inevitable process of destruction.

Central to Rita's torment is the cultural and epistemological schism between whites and Indians, represented in its extreme form by the contrast between the mechanical, life-denying pseudo-rationalism of the Magistrate and the humane, intuitive impressionism of David Joe. These ways of seeing and understanding the world are so fundamentally different that the results of their clashes are sometimes comical. When Rita claims to have seen God in the sky she's told to call the Air Force. When Jaimie Paul sees a TV commercial that shows a knife "cutting up good shoes like they were potatoes," he reacts with comic bewilderment (edged with the bitter irony that he and Rita have nothing to eat). But Rita's inability to assimilate is also the real crime of which the white Witnesses along with the Teacher and Priest, the Magistrate and Mr. Homer take turns accusing her. In court, while the Magistrate rambles on about "the process of legal argument," Rita asks him if she can bum a cigarette; in the stage direction the Policeman "smiles and exits"—he rests his case. Later the Magistrate tells Rita, "the obstacles to your life are here ... in your thoughts ... possibly even in your culture," and he suggests that she fix her hair, tame her accent, "perhaps even change your name."

But Rita won't be helped and can't be saved. She certainly gets no help from the hollow paternalism of the Priest, the Magistrate or the ironically named Mr. Homer. Nor can Rita be aided by her own father. For all the sympathy Ryga invests in him, David Joe is impotent to save his people, just as Jaimie Paul says. And when he comes to take Rita home to the reserve from the city, she refuses to go. Rita is trapped. The rural past, though pastoral in her memory, she knows is a dead-end. The urban present holds only degradation and the promise of an early death. And what about the future? The circular ramp that comprises the set traces Rita's futile journey through the play; the shadowy Murderers who appear and reappear symbolize her doom, immanent from the start; the Brechtian Singer who sings of the fate of Rita and Jaimie forecloses any hope of salvation. The one rich fantasy she and Jaimie indulge turns quickly sour: their dream of having children in the city collides with the ugly fact that Clara Hill has had to give hers away. The scene that begins with the implied promise of lovemaking in Jaimie's room ends in frustration, disgust and despair.

Is Rita Joe tragic? Does she retain her selfhood with a stubborn persistence that somehow transforms her death from a sordid ritual of rape and murder into the "ecstasy" of a martyr? Or is she a passive victim doomed by birth, culture and her own feeble resignation? The play's articulation of these questions is complicated by the problems inherent in a white male writer's depiction of a Native woman's experience—a character represented onstage in the original production by a classically trained white actress. Not until 1981 would a production of the play use Native performers in all the Native roles. By the mid-1980s an increasingly strong contingent of Native actors and playwrights would begin telling their theatrical stories themselves. But George Ryga's probing of this terrible wound near the heart of Canadian society, radical in 1967, continues to resonate with its own dark truths.

The Ecstasy of Rita Joe opened at the Playhouse Theatre Centre, Vancouver, on November 23, 1967, with the following cast:

RITA JOE	Frances Hyland
JAIMIE PAUL	August Schellenberg
DAVID JOE	Chief Dan George
MAGISTRATE	Henry Ramer
MR. HOMER	Walter Marsh
PRIEST	Robert Clothier
EILEEN JOE	Patricia Gage
OLD INDIAN WOMAN	Rae Brown
TEACHER	Claudine Melgrave
POLICEMAN	Bill Clarkson
WITNESS; MURDERER	Merv Campone
WITNESS; MURDERER	Alex Bruhanski
WITNESS	Jack Leaf
MURDERER	Jack Buttrey
YOUNG INDIAN MEN	Leonard George, Robert Hall, Frank Lewis, Paul Stanley
GUITARIST	Willy Dunn
SINGER	Ann Mortifee

Directed by George Bloomfield
Set and Lighting Design by Charles Evans
Costume Design by Margaret Ryan
Music by Willy Dunn and Ann Mortifee
Lyrics by George Ryga
Choreography by Norbert Vesak

THE ECSTASY OF RITA JOE

CHARACTERS

RITA JOE
JAIMIE PAUL
DAVID JOE, *Rita's father*
MAGISTRATE
MR. HOMER
FATHER ANDREW, *a priest*
EILEEN JOE, *Rita's sister*
OLD INDIAN WOMAN
MISS DONOHUE, *a teacher*
POLICEMAN
WITNESSES
MURDERERS
YOUNG INDIAN MEN
SINGER

SET

A circular ramp beginning at floor level stage left and continuing downward below floor level at stage front, then rising and sweeping along stage back at two-foot elevation to disappear in the wings of stage left. This ramp dominates the stage by wrapping the central and forward playing area. A short approach ramp, meeting with the main ramp at stage right, expedites entrances from the wings of stage right. The MAGISTRATE's chair and representation of court desk are situated at stage right, enclosed within the sweep of the ramp. At the foot of the desk is a lip on stage right side. The SINGER sits here, turned away from the focus of the play. Her songs and accompaniment appear almost accidental. She has all the reactions of a white liberal folklorist with a limited concern and understanding of an ethnic dilemma which she touches in the course of her research and work in compiling and writing folk songs. She serves too as an alter ego to RITA JOE.

No curtain is used during the play. At the opening, intermission and conclusion of the play, the curtain remains up. The onus for isolating scenes from the past and present in RITA JOE's life falls on highlight lighting.

Backstage, there is a mountain cyclorama. In front of the cyclorama there is a darker maze curtain to suggest gloom and confusion, and a cityscape.

ACT ONE

The house lights and stage work lights remain on. Backstage, cyclorama, and maze curtains are up, revealing wall back of stage, exit doors, etc.

CAST and SINGER enter offstage singly and in pairs from the wings, the exit doors at the back of the theatre, and from the auditorium side doors. The entrances are workmanlike and untheatrical. When all the CAST is on stage, they turn to face the audience momentarily. The house lights dim.

The cyclorama is lowered into place. The maze curtain follows. This creates a sense of compression of stage into the auditorium. Recorded voices are heard in a jumble of mutterings and throat clearings. The MAGISTRATE enters as the CLERK begins.

CLERK: *(recorded)* This court is in session. All present will rise …

The shuffling and scraping of furniture is heard. The CAST repeat "Rita Joe, Rita Joe." A POLICEMAN brings on RITA JOE.

MAGISTRATE: Who is she? Can she speak English?

POLICEMAN: Yes.

MAGISTRATE: Then let her speak for herself!

He speaks to the audience firmly and with reason.

MAGISTRATE: To understand life in a given society, one must understand laws of that society. All relationships …

CLERK: *(recorded)* Man to man … man to woman … man to property … man to the state …

MAGISTRATE: … are determined and enriched by laws that have grown out of social realities. The quality of the law under which you live and function determines the real quality of the freedom that was yours today.

The rest of the CAST slowly move out.

MAGISTRATE: Your home and your well-being were protected. The roads of the city are open to us. So are the galleries, libraries, the administrative and public buildings. There are buses, trains … going in and coming out. Nobody is a prisoner here.

RITA: *(with humour, almost a sad sigh)* The first time I tried to go home I was picked up by some men who gave me five dollars. An' then they arrested me.

The POLICEMAN retreats into the shadows. The SINGER crosses down.

MAGISTRATE: Thousands leave and enter the city every day …

RITA: It wasn't true what they said, but nobody'd believe me …

SINGER: *(singing a recitivo searching for a melody)*
Will the winds not blow
My words to her
Like the seeds
Of the dandelion?

MAGISTRATE: *(smiling, as at a private joke)* Once … I saw a little girl in the Cariboo country. It was summer then and she wore only a blouse and skirt. I wondered what she wore in winter?

The MURDERERS hover in the background on the upper ramp. One whistles and one lights a cigarette—an action which will be repeated at the end of the play.

RITA: *(moving to him, but hesitating)* You look like a good man. Tell them to let me go, please!

The MAGISTRATE goes to his podium.

MAGISTRATE: Our nation is on an economic par with the state of Arkansas … We are a developing country, but a buoyant one. Still … the summer report of the Economic Council of Canada predicts a reduction in the gross national product unless we utilize our manpower for greater efficiency. Employed, happy people make for a prosperous, happy nation …

RITA: *(exultantly)* I worked at some jobs, mister!

The MAGISTRATE turns to face RITA JOE. The MURDERERS have gone.

MAGISTRATE: Gainful employment. Obedience to the law …

RITA: *(to the MAGISTRATE)* Once I had a job …

He does not relate to her. She is troubled. She talks to the audience.

RITA: Once I had a job in a tire store … an' I'd worry about what time my boss would come … He was always late … and so was everybody. Sometimes I got to thinkin' what would happen if he'd not come. And nobody else would come. And I'd be all day in this big room with no lights on an' the telephone ringing an' people asking for other people that weren't there … What would happen?

As she relates her concern, she laughs. Towards the end of her monologue she is so amused by the absurdity of it all that she can hardly contain herself.

Lights fade on the MAGISTRATE who broods in his chair as he examines his court papers.

Lights up on JAIMIE PAUL approaching on the backstage ramp from stage left. He is jubilant, his laughter blending with her laughter. At the sound of his voice, RITA JOE runs to him, to the memory of him.

JAIMIE: I seen the city today and I seen things today I never knew was there, Rita Joe!

RITA: *(happily)* I seen them too, Jaimie Paul!

He pauses above her, his mood light and childlike.

JAIMIE: I see a guy on top of a bridge, talkin' to himself … an' lots of people on the beach watchin' harbour seals … Kids feed popcorn to seagulls … an' I think to myself … Boy! Pigeons eat pretty good here!

RITA: In the morning, Jaimie Paul … very early in the morning … the air is cold like at home …

JAIMIE: Pretty soon I seen a little woman walkin' a big black dog on a rope … Dog is mad … Dog wants a man!

JAIMIE PAUL moves to RITA JOE. They embrace.

RITA: Clouds are red over the city in the morning. Clara Hill says to me if you're real happy … the clouds make you forget you're not home …

They laugh together. JAIMIE PAUL breaks from her. He punctuates his story with wide, sweeping gestures.

JAIMIE: I start singin' and some hotel windows open. I wave to them, but nobody waves back! They're watchin' me, like I was a harbour seal! *(He laughs.)* So I stopped singin'!

RITA: I remember colours, but I've forgot faces already …

JAIMIE PAUL looks at her as her mood changes. Faint light on the MAGISTRATE brightens.

RITA: A train whistle is white, with black lines … A sick man talkin' is brown like an overcoat with pockets torn an' string showin … A sad woman is a room with the curtains shut …

MAGISTRATE: Rita Joe?

She becomes sobered, but JAIMIE PAUL continues laughing. She nods to the MAGISTRATE, then turns to JAIMIE PAUL.

RITA: Them bastards put me in jail. They're gonna do it again, they said … Them bastards!

JAIMIE: Guys who sell newspapers don't see nothin' …

RITA: They drive by me, lookin' …

JAIMIE: I'm gonna be a carpenter!

RITA: I walk like a stick, tryin' to keep my ass from showin' because I know what they're thinkin' … Them bastards!

JAIMIE: I got myself boots an' new shirt … See!

RITA: *(worried now)* I thought their jail was on fire … I thought it was burning.

JAIMIE: Room I got costs me seven bucks a week …

RITA: I can't leave town. Every time I try, they put me in jail.

A POLICEMAN enters with a file folder.

JAIMIE: They say it's a pretty good room for seven bucks a week …

JAIMIE PAUL begins to retreat backwards from her, along the ramp to the wings of stage left. She is isolated in a pool of light away from the MAGISTRATE. The light isolation between her

and JAIMIE PAUL deepens, as the scene turns into the courtroom again.

MAGISTRATE: Vagrancy … You are charged with vagrancy.

JAIMIE: *(with enthusiasm, boyishly)* First hundred bucks I make, Rita Joe … I'm gonna buy a car so I can take you every place!

RITA: *(moving after him)* Jaimie!

He retreats, dreamlike, into the wings. The spell of memory between them is broken. Pools of light between her and the MAGISTRATE spread and fuse into a single light area. She turns to the MAGISTRATE, worried and confused.

MAGISTRATE: *(reading the documents in his hand)* The charge against you this morning is vagrancy …

The MAGISTRATE continues studying the papers he holds. She looks up at him and shakes her head helplessly, then blurts out to him.

RITA: I had to spend last night in jail … Did you know?

MAGISTRATE: Yes. You were arrested.

RITA: I didn't know when morning came … there was no windows … The jail stinks! People in jail stink!

MAGISTRATE: *(indulgently)* Are you surprised?

RITA: I didn't know anybody there … People in jail stink like paper that's been in the rain too long. But a jail stinks worse. It stinks of rust … an' old hair …

The MAGISTRATE looks down at her for the first time.

MAGISTRATE: You … are Rita Joe?

She nods quickly. A faint concern shows in his face. He watches her for a long moment.

MAGISTRATE: I know your face … yet … it wasn't in this courtroom. Or was it?

RITA: I don't know …

MAGISTRATE: *(pondering)* Have you appeared before me in the past year?

RITA: *(turning away from him, shrugging)* I don't know. I can't remember …

The MAGISTRATE throws his head back and laughs. The POLICEMAN joins in.

MAGISTRATE: You can't remember? Come now …

RITA: *(laughing with him and looking to the POLICEMAN)* I can't remember …

MAGISTRATE: Then I take it you haven't appeared before me. Certainly you and I would remember if you had.

RITA: *(smiling)* I don't remember …

The MAGISTRATE makes some hurried notes, but he is watching RITA JOE, formulating his next thought.

RITA: *(naively)* My sister hitchhiked home an' she had no trouble like I …

MAGISTRATE: You'll need witnesses, Rita Joe. I'm only giving you eight hours to find witnesses for yourself …

RITA: Jaimie knows …

She turns to where JAIMIE PAUL had been, but the back of the stage is in darkness. The POLICEMAN exits suddenly.

RITA: Jaimie knew …

Her voice trails off pathetically. The MAGISTRATE shrugs and returns to studying his notes. RITA JOE chafes during the silence which follows. She craves communion with people, with the MAGISTRATE.

RITA: My sister was a dressmaker, mister! But she only worked two weeks in the city … An' then she got sick and went back to the reserve to help my father catch fish an' cut pulpwood. *(smiling)* She's not coming back … that's for sure!

MAGISTRATE: *(with interest)* Should I know your sister? What was her name?

RITA: Eileen Joe.

EILEEN JOE appears spotlit behind, a memory crowding in.

MAGISTRATE: Eileen … that's a soft, undulating name.

RITA: Two weeks, and not one white woman came to her to leave an order or old clothes for her to fix. No work at all for two weeks, an' her money ran out … Isn't that funny?

The MAGISTRATE again studies RITA JOE, his mind elsewhere.

MAGISTRATE: Hmmmmm …

EILEEN JOE disappears.

RITA: So she went back to the reserve to catch fish an' cut pulpwood!

MAGISTRATE: I do know your face … yes! And yet …

RITA: Can I sit someplace?

MAGISTRATE: *(excited)* I remember now … Yes! I was on holidays three summers back in the Cariboo country … driving over this road with not a house or field in sight … just barren land, wild and wind-blown. And then I saw this child beside the road, dressed in a blouse and skirt, barefooted …

RITA: *(looking around)* I don't feel so good, mister.

MAGISTRATE: My God, she wasn't more than three or four years old … walking towards me beside the road. When I'd passed her, I stopped my car and then turned around and drove back to where I'd seen her, for I wondered what she could possibly be doing in such a lonely country at that age without her father or mother walking with her … Yet when I got back to where I'd seen her, she had disappeared. She was nowhere to be seen. Yet the land was flat for over a mile in every direction … I had to see her. But I couldn't …

He stares down at RITA JOE for a long moment.

MAGISTRATE: You see, what I was going to say was that this child had your face! isn't that strange?

RITA: *(with disinterest)* Sure, if you think so, mister …

MAGISTRATE: Could she have been … your daughter?

RITA: What difference does it make?

MAGISTRATE: Children cannot be left like that … It takes money to raise children in the woods as in the cities … There are institutions and people with more money than you who could …

RITA: Nobody would get my child, mister!

She is distracted by EILEEN JOE's voice in her memory. EILEEN's voice begins in darkness, but as she speaks, a spotlight isolates her in front of the ramp, stage left. EILEEN is on her hands and knees, two buckets beside her. She is picking berries in mime.

EILEEN: First was the strawberries an' then the blueberries. After the frost ... we picked the cranberries ...

She laughs with delight.

RITA: *(pleading with the MAGISTRATE, but her attention on EILEEN)* Let me go, mister ...

MAGISTRATE: I can't let you go. I don't think that would be of any use in the circumstances. Would you like a lawyer?

Even as he speaks, RITA JOE has entered the scene with EILEEN picking berries. The MAGISTRATE's light fades on his podium.

RITA: You ate the strawberries an' blueberries because you were always a hungry kid!

EILEEN: But not cranberries! They made my stomach hurt.

RITA JOE goes down on her knees with EILEEN.

RITA: Let me pick ... You rest. *(holding out the bucket to EILEEN)* Mine's full already ... Let's change. You rest ...

During the exchange of buckets, EILEEN notices her hands are larger than RITA JOE's. She is both delighted and surprised by this.

EILEEN: My hands are bigger than yours, Rita ... Look! *(taking RITA JOE's hands in hers)* When did my hands grow so big?

RITA: *(wisely and sadly)* You've worked so hard ... I'm older than you, Leenie ... I will always be older.

The two sisters are thoughtful for a moment, each watching the other in silence. Then RITA JOE becomes animated and resumes her mime of picking berries in the woods.

RITA: We picked lots of wild berries when we were kids, Leenie!

They turn away from their work and lie down alongside each other, facing the front of the stage. The light on them becomes summery, warm.

RITA: In the summer, it was hot an' flies hummed so loud you'd go to sleep if you sat down an' just listened.

EILEEN: The leaves on the poplars used to turn black an' curl together with the heat ...

RITA: One day you and I were pickin' blueberries and a big storm came ...

A sudden crash of thunder and a lightning flash. The lights turn cold and blue. The three MURDERERS stand in silhouette on a riser behind them. EILEEN cringes in fear, afraid of the storm, aware of the presence of the MURDERERS behind them. RITA JOE springs to her feet, her being attached to the wildness of the atmosphere. Lightning continues to flash and flicker.

EILEEN: Oh, no!

RITA: *(shouting)* It got cold and the rain an' hail came ... the sky falling!

EILEEN: *(crying in fear)* Rita!

RITA: *(laughing, shouting)* Stay there!

A high flash of lightning, silhouetting the MURDERERS harshly. They take a step forward on the lightning flash. EILEEN dashes into the arms of RITA JOE. She screams and drags RITA JOE down with her. RITA JOE struggles against EILEEN.

RITA: Let me go! What in hell's wrong with you? Let me go!

MAGISTRATE: I can't let you go.

The lightning dies, but the thunder rumbles off into the distance. EILEEN subsides, and pressing herself into the arms of RITA JOE as a small child to her mother, she sobs quietly.

RITA: There, there ... *(with infinite tenderness)* You said to me, "What would happen if the storm hurt us an' we can't find our way home, but are lost together so far away in the bush?"

EILEEN looks up, brushing away her tears and smiling at RITA JOE.

RITA and EILEEN: *(in unison)* Would you be my mother then?

RITA: Would I be your mother?

RITA JOE releases EILEEN who looks back fearfully to where the MURDERERS had stood.

They are gone. She rises and, collecting the buckets, moves hesitantly to where they had been. Confident now, she laughs softly and nervously to herself and leaves the stage, RITA JOE rises and talks to EILEEN as she departs.

RITA: We walked home through the mud an' icy puddles among the trees. At first you cried, Leenie ... and then you wanted to sleep. But I held you up an' when we got home you said you were sure you would've died in the bush if it hadn't been for us being together like that.

EILEEN disappears from the stage. The MAGISTRATE's light comes up. RITA JOE shakes her head sadly at the memory, then comes forward to the apron of the stage. She is proud of her sister and her next speech reveals this pride.

RITA: She made a blouse for me that I wore every day for one year, an' it never ripped at the armpits like the blouse I buy in the store does the first time I stretch. *(She stretches languidly.)* I like to stretch when I'm happy! It makes all the happiness go through me like warm water ...

The PRIEST, the TEACHER, and a YOUNG INDIAN MAN cross the stage directly behind her. The PRIEST wears a Roman collar and a checked bush-jacket of a worker-priest. He pauses before passing RITA JOE and goes to meet her.

PRIEST: Rita Joe? When did you get back? How's life?

RITA JOE shrugs noncommittally.

RITA: You know me, Father Andrew ... could be better, could be worse ...

PRIEST: Are you still working?

RITA JOE is still noncommittal. She smiles at him. Her gestures are not definite.

RITA: I live.

PRIEST: *(serious and concerned)* It's not easy, is it?

RITA: Not always.

The TEACHER and the YOUNG INDIAN MAN exit.

PRIEST: A lot of things are different in the city. It's easier here on the reserve ... life is simpler. You can be yourself. That's important to remember.

RITA: Yes, Father ...

The PRIEST wants to ask and say more, but he cannot. An awkward moment between them and he reaches out to touch her shoulder gently.

PRIEST: Well ... be a good girl, Rita Joe ...

RITA: *(without turning after him)* Goodbye, Father.

MAGISTRATE: *(more insistently)* Do you want a lawyer?

The PRIEST leaves stage right. As he leaves, cross light to where a happy JAIMIE PAUL enters from stage left. JAIMIE PAUL comes down to join RITA JOE.

JAIMIE: This guy asked me how much education I got, an' I says to him, "Grade six. How much education a man need for such a job?" ... An' the bum, he says it's not good enough! I should take night school. But I got the job, an' I start next Friday ... like this ...

JAIMIE PAUL does a mock sweeping routine as if he was cleaning a vast office building. He and RITA JOE are both laughing.

JAIMIE: Pretty good, eh?

RITA: Pretty good.

JAIMIE: Cleaning the floors an' desks in the building ... But it's a government job, and that's good for life. Work hard, then the government give me a raise ... I never had a job like that before ...

RITA: When I sleep happy, I dream of blueberries an' sun an' all the nice things when I was a little kid, Jaimie Paul.

The sound of an airplane is heard. JAIMIE PAUL looks up. RITA JOE also stares into the sky of her memory. JAIMIE PAUL's face is touched with pain and recollection. The TEACHER, RITA JOE's FATHER, an OLD WOMAN, four YOUNG INDIAN MEN and EILEEN JOE come into the background quietly, as if at a wharf watching the airplane leave the village. They stand looking up until the noise of the aircraft begins to diminish.

JAIMIE: That airplane ... a Cessna ...

He continues watching the aircraft and turns, following its flight path.

JAIMIE: She said to me, maybe I never see you again, Jaimie Paul.

There is a faint light on the MAGISTRATE in his chair. He is thoughtful, looking down at his hands.

MAGISTRATE: Do you want a lawyer?

RITA: *(to JAIMIE PAUL)* Who?

JAIMIE: Your mother ... I said to her, they'll fix you up good in the hospital. Better than before ... It was a Cessna that landed on the river an' took her away ... Maybe I never see you again, Jaimie, she says to me. She knew she was gonna die, but I was a kid and so were you ... What the hell did we know? I'll never forget ...

JAIMIE PAUL joins the village group on the upper level.

SINGER: *(singing an indefinite melody developing into a square-dance tune)*
There was a man in a beat-up hat
Who runs a house in the middle of town,
An' round his stove-pipe chimney house
The magpies sat, just a-lookin' round.

The Indian village people remain in the back of the stage, still watching the airplane which has vanished. JAIMIE PAUL, on his way, passes MR. HOMER, a white citizen who has the hurried but fulfilled appearance of the socially responsible man. MR. HOMER comes to the front of the stage beside RITA JOE. He talks directly to the audience.

MR. HOMER: Sure, we do a lot of things for our Indians here in the city at the Centre ... Bring 'em in from the cold an' give them food ... The rest ... well, the rest kinda take care of itself.

RITA JOE lowers her head and looks away from him. MR. HOMER moves to her and places his hand on her shoulders possessively.

MR. HOMER: When your mother got sick we flew her out ... You remember that, Rita Joe?

RITA: *(nodding, looking down)* Yes, Mr. Homer ... Thank you.

MR. HOMER: And we sent her body back for the funeral ... Right, Rita Joe?

The people of the village leave except for the YOUNG INDIAN MEN who remain and mime drinking.

MR. HOMER: And then sometimes a man drinks it up an' leaves his wife an' kids and the poor dears come here for help. We give them food an' a place to sleep ... Right, Rita?

RITA: Yes.

MR. HOMER: Clothes too ... White people leave clothes here for the Indians to take if they need 'em. Used to have them all up on racks over there ... just like in a store ... *(pointing)* But now we got them all on a heap on a table in the basement.

He laughs and RITA JOE nods with him.

MR. HOMER: Indian people ... 'specially the women ... get more of a kick diggin' through stuff that's piled up like that ...

MR. HOMER chuckles and shakes his head. There is a pale light on the MAGISTRATE, who is still looking down at his hands.

MAGISTRATE: There are institutions to help you ...

MR. HOMER again speaks to the audience, but now he is angry over some personal beef.

MR. HOMER: So you see, the Centre serves a need that's real for Indians who come to the city. *(wagging his finger at the audience angrily)* It's the do-gooders burn my ass, you know! They come in from television or the newspaper ... hang around just long enough to see a drunken Indian ... an' bingo!

JAIMIE: Bingo!

MR. HOMER: That's their story! Next thing, they're seeing some kind of Red Power ...

The YOUNG INDIAN MEN laugh and RITA JOE gets up to join them.

MR. HOMER: ... or beatin' the government over the head! Let them live an' work among the Indians for a few months ... then they'd know what it's really like ...

The music comes up sharply.

SINGER:
Round and round the cenotaph,
The clumsy seagulls play.
Fed by funny men with hats
Who watch them night and day.

The four YOUNG INDIAN MEN join with RITA JOE and dance. Leading the group is JAIMIE PAUL. He is drunk, dishevelled. Light spreads before them as they advance onstage. They are laughing rowdily. RITA JOE moves to them.

RITA: Jaimie Paul?

MR. HOMER leaves. JAIMIE PAUL is overtaken by two of his companions who take him by the arms, but he pushes them roughly away.

JAIMIE: Get the hell outa my way! … I'm as good a man as him any time …

JAIMIE PAUL crosses downstage to confront a member of the audience.

JAIMIE: You know me? … You think I'm a dirty Indian, eh? Get outa my way!

He puts his hands over his head and continues staggering away.

JAIMIE: Goddamnit, I wanna sleep …

The YOUNG INDIAN MEN and JAIMIE PAUL exit. RITA JOE follows after JAIMIE PAUL, reaching out to touch him, but the SINGER stands in her way and drives her back, singing …

Music up tempo and volume.

SINGER:
Oh, can't you see that train roll on,
Its hot black wheels keep comin' on?
A Kamloops Indian died today.
Train didn't hit him, he just fell.
Busy train with wheels on fire!

The music dies. A POLICEMAN enters.

POLICEMAN: Rita Joe!

He repeats her name many times. The TEACHER enters ringing the school handbell and crosses through.

TEACHER: *(calling)* Rita Joe! Rita Joe! Didn't you hear the bell ring? The class is waiting … The class is always waiting for you.

The TEACHER exits.

MAGISTRATE and POLICEMAN: *(sharply, in unison)* Rita Joe!

The POLICEMAN grabs and shakes RITA JOE to snap her out of her reverie.

Light up on the MAGISTRATE who sits erect, with authority.

MAGISTRATE: I ask you for the last, time, Rita Joe … Do you want a lawyer?

RITA: *(defiantly)* What for? … I can take care of myself.

MAGISTRATE: The charge against you this morning is prostitution. Why did you not return to your people as you said you would?

The light on the backstage dies. RITA JOE stands before the MAGISTRATE and the POLICEMAN. She is contained in a pool of light before them.

RITA: *(nervous, with despair)* I tried … I tried …

The MAGISTRATE settles back into his chair and takes a folder from his desk, which he opens and studies.

MAGISTRATE: Special Constable Eric Wilson has submitted a statement to the effect that on June 18th he and Special Constable Schneider approached you on Fourth Avenue at nine-forty in the evening …

POLICEMAN: We were impersonating two deckhands newly arrived in the city …

MAGISTRATE: You were arrested an hour later on charges of prostitution.

The MAGISTRATE holds the folder threateningly and looks down at her. RITA JOE is defiant.

RITA: That's a goddamned lie!

MAGISTRATE: *(sternly, gesturing to the POLICE-MAN)* This is a police statement. Surely you don't think a mistake was made?

RITA: *(peering into the light above her, shuddering)* Everything in this room is like ice … How can you stay alive working here? … I'm so hungry I want to throw up …

MAGISTRATE: You have heard the statement, Rita Joe … Do you deny it?

RITA: I was going home, trying to find the highway … I knew those two were cops, the moment I saw them … I told them to go f … fly a kite! They got sore then an' started pushing me around …

MAGISTRATE: *(patiently now, waving down the objections of the POLICEMAN)* Go on.

RITA: They followed me around until a third cop drove up. An' then they arrested me.

MAGISTRATE: Arrested you … Nothing else?

RITA: They stuffed five dollar bills in my pockets when they had me in the car ... I ask you, mister, when are they gonna charge cops like that with contributing to ...

POLICEMAN: Your worship ...

MAGISTRATE: (irritably, indicating the folder on the table before him) Now it's your word against this! You need references ... people who know you ... who will come to court to substantiate what you say ... today! That is the process of legal argument!

RITA: Can I bum a cigarette someplace?

MAGISTRATE: No. You can't smoke in court.

The POLICEMAN smiles and exits.

RITA: Then give me a bed to sleep on, or is the sun gonna rise an' rise until it burns a hole in my head?

Guitar music cues softly in the background.

MAGISTRATE: Tell me about the child.

RITA: What child?

MAGISTRATE: The little girl I once saw beside the road!

RITA: I don't know any girl, mister! When do I eat? Why does an Indian wait even when he's there first thing in the morning?

The pool of light tightens around the MAGISTRATE and RITA JOE.

MAGISTRATE: I have children ... two sons ...

RITA: (nodding) Sure. That's good.

The MAGISTRATE gropes for words to express a message that is very precious to him.

MAGISTRATE: My sons can go in any direction they wish ... into trades or university ... But if I had a daughter, I would be more concerned ...

RITA: What's so special about a girl?

MAGISTRATE: I would wish ... well, I'd be concerned about her choices ... her choices of living, school ... friends ... These things don't come as lightly for a girl. For boys it's different ... But I would worry if I had a daughter ... Don't hide your child! Someone else can be found to raise her if you can't!

RITA JOE shakes her head, a strange smile on her face.

MAGISTRATE: Why not? There are people who would love to take care of it.

RITA: Nobody would get my child ... I would sooner kill it an' bury it first! I am not a kind woman, mister judge!

MAGISTRATE: (at a loss) I see ...

RITA: (a cry) I want to go home ...

Quick up tempo music is heard. Suddenly, the lights change.

JAIMIE PAUL and the YOUNG INDIAN MEN sweep over the backstage ramp, the light widening for them. RITA JOE moves into this railway station crowd. She turns from one man to another until she sees JAIMIE PAUL.

EILEEN JOE and an OLD WOMAN enter.

RITA: Jaimie!

EILEEN: (happily, running to him) Jaimie Paul! God's sakes ... When did you get back from the north? ... I thought you said you wasn't coming until breakup ...

JAIMIE: (turning to EILEEN) I was comin' home on the train ... had a bit to drink and was feeling pretty good ... Lots of women sleeping in their seats on the train ... I'd lift their hats an' say, "Excuse me, lady ... I'm lookin' for a wife!" (turning to the OLD WOMAN) One fat lady got mad, an' I says to her, "That's alright, lady ... You got no worries ... You keep sleepin'!"

Laughter.

JAIMIE PAUL and the OLD WOMAN move away. EILEEN sees RITA JOE who is standing watching.

EILEEN: Rita! ... Tom an' I broke up ... did I tell you?

RITA: No, Leenie ... you didn't tell me!

EILEEN: He was no good ... He stopped comin' to see me when he said he would. I kept waiting, but he didn't come ...

RITA: I sent you a pillow for your wedding!

EILEEN: I gave it away ... I gave it to Clara Hill.

RITA: (laughing bawdily and miming pregnancy) Clara Hill don't need no pillow now!

JAIMIE: *(smiling, crossing to her and exiting)* I always came to see you, Rita Joe ...

RITA JOE looks bewildered.

OLD WOMAN: *(exiting)* I made two Saskatoon pies, Rita ... You said next time you came home you wanted Saskatoon pie with lots of sugar ...

EILEEN and the OLD WOMAN drift away. JAIMIE PAUL moves on to the shadows. The THREE MURDERERS enter in silhouette; one whistles. RITA JOE rushes to the YOUNG INDIAN MEN downstage.

RITA: This is me, Rita Joe, God's sakes ... We went to the same school together ... Don't you know me now, Johnny? You remember how tough you was when you was a boy? ... We tied you up in the Rainbow Creek and forgot you was there after recess ... An' after school was out, somebody remembered. *(laughing)* And you was blue when we got to you. Your clothes was wet to the chin, an' you said, "That's a pretty good knot ... I almost gave up trying to untie it!"

The music continues. RITA JOE steps among the YOUNG INDIAN MEN and they mime being piled in a car at a drive-in.

Steve Laporte? ... You remember us goin' to the drive-in and the cold rain comin' down the car windows so we couldn't see the picture show anyhow?

She sits beside STEVE LAPORTE. They mime the windshield wipers.

A cold white light comes up on the playing area directly in front of the MAGISTRATE's chair. A MALE WITNESS of dishevelled, dirty appearance steps into the light and delivers testimony in a whining, defensive voice. He is one of the MURDERERS, but apart from the other three, he is nervous.

FIRST WITNESS: I gave her three bucks ... an' once I got her goin' she started yellin' like hell! Called me a dog, pig ... some filthy kind of animal ... So I slapped her around a bit ... Guys said she was a funny kind of bim ... would do it for them standing up, but not for me she wouldn't ... So I slapped her around ...

The MAGISTRATE nods and makes a notation. The light on the FIRST WITNESS dies. RITA JOE speaks with urgency and growing fear to STEVE LAPORTE.

RITA: Then you shut the wipers off an' we were just sitting there, not knowing what to do ... I wish ... we could go back again there an' start livin' from that day on ... Jaimie!

RITA JOE looks at STEVE LAPORTE as at a stranger. She stands and draws away from him. JAIMIE PAUL enters behind RITA JOE.

There is a cold light before the MAGISTRATE again and another MALE WITNESS moves into the light, replacing the FIRST WITNESS. He too is one of the MURDERERS. This SECOND WITNESS testifies with full gusto.

SECOND WITNESS: Gave her a job in my tire store ... took her over to my place after work once ... She was scared when I tried a trick, but I'm easy on broads that get scared, providin' they keep their voices down ... After that, I slipped her a fiver ... Well, sir, she took the money, then she stood in front of the window, her head high an' her naked shoulders shakin' like she was cold. Well, sir, she cried a little an' then she says, "Goddamnit, but I wish I was a school teacher ..."

He laughs and everyone onstage joins in the laughter. The light dies out on the SECOND WITNESS. JAIMIE PAUL enters and crosses to RITA JOE. They lie down and embrace.

RITA: You always came to see me, Jaimie Paul ... The night we were in the cemetery ... you remember, Jaimie Paul? I turned my face from yours until I saw the ground ... an' I knew that below us ... they were like us once, and now they lie below the ground, their eyes gone, the bones showin' ... They must've spoke and touched each other here ... like you're touching me, Jaimie Paul ... an' now there was nothing over them, except us ... an' wind in the grass an' a barbwire fence creaking. An' behind that, a hundred acres of barley.

JAIMIE PAUL stands.

RITA: That's something to remember, when you're lovin', eh?

The sound of a train whistle is heard. JAIMIE PAUL goes and the lights onstage fade.

The music comes up and the SINGER sings. As JAIMIE PAUL passes her, the SINGER pursues him up the ramp, and RITA JOE runs after them.

SINGER:
Oh, can't you see that train roll on,
Gonna kill a man, before it's gone?
Jaimie Paul fell and died.
He had it comin', so it's alright.
Silver train with wheels on fire!

The music dies instantly. RITA JOE's words come on the heels of the music as a bitter extension of the song.

She stands before the MAGISTRATE, again in the court, but looks back to where JAIMIE PAUL had been in the gloom. The POLICEMAN enters where JAIMIE PAUL has exited, replacing him, for the fourth trial scene.

RITA: Jaimie, why am I here? … Is it … because people are talkin' about me and all them men … Is that why? I never wanted to cut cordwood for a living … *(with great bitterness)* Never once I thought … it'd be like this …

MAGISTRATE: What are we going to do about you, Rita Joe? This is the seventh charge against you in one year … Laws are not made to be violated in this way … Why did you steal?

RITA: I was hungry. I had no money.

MAGISTRATE: Yet you must have known you would be caught?

RITA: Yes.

MAGISTRATE: Are you not afraid of what is happening to you?

RITA: I am afraid of a lot of things. Put me in jail. I don't care …

MAGISTRATE: *(with forced authority)* Law is a procedure. The procedure must be respected. It took hundreds of years to develop this process of law.

RITA: I stole a sweater … They caught me in five minutes!

She smiles whimsically at this. The MAGISTRATE is leafing through the documents before him. The POLICEMAN stands to one side of him.

MAGISTRATE: The prosecutor's office has submitted some of the past history of Rita Joe …

POLICEMAN: She was born and raised on a reservation. Then came a brief period in a public school off the reservation … at which time Rita Joe established herself as something of a disruptive influence …

RITA: What's that mean?

MAGISTRATE: *(turning to her, smiling)* A trouble maker!

RITA JOE becomes animated, aware of the trap around her closing even at moments such as this.

RITA: Maybe it was about the horse, huh?

She looks up at the MAGISTRATE who is still smiling, offering her no help.

RITA: There was this accident with a horse … It happened like this … I was riding a horse to school an' some of the boys shot a rifle an' my horse bucked an' I fell off. I fell in the bush an' got scratched … The boys caught the horse by the school and tried to ride him, but the horse bucked an' pinned a boy against a tree, breaking his leg in two places …

She indicates the place the leg got broken.

RITA: They said … an' he said I'd rode the horse over him on purpose!

MAGISTRATE: Well … did you?

RITA: It wasn't that way at all, I tell you! They lied!

The POLICEMAN and the SINGER laugh.

MAGISTRATE: Why should they lie, and Rita Joe alone tell the truth? … Or are you a child enough to believe the civilization of which we are a part …

He indicates the audience as inclusive of civilization from his point of view.

MAGISTRATE: … does not understand Rita Joe?

RITA: I don't know what you're saying.

MAGISTRATE: *(with a touch of compassion)* Look at you, woman! Each time you come before me you are older. The lines in your face are those of …

RITA: I'm tired an' I want to eat mister! I haven't had grub since day before yesterday … This room is like a boat on water … I'm so dizzy …

What the hell kind of place is this won't let me go lie down on grass?

She doubles over to choke back her nausea.

MAGISTRATE: This is not the reservation, Rita Joe. This is another place, another time ...

RITA: *(straining to remember, to herself)* I was once in Whitecourt, Alberta. The cops are fatter there than here. I had to get out of Whitecourt, Alberta ...

MAGISTRATE: Don't blame the police, Rita Joe! The obstacles to your life are here ... *(He touches his forefinger to his temples.)* ... in your thoughts ... possibly even in your culture ...

RITA JOE turns away from him, searching the darkness behind her.

MAGISTRATE: What's the matter?

RITA: I want to go home!

MAGISTRATE: But you can't go now. You've broken a law for which you will have to pay a fine or go to prison ...

RITA: I have no money.

MAGISTRATE: *(with exasperation)* Rita Joe ... It is against the law to solicit men on the street. You have to wash ...

RITA JOE begins to move away from him, crossing the front of the stage along the apron, her walk cocky. The light spreads and follows her.

MAGISTRATE: You can't walk around in old clothes and running shoes made of canvas ... You have to have some money in your pockets and an address where you live. You should fix your hair ... perhaps even change your name. And try to tame that accent that sounds like you have a mouthful of sawdust ... There is no peace in being extraordinary!

The light dies on the MAGISTRATE and the POLICEMAN.

RITA JOE is transported into another memory. JAIMIE PAUL enters and slides along the floor, left of centre stage. He is drunk, counting the fingers on his outstretched hands. MR. HOMER has entered with a wagon carrying hot soup and mugs. Four YOUNG INDIAN MEN come in out of the cold. MR. HOMER speaks to the audience in a matter-of-fact informative way.

MR. HOMER: *(dispensing soup to the YOUNG INDIAN MEN)* The do-gooders make something special of the Indian ... There's nothing special here ... At the centre here the quick cure is a bowl of stew under the belt and a good night's sleep.

JAIMIE: Hey, Mister Homer! How come I got so many fingers? Heh?

He laughs. MR. HOMER ignores JAIMIE PAUL and continues talking to the audience.

MR. HOMER: I wouldn't say they were brothers or sisters to me ... no sir! But if you're ...

JAIMIE PAUL gets up and embraces RITA JOE.

JAIMIE: I got two hands an' one neck ... I can kill more than I can eat ... If I had more fingers I would need mittens big as pie plates ... Yeh?

MR. HOMER: *(to JAIMIE PAUL)* Lie down, Jaimie Paul, an' have some more sleep. When you feel better, I'll get you some soup.

RITA JOE laughs. JAIMIE PAUL weaves his way uncertainly to where MR. HOMER stands.

JAIMIE: *(laughing)* I spit in your soup! You know what I say? ... I say I spit in your soup, Mister Homer ...

He comes to MR. HOMER and seems about to do just what he threatens.

MR. HOMER: *(pushing him away with good humour)* I'll spit in your eyeball if you don't shut up!

JAIMIE: *(breaking away from MR. HOMER, taunting)* You ... are not Mister Homer!

MR. HOMER: I'm not what?

JAIMIE: You're not Mister Homer ... You're somebody wearing his pants an' shirt ... *(stumbling away)* But you're not Mister Homer ... Mister Homer never gets mad ... No sir, not Mister Homer!

MR. HOMER: I'm not mad ... What're you talkin' about?

JAIMIE PAUL turns and approaches the YOUNG INDIAN MEN. He threatens to fall off the apron of the stage.

JAIMIE: No ... not Mister Homer! An' I got ten fingers ... How's that?

MR. HOMER: For Chris' sake, Jaimie ... go to sleep.

JAIMIE PAUL stops and scowls, then grins knowingly. He begins to mime a clumsy paddler paddling a boat.

JAIMIE: *(laughing again)* I know you ... Hey? I know you! ... I seen you up Rainbow Creek one time ... I seen you paddling!

He breaks up with laughter.

MR. HOMER: *(amused, tolerant)* Oh, come on ... I've never been to Rainbow Creek.

JAIMIE: *(controlling his laughter)* Sure you been to Rainbow Creek ... *(He begins to mime paddling again.)* Next time you need a good paddler, you see me. I have a governmen' job, but screw that. I'm gonna paddle! I seen you paddle ...

Again he breaks up in laughter as he once more demonstrates the quality of paddling he once saw.

RITA JOE is fully enjoying the spectacle. So are the YOUNG INDIAN MEN. MR. HOMER is also amused by the absurdity of the situation. JAIMIE PAUL turns, but chokes up with laughter after saying ...

JAIMIE: I have seen some paddlers ... but you!

JAIMIE PAUL turns and waves his hand derisively, laughing.

MR. HOMER: It must've been somebody else ... I've never been to Rainbow Creek.

JAIMIE: Like hell, you say!

JAIMIE PAUL paddles the soup wagon out. Guitar music comes in with an upbeat tempo. RITA JOE and the YOUNG INDIAN MEN dance to the beat. The YOUNG INDIAN MEN then drift after MR. HOMER.

The light fades slowly on centre stage and the music changes.

RITA JOE, happy in her memory, does a circling butch walk in the fading light to the song of the SINGER. At the conclusion of the song, she is on the apron, stage right, in a wash of light that includes the MAGISTRATE and the SINGER.

SINGER:
I woke up at six o'clock
Stumbled out of bed,

Crash of cans an' diesel trucks
Damned near killed me dead.

Sleepless hours, heavy nights,
Dream your dreams so pretty.
God was gonna have a laugh
An' gave me a job in the city!

RITA JOE is still elated at her memory of JAIMIE PAUL and his story. With unusual candour, she turns girlishly before the MAGISTRATE, and in mild imitation of her own moment of drunkenness, begins telling him a story.

Faint guitar music in the background continues.

RITA: One night I drank a little bit of wine, an' I was outside lookin' at the stars ... thinking ... when I was a little girl how much bigger the trees were ... no clouds, but suddenly there was a light that made the whole sky look like day ...

Guitar out.

RITA: ... just for a moment ... an' before I got used to the night ... I saw animals, moving across the sky ... two white horses ... A man was takin' them by the halters, and I knew the man was my grandfather ...

She stares at the MAGISTRATE, unsure of herself now.

MAGISTRATE: Yes! Is that all?

RITA: No ... But I never seen my grandfather alive, and I got so sad thinkin' about it I wanted to cry. I wasn't sure it was him, even ... *(She begins to laugh.)* I went an' telephoned the police and asked for the chief, but the chief was home and a guy asks what I want.

MAGISTRATE: *(mildly amused)* You ... called the police?

RITA: I told the guy I'd seen God, and he says, "Yeh? What would you like us to do about it?" An' I said, "Pray! Laugh! Shout!"

MAGISTRATE: Go on ...

RITA: He ... asked where I'd seen God, an' I told him in the sky. He says you better call this number ... It's the Air Force. They'll take care of it!

She laughs and the MAGISTRATE smiles.

RITA: I called the number the guy gave me, but it was nighttime and there was no answer! If God was to come at night, after office hours, then ...

A terrible awkwardness sets in. There is a harsh light on her. She turns away, aware that she is in captivity.

The MAGISTRATE stirs with discomfort.

RITA: *(with great fear)* How long will this be? Will I never be able to ...

MAGISTRATE: *(annoyed at himself, at her)* There is nothing here but a record of your convictions ... nothing to speak for you and provide me with any reason to moderate your sentence! What the hell am I supposed to do? Violate the law myself because I feel that somehow ... I've known and felt ... No! *(turning from her)* You give me no alternative ... no alternative at all!

The MAGISTRATE packs up his books.

RITA: I'll go home ... jus' let me go home. I can't get out of jail to find the highway ... or some kind of job!

MAGISTRATE: *(standing)* Prison and fines are not the only thing ... Have you, for instance, considered that you might be an incurable carrier? There are people like that ... They cannot come into contact with others without infecting them. They cannot eat from dishes others may use ... They cannot prepare or touch food others will eat ... The same with clothes, cars, hospital beds!

The MAGISTRATE exits.

RITA JOE shakes her head with disbelief. The idea of perpetual condemnation is beyond her comprehension. She falls to the floor. Guitar music is heard in the background.

She turns away from the MAGISTRATE and the light comes up over the ramp at the back of the stage. Another light comes up on centre stage left. Here, EILEEN JOE and the OLD WOMAN are miming clothes washing using a scrubbing board and placing the wash into woven baskets. The woman and the girl are on their knees, facing each other.

On the ramp above them, JAIMIE PAUL is struggling with a POLICEMAN who is scolding him softly for being drunk, abusive and noisy. JAIMIE PAUL is jocular; the POLICEMAN, harassed and worried. They slowly cross the ramp from stage left.

SINGER:
Four o'clock in the morning,
The sailor rides the ship
An' I ride the wind!

Eight o'clock in the morning,
My honey's scoldin' the sleepyheads
An' I'm scoldin' him.

JAIMIE: *(to the POLICEMAN)* On the Smoky River ... four o'clock in the morning ... Hey? There was nobody ... just me ... You know that?

POLICEMAN: No, I don't. Come on. Let's get you home.

JAIMIE PAUL moves forward and embraces the POLICEMAN.

JAIMIE: You wanna see something?

JAIMIE PAUL takes out a coin to do a trick.

OLD WOMAN: *(to EILEEN)* Your father's been very sick.

EILEEN: He won't eat nothing ...

OLD WOMAN: Jus' sits and worries ... That's no good.

JAIMIE PAUL: *(finishing his coin trick)* You like that one? Hey, we both work for the government, eh?

They exit laughing.

JAIMIE PAUL: Watch the rough stuff ... just don't make me mad.

OLD WOMAN: If Rita Joe was to come and see him ... maybe say goodbye to him ...

RITA: *(calling from her world to the world of her strongest fears)* But he's not dying! I saw him not so long ago ...

The women in her memory do not hear her. They continue discussing her father.

OLD WOMAN: He loved her an' always worried ...

RITA: I didn't know he was sick!

OLD WOMAN: You were smart to come back, Eileen Joe.

RITA: *(again calling over the distance of her soul)* Nobody told me!

SINGER:
Nine o'clock in the evening,
Moon is high in the blueberry sky
An' I'm lovin' you.

JAIMIE: *(now passing along the apron beside RITA JOE, talking to the POLICEMAN)* You seen where I live? Big house with a mongolia in front … Fancy place! You wanna see the room I got?

POLICEMAN: *(gruffly, aware that JAIMIE PAUL can become angry quickly)* When I get holidays, we'll take a tour of everything you've got … but I don't get holidays until September!

From the apron they cross upstage diagonally, between the OLD WOMAN with EILEEN, and RITA JOE.

JAIMIE: You're a good man … good for a laugh. I'm a good man … you know me!

POLICEMAN: Sure, you're first class when you're sober!

JAIMIE: I got a cousin in the city. He got his wife a stove an' washing machine! He's a good man … You know my cousin maybe?

Fading off. They leave the stage.

The OLD WOMAN has risen from her knees and wearily collected one basket of clothes. She climbs the ramp and moves to the wings, stage right. EILEEN is thoughtful and slower, but she also prepares her clothes wash and follows.

OLD WOMAN: Nothing in the city I can see … only if you're lucky. A good man who don't drink or play cards … that's all.

EILEEN: And if he's bad?

OLD WOMAN: Then leave him. I'm older than you, Eileen … I know what's best.

The OLD WOMAN exits. The guitar music dies out. JAIMIE PAUL's laughter and voice is heard offstage.

JAIMIE: *(offstage, loud, boisterous)* We both work for the gov'ment! We're buddies, no? … You think we're both the same?

Laughter. The lights on the ramp and centre stage die.

RITA: *(following JAIMIE PAUL's laughter)* Good or bad, what difference? So long as he's a livin' man!

RITA JOE and EILEEN giggle. The light spreads around her into pale infinity.

The TEACHER enters on the ramp. She rings a handbell and stops a short distance from the wings to peer around. She is a shy, inadequate woman who moves and behaves jerkily, the product of incomplete education and poor job placement.

TEACHER: *(in a scolding voice)* Rita! Rita Joe!

The bell rings.

TEACHER: The class is waiting for you. The class is always waiting.

RITA JOE is startled to hear the bell and see the woman. She comes to her feet, now a child before the TEACHER, and runs to join EILEEN. JAIMIE PAUL and YOUNG INDIAN MEN have entered with the bell and sit cross-legged on the floor as school children.

RITA: The sun is in my skin, Miss Donohue. The leaves is red and orange, and the wind stopped blowin' an hour ago.

The TEACHER has stopped to listen to this. RITA JOE and EILEEN, late again, slip into class and sit on the floor with the others.

TEACHER: Rita! What is a noun?

No answer. The kids poke RITA JOE to stand up.

TEACHER: Did you hear what I asked?

RITA: *(uncertain)* No … yes?

TEACHER: There's a lot you don't know … That kind of behaviour is exhibitionism! We are a melting pot!

RITA: A melting pot?

TEACHER: A melting pot! Do you know what a melting pot is?

RITA: It's … *(She shrugs.)* … a melting pot!

The class laughs.

TEACHER: Precisely! You put copper and tin into a melting pot and out comes bronze … It's the same with people!

RITA: Yes, Miss Donohue … out comes bronze …

Laughter again. The TEACHER calls RITA JOE over to her. The light fades on the other children.

TEACHER: Rita, what was it I said to you this morning?

RITA: You said … wash my neck, clean my fingernails …

TEACHER: (cagey) No, it wasn't, Rita!

RITA: I can't remember. It was long ago.

TEACHER: Try to remember, Rita.

RITA: I don't remember, Miss Donohue! I was thinkin' about you last night, thinkin' if you knew some …

TEACHER: You are straying off the topic! Never stray off the topic!

RITA: It was a dream, but now I'm scared, Miss Donohue. I've been a long time moving about … trying to find something! … I must've lost …

TEACHER: No, Rita. That is not important.

RITA: Not important?

TEACHER: No, Rita … Now you repeat after me like I said or I'm going to have to pass you by again. Say after me …

RITA: Sure. Say after you …

TEACHER: Say after me … "A book of verse underneath the spreading bough … "

RITA: "A book of verse underneath the spreading bough … "

TEACHER: "A jug of wine, a loaf of bread and thou beside me … singing in the wilderness."

RITA: (the child spell broken, she laughs bawdily) Jaimie said, "To heck with the wine an' loaf … Let's have some more of this here thou!"

Her laughter dies. She wipes her lips, as if trying to erase some stain there.

TEACHER: (peevish) Alright, Rita … Alright, let's have none of that!

RITA: (plaintively) I'm sorry, Miss Donohue … I'm sure sorry!

TEACHER: That's alright.

RITA: I'm sorry!

TEACHER: Alright …

RITA: Sorry …

TEACHER: You will never make bronze! Coming from nowhere and going no place! Who am I to change that?

RITA JOE grips the edge of the desk with both hands, holding on tightly.

RITA: No! They said for me to stay here, to learn something!

TEACHER: (with exasperation) I tried to teach you, but your head was in the clouds, and as for your body … Well! I wouldn't even think what I know you do!

The TEACHER crosses amongst the other children.

RITA: I'm sorry … please! Let me say it after you again … (blurting it out) "A book of verse underneath the spreading … "

TEACHER: Arguing … always trying to upset me … and in grade four … I saw it then … pawing the ground for men like a bitch in heat!

RITA: (dismayed) It … isn't so!

TEACHER: You think I don't know? I'm not blind … I can see out of the windows.

The TEACHER marches off into the wings and the class runs after her leaving RITA JOE alone onstage.

RITA: That's a lie! For God's sake, tell the judge I have a good character … I am clean an' honest … Everything you said is right, I'm never gonna argue again … I believe in God … an' I'm from the country and lost like hell! Tell him!

She shakes her head sadly, knowing the extent of her betrayal.

RITA: They only give me eight hours to find somebody who knows me … An' seven and a half hours is gone already!

The light on the scene dies.

SINGER: (recitivo)
Things that were …
Life that might have been …

A pale backlight on the back of the ramp comes up. Recorded sounds of crickets and the distant sound of a train whistle are heard.

RITA JOE's FATHER and JAIMIE PAUL enter on the ramp from stage left. The FATHER leads the way.

JAIMIE PAUL is behind, rolling a cigarette. They walk slowly, thoughtfully, following the ramp across and downstage. RITA JOE stands separate, watching.

SINGER:
The blue evening of the first
Warm day
Is the last evening.
There'll not be another
Like it.

JAIMIE: No more handouts, David Joe ... We can pick an' can the berries ourselves.

FATHER: We need money to start a cooperative like that.

JAIMIE: Then some other way!

The old man listens, standing still, to the sounds of the train and the night.

FATHER: You're a young man, Jaimie Paul ... young an' angry. It's not good to be that angry.

JAIMIE: We're gonna work an' live like people ... not be afraid all the time ... stop listening to an old priest an' Indian Department guys who're working for a pension!

FATHER: You're a young man, Jaimie Paul ...

JAIMIE: I say stop listening, David Joe! ... In the city they never learned my name. It was "Hey, fella" ... or "You, boy" ... that kind of stuff.

Pause. The sound of the train whistle is heard.

FATHER: A beautiful night, Jaimie Paul.

JAIMIE: We can make some money. The berries are good this year!

JAIMIE PAUL is restless, edgy, particularly on the train whistle sound.

FATHER: Sometimes ... children ... you remember every day with them ... Never forget you are alive with children.

JAIMIE PAUL turns away and begins to retrace his steps.

JAIMIE: You want us all to leave an' go to the city? Is that what you want?

The FATHER shakes his head. He does not wish for this, but the generation spread between them is great now. JAIMIE PAUL walks away with a gesture of contempt.

The sounds die. The light dies and isolates the FATHER and RITA JOE.

RITA: You were sick, an' now you're well.

FATHER: *(in measured speech, turning away from RITA JOE, as if carefully recalling something of great importance)* You left your father, Rita Joe ... never wrote Eileen a letter that time ... Your father was pretty sick man that time ... pretty sick man ... June ninth he got the cold, an' on June twenty he ...

RITA: But you're alive! I had such crazy dreams I'd wake up laughing at myself!

FATHER: I have dreams too ...

RITA JOE moves forward to him. She stops talking to him, as if communicating thoughts rather than words. He remains standing where he is, facing away from her.

RITA: I was in a big city ... so many streets I'd get lost like nothin' ... When you got sick I was on a job ...

FATHER: June ninth I got the cold ...

RITA: Good job in a tire store ... Jaimie Paul's got a job with the government, you know?

FATHER: Pretty sick man, that time ...

RITA: A good job in a tire store. They was gonna teach me how to file statements after I learned the telephone. Bus ticket home was twenty dollars ... But I got drunk all the same when I heard an' I went in and tried to work that day ... *(smiling and shaking her head)* Boy, I tried to work! Some day that was!

FATHER: I have dreams ... Sometimes I'm scared ...

They finally look at each other.

RITA: *(shuddering)* I'm so cold ...

FATHER: Long dreams ... I dream about Rita Joe ... *(sadly)* Have to get better. I've lived longer, but I know nothing ... nothing at all. Only the old stories.

RITA JOE moves sideways to him. She is smiling happily.

RITA: When I was little, a man came out of the bush to see you. Tell me why again!

The FATHER hesitates, shaking his head, but he is also smiling. The light of their separate yearnings fades out and the front of the stage is lit with the two of them together. The FATHER turns and comes forward to meet her.

FATHER: You don't want to hear that story again.

He sits on the slight elevation of the stage apron. RITA JOE sits down in front of him and snuggles between his knees. He leans forward over her.

RITA: It's the best story I ever heard!

FATHER: You were a little girl ... four years old already ... an' Eileen was getting big inside your mother. One day it was hot ... sure was hot. Too hot to try an' fish in the lake, because the fish was down deep where the water was cold.

RITA: The dog started to bark ...

FATHER: The dog started to bark ... How!

FATHER and RITA: *(in unison)* How! How! How!

FATHER: Barking to beat hell an' I says to myself why ... on such a hot day? Then I see the bushes moving ... somebody was coming to see us. Your mother said from inside the house, "What's the matter with that dog?" An' I says to her, "Somebody coming to see me." It was big Sandy Collins, who ran the sawmill back of the reserve. Business was bad for big Sandy then ... but he comes out of that bush like he was being chased ... his clothes all wet an' stickin' to him ... his cap in his hands, an' his face black with the heat and dirt from hard work ... He says to me, "My little Millie got a cough last night an' today she's dead." ... "She's dead," big Sandy says to me. I says to him, "I'm sorry to hear that, Sandy. Millie is the same age as my Rita." And he says to me, "David Joe ... look, you got another kid coming ... won't make much difference to you ... Sell me Rita Joe like she is for a thousand dollars!"

RITA JOE giggles. The FATHER raises his hand to silence her.

FATHER: "A thousand dollars is a lot of money, Sandy," I says to him ... "Lots of money. You got to cut a lot of timber for a thousand dollars." Then he says to me, "Not a thousand cash at once, David Joe. First I give you two hundred fifty dollars ... When Rita Joe comes ten years old and she's still alright, I give you the next two hundred

fifty ... An' if she don't die by fifteen, I guarantee you five hundred dollars cash at once!"

RITA JOE and the FATHER break into laughter. He reaches around her throat and draws her close.

FATHER: So you see, Rita Joe, you lose me one thousand dollars from big Sandy Collins!

They continue laughing.

A harsh light on the MAGISTRATE, who enters and stands on his podium.

MAGISTRATE: Rita Joe, when was the last time you had dental treatment?

RITA JOE covers her ears, refusing to surrender this moment of security in the arms of her FATHER.

RITA: I can't hear you!

MAGISTRATE: *(loudly)* You had your teeth fixed ever?

RITA: *(coming to her feet and turning on him)* Leave me alone!

MAGISTRATE: Have you had your lungs X-rayed recently?

RITA: I was hungry, that's all!

MAGISTRATE: *(becoming staccato, machine-like in his questions)* When was your last Wasserman taken?

RITA: What's that?

RITA JOE hears the TEACHER's voice. She turns to see the approaching TEACHER give the MAGIS-TRATE testimony. The stage is lit in a cold blue light now.

TEACHER: *(crisply to the MAGISTRATE as she approaches, her monologue a reading)* Dear Sir ... In reply to your letter of the twelfth, I cannot in all sincerity provide a reference of good character for one Rita Joe ...

The WITNESSES do not see her and the testimony takes on the air of a nightmare for RITA JOE. She is baffled and afraid. The TEACHER continues to quietly repeat her testimony. RITA JOE appeals to the MAGISTRATE.

RITA: Why am I here? What've I done?

MAGISTRATE: You are charged with prostitution.

Her FATHER stands and crosses upstage to the ramp to observe. He is joined by EILEEN JOE, the OLD WOMAN and the PRIEST. MR. HOMER approaches briskly from stage left.

MR. HOMER: She'd been drinking when she comes into the centre ... Nothing wrong in that I could see, 'specially on a Friday night. So I give her some soup an' a sandwich. Then all of a sudden in the middle of a silly argument, she goes haywire ... an' I see her comin' at me ... I'll tell you, I was scared! I don't know Indian women that well!

MAGISTRATE: Assault!

RITA JOE retreats from him. The TEACHER and MR. HOMER now stand before the MAGISTRATE as if they were frozen. MR. HOMER repeats his testimony under the main dialogue. JAIMIE PAUL staggers in from stage right, over the ramp, heading to the wings of lower stage left.

JAIMIE: *(to himself)* What the hell are they doing?

RITA: *(running to him)* Say a good word for me, Jaimie!

JAIMIE: They fired me yesterday ... What the hell's the use of living?

JAIMIE PAUL leaves the stage as the SCHOOL BOARD CLERK enters to offer further testimony to the MAGISTRATE.

SCHOOL BOARD CLERK: I recommended in a letter that she take school after grade five through correspondence courses from the Department of Education ... but she never replied to the form letter the school division sent her ...

RITA: *(defending herself to the MAGISTRATE)* That drunken bastard Mahoney used it to light fire in his store ... He'd never tell Indians when mail came for us!

SCHOOL BOARD CLERK: I repeat ... I wish our position understood most clearly ... No reply was ever received in this office to the letter we sent Rita Joe!

RITA: One letter ... one letter for a lifetime?

TEACHER: Say after me! "I wandered lonely as a cloud, that floats on high o'er vales and hills ... When all at once I saw a crowd ... a melting pot ... "

A POLICEMAN and a MALE WITNESS enter. The PRIEST crosses downstage. The testimonies are becoming a nightmare babble.

RITA JOE is stung, stumbling backward from all of them as they face the MAGISTRATE with their condemnations.

POLICEMAN: We were impersonating two deck-hands ...

The PRIEST is passing by RITA JOE. He makes the sign of the cross and offers comfort in a thin voice, lost in the noise.

PRIEST: Be patient, Rita ... The young are always stormy, but in time, your understanding will deepen ... There is an end to all things.

WITNESS: I gave her a job, but she was kind of slow ... I can't wait around, there's lots of white people goin' lookin' for work ... so I figure, to hell with this noise ...

MAGISTRATE: *(loudly over the voices)* Have your ears ached?

RITA: No!

MAGISTRATE: Have you any boils on your back? Any discharge? When did you bathe last?

The MURDERERS appear and circle RITA JOE.

MAGISTRATE: Answer me! Drunkenness! Shop-lifting! Assault! Prostitution, prostitution, prostitution!

RITA: *(her voice shrill, cutting over the babble)* I don't know what happened ... but you got to listen to me and believe me, mister!

The babble ceases abruptly. RITA JOE pleads with them as best she knows.

RITA: You got rules here that was made before I was born ... I was hungry when I stole something ... an' I was hollerin' I was so lonely when I started whoring ...

The MURDERERS come closer.

MAGISTRATE: Rita Joe ... has a doctor examined you? ... I mean, really examined you? Rita Joe ... you might be carrying and transmitting some disease and not aware of it!

RITA: *(breaking away from the MURDERERS)* Bastards! *(to the MAGISTRATE)* Put me in jail ... I don't care ... I'll sign anything. I'm so goddamn hungry I'm sick ... Whatever it is, I'm guilty!

She clutches her head and goes down in a squat of defeat.

MAGISTRATE: Are you free of venereal disease?

RITA: I don't know. I'm not sick that way.

MAGISTRATE: How can you tell?

RITA: *(lifting her face to him)* I know ... A woman knows them things ...

Pause.

MAGISTRATE: Thirty days!

The POLICEMAN leads RITA JOE off and the house lights come up. The ACTORS and the SINGER walk off the stage, leaving emptiness as at the opening of the act.

ACT TWO

The house lights dim. A POLICEMAN brings RITA JOE in downstage centre. She curls up in her jail cell and sleeps. RITA JOE's FATHER enters on the ramp and crosses down to the audience.

The stage worklights die down. Lights isolate RITA JOE's FATHER. Another light with prison bar shadows isolates RITA JOE in her area of the stage.

FATHER: *(looking down on RITA JOE)* I see no way ... no way ... It's not clear like trees against snow ... not clear at all ...

To the audience.

FATHER: But when I was fifteen years old, I leave the reserve to work on a threshing crew. They pay a dollar a day for a good man ... an' I was a good strong man. The first time I got work there was a girl about as old as I ... She'd come out in the yard an' watch the men working at the threshing machine. She had eyes that were the biggest I ever seen ... like fifty-cent pieces ... an' there was always a flock of geese around her. Whenever I see her I feel good. She used to stand an' watch me, an' the geese made a helluva lot of noise. One time I got off my rick an' went to get a drink of water ... but I walked close to where she was watching me. She backed away, and then ran from me with the geese chasin' after her,

their wings out an' their feet no longer touching the ground ... They were white geese ... The last time Rita Joe come home to see us ... the last time she ever come home ... I watched her leave ... and I seen geese running after Rita Joe the same way ... white geese ... with their wings out an' their feet no longer touching the ground. And I remembered it all, an' my heart got so heavy I wanted to cry ...

The light fades to darkness on the FATHER, as he exits up the ramp and off. RITA JOE wakes from her dream, cold, shaking, desperate.

SINGER:
The blue evening of the
First warm day
Is the last evening.
There'll not be another
Like it.

The PRIEST enters from darkness with the POLICEMAN. He is dressed in a dark suit which needs pressing. He stops in half shadow outside RITA JOE's prison light.

The scene between them is played out in the manner of two country people meeting in a time of crisis. Their thoughts come slowly, incompletely. There is both fear and helplessness in both characters.

PRIEST: I came twice before they'd let me see you ...

RITA JOE jumps to her feet. She smiles at him.

RITA: Oh, Father Andrew!

PRIEST: Even so, I had to wait an hour.

A long pause. He clumsily takes out a package of cigarettes and matches from his pocket and hands them to her, aware that he is possibly breaking a prison regulation.

PRIEST: I'm sorry about this, Rita.

RITA JOE tears the package open greedily and lights a cigarette. She draws on it with animal satisfaction.

RITA: I don't know what's happening, Father Andrew.

PRIEST: They're not ... hurting you here?

RITA: No.

PRIEST: I could make an appointment with the warden if there was something ...

RITA: What's it like outside? ... Is it a nice day outside? I heard it raining last night ... Was it raining?

PRIEST: It rains a lot here ...

RITA: When I was a kid, there was leaves an' a river ... Jaimie Paul told me once that maybe we never see those things again.

A long pause. The PRIEST struggles with himself.

PRIEST: I've never been inside a jail before ... They told me there was a chapel ...

He points indefinitely back.

RITA: What's gonna happen to me? ... That judge sure got sore ...

She laughs.

PRIEST: *(with disgust, yet unsure of himself)* Prostitution this time?

RITA: I guess so ...

PRIEST: You know how I feel ... City is no place for you ... nor for me ... I've spent my life in the same surroundings as your father!

RITA: Sure ... but you had God on your side!

She smiles mischievously. The PRIEST angers.

PRIEST: Rita, try to understand ... Our Lord Jesus once met a woman such as you beside the well ... He forgave her!

RITA: I don't think God hears me here ... Nobody hears me now, nobody except cops an' pimps an' bootleggers!

PRIEST: I'm here. I was there when you were born.

RITA: You've told me lots of times ... I was thinkin' about my mother last night ... She died young ... I'm older than she was ...

PRIEST: Your mother was a good, hard-working woman. She was happy ...

A pause between them.

RITA: There was frost on the street at five o'clock Tuesday morning when they arrested me ... Last night I remembered things flyin' and kids runnin' past me trying to catch a chocolate wrapper that's blowin' in the wind ... *(She presses her hands against her bosom.)* It hurts me here to think about them things!

PRIEST: I worry about you ... Your father worries too ... I baptized you ... I watched you and Leenie grow into women!

RITA: Yes ... I seen God in what you said ... in your clothes! In your hair!

PRIEST: But you're not the woman I expected you to be ... Your pride, Rita ... your pride ... may bar you from heaven.

RITA: *(mocking him)* They got rules there too ... in heaven?

PRIEST: *(angry)* Rita! ... I'm not blind ... I can see! I'm not deaf ... I know all about you! So does God!

RITA: My uncle was Dan Joe ... He was dyin' and he said to me, "Long ago the white man come with Bibles to talk to my people, who had the land. They talk for hundred years ... then we had all the Bibles, an' the white man had our land ...

PRIEST: Don't blame the Church! We are trying to help ...

RITA: *(with passion)* How? I'm looking for the door ...

PRIEST: *(tortured now)* I ... will hear your confession ...

RITA: But I want to be free!

PRIEST: *(stiffly)* We learn through suffering, Rita Joe ... We will only be free if we become humble again. *(Pause.)* Will you confess, Rita Joe? *(A long pause.)* I'm going back on the four o'clock bus. *(He begins walking away into the gloom.)* I'll tell your father I saw you, and you looked well.

He is suddenly relieved.

RITA: *(after him as he leaves)* You go to hell!

The PRIEST turns sharply.

RITA: Go tell your God ... when you see him ... tell him about Rita Joe an' what they done to her! Tell him about yourself too! ... That you were not good enough for me, but that didn't stop you tryin'! Tell him that!

The PRIEST hurries away. Guitar in. RITA JOE sits down, brooding.

SINGER:
I will give you the wind and a sense of wonder
As the child by the river, the reedy river.
I will give you the sky wounded by thunder
And a leaf on the river, the silver river.

A light comes up on the ramp where JAIMIE PAUL appears, smiling and waving to her.

JAIMIE: *(shouting)* Rita Joe! I'm gonna take you dancing after work Friday … That job's gonna be alright!

RITA JOE springs to her feet, elated.

RITA: Put me back in jail so I can be free on Friday!

A sudden burst of dance music. The stage lights up and JAIMIE PAUL approaches her. They dance together, remaining close downstage centre.

SINGER:
Round an' round the cenotaph,
The clumsy seagulls play.
Fed by funny men with hats
Who watch them night and day.

Sleepless hours, heavy nights,
Dream your dreams so pretty.
God was gonna have a laugh
An' gave me a job in the city!

The music continues for the interlude.

Some YOUNG INDIAN MEN run onto the stage along the ramp and join JAIMIE PAUL and RITA JOE in their dance. The MURDERERS enter and elbow into the group, their attention specifically menacing towards JAIMIE PAUL and RITA JOE. A street brawl begins as a POLICEMAN passes through on his beat. The MURDERERS leave hastily.

I woke up at six o'clock,
Stumbled out of bed.
Crash of steel and diesel trucks
Damned near killed me dead.

Sleepless hours, heavy nights,
Dream your dreams so pretty.
God was gonna have a laugh
An' gave me a job in the city!

Musical interlude. RITA JOE and JAIMIE PAUL continue dancing languidly. The YOUNG INDIAN MEN exit.

I've polished floors an' cut the trees,
Fished and stooked the wheat.
Now "Hallelujah, Praise the Lord,"
I sing before I eat!

Sleepless hours, heavy nights,
Dream your dreams so pretty.
God was gonna have a laugh
An' gave me a job in the city!

Musical interlude.

The music dies as the YOUNG INDIAN MEN wheel in a brass bed, circle it around and exit. The stage darkens except for a pool of light where RITA JOE and JAIMIE PAUL stand, embracing. JAIMIE PAUL takes her hand and leads her away.

JAIMIE: Come on, Rita Joe … you're slow.

RITA: *(happy in her memories, not wishing to forget too soon, hesitating)* How much rent … for a place where you can keep babies?

JAIMIE: I don't know … maybe eighty dollars a month.

RITA: That's a lot of money.

JAIMIE: It costs a buck to go dancin' even …

They walk slowly along the apron to stage left, as if following a street to JAIMIE PAUL's rooming house.

JAIMIE: It's a good place … I got a sink in the room. Costs seven bucks a week, that's all!

RITA: That's good … I only got a bed in my place …

JAIMIE: I seen Mickey an' Steve Laporte last night.

RITA: How are they?

JAIMIE: Good … We're goin' to a beer parlour Monday night when I get paid … the same beer parlour they threw Steve out of! Only now there's three of us goin' in!

They arrive at and enter his room. A spot illuminates the bed near the wings of stage left. It is old, dilapidated. JAIMIE PAUL and RITA JOE enter the area of light around the bed. He is aware that the room is more drab than he would wish it.

JAIMIE: How do you like it … I like it!

RITA: *(examining room critically)* It's … smaller than my place.

JAIMIE: Sit down.

She sits on the edge of the bed and falls backward into a springless hollow. He laughs nervously. He is awkward and confused. The ease they shared walking to his place is now constricted.

JAIMIE: I was gonna get some grub today, but I was busy … Here …

He takes a chocolate bar out of his shirt pocket and offers it to her. She opens it, breaks off a small piece, and gives the remainder to him. He closes the wrapper and replaces the bar in his pocket. She eats ravenously. He walks around the bed nervously.

JAIMIE: No fat d.p.'s gonna throw me or the boys out of that beer parlour or he's gonna get this!

He holds up a fist in a gesture that is both poignant and futile. She laughs and he glowers at her.

JAIMIE: I'm tellin' you!

RITA: If they want to throw you out, they'll throw you out.

JAIMIE: Well, this is one Indian guy they're not pushing around no more!

RITA: God helps them who help themselves.

JAIMIE: That's right! *(laughing)* I was lookin' at the white shirts in Eaton's and this bugger comes an' says to me, you gonna buy or you gonna look all day?

RITA: *(looking around her)* It's a nice room for a guy, I guess …

JAIMIE: It's a lousy room!

RITA JOE lies back lengthwise in the bed. JAIMIE PAUL sits on the bed beside her.

RITA: You need a good job to have babies in the city … Clara Hill gave both her kids away they say …

JAIMIE: Where do kids like that go?

RITA: Foster homes, I guess.

JAIMIE: If somebody don't like the kid, back they go to another foster home?

RITA: I guess so … Clara Hill don't know where her kids are now.

JAIMIE: *(twisting sharply in his anger)* Goddamn it!

RITA: My father says …

JAIMIE PAUL rises, crosses round the bed to the other side.

JAIMIE: *(harshly)* I don't want to hear what your father got to say! He's like … like the kind of Indian a white man likes! He's gonna look wise and wait forever … for what? For the kids they take away to come back?

RITA: He's scared … I'm scared … We're all scared, Jaimie Paul.

JAIMIE PAUL lies face down and mimes a gun through the bars.

JAIMIE: Sometimes I feel like takin' a gun and just …

He waves his hand as if to liquidate his environment and all that bedevils him. He turns over on his back and lies beside RITA JOE

JAIMIE: I don't know … Goddamnit, I don't know what to do. I get mad an' then I don't know what I'm doing or thinkin' … I get scared sometimes, Rita Joe.

RITA: *(tenderly)* We're scared … everybody …

JAIMIE: I'm scared of dyin' … in the city. They don't care for one another here … You got to be smart or have a good job to live like that.

RITA: Clara Hill's gonna have another baby …

JAIMIE: I can't live like that … A man don't count for much here … Women can do as much as a man … There's no difference between men and women. I can't live like that.

RITA: You got to stop worrying, Jaimie Paul. You're gonna get sick worryin'.

JAIMIE: You can't live like that, can you?

RITA: No.

JAIMIE: I can't figure out what the hell they want from us!

RITA: *(laughing)* Last time I was in trouble, the judge was asking me what I wanted from him! I could've told him, but I didn't!

They both laugh. JAIMIE PAUL becomes playful and happy.

JAIMIE: Last night I seen television in a store window. I seen a guy on television showing this knife that cuts everything it's so sharp ... He was cutting up good shoes like they were potatoes ... That was sure funny to see!

Again they laugh in merriment at the idea of such a demonstration. JAIMIE PAUL continues with his story, gesturing with his hands.

JAIMIE: Chop ... chop ... chop ... A potful of shoes in no time! What's a guy gonna do with a potful of shoes? Cook them?

They continue laughing and lie together again. Then JAIMIE PAUL sobers. He rises from the bed and walks around it. He offers his hand to RITA JOE, who also rises.

JAIMIE: *(drily)* Come on. This is a lousy room!

SINGER: *(reprise)*
God was gonna have a laugh,
And gave me a job in the city!

The light goes down on RITA JOE and JAIMIE PAUL. The YOUNG INDIAN MEN clear the bed. Cross fade to the rear ramp of the stage. RITA JOE's FATHER and the PRIEST enter and cross the stage.

PRIEST: She got out yesterday, but she wouldn't let me see her. I stayed an extra day, but she wouldn't see me.

FATHER: *(sadly)* I must go once more to the city ... I must go to see them.

PRIEST: You're an old man ... I wish I could persuade you not to go.

FATHER: You wouldn't say that if you had children, Andrew ...

The lights go down on them.

The lights come up downstage centre. Three YOUNG INDIAN MEN precede MR. HOMER, carrying a table between them. MR. HOMER follows with a hamper of clothes under his arm.

MR. HOMER: Yeh ... right about there is fine, boys. Got to get the clutter out of the basement ... There's mice coming in to beat hell.

MR. HOMER empties the clothes hamper on the table. The YOUNG INDIAN MEN step aside and converse in an undertone.

On the ramp, a YOUNG INDIAN MAN weaves his way from stage left and down to centre stage where the others have brought the table. He is followed by JAIMIE PAUL and RITA JOE, who mime his intoxicated progress.

MR. HOMER: *(speaking to the audience)* The Society for Aid to the Indians sent a guy over to see if I could recommend someone who'd been ... well, through the mill, like they say ... an' then smartened up an' taken rehabilitation. The guy said they just wanted a rehabilitated Indian to show up at their annual dinner. No speeches or fancy stuff ... just be there.

The YOUNG INDIAN MAN lies down carefully to one side of MR. HOMER.

MR. HOMER: Hi, Louie. Not that I would cross the street for the Society ... They're nothing but a pack of do-gooders out to get their name in the papers ...

The YOUNG INDIAN MAN begins to sing a tuneless song, trailing off into silence.

MR. HOMER: Keep it down, eh, Louie? I couldn't think of anybody to suggest to this guy ... so he went away pretty sore ...

RITA JOE begins to rummage through the clothes on the table. She looks at sweaters and holds a red one thoughtfully in her hands. JAIMIE PAUL is in conversation with the YOUNG INDIAN MEN to one side of the table. MR. HOMER turns from the audience to see RITA JOE holding the sweater.

MR. HOMER: Try it on, Rita Joe ... That's what the stuff's here for.

JAIMIE PAUL turns. He is in a provocative mood, seething with rebellion that makes the humour he triggers both biting and deceptively innocent. The YOUNG INDIAN MEN respond to him with strong laughter. JAIMIE PAUL takes a play punch at one of them.

JAIMIE: Whoops! Scared you, eh?

He glances back at MR. HOMER, as if talking to him.

JAIMIE: Can't take it, eh? The priest can't take it. Indian Department guys can't take it ... Why listen to them? Listen to the radio if you want to hear something.

The YOUNG INDIAN MEN laugh.

JAIMIE: Or listen to me! You think I'm smart?

YOUNG INDIAN MAN: You're a smart man, Jaimie Paul.

JAIMIE: Naw ... I'm not smart ... *(pointing to another YOUNG INDIAN MAN)* This guy here ... calls himself squaw-humper ... he's smart! ... Him ... he buys extra big shirts ... more cloth for the same money ... That's smart! *(laughter)* I'm not smart. *(seriously)* You figure we can start a business an' be our own boss?

YOUNG INDIAN MAN: I don't know about that ...

JAIMIE PAUL leaves them and goes to lean over the YOUNG INDIAN MAN who is now asleep on the floor.

JAIMIE: Buy a taxi ... be our own boss ...

He shakes the sleeping YOUNG INDIAN MAN, who immediately begins his tuneless song.

JAIMIE: Aw, he's drunk

JAIMIE PAUL goes over to the table and stares at the YOUNG INDIAN MAN beyond the table.

JAIMIE: *(soberly)* Buy everything we need ... Don't be bums! Bums need grub an' clothes ... Bums is bad for the country, right Mr. Homer?

MR. HOMER: *(nodding)* I guess so ... *(to RITA JOE who is now wearing the old sweater)* Red looks good on you, Rita Joe ... Take it!

JAIMIE PAUL goes over and embraces RITA JOE, then pushes her gently away.

JAIMIE: She looks better in yellow. I never seen a red dandelion before.

He and the YOUNG INDIAN MEN laugh, but the laughter is hollow.

MR. HOMER: Come on, Jaimie! Leave the girl alone. That's what it's here for ... Are you working?

JAIMIE: *(evasive, needling)* Yeh! ... No! ... "Can you drive?" the guy says to me. "Sure, I can drive," I says to him. "Okay," he says, "then drive this broom until the warehouse is clean."

They all laugh.

MR. HOMER: That's a good one ... Jaimie, you're a card ... Well, time to get some food for you lot ...

MR. HOMER leaves. RITA JOE feels better about the sweater. She looks to one of the YOUNG INDIAN MEN for approval. JAIMIE PAUL becomes grim-faced.

RITA: Do you like it?

YOUNG INDIAN MAN: Sure. It's a nice sweater ... Take it.

JAIMIE: Take it where? Take it to hell ... Be men! *(pointing after MR. HOMER)* He's got no kids ... Guys like that get mean when they got no kids ... We're his kids an' he means to keep it that way! Well, I'm a big boy now! *(to RITA JOE)* I go to the employment office. I want work an' I want it now. "I'm not a goddamned cripple," I says to him. An' he says he can only take my name! If work comes he'll call me! "What the hell is this," I says to him. "I'll never get work like that ... There's no telephone in the house where I got a room!"

MR. HOMER returns pushing a wheeled tray on which he has some food for sandwiches, a loaf of bread and a large cutting knife. He begins to make some sandwiches.

RITA: *(scolding JAIMIE PAUL)* You won't get work talking that way, Jaimie Paul!

JAIMIE: Why not? I'm not scared. He gets mad at me an' I say to him ... "You think I'm some stupid Indian you're talkin' to? Heh? You think that?"

JAIMIE PAUL struts and swaggers to demonstrate how he faced his opponent at the employment office.

MR. HOMER: *(cutting bread)* You're a tough man to cross, Jaimie Paul.

JAIMIE: *(ignoring MR. HOMER, to the YOUNG INDIAN MEN)* Boy, I showed that bastard who he was talkin' to!

RITA: Did you get the job?

JAIMIE: *(turning to her, laughing boyishly)* No! He called the cops an' they threw me out!

They all laugh. The YOUNG INDIAN MEN go to the table now and rummage through the clothes.

MR. HOMER: Take whatever you want, boys … there's more clothes comin' tomorrow.

JAIMIE PAUL impulsively moves to the table where the YOUNG INDIAN MEN are fingering the clothes. He pushes them aside and shoves the clothes in a heap leaving a small corner of the table clean. He takes out two coins from his pockets and spits in his hands.

JAIMIE: I got a new trick … Come on, Mister Homer … I'll show you! See this!

He shows the coins, then slams his hands palms down on the table.

JAIMIE: Which hand got the coins?

MR. HOMER: Why … one under each hand …

JAIMIE: Right! *(turning up his hands)* Again? *(He collects the coins and slaps his hands down again.)* Where are the coins now? Come on, guess!

MR. HOMER is confident now, and points to the right hand with his cutting knife. JAIMIE PAUL laughs and lifts his hands. The coins are under his left hand.

MR. HOMER: Son of a gun.

JAIMIE: You're a smart man.

He puts the coins in his pockets and, laughing, turns to RITA JOE who stands uncertainly, dressed in the red sweater. She likes the garment, but she is aware JAIMIE PAUL might resent her taking it. The YOUNG INDIAN MEN again move to the table, and MR. HOMER returns to making sandwiches.

MR. HOMER: There's a good pair of socks might come in handy for one of you guys!

A YOUNG INDIAN MAN pokes his thumbs through the holes in the socks, and laughs.

JAIMIE: Sure … take the socks! Take the table!

He slaps the table with his hands and laughs.

JAIMIE: Take Mister Homer cutting bread! Take everything!

MR. HOMER: Hey, Jaimie!

JAIMIE: Why not? There's more comin' tomorrow, you said!

RITA: Jaimie!

MR. HOMER: You're sure in a smart-assed mood today, aren't you?

JAIMIE: *(pointing to the YOUNG INDIAN MAN with the socks, but talking to MR. HOMER)* Mister, friend Steve over there laughs lots … He figures … the way to get along an' live is to grab his guts an' laugh at anything anybody says. You see him laughing all the time. A dog barks at him an' he laughs … *(laughter from the YOUNG INDIAN MAN)* Laughs at a fence post fallin' … *(laughter)* Kids with funny eyes make him go haywire … *(laughter)* Can of meat an' no can opener …

MR. HOMER watches the YOUNG INDIAN MEN and grins at JAIMIE PAUL.

MR. HOMER: Yeh … he laughs quite a bit …

JAIMIE: He laughs at a rusty nail … Nice guy … laughs all the time.

MR. HOMER: *(to JAIMIE PAUL, holding the knife)* You wanted mustard on your bread or just plain?

JAIMIE: I seen him cut his hand and start laughin' … isn't that funny?

The YOUNG INDIAN MEN laugh, but with less humour now.

MR. HOMER: *(to JAIMIE PAUL)* You want mustard? … I'm talkin' to you!

JAIMIE: I'm not hungry.

The YOUNG INDIAN MEN stop laughing altogether. They become tense and suspicious of JAIMIE PAUL, who is watching them severely.

MR. HOMER: Suit yourself. Rita?

She shakes her head slowly, her gaze on JAIMIE PAUL's face.

RITA: I'm not hungry.

MR. HOMER looks from RITA JOE to JAIMIE PAUL, then to the YOUNG INDIAN MEN. His manner stiffens.

MR. HOMER: I see …

JAIMIE PAUL and RITA JOE touch hands and come forward to sit on the apron of the stage, front. A pale light is on the two of them. The stage lights behind them fade. A low light that is diffused and shadowy remains on the table where

MR. HOMER has prepared the food. The YOUNG INDIAN MEN move slowly to the table and begin eating the sandwiches MR. HOMER offers to them. The light on the table fades very low. JAIMIE PAUL hands a cigarette to RITA JOE and they smoke.

Light comes up over the rear ramp. RITA JOE's FATHER enters onto the ramp from the wings of stage right. His step is resolute. The PRIEST follows behind him a few paces. They have been arguing. Both are dressed in work clothes: heavy trousers and windbreakers.

JAIMIE: When I'm laughing, I got friends.

RITA: I know, Jaimie Paul ...

PRIEST: That was the way I found her, that was the way I left her.

JAIMIE: *(bitterly)* When I'm laughing, I'm a joker ... a funny boy!

FATHER: If I was young ... I wouldn't sleep. I would talk to people ... let them all know!

JAIMIE: I'm not dangerous when I'm laughing ...

PRIEST: You could lose the reserve and have nowhere to go!

FATHER: I have lost more than that! Young people die ... young people don't believe me ...

JAIMIE: That's alright ... that's alright ...

The light dies out on JAIMIE PAUL and RITA JOE. The light also dies out on MR. HOMER and the YOUNG INDIAN MEN.

PRIEST: You think they believe that hot-headed ... that troublemaker?

FATHER: *(turning to face the PRIEST)* Jaimie Paul is a good boy!

PRIEST: David Joe ... you and I have lived through a lot. We need peace now, and time to consider what to do next.

FATHER: Eileen said to me last night ... she wants to go to the city. I worry all night ... What can I do?

PRIEST: I'll talk to her, if you wish.

FATHER: *(angry)* And tell her what? ... Of the animals there ... *(gesturing to the audience)* who sleep with sore stomachs because ... they eat too much?

PRIEST: We mustn't lose the reserve and the old life, David Joe ... Would you ... give up being chief on the reserve?

FATHER: Yes!

PRIEST: To Jaimie Paul?

FATHER: No ... to someone who's been to school ... maybe university ... who knows more.

PRIEST: *(relieved by this, but not reassured)* The people here need your wisdom and stability, David Joe. There is no man here who knows as much about hunting and fishing and guiding. You can survive ... What does a youngster who's been away to school know of this?

FATHER: *(sadly)* If we only fish an' hunt an' cut pulpwood ... pick strawberries in the bush ... for a hundred years more, we are dead. I know this, here ... *(He touches his breast.)*

The light dies on the ramp.

A light rises on stage front, on JAIMIE PAUL and RITA JOE sitting at the apron of the stage. MR. HOMER is still cutting bread for sandwiches. The three YOUNG INDIAN MEN have eaten and appear restless to leave. The fourth YOUNG INDIAN MAN is still asleep on the floor. RITA JOE has taken off the red sweater, but continues to hold it in her hand.

JAIMIE: *(to MR. HOMER)* One time I was on a trapline five days without grub. I ate snow an' I walked until I got back. You think you can take it like me?

MR. HOMER approaches JAIMIE PAUL and holds out a sandwich to him.

MR. HOMER: Here ... have a sandwich now.

JAIMIE PAUL ignores his hand.

RITA: Mister Homer don't know what happened, Jaimie Paul.

MR. HOMER shrugs and walks away to his sandwich table.

JAIMIE: Then he's got to learn ... Sure he knows! *(to MR. HOMER)* Sure he knows! He's feedin' sandwiches to Indian bums ... He knows. He's the worst kind!

The YOUNG INDIAN MEN freeze and MR. HOMER stops.

MR. HOMER: *(coldly)* I've never yet asked a man to leave this building.

RITA JOE and JAIMIE PAUL rise to their feet. RITA JOE goes to the clothes table and throws the red sweater back on the pile of clothes. JAIMIE PAUL laughs sardonically.

MR. HOMER: *(to RITA JOE)* Hey, not you, girl ... You take it!

She shakes her head and moves to leave.

RITA: I think we better go, boys.

The sleeping YOUNG INDIAN MAN slowly raises his head, senses there is something wrong, and is about to be helped up when ...

JAIMIE: After five days without grub, the first meal I threw up ... stomach couldn't take it ... But after that it was alright ... *(to MR. HOMER, with intensity)* I don't believe nobody ... no priest nor government ... They don't know what it's like to ... to want an' not have ... to stand in line an' nobody sees you!

MR. HOMER: If you want food, eat! You need clothes, take them. That's all ... But I'm runnin' this centre my way, and I mean it!

JAIMIE: I come to say no to you ... That's all ... that's all!

He throws out his arms in a gesture that is both defiant and childlike. The gesture disarms some of MR. HOMER's growing hostility.

MR. HOMER: You've got that right ... no problems. There's others come through here day an' night ... No problems.

JAIMIE: I don't want no others to come. I don't want them to eat here! *(indicating his friends)* If we got to take it from behind a store window, then we break the window an' wait for the cops. It's better than ... than this!

He gestures with contempt at the food and the clothes on the table.

MR. HOMER: Rita Joe ... where'd you pick up this ... this loudmouth anyway?

RITA: *(slowly, firmly)* I think ... Jaimie Paul's ... right.

MR. HOMER looks from face to face. The three YOUNG INDIAN MEN are passive, staring into the distance. The fourth is trying hard to clear his head. JAIMIE PAUL is cold, hostile. RITA JOE is determined.

MR. HOMER: *(decisively)* Alright! You've eaten ... looked over the clothes ... Now clear out so others get a chance to come in! Move!

He tries to herd everyone out and the four YOUNG INDIAN MEN begin to move away. JAIMIE PAUL mimics the gestures of MR. HOMER and steps in front of the YOUNG INDIAN MEN herding them back in.

JAIMIE: Run, boys, run! Or Mister Homer gonna beat us up!

RITA JOE takes JAIMIE PAUL's hand and tries to pull him away to leave.

RITA: Jaimie Paul ... you said to me no trouble!

JAIMIE PAUL pulls his hand free and jumps back of the clothes table. MR. HOMER comes for him, unknowingly still carrying the slicing knife in his hand. An absurd chase begins around the table. One of the YOUNG INDIAN MEN laughs, and stepping forward, catches hold of MR. HOMER's hand with the knife in it.

YOUNG INDIAN MAN: Hey! Don't play with a knife, Mister Homer!

He gently takes the knife away from MR. HOMER and drops it on the food table behind. MR. HOMER looks at his hand, an expression of shock on his face. JAIMIE PAUL gives him no time to think about the knife and what it must have appeared like to the YOUNG INDIAN MEN. He pulls a large brassiere from the clothes table and mockingly holds it over his breasts, which he sticks out enticingly at MR. HOMER. The YOUNG INDIAN MEN laugh. MR. HOMER is exasperated and furious. RITA JOE is frightened.

RITA: It's not funny, Jaimie!

JAIMIE: It's funny as hell, Rita Joe. Even funnier this way!

JAIMIE PAUL puts the brassiere over his head, with the cups down over his ears and the straps under his chin. The YOUNG INDIAN MEN are all laughing now and moving close to the table. MR. HOMER makes a futile attempt at driving them off.

Suddenly JAIMIE PAUL's expression turns to one of hatred. He throws the brassiere on the table and gripping its edge, throws the table and clothes over, scattering the clothes. He kicks at them. The YOUNG INDIAN MEN all jump in and, picking up the clothes, hurl them over the ramp.

RITA JOE runs in to try and stop them. She grips the table and tries lifting it up again.

MR. HOMER: *(to JAIMIE PAUL)* Cut that out, you sonofabitch!

JAIMIE PAUL stands watching him. MR. HOMER is in a fury. He sees RITA JOE struggling to right the table. He moves to her and pushes her hard.

MR. HOMER: You slut! ... You breed whore!

RITA JOE recoils. With a shriek of frustration, she attacks MR. HOMER, tearing at him. He backs away, then turns and runs. JAIMIE PAUL over-turns the table again. The others join in the melee with the clothes. A POLICEMAN enters and grabs JAIMIE PAUL. RITA JOE and the four YOUNG INDIAN MEN exit, clearing away the tables and remaining clothes.

A sharp, tiny spotlight comes up on the face and upper torso of JAIMIE PAUL. He is wild with rebellion as the POLICEMAN forces him, in an arm lock, down towards the audience.

JAIMIE: *(screaming defiance at the audience)* Not jus' a box of cornflakes! When I go in I want the whole store! That's right ... the whole god-damned store!

Another sharp light on the MAGISTRATE standing on his podium looking down at JAIMIE PAUL.

MAGISTRATE: Thirty days!

JAIMIE: *(held by POLICEMEN)* Sure, sure ... Anything else you know?

MAGISTRATE: Thirty days!

JAIMIE: Gimme back my truth!

MAGISTRATE: We'll get larger prisons and more police in every town and city across the country!

JAIMIE: Teach me who I really am! You've taken that away! Give me back the real me so I can live like a man!

MAGISTRATE: There is room for dialogue. There is room for disagreement and there is room for

social change ... but within the framework of institutions and traditions in existence for that purpose!

JAIMIE: *(spitting)* Go to hell! ... I can die an' you got nothing to tell me!

MAGISTRATE: *(in a cold fury)* Thirty days! And after that, it will be six months! And after that ... God help you!

The MAGISTRATE marches off his platform and offstage. JAIMIE PAUL is led off briskly in the other direction offstage.

The lights change. RITA JOE enters, crossing the stage, exchanging a look with the SINGER.

SINGER:
Sleepless hours, heavy nights,
Dream your dreams so pretty.
God was gonna have a laugh
An' gave me a job in the city!

RITA JOE walks the street. She is smoking a cigarette. She is dispirited.

The light broadens across the stage. RITA JOE's FATHER and JAIMIE PAUL enter the stage from the wings of centre stage left. They walk slowly towards where RITA JOE stands. At the sight of her FATHER, RITA JOE moans softly and hurriedly stamps out her cigarette. She visibly straightens and waits for the approaching men, her expression one of fear and joy.

FATHER: I got a ride on Miller's truck ... took me two days ...

JAIMIE: It's a long way, David Joe.

The FATHER stops a pace short of RITA JOE and looks at her with great tenderness and concern.

FATHER: *(softly)* I come ... to get Rita Joe.

RITA: Oh ... I don't know ...

She looks to JAIMIE PAUL for help in deciding what to do, but he is sullen and uncommunicative.

FATHER: I come to take Rita Joe home ... We got a house an' some work sometime ...

JAIMIE: She's with me now, David Joe.

RITA: *(very torn)* I don't know ...

JAIMIE: You don't have to go back, Rita Joe.

RITA JOE looks away from her FATHER with humility. The FATHER turns to JAIMIE PAUL. He stands ancient and heroic.

FATHER: I live ... an' I am afraid. Because ... I have not done everything. When I have done everything ... know that my children are safe ... then ... it will be alright. Not before.

JAIMIE: *(to RITA JOE)* You don't have to go. This is an old man now ... He has nothing to give ... nothin' to say!

RITA JOE reacts to both men, her conflict deepening.

FATHER: *(turning away from JAIMIE PAUL to RITA JOE)* For a long time ... a very long time ... she was in my hands ... like that! *(He cups his hands into the shape of a bowl.)* Sweet ... tiny ... lovin' all the time and wanting love ... *(He shakes his head sadly.)*

JAIMIE: *(angrily)* Go tell it to the white men! They're lookin' for Indians that stay proud even when they hurt ... just so long's they don't ask for their rights!

The FATHER turns slowly, with great dignity, to JAIMIE PAUL. His gestures show JAIMIE PAUL to be wrong; the old man's spirit was never broken. JAIMIE PAUL understands and looks away.

FATHER: You're a good boy, Jaimie Paul ... a good boy ... *(to RITA JOE, talking slowly, painfully)* I once seen a dragonfly breakin' its shell to get its wings ... it floated on water an' crawled up on a log where I was sitting ... It dug its feet into the log an' then it pulled until the shell bust over its neck. Then it pulled some more ... an' slowly its wings slipped out of the shell ... like that!

He shows with his hands how the dragonfly got his freedom.

JAIMIE: *(angered and deeply moved by the FATHER)* Where you gonna be when they start bustin' our heads open an' throwing us into jails right across the goddamned country?

FATHER: Such wings I never seen before ... folded like an accordion so fine, like thin glass an' white in the morning sun ...

JAIMIE: We're gonna have to fight to win ... there's no other way! They're not listenin' to you, old man! Or to me.

FATHER: It spread its wings ... so slowly ... an' then the wings opened an' began to flutter ... just like that ... see! Hesitant at first ... then stronger ... an' then the wings beatin' like that made the dragonfly's body quiver until the shell on its back falls off ...

JAIMIE: Stop kiddin' yourself! We're gonna say no pretty soon to all the crap that makes us soft an' easy to push this way ... that way!

FATHER: ... An' the dragonfly ... flew up ... up ... up ... into the white sun ... to the green sky ... to the sun ... faster an' faster ... Higher ... higher!

The FATHER reaches up with his hands, releasing the imaginary dragonfly into the sun, his final words torn out of his heart. RITA JOE springs to her feet and rushes against JAIMIE PAUL, striking at him with her fists.

RITA: *(savagely)* For Chris' sakes, I'm not goin' back! ... Leave him alone ... He's everything we got left now!

JAIMIE PAUL stands, frozen by his emotion which he can barely control. The FATHER turns. RITA JOE goes to him. The FATHER speaks privately to RITA JOE in Indian dialect. They embrace. He pauses for a long moment to embrace and forgive her everything. Then he goes slowly offstage into the wings of stage left without looking back.

FATHER: Goodbye, Rita Joe ... Goodbye, Jaimie Paul ...

RITA: Goodbye, Father.

JAIMIE PAUL watches RITA JOE who moves away from him to the front of the stage.

JAIMIE: *(to her)* You comin'?

She shakes her head to indicate no, she is staying. Suddenly JAIMIE PAUL runs away from her diagonally across to the wings upstage. As he nears the wings, the four YOUNG INDIAN MEN emerge, happily on their way to a party. They stop him at his approach. He runs into them, directing them back, his voice breaking with feelings of love and hatred intermingling.

JAIMIE: *(shouting at them)* Next time ... in a beer parlour or any place like that ... I'll go myself or you guys take me home ... No more white buggers pushin' us out the door or he gets this!

He raises his fist. The group of YOUNG INDIAN MEN, elated by their newly-found determination, surround JAIMIE PAUL and exit into the wings of the stage. The light dies in back and at stage left.

The MAGISTRATE enters. There is a light on RITA JOE where she stands. There is also a light around the MAGISTRATE. The MAGISTRATE's voice and purpose are leaden. He has given up on RITA JOE. He is merely performing the formality of condemning her and dismissing her from his conscience.

MAGISTRATE: I sentence you to thirty days in prison.

RITA: *(angry, defiant)* Sure, sure ... Anything else you know?

MAGISTRATE: I sentence you to thirty days in prison, with a recommendation you be examined medically and given all necessary treatment at the prison clinic. There is nothing ... there is nothing I can do now.

RITA: *(stoically)* Thank you. Is that right? To thank you?

MAGISTRATE: You'll be back ... always be back ... growing older, tougher ... filthier ... looking more like stone and prison bars ... the lines in your face will tell everyone who sees you about prison windows and prison food.

RITA: No child on the road would remember you, mister!

The MAGISTRATE comes down to stand before her. He has the rambling confidence of detached authority.

MAGISTRATE: What do you expect? We provide schools for you and you won't attend them because they're out of the way and that little extra effort is too much for you! We came up as a civilization having to ... yes, claw upwards at times ... There's nothing wrong with that ... We give you X-ray chest clinics ...

He turns away from her and goes to the apron of the stage and speaks directly to the audience.

MAGISTRATE: We give them X-ray chest clinics and three-quarters of them won't show up ... Those that do frequently get medical attention at one of the hospitals ...

RITA: *(interjecting)* My mother died!

MAGISTRATE: *(not hearing her)* But as soon as they're released they forget they're chronically ill and end up on a drinking party and a long walk home through the snow ... Next thing ... they're dead!

RITA: *(quietly)* Oh, put me in jail an' then let me go.

MAGISTRATE: *(turning to her)* Some of you get jobs ... There are jobs, good jobs, if you'd only look around a bit ... and stick with them when you get them. But no ... you get a job and promise to stay with it and learn, and two weeks later you're gone for three, four days without explanation ... Your reliability record is ruined and an employer has to regard you as lazy, undependable ... What do you expect!

RITA: I'm not scared of you now, bastard!

MAGISTRATE: You have a mind ... you have a heart. The cities are open to you to come and go as you wish, yet you gravitate to the slums and skid rows and the shanty-town fringes. You become a whore, drunkard, user of narcotics ... At best, dying of illness or malnutrition ... At worst, kicked or beaten to death by some angry white scum who finds in you something lower than himself to pound his frustrations out on! What's to be done! You Indians seem to be incapable of taking action to help yourselves. Someone must care for you ... Who! For how long!

RITA: You don't know nothin'!

MAGISTRATE: I know ... I know ... It's a struggle just to stay alive. I know ... I understand. That struggle is mine, as well as yours, Rita Joe! The jungle of the executive has as many savage teeth ready to go for the throat as the rundown hotel on the waterfront ... Your days and hours are numbered, Rita Joe ... I worry for the child I once saw ... I have already forgotten the woman!

He turns away from her and exits into the wings stage right.

The lights on RITA JOE fade. Lights of cold, eerie blue wash the backdrop of the stage faintly. RITA JOE stands in silhouette for a long moment.

Slowly, ominously, the three MURDERERS appear on the ramp backstage, one coming from the wings of stage right; one from the wings of stage left; and one rising from the back of the ramp, climbing it. One of the MURDERERS is whistling, a soft nervous noise throughout their scene onstage.

RITA JOE whimpers in fear, and as the MURDERERS loom above her, she runs along the apron to stage left. Here she bumps into JAIMIE PAUL who enters. She screams in fear.

JAIMIE: Rita Joe!

RITA: *(terrorized)* Jaimie! They're comin'. I seen them comin'!

JAIMIE: Who's coming! What's the matter, Rita Joe?

RITA: Men I once dreamed about … I seen it all happen once before … an' it was like this …

JAIMIE PAUL laughs and pats her shoulders reassuringly. He takes her hand and tries to lead her forward to the apron of the stage, but RITA JOE is dead, her steps wooden.

JAIMIE: Don't worry … I can take care of myself!

A faint light on the two of them.

RITA: You been in jail now too, Jaimie Paul …

JAIMIE: So what! Guys in jail was saying that they got to put a man behind bars or the judge don't get paid for being in court to make the trial … Funny world, eh, Rita Joe!

RITA: *(nodding)* Funny world.

The light dies on them. They come forward slowly.

JAIMIE: I got a room with a hot plate … We can have a couple of eggs and some tea before we go to see the movie.

RITA: What was it like for you in jail?

JAIMIE: So so …

JAIMIE PAUL motions for RITA JOE to follow him and moves forward from her. The distant sound of a train approaching is heard. She is wooden, coming slowly after him.

RITA: It was different where the women were … It's different to be a woman … Some women was wild … and they shouted they were riding black horses into a fire I couldn't see … There was no fire there, Jaimie!

JAIMIE: *(turning to her, taking her arm)* Don't worry … we're goin' to eat and then see a movie … Come on, Rita Joe!

She looks back and sees the MURDERERS rise and slowly approach from the gloom. Her speech becomes thick and unsteady as she follows JAIMIE PAUL to the front of the ramp.

RITA: One time I couldn't find the street where I had a room to sleep in … forgot my handbag … had no money … An old man with a dog said hello, but I couldn't say hello back because I was worried an' my mouth was so sticky I couldn't speak to him …

JAIMIE: Are you comin'?

RITA: When you're tired an' sick, Jaimie, the city starts to dance …

JAIMIE: *(taking her hand, pulling her gently along)* Come on, Rita Joe.

RITA: The street lights start rollin' like wheels an' cement walls feel like they was made of blanket cloth …

The sound of the train is closer now. The lights of its lamps flicker in back of the stage. RITA JOE turns to face the MURDERERS, one of whom is whistling ominously. She whimpers in fear and presses herself against JAIMIE PAUL. JAIMIE PAUL turns and sees the MURDERERS hovering near them.

JAIMIE: Don't be scared … Nothing to be scared of, Rita Joe … *(to the MURDERERS)* What the hell do you want?

One of the MURDERERS laughs. JAIMIE PAUL pushes RITA JOE back behind himself. He moves towards the MURDERERS, taunting them.

JAIMIE: You think I can't take care of myself?

With deceptive casualness, the MURDERERS approach him. One of them makes a sudden lurch at JAIMIE PAUL as if to draw him into their circle. JAIMIE PAUL anticipates the trap and takes a flying kick at the MURDERER, knocking him down.

They close around JAIMIE PAUL with precision, then attack. JAIMIE PAUL leaps, but is caught mid-air by the other two. They bring him down and put the boots to him. RITA JOE screams and runs to him. The train sound is loud and immediate now.

One of the MURDERERS has grabbed RITA JOE. The remaining two raise JAIMIE PAUL to his feet and one knees him viciously in the groin. JAIMIE PAUL screams and doubles over. The lights of the train are upon them. The MURDERERS leap off the ramp leaving JAIMIE PAUL in the path of the approaching train. JAIMIE PAUL's death cry becomes the sound of the train horn. As the train sound roars by, the MURDERERS return to close in around RITA JOE.

One MURDERER springs forward and grabs RITA JOE. The other two help to hold her, with nervous fear and lust. RITA JOE breaks free of them and runs to the front of the stage. The three MURDERERS come after her, panting hard. They close in on her leisurely now, playing with her, knowing that they have her trapped.

Recorded and overlapping voices.

CLERK: The court calls Rita Joe ...

MAGISTRATE: Who is she? ... Let her speak for herself ...

RITA: In the summer it was hot, an' flies hummed ...

TEACHER: A book of verse, a melting pot ...

MAGISTRATE: Thirty days!

FATHER: Barkin' to beat hell ... How! How!

JAIMIE: *(laughing, defiant, taunting)* You go to hell!

PRIEST: A confession, Rita Joe ...

Over the voices she hears, the MURDERERS attack. Dragging her down backwards, they pull her legs open and one MURDERER lowers himself on her.

RITA: Jaimie! Jaimie! Jaimie!

RITA JOE's head lolls over sideways. The MURDERERS stare at her and pull back slightly.

MURDERER: *(thickly, rising off her twisted, broken body)* Shit ... she's dead ... We hardly touched her.

He hesitates for a moment, then runs, joined by the SECOND MURDERER.

SECOND MURDERER: Let's get out of here!

They run up onto the ramp and watch as the THIRD MURDERER piteously climbs onto the dead RITA JOE.

Sounds of a funeral chant. MOURNERS appear on riser backstage. RITA JOE's FATHER enters from the wings of stage left, chanting an ancient Indian funeral chant, carrying the body of JAIMIE PAUL. The MURDERER hesitates in his necrophilic rape and then runs away.

The YOUNG INDIAN MEN bring the body of JAIMIE PAUL over the ramp and approach. The body is placed down on the podium, beside RITA JOE's. All the Indians, young and old, kneel around the two bodies. The FATHER continues his death chant. The PRIEST enters from the wings of stage right reciting a prayer. The TEACHER, SINGER, POLICEMAN and MURDERERS come with him forming the outside perimeter around the Indian funeral.

PRIEST: Hail Mary, Mother of God ... pray for us sinners now and at the hour of our death.

Repeated until finally EILEEN JOE slowly rises to her feet and, turning to the PRIEST and WHITE MOURNERS, says softly ...

EILEEN: *(over the sounds of chanting and praying)* No! ... No! ... No more!

The YOUNG INDIAN MEN rise one after another facing the outer circle defiantly, and the CAST freezes on stage, except for the SINGER.

SINGER:
Oh, the singing bird
Has found its wings
And it's soaring!
My God, what a sight!
On the cold fresh wind of morning! ...

During the song, EILEEN JOE steps forward to the audience and as the song ends, says ...

EILEEN: When Rita Joe first come to the city, she told me ... the cement made her feet hurt.

END

JOHN HERBERT

(b. 1926)

Although John Herbert Brundage was a prime mover in the creation of Toronto's alternate theatre in the 1960s—"the single most important figure of the decade," according to Bill Glassco—his success as a playwright, to a much greater extent even than George Ryga's, happened outside of Canada. And more so than Ryga's it rests on a single play. At last count *Fortune and Men's Eyes* had been performed in over a hundred countries in at least forty different translations. It has sold, in an American edition, more copies than any other published Canadian play. It even led to the founding of the Fortune Society, an organization devoted to prison reform in the United States. Yet *Fortune* was an established international success for nearly eight years before Herbert got to see a professional production in his home and native city, "cold, bitter, suspicious Toronto," as he entitled a 1971 magazine article.

Herbert's bitterness about Toronto stems in part from an incident in 1946 when, as he tells it, he was beaten and robbed by a street gang. Instead of laying charges against his assailants, the police charged Herbert with having sexually propositioned them and he was convicted of gross indecency. The six months he spent in Guelph reformatory would later become the basis for *Fortune and Men's Eyes*. The vivid third-person description of his time in prison that Herbert contributed to Geraldine Anthony's *Stage Voices* makes clear that the characters of both Mona and Queenie in *Fortune* are projections of his own experience behind bars.

Herbert's theatrical career began in 1955 when he enrolled in the New Play Society School of Drama, studying acting, directing and production for three years followed by two years of dance training at the National Ballet school. In 1960 he founded Adventure Theatre in Toronto and from 1962–65 was artistic director of the New Venture Players with whom he produced and directed his own early plays "Private Club," "A Household God" and an adaptation from Dumas, "A Lady of Camellias." In 1965 he opened a fifty-seat theatre over a pizzeria on Yonge Street. The Garret Theatre ran off and on until 1970, subsidized by Herbert's labours as a waiter. Among its productions were his plays "Closer to Cleveland" and "World of Woyzeck," adapted from Büchner.

Meanwhile Herbert had written *Fortune and Men's Eyes* in 1964, and while serving drinks at the University Club he had mentioned it to Robertson Davies who suggested submitting the play to a summer workshop at Stratford. *Toronto Star* critic Nathan Cohen got wind of the 1965 workshop production, read the script and sent it to New York producer David Rothenberg. *Fortune and Men's Eyes* opened off-Broadway in 1967, and within a few years it was making its way around the world.

The international success of *Fortune* did little, however, for Herbert's fortunes in Canada. Unable to get a major Canadian production of the play and with the Garret devouring his foreign royalties, Herbert closed the theatre permanently in 1970 (deeding its equipment to Ken Gass who promptly set up the Factory Lab) and left in frustration to live in England. But two years later he was back in Toronto to stay, trying again to establish his presence in the Canadian theatre. Between 1972 and 1974 he staged two ambitious new plays, *Born of Medusa's Blood* and *Omphale and the Hero*, and four one-acts under the title *Some Angry Summer Songs*, but no one seemed to be listening. By 1975, when *Fortune* won the Chalmers Award for its first professional production in Toronto, Herbert had pretty well retired from the theatre. He has since written a novel (*The House That Jack Built*), taught drama and creative writing, worked as an art and theatre critic, and served as Associate Editor of *Onion*, a Toronto arts newsletter.

All Herbert's full-length plays and many of his one-acts concern relationships characterized by selfishness and betrayal usually resulting in destruction. At the centre of both *Born of Medusa's Blood* and *Omphale and the Hero* are female redeemer/whore figures destroyed by perverse machismo and a corrupt social order. *Fortune and Men's Eyes* uses the same formula but in a much more dramatically compelling way. The prison environment enforces a distinctive kind of garrison mentality among its inhabitants whose struggle for survival involves not just their physical well-being but their ethical and sexual identities as well.

Fortune and Men's Eyes (originally titled *The Christmas Concert*) has the structure of a morality play. Smitty, as his name suggests, is Everyman. He enters the prison world an innocent and is immediately confronted by a distorted value system which demands from him a series of unpalatable choices. As represented by his three cellmates, his options are to accept, reject or accommodate himself to the prison's values. Rocky has clearly adopted those values as his own. His authoritarianism and racism, his blackmail of the guard and manipulation of Catso show him to be completely at home in the prison system, the jungle in which he calls himself king. At the other extreme is Mona who transcends "her" surroundings by separating body and spirit, preserving—at a terrible price—what the play suggests is an essentially "feminine" gentleness and sensitivity inimical to the perverted masculinity of the prison that expresses itself through homosexual gang rapes and brutal beatings. In between these two is Queenie. He knows the prison game even better than Rocky and can be just as vicious; yet like Mona he has not entirely lost himself to the system. His outrageous drag routines are a personal signature marking his distance from the prison's drab conformity (and making him the play's most entertaining character). But behind the personae of the clown and the helpful "mother" that Queenie plays in the prison's travesty of domestic order is just one more sad, damaged boy.

"I feel like I'm in another country," Smitty says when he first enters the cellblock. But it's not long before he's forced to adopt native customs, and by Scene Two he's already speaking the language. He comes under the influence first of Rocky, then of Queenie, learning the rules of the game so well that by the end he is almost too far gone to embrace the possibility of salvation held out by Mona and amplified in the Shakespeare sonnet from which the play's title comes. After their moment of communion is shattered by the brutality of the others and the prison's injustice, Smitty shows that he has become another Rocky: cruel, desensitized, irrevocably lost.

Although *Fortune and Men's Eyes* is certainly an exposé of the brutalizing effects of prison life, environment is not the only operative factor in the play. Herbert's naturalism also encompasses the other traditional element, heredity. In his study *Modern Tragedy*, Raymond Williams describes how "in Ibsen, the hero defines an opposing world, full of lies and compromises and dead positions, only to find, as he struggles against it, that as a man he belongs to this world and has its destructive inheritance in himself." Smitty too carries within him a destructive inheritance. Like his father, the practical businessman who turns out to be a "hardhearted bastard," Smitty reveals a cold-blooded pragmatism that leaves him emotionally crippled. He no sooner complains that his father treats his mother like a prostitute than he offers Mona the same treatment. Just as Rocky is an inevitable product and victim of his criminal family, Queenie of his mother's abandonment, and Mona of an effeminate physical appearance, Smitty is doomed by a condition more devastating than anything symbolized by the final slamming shut of the jail door.

Fortune and Men's Eyes opened at the Actors Playhouse in New York on February 23, 1967.

ROCKY	Victor Arnold
MONA	Robert Christian
QUEENIE	Bill Moor
GUARD	Clifford Pellow
SMITTY	Terry Kiser

Directed by Mitchell Nestor
Setting by C. Murawski
Costumes by Jan
Music and Sound Effects by Terry Ross

FORTUNE AND MEN'S EYES

CHARACTERS

SMITTY, a good-looking, clean-cut youth of clear intelligence, aged seventeen years. He has the look of a collegiate athlete. The face is strong and masculine with enough sensitivity in feature and expression to soften the sharp outline. He is of a type that everyone seems to like, almost on sight.

ROCKY, a youth of nineteen years who seems older and harder than his age should allow, though there is an emotional immaturity that reveals itself constantly. He has a nature, driven by fear, that uses hatred aggressively to protect itself, taking pride in harbouring no soft or gentle feelings. He lives like a cornered rat, vicious, dangerous and unpredictable. He is handsome in a lean, cold, dark, razor-featured way.

QUEENIE, a large, heavy-bodied youth of nineteen or twenty with the strength of a wrestler but the soft white skin of a very blond person. Physical appearance is a strange combination of softness and hulking strength. For a large person he moves with definite grace and fine precision, almost feminine in exactness, but in no way frivolous or fluttery. Movements, when exaggerated purposely, are big, showy and extravagant. The face is dainty in features as a "cupie-doll's"—plump-cheeked and small-nosed. The mouth has a pouting, self-indulgent look, but the eyes are hard, cold, and pale blue like ice. The hair is fair, fine, and curly, like a baby's. One looks at him and thinks of a madam in a brothel ... coarse, cruel, tough and voluptuously pretty.

MONA, a youth of eighteen or nineteen years, of a physical appearance that arouses resentment at once in many people, men and women. He seems to hang suspended between the sexes, neither boy nor woman. He is slender, narrow-shouldered, long-necked, long-legged, but never gauche or ungainly. He moves gracefully, but not self-consciously. His nature seems almost more feminine than effeminate because it is not mannerism that calls attention to an absence of masculinity so much as the sum of his appearance, lightness of movement, and gentleness of action. His effeminacy is not aggressive ... just exists. The face is responsible for his nickname of "Mona Lisa." Features are madonna-like, straight-nosed, patrician-mouthed and sad-eyed. Facial contour is oval and the expression enigmatic. If he had been a woman, some would have described him as having a certain ethereal beauty.

GUARD, a rugged-faced man of about forty-five to fifty, who looks like an ex-army officer. He has a rigid military bearing, a look of order and long acquaintance with discipline. He presents an impressive exterior of uniformed law enforcement, but one senses behind the unsmiling features some nagging doubt or worry, as if something of his past returned occasionally to haunt him, when he would prefer it forgotten. At these moments, his actions are uneasy and he does not seem so impressive, in spite of his uniform. He has a stomach ulcer that causes him much physical discomfort, manifesting itself in loud belching.

SCENE

A Canadian reformatory, prep school for the penitentiary. The inmates are usually young, but there are often older prisoners, as indicated by the dialogue in places. We are primarily concerned here with four who are young, though they tell us others exist. The overwhelming majority of prisoners in a reformatory are in the late teens and early twenties. Those who are older have been convicted of offenses that do not carry a sentence large enough to warrant sending them to a penitentiary.

SET

The setting is a dormitory with four beds and two doorways. One door leads to the corridor, but we do not see it. There is a stone alcove, angled so that we get the impression of a short hall. We hear the guard's key open this unseen door whenever he or the four inmates enter or exit. The whole upstage wall is barred so that we look into the corridor where the guard and inmates pass in entrance and exit. Another doorway leads to the toilet and shower room.

ACT ONE

Scene One

Mid-October, evening.

Overture: 3 songs—"Alouette" (sung by Group of Boys' Voices); "Down in the Valley" (One Male Voice); "Jesus Loves Me" (sung by Group of Boys' Voices).

ROCKY is stretched on his bed like a prince at rest; QUEENIE sits on his own bed upstage; MONA leans against the wall of bars, upstage of QUEENIE. In the distance we hear the clang of metal doors, and a gruff voice issuing orders. MONA turns at the sounds, and looks along the hall.

Just before lights come up, after curtain has opened, a BOY's VOICE is heard singing, at a distance—as if farther along a corridor.

BOY'S VOICE: *(singing)*
Oh, if I had the wings of an angel
Over these prison walls would I fly—

Sound of metal doors clanging open and shut. And sound of heavy boots marching along corridor.

VOICE: *(English accent)* Halt! Attention! Straighten that line! Guard! Take this one down and put him in Observation!

GUARD: Yes sir! Smith! Step out—and smartly!

Lights come up.

BOY'S VOICE: *(singing)*
Oh, if I had the wings of—

QUEENIE: *(on stage)*
Oh, if I had the wings of an angel
And the ass of a big buffalo,
I would fly to the heavens above me,
And crap on the people below.

VOICE: *(English accent, raised now, the voice is not only gruff as before but high and shrill in overtone, like Hitler's recorded speech)* And you, Canary-Bird—shut that bloody row, or I shall cut off your seed supply.

Repeated sound of metal doors, and of boots marching away.

QUEENIE: Oh, oh! That's Bad Bess. The Royal Sergeant don't come this close to the common folk, except when they're bringin' in a batch o' fish.

ROCKY: What's the action out there, Queenie?

MONA: *(standing nearest the bars)* It's the new arrivals.

ROCKY: Anybody ask you to open your mouth, fruity?

QUEENIE: Oh, lay off the Mona Lisa, for Christ sake, Rocky.

ROCKY: Always getting her jollies looking out that hole.

QUEENIE: Does Macy's bother Gimbel's?

ROCKY: They got their own corners.

QUEENIE: Well she ain't in yours, so dummy up!

ROCKY: Don't mess with the bull, Queenie!

QUEENIE: Your horn ain't long enough to reach me, Ferdinand.

ROCKY: You might feel it yet.

QUEENIE: Worst offer I've had today, but it's early.

ROCKY: Screw off! *(turning toward MONA)* Look at the queer watchin' the fish! See anything you can catch, Rosie?

QUEENIE: How's the new stock, Mona? Anything worth shakin' it for?

MONA: They're all so young.

QUEENIE: That'll suit Rocky. If he could coop a new chicken in his yard, he might not be so salty.

ROCKY: Where'd you get all that mouth ... from your mother?

QUEENIE: The better to gobble you up with, Little Red Riding Wolf!

ROCKY: Tell it to your old man.

QUEENIE: Which one? Remember me? I'm my own P.I.

ROCKY: You got a choice?

QUEENIE: I don't mean pimp, like you, I mean political influence, like me!

ROCKY: So you got a coupla wheels in the office! Big deal!

QUEENIE: I like it that way ... makes it so I don't have to take no crap from a would-be hippy like you.

MONA: They're coming this way.

QUEENIE: Hell! And I didn't set my hair in toilet paper curls last night. Oh well! I'll try to look seductive.

ROCKY: You better turn around then.

QUEENIE: Well, my backside looks better than your face, if that's what you wanta say.

ROCKY: (with disdain) Queers!

Enter GUARD with a youth who is about seventeen.

ROCKY: Hi, screw! What's that ... your new baby?

GUARD: You planning a return trip to the tower, smart boy?

ROCKY: Just bein' friendly, Captain! I like to make the kids feel at home.

GUARD: So I've noticed. (to the new boy) Okay, Smith, this is your dormitory for now. Try to get along with the others and keep your nose clean. Do as you're told, keep your bunk tidy, and no talking after lights out. You'll be assigned your work tomorrow. Meanwhile, follow the others to washup and meals. Pick up the routine and don't spend too much time in the craphouse, or you'll end up in an isolation cell.

ROCKY: He means Gunsel's Alley. Too bad all the queers don't make it there.

QUEENIE: (to the GUARD) Now he wants a private room. Take him away, Nurse!

GUARD: Okay you two! Turn off the vaudeville. You'll get your chance to do your number at the Christmas concert.

He exits.

QUEENIE: The Dolly Sisters! After you got your royal uniform, in the delousing room, did Bad Bess challenge you to a duel?

SMITTY: Who?

QUEENIE: Little Sergeant Gritt—that chalk-faced, pea-eyed squirt in the rimless goggles! He's always goin' on about the "Days of Empire" and "God and Country" and all suchlike Bronco Bullcrap.

SMITTY: Oh, yes! He did most of the talking.

QUEENIE: That's our Cockney cunt—never closes her hole. Didn't he want you to square off for fisticuffs, old chap? Sporting chance an' all that stale roast beef an' Yorkshire pudding?

SMITTY: Well, he did say he'd been boxing champion at some school in England, and that, if any of us thought we were tough, this was our chance to prove it—man to man, with no interference.

QUEENIE: Yeah—that's his usual pitch. Corny, ain't it? It makes him feel harder than those stone lions out front o' Buckingham Palace. Yellow-bellied little rat! When he's outa that uniform, he's scared to death o' any eleven-year-old kid he meets on the street. Did his Lordship get any challengers?

SMITTY: Well, no! I wasn't surprised at that. I felt sure it was just a way of letting the prisoners know who's boss.

QUEENIE: I must say—you ain't exactly a idiot.

ROCKY: One o' these farty Fridays, he's gonna get it good, from some guy faster'n that goddam Indian.

QUEENIE: How stupid kin a Iroquois be? Imagine this jerky Indian from Timmins, takin' that fish-faced little potato chip at his word. The only one ever took the chance—far as I know.

SMITTY: He'd have to have a lot of guts.

QUEENIE: Oh yeah—and they showed them to him fast. He was a brave brave all right—an' stupid as a dead buffalo. The second he an' Bad Bess squared off at each other, two guards jumped Big Chief Running Blood, an' the three British bully boys beat the roaring piss outa him. Heroes all!

ROCKY: What a mess they made o' that squaw-banger!

QUEENIE: You couldn't exactly put that profile on a coin no more—not even a cheap little copper. Oh, well—let's look on the bright side o' the penny; he's in pretty good shape for the shape he's in. After all, he got a free nose-bob an' can pass for a pale nigger now. A darkie can get a better job 'n a redskin any day.

ROCKY: Whoever heard of a Indian what worked? They git government relief.

QUEENIE: Howdya think he got here, Moronia? He was one o' them featherheads from Matachewan Reservation, tryin' t' get a job in the mines. There was this great big ol' riot, an' the cowboys won again. Pocahontas' husband is up here because he tried t' scalp some Timmins cop. An', believe you me, that's the wrong way to get yourself a wig in that tin town.

ROCKY: An' you believe that crap, like he tells you his stories about how some stinkin' bird got its name? Jeez! Maybe you should git yerself a blanket an' become a squaw—you dig these teepee tales so much.

QUEENIE: I dig all kinds o' tail, pale-ass—except yours.

ROCKY: All Indians is screwin' finks an' stoolies, an' I woulden trust 'em with a bottle o' cheap shavin' lotion; and that Blackfeet bum probably slugged some ol' fairy in a public crapper, t' git a bottle o' wine.

QUEENIE: Always judgin' everybody by yourself! Tch! Tch! That's the sign of a slow con man, Sweetie.

MONA: *(to new boy)* What's your name? I'm Jan.

SMITTY: Smith.

QUEENIE: But you can call her Mona, and I'm Queenie.

ROCKY: Look at the girls givin' the new boy a fast cruise. Give him time to take his pants off, Queenie.

QUEENIE: So you can get into them, Daddy-O? Don't let him bug you, Smitty. He thinks he's the big rooster here.

ROCKY: You know it too. Welcome home punk!

SMITTY: This is my first time.

ROCKY: Braggin' or complainin'?

SMITTY: Neither. It's just a fact.

ROCKY: Well, that's nice. You shouldn't be here at all I guess. Got a bum beef?

SMITTY: A ... a what?

ROCKY: Crap! A beef! A rap! Whose cookies did you boost ... your mother's?

QUEENIE: What the judge wants to know, honey, is what special talent brought you this vacation—are you a store-counter booster or like myself do you make all your house calls when nobody's home?

SMITTY: Neither!

QUEENIE: Rolled a drunk ... autographed somebody's cheques ... raped the girl next door?

SMITTY: No, and I ... I don't want to talk about it.

QUEENIE: You might as well spill it, kid. I can't stand suspense. Ask Mona ... she screwed all around the mulberry bush until I finally had to go find out in the office.

ROCKY: I coulda saved you the trouble and told you she reached for the wrong joy stick. Did you ever get one you didn't like, Mona?

MONA: *(to SMITTY)* I've learned it doesn't matter what you've done. If you don't say, everyone assumes it's something far worse, so you might as well get it over with.

SMITTY: I just can't.

QUEENIE: Okay Smitty ... skip it! I'll find out on the Q.T., but I won't spill it.

ROCKY: Ottawa's First Lady! How did you do it, Ladybird?

QUEENIE: Well ... I lifted my left leg and then my right, and between the two of them, I rose right to the top.

ROCKY: Of a pile of bull!

MONA: How long is your sentence?

SMITTY: Six months.

MONA: Same as mine. I have a few to go.

SMITTY: Does ... does it seem as long as ... as ...

MONA: Not after a while. You get used to the routine, and there are diversions.

ROCKY: That's an invitation to the crapper.

MONA: Do you like to read?

SMITTY: I never did ... much.

MONA: Well, this is a good place to acquire the habit.

ROCKY: Yeah! Let Mona the fruit teach you her habits, then you can go and make yourself an extra pack of weed a week.

QUEENIE: She don't go as cheap as you, Rocky. We're tailor-made cigarette girls or nothin'.

ROCKY: I get what I want without bending over.

QUEENIE: Sure! You can always con some stupid chicken into doing it for you. How many left in your harem now, Valentino?

ROCKY: My kids wouldn't spit on the best part of you.

QUEENIE: Who's interested in a lot of little worn-out punks? I've seen them all hustling their skinny asses in the Corner Cafeteria, and if it wasn't for the old aunties who feel them up in the show and take them for a meal, they'd starve to death. Did you tell them before they left that you'd provide them with a whole bus terminal to sleep in when you get out?

ROCKY: After I smarten them up, they don't have to flop in your hunting grounds. They go where the action is and cruise around in Cadillacs.

QUEENIE: Yours, of course?

ROCKY: What I *take*, you can call *mine*.

QUEENIE: What a pity you couldn't get a judge to see it the same way.

ROCKY: You're cruisin' for a bruisin', bitch!

QUEENIE: Thanks awfully, but I'm no maso-sissy, sad-ass. I always kick for the balls when attacked.

He sings to the tune of "Habanera" from Carmen:

My name is Carmen,
I am a whore,
And I go knocking
From door to door.

ROCKY: I'll meet you in front of the city hall next Christmas.

QUEENIE: Lovely, but don't ask me for a quarter, like last time.

ROCKY: Since when did you walk on the street with more than a dime?

QUEENIE: After I stopped letting bums like you roost at my place overnight.

ROCKY: Cripes! You'll never forget you played Sally Ann to me once. When you sobered up and felt like a little fun, did you miss me?

QUEENIE: Yeah—also my marble clock, my garnet ring, and eleven dollars.

ROCKY: *(laughing)* Oh jeez, I wish I coulda seen your face. Was your mascara running?

QUEENIE: He's having such a good time, I hate to tell him I like Bob Hope better. So where did you come from Smitty ... the big corner?

MONA: That means the city ... it's a slang term. You'll get used to them.

SMITTY: I feel like I'm in another country.

ROCKY: What's your ambition, kid? You wanna be a Square John ... a brown nose?

QUEENIE: Ignore the ignoramus. He loves to play the wise guy.

SMITTY: I'm willing to catch on.

QUEENIE: You will, but you gotta watch yourself ... play it cool and listen to the politicians.

SMITTY: Politicians?

QUEENIE: The hep guys ... hippos, who are smart enough to make it into the office. They get the best of it ... good grub, new shirts and jeans, lightweight booties and special privileges ... extra gym, movie shows, and sometimes even tailor-made cigarettes. Like to get in on that?

SMITTY: I don't smoke.

QUEENIE: Well for cripes' sake don't tell them. Take your deck of weed and give it to your mother.

SMITTY: My ...

QUEENIE: Me, honey! Who else!

SMITTY: Oh! Okay!

MONA: Tailor-made cigarettes are contraband, but your package of tobacco is handed out with a folder of cigarette papers and a razor blade when you go for clothing change once a week ... it's sort of a payday!

ROCKY: Listen to our little working girl. She works in the gash-house sewing pants together for the guys to wear. Her only complaint is there's nothing in 'em when they're finished.

SMITTY: Is that what I'll be doing … ?

QUEENIE: No baby, you won't. The tailor shop and the laundry are especially for us girls. They can make sure, that way, we don't stray behind a bush. But I like the laundry since they made me forelady. It's a sweet act of fate because it's the only place in the joint where I can get Javex—to keep myself a natural blonde.

ROCKY: And it's easier to show your ass bending over a tub than under a sewing machine or a wheelbarrow.

QUEENIE: You've got a one-track mind, and it's all dirt.

ROCKY: My shovel's clean.

QUEENIE: I don't know how. Every time you get in a shower, you've got it in somebody's ditch.

ROCKY: Don't be jealous. I'll get around to shovelling in yours.

QUEENIE: Be sure you can fill it with diamonds when you come callin'.

ROCKY: You'd be happy with a fistful of chocolates.

QUEENIE: Feed the Lauras to your chickens at jug-up, eh Smitty?

SMITTY: Jug-up?

QUEENIE: Meals! Didn't they yell jug-up at you before you ate today?

SMITTY: I wasn't hungry. I thought the food would be the same as at the city jail, and it always made me sick after.

QUEENIE: Don't remind me of that sewage dump on the River. I think they bought that bloody old baloney and those withered wieners once a year … and you could put up wallpaper forever with that goddam porridge. Don't worry … the pigs they keep here are fed better than that.

MONA: Yes, the meals are good, Smitty. This place has its own farm, so the animals and vegetables are all raised by the prisoners.

SMITTY: I once worked on a farm, between school terms. I wouldn't mind if they put me on that … the time would go fast.

QUEENIE: That's the idea, honey! I'll try to wangle you a good go so you don't hafta do hard time. I got some pull in the office.

ROCKY: You'll have to serve a little keester to the politicians who wanna put you in the barn.

SMITTY: What?

ROCKY: But I guess you been in the hay before. Queenie's all for fixin' you up with an old man. You're ripe for tomato season.

QUEENIE: One thing about it, Rockhead. It'll be a hippy who's got it made, and no crap disturber like you that picks him off my vine.

SMITTY: I don't want to hurt anybody's feelings, but I'm not … queer. I've got a girl friend: she even came to court.

ROCKY: You shoulda brought her with you. I'da shared my bunk with her.

SMITTY: You don't understand, she's not that kind of …

MONA: It's all right, Smitty; he's just teasing you. Life inside is different, but you still don't have to do anything you don't want to, not if you—

QUEENIE: I'm tryin' to smarten him up, Mona, and you try to queer the play. Has sittin' outside the fence got you anything? At jug-up some punk's always grabbin' the meat off your plate and you're scared to say boo.

MONA: I get enough to eat. If anybody's that hungry, I don't begrudge it.

QUEENIE: And look at your goddam rags. They give you that junk on purpose, to make a bloody clown outa you. You ain't had a garment that fits since you come in.

MONA: I can fix them to look better at the shop when the guard's not looking.

QUEENIE: Well I like everything new. I can't feel sexy in rags.

MONA: I don't really care what I look like here.

QUEENIE: (sigh of despair) See, Smitty! I try to sharpen the girls I like and she don't listen to a screwin' word I say. I coulda got her a real good old man, but she told him she liked her "independence" if you can picture it.

SMITTY: I can understand that.

QUEENIE: Yeah? So what happens? One day in the gym a bunch of hippos con her into the storeroom to get something for the game, and teach her another one instead. They make up the team, but she's the only basket. They all took a whack, now she's public property. You can't say no around here unless you got somebody behind you. Take it from your mother ... I know the score.

SMITTY: I'll have to think about it.

QUEENIE: Well don't wait until they give you a gang splash in the storeroom. Mona had to hold onto the wall to walk, for a week.

MONA: They won't do it to him. He doesn't look gay, and he's probably not here on a sex charge. They felt I had no rights.

SMITTY: That doesn't seem fair.

MONA: I didn't think so either. It takes a while to get used to the rules of the game, and I've made a few concessions since ... just to make life bearable. One thing, Smitty; don't depend on protection from the guards, and don't ever go to them. You have to solve your own problems.

ROCKY: And Mona'll show you her scars to prove it ... fink! Squealed to a goddam screw! Cut you up pretty good after that, didn't we, bitch?

SMITTY: But how could they get away with it?

QUEENIE: The usual way ... it was an "accident."

SMITTY: Jan?

MONA: Everyone agreed it was an accident including me. Be careful, Smitty!

QUEENIE: Now Mona's givin' you some smart news. There's only two kinds of guards: the ones you can use like Holy Face who brought you in— and the fink screws that go straight to the General. When you see one comin' give six so we can play it safe.

SMITTY: Six?

QUEENIE: Say "six" instead of "nix" ... a warning!

SMITTY: Oh, I get it.

QUEENIE: It's no game, Honey! They got a nice cold tower here with no blankets or mattresses on the iron bunks and a diet of bread and water to tame you. If that don't work, there's a little machine that fastens your hips and ankles, while some sad-ass screw that's got a rod on for you bangs you across the ass with a leather belt fulla holes, and some other son of a bitch holds your arms over your head, twisted in your shirt. They can make you scream for God and your mother before they let you go.

SMITTY: *(aghast)* It sounds like the late late show.

QUEENIE: It's no Hollywood horror-vision. Ask Mona; she was in a fog for a month after.

SMITTY: Mona? ... Jan?

MONA: I don't want to talk about that, Smitty.

ROCKY: No. She'd rather dream about it.

QUEENIE: She wakes the whole place in the middle of the night with those bloody awful screams—"Mother! Mother!" Crap!

SMITTY: *(petrified)* You're only trying to scare me ... all of you.

MONA: *(gently)* No, we're not, Smitty ... someone's always waiting for you to make a misstep. Please be careful.

SMITTY: I've heard of lashes, but I thought it was only in very special cases.

MONA: *(bitterly)* They don't keep those little goodies because they have to but because they want to. Learn to look into their eyes before you stick out a hand.

SMITTY: Thanks, Mona. I'll remember.

QUEENIE: Well, now we're gettin' someplace. You see what a wise girl Mona's gettin' to be? She'll know the ropes better than me next time around.

SMITTY: Same thing happen to you?

QUEENIE: Well not exactly, but then I handle myself a little different. Mona's a girl who's gotta learn the hard way. I always see the trap before it springs. But then I have the advantage of early training. I was a Children's Aid ward, and shuffled around from foster homes to farms, to God knows what. I been locked in closets so my foster mother could drink and play cards unseen; I had farmers treat me worse'n their dogs, and I learned before I was twelve that nobody gives a crap about you in this cruddy world. So I decided to do something about it. Queenie looks after Queenie, and pretty good too let me tellya.

SMITTY: Sounds like you've had a rough time.

QUEENIE: Skip it! I wouldn't trade places with any soft son of a bitch who needs a goddam mother to tell it what to do and a lousy house in some phony suburb with home-baked pies, and a lot of chitchat around a kitchen table. I've seen what that does to people, and I hate them gutless bastards who go to work eight hours a day, to parties and shows the rest of the time, and walk around with their noses in the air like their own crap don't stink.

MONA: Queenie's never been able to find her mother. The Children's Aid wouldn't give the address because of her criminal record.

QUEENIE: Who wants it anyway? She's probably a pukin' prostitute somewhere, walkin' around the street with a gutful of gin. What dirty bitch would leave a kid before its eyes was open to be pushed around by a buncha bastards who only want some sucker to do the housework for them? I bailed myself outa that crap when I was lucky thirteen and found out somebody liked my body. I been renting it out ever since.

ROCKY: But the offers are gettin' fewer and the rates are gettin' lower. Next year you'll be dishwasher at the corner lunch.

QUEENIE: Listen, asshole, as long as there's houses fulla jewelry an' furs, this girl's hands will help to keep the insurance companies in business, and don't you forget it. It's you stinkin' pimps who better move fast an' get it made before your hair an' teeth rot out on the sidewalk. I'll wave at your bench as I ride past the park in my limousine.

MONA: *(seeing the GUARD approach)* Six!

Enter the GUARD called "Holy Face."

GUARD: Book-up! Okay Curlylocks, it's your turn to wheel the library around, I'm advised from the office, so try not to spend too much time visiting your friends en route ... everybody's entitled to a book, too. Your pram's in the corridor.

QUEENIE: Thanks Daddy-O, I'll save you a Baby Bunting book.

QUEENIE combs his hair in preparation for the excursion.

GUARD: We have another nice little detail in the V.D. ward. A new patient just puked all over his cell, but he's too weak to mop it up.

MONA: The poor kid!

GUARD: Okay, beautiful. I figure even you might be trusted up there.

QUEENIE: Always the little mother, but don't go giving any kisses till he's had his shots, Nurse.

QUEENIE exits into the corridor wheeling the library cart.

QUEENIE: Cigars, cigarettes, vaseline! Everything for the home!

ROCKY: Thanks, Captain! I was just about to bash their heads together when you made the scene. You saved me a trip to the tower.

GUARD: It's temporary, believe me. You've been getting closer to it every day. Don't start brooding, Smith ... that doesn't help in here. Get yourself a book or something before lights out.

SMITTY: Yes sir.

ROCKY: My, my! What a polite little chap. Isn't he sweet, Officer?

GUARD: Lay off him Tibber, or I'll have you moved to a stricter dormitory. Can't you get along anywhere?

ROCKY: Sure, outside!

GUARD: Is that why we're honoured by your presence so often?

ROCKY: Well the law don't like to see a smart guy get ahead. They want suckers who'll take a few cents a week, a row of brass buttons, and call it a living.

GUARD: But we can walk home when the work's done without an armed escort. Think about that, big shot!

ROCKY: I'm thinkin'.

He gives the GUARD a look that seems to make the GUARD uneasy,

ROCKY: You wanta stay nice an' honest—and keep it that way. Like, I mean next year ya kin take off wit' yer pension, ain't it? That is—if nothing don't go wrong.

GUARD: Lights out at eight o'clock, Smith! Be ready for bed by then.

SMITTY: Eight?

GUARD: That's right. You're up at six. It won't seem so early when you get used to the idea that, in the evening, there's no place to go.

SMITTY: I guess so.

GUARD: Okay, Florence Nightingale—on the double!

He exits with MONA.

ROCKY: Oh boy! That sucker's ulcer's gonna kill'im afore he gits the chance t'sit at home in a rockin' chair.

SMITTY: He sure did look sick when he went out.

ROCKY: He's sick an' he makes me sick. You ain't smart, ya know, Smitty!

SMITTY: How come?

ROCKY: Fruits always get ya in the deep crap.

SMITTY: I don't know; I never knew any before.

ROCKY: You ain't been around.

SMITTY: No, I guess not.

ROCKY: They'll screw you up every time.

SMITTY: How?

ROCKY: 'Cause they're all phonies ... gutless; they're all finks.

SMITTY: You sound like you've had experience with them.

ROCKY: An overdose! But no more! I gotta get me one when I get outa the joint. I'm gonna break both her legs ... then I'm gonna put a coupla sharp chicks out on the hustle for me. That's the real dough.

SMITTY: You mean ... women?

ROCKY: Let me tell ya! They were fallin' all over Rocky for me to be their boy, but I latched on to this one homo first to make a fast buck. Took him for everything he had ... almost!

SMITTY: The homo?

ROCKY: Fag!

SMITTY: Oh—queer.

ROCKY: More money than bloody brains! Crazy about me! Old man's a big shot millionaire—stock exchange, race horses—the whole bit, but his one son was real fruit. It took some connin', but I got in solid ... weekly allowance, swell apartment, lotsa booze and company and a Cadillac convertible.

SMITTY: All yours?

ROCKY: Except the heap! That's how she got me. I was browned off with the freak and split. Sold the works ... television set, cut-glass decanters and whisky glasses, paintin's and statoos ... all that crap! I split in the Caddy with a roll would choke an elephant an' had me a ball ... hotel rooms an' motels from Montreal to Windsor ... Forty-two Street, Frisco ... dames, cards, booze! Man, was I livin' high!

SMITTY: Money run out?

ROCKY: Hell no! When ya got it, ya can always make it, but that fruit had the brass to call the bulls and get me picked up for takin' the Caddy.

SMITTY: Because it wasn't yours?

ROCKY: What I take is mine—that's my motto. But these queers always like one string to keep ya in line. This bastard kept the car in her name so she could screw me up when the time came.

SMITTY: So he ... she laid a charge?

ROCKY: Hell, no! She wanted me back, that's all! We agreed on a story to cover all the crap stirred up, but her old man and the bulls stepped in anyways and fixed me good. They tried to throw the book at me. Now, I'm gonna fix her, an' when I'm finished she won't be able to cruise no more little boys for about a year, except out a window or on a stretcher!

SMITTY: If you do that, maybe they'll send you back again.

ROCKY: You sure are dumb. After you do a job, like I'm gonna, on somebody, they're scared crapless ... glad to give ya both sides o' the street. Never let a fruit scare ya ... the cops don't like them either, so underneath they're yellow as a broken egg. Don't ever forget that.

SMITTY: I'll remember.

ROCKY: Ya know, I could make a real sharp guy outa you. Ya got a head an' ya don't shoot your mouth too much.

SMITTY: I don't know too much.

ROCKY: You'll learn, kid! You'll learn. Listen to old Rocky an' you'll get to sit on the sunny side of the yard. See ... I'm in this dormitory because I raise hell a bit. That's why they put me with these two fruits—to watch me. But there's bigger an' better dorms with more guys, an' that's where I'll be goin' back to ... an' so could you, if you play along with Rocky.

SMITTY: How do you mean?

ROCKY: Well ya gotta have a buddy, see? Ya can't get chummy with the whole joint, an' specially no fruits. If ya get that name, your ass is cooked when you get to a good dorm. Why d'ya think I give 'em a hard time here? If you're smart, you'll do the same thing. There's real guys in some corridors, so ya wanna keep your nose clean.

SMITTY: I sure don't want anybody to think I'm queer.

ROCKY: Good! That's what I like t'hear.

SMITTY: Why would they put me in this particular dormitory, I wonder? To watch me, too?

ROCKY: Ya musta done somethin' goofy before your bit here ... took a poke at a copper or some- thin' like that. They won't leave ya here if Rocky can swing somethin' for us. The other blocks are probably filled up, but we'll be movin' soon. Would you go for that, kid?

SMITTY: Maybe it would be better.

ROCKY: Stick with the Rock an' you'll be looked up at. That ain't easy in the joint. Every jerk's lookin' for your jellyspot. I didn't get the name I got by takin' it off these goons. Even the screws step easy on me. See how I talk to Holy Face? His blood turns to crap around Rocky.

SMITTY: He doesn't seem to stop you too much.

ROCKY: Nobody stops this boy. Besides I got somethin' on Holy Face. I'll tell you if you make up your mind who your buddy's gonna be. Remember what happened to Mona. You're sittin' duck for a gang splash if ya ain't got a old man. I'm offerin' to be your old man, kid, an' if you're wise you'll think fast. Whadda ya say?

SMITTY: Would it keep me from ... what happened to Mona ... in the storeroom?

ROCKY: Ya wouldn't want all those goons to pile on ya, would ya now?

SMITTY: No ... for God's sake, no!

ROCKY: Am I your old man then?

SMITTY: Like ... a buddy, you mean?

ROCKY: Sure, that's the score. I'll kill any son of a bitch lays a hand on ya.

SMITTY: Okay ... and ... thanks!

ROCKY: (tossing SMITTY his cigarette lighter) Here's a firebox for ya, kid. Keep it! We're gonna get along good, Smitty. Ya wanna know what I got on Holy Face?

SMITTY: Well, sure!

ROCKY: He took a pigeon outa the joint for a pal o' mine, so I know all about it, an' he knows I got the goods on him. I throw him a hint every once in a while when he thinks he's gonna push me around.

SMITTY: A pigeon?

ROCKY: A letter ... a message! Jailbird lingo for stuff that ain't allowed— (with a confiding wink) like a punk kid is a chicken an' if he gives ya a kiss, that's a bluebird. Everythin' you write's gotta go through a censor in the office, but if ya got somethin' goin' for ya, ya can allays buy some screw. One o' my buddies gave Holy Face fifty bucks t' get a pigeon out for him. That's about as much dough as a lousy screw makes in a week, an' Holy Face ain't so holy as he acts when it comes to makin' hisself a buck.

SMITTY: But there's no money in here. They kept mine at the office.

ROCKY: You're green, kid. There's all kinds of lines goin' around the joint.

SMITTY: But how?

ROCKY: Easy! Some relative calls in for a Sunday visit, slips Holy Face the dough, an' next chance he's got, he divvies up, takes out his half-C note and posts your pigeon.

SMITTY: Why not get the relatives to take a message for nothing?

ROCKY: There's things some relatives won't do. This was a junk deal … dope … big-time stuff!

SMITTY: What kind of excuse could you give to ask fifty dollars from a relative … here?

ROCKY: Plenty! Tell 'em the meals are crap an' cash could get ya candy, magazines, or nice face soap … some story like that. Say ya can only get stuff through a good-hearted screw who's takin' a chance for ya. Play it hearts and flowers … works good on most relatives.

SMITTY: I guess so.

ROCKY: So come on, baby, let's me and you take a shower before bedtime.

SMITTY: A shower?

ROCKY: Sure! I like one every night before lights out!

SMITTY: Go ahead! I had one this afternoon when they brought me in and gave me a uniform.

ROCKY: It ain't gonna kill ya t'take another. I like company.

SMITTY: Tomorrow, Rocky.

ROCKY: Right now!

SMITTY: No … thanks!

ROCKY: I like my kids clean.

SMITTY: I'm clean.

ROCKY: Get up!

SMITTY: What …

ROCKY: Get movin' … into that shower room.

SMITTY: Rocky, you're not …

ROCKY: I said *move*, boy!

SMITTY: No! I changed my mind. I don't want an old man.

ROCKY: You got a old man, an' that's better than the storeroom, buddy boy!

SMITTY: I'll take a chance.

ROCKY: I'll make sure it's no chance. It's me or a gang splash. Now move your ass fast. I'm not used to punks tellin' me what they want.

He grabs SMITTY's arm, twisting it behind the boy's back. SMITTY gives a small cry of pain, but ROCKY throws a hand over his mouth, pushing him toward the shower room. SMITTY pulls his face free.

SMITTY: Rocky … please … if you like me …

ROCKY: I like you … an' you're gonna like me!

Blackout.

Scene Two

Three weeks later, evening.

As the scene opens, SMITTY and MONA are lying or sitting on their own cots, each reading his own book. ROCKY can be heard offstage, singing in the shower room. QUEENIE and the GUARD are both absent.

ROCKY: *(singing)* Oh, they call me The Jungle King, The Jungle King … *(shouting)* Hey-y Smitty!

SMITTY: Yeah?

He continues reading.

ROCKY: *(offstage)* Hey Smitty!

SMITTY: Yeah, Rocky.

ROCKY: *(offstage)* Roll me some smokes!

SMITTY: Okay, okay.

He moves, still reading, to ROCKY's cot, where he finds packages of tobacco, but no papers.

ROCKY: *(still offstage and singing)* Oh, the Lion and the Monkey …

SMITTY: What you got there, Jan? You must have had thirty takeouts in three weeks.

MONA: It's a book of poems.

SMITTY: Any good?

MONA: Yes, but it's not exactly what I wanted.

SMITTY: I've got something better; well, more useful, anyway. Come here; have a look.

MONA: *(after crossing to join SMITTY on ROCKY's bed)* "Advanced Automobile Mechanics." Very practical!

SMITTY: I'm a practical guy. You see, I figure I might not be able to get a job in an office, because—well—bonding, and all that. You know what I mean. Anyway, I worked evenings after school and all day Saturday in my fath—in a garage. I learned a lot about car motors, so I might as well put it to use. Mechanics are paid pretty good, you know.

MONA: That's wonderful, Smitty. This way, your time won't be wasted. You can make your six months really tell, and then after ...

ROCKY: *(entering singing and combing his hair)* The Jungle King, the Jungle King ... Say-y! Whadya call this here scene—squatters' rights? Let me tellya somethin'—quick! In good ol' Cabbage-town, there's a li'l joint where me gang hangs out; it's called the Kay Won Cafe. Guess who runs it?

SMITTY: A Chinaman?

ROCKY: Wrong! Charlie owns it, but Rocky runs it. A pretty-boy comes in there 'n' I don't like his face much—me boys wait fer 'im outside, an' grab aholt his arms 'n' legs, an' Rock, who's welterweight champ 'round there, changes the smart guy's kisser a li'l.

SMITTY: You don't like your punching bag to swing too free. Your toughs have to hold him, eh?

ROCKY: I do things *my* way. There's another spot, on the roughest corner in town, called Eddie's Poolroom. Now—guess who runs it?

SMITTY: Eddie?

ROCKY: Oh boy, do you learn slow! Same story. Eddie owns the shack, but ya kin bet yer sweet billiard cue The Rock says who's behin' the eight ball 'round there.

MONA: *(rising from ROCKY's bed)* All right, Rocky—I get the point.

ROCKY: Ya better see it, Pinhead—or I'll give ya a fat eye t' wear. Now beat it!

SMITTY: Leave him alone.

ROCKY: Oh, you ain't talkin' t' me.

SMITTY: Just don't touch him.

ROCKY: Whadya think he is—precious or somethin'?

SMITTY: Lay off, that's all.

ROCKY: How come ya talk t' me like that? Ain't I good t'ya kid? Don't I getya cookies outa the kitchen? An' rubber t' chew, off Holy Face?

SMITTY: You're so good to me—and I'm so sick of it all.

ROCKY: Now, now! That ain't a nice way t' talk, when I just bin fixin' it up with Baldy t' git us in "D" Dorm. Ain't that whatya wanted all along?

SMITTY: Let's not overdo this "togetherness."

ROCKY: Sad—sad—sad! We-ell—I guess I'll just hafta 'range us a li'l extra gym, so's ya don't feel too neglected. The boys'll wanna meet ya before we move inta their Big Dorm. Tomorrow afternoon, Smitty? Get together wit de gang—just like at Eddie's or the Kay Won?

SMITTY: No, Rocky—no!

ROCKY: No what? No ketchup or no apple-sauce?

SMITTY: No—no extra gym.

MONA: Please, Rocky—we were only ...

ROCKY: Shut up, ya wall-eyed whore!

MONA: I only ...

QUEENIE is heard singing, approaching in corridor.

SMITTY: Six! Six! Forget it!

QUEENIE: *(offstage, singing)*
I'm a big girl now,
I wanna be handled like a big girl now;
I'm tired a stayin' home each evenin' after dark,
Tired a bein' dynamite without a spark ...

Let me in. *(stamping his feet)* Let me in this cell!

QUEENIE and the GUARD called Holy Face enter, QUEENIE carrying a small, white, cone-shaped Dixie cup. He continues singing.

QUEENIE: I wanna learn what homos do in old Queen's Park ...

GUARD: I wanna learn what you do up in that hospital so often.

QUEENIE: I show the surgeon my stretch marks.

GUARD: I know it can't be only for that coneful of cold cream. I'll bet if I gave you a frisk, I'd find scissors or a scalpel tucked in the seam of your shirt. I oughta search you every time out.

QUEENIE: *(throwing open his arms)* Oh do, Daddy-O! I just can't wait t' feel your big callous hands on m' satin-smooth bod-ee!

GUARD: I'd as soon have syphilis.

QUEENIE: Who's she? Any relation to Gonorita?

GUARD: Cut it! Let's have a little common decency.

QUEENIE: What's that—somethin' ya eat? Ya know, you're not well at all; the way you been belchin' and turnin' green around here lately. Maybe that ulcer of yours has soured into cancer, an' you'll never make that first pension cheque.

GUARD: I'll live to collect it all, and my stomach will sweeten considerably next winter, when I'm down in Florida—away from you bunch of bums.

GUARD belches loudly.

QUEENIE: Pardon *you!* Will the rest be up in a minute? Maybe if the Doc finds out you ain't fit to work, they'll fire ya. Part-pension won't pay the shot for Palm Beach.

GUARD: One thing—I'm going to find out what you do with all those gobs of goo from the dispensary. I suspect it's got somethin' to do with the backside of decency.

GUARD exits to shower room.

QUEENIE: How gross of you, Gertrude. No secret at all! I mix the cold cream with coal dust off the window sills, an' sell it to the screws for mascara. Helen Roobenbitch ain't got nothin' on me.

He exits to shower room. Sound of a slap.

QUEENIE: *(offstage)* Brutality! Brutality!

GUARD: *(entering)* Next stop for that one is the bug wing. It might as well wear its jacket the same way it does everything else—backwards!

ROCKY: Take it an' tie it up an' don't never ever bring it back no more.

GUARD: Okay. Book-up time. Anybody want a trip to the library?

ROCKY: Yeah! I'll take a book of matches—t' the works.

GUARD: Pyromania would become you, Tibber; you got all the other bugs.

ROCKY: It bugs me sometimes watchin' noses stuck into sheets o' paper day 'n' night. Ain't that right, Smitty?

GUARD: Keep right on reading, Smith! There's no safer pastime around here. Tibber never got past Super-Rat. Well—if that's it, I'll head for a smoke in the lock—

MONA: I'd like to go to the library.

GUARD: Again? You're there every time the doors open. Can't you wait for the cart to come around?

MONA: It won't have what I'm looking for.

GUARD: Cripes! if there wasn't bars on that book room, you'd be breakin' in.

MONA: Mr. Benson said that I could find something to do for the Christmas concert.

He shows GUARD a library pass-card.

GUARD: I thought Benson ran the orchestra. Why don't he get you to play the skin flute?

ROCKY: Yah! Yah! The Minnie-Lousy could give him lessons.

MONA: Mr. Benson's in charge of drama for the concert, too. I'm going to do something like that.

GUARD: Why don't you do "I'm a Big Girl Now"? Sassy-face in there could teach you the words.

MONA: I don't sing.

GUARD: Oh, hell! Come on, Hortense; your carriage awaits without.

MONA: Thank you.

SMITTY: See you after, Jan.

MONA: See you, Smitty.

GUARD and MONA exit.

ROCKY: *(singing introduction to "I'm a Big Girl Now")*
Me 'n' my chilehood sweetheart
Ha' come t' de partin' o' de ways …

SMITTY: Oh, you're really funny.

QUEENIE: *(entering from shower room singing)*
He still treats me like he did In our bab-ee days,
But I'm a little bit older
And a little bit bolder
Since both of us were three …

ROCKY: Put down that bloody book, kid!

SMITTY does so, and sits looking at ROCKY.

QUEENIE: *(still singing)*
I'm a little more padded
Somethin' new has been added …

ROCKY: I got best bunk in this joint; can see everything comin' at us down the hall. I wantya t' know I'm real particular who uses it. That thing don't sit on my bunk no more.

SMITTY: *(rising)* That'll make two of us …

ROCKY: *(pushing him back)* What's mine is yours, kid.

QUEENIE: An' what's urine is my-un.

SMITTY: Keep it! I only want what's mine.

He gets up again and goes to lie face down on his own cot.

ROCKY: Come again on them mashed potatoes.

SMITTY: You heard me.

ROCKY: Watchit! I warned ya 'bout the tomato sauce. Be a good kid now, an' roll me a smoke.

SMITTY casually rolls a cigarette, as though it is second nature to do so for ROCKY.

QUEENIE: And when you've done that, Cinderella—mop the floor, wash the windows, shake the rugs and …

SMITTY: Aw, cut it, Queenie!

ROCKY: Smitty likes to keep the old man happy, don't you, kid?

SMITTY: Sure!

QUEENIE: *(singing to the tune of "Old Man River")*
Far far be it from me to free the slaves;
I'm not honest, and my name ain't Abe.
He just keeps rollin'—rollin' those ciggie-boos.

ROCKY: Yer name'll be mud if you keep that up.

QUEENIE: Queen Mud to you, peasant!

ROCKY: I think she's jealous, Smitty.

QUEENIE: Of what, for crap's sake?

ROCKY: 'Cause me an' Smitty is such good buddies. Bugs you, don't it?

QUEENIE: I don't give a damn if you legalize it in church-up next Sunday, and have fourteen babies. It ain't green you see in my eye, it's red, 'cause I hate to see a guy who could be a hippo playin' bumboy to a haywire loony who'll get him an assbeat or a trip to the tower before his time's up.

ROCKY: You're really askin' for it, ain't ya?

QUEENIE: I'd like nothin' better than for you to take a swing at me, rockhead. Then we'll see who's gonna be called mud!

ROCKY: I'll find a better way, and you can believe it.

QUEENIE: It'll have to be while I'm asleep, 'cause I can see your next move like you drew me a map.

ROCKY: How come you're so smart … for a queer?

QUEENIE: 'Cause I get to bed bright an' early, and I'm up with the jailbirds—fresh as a pansy! We can't all be as dumb as you, Dora; it makes for bad publicity.

ROCKY: When you find me underneath, class me with you. For now you call me Mister!

QUEENIE: How'd you like to say hello to your dear old friend Baldy in the office? He tells me he knows you from your first semester here, when you were chicken, like Smitty. I believe he gave your coming out party, and made you debutante of the year.

ROCKY: I ain't interested in no old fairy's tales.

QUEENIE: May I quote you, or don't you want Baldy to pick you out a nice private room, where you can count your belly button and say your prayers, to pass the time?

ROCKY: Shoot off your mouth any way you want. Baldy an' me get along just fine.

QUEENIE: Yeah, he's got a soft spot in his head for you … except when he sees Smitty. Your sonny outshines you, it seems.

ROCKY: If he likes me, he's gotta like my buddy too.

QUEENIE: He does. Oh yes indeedy, *how* he does!

SMITTY: Why don't you two turn it off? What am I anyways, a piece of goods on the bargain counter?

QUEENIE: That's up to you, honey. If you smartened up, you could be as high-priced as you want.

SMITTY: I just don't want to be bugged, that's all. Let me do my time the easy way.

QUEENIE: Like the Mona Lisa?

SMITTY: What's Mona Lisa got to do with it?

QUEENIE: Well, she don't believe in wheelin' and dealin' either, and you see what she gets. You gotta hustle inside too, you know, or you could end up like a chippy-ass, wipin' up somebody's puke.

SMITTY: I thought you were Mona's friend.

QUEENIE: I am, and I guess I like her 'cause she's different from me. But that don't mean a comer like you has to settle for the crappy end of the stick. You could have it all your own way ... by just reachin' for it. You can't park your keester in a corner 'round here.

SMITTY: I'm satisfied to sit it out.

QUEENIE: Okay. Play it safe, but don't be sorry later. Nobody'll bother you while you got a old man, but you'll be anybody's baby when he drops you for a new chicken.

ROCKY sings first two lines of "Jalousie".

QUEENIE: It's Catso-Ratso, your old gearbox buddy who's got the greenies. That Wop's gonna get you good.

ROCKY: No macaroni scares me, sister!

Sound of metal door opening and closing at a distance.

VOICE: *(at distance along corridor)* Tower up!

SECOND VOICE: Tower screw!

THIRD VOICE: *(closer)* Hack from Tower!

FOURTH VOICE: Holy Face with hack!

FIFTH VOICE: *(nearby)* Who they after?

SIXTH VOICE: *(next cell)* They're still comin'. Must be after Rocky! *(same)* Hey Rocky! What'd ya do now?

GUARD: *(offstage)* Shut those goddam traps!

VOICE: *(at distance)* Holy Face is a stinkin' lush.

Onstage cell inmates pick it up.

ROCKY: Beats his wife an' bangs his daughter.

QUEENIE: Not our Holy Face! He does it on his dear ol' granny.

GUARD: *(offstage)* Who in hell said that?

A short silence.

VOICE: *(at distance)* It was me, Sir—GAWD! Ain't you ashamed o' yerself?

General laughter from all voices along corridor and on stage.

GUARD: *(to unseen tower guard)* Jenkins! Go get those bastards!

Sound of a heavy stick banging on metal doors, fading into distance—then silence. GUARD appears.

ROCKY: *(singing old hymn)*
Rock of ages, cleft for me-ee
Let me hide meself in thee-hee—

GUARD: *(entering cell)* That's just lovely— Tibber! I can hardly wait to hear the rest at the Christmas concert.

ROCKY: Thanks, Cap! Bring the wife and kids. They deserve a treat for living with you all year.

GUARD: I'd as soon see them into a monkey cage at the zoo.

ROCKY: Fine sense of loyalty to your students, professor! Tch-tch ... You hurt my feelin's.

QUEENIE: How do you think the monkeys must feel? Speakin' of monkeys, where in hell's the Mona Lisa?

GUARD: I took it over to the library. It's trying to find some book it needs for a number in the Christmas concert.

QUEENIE: I don't need no book for my act! What's she gonna do ... read "Alice in Wonderland"?

GUARD: I believe it's hunting on the Shakespeare shelf.

QUEENIE: Oh no, who does she think she is ... Bette Davis?

GUARD: As long as it doesn't ask me to play Romeo, I couldn't care less.

QUEENIE: "But soft, what balcony from yonder Juliet breaks … "

SMITTY: Mona shouldn't try to do Shakespeare here. They'd probably laugh, and …

QUEENIE: And what? Don't you think we could use a good laugh around this dump? Let her do it if she's fool enough. She'd be worse tryin' to do my act.

SMITTY: But they might hurt her feelings …

QUEENIE: Yeah? Maybe *you* should play Romeo. What do you think, Captain?

GUARD: I suppose a little Shakespeare's all right. We've never had the classics before. Maybe it'll start a whole new trend in Christmas concerts.

QUEENIE: Well, I'll stick to song and dance and a few bumps and grinds.

SMITTY: *(thinking aloud)* But why?

QUEENIE: Why bumps and grinds?

SMITTY: Huh? No … no I was thinking of something else.

GUARD: Come on Tibber … on your feet! They want you in the big office.

ROCKY: What in hell for?

GUARD: Well, I'm reasonably sure it's not to give you the Nobel Peace Prize.

ROCKY: I ain't done nothin'.

GUARD: I wouldn't know. I got a few dozen other characters to watch besides you. Make it fast. I've got to bring the Shakespearean actress back before lights out.

ROCKY: Crap! Roll me some smokes for later, Smitty!

SMITTY: Yeah! I'll try to keep busy so I don't miss you.

ROCKY and GUARD exit.

QUEENIE: *(singing first three lines of "I'll See You Again" after them)* You don't smoke, an' you spend half your time rollin' smokes for that haywire goon. What's the matter with you?

SMITTY: *(dryly)* We're "buddies."

QUEENIE: I'd like to know how he got you to make a mistake like that! I had an idea when I first saw you that you're the kind of guy who'd like to be on top.

SMITTY: Of what?

QUEENIE: Of everything. You're no lolliflier—you don't have to play it the way I do. Whatever you're gonna be here … you gotta be it in a big way. My way, I'm happy. The hippos know I'm a mean bitch, so I got no questions to answer. But I'm nobody's punk, and you shouldn't be either.

SMITTY: So what am I supposed to do … let you pick me an old man? How the hell would that make any difference?

QUEENIE: You don't need a old man, you could be a hippo, if you play your cards right.

SMITTY: So deal me a hand, and see if it comes up a winner.

QUEENIE: Okay. Here's a straight. Rocky's nowhere near top dog in this joint … just a hard crap disturber who gets a wide berth from everybody. He ain't in at all, and as long as you're with him, you ain't either. If you get out from under Rocky, and I spread the news you're boss in this block, they'll listen.

SMITTY: So how do I do it? Give him to some sucker for Christmas?

QUEENIE: Who'd take him as a gift? You could wrap him up, just the same.

SMITTY: I'm tempted. What would I use, crap paper?

QUEENIE: You ain't scared of Rocky?

SMITTY: Hell, no! I just figured he helped to keep me out of the storeroom. He said if I was asked to that party, I wouldn't be a guest, and I didn't like the idea of providing entertainment for anybody's wolf pack.

QUEENIE: So that's how he caught you … the cagey bastard.

SMITTY: You going to sound off about that?

QUEENIE: Not on your life! It wouldn't do me any good to broadcast how Rocky conned you into his nest. When I tipped you off to the storeroom gang splash, it was a cue to get next to the politicians who can do you some good. You shouldn't have give in so soon, or so easy.

SMITTY: Were you here?

QUEENIE: No, damn it!

SMITTY: Well, let me tell you, it wasn't so easy.

QUEENIE: Yeah? Can you go?

SMITTY: You think I didn't fight?

QUEENIE: So how come Rocky won?

SMITTY: With his mouth! Every time he said storeroom, I remembered about Mona, and my fists melted like candy floss.

QUEENIE: *(excited)* You takin' a shower tonight?

SMITTY: I don't know. I try to make them few and far between. If I had a choice, I'd be dirty as a craphouse rat before taking a shower with Rocky.

QUEENIE: Take one tonight, and I'll give six. One thing about Rocky, he don't squeal.

SMITTY: What did you say?

QUEENIE: I'll ... give ... *six!*

SMITTY: Well! How do you think I should play it?

QUEENIE: You want to be on top, don't ya? I ain't interested in no stars can't live up to their billing. If I put it out that you're telling me an' Rocky what to do, I gotta believe half of it.

SMITTY: I begin to read you. You want me to punch his head in. Right?

QUEENIE: Have you got what it takes?

SMITTY: All stored up!

QUEENIE: Then let it go.

SMITTY: In the crapper?

QUEENIE: I'll give you six in case Holy Face is hangin' around, but try and make it fast. Turn on a coupla showers to cover the slammin'.

SMITTY: You're on! Oh! Oh! Hold it a minute! What about after?

QUEENIE: What about it?

SMITTY: What will I owe you? You're not doing this out of sweet charity.

QUEENIE: Am I so hard to be nice to?

SMITTY: That depends ...

QUEENIE: I mean ... when you want and how you want—I'm nobody's old man, if you know what I mean.

SMITTY: It'd be a change, anyway.

QUEENIE: Whatever you want. You'll be top dog in this corner.

SMITTY: Six!

Sound of key in corridor door ... enter GUARD and ROCKY.

GUARD: Slipped out of that one like a snake, didn't you, Tibber?

ROCKY: Sure! I don't let no finks hang me on the hook.

GUARD: You'll get caught one day, and when you do, I want to be there.

ROCKY: And here I thought you was my true friend.

GUARD: You make no friends, Tibber!

ROCKY: I got Smitty. I tell him everything ... but everything, screw.

GUARD: That's his business.

ROCKY: Now, don't ya wish ya hadn't slapped me across the mouth three years ago, Mr. Screw?

GUARD: If I had to worry about every mouth I slapped around here, I'd be better off working as a wet nurse.

ROCKY: Well, maybe ya slug so many, ya forgot, but I ain't. It was my first day in the joint, an' I didn't call you "sir."

GUARD: You always were a nervy little brat.

ROCKY: So you said, an' ya smashed me across the jaw wit' both sides o' your big mitt, an' when I says, "Ain't y'afraid I'll tell the Warden?" ya says, why should ya be; twenty years ago ya smacked me father in the mouth, an' he was a thief an' a pimp just like me. Ain't that so, Hack?

GUARD: Yeah, that's it all right.

ROCKY: So-o, how's it feel t' have yer own arse roastin' over the pit—an' fer a little fifty-buck boo-boo?

GUARD: You bastard!

He exits.

ROCKY: Oh, how sweet it is. *(laughing)* See how I shake 'em up, Smitty old kid? *(stretching out on his bed)* Say, where's my weeds, pal?

SMITTY: Roll your own—pal.

ROCKY rolls a cigarette without taking his eyes from SMITTY's face.

ROCKY: Gimme a light, kid!

SMITTY: *(tossing a lighter to ROCKY)* Light on your ass!

ROCKY: *(carefully)* You two take a shower while The Rock was out on business?

QUEENIE: *(coyly)* I should be so lucky.

ROCKY: Smitty, come here. I'm gonna to tell you what happens to jokers what try to give Rocky the dirty end.

SMITTY: I can hear you.

ROCKY: That phony Wop, Catsolino, finked to a shop screw on me, an' now he's all wrapped up in the General's office ... wishin' he'd kept his hole closed.

QUEENIE: I thought good old Catso was your machine-shop buddy.

ROCKY: Think again. He mouthed off to the machine-shop screw I lifted his lousy firebox, so they hauled me up to the General, give me a quick frisk, an' when they couldn't find nothin', put the pressure on me. I took it good for you, Smitty.

SMITTY: For me?

ROCKY: Sure! Where d'ya think you got your screwin' firebox—from Ronson's?

SMITTY: But I didn't want the bloody lighter. All I used it for was to light your crappin' smokes when you ask me to come on like your butler.

ROCKY: Alla same, I took it good so's they wouldn't put you on the spot, kid.

QUEENIE: My hero! They make medals for people like you and Saint Joan.

ROCKY: Can it! One thing about it, old Catso's headed for the tower as sure as Christ made little apples an' his mother's ass. His Wop temper got riled up when the screws started shovin' him, and he gave old Sad-Ass Shriker a punch in the mouth. He sure picked the wrong target. Shriker's had a rod-on for that Wop a mile long. Shriker don't like no sissies, Micks, Wops, or Kikes, an' when he gets ahold of one, he's just gotta get 'em into the butcher shop so he can have his jollies.

QUEENIE: That's Mona's dearest boy friend ... the one who slapped her little keester for her. I think she still dreams about him.

SMITTY: That's not funny, Queenie.

QUEENIE: Who says so? It gives me a laugh.

ROCKY: Six!

Sound of key in the door. Enter GUARD and MONA.

GUARD: Make way for the great Sarah Bernhardt ... or is it Heartburn?

He exits.

QUEENIE: Don't stand up; she's just passing through. No autographs, no interviews, no pictures, and please desist from climbing up on her balcony. Cripes! Look at the expression. She's takin' this tragic stuff serious. Pardon me, madam ... do we perchance breathe the same air?

SMITTY: Leave her alone, Queenie. You look upset, Mona, what's eating you?

MONA: *(trembling)* I ... I saw something awful as I passed the hospital door.

QUEENIE: Don't tell me one of the boys was havin' a baby?

MONA: Tony ...

QUEENIE: *(quickly interested)* Catsolino?

MONA: Yes, he ...

ROCKY: Cripes! Those screws musta really marked him up. That circus troupe he calls his family'll be cut off from Sunday visits while old Catso's walkin' around lookin' like a road map.

MONA: It wasn't just that.

SMITTY: What then, for God's sake?

MONA: The doctor was holding a stethoscope to his heart.

ROCKY: Maybe they wanted t' see if Wops has got one.

QUEENIE: I know what she means, an' so do you, rat. Some buddy you are to let him get it. See where Rocky takes his pals, Smitty?

SMITTY: What? Let me in on it.

QUEENIE: You wouldn't know of course. The butcher always tests your heart before he lets 'em cut you up in the kitchen.

SMITTY: What are you blowing about?

QUEENIE: There's a little room off the kitchen where they keep a machine an' a coupla long pieces of cowhide … only that torture chamber ain't for the dumb animals.

SMITTY: They're not going to …

QUEENIE: You're goddam right they are. You don't slug a screw in the chops an' get off light. Catso's going to get the cat-o'-nine-tails.

SMITTY: God help him.

QUEENIE: Shall we pray?

ROCKY: The only time you get on your knees, bitch, it ain't to pray.

SMITTY: Over a lousy little firebox …

QUEENIE: Ease off Smitty. It ain't your beef.

SMITTY: The lighter was lifted for me.

ROCKY: That ain't what he's getting a ass-beat for. I got no sympathy for a bloody fink. All squealers oughta be shot.

SMITTY: Because of me …

ROCKY: You're buggy …

SMITTY: (to MONA) What are you doing that for?

MONA is standing close to the upstage bars at the extreme end of the wall, near the exit hall, poised in a position of straining to hear some sound from a great distance away. He seems completely occupied with the effort, unaware of the others in the room.

QUEENIE: She's listening for the screams. Sometimes the screws leave the kitchen door open, an' you can just hear from that corner. Once I even heard the bloody slaps of the belt. Musta been old Shriker swingin'.

MONA: Oh-h-h …

He does not seem to hear or see SMITTY.

QUEENIE: Oh, let her get 'er kicks. I think she's a goddam masochist.

SMITTY crosses to pull MONA from the bars almost brutally, but the boy does not seem to care. He only covers his ears with both hands, as though to shut out some sound.

SMITTY: (voice shaking) What do you want to do that for? You trying to bug me? Make me feel guilty?

MONA: (dazed) I'm sorry … I'm sorry.

He sits in a trance on his bed.

ROCKY: I'm sick of this crap. Come on, Smitty, let's take a shower. For some reason I feel real good tonight.

SMITTY: Glad to hear it!

ROCKY: Jesus! Don't tell me you're actual gettin' co-operative?

SMITTY: I am … tonight.

ROCKY: We-ll, it's about time! Give us six, Mona, if you can come outa that stupor.

QUEENIE: Don't bug her! I'll give you six tonight.

ROCKY: When did you get so friendly? I had the impression you didn't exactly like us leavin' you alone, Mother dear.

QUEENIE: (sweetly) Tonight I like it. I'll baby-sit.

ROCKY: I smell a sardine, or two.

QUEENIE: What are ya worried about, Rocky? You must have a guilty conscience!

ROCKY: I got no conscience an' no fat fruit worries me either. Come on, buddy boy.

SMITTY: You can call me Smith.

ROCKY: I don't care what I call you as long as y' do like you're told. Now move your ass.

SMITTY walks into the shower room. ROCKY turns a questioning look on QUEENIE who smiles in reply like the Cheshire cat. ROCKY goes out to the shower room and QUEENIE crosses to stand near the door to the corridor, without looking toward the shower room door.

MONA: *(starting)* Something's wrong in there. What's that?

QUEENIE: Mind your own screwin' business.

MONA: But Smitty …

QUEENIE: Can take care of himself. He's my boy now, and don't you forget it.

MONA: But Rocky …

QUEENIE: Is getting a lesson he's needed for a long time.

MONA: How do you … ?

QUEENIE: Because I can pick 'em real good, honey. I know a born hippo when I see one. I ain't spent time around these joints since I was fourteen for nothing. Smitty's got everythin' it takes to run his own show, but he needs me t' help him. I'm big-hearted that way.

MONA: There's no sound now …

QUEENIE: I said make it fast. You give me six. I'm gonna check the damage.

QUEENIE goes to shower room, returning almost at once.

QUEENIE: You still got that alcohol an' bandages I give you t' hide under your mattress?

MONA: You planned this—to get Smitty.

QUEENIE: Right where I can see him—like I got all the other suckers on this street.

MONA: He could have been caught—or killed. You're not even on his side.

QUEENIE: If he's got a side! Shut your nellie jaw, before I blind you, bitch—an' get me that goddam medicine bag.

MONA: Yes—I'll get it. *(He does so.)*

QUEENIE: An' get ready to bow low, Miss Shakespeare. This block had a good queen; all it needed was a king.

He exits triumphantly, leaving MONA looking lost and alone.

Curtain.

ACT TWO

Christmas Eve.

At the end of the dormitory, ROCKY lies smoking on his bed; at the other end, SMITTY is propped up on his with a book, reading; the GUARD, Holy Face, sits on a high stool upstage, and a portable record player is going, the music filling the dormitory with something of a night-club atmosphere.

ROCKY: Crap, Captain! The Christmas stunt is lousy enough, without havin' t' watch stinkin' rehearsals.

GUARD: We could always arrange to reserve you a private room, Mr. Tibber. There's a vacancy right now in Gunsel's Alley …

ROCKY: Screw off!

GUARD: If you think this is any treat for me, guess again. I got a television when I want to be entertained. The tumblers and acrobats and what-have-you are using up the stage and gym floor, so the leading ladies will just have to practise here at home, with the family. You are what might be described as a captive audience. *(walking toward shower room door)* Move it, girls … you're on! These critics of yours will be asleep before you get into those costumes.

QUEENIE: *(calling from shower room)* Thank you, Mr. Sullivan. A little cruisin' music, please, while I remove my jock. I'll take it from the top … as we used to say at the Casino.

The GUARD crosses to reset the record, and QUEENIE enters, looking like a combination of Gorgeous George, Sophie Tucker and Mae West. He wears a platinum-blond wig, spangled sequin dress, long black gloves, large rhinestone jewelry on ears, neck and wrists, heavy make-up, and is carrying a large feather fan. There is no self-consciousness or lack of confidence: movements are large, controlled, voluptuous and sure. He throws open the fan, as ROCKY, SMITTY and the GUARD watch, bending his knees in a slow dip, so the tight gown pulls across his heavy, rounded body, giving the look of an overweight strip teaser beginning the act; slowly he undulates the hips forward and upward in a series of professionally controlled bumps and grinds, the meat and muscle of burlesque dancing. As the record plays the opening to a song, an old night-club favorite,

QUEENIE prepares the way with these bold, sex-conscious movements.

SMITTY: Holy mother of … you look as sexy as hell. Look what we had here, and didn't know it.

QUEENIE: It's all yours, honey—every precious pound.

He picks up the melody from the recording, a parody of "A Good Man Is Hard to Find."

Here is a story, without morals
An' all you fags better pay some mind
'Cause if ya find a man worth keepin'
Be satisfied—and treat him kind.

A hard man is good to find
I always get the other kind
Just when I think that he's my pal
I turn around an' find him actin' like somebody's gal
And then I rave; I even crave
To see him lyin' dead in his grave.
So if your hippo's nice
Take my advice
Hug him in the shower, kiss him every night
Give him plenty oompah, treat him right
'Cause a hard man nowadays is good to find.

There is spontaneous applause, from even ROCKY and the GUARD, for there is an all-embracing extrovert quality to QUEENIE's performance that is somehow contagious, partly because of a warmth generated by a feeling that QUEENIE seems completely happy with himself and his surroundings.

ROCKY: Come on, Queenie … give us another one … real lowdown and dirty.

SMITTY: Yeah, Queenie … sing it for Daddy, and don't forget I like the wiggle accompaniment.

QUEENIE: *(like a famous star)* Sorry, boys … that's gotta wait for the show. Get your tickets early, before the front seats are sold out. I wouldn't wantya t' miss anything headed your way.

SMITTY: Throw it here, kid; I don't need a catcher's mitt.

ROCKY: Turn that stuff on again, Queenie; I might get in the mood.

QUEENIE: Put your gloves on, boys. We ain't got that much time before the show starts, an' this is more or less a costume an' make-up rehearsal. We got our numbers down already, but they didn't get these Christmas decorations in till today. Ain't this gown a flip?

SMITTY: Fits like a second skin. What did you do … grow into it?

QUEENIE: I hadda get Mona to shove me with a shoehorn.

SMITTY: What you hiding under there?

QUEENIE: Nothing, baby—but your Christmas box.

ROCKY: I'll look after the diamonds for ya.

QUEENIE: They musta took a chandelier apart to get all this glass. Feels good, but you couldn't hock it for a plate o' beans.

ROCKY: Looks like they shot a ostrich for ya, too.

QUEENIE: *(waving the fan)* I hope it ain't moulting season in Africa.

SMITTY: You sprung those curls awful fast.

QUEENIE: My teeth an' my ass are my own, Honey!

GUARD: *(caught in the mood)* If my wife could see me now, she'd start divorce proceedings.

QUEENIE: Never mind, baby; think of the beautiful music you an' me could make while she's in Mexico.

ROCKY: As long as you're spreadin' it around, Queenie … my pad's over here. Holy Face ain't got anythin' I can't better.

QUEENIE: *(enjoying every moment)* What am I bid? Line up the Cadillacs on stage left an' the mink coats on the right. What's your offer, Smitty?

SMITTY: All I got is this book on auto mechanics.

QUEENIE: *(with a wink)* Oh, that ain't all you got, Honey.

SMITTY: *(laughing)* You've been peeking again.

ROCKY: Turn on the walkin' music, Queenie, an' give us a the strip you did at the last Christmas concert.

QUEENIE: Are you kidding? I did a week in the tower for that surprise performance. I could hear the boys still whistlin', when they turned the key on your mother. Oh well, the bread an' water was good for my figure. I started the New Year lookin' like a cover off *Vogue!*

GUARD: No more surprises like that one, Queenie, or your concert days will be over. The conveners of this one had a hell of a time getting the General to trust you again.

QUEENIE: Oh, I told them how to fix that up.

GUARD: That's news to me. What did you do?

QUEENIE: I promised the General a little bit.

ROCKY, SMITTY and the GUARD laugh uproari-ously. At this moment, MONA enters, wearing a makeshift costume for Portia's court scene in The Merchant of Venice. *It is a converted red velvet curtain and becomes him somewhat, but contrast between the graceful, almost classic costume and Queenie's glittering ensemble seems incongruous.*

ROCKY: Flyin' crap! What's that supposed to be? Your bathrobe an' nightcap? What're you gonna do ... "The Night Before Christmas"?

QUEENIE: *(in impresario fashion)* Ladies and gentlemen, I want you all to meet Tillie—The Birdwoman, God's gift to the Tree People.

ROCKY, SMITTY and GUARD howl at the announcement, but MONA remains as enigmatic in expression as the painting he is named for.

QUEENIE: What kinda music do you want, Tillie a slow waltz or a minuet? You'll never get those window drapes off the ground.

MONA: I won't need music.

QUEENIE: Well, you need something. *(proffering the fan)* How about these feathers? If you wave 'em hard enough, they might lift you up on your toes; you could call it "The Dying Duck" ballet.

ROCKY: Maybe she oughta have a window to hang herself in.

QUEENIE: You better not do a strip, 'cause you'd hafta have red flannel underwear to go with that smock.

MONA: It's from *The Merchant of Venice.*

QUEENIE: Well, I'd take it back to him, dearie; you got gypped, whatever you paid.

MONA: This costume is for the courtroom scene ...

QUEENIE: Oh, I get it. You're gonna play a judge. That should go over big in this joint.

MONA: It's Portia ...

QUEENIE: It's poor something.

SMITTY: *(sober and fierce suddenly)* Cut it, Queenie!

QUEENIE: What's biting your backside, big boy? She oughta be able to take a little fun.

SMITTY: You go past the point where it's funny.

QUEENIE: When I want you to tell me what to laugh at, I'll write you a certificate of authority.

GUARD: *(standing)* Okay, children ... cool it! Or we cut the run-through right here.

QUEENIE: Let's have Miss Shakespeare's num-ber. I'm sure Rocky and the other boys will just love it, especially the ones who write poems on the wall of the crapper.

SMITTY: I know the scene, Mona; we took it in high-school English. It's where Portia goes to court for her boyfriend. Isn't that the part?

MONA: *(attention on SMITTY only)* Yes ... it is the plea she makes in the name of human chari-ty and ...

SMITTY: *(gently)* Mercy?

MONA: Yes.

SMITTY: I'd like to hear it again. Will you say it for me?

QUEENIE: Oh mercy my me.

The others move into the background, sitting on beds; the GUARD returns to his stool. They watch, as though at some amusing spectacle where one should not laugh but cannot resist, QUEENIE pokes ROCKY in the ribs with his elbow, then opens the fan over his face, holding it as a shield. ROCKY casually lights a cigarette and the GUARD yawns with indifference. Only SMITTY moves to hear MONA, looking into the serious, sad face.

MONA begins very hesitantly, stuttering (with comic pathos and badly spoken) —as the others giggle and roll eyes, etc.

QUEENIE and ROCKY interrupt MONA's speech throughout.

MONA: The quality of mercy is not strained,
It droppeth, as the gentle rain from heaven
Upon the place beneath: it is twice blessed;
It blesseth him that gives, and him that takes:
'Tis mightiest in the mightiest; it becomes
The throned monarch better than his crown;
His sceptre shows the force of temporal power
The attribute to awe and majesty,
Wherein doth sit the dread and fear of kings;
But mercy is above this sceptred sway,
It is enthroned in the hearts of kings,
It is an attribute of God himself;
And earthly power doth then show likest God's,
When mercy seasons justice.

QUEENIE: *(to SMITTY, standing)* Down in front.

SMITTY sits and MONA strives to continue.

QUEENIE: *(with finality)* Thank you!

MONA continues.

ROCKY: Take it off.

QUEENIE: Put it on.

ROCKY: Ya dropped yer lunch.

QUEENIE: Encore!

ROCKY: Turn off the lights.

QUEENIE: Gee, you're pretty, lady!

ROCKY: Pretty ugly.

QUEENIE: Would you mind terribly—coming out of a cake?

MONA falters and seems unable to continue.

QUEENIE: Oh, she doesn't know it by heart.

SMITTY: *(turning to the GUARD)* Will you make them shut up?

GUARD: Okay. Good enough! The guys are waitin' and they won't know them words any better 'n you do. Let's go, Christmas dolls! Come on, Shirley, Dimples—and you too, Raggedy Ann!

QUEENIE: *(grabbing MONA away from SMITTY)* Laws has muhcy, Miss Melanie—de Yankees is hyeah. Ain't you skeered dey gonna find yoah sissy brudder in dat closet? *(propelling MONA toward corridor and concert)* Run foh yoah life; all Atlanta am on fiyah!

They exit.

GUARD: *(to ROCKY and SMITTY)* You bums get busy with a boot brush, and button up those shirt fronts. The General's wife and the Salvation Army are out there tonight.

He exits

ROCKY: *(shouting after him)* Yeah! I'll wear me best tie—de one wit' stripes. Queenie's browned off with you, Smitty.

SMITTY: Who gives a screw?

ROCKY: Mona … maybe?

SMITTY: How come Mona bothers you so much? You got a rod-on for her?

ROCKY: I got something I'd like t' give all fruits, but it ain't what they're looking for.

SMITTY: Seems to me that Mona doesn't know you're alive.

ROCKY: Oh, the Mona knows I'm here all right, only it's too lily-livered to look.

SMITTY: For a joker who claims he doesn't go in that direction, it looks to me like you ride the train awful hard.

ROCKY: You tryin' t' prove somethin', wise guy?

SMITTY: I don't have to. You prove the point every time you open your trap … it snaps shut on what you are.

ROCKY: Don't ever get the idea I'm a pansy, punker!

SMITTY: Watch your words there, Rocky. I'm nobody's punker these days, or have you forgotten what the floor of the crapper smells like … up close?

ROCKY: I ain't forgot.

SMITTY: Don't make me remind you too often.

ROCKY: Y'use yer meat hooks pretty good, but that don't make you big time, Mister. Queenie tells me you're doing a lousy little joy-ride rap. That's kid stuff.

SMITTY: It's big enough for me.

ROCKY: Ya didn't know yer ass from a hole in the ground before ya hit this joint here. It took me and Queenie t' smarten y' up.

SMITTY: I'm not interested in getting smart like you or Queenie. Did you get a chance to keep any of the stuff you got knocked off for? I guess not. And it must have taken a lot of Queenie's guts to smash a little old lady over the head for a closetful of diamonds and furs.

ROCKY: I'da got away clean if the lousy heap didn't run outa stinkin' gas, but Queenie screwed herself ... she hadda play the actress before sluggin' some old bitch, by standin' in the hall singin' "Happy Birthday" to cover up the screams. Too bad the next-door neighbour knew it wasn't the old dame's birthday, and called the cops. Crap! I'da gave my right eye to a' seen Queenie's face when they put the arm on her with that load of mink coats and diamonds. I'll bet she was plannin' to wear 'em, like Queen Elizabeth, on Hallowe'en.

SMITTY: So today she's wearing a neckload of cheap glass and singing her songs to a gymnasium full of pickpockets and petty boosters.

ROCKY: Well, I ain't in that class. When my bit's up here, my real old man'll be outta Kingston, and me and him's gonna hit the big time together. I guess a pun ... (thinking better of using the term) ... a joy-rider like you don't know who Tiger Tibber is.

SMITTY: Sure ... I've read about your father ... the high priest of pipe dreams.

ROCKY: But you wouldn't know what kind of cash a guy gets, dealin' out the junk.

SMITTY: Look Rocky. I don't give a crap what you and your old man do to get back here or someplace else. Queenie's always telling me what a big thing it is to pry open somebody's door or window, and you want to impress me by telling me your father peddles dope and your mother sells bingo to wine-hounds. Well, it cuts no ice with me. If I was to choose a racket it wouldn't be lousy drugs and cheap booze.

ROCKY: Well, ya better find somethin', buddy boy, 'cause y'ain't gonna be able t' git a decent job no more—maybe not even a half-assed one. Lookit Queenie! She was workin' the counter o' a Chinatown restaurant, after her first bit here. She wuzn't there two weeks when Seven-Foot Tiny o' the Morality Squad steps inta the kitchen t' scoff a free cuppa coffee. He catches sight o' sweet Queenie playin' tea maid t' all them tourists n' square Chinks, so sends down t' the cash register for the manager. He asks him does he know he's got a queer an' a thief workin' fer 'im. Dear Queenie, who planned on gittin' fat that winter, wuz out in the alley wit' the rest o' the cats— before Big Tiny finishes his bummy cuppa coffee.

SMITTY: So? Queenie made a try, anyway. It was probably better than selling bingo to wine-hounds. You pick your form of animal life; I'll find mine.

ROCKY: You keep my old lady outa it. When she was a big-time bootlegger she use'ta eat little boys like you for breakfast.

SMITTY: I can believe it!

ROCKY: And she still rakes in more dough in a day than you seen in a year.

SMITTY: I hope she saves it to pay her fines. They must love her at City Hall.

ROCKY: Can it.

SMITTY: You started this bomb rolling, big mouth.

ROCKY: That's what I get for tryin' to level withya about Queenie! She's bugged by you playin' nursemaid to Mona.

SMITTY: I don't like to see somebody shoved around by a couple of yellow-bellied crapheads.

ROCKY: You tangled with Queenie yet?

SMITTY: I'm ready when it comes!

ROCKY: I got news for you. Queenie's in solid with the politicians. She keeps old Baldy fixed up with punkers, and he pays by takin' the jokers she fingers, and locking 'em up in Gunsel's Alley.

SMITTY: I'm worried sick; notice how my nails are chewed to the elbow.

ROCKY: You ain't done hard time till they make you sit it out in Gunsel's Alley. Y'eat, crap, wash, jerk an' flop ... all in a lonely little six-by-six. It's real cozy if ya don't go haywire the first month. A couple of goons smashed their own heads on the brick wall ... wide open like eggs. They figgered they was better off in the hospital than locked up alone in a cage, like a screwin' canary.

SMITTY: I'd sing all day long, if I thought I wouldn't have to look at your ugly map for the rest of my time.

ROCKY: Yeah? Well they don't let little Mona drop in for visits, y'know.

SMITTY: Let's take a shower, Rocky!

ROCKY: I'm nice and clean right now, thanks.

SMITTY: Well don't rub any more of your dirt on me, 'cause I'll get the urge to clean it off … on you. Dig me, punk?

GUARD: (entering with MONA) Okay Hans and Fritz! Patch it up and come on to the Christmas concert. They've got a bag of candies and an orange waiting for you at the door.

SMITTY: Why aren't you backstage, Mona? It's about time to start.

MONA: They decided I shouldn't do any Shakespeare.

SMITTY: Who decided?

MONA: Mr. Benson said they would only laugh at me and make life more unpleasant afterwards.

SMITTY: Well come on and watch with me, then.

GUARD: No, leave it here! Whenever that one gets into an assembly, there's trouble. Last time it was at church-up … somebody split its pants down the back with a razor blade.

SMITTY: You wouldn't call that his fault.

GUARD: Look, Junior! If you had a bunch of hunters waving rifles around, you wouldn't throw a bird in the air, and expect nobody to shoot, would ya? It stays here.

SMITTY: This is Christmas!

GUARD: I don't care if it's the day of the Second Coming, the target stays here. Anyhow, it's got the whole corridor to roam around in tonight. The cell doors are all open, an' silly-bitch can go sniffin' around the empty beds for entertainment.

SMITTY: Isn't there a rule that says everybody attends the Christmas concert?

GUARD: You ask too many questions, Smith.

SMITTY: I thought you went by *all* the rules.

GUARD: (uneasy, as sometimes with ROCKY's words) Yeah! Come on, let's go.

SMITTY: I'll celebrate right here.

GUARD: Pick the kind of company you want, Smitty, but take my advice … don't get caught. Come on, Tibber.

ROCKY: Let's move! The concert can't be as corny as this act. So long, sweethearts.

GUARD and ROCKY exit.

In the distance, BOYS' voices can be heard singing a round of:

Row, row, row your boat,
Gently down the stream
Merrily, merrily, merrily, merrily,
Life is but a dream …

Sounds are from gathering in the auditorium.

SMITTY: I hate that son of a bitch, and I'm soon going to show him how much. Then, he'll know the shower of knuckles I gave him was only a baptism.

MONA: Rocky can destroy himself soon enough.

SMITTY: He ought to be squashed—like a bedbug.

MONA: What would you expect of him? Do you know that his father …

SMITTY: Hell, yes! He takes great pride in his parents—the famous dope-peddler and the fabulous bootlegger. He sure rounds out that family circle.

MONA: Before he came here, this time, his mother was sent to jail. She's been convicted so many times, the court wouldn't accept another fine.

SMITTY: My heart beats for the dear, lost lady and her deprived offspring. Who'll make the pancakes now and run the still?

MONA: Rocky's sixteen-year-old brother took over the bootlegging and began, besides, to sell his teenage girlfriends to anybody who has five dollars.

SMITTY: Say! Outside, did you live near that slum?

MONA: No, I probably wouldn't have lived this long, or, at least, my nose would be a different shape.

SMITTY: How come you know so much about the rockhead?

MONA: I listen to him and read between the lines.

SMITTY: What a waste of time! That's their mess—not ours. I'm interested in you and me. You make excuses for them, but you keep your secrets, like Greta Garbo—under a hat.

MONA: You haven't said much about your life outside.

SMITTY: I'm forgetting, that's why—I'm going to spend the rest of my life forgetting my father. He put me here. To hell with him! Who put you in?

MONA: No one—really! It just—happened.

SMITTY: Happened? How can a thing like getting here just happen?

MONA: My life—like that from the start; I expect what comes.

SMITTY: That tells me a lot.

MONA: It's just that I can't …

SMITTY: So shove it, then!

MONA: A gang—of guys—in the neighbour-hood—that night—pushed me around. My payday—had it on me—they knew. Next thing—I'm on the ground—kicking me—kicking. I look up—all those legs, but there's a big cop. Thank God! Thank God! Bleeding—numb—on my feet at last! Then—he looked at me, and I saw his sympathy shift—to the gang. Forgot my money—excited, asked were they mixed up with me—sexually. Smitty?

SMITTY: Don't get off the damn pot! Crap it out!

MONA: A—a huddle—like a football game—formation; all came out, laid charges—said I made passes. Four gave witness in court. Only voice for me—my poor, shocked mother, and sitting out there, trying to smile at me—eyes dark, afraid—God help her—my younger sister!

SMITTY: But you should have had a lawyer.

MONA: Oh, I had one—or did I? Yeah—too late, after he got his money—we saw he didn't care—to tarnish his reputation. No real defense. A deal. Magistrate's court is like trial in a police station—all pals, lawyers and cops together! Threw me on the mercy of the court. Oh Christ—that judge, with his hurry-up face, heard the neat police evidence and my lawyer's silly, sugar-sweet plea. So

half-hearted—I wanted to shout, "Let me speak; leave me some damn dignity!" The fat, white-haired frown looked down on me—"Go to jail for six months!"—like I'd dirtied his hands, and that would wipe them clean. Six months! Six thousand would have sounded the same.

SMITTY: Well, things are going to be a lot different by next month. There's a brand new year on the way.

MONA: How—"different"?

SMITTY: I mean, you're not going to be pushed around by anybody—goons, like Rocky and Queenie. They taught me more than was good for them. I'm on my way to being a politician, and I don't plan to do any more hard time because of anybody. We've had it rough lately, but I'm about to even the score.

MONA: I don't know how that can be done.

SMITTY: Hell, kid! What I'm saying is we're going to wear the best of everything—new shirts, fresh from the tailor shop, and lightweight boots. We'll get extra grub—candy and fresh fruit—everything good that's going around. What do you say to that?

MONA: What do you expect me to say—about those things?

SMITTY: Well, for cripe's sake you might say "thanks." I'll have to. Or, "I like you, Smitty," or even—you might—

MONA: What's happened to you, Smitty?

SMITTY: I've discovered I'm human. You're not blind. Who's been acting like your old man lately?

MONA: I don't have any old man. I thought you understood that.

SMITTY: You only think you don't. Look, Jan, when I came to this joint, I didn't know up from down. I've made a few mistakes since the one that got me here, and that's the only one I'm not sorry for. I stole a car—to get my mother out of town, away from my drunken slob of a father. I had to—he had the keys. I was helping her to run away with Ben—Ben's a nice guy. They tried to get me out of this jackpot, together, but I slugged a cop when they were arresting me. My dear father got back at us all. He didn't have a good word for me in court. After all, he was the respectable married man, a substantial citizen with his own business—the hardhearted bastard! Hard is a good word for him. He likes hard women, hard liquor, and hard words. For all he wanted from my mother, he might as well have hired a housekeeper and visited a prostitute regularly. Screw him! What I'm saying is you've got to work at it to make things go your way.

MONA: I can see you're not going to park your keester in a corner. Your father and Queenie have taught you well.

SMITTY: And I'm sick of that fat whore treating me like a piece of her property. I'll pick my own bedmate from here in. I shouldn't have to give you all this jazz, you know what I need. Haven't you any feelings after all?

MONA: Yes—some, but not the kind you're getting at—at least, not with you.

SMITTY: What did you say?

MONA: I said—not with you, Smitty.

SMITTY: Saving yourself for those dirty bastards in the gym? Is that what you enjoy—being forced into a corner?

MONA: It's better that way.

SMITTY: Better? Are you playing hard to get or something? Because I know different; anybody who grabs you, gets you.

MONA: Slicings—patterns—blind and empty release; sure, I'll go on being a party to it.

SMITTY: Do you like that? I thought you liked me.

MONA: I do, Smitty—a great deal.

SMITTY: I knew you put up with what you got because you had no choice; that you really went for me. You showed it in a hundred ways, so now, while we're alone—a chance—

MONA: Just a minute! How do you feel with Queenie—afterward?

SMITTY: I could spit on her.

MONA: It would be the same with me; it's not in your nature.

SMITTY: I came to you.

MONA: No! Just circumstance! You're looking for a girl—not for me.

SMITTY: Do I smell or something? What's wrong with *my* body?

MONA: Nothing—it's very—Smitty, don't ask me to.

SMITTY: Should I ask you to do it with somebody else? Keep on being public property? I guess you like change—a different one every day, for variety. What do you do? Make comparisons?

MONA: I—separate! Yes, that's right. I separate things in order to live with others and myself. What my body does and feels is one thing, and what I think and feel apart from that is something else.

SMITTY: You're crazy.

MONA: It's to the world I dream in you belong. It endures better. I won't let you move over, into the other, where I would become worthless to you—and myself. I have a right to save something.

SMITTY: I was afraid of everyone—everything—except you—until now. You're trying to shake me.

MONA: You're trying to kill me. You think I can be just used any old way—even by you.

SMITTY: To hell with me then!

MONA: No—listen! it's the sight of myself I can't stand—the way you throw it back.

SMITTY: Where do you get the goddam gall to tell me how I see you?

MONA: The right to say or be anything or everything or nothing to myself—and not a tame little fruit. Wasn't that it—soft, worshipping, harmless? Now you've flexed your muscles and found power, I'm an easy convenience. Not a Queenie! Oh no; I'd never turn on you. If I mattered, you'd be afraid of my feelings—not sure of them. You're offering me—indifference. Well, I don't want it.

SMITTY: Did you think I wanted your body? You make me sick. I wanted some kind of reaction to me, and only because I'm caught in this hellhole, you filthy fairy! You cocksucker!

MONA: You see? You see?

SMITTY: *(running to the bars)* Let me out of here! I'll go to the bloody concert—anywhere—where there's life—

He bangs wildly on the bars with his fists. MONA follows to stand behind SMITTY, puts out a hand gently, but not touching him, then with difficulty punches him on the shoulder. SMITTY reacts violently, turning on MONA.

MONA: No! Wait a minute!

He goes to SMITTY's bunk, picks up a book and holds it out.

MONA: Look—listen—you read it.

SMITTY goes slowly to sit beside MONA and begins to read, clumsily, haltingly. They laugh, embarrassed, and continue to read until they are in a slight hysteria of laughter that causes them to break up and fall against each other.

When in disgrace with fortune and men's eyes
I, all alone, beweep my outcast state,
And trouble deaf heaven with my bootless cries,
And look upon myself, and curse my fate,
Wishing me like to one more rich in hope,
Featur'd like him, like him with friends possess'd,
Desiring this man's art, and that man's scope,
With what I most enjoy, contented least;
Yet in these thoughts myself almost despising,
Haply I think on thee, and then my soul
(Like to the lark at break of day arising,
From sullen earth) sings hymns at heaven's gate;
For thy sweet love remembered such wealth brings,
That then I scorn to share my state with kings.

SMITTY and MONA are laughing, heads close together, when QUEENIE and ROCKY enter.

QUEENIE: I'll give the bitch a bluebird!

He smashes his fist into MONA's cheek.

ROCKY: Give it to the dirty little fruit.

SMITTY has leaped up, fists ready to swing. He punches QUEENIE on the jaw.

SMITTY: Screw off, bastard!

QUEENIE: *(backing away, but preparing to fight)* I'll take the punk, Rocky. Put your boots to the bitch.

SMITTY turns to take ROCKY, and QUEENIE uses the advantage to put a wrestling hold on SMITTY, pinning his arms behind his back.

QUEENIE: I got him. Go, Rocky! Go!

ROCKY: *(shaking MONA as though he were a rag doll)* I'm gonna smash your face, fairy.

He throws MONA to the floor, raising his foot to kick, but SMITTY breaks from QUEENIE, hurling the heavy blond to the floor, and kicks ROCKY in the groin. ROCKY screams, doubling over with pain. SMITTY then goes after QUEENIE just as the GUARD comes in, gun drawn.

GUARD: To the wall fast, or I cut your feet off.

All except MONA, who lies on the floor, move toward the wall.

Raise those mitts, children!

The three raise their hands.

Okay, crap-disturbers, what's the score here?

QUEENIE and ROCKY and SMITTY: *(together)* That dirty little bitch ... The goddam fruit ... These filthy bastards ...

GUARD: Cut it! One at a time! *(to QUEENIE)* You Goldilocks, what's your story?

QUEENIE: When me an' Rocky come in from the concert, that lolliflier on the floor was tryin' to make the kid here. *(wide-eyed)* We done it for his own good, Cap!

GUARD: Yeah! I can just imagine your motives. *(to ROCKY)* Okay, you now, Terrible Tibber! Let's hear your phony. Who were you saving?

ROCKY: Queenie gave it to you straight, Cap; an' I'm sticking with that story. The fruit was gropin' pretty good when we made the scene. We don't want that kinda stuff in here. You know how it is. Just turn your back an' that little queer's reachin' ...

GUARD: Okay, turn it off, Tibber! Next thing you'll be telling me you want to go to church next Sunday to pray. *(to SMITTY)* All right, Romeo! Let's have your version of the balcony scene.

SMITTY: My name is Smith.

GUARD: Well, well! May I call you Mister Smith? Names don't mean a damned thing in here, sonny. Actions mean everything. Did that thing on the floor make a pass at you?

SMITTY: Nobody made a pass.

GUARD: Oh, now, this isn't your mother or a judge you're talking to, Smarty Smith. We know by now a pass was made. I'm not asking you if you liked it. I want to know who made a the pass.

SMITTY: Nobody made a pass at anybody.

GUARD: Real stubborn, aren't you?

SMITTY: You asked me. I can't help it that you don't believe me. We were talking when these haywire goons hit the block. They started the hey rube and I took over, since they seemed to want to play.

GUARD: You're not only getting too smart, Smith, you're becoming arrogant as well. Where do you think this attitude's going to lead you?

SMITTY: Into the office, where I can put an end to this crap.

GUARD: You're right ... the General's office, where you'll need some much smarter answers.

SMITTY: I've got them.

GUARD: Your answers aren't worth much when you get hauled up on the big guy's carpet, kid.

SMITTY: Says you! Don't you think they might be worth about ... fifty bucks?

The GUARD is stunned into silence. He steals a quick accusing look at ROCKY, who averts his eyes carefully.

GUARD: *(shakily)* I don't think you know what you're talking about. What is this ... some kind of bluff?

SMITTY: I don't say anything I can't back up with the facts ... like names, dates and letters. Dig me, screw?

GUARD: *(enraged but cornered)* You crapping fink! Learned it all, haven't you? Found a way to save your precious little hide? *(to ROCKY)* I ought to shoot you a second mouth, Tibber.

ROCKY just grins in reply, now enjoying the GUARD's discomfiture.

GUARD: There's one hide's not gonna get off so easy. *(pushing MONA with his foot)* Up off your ass, you little pansy! You know what you got the last time this happened, don't you?

He pushes MONA ahead of him, toward the corridor door.

GUARD: You can bend over all you want, in the kitchen.

MONA: *(realizing)* No! Oh, no, no, no, no ...

His protests mount to screams offstage.

SMITTY: *(running to the bars)* Stop it! Stop it! I did it! I made the pass. *(shouting after them)* Do you hear? I made the pass ... I made the ...

QUEENIE and ROCKY begin to laugh in derision.

SMITTY: *(turning vicious)* Shut up you yellow bastards! I'll wipe the floor with your rotten guts. One more laugh out of your ugly kissers and I'll spray teeth from here to hell.

QUEENIE: We didn't mean anything, Smitty. What are you so hot about? That little ...

SMITTY: Shut your filthy hole, you fat whore!

ROCKY: Jeez, Smitty, that thing ain't worth ...

SMITTY: Listen to me, Rock-ass! Before I leave this stinking joint I'm going to demolish your mug so bad that no fruit will ever look at you again ... let alone a woman. When will depend on you. Ask for it once and you've got it. This is my show from now on. I got that lousy screw over a barrel, and I'm going to keep him there. Also, Baldy's making me a politician ... a wheel in the office. You see, Queenie, I wasn't hustling my little ass in the park at thirteen for peanuts. I went to school; I got typing and bookkeeping, so Baldy's put me where I can make things move my way. If you'd learned to write, maybe you'd be better off ... but you'll swallow chicken crap when I make up the menu. And you, monkey; would you like to be my punchin' bag around here or should I ship you into Gunsel's Alley for safekeeping? Choose fast!

ROCKY: I ... I'll take it off you.

SMITTY: Okay. You'll volunteer to be my sparring partner in the gym every time I want to box somebody, and sweetie, I'm gonna knock you senseless. Now get into that goddam crapper and stick your heads into a coupla bowls till I yell for you to come out. That'll be after lights out, 'cause I don't want to see your ugly maps again today.

ROCKY and QUEENIE look at each other, dazed,

SMITTY: You know who Baldy is? You know what he can do? Well, I'm his boy now.

QUEENIE: Ain't it the bitter truth? *(pulling ROCKY away)* Come on, Snake-Eyes; we rolled too low in the game—this time around.

SMITTY: So move, goddam it!

He takes a step toward them. In their haste to get out, the two bump into each other, ridiculous and clumsy in their new roles. SMITTY laughs loudly, revealing a cruelty that fills the room with its sound. Suddenly his head turns in another direction as though just recalling something. He steals a quick look toward the shower room, then stealthily and lithely as a cat, he moves to the corner of the dorm where MONA had listened to the sound of Catsolino's beating. From an attitude of strained listening, SMITTY suddenly contorts in pain as MONA had done before, but there is no sound from his distorted mouth. He seems to be whipped by unseen strokes of a lash, until he is spread-eagled across the upstage bars. When it seems he can bear no more he covers his ears with both hands, stumbling blindly downstage. Standing thus, head and shoulders down, he rises slowly out of the hunched position to full height, hands lowering. His face now seems to be carved of stone, the mouth narrow, cruel and grim, the eyes corresponding slits of hatred. He speaks in a hoarse, ugly whisper.

I'm going to pay them back.

He then walks, almost casually, down to ROCKY's bunk where cigarettes, which we have not seen him use before, and a lighter lie on the side table. He picks up a cigarette, lights it, then stretches out on ROCKY's bed, torso upright against the back of it. Looking coolly out to the audience with a slight, twisted smile that is somehow cold, sadistic and menacing, he speaks his last line.

I'll pay you all back.

Light fades to black, and there is heard a final slam of the jail door.

END

MICHEL TREMBLAY (b. 1942)

When Michel Tremblay saw his first play, *Le Train*,[1] televised in 1964, he realized he had written "a bad French play." As he recalls in *Stage Voices*, "When I began to write drama, I wrote bad *French* plays because what I had seen on TV were good *French* plays!" He resolved to write about the people he knew in ways that would reflect their lives and experience as Quebeckers, and in the language they really spoke—not French or even "French-Canadian," but *québécois*. With the tremendous success of *Les Belles-Soeurs* in 1968 Tremblay changed the face of theatre in Quebec, becoming an icon of *québécois* nationalism and launching a career that would make him Quebec's—and Canada's—foremost dramatist.

The attempt to write modern Quebec onto the stage had really begun in 1948 with Gratien Gélinas' *Tit-Coq*, a well-made, sentimental melodrama that pitted an outsider (the "little rooster" of the title, a young soldier played by Gélinas himself) against the established order in the form of church and family. Tit-Coq's illegitimacy, his colloquial language, the realist backdrop of working-class Montreal—all these struck powerful chords in the Quebec audience and made the play an unprecedented success. Led by writers like Gélinas and Marcel Dubé, whose *Zone* (1953) depicted the tragedy of a teenage gang in the Montreal slums, indigenous theatre thrived in 1950s Quebec, aided by the popularity of television drama. But by the end of the decade Gélinas, Dubé and the other mainstays of the new theatre seemed to have abandoned *québécois* idioms for more standardized Parisian language and style, writing the "good French plays" Tremblay inadvertently took as his own early models. It remained for Tremblay to break the mould by grounding his plays in a radically localized, deromanticized Montreal milieu. Beginning with *Les Belles-Soeurs*, his characters would speak not in "proper French" but, for the first time ever on the stage, entirely in *joual*, the bastardized local slang that was for some Quebeckers an embarrassing sign of their cultural degradation, but for others a symbol of their uniqueness as a people.

Tremblay wrote *Le Train* in 1959, his playwriting debut coinciding with the death of Premier Maurice Duplessis and the end of the deeply conservative political regime that had ruled Quebec through the entire post-war era. *Les Belles-Soeurs* premiered the same year René Lévesque founded the nationalist Parti Québécois. The decade framed by these two plays saw the beginning of the period of social renaissance dubbed the Quiet Revolution, as well as the not so quiet revolutionary campaign for Quebec independence mounted by the FLQ, and French President Charles de Gaulle's famous "Vive le Québec libre" speech in Montreal. As the redefinition of Quebec's political identity intensified, the articulation of its culture played an increasingly important role in the ferment of the times. Michel Tremblay was right in its midst.

He grew up in a working class neighbourhood in east end Montreal, the Plateau Mont-Royal, raised by an extended family of women. Though a gifted student, Tremblay eventually left school to work as a printer, his father's profession, before turning to writing full time. In 1964 he met the young director André Brassard who became his lifelong collaborator and primary dramatic interpreter. The next year Brassard staged several short stories from what would be Tremblay's first published book, *Stories for Late Night Drinkers* (1966). Tremblay wrote *Les Belles-Soeurs* in 1965, and during the three years it took to get produced, he revised and expanded some earlier one-acts into *En Pièces Détachées*, which opened in 1969 at Théâtre de Quat'Sous, the Montreal venue that has become most closely identified with his work. (All Tremblay's plays have premiered in Montreal or at Ottawa's National Arts Centre.)

By this time the parameters of Tremblay's dramatic world had been clearly laid out. The unhappy women of *Les Belles-Soeurs* and *En Pièces Détachées*, and the broken men of the latter play, live on a street very much like the rue Fabre on which Tremblay himself grew up, festering in what we would today call severely dysfunctional families, sexually and emotionally frustrated, and desperate to escape their alienation. Their fantasies of escape are often directed at another street: boulevard St. Laurent, or "The Main," a fringe society of clubs and bars, hookers and drag queens, where anything seems possible. But ultimately it proves to be a world of false glamour and shattered dreams. Eventually the "Cycle of Les Belles-Soeurs" would comprise more than a dozen plays mapping the rich human territory around these two streets.

La Duchesse de Langeais (1969), the lengthy monologue of an ageing transvestite, provides Tremblay's first direct introduction to the world of The Main, elaborated again in the musical *Demain matin, Montreal m'attend* (1970), and *Hosanna* (1973), one of his most popular and enduring plays. The poignant story of a hairdresser *cum* drag queen with a biker lover and the burning desire to be Elizabeth Taylor in *Cleopatra*, the play had productions in Paris, New York and London between 1978 and 1981, and has been frequently revived in English Canada and Quebec. An engaging human drama, *Hosanna* also functions as cultural allegory. "We submitted to a foreign culture and this turned us into transvestites," Tremblay has said. "Finally, in the Sixties, we began taking off our foreign clothes and trying to rediscover the centre of our Quebec reality ... "

The family plays, too, speak to Tremblay's sense of the broader *québécois* condition. *Forever Yours, Marie-Lou* (1971) is his most brutal portrait of the self-destructive family, an image of colonized Quebec with its internecine warfare and self-hatred. In the play two sisters, Carmen and Manon, live haunted by the ghosts of their dead parents, paralyzed by the dead hand of the past. Carmen flees to the clubs of The Main and becomes a country singer, returning in Tremblay's *Sainte-Carmen of the Main* (1976) as a martyr to cultural authenticity. Manon (whom Tremblay has said he loves most of all his characters) becomes a religious fanatic, appearing again in *Damnée Manon, Sacrée Sandra* (1977) along with her alter ego, the transvestite Sandra, Hosanna's arch-rival. In 1991 the three plays appeared together in Montreal under the title *La Trilogie des Brassard*.

Forever Yours, Marie-Lou initiated the popularization of Tremblay's plays in English, premiering at Toronto's Tarragon Theatre in 1972, directed by Bill Glassco in a translation by Glassco and John Van Burek. Five years later it became his first play to get an English-language production in Quebec when the election of the Parti Québécois prompted Tremblay to lift his prohibition against such productions. By that time *En Pièces Détachées, Les Belles-Soeurs* and *Hosanna* had also entered the English-Canadian repertoire, as had *Bonjour, là, Bonjour* (1974), in which brother-sister incest and the ability of a son to say "I love you" to his father indicated Tremblay's more positive feelings about the possibilities of healing within both the micro- and macrocosms of modern Quebec. It quickly became one of his most popular plays, produced across the United States in the late 1970s and early 1980s.

After *Damnée Manon*, Tremblay felt he had temporarily said all he had to say in drama and turned his attention to a semi-autobiographical cycle of novels set on the same rue Fabre from the 1940s to the early 1960s. *The Fat Lady Next Door Is Pregnant* (1978) —the title character is Tremblay's mother, pregnant with him—*Thérèse and Pierrette and the Little Hanging Angel* (1980), *The Duchess and the Commoner* (1982), *News from Édouard* (1984), *The First Quarter of the Moon* (1989) and *A Thing of Beauty* (1998) comprise the magic-realist "Chronicles of Plateau Mont-Royal." Another novel, *The Heart Laid Bare* (1986), is a gay love story.

But he was far from through with the stage. After a brief theatrical detour into the bourgeois drawing room of four sisters (whose discussions include the scandalous opening night of *Les Belles-Soeurs*) in *The Impromptu of Outremont* (1980), and an artsy gay couple in *Remember Me* (1981), he returned to the gritty emotional landscapes of his early plays with *Albertine in Five Times* (1984), in which five actresses simultaneously play the desperate Albertine at different decades in her life. In *The Real World?* (1987) Tremblay metatheatrically examines the ways he exploited his own family for his dramatic art, and *La Maison Suspendue* (1990) celebrates reconciliation and the imagination in a dreamy, sentimental weaving together of three generations from both the play and novel cycles. *Marcel Pursued by the Hounds* (1992), a prequel of sorts to *En Pièces Détachées*, once again finds the tawdry Main a beacon of hope for escape from the misery of family and neighbourhood. Paying homage to his late mother, *For the Pleasure of Seeing Her Again* (1998) proved a great popular and critical success in both French and English, winning Tremblay another Chalmers Award twenty years after the production of *Les Belles-Soeurs*.

Tremblay's substantial opus also includes successful stage adaptations of plays by Aristophanes, Tennessee Williams, Paul Zindel, Dario Fo, Chekhov and Gogol. (The latter, *Les Gars de Québec* [1985], set *The Inspector General* in rural Quebec during the Duplessis era.) He has written a *québécois* pop opera, *Nelligan* (1990); two autobiographical memoirs, *Bambi and Me* (1990) and *Douze coups de théâtre* (1992); and a number of films, including *Il était une fois dans l'est* (1974), an extension of his early dramatic material in collaboration with André Brassard. Tremblay's numerous honours include six Chalmers Awards for best Canadian play in Toronto, the Governor General's Performing Arts Award, the Ontario Lieutenant Governor's Medal, and the Prix France-Québec (twice). In 1984 France named him Chevalier de l'Ordre des Arts et des Lettres, and he has since received honourary degrees from Concordia, McGill, Windsor and the University of Stirling in Scotland.

Les Belles-Soeurs remains his most celebrated work, both in French and in translation. From 1991–93 alone, it played in English at Stratford, in Spanish in Buenos Aires, in Yorkshire dialect in Sheffield, and in French, Yiddish and Scots in Montreal. As *The Guid Sisters* it has been one of Scotland's most popular plays since 1988. France's prestigious literary magazine *Lire* named *Les Belles-Soeurs* one of the 49 plays in its ideal repertoire of world theatre since antiquity. But initially it met with great resistance. Rejected by the Dominion Drama Festival for its 1967 all-Canadian showcase, the play finally gained public attention through a reading at Montreal's Centre d'Essai des Auteurs Dramatiques, the most important laboratory for new play development in Quebec since its founding in 1965.

The premiere of *Les Belles-Soeurs*, directed by André Brassard at the Théâtre du Rideau-Vert in August 1968, elicited howls of protest and torrents of praise. The protesters complained of the play's unflattering portrayal of *québécoise* womanhood, family and religion. But they focused their attacks on the use of *joual* with its crudity and vulgarity ("a filthy bathroom language," wrote one reviewer), its incorporation of English words and phrases, and its implications of Quebec's inferiority to the imperial French standard of language and culture. (The play itself anticipated these criticisms in the affected character of Lisette de Courval, gushing over how refined and polite Europeans are, and how beautifully everyone speaks in Paris: "There they talk *real* French ... Not like here.") For Tremblay, the language established his characters' authenticity. It reflected the frustrations of their daily existence and emblemized Quebec's historical legacy of bitterness and defeat echoed at the end of the play in the ironic singing of "O Canada" ("an anthem of submission," in Tremblay's words).

In short order the play's champions overcame its critics. Following two popular revivals in Montreal, *Les Belles-Soeurs* had a triumphant production in Paris in 1973, and that same year Brassard directed its English-language debut at Toronto's St. Lawrence Centre to rave reviews. Seattle hosted the American premiere in 1979. The play's successes in English have come despite the severe difficulties of translating a language whose precise flavour and cultural particularities can only be roughly approximated.

Literally translated, "les belles-soeurs" means "the sisters-in-law." Like the creators of other well-known stage "sisters," Anton Chekhov and Tomson Highway, and like his favourite playwright, Samuel Beckett, Tremblay writes tragicomedy. He satirizes the manners and dissects the values of the female society gathered in Germaine Lauzon's kitchen on the rue Fabre—their philistine tastes, greed and envy, social and religious hypocrisy—through sharply comic character portraits and often hilarious ensembles like the "Ode to Bingo." But at the same time he details the fifteen women's painfully repressed desires and thwarted aspirations. They span three generations, but profound unhappiness and pessimism is their common lot. Lacking joy ("I've never laughed in my life"), desperate for affection ("I need ... to love someone"), resigned to futility ("Do I look like someone who's ever won anything?"), they turn their bitterness to resentment. No one can be allowed to snatch a little happiness, not friend or sister, mother-in-law or daughter. The lives of the young—Linda, Lise and Ginette—promise only to repeat the patterns of the old. The clubs on the Main offer the illusion of hope but no long-term escape, as Pierrette's sad story reveals. Even Germaine's apparent good fortune only leads her down the classic tragic path through pride to a fall, complete with dramatic irony. No one ever gets to Moscow and Godot never comes.

Tremblay's admiration for the Greek tragic chorus is reflected in the play's choral interludes. In typical Tremblayan fashion the chorus lamenting "this stupid, rotten life" combines pain ("My husband bitches. The kids scream. We all fight") and comic painkiller ("But at night we watch TV"). But Tremblay suggests that this chorus has yet another function: "One woman saying she is unhappy with her life is pitiful, but five women saying at the same time that they are unhappy with their lives is the beginning of a revolution" (*Stage Voices*). The kitchen setting and the absence of men in the play (the image, in one sense, of a politically emasculated Quebec) provide the women a comfortably feminized space in which to voice their complaints and frustrations, many of them regarding sex or domestic oppression linked directly to gender. But they fail to find allies in each other. Their solo turns, when they come downstage to speak to the audience in monologue, occur far more frequently than choral solidarity. "They're women who should have rebelled but it was still too early in our history for that to happen," Tremblay told Donald Smith in 1986. "They know why they're unhappy and they'd like it to change, but they still don't have the means to do it. All they can do is give in and go on accepting it."

NOTES

1. All titles are those of the published English translation unless the work has remained untranslated. Many of the plays have the same title in English and French. Dates in parentheses denote the first French-language production for a play or publication date for a book.

Les Belles-Soeurs was first produced at Le Théâtre du Rideau-Vert in Montreal on August 8, 1968, with the following cast:

GERMAINE LAUZON	Denise Proulx
LINDA LAUZON	Odette Gagnon
ROSE OUIMET	Denise Filiatrault
GABRIELLE JODOIN	Lucille Bélair
LISETTE DE COURVAL	Hélène Loiselle
MARIE-ANGE BROUILLETTE	Marthe Choquette
YVETTE LONGPRÉ	Sylvie Heppel
DES-NEIGES VERRETTE	Denise de Jaguère
THÉRÈSE DUBUC	Germaine Giroux
OLIVINE DUBUC	Nicole Leblanc
ANGÉLINE SAUVÉ	Anne-Marie Ducharme
RHÉAUNA BIBEAU	Germaine Lemyre
LISE PAQUETTE	Rita Lafontaine
GINETTE MENARD	Josée Beauregard
PIERRETTE GUÉRIN	Luce Guilbeault

Directed and designed by André Brassard

Les Belles-Soeurs was first performed in English, translated by John Van Burek and Bill Glassco, at the St. Lawrence Centre in Toronto on April 3, 1973:

GERMAINE LAUZON	Candy Kane
LINDA LAUZON	Elva-May Hoover
ROSE OUIMET	Monique Mercure
GABRIELLE JODOIN	Araby Lockhart
LISETTE DE COURVAL	Mia Anderson
MARIE-ANGE BROUILLETTE	Deborah Packer
YVETTE LONGPRÉ	Louise Nichol
DES-NEIGES VERRETTE	Maureen Fitzgerald
THÉRÈSE DUBUC	Irene Hogan
OLIVINE DUBUC	Lilian Lewis
ANGÉLINE SAUVÉ	Patricia Hamilton
RHÉAUNA BIBEAU	Nancy Kerr
LISE PAQUETTE	Trudy Young
GINETTE MENARD	Suzette Couture
PIERRETTE GUÉRIN	Melanie Morse

Directed and designed by André Brassard

LES BELLES-SOEURS
Translated by John Van Burek and Bill Glassco

CHARACTERS

GERMAINE LAUZON
LINDA LAUZON, *Germaine's daughter*
ROSE OUIMET, *Germaine's sister*
GABRIELLE JODOIN, *another sister*
LISETTE DE COURVAL
MARIE-ANGE BROUILLETTE } *neighbours*
YVETTE LONGPRÉ
DES-NEIGES VERRETTE
THÉRÈSE DUBUC, *Germaine's sister-in-law*
OLIVINE DUBUC, *Thérèse's mother-in-law*
ANGÉLINE SAUVÉ }
RHÉAUNA BIBEAU } *neighbours*
LISE PAQUETTE }
GINETTE MENARD } *Linda's friends*
PIERRETTE GUÉRIN, *Germaine's youngest sister*

SCENE

The kitchen of a Montreal tenement, 1965. Four enormous boxes occupy centre stage.

ACT ONE

LINDA LAUZON enters. She sees four boxes in the middle of the kitchen.

LINDA: God, what's that? Ma!

GERMAINE: *(offstage)* Is that you, Linda?

LINDA: Yeah! What are all these boxes in the kitchen?

GERMAINE: *(offstage)* They're my stamps.

LINDA: Already? Jeez, that was fast.

GERMAINE LAUZON enters.

GERMAINE: Yeah, it surprised me too. They came this morning right after you left. The door-bell rang. I went to answer it and there's this big fellow standing there. Oh, you'd have liked him, Linda. Just your type. About twenty-two, twenty-three, dark curly hair. Nice little moustache. Real handsome. Anyway, he says to me, "Are you the lady of the house, Mme Germaine Lauzon?" I said, "Yes that's me." And he says, "Good, I've brought your stamps." Linda, I was so excited. I didn't know what to say. Next thing I knew, two guys are bringing in the boxes and the other one's giving me this speech. Linda, what a talker. And such manners. I'm sure you would have liked him.

LINDA: So, what did he say?

GERMAINE: I can't remember. I was so excited. He told me the company he works for was real happy I'd won the million stamps. That I was real lucky ... Me, I was speechless. I wish your father had been here, he could have talked to him. I don't even know if I thanked him.

LINDA: That's a lot of stamps to glue. Four boxes! One million stamps, that's no joke!

GERMAINE: There's only three boxes. The other one's booklets. But I had an idea, Linda. We're not gonna do all this alone! You going out tonight?

LINDA: Yeah, Robert's supposed to call me ...

GERMAINE: You can't put it off till tomorrow? Listen, I had an idea. I phoned my sisters, your father's sister and I went to see the neighbours. And I've invited them all to come and paste stamps with us tonight. I'm gonna give a stamp-pasting party. Isn't that a great idea? I bought some peanuts, and your little brother went out to get some Coke ...

LINDA: Ma, you know I always go out on Thursdays! It's our night out. We're gonna go to a show.

GERMAINE: You can't leave me alone on a night like this. I've got fifteen people coming ...

LINDA: Are you crazy! You'll never get fifteen people in this kitchen! And you can't use the rest of the house. The painters are here. Jesus, Ma! Sometimes you're really dumb.

GERMAINE: Sure, that's right, put me down. Fine, you go out, do just as you like. That's all you ever do anyway. Nothing new. I never have any pleasure. Someone's always got to spoil it for me. Go ahead Linda, you go out tonight, go to your goddamned show. Jesus Christ Almighty, I'm so fed up.

LINDA: Come on, Ma, be reasonable …

GERMAINE: I don't want to be reasonable, I don't want to hear about it! I kill myself for you and what do I get in return? Nothing! A big fat nothing! You can't even do me a little favour! I'm warning you, Linda, I'm getting sick of waiting on you, you and everyone else. I'm not your servant, you know. I've got a million stamps to paste and I'm not about to do it myself. Besides, those stamps are for the whole family, which means everybody's gotta do their share. Your father's working tonight but if we don't get done he says he'll help tomorrow. I'm not asking for the moon. Help me for a change, instead of wasting your time with that jerk.

LINDA: Robert is not a jerk.

GERMAINE: Sure, he's a genius! Boy, I knew you were stupid, but not that stupid. When are you going to realize your Robert is a bozo? He doesn't even make sixty bucks a week. All he can do is take you to the local movie house Thursday nights. Take a mother's advice, Linda, keep hanging around with that dope and you'll end up just like him. You want to marry a shoe-gluer and be a strapper all your life?

LINDA: Shut up, Ma! When you get sore, you don't know what you're saying. Anyway, forget it … I'll stay home … just stop screaming, okay? And by the way, Robert's due for a raise soon and he'll be making lots more. He's not as dumb as you think. Even the boss told me he might start making big money 'cause they'll put him in charge of something. You wait. Eighty bucks a week is nothing to laugh at. Anyway … I'm gonna go phone him and tell him I can't go to the show … Hey, why don't I tell him to come and glue stamps with us?

GERMAINE: Mother of God, I just told you I can't stand him and you want to bring him home tonight. Where the hell are your brains? What did I do to make God in heaven send me such idiots? Just this afternoon, I send your brother to get me a bag of onions and he comes home with a quart of milk. It's unbelievable! You have to repeat everything ten times around here. No wonder I lose my temper. I told you, Linda. The party's for girls. Just girls. Your Robert's not queer, is he?

LINDA: Okay Ma, okay, don't flip your wig. I'll tell him not to come. Jesus, you can't do a thing around here. You think I feel like gluing stamps after working all day. (She starts to dial a number.) Why don't you go dust in the living room, eh? You don't have to listen to what I'm going to say … Hello, may I speak to Robert? When do you expect him? … Okay, will you tell him Linda phoned? … Fine, Mme Bergeron, and you? … That's good … Okay, thanks a lot. Bye. (She hangs up. The phone rings right away.) Hello? … Ma, it's for you.

GERMAINE: Twenty years old and you still can't say "One moment please" when you answer a phone.

LINDA: It's only Aunt Rose. Why should I be polite to her?

GERMAINE: (putting her hand over the receiver) Will you be quiet! What if she heard you?

LINDA: Who gives a shit?

GERMAINE: Hello? Oh, it's you, Rose … Yeah, they're here … How 'bout that? A million of 'em! They're sitting right in front of me and I still can't believe it. One million! One million! I don't know how much that is, but who cares. A million's a million … Sure, they sent a catalogue. I already had one but this one's for this year, so it's a lot better. The old one was falling apart … They've got the most beautiful stuff, wait till you see it. It's unbelievable! I think I'll be able to take everything they've got. I'll re-furnish the whole house. I'm gonna get a new stove, new fridge, new kitchen table and chairs. I think I'll take the red one with the gold stars. I don't think you've seen that one … Oh, it's so beautiful, Rose. I'm getting new pots, new cutlery, a full set of dishes, salt and pepper shakers … Oh, and you know those glasses with the "caprice" design. Well, I'm taking a set of those, too. Mme de Courval got a set last year and she paid a fortune for them, but mine will be free. She'll be mad as hell … What? … Yeah, she'll be here tonight. They've got those chrome tins for flour and sugar, coffee and stuff … I'm taking it all. I'm getting a Colonial bedroom suite with full accessories. There's curtains, dresser-covers, one of those things you put on the floor beside the bed … No, dear, not that … New wallpaper … Not the floral, Henri can't sleep with flowers … I'm telling you Rose, it's gonna be one beautiful bedroom. And the living room! Wait till you hear this … I've got a big TV with a built-in stereo, a synthetic nylon carpet, real paintings ... You know those Chinese paintings I've always wanted, the ones with the velvet? ... Aren't they though? Oh, now get a load of this ... I'm gonna have the same crystal platters as your sister-in-law, Aline! I'm not sure, but I think mine are even nicer. There's ashtrays and lamps ... I guess that's about it for the living room ... there's an electric razor for Henri to shave with, shower curtains. So what? We'll put one in. It all comes with the stamps. There's a sunken bathtub, a new sink, bathing suits for everyone ... No, Rose, I am not too fat. Don't get smart. Now listen, I'm gonna re-do the kid's room, completely. Have you seen what they've got for kids' bedrooms? Rose, it's fabulous! They've got Mickey Mouse all over everything. And for Linda's room ... Okay, sure, you can just look at the catalogue. But come over right away, the others will be here any minute. I told them to come early. I mean it's gonna take forever to paste all those stamps.

MARIE-ANGE BROUILLETTE enters.

GERMAINE: Okay, I've gotta go. Mme Brouillette's just arrived. Okay, yeah ... Yeah ... Bye! *(hangs up the phone)*

MARIE-ANGE: Mme Lauzon, I just can't help it, I'm jealous.

GERMAINE: Well, I know what you mean. It's quite an event. But excuse me for a moment, Mme Brouillette, I'm not quite ready. I was talking to my sister, Rose. We can see each other across the alley, it's handy.

MARIE-ANGE: Is she gonna be here?

GERMAINE: You bet! She wouldn't miss this for love nor money. Here, have a seat and while you're waiting look at the catalogue. You won't believe all the lovely things they've got. And I'm getting them all, Mme Brouillette. The works! The whole catalogue. *(She goes into her bedroom.)*

MARIE-ANGE: You wouldn't catch me having luck like that. Fat chance. My life is shit and it always will be. A million stamps! A whole house. If I didn't bite my tongue, I'd scream. Typical. The ones with all the luck least deserve it. What did Mme Lauzon do to deserve this, eh? Nothing. Absolutely nothing! She's no better looking than me. In fact, she's no better period. These contests shouldn't be allowed. The priest the other day was right. They ought to be abolished. Why should she win a million stamps and not me?

Why? It's not fair. I work too, I've got kids, too, I have to wipe their asses, just like her. If anything, my kids are cleaner than hers. I work like a slave, it's no wonder I'm all skin and bones. Her, she's fat as a pig. And now, I'll have to live next door to her and the house she gets for free. It burns me up, I can't stand it. What's more, there'll be no end to her smart-assed comments 'cause it'll all go straight to her head. She's just the type, the loud-mouthed bitch. We'll be hearing about her goddamned stamps for years. I've a right to be angry. I don't want to die in this shit while madame Fatso here goes swimming in velvet! It's not fair! I'm sick of knocking myself out for nothing! My life is nothing. A big fat zero. And I haven't a cent to my name. I'm fed up. I'm fed up with this stupid, rotten life.

During the monologue, GABRIELLE JODOIN, ROSE OUIMET, YVETTE LONGPRÉ and LISETTE DE COURVAL have entered. They take their places in the kitchen without paying attention to MARIE-ANGE. The five women get up and turn to the audience. The lighting changes.

THE FIVE WOMEN: *(together)* This stupid, rotten life! Monday!

LISETTE: When the sun with his rays starts caressing the little flowers in the fields and the little birdies open wide their little beaks to send forth their little cries to heaven ...

THE OTHERS: I get up and I fix breakfast. Toast, coffee, bacon, eggs. I nearly go nuts trying to get the others out of bed. The kids leave for school, my husband goes to work.

MARIE-ANGE: Not mine, he's unemployed. He stays in bed.

THE FIVE WOMEN: Then I work. I work like a demon. I don't stop till noon. I wash ... Dresses, shirts, stockings, sweaters, pants, underpants, bras. The works. I scrub it, wring it out, scrub it again, rinse it ... My hands are chapped. My back is sore. I curse like hell. At noon, the kids come home. They eat like pigs, they wreck the house, they leave. In the afternoon I hang out the wash, the biggest pain of all. When that's finished, I start the supper. They all come home. They're tired and grumpy. We all fight. But at night, we watch TV. Tuesday ...

LISETTE: When the sun with his rays ...

THE OTHERS: I get up and I fix breakfast. The same goddamn thing. Toast, coffee, bacon, eggs. I drag the others out of bed and I shove them out the door. Then it's the ironing. I work, I work, I work and I work. It's noon before I know it and the kids are mad because lunch isn't ready. I make 'em baloney sandwiches. I work all afternoon. Suppertime comes, we all fight. But at night, we watch TV. Wednesday … Shopping day. I walk all day, I break my back carrying parcels this big, I come back home exhausted. But I've still got to make supper. When the others get home I look like I'm dead. I am. My husband bitches, the kids scream. We all fight. But at night, we watch TV. Thursday and Friday … Same thing … I work. I slave. I kill myself for my pack of morons. Then I spend the day Saturday tripping over the kids and we all fight. But at night, we watch TV. Sunday we go out, the whole family, we get on the bus and go for supper with the mother-in-law. I have to watch the kids like a hawk, laugh at the old man's jokes, eat the old lady's food, which everyone says is better than mine … At night, we watch TV. I'm fed up with this stupid, rotten life! This stupid, rotten life! This stupid, rotten life. This stup …

The lights return to normal. They sit down suddenly.

LISETTE: On my last trip to Europe …

ROSE: There she goes with her Europe again. We're in for it now. Once she gets started, there's no shutting her up!

DES-NEIGES VERRETTE comes in. Discreet little greetings are heard.

LISETTE: I only wished to say that in Europe they don't have stamps. I mean, they have stamps, but not like these ones. Only letter stamping stamps.

DES-NEIGES: That's no fun! So they don't get presents like us? Sounds pretty dull to me, Europe.

LISETTE: Oh no, it's very nice despite that …

MARIE-ANGE: Mind you, I've got nothing against stamps, they're useful. If it weren't for the stamps, I'd still be waiting for that thing to grind my meat with. What I don't like is the contests.

LISETTE: But why? They can make families happy.

MARIE-ANGE: Maybe, but they're a pain in the ass for the people next door.

LISETTE: Mme Brouillette, your language! I speak properly, and I'm none the worse for it.

MARIE-ANGE: I talk the way I talk, and I say what I got to say. I never went to Europe, so I can't afford to talk like you.

ROSE: Hey, you two, cut it out! We didn't come here to fight. You keep it up, I'm crossing the alley and going home.

GABRIELLE: What's taking Germaine so long? Germaine!

GERMAINE: *(from the bedroom)* Be there in a minute. I'm having a hard time getting into my … Well, I'm having a hard time … Is Linda there?

GABRIELLE: Linda! Linda! No, she's not here.

MARIE-ANGE: I think I saw her go out a while ago.

GERMAINE: Don't tell me she's snuck out, the little bugger.

GABRIELLE: Can we start pasting stamps in the meantime?

GERMAINE: No wait! I'm going to tell you what to do. Don't start yet, wait till I get there. Chat for a bit.

GABRIELLE: "Chat for a bit?" What are we going to chat about …

The telephone rings.

ROSE: My God, that scared me! Hello … No, she's out, but if you want to wait I think she'll be back in a few minutes. *(She puts the receiver down, goes out on the balcony and shouts.)* Linda! Linda, telephone!

LISETTE: So, Mme Longpré, how does marriage agree with your daughter Claudette?

YVETTE: Oh she loves it. She's having a ball. She told me about her honeymoon, you know.

GABRIELLE: Where did they go to?

YVETTE: Well, he won a trip to the Canary Islands, eh? So you see, they had to put the wedding ahead a bit …

ROSE: *(laughing)* The Canary Islands! A honeymoon in bird shit, eh?

GABRIELLE: Come on, Rose!

ROSE: What?

DES-NEIGES: The Canary Islands, where's that?

LISETTE: We stopped by there, my husband and I, on our last trip to Europe. It's a real ... It's a very pleasant country. The women only wear skirts.

ROSE: The perfect place for my husband!

LISETTE: And I'm afraid the natives are not very clean. Of course, in Europe, people don't wash.

DES-NEIGES: It shows, too. Look at those Italians next door to me. You wouldn't believe how that woman stinks.

They all burst out laughing.

LISETTE: *(insinuating)* Did you ever notice her clothesline, on Monday?

DES-NEIGES: No, why?

LISETTE: Well, all I know is this ... Those people don't have any underwear.

MARIE-ANGE: You're kidding!

ROSE: I don't believe it!

YVETTE: You gotta be joking!

LISETTE: It's the God's truth! Take a look for yourselves next Monday. You'll see.

YVETTE: No wonder they stink.

MARIE-ANGE: Maybe she's too modest to hang them outside.

The others laugh.

LISETTE: Modest! A European? They don't know what it means. Just look at their movies you see on TV. It's appalling. They stand right in the middle of the street and kiss. On the mouth, too! It's in their blood, you know. Take a look at that Italian's daughter when she brings her friends around ... Her boyfriends, that is ... It's disgusting what she does, that girl. She has no shame! Which reminds me, Mme Ouimet. I saw your Michel the other day ...

ROSE: Not with that slut, I hope!

LISETTE: I'm afraid so.

ROSE: You must be mistaken. It couldn't have been him.

LISETTE: I beg your pardon, but the Italians are my neighbours, too. The two of them were on the front balcony ... I suppose they thought no one could see them ...

DES-NEIGES: It's true, Mme Ouimet, I saw them myself. I tell you, they were necking like crazy.

ROSE: The little bastard! As if one pig in the family's not enough. By pig I mean my husband. Can't even watch a girl on TV without getting a ... Without getting worked up. Goddamn sex! They never get enough, those Ouimets. They're all alike, they ...

GABRIELLE: Rose, you don't have to tell the whole world ...

LISETTE: But we're very concerned ...

DES-NEIGES and MARIE-ANGE: Yes, we are ...

YVETTE: To get back to my daughter's honeymoon ...

GERMAINE: *(entering)* Here I am, girls! *(greetings, "how are you's," etc.)* So, what have you all been talking about?

ROSE: Oh, Mme Longpré was telling us about her daughter Claudette's honeymoon ...

GERMAINE: Really? *(to YVETTE)* Hello, dear ... *(to ROSE)* And what was she saying?

ROSE: Sounds like they had a great trip. They met all these people. They went on a boat. They were visiting islands, of course, the Canary Islands ... They went fishing and they caught fish this big. They ran into some couples they knew ... Old friends of Claudette's. Then they came back together and, oh yes, they stopped over in New York. Mme Longpré was giving us all the details ...

YVETTE: Well ...

ROSE: Eh, Mme Longpré, isn't that right?

YVETTE: Well, as a matter of fact ...

GERMAINE: You tell your daughter, Mme Longpré, that I wish her all the best. Of course, we weren't invited to the wedding, but we wish her well anyway.

There is an embarrassed silence.

GABRIELLE: Hey! It's almost seven! The rosary!

GERMAINE: Dear God, my novena for Ste-Thérèse. I'll get Linda's radio. *(She goes out.)*

ROSE: What does she want with Ste-Thérèse, especially after winning all that?

DES-NEIGES: Maybe she's having trouble with her kids …

GABRIELLE: No, she would have told me …

GERMAINE: *(from the bedroom)* Goddamn it! Where did she put that frigging radio?

ROSE: I don't know, Gaby. Our sister usually keeps things to herself.

GABRIELLE: Not with me. She tells me everything. You, you're such a blabbermouth …

ROSE: You've got a lot of nerve! What do you mean, blabbermouth? Gabrielle Jodoin! My mouth's no bigger than yours.

GABRIELLE: Come off it, you know you can't keep a secret!

ROSE: Well, I never … If you think …

LISETTE: Wasn't it you, Mme Ouimet, who just said we didn't come here to quarrel?

ROSE: Hey, you mind your own business. Besides, I didn't say "quarrel." I said "fight."

GERMAINE comes back in with a radio.

GERMAINE: What's going on? I can hear you at the other end of the house!

GABRIELLE: Nothing, it's our sister again …

GERMAINE: Settle down, Rose. You're supposed to be the life of the party … No fighting tonight.

ROSE: You see! In our family we say "fight."

GERMAINE turns on the radio. We hear a voice saying the rosary. All the women get down on their knees. After a few "Hail Marys" a great racket is heard outside. The women scream and run to the door.

GERMAINE: Oh my God! My sister-in-law Thérèse's mother-in-law just fell down three flights of stairs!

ROSE: Did you hurt yourself, Mme Dubuc?

GABRIELLE: Rose, shut up! She's probably dead!

THÉRÈSE: *(from a distance)* Are you all right, Mme Dubuc? *(A faint moan is heard.)* Wait a minute. Let me get the wheelchair off you. Is that better? Now I'm gonna help you get back in your chair. Come on, Mme Dubuc, make a little effort. Don't be so limp! Ouch!

DES-NEIGES: Here, Mme Dubuc. Let me give you a hand.

THÉRÈSE: Thanks Mlle Verrette. You're so kind.

The other women come back into the room.

ROSE: Germaine, shut off the radio. I'm a nervous wreck!

GERMAINE: What about my novena?

ROSE: How far have you gotten?

GERMAINE: I'm only up to seven, but I promised to do nine.

ROSE: So, pick it up tomorrow and you'll be finished on Saturday.

GERMAINE: It's not for nine days, it's for nine weeks.

THÉRÈSE DUBUC and DES-NEIGES VERRETTE enter with OLIVINE DUBUC, who is in a wheelchair.

GERMAINE: My God, she wasn't hurt bad, I hope.

THÉRÈSE: No, no, she's used to it. She falls out of her chair ten times a day. Whew! I'm all out of breath. It's no joke, hauling this thing up three flights of stairs. You got something to drink, Germaine?

GERMAINE: Gaby, give Thérèse a glass of water. *(She approaches OLIVINE DUBUC.)* And how are you today, Mme Dubuc?

THÉRÈSE: Don't get too close, Germaine. She's been biting lately.

In fact, OLIVINE DUBUC tries to bite GERMAINE's hand.

GERMAINE: My god, you're right! She's dangerous! How long has she been doing that?

THÉRÈSE: Shut off the radio, Germaine, it's getting on my nerves. I'm too upset after what's happened.

GERMAINE: *(reluctantly shuts off the radio)* It's alright, Thérèse, I understand.

THÉRÈSE: Honestly, you don't know what it's like, I'm at the end of my tether! You can't imagine my life since I got stuck with my mother-in-law. It's not that I don't love her, the poor woman, I pity her. But she's sick, and so temperamental. I've gotta watch her like a hawk!

DES-NEIGES: How come she's out of the hospital?

THÉRÈSE: Well, you see, Mlle Verrette, three months ago my husband got a raise, so welfare stopped paying for his mother. If she'd stayed there, we would have had to pay all the bills ourselves.

MARIE-ANGE: My, my, my …

YVETTE: That's awful.

DES-NEIGES: Dreadful!

During THÉRÈSE's speech, GERMAINE opens the boxes and distributes the stamps and books.

THÉRÈSE: We had to bring her home. It's some cross to bear, believe me! Don't forget, that woman's ninety-three years old. It's like having a baby in the house. I have to dress her, undress her, wash her …

DES-NEIGES: God forbid!

YVETTE: You poor thing.

THÉRÈSE: No, it's no fun. Why only this morning, I said to Paul … he's my youngest … "Maman's going shopping, so you stay here and take good care of Granny." Well, when I got home, Mme Dubuc had dumped a quart of molasses all over herself and was playing in it like a kid. Of course, Paul was nowhere to be seen. I had to clean the table, the floor, the wheelchair …

GERMAINE: What about Mme Dubuc?

THÉRÈSE: I left her like that for the rest of the afternoon. That'll teach her. If she's gonna act like a baby, I'll treat her like one. Do you realize I have to spoon feed her?

GERMAINE: My poor Thérèse. How I feel for you.

DES-NEIGES: You're too good, Thérèse.

GABRIELLE: Much too good, I agree.

THÉRÈSE: What can you do, we all have our crosses to bear.

MARIE-ANGE: If you ask me, Thérèse, you've got a heavy one!

THÉRÈSE: Oh well, I don't complain. I just tell myself that our Lord is good and He's gonna help me get through.

LISETTE: I can't bear it, it makes me want to weep.

THÉRÈSE: Now, Mme de Courval, don't overdo it.

DES-NEIGES: All I can say, Mme Dubuc, is you're a real saint.

GERMAINE: Well, now that you've got stamps and booklets, I'll put a little water in some saucers and we can get started, eh? We don't want to spend the night yacking.

She fills a few saucers and passes them around. The women start pasting stamps in the books. GERMAINE goes out on the balcony.

GERMAINE: If Linda were here, she could help me! Linda! Linda! Richard, have you seen Linda? I don't believe it! She's got the nerve to sit and drink Coke while I'm slaving away! Be an angel, will you, and tell her to come home right away? Come see Mme Lauzon tomorrow and she'll give you some peanuts and candy, if there's any left, okay? Go on, sweetie, and tell her to get home this minute! *(She comes back inside.)* The little bitch. She promised to stay home.

MARIE-ANGE: Kids are all the same.

THÉRÈSE: You can say that again! They got no respect.

GABRIELLE: You're telling me. At our house, it's unbearable. Ever since my Raymond started his *cours classique* he's changed something awful … We don't recognize him! He walks around with his nose in the air like he's too good for us. He speaks Latin, at the table! We have to listen to his awful music. Can you imagine, classical music in the middle of the afternoon? And when we don't want to watch his stupid TV concerts, he throws a fit. If there's one thing I hate it's classical music.

ROSE: Ah! You're not the only one.

THÉRÈSE: I agree. It drives me crazy. Clink! Clank! Bing, Bang, Bong!

GABRIELLE: Of course, Raymond says we don't understand it. As if there's something to understand! Just because he's learning all sorts of nonsense at school, he thinks he can treat us like dirt. I've got half a mind to yank him out and put him to work.

ALL THE WOMEN: Kids are so ungrateful! Kids are so ungrateful!

GERMAINE: Be sure to fill those books, eh, girls? Stamps on every page.

ROSE: Relax, Germaine, you'd think we'd never done it before.

YVETTE: Isn't it getting a little warm in here? Maybe we could open the window a bit ...

GERMAINE: No, no, not with the stamps. It'll make a draft.

ROSE: Come on, Germaine, they're not birds. They won't fly away. Oh, speaking of birds, last Sunday I went to see Bernard, my oldest. Well, you've never seen so many birds in one house. The house is one big bird cage. And it's her doing, you know. She's nuts about birds! And she doesn't want to kill any. Too soft-hearted, but surely to God there's a limit. Listen to this, it's a scream.

Spotlight on ROSE OUIMET.

ROSE: I'm telling you the woman's nuts. I joke about it but really, it's not funny. Anyway, last Easter, Bernard picked up this bird cage for the two kids. Some guy at the tavern needed money, so he sold it to him cheap ... Well, the minute he got it in the house, she went bananas. Fell head over heels in love with his birds. No kidding. She took better care of them than she did her kids. Of course, in no time at all the females were laying eggs ... And when they started to hatch, Manon thought they were so cute. She didn't have the heart to get rid of them. You've got to be crazy, eh? So she kept them! The whole flock! God knows how many she's got. I never tried to count 'em ... But, believe me, every time I set foot in the place I nearly go out of my mind! But wait, you haven't heard anything yet. Every day around two, she opens up the cage and out come her stupid birds. What happens? They fly all over the house. They shit all over everything, including us, and we run after them cleaning it all up. Of course, when it's time to get them back in the cage, they don't want to go. They're having too much fun! So Manon starts screaming at the kids, "Catch Maman's little birdies, Maman's too tired." So the kids go charging after the birds and the place is a frigging circus. Me, I get the hell out! I go sit on the balcony and wait till they've all been caught. *(The women laugh.)* And those kids! God, what brats! Oh, I like them okay, they're my grandchildren. But Jesus, do they drive me nuts. Our kids weren't like that. Say what you like. Young people today, they don't know how to bring up their kids.

GERMAINE: You said it!

YVETTE: That's for sure.

ROSE: I mean, take the bathroom. Now we wouldn't have let our kids play in there. Well, you should have seen it on Sunday. The kids went in there like they were just going about their business and in no time flat they'd turned the place upside down. I didn't say a word! Manon always says I talk too much. But I could hear them alright and they were getting on my nerves. You know what they were doing? They took the toilet paper, and they unrolled the whole goddamn thing. Manon just yelled "Look, you kids, Maman's gonna get angry." A lot of good that did. They didn't pay any attention. They kept right on going. I would've skinned 'em alive, the little buggers. And were they having a ball! Bruno, the youngest ... Can you imagine calling a kid "Bruno"? ... Anyway, Bruno climbed into the bathtub fully dressed and all rolled up in toilet paper and turned on the water. Listen, he was laughing so hard he nearly drowned! He was making boats out of soggy paper and the water was running all over the place. A real flood! Well, I had to do something. I mean, enough is enough, so I gave them a licking and sent them off to bed.

YVETTE: That's exactly what they needed!

ROSE: Their mother raised a stink, of course, but I'll be damned if I was gonna let them carry on like that. Manon, the dim-wit, she just sits there peeling potatoes and listening to the radio. Oh, she's a winner, that one! But I guess she's happy. The only thing she worries about is her birds. Poor Bernard! At times I really feel sorry for him, being married to that. He should have stayed home with me. He was a lot better off ... *(She bursts out laughing.)*

Lights return to normal.

YVETTE: Isn't she a riot! There's no stopping her.

GABRIELLE: Yeah, there's never a dull moment with Rose.

ROSE: I always say, when it's time to laugh, might as well have a good one. Every story has a funny side, you know? Even the sad ones …

THÉRÈSE: You're damn lucky if you can say that, Mme Ouimet. It's not everyone …

DES-NEIGES: We understand, dear. It must be hard for you to laugh with all your troubles. You're far too good, Mme Dubuc! You're always thinking of others …

ROSE: That's right, you should think of yourself sometimes. You never go out.

THÉRÈSE: I don't have time! When would you have me go out? I have to take care of her … Ah! if only that was all …

GERMAINE: Thérèse, don't tell me there's more.

THÉRÈSE: If you only knew! Now that my husband's making some money the family thinks we're millionaires. Why only yesterday, a sister-in-law of my sister-in-law's came to the door with her hand out. Well, you know me. When she told me her story it just broke my heart. So I gave her some old clothes I didn't need anymore … Ah, she was so happy … weeping with gratitude … she even kissed my hands.

DES-NEIGES: I'm not surprised. You deserve it!

MARIE-ANGE: Mme Dubuc, I really admire you.

THÉRÈSE: Oh, don't say that …

DES-NEIGES: No, no, no. You deserve it.

LISETTE: You certainly do, Mme Dubuc. You deserve our admiration and I assure you, I shan't forget you in my prayers.

THÉRÈSE: Well, I always say, "If God put poor people on this earth, they gotta be encouraged."

GERMAINE: When you're through filling your books there instead of piling them on the table, why don't we put them back in the box? … Rose, give me a hand. We'll take out the empty books and put in the full ones.

ROSE: Good idea. My God! Look at all these books. We gotta fill all them tonight?

GERMAINE: Sure, why not? Besides, everyone's not here yet, so we …

DES-NEIGES: Who else is coming, Mme Lauzon?

GERMAINE: Rhéauna Bibeau and Angéline Sauvé are supposed to come by after the funeral parlour. One of Mlle Bibeau's old girlfriends has a daughter whose husband died. His name was … Baril, I think …

YVETTE: Not Rosaire Baril.

GERMAINE: Yeah, I think that's it …

YVETTE: But I knew him well! I used to go out with him for Godsake. How do you like that! I'd have been a widow today.

GABRIELLE: Guess what, girls? I got the eight mistakes in last Saturday's paper. It's the first time I ever got 'em all and I've been trying for six months … I sent in the answer …

YVETTE: Did you win anything yet?

GABRIELLE: Do I look like someone who's ever won anything?

THÉRÈSE: Hey, Germaine, what are you going to do with all these stamps?

GERMAINE: Didn't I tell you? I'm going to redecorate the whole house. Wait a minute … Where did I put the catalogue? … Ah, here it is. Look at that, Thérèse. I'm gonna have all that for nothing.

THÉRÈSE: For nothing! You mean it's not going to cost you a cent?

GERMAINE: Not a cent! Aren't these contests wonderful?

LISETTE: That's not what Mme Brouillette said a while ago …

GERMAINE: What do you mean?

MARIE-ANGE: Mme de Courval, really!

ROSE: Well, come on, Mme Brouillette. Don't be afraid to say what you think. You said earlier you don't like these contests because only one family wins.

MARIE-ANGE: Well, it's true! All these lotteries and contests are unfair. I'm against them.

GERMAINE: Just because you never won anything.

MARIE-ANGE: Maybe, maybe, but they're still not fair.

GERMAINE: Not fair, my eye! You're jealous, that's all. You said so yourself the minute you walked in. Well, I don't like jealous people, Mme Brouillette. I don't like them one bit! In fact, if you really want to know, I can't stand them!

MARIE-ANGE: Well! In that case, I'm leaving!

GERMAINE: No, no don't go! Look I'm sorry ... I'm all nerves tonight, I don't know what I'm saying. We'll just forget it, okay? You have every right to your opinions. Every right. Just sit back down and keep pasting.

ROSE: Our sister's afraid of losing one of her workers.

GABRIELLE: Shut up, Rose! You're always sticking your nose where it don't belong.

ROSE: What's eating you? I can't even open my mouth?

MARIE-ANGE: Alright, I'll stay. But I still don't like them.

From this point on, MARIE-ANGE BROUILLETTE will steal all the books she fills. The others will see what she's doing right from the start, except for GERMAINE, obviously, and they will decide to follow suit.

LISETTE: Well, I figured out the mystery charade in last month's *Chatelaine*. It was very easy ... My first syllable is a Persian king ...

ROSE: Onassis?

LISETTE: No, a *Persian* king ... It's a "shah" ...

ROSE: That's a Persian?

LISETTE: Why, of course ...

ROSE: *(laughing)* That's his tough luck!

LISETTE: My second is for killing bugs ... No one? ... Oh, well, "Raid" ...

ROSE: My husband's a worm, do you think it would work on him? ... She's really nuts with all this stuff, eh?

LISETTE: And the whole thing is a social game ...

ROSE: Spin the bottle!

GABRIELLE: Rose, will you shut up for Godsake! *(to LISETTE)* Scrabble?

LISETTE: Oh, come now, it's simple ... Shahraid ... Charade!

YVETTE: Ah ... What's a charade?

LISETTE: Of course, I figured it out in no time ... It was so easy ...

YVETTE: So, did you win anything?

LISETTE: Oh, I didn't bother to send it in. I just did it for the challenge ... Besides, do I look like I need to win things?

ROSE: Well, I like mystery words, hidden words, crosswords, turned-around words, bilingual words. All that stuff with words. It's my specialty. I'm a champ, you know, I've broken all the records! Never miss a contest ... Costs me two bucks a week just for stamps!

YVETTE: So did you win yet?

ROSE: *(looking at GERMAINE)* Do I look like somebody who's ever won anything?

THÉRÈSE: Mme Dubuc, will you let go of my saucer? ... There, now you've done it! You've spilled it! That's the last straw!

She socks her mother-in-law on the head and the latter settles down a little.

GABRIELLE: Wow! You don't fool around! Aren't you afraid you'll hurt her?

THÉRÈSE: No, no. She's used to it. It's the only way to shut her up. My husband figured it out. If you give her a good bash on the head, it seems to knock her out a while. That way she stays in her corner and we get some peace.

Blackout. Spotlight on YVETTE LONGPRÉ.

YVETTE: When my daughter Claudette got back from her honeymoon, she gave me the top part of her wedding cake. I was so proud! It's such a lovely piece. A miniature sanctuary all made of icing. It's got a red velvet stairway leading up to a platform and on top of the platform stand the bride and groom. Two little dolls all dressed up like newly-weds. There's even a priest to bless them and behind him there's an altar. It's *all* icing. I've never seen anything so beautiful. Of course, we paid a lot for the cake. After all, six levels! It wasn't *all* cake though. That would have cost a fortune. Just the first two levels were cake. The rest was wood. But it's amazing, eh? You'd never have guessed. Anyway, when my daughter gave me the top part, she had it put under this glass bell. It looked so pretty, but I was afraid it would spoil ... you know, without air. So I took my husband's glass knife ... He's got a special knife for cutting glass ... And I cut a hole in the top of the bell. Now the air will stay fresh and the cake won't go bad.

Lights up.

DES-NEIGES: Me too. I took a stab at a contest a few weeks ago. You had to find a slogan for some bookstore ... I think it was Hachette or something ... Anyway, I gave it a try ... I came up with "Hachette will chop the cost of your books." Not bad, eh?

YVETTE: Yeah, but did you win anything?

DES-NEIGES: Do I look like somebody who's ever won anything?

GERMAINE: By the way, Rose, I saw you cutting your grass this morning. You should buy a lawn-mower.

ROSE: What for? I get along fine with scissors. Besides it keeps me in shape.

GERMAINE: You were puffing away like a steam engine.

ROSE: I'm telling you, it's good for me. Anyway, I can't afford a lawn-mower. Even if I could, that's the last thing I'd buy.

GERMAINE: I'll be getting a lawn-mower with my stamps ...

DES-NEIGES: Her and her stamps, she's starting to get on my nerves! *(She hides a booklet in her purse.)*

ROSE: What are you gonna do with a lawn-mower on the third floor?

GERMAINE: You never know, it might come in handy. And who knows, we might move someday.

DES-NEIGES: I suppose she's going to tell us she needs a new house for all the stuff she's gonna get with her lovely stamps.

GERMAINE: You know, we probably will need a bigger place for all the stuff I'm gonna get with my stamps.

DES-NEIGES VERRETTE, MARIE-ANGE BROUILLETTE and THÉRÈSE DUBUC all hide two or three books each.

GERMAINE: Rose, if you want, you can borrow my lawn-mower.

ROSE: No way! I might bust it. I'd be collecting stamps for the next two years just to pay you back.

The women laugh.

GERMAINE: Don't be smart.

MARIE-ANGE: Isn't she something! Can you beat that!

THÉRÈSE: Hey, I forgot to tell you. I guessed the mystery voice on the radio ... It was Duplessis ... My husband figured it out 'cause it was an old voice. I sent in twenty-five letters just to be sure they'd get it. And for extra luck, I signed my youngest boy's name, Paul Dubuc ...

YVETTE: Did you win anything yet?

THÉRÈSE: *(looking to GERMAINE)* Do I look like someone who's ever won anything?

GABRIELLE: Say, do you know what my husband's gonna get me for my birthday?

ROSE: Same as last year. Two pairs of nylons.

GABRIELLE: No sir-ee! A fur coat. Of course, it's not real fur, but who cares? I don't think real fur's worth buying anymore. The synthetics they make nowadays are just as nice. In fact, sometimes nicer.

LISETTE: Oh, I disagree ...

ROSE: Sure, we all know who's got a fat mink stole!

LISETTE: Well, if you ask me, there's no substitute for authentic, genuine fur. Incidentally, I'll be getting a new stole in the autumn. The one I have now is three years old and it's starting to look ... well, a bit ratty. Mind you, it's still mink, but ...

ROSE: Shut your mouth, you bloody liar! We know goddamn well your husband's up to his ass in debt because of your mink stoles and trips to Europe! She's got no more money than the rest of us and she thinks her farts smell like perfume!

LISETTE: Mme Jodoin, if your husband wants to buy my stole, I'll sell it to him cheap. Then you'll have real mink. After all, between friends …

YVETTE: You know the inflated objects game in the paper, the one where you're supposed to guess what the objects are? Well, I guessed them. There was a screw, a screw-driver and some kind of bent up hook.

THE OTHERS: So …

YVETTE sits down.

GERMAINE: You know Daniel, Mme Robitaille's little boy? He fell off the second floor balcony the other day. Not even a scratch! How 'bout that?

MARIE-ANGE: Don't forget he landed on Mme Turgeon's hammock. And Monsieur Turgeon was in it at the time …

GERMAINE: That's right. He's in hospital for three months.

DES-NEIGES: Speaking of accidents, I heard a joke the other day …

ROSE: Well, aren't you gonna tell us?

DES-NEIGES: Oh, I couldn't. It's too racy …

ROSE: Come on, Mlle Verrette! We know you've got a stack of them …

DES-NEIGES: No. I'm too embarrassed. I don't know why, but I am …

GABRIELLE: Don't be such a tease, Mlle Verrette. You know darn well you're gonna tell us anyway …

DES-NEIGES: Well … Alright … There was this nun who got raped in an alley …

ROSE: Sounds good!

DES-NEIGES: And the next morning they found her lying in the yard, a real mess, her habit pulled over her head, moaning away … So this reporter comes running over and he says to her, "Excuse me, Sister, but could you tell us something about this terrible thing that's happened to you?" Well, she opens her eyes, looks up at him and in a very small voice she says, "Again, please."

All the women burst out laughing except for LISETTE DE COURVAL who appears scandalized.

ROSE: Christ Almighty, that's hysterical! I haven't heard such a good one for ages. I'm gonna pee my pants! Mlle Verrette, where in the world do you get them?

GABRIELLE: You know where, from her travelling salesman …

DES-NEIGES: Mme Jodoin, please!

ROSE: That's right too. Her travelling salesman …

LISETTE: I don't understand.

GABRIELLE: Mlle Verrette has a travelling salesman who comes to sell her brushes every month. I think she likes him more than his brushes.

DES-NEIGES: Mme Jodoin, honestly!

ROSE: One thing's for sure, Mlle Verrette has more brushes than anyone in the parish. Hey, I saw your boyfriend the other day … He was sitting in the restaurant … He must have been to see you, eh?

DES-NEIGES: Yes, he was—but I assure you, there's nothing between us.

ROSE: That's what they all say.

DES NEIGES: Really, Mme Ouimet, you're always twisting things to make people look bad. Monsieur Simard is a very nice man.

ROSE: Yeah, but who's to say you're a nice lady? Now, now, Mlle Verrette, don't get angry. I'm only pulling your leg.

DES-NEIGES: Then don't say things like that. Of course, I'm a nice lady, a thoroughly respectable one too. By the way, the last time he was over, Henri … er … Monsieur Simard was telling me about a project he has in mind … And he asked me to extend you all an invitation. He wants me to organize a demonstration next week … at my house. He chose me because he knows my house … It'd be for a week Sunday, right after the rosary. I need at least ten people if I'm gonna get my gift … You know, they give away those fancy cups to the one who holds the demonstration … Fantasy Chinaware … You should see them, they're gorgeous. They're souvenirs he brought back from Niagara Falls … They must have cost a fortune.

ROSE: You bet, we'll go, eh, girls? I love demonstrations! Any door prizes?

DES-NEIGES: I don't know. I suppose. Maybe … Anyway, I'll provide snacks …

ROSE: That's more than you get around here. We'll be lucky to see a glass of water!

OLIVINE DUBUC tries to bite her daughter-in-law.

THÉRÈSE: Mme Dubuc, if you don't stop that I'm gonna lock you in the bathroom and you can stay there for the rest of the evening.

Blackout. Spotlight on DES-NEIGES VERRETTE.

DES-NEIGES: The first time I saw him I thought he was ugly ... it's true. He's not good-looking. When I opened the door he took off his hat and said, "Would you be interested in buying some brushes, Madame?" I slammed the door in his face. I never let a man in the house! Who knows what might happen ... The only one who gets in is the paper boy. He's still too young to get any wrong ideas. Well, a month later my friend with the brushes came back. There was a terrible snowstorm outside, so I let him stand in the hall. Once he was in the house, I was frightened, but I told myself he didn't look dangerous, even if he wasn't good looking ... He's always well-dressed ... Not a hair out of place ... He's a real gentleman ... And so polite! Well, he sold me a couple of brushes and then he showed me his catalogue. There was one that I wanted, but he didn't have it with him, so he said I could place an order. Ever since then, he's come back once a month. Sometimes I don't buy a thing. He just comes in and we chat for a while. He's such a nice man. When he speaks, you forget he's ugly. And he knows so many interesting things! The man must travel all over the province! I think ... I think I'm in love with him ... I know it's crazy. I only see him once a month, but it's so nice when we're together. I'm so happy when he comes. I've never felt this way before. Never. Men never paid much attention to me. I've always been ... unattached. But he tells me about his trips, and all kinds of stories ... Sometimes they're a bit risqué, but honestly, they're so funny! I must admit, I've always liked stories that are a bit off-colour ... And it's good for you to tell them sometimes. Not all his jokes are dirty, mind you. Lots of them are clean. And it's only lately that he's been telling me the spicy ones. Sometimes they're so dirty I blush! The last time he came he took my hand when I blushed. I nearly went out of my mind. My insides went all funny when he put his big hand on mine. I need him so badly! I don't want

him to go away! Sometimes, just sometimes, I dream about him. I dream ... that we're married. I need him to come and see me. He's the first man that ever cared about me. I don't want to lose him! I don't want to! If he goes away, I'll be all alone again, and I need ... someone to love ... *(She lowers her eyes and murmurs.)* I need a man.

The lights come on again. LINDA LAUZON, GINETTE MENARD and LISE PAQUETTE enter.

GERMAINE: Ah, there you are!

LINDA: I was at the restaurant.

GERMAINE: I know you were at the restaurant. You keep hanging around there, you're gonna end up like your Aunt Pierrette ... In a whorehouse.

LINDA: Lay off, Ma! You're making a stink over nothing.

GERMAINE: I asked you to stay home ...

LINDA: Look, I went to get cigarettes and I ran into Lise and Ginette ...

GERMAINE: That's no excuse. You knew I was having company, why didn't you come right home. You do it on purpose, Linda. You do it just to make my blood boil. You want me to blow my stack in front of my friends? Is that it? You want me to swear in public? Well, Jesus Christ Almighty, you've succeeded! But don't think you're off the hook yet, Linda Lauzon. I'll take care of you later.

ROSE: This is no time to bawl her out, Germaine!

GABRIELLE: Rose, you mind your own business.

LINDA: So, I'm a little late, my God, it's not the end of the world!

LISE: It's our fault, Mme Lauzon.

GINETTE: Yeah, it's our fault.

GERMAINE: I know it's your fault. And I've told Linda a hundred times not to run around with tramps. But you think she gives a damn? Sometimes I'd like to strangle her!

ROSE: Now, Germaine ...

GABRIELLE: Rose, I told you, stay out of this! You got that? It's their business. It's nothing to do with you.

ROSE: Hey, get off my back! What's with you anyway? Linda's getting bawled out and she hasn't done a goddamn thing!

GABRIELLE: It's none of our business!

LINDA: Leave her alone, Aunt Gaby. She's only trying to defend me.

GABRIELLE: Don't you tell me what to do! I'm your Godmother!

GERMAINE: You see what she's like! Day in and day out! I never brought her up to act this way.

ROSE: Now that you mention it, how do you bring up your kids?

GERMAINE: Hah! You should talk! ... Your kids ...

LINDA: Go on, Aunt Rose, tell her. You're the only one who can give it to her good.

GERMAINE: So, you're siding with your Aunt Rose now are you? You've forgotten what you said when she phoned a while ago, eh? You've forgotten about that? Come on, Linda, tell Aunt Rose what you said about her.

LINDA: That was different ...

ROSE: Why, what did she say?

GERMAINE: Well, she answered the phone when you called, right? And she was too rude to say, "One moment, please," so I told her to be more polite with you ...

LINDA: Will you shut up, Ma! That has nothing to do with it.

ROSE: I want to know what you said, Linda.

LINDA: It's not important, I was mad at her.

GERMAINE: She said, "It's only Aunt Rose. Why should I be polite to her?"

ROSE: I don't believe it ... You said that?

LINDA: I told you, I was mad at her!

ROSE: I never thought that of you, Linda. There, you've let me down. You've really let me down.

GABRIELLE: Let them fight it out themselves, Rose.

ROSE: You bet I'll let 'em fight. Go on, Germaine. Knock her silly, the little brat! You wanna know something, Linda? Your mother's right. If you're not careful, you'll end up like your Aunt Pierrette. I've got a good mind to slap your face!

GERMAINE: Just you try it! You don't lay a hand on my kids! if they need a beating, I'll do it. Nobody else!

THÉRÈSE: Will you please stop bickering, I'm tired!

DES-NEIGES: Lord, yes, you're wearing us out.

THÉRÈSE: You'll wake up my mother-in-law and get her going again.

GERMAINE: She's your problem, not mine! Why didn't you leave her at home?

THÉRÈSE: Germaine Lauzon!

GABRIELLE: Well, she's right. You don't go out to parties with a ninety-three year old cripple.

LISETTE: Mme Jodoin, didn't I just hear you tell your sister to mind her own business?

GABRIELLE: Keep your big nose out of this you stuck up bitch! Shut your yap and keep pasting or I'll shut it for you.

LISETTE: (getting up) Gabrielle Jodoin!

OLIVINE DUBUC spills the saucer she has been playing with.

THÉRÈSE: Mme Dubuc, for Godsake!

GERMAINE: Aw, shit, my tablecloth!

ROSE: She's soaked me, the old bag!

THÉRÈSE: That's not true! You weren't even close!

ROSE: Sure, call me a liar right to my face!

THÉRÈSE: Rose Ouimet, you are a liar!

GERMAINE: Look out, she's falling out of her chair!

DES-NEIGES: Oh, no, she's on the floor, again!

THÉRÈSE: Somebody give me a hand.

ROSE: Not me, no way!

GABRIELLE: Pick her up yourself.

DES-NEIGES: Here, I'll help you, Mme Dubuc.

THÉRÈSE: Thank you, Mlle Verrette.

GERMAINE: And you, Linda, you watch your step for the rest of the evening.

LINDA: I feel like going back to the restaurant.

GERMAINE: Do that and you won't set foot in this house again, you hear?

LINDA: Sure, I've heard it a thousand times.

LISE: Can it, Linda …

THÉRÈSE: For Godsake, Mme Dubuc, make a little effort. You go limp like that on purpose.

MARIE-ANGE: I'll hold the chair.

THÉRÈSE: Thank you …

ROSE: If it was me, I'd take that lousy chair and …

GABRIELLE: Rose, don't start again!

THÉRÈSE: Whew! What I go through …

GABRIELLE: Hey, will you get a load of de Courval, still pasting her stamps … The bloody snob. As if nothing had happened! I guess we're not good enough for her.

Blackout. Spotlight on LISETTE DE COURVAL.

LISETTE: It's like living in a barnyard. Léopold told me not to come and he was right. I should have stayed home. We don't belong with these people. Once you've tasted life on an ocean liner and have to return to this, well … It's enough to make you weep … I can still see myself, stretched out on the deck chair, a Book-of-the-Month in my lap … And that lieutenant who was giving me the eye … My husband says he wasn't, but he didn't see what I saw … Mmmmm … That was some man. Maybe I should have encouraged him a little more … *(She sighs.)* … And Europe! Everyone there is so refined! So much more polite than here. You'd never meet a Germaine Lauzon in Europe. Never! Only people of substance. In Paris, you know, everyone speaks so beautifully and there they talk *real* French … Not like here … I despise every one of them. I'll never set foot in this place again! Léopold was right about these people. These people are *cheap*. We shouldn't mix with them. Shouldn't talk about them … They should be hidden away somewhere. They don't know how to live! We broke away from this and we must never, ever go back. Dear God, they make me so ashamed!

The lights come back up.

LINDA: I've had it. I'm leaving …

GERMAINE: The hell you are! I'm warning you Linda! …

LINDA: "I'm warning you, Linda!" Is that all you know how to say?

LISE: Linda, don't be stupid.

GINETTE: Let's stay.

LINDA: No, I'm leaving. I've listened to enough crap for one night.

GERMAINE: Linda, I forbid you to leave!

VOICE OF A NEIGHBOUR: Will you stop screaming up there. We can't hear ourselves think!

ROSE: *(going out on the balcony)* Hey, you! Get back in your house.

NEIGHBOUR: I wasn't talking to you!

ROSE: Oh yes, you were. I'm just as loud as the rest of them!

GABRIELLE: Rose, get in here!

DES-NEIGES: *(referring to the neighbour)* Don't pay any attention to her.

NEIGHBOUR: I'm gonna call the cops!

ROSE: Go right ahead, we need some men up here.

GERMAINE: Rose Ouimet, get back in this house! And you, Linda …

LINDA: I'm leaving. See ya! *(She goes out with GINETTE and LISE.)*

GERMAINE: She's gone! Gone! Walked right out! I don't believe it! That kid will be the death of me. I'm gonna smash something. I'm gonna smash something!

ROSE: Germaine, control yourself.

GERMAINE: Making a fool of me in front of everyone! *(She starts sobbing.)* My own daughter … I'm so ashamed!

GABRIELLE: Come on, Germaine. It's not that bad …

LINDA'S VOICE: Hey, if it isn't Mlle Sauvé. How are you doing?

ANGÉLINE'S VOICE: Hello, sweetheart, how are you?

ROSE: Germaine, they're here. Blow your nose and stop crying.

LINDA'S VOICE: Not bad, thanks.

RHÉAUNA'S VOICE: Where are you off to?

LINDA'S VOICE: I was gonna go to the restaurant, but now that you're here, I think I'll stay.

LINDA, GINETTE and LISE enter with ANGÉLINE and RHÉAUNA.

ANGÉLINE: Hello, everybody.

RHÉAUNA: Hello.

THE OTHERS: Hello, hello. Come on in, how have you been … *etc.*

RHÉAUNA: What an awful climb, Mme Lauzon. I'm all out of breath.

GERMAINE: Well, have a seat …

ROSE: You're out of breath? Don't worry, my sister's getting an elevator with her stamps.

They all laugh except RHÉAUNA and ANGÉLINE who don't understand.

GERMAINE: Very funny, Rose! Linda, go get some more chairs …

LINDA: Where? There aren't any more.

GERMAINE: Go ask Mme Bergeron if she'll lend us some …

LINDA: *(to the girls)* Come on, guys …

GERMAINE: *(low to LINDA)* We make peace for now, but wait till the others have gone …

LINDA: I'm not scared of you. If I came back it's because Mlle Sauvé and Mlle Bibeau showed up, not because of you. *(LINDA goes out with her friends.)*

DES-NEIGES: Here, take my seat, Mlle Bibeau …

THÉRÈSE: Yes, come and sit next to me …

MARIE-ANGE: Sit down here, Mlle Bibeau …

ANGÉLINE and RHÉAUNA: Thank you. Thanks very much.

RHÉAUNA: I see you're pasting stamps.

GERMAINE: We sure are. A million of 'em!

RHÉAUNA: Dear God, a million! How are you getting on?

ROSE: Not bad … But my tongue's paralyzed.

RHÉAUNA: You've been doing it with your tongue?

GABRIELLE: Of course not, she's just being smart.

ROSE: Good old Bibeau. Sharp as a tack!

ANGÉLINE: Why don't we give you a hand?

ROSE: Okay. As long as you don't give us some tongue! *(She bursts out laughing.)*

GABRIELLE: Rose, don't be vulgar!

GERMAINE: So, how was the funeral parlour?

Blackout. Spotlight on ANGÉLINE and RHÉAUNA.

RHÉAUNA: I tell you, it came as a shock …

ANGÉLINE: But I thought you hardly knew him.

RHÉAUNA: I knew his mother. So did you. Remember, we went to school together. I watched that man grow up …

ANGÉLINE: Such a shame. Gone, just like that. And us, we're still here.

RHÉAUNA: Ah, but not for long …

ANGÉLINE: Rhéauna, please …

RHÉAUNA: I know what I'm talking about. You can tell when the end is near. I've suffered. I know.

ANGÉLINE: Ah, when it comes to that, we've both had our share. I've suffered, too.

RHÉAUNA: I've suffered a lot more than you, Angéline. Seventeen operations! A lung, a kidney, one of my breasts … Gone! I'm telling you, there's not much left.

ANGÉLINE: And me with my arthritis that won't let up. But Mme … What was her name … You know, the wife of the deceased … She gave me a recipe … She says it works wonders.

RHÉAUNA: But you've tried everything. The doctors have all told you, there's nothing you can do. There's no cure for arthritis.

ANGÉLINE: Doctors, doctors! ... I've had it with doctors. All they think about is money. They bleed you to death and go to California for the winter. You know, Rhéauna, the doctor said he'd get well, Monsieur ... What was his name again? The one who died?

RHÉAUNA: Monsieur Baril ...

ANGÉLINE: That's it. I can never remember it. It's easy enough, too. Anyhow, the doctor told Monsieur Baril that he had nothing to worry about ... And look what happened ... Only forty years old ...

RHÉAUNA: Forty years old! That's young to die.

ANGÉLINE: He sure went fast ...

RHÉAUNA: She told me how it happened. It's so sad ...

ANGÉLINE: Really? I wasn't there. How did it happen?

RHÉAUNA: When he got home from work on Monday night, she thought he was looking a bit strange. He was white as a sheet, so she asked him how he felt. He said he felt okay and they started supper ... Well, now, the kids were making a fuss at the table and Monsieur Baril got mad and had to punish Rolande. That's his daughter ... Of course, after that, he looked like he was ready to drop ... she didn't take her eyes off him for a second ... But she told me later that it happened so fast she didn't have time to do a thing. All of a sudden he said he felt funny and over he went ... His face right in the soup. That was it!

ANGÉLINE: Lord, have mercy. So sudden! I tell you, Rhéauna, it's frightening. It gives me the shivers.

RHÉAUNA: Isn't it the truth? We never know when God's going to come for us. He said it Himself, "I'll come like a thief."

ANGÉLINE: Don't talk like that, it scares me. I don't want to die that way. I want to die in my bed ... have time to make my confession ...

RHÉAUNA: Oh, God forbid that I should die before confessing! Angéline, promise me you'll call the priest the minute I'm feeling weak. Promise me that.

ANGÉLINE: You know I will. You've asked me a hundred times. Didn't I get him there for your last attack? You had Communion and everything.

RHÉAUNA: I'm so afraid to die without the last rites.

ANGÉLINE: But what do you have to confess, Rhéauna?

RHÉAUNA: Don't say that, Angéline. Don't ever say that! We're never too old to sin.

ANGÉLINE: If you ask me, Rhéauna, you'll go straight to heaven. You've got nothing to worry about. Hey! Did you notice Baril's daughter? The way she's changed! She looks like a corpse.

RHÉAUNA: Isn't it the truth. Poor Rolande. She's telling everyone that she killed her father. It's because of her that he got mad, you see, at supper ... Oh I feel so sorry for her ... And her mother. What a tragedy! Such a loss for everyone. They'll miss him so ...

ANGÉLINE: You're telling me ... The father. Mind you, it's not as bad as the mother, but still ...

RHÉAUNA: True. Losing the mother is worse. You can't replace a mother.

ANGÉLINE: Did you see how nice he looked? ... Like a young man. He was even smiling ... I could have sworn he was asleep. But I still think he's better off where he is ... You know what they say, it's the ones who stay behind who most deserve the pity. Him, he's fine now ... Ah, I still can't get over how good he looked. Almost like he was breathing.

RHÉAUNA: Yeah! But he wasn't.

ANGÉLINE: But I can't imagine why they put him in that suit ...

RHÉAUNA: What do you mean?

ANGÉLINE: Didn't you notice? He was wearing a blue suit. You don't do that when you're dead. A blue suit is much too light. Now, navy-blue would be okay, but powder blue ... Never! When you're dead, you wear a black suit.

RHÉAUNA: Maybe he didn't have one. They're not that well off, you know.

ANGÉLINE: Dear God, you can rent a black suit! And look at Mme Baril's sister! In green! At a funeral parlour! And did you notice how much she's aged? She looks years older than her sister …

RHÉAUNA: She is older.

ANGÉLINE: Don't be silly, Rhéauna, she's younger.

RHÉAUNA: No, she isn't.

ANGÉLINE: Why sure, Rhéauna, listen! Mme Baril is at least thirty-seven, but her sister …

RHÉAUNA: She's well over forty!

ANGÉLINE: Rhéauna, she isn't!

RHÉAUNA: She's at least forty-five …

ANGÉLINE: That's what I'm telling you. She's aged so much, she looks a lot older than she is … Listen, my sister-in-law, Rose-Aimée, is thirty-six and the two of them went to school together …

RHÉAUNA: Well, anyway, it doesn't surprise me she's aged so fast … What with the life she leads …

ANGÉLINE: I'm not sure they're true, all those stories.

RHÉAUNA: They must be! Mme Baril tries to hide it 'cause it's her sister … But the truth always comes out. It's like Mme Lauzon and her sister, Pierrette. Now, if there's one person I can't stand, it's Pierrette Guérin. A shameless hussy! Nothing but shame to her whole family. I tell you, Angéline, I wouldn't want to see her soul. It must be black as coal.

ANGÉLINE: You know, Rhéauna, deep down inside, Pierrette isn't all bad.

Spotlight on GERMAINE LAUZON.

GERMAINE: My sister, Pierrette, I've had nothing to do with her for a long time. Not after what she did. When she was young, she was so good, and so pretty. But now, she's nothing but a whore. My sisters and I were nuts about her. We spoiled her rotten. And look what it got us … I don't understand. I don't understand. Papa used to call her his pepper pot. He was so crazy about his little Pierrette. When he'd put her on his knee, you could tell he was happy. And the rest of us weren't even jealous …

ROSE: We'd say, "She's the youngest. It's always that way, it's the youngest who gets the attention." When she started school, we dressed her like a princess. I was already married, but I remember as if it were yesterday. Oh, she was so pretty! Like Shirley Temple! And so quick at school. A lot better than me, that's for sure. I was lousy at school … I was the class clown, that's all I was ever good for … But her, the little bugger, always coming home with prizes. First in French, first in Arithmetic, first in Religion … Yeah, Religion! She was pious as a nun, that kid. I tell you, the Sisters were nuts about her! But to see her today … I almost feel sorry for her. She must need help sometimes … She must get so lonely …

GABRIELLE: When she finished school, we asked her what she wanted to do. She wanted to be a teacher. She was all set to begin her training … And then she met her Johnny.

THE THREE SISTERS: Goddamn Johnny! He's a devil out of hell! It's all his fault she turned out the way she did. Goddamn Johnny! Goddamn Johnny!

RHÉAUNA: What do you mean, not all bad! You've got to be pretty low to do what she did. Do you know what Mme Longpré told me about her?

ANGÉLINE: No, what?

THÉRÈSE: Ow!!!

The lights come back up. THÉRÈSE DUBUC gives her mother-in-law a sock on the head.

GERMAINE: Beat her brains out if you have to, Thérèse, but do something!

THÉRÈSE: Sure, beat her brains out! Look, I'm doing all I can to keep her quiet. I'm not about to kill her just to make you happy.

ROSE: If it was up to me, I'd shove her off the balcony …

THÉRÈSE: What? Say that again, Rose. I didn't hear you!

ROSE: I was talking to myself.

THÉRÈSE: You're scared, eh?

ROSE: Me, scared?

THÉRÈSE: Yes, Rose. Scared!

MARIE-ANGE: Don't tell me there's gonna be another fight.

ANGÉLINE: Has there been a fight?

RHÉAUNA: Oh, who was fighting?

ANGÉLINE: We should have come sooner.

THÉRÈSE: I won't stand for that. She insulted my mother-in-law! My husband's mother!

LISETTE: There they go again!

ROSE: She's so old! She's useless!

GERMAINE: Rose!

GABRIELLE: Rose, that's cruel! Aren't you ashamed?

THÉRÈSE: Rose Ouimet, I'll never forgive you for those words! Never!

ROSE: Ah, piss off!

ANGÉLINE: Who had a fight?

ROSE: You want to know everything, eh, Mademoiselle Sauvé? You want all the gory details?

ANGÉLINE: Mme Ouimet!

ROSE: So you can blab it all over town, eh? Isn't that it?

RHÉAUNA: Rose Ouimet, I don't lose my temper often, but I will not allow you to insult my friend.

MARIE-ANGE: (to herself) I'll just grab a few more while no one's looking.

GABRIELLE: (who has seen her) What are you doing there, Mme Brouillette?

ROSE: Fine, I've said enough. I'll shut up.

MARIE-ANGE: Shhhh! Take these and keep quiet!

LINDA, GINETTE and LISE arrive with the chairs. There is a great hullabaloo. All the women change places, taking advantage of the occasion to steal more stamps.

MARIE-ANGE: Don't be afraid, take them!

DES-NEIGES: Aren't you overdoing it?

THÉRÈSE: Hide these in your pocket, Mme Dubuc ... No! Damn it! Hide them!

GERMAINE: You know that guy who runs the meat shop, what a thief!

The door opens suddenly and PIERRETTE GUÉRIN comes in.

PIERRETTE: Hi, everybody!

THE OTHERS: Pierrette!

LINDA: Great! It's Aunt Pierrette!

ANGÉLINE: Oh my God, Pierrette!

GERMAINE: What are you doing here? I told you I never wanted to see you again.

PIERRETTE: I heard that my big sister, Germaine, had won a million stamps, so I decided to come over and have a look. (She sees ANGÉLINE.) Well, I'll be goddamned! Angéline! What are you doing here?

Everyone looks at ANGÉLINE. Blackout.

ACT TWO

The second act begins with PIERRETTE's entrance. Hence the last six speeches of Act One are repeated now. The door opens suddenly and PIERRETTE GUÉRIN comes in.

PIERRETTE: Hi, everybody!

THE OTHERS: Pierrette!

LINDA: Great! It's Aunt Pierrette!

ANGÉLINE: Oh, my God, Pierrette!

GERMAINE: What are you doing here? I told you I never wanted to see you again.

PIERRETTE: I heard that my big sister, Germaine, had won a million stamps, so I decided to come over and have a look. (She sees ANGÉLINE.) Well, I'll be goddamned! Angéline! What are you doing here?

Everyone looks at ANGÉLINE.

ANGÉLINE: My God! I'm caught.

GERMAINE: What do you mean, Angéline?

GABRIELLE: How come you're talking to Mlle Sauvé?

ROSE: You oughta be ashamed!

PIERRETTE: Why? We're real good friends, eh, Géline?

ANGÉLINE: Oh! I think I'm going to faint! *(She pretends to faint.)*

RHÉAUNA: Good heavens, Angéline!

ROSE: She's dead!

RHÉAUNA: What?

GABRIELLE: Don't be ridiculous! Rose, you're getting carried away again.

PIERRETTE: She hasn't even fainted. She's only pretending. *(PIERRETTE approaches ANGÉLINE.)*

GERMAINE: Don't you touch her!

PIERRETTE: Mind your own business! She's my friend.

RHÉAUNA: What do you mean, your friend?

GERMAINE: Don't try to tell us Mlle Sauvé is a friend of yours!

PIERRETTE: Of course she is! She comes to see me at the club almost every Friday night.

ALL THE WOMEN: What!

RHÉAUNA: That's impossible.

PIERRETTE: Ask her! Hey, Géline, isn't it true what I'm saying? Come on, stop playing dead and answer me. Angéline, we all know you're faking! Tell them. Isn't it true you come to the club?

ANGÉLINE: *(after a silence)* Yes, it's true.

RHÉAUNA: Oh, Angéline! Angéline!

SOME OF THE WOMEN: Dear God, this is dreadful!

SOME OTHER WOMEN: Dear God, this is horrible!

LINDA, GINETTE and LISE: Holy shit, that's great!

The lights go out.

RHÉAUNA: Angéline! Angéline!

Spotlight on ANGÉLINE and RHÉAUNA.

ANGÉLINE: Rhéauna, you must understand …

RHÉAUNA: Don't you touch me! Get away!

THE WOMEN: Who would have thought … Such a horrible thing!

RHÉAUNA: I'd never have thought this of you. You, in a club. And every Friday night! It's not possible. It can't be true.

ANGÉLINE: I don't do anything wrong, Rhéauna. All I have is a Coke.

THE WOMEN: In a club! In a night club!

GERMAINE: God only knows what she does there.

ROSE: Maybe she tries to get picked up.

ANGÉLINE: But I tell you, I don't do anything wrong!

PIERRETTE: It's true. She doesn't do anything wrong.

ROSE, GERMAINE, and GABRIELLE: Shut up, you demon. Shut up!

RHÉAUNA: You're no longer my friend, Angéline. I don't know you.

ANGÉLINE: Listen to me, Rhéauna, you must listen! I'll explain everything and then you'll see!

ROSE, GERMAINE and GABRIELLE: A club! the fastest road to hell!

ALL THE WOMEN: *(except the girls)* The road to hell, the road to hell! If you go there, you'll lose your soul! Cursed drink, cursed dancing! That's the place where our men go wrong and spend their money on women of sin!

ROSE, GERMAINE and GABRIELLE: Women of sin like you, Pierrette!

ALL THE WOMEN: *(except the girls)* Shame on you, Angéline Sauvé, to spend your time in this sinful way!

RHÉAUNA: But Angéline, a club! It's worse than hell!

PIERRETTE: *(laughing heartily)* If hell's anything like the club I work in, I wouldn't mind eternity there!

ROSE, GERMAINE and GABRIELLE: Shut up, Pierrette. The devil has your tongue!

LINDA, GINETTE and LISE: The devil? Come on! Get with the times! The clubs are not the end of the world! They're no worse than any place else. They're fun! They're lots of fun. The clubs are lots of fun.

THE WOMEN: Ah! Youth is blind! Youth is blind! You're gonna lose yourselves and then you'll come crying to us. But it'll be too late! It'll be too late! Watch out! You be careful of these cursed places! We don't always know when we fall, but when we get back up, it's too late!

LISE: Too late! It's too late! Oh my God, it's too Late!

GERMAINE: I hope at least you'll go to confession, Angéline Sauvé!

ROSE: And to think that every Sunday I see you at Communion ... Communion with a sin like that on your conscience!

GABRIELLE: A mortal sin!

ROSE, GERMAINE and GABRIELLE: How many times have we been told ... It's a mortal sin to set foot in a club!

ANGÉLINE: That's enough. Shut up and listen to me!

THE WOMEN: Never! You've no excuse!

ANGÉLINE: Rhéauna, will you listen to me! We're old friends. We've been together for thirty-five years. You mean a lot to me, but there are times when I want to see other people. You know how I am. I like to have fun. I grew up in church basements and I want to see other things. Clubs aren't all bad, you know. I've been going for four years and I never did anything wrong. And the people who work there, they're no worse than us. I want to meet people, Rhéauna! Rhéauna, I've never laughed in my life!

RHÉAUNA: There are better places to laugh. Angéline, you're going to lose your soul. Tell me you won't go back.

ANGÉLINE: Listen, Rhéauna, I can't! I like to go there, don't you understand? I like it!

RHÉAUNA: You must promise or I'll never speak to you again. It's up to you. It's me or the club. If you only knew how much that hurts, my best friend sneaking off to a night club. How do you think that looks, Angéline? What will people say when they see you going there? Especially where Pierrette works. It's the lowest of them all! You must never go back, Angéline, you hear? If you do, it's finished between us. Finished! You ought to be ashamed!

ANGÉLINE: Rhéauna, you can't ask me not to go back ... Rhéauna, answer me!

RHÉAUNA: Until you promise, not another word!

The lights come up. ANGÉLINE sits in a comer. PIERRETTE joins her.

ANGÉLINE: Why did you have to come here tonight?

PIERRETTE: Let them talk. They love to get hysterical. They know damn well you don't do anything wrong at the club. In five minutes, they'll forget all about it.

ANGÉLINE: You think so, eh? Well, what about Rhéauna? You think she'll forgive me just like that? And Mme de Courval who's in charge of recreation for the parish, also President of the Altar Society at Our Lady of Perpetual Help! You think she'll continue speaking to me? And your sisters who can't stand you because you work in a club! I'm telling you it's hopeless! Hopeless!

GERMAINE: Pierrette!

PIERRETTE: Listen, Germaine, Angéline feels bad enough. So let's not fight, eh? I came here to see you and paste stamps and I want to stay. And I don't have the plague, okay? Just leave us alone. Don't worry. The two of us'll stay out of your way. After tonight, if you want, I'll never come back again. But I can't leave Angéline alone.

ANGÉLINE: You can leave if you want, Pierrette ...

PIERRETTE: No, I want to stay.

ANGÉLINE: Okay, then I'll go.

LISETTE: Why don't they both leave!

ANGÉLINE gets up.

ANGÉLINE: *(to RHÉAUNA)* Are you coming? *(RHÉAUNA doesn't answer.)* Okay. I'll leave the door unlocked ...

She goes towards the door. The lights go out. Spotlight on ANGÉLINE SAUVÉ.

It's easy to judge people. It's easy to judge them, but you have to look at both sides of the coin. The people I've met in that club are my best friends. No one has ever treated me so well ... Not even Rhéauna. I have fun with those people. I can laugh with them. I was brought up by nuns in the parish halls who did the best they could, poor souls, but knew nothing. I was fifty-five years old when I learned to laugh. And it was only by chance. Because Pierrette took me to her club one night. Oh, I didn't want to go. She had to drag me there. But, you know, the minute I got in the door, I knew what it was to go through life without having any fun. I suppose clubs aren't for everyone, but me, I like them. And of course, it's not true that I only have a Coke. Of course, I drink liquor! I don't have much, but still, it makes me happy. I don't do anyone any harm and I buy myself two hours of pleasure every week. But this was bound to happen someday. I knew I'd get caught sooner or later. I knew it. What am I going to do now? Dear God, what am I going to do? *(Pause.)* Damn it all! Everyone deserves to get some fun out of life! *(Pause.)* I always said that if I got caught I'd stop going ... But I don't know if I can ... And Rhéauna will never go along with that. *(Pause.)* Ah, well, I suppose Rhéauna is worth more than Pierrette. *(She gives a long sigh.)* I guess the party's over ...

She goes off. Spotlight on YVETTE LONGPRÉ.

YVETTE: Last week, my sister-in-law, Fleur-Ange, had a birthday. They had a real nice party for her. There was a whole gang of us there. First there was her and her family, eh? Oscar David, her husband, Fleur-Ange David, that's her, and their seven kids: Raymonde, Claude, Lisette, Fernand, Réal, Micheline and Yves. Her husband's parents, Aurèle David and his wife, Ozéa David, were there too. Next, there was my sister-in-law's mother, Blanche Tremblay. Her father wasn't there 'cause he's dead ... Then there were the other guests: Antonio Fournier, his wife Rita, Germaine Gervais, also Wilfred Gervais, Armand Campeau, Daniel Lemoyne and his wife, Rose-Aimée, Roger Joly, Hormidas Guay, Simmone Laflamme, Napoleon Gauvin, Anne-Marie Turgeon, Conrad Joanette, Léa Liasse, Jeanette Landreville, Nona Laplante, Robertine Portelance, Gilbert Morrissette, Lilianne Beaupré, Virginie Latour, Alexandre Thibodeau, Ovila Gariépy, Roméo Bacon and his wife Juliette, Mimi Bleau, Pit Cadieux, Ludger Champagne, Rosaire Rouleau, Roger Chabot, Antonio Simard, Alexandrine Smith, Philémon Langlois, Eliane Meunier, Marcel Morel, Grégoire Cinq-Mars, Théodore Fortier, Hermine Héroux and us, my husband, Euclide, and me. And I think that's just about everyone ...

The lights come back up.

GERMAINE: Okay, now let's get back to work, eh?

ROSE: On your toes, girls. Here we go!

DES-NEIGES: We're not doing badly, are we? Look at all I've pasted ...

MARIE-ANGE: What about all you've stolen ...

LISETTE: You want to hand me some more stamps, Mme Lauzon.

GERMAINE: Sure ... coming right up ... Here's a whole bunch.

RHÉAUNA: Angéline! Angéline! It can't be true!

LINDA: *(to PIERRETTE)* Hi, Aunt Pierrette.

PIERRETTE: Hi! How're you doing?

LINDA: Oh, not too hot. Ma and I are always fighting and I'm really getting sick of it. She's always bitching about nothing, you know? I'd sure like to get out of here.

GERMAINE: The retreats will be starting pretty soon, eh?

ROSE: Yeah! That's what they said last Sunday.

MARIE-ANGE: I hope we won't be getting the same priest as last year ...

GERMAINE: Me too! I didn't like him either. What a bore.

PIERRETTE: Well, what's stopping you? You could come and stay with me ...

LINDA: Are you kidding? They'd disown me on the spot!

LISETTE: No, we've got a new one coming this year.

DES-NEIGES: Oh yeah? Who's it gonna be?

LISETTE: A certain Abbé Rochon. They say he's excellent. I was talking to l'Abbé Gagné the other day and he tells me he's one of his best friends ...

ROSE: *(to GABRIELLE)* There she goes again with her l'Abbé Gagné. We'll be hearing about him all night! You'd think she was in love with him. L'Abbé Gagné this, l'Abbé Gagné that. Well, if you want my opinion, I don't like l'Abbé Gagné.

GABRIELLE: I agree. He's too modern for me. It's okay to take care of parish activities, but he shouldn't forget he's a priest! A man of God!

LISETTE: Oh, but the man is a saint … You should get to know him, Mme Dubuc. I'm sure you'd like him … When he speaks, you'd swear it was the Lord himself talking to us.

THÉRÈSE: Don't overdo it …

LISETTE: And the children! They adore him. Oh, that reminds me, the children in the parish are organizing a variety night for next month. I hope you can all make it because it should be very impressive. They've been practicing for ages …

DES-NEIGES: What's on the programme?

LISETTE: Well, it's going to be very good. There'll be all sorts of things. Mme Gladu's little boy is going to sing …

ROSE: Again! I'm getting sick of that kid. Besides, since he went on television, his mother's got her nose in the air. She thinks she's a real star!

LISETTE: But the child has a lovely voice.

ROSE: Oh yeah? Well, he looks like a girl with his mouth all puckered up like a turkey's ass.

GABRIELLE: Rose!

LISETTE: Diane Aubin will give a demonstration of aquatic swimming … We'll be holding the event next door to the city pool, it will be wonderful …

ROSE: Any door prizes?

LISETTE: Oh yes, lots. And the final event of the evening will be a giant bingo.

THE OTHER WOMEN: *(except the girls)* A bingo!

Blackout. When the lights come back up, the women are all at the edge of the stage.

LISETTE: Ode to Bingo!

While ROSE, GERMAINE, GABRIELLE, THÉRÈSE and MARIE-ANGE recite the Ode to Bingo, the four other women call out bingo numbers in counterpoint.

ROSE, GERMAINE, GABRIELLE, THÉRÈSE and MARIE-ANGE: Me, there's nothing in the world I like more than bingo. Almost every month we have one in the parish. I get ready two days ahead of time; I'm all wound up, I can't sit still, it's all I can think of. And when the big day arrives, I'm so excited, housework's out of the question. The minute supper's over, I get all dressed up, and a team of wild horses couldn't hold me back. I love playing bingo! I adore playing bingo! There's nothing in the world can beat bingo! When we arrive at the apartment where we're going to play we take off our coats and head straight for the tables. Sometimes it's the living room the lady's cleared, sometimes it's the kitchen. Sometimes it's even the bedroom. We sit at the tables, distribute the cards, set up the chips and the game begins!

The women who are calling the numbers continue alone for a moment.

I'm so excited, I go bananas. I get all mixed up, I sweat like a pig, screw up the numbers, put my chips in the wrong squares, make the caller repeat the numbers, I'm in an awful state! I love playing bingo! I adore playing bingo! There's nothing in the world can beat bingo! The game's almost over. I've got three more tries. Two down and one across. I'm missing the B14! I need the B14! I want the B14! I look at the others. Shit, they're as close as I am. What am I gonna do? I've gotta win! I've gotta win! I've gotta win!

LISETTE: B14!

THE OTHERS: Bingo! Bingo! I've won! I knew it! I knew I couldn't lose! I've won! Hey, what did I win?

LISETTE: Last month we had Chinese dog door stops. But this month, this month, we've got ashtray floor lamps!

THE OTHERS: I love playing bingo! I adore playing bingo! There's nothing in the world beats bingo! What a shame they don't have 'em more often. The more they have, the happier it makes me! Long live the Chinese dogs! Long live the ashtray floor lamps! Long live bingo!

Lights to normal.

ROSE: I'm getting thirsty.

GERMAINE: Oh, God, I forgot the drinks! Linda, get out the Cokes.

OLIVINE: Coke … Coke … Yeah … Yeah, Coke …

THÉRÈSE: Relax, Mme Dubuc. You'll get your Coke like everyone else. But drink it properly! No spilling it like last time.

ROSE: She's driving me up the wall with her mother-in-law …

GABRIELLE: Forget it, Rose. There's been enough fighting already.

GERMAINE: Yeah! Just keep quiet and paste. You're not doing a thing!

Spotlight on the refrigerator. The following scene takes place by the refrigerator door.

LISE: *(to LINDA)* I've got to talk to you, Linda …

LINDA: I know, you told me at the restaurant … But it's hardly a good time …

LISE: It won't take long and I've got to tell somebody, I can't hide it much longer. I'm too upset. And Linda, you're my best friend … Linda, I'm going to have a baby.

LINDA: What! But that's crazy! Are you sure?

LISE: Yes, I'm sure. The doctors told me.

LINDA: What are you gonna do?

LISE: I don't know. I'm so depressed! I haven't told my parents yet. My father'll kill me, I know he will. When the doctor told me, I felt like jumping off the balcony …

PIERRETTE: Listen, Lise …

LINDA: You heard?

PIERRETTE: Yeah! I know you're in a jam, kid, but … I might be able to help you …

LISE: Yeah? How?

PIERRETTE: Well, I know a doctor …

LINDA: Pierrette, she can't do that!

PIERRETTE: Come on, it's not dangerous … He does it twice a week, this guy.

LISE: I've thought about it already, Linda … But I didn't know anyone … And I'm scared to try it alone.

PIERRETTE: Don't ever do that! It's too dangerous! But with this doctor … I can arrange it, if you like. A week from now you'll be all fixed up.

LINDA: Lise, you can't do that!

LISE: What else can I do? It's the only way out. I don't want the thing to be born. Look what happened to Manon Belair. She was in the same boat and now her life's all screwed up because she's got that kid on her hands.

LINDA: What about the father? Can't he marry you?

LISE: Are you kidding! I don't even know where he is. He just took off somewhere. Sure, he promised me the moon. We were gonna be happy. He was raking it in, I thought everything was roses. One present after another. No end to it. It was great while it lasted … but Goddamn it, this had to happen. It just had to. Why is it always me who ends up in the shit? All I ever wanted was a proper life for myself. I'm sick of working at Kresges. I want to make something of myself, you know, I want to be somebody. I want a car, a decent place to live, nice clothes. My uniforms for the restaurant are all I own, for Chrissake. I never have any money, I always have to scrounge, but I want that to change. I don't want to be cheap anymore. I came into this world by the back door, but by Christ I'll go out by the front! Nothing's gonna stop me. Nothing. You watch, Linda, you'll see I was right. Give me two or three years and you'll see that Lise Paquette is a somebody. And money, she's gonna have it, okay?

LINDA: You're off to a bad start.

LISE: That's just it! I've made a mistake and I want to correct it. After this I'll start fresh. You understand, don't you, Pierrette?

PIERRETTE: Sure, I do. I know what it is to want to be rich. Look at me. When I was your age, I left home because I wanted to make some money. But I didn't start by working in a dime store. Oh, no! I went straight to the club. Because that's where the money was. And it won't be long now before I hit the jackpot. Johnny's promised me …

ROSE, GERMAINE and GABRIELLE: Goddamn Johnny! Goddamn Johnny!

GINETTE: What's going on over here?

LISE: Nothing, nothing. *(to PIERRETTE)* We'll talk about it later …

GINETTE: Talk about what?

LISE: Forget it. It's nothing!

GINETTE: Can't you tell me?

LISE: Look, will you leave me alone?

PIERRETTE: Come on, we can talk over here …

GERMAINE: What's happening to those Cokes?

LINDA: Coming, coming …

The lights come back up.

GABRIELLE: Hey, Rose, you know that blue suit of yours? How much did you pay for it?

ROSE: Which one?

GABRIELLE: You know, the one with the white lace around the collar?

ROSE: Oh, that one … I got it for $9.98.

GABRIELLE: That's what I thought. Imagine, today I saw the same one at Reitman's for $14.98.

ROSE: No kidding! I told you I got it cheap, eh?

GABRIELLE: I don't know how you do it. You always find the bargains.

LISETTE: My daughter Micheline just found a new job. She's started to work with those F.B.I. machines.

MARIE-ANGE: Oh yeah! I hear those things are tough on the nerves. The girls who work them have to change jobs every six months. My sister-in-law, Simonne's daughter, had a nervous breakdown over one. Simonne just called today to tell me about it.

ROSE: Oh my God, I forgot, Linda, you're wanted on the phone!

LINDA runs to the phone.

LINDA: Hello? Robert? How long have you been waiting?

GINETTE: Tell me.

LISE: No. Beat it, will you? I want to talk to Pierrette … Go on, get lost!

GINETTE: Okay, I get the message! You're happy to have me around when there's nobody else, eh? But when someone more interesting comes along …

LINDA: Listen, Robert, how many times do I have to tell you, it's not my fault! I just found out!

THÉRÈSE: Here, Mme Dubuc, hide these!

ROSE: How are things at your place, Ginette?

GINETTE: Oh, same as usual, they fight all day long … Nothing new. My mother still drinks … And my father gets mad … And they go on fighting …

ROSE: Poor kid … And your sister?

GINETTE: Suzanne? Oh, she's still the brainy one. She can't do anything wrong, you know? "Now there's a girl who uses her head. You should be more like her, Ginette. She's making something of her life" … Nobody else even counts, especially me. But they always did like her best. And, of course, now she's a teacher, you'd think she was a saint or something.

ROSE: Hey, come on, Ginette. Isn't that a bit much?

GINETTE: No, I'm serious … My mother's never cared about me. It's always, "Suzanne's the prettiest. Suzanne's the nicest" … Day in, day out till I'm sick of it! Even Lise doesn't like me anymore!

LINDA: *(on the phone)* Oh, go to hell! If you're not gonna listen, why should I talk? Call me back when you're in a better mood! *(She hangs up.)* For Chrissake, Aunt Rose, why didn't you tell me I was wanted on the phone? Now he's pissed off at me!

ROSE: Isn't she polite! You see how polite she is?

Spotlight on PIERRETTE GUÉRIN.

PIERRETTE: When I left home, I was head over heels in love, I couldn't even see straight. No one existed for me but Johnny. He made me waste ten years of my life, the bastard. I'm only thirty now and I feel like sixty. The things that guy got me to do! And me, the idiot, I listened to him. Did I ever. Ten years I worked his club for him. I was a looker, I brought in the customers, and that was fine as long as it lasted … But now … now I'm fucked. I feel like jumping off a bridge. All I got left is the bottle. And that's what I've been doing since Friday. Poor Lise, she thinks she's done for just 'cause she's pregnant. She's young, I'll give her my doctor's name … He'll fix her up. It'll be easy for her to start over. But not me. Not me. I'm too old. A girl who's been at it for ten years is washed up. Finished. And try telling that to my sisters. They'll never understand. I don't know what I'm gonna do now. I don't know.

LISE: I don't know what I'm gonna do now. I don't know. An abortion, that's serious. I've heard enough stories to know that. But I guess I'm better off going to see Pierrette's doctor than trying to do it myself. Ah, why do these things always happen to me? Pierrette, she's lucky. Working in the same club for ten years, making a bundle … And she's in love! I wouldn't mind being in her shoes. Even if her family can't stand her, at least she's happy on her own.

PIERRETTE: He dumped me, just like that! "It's finished," he said. "I don't need you anymore. You're too old and too ugly. So pack your bags and beat it." That son-of-a-bitch! He didn't leave me a nickel! Not a goddamn nickel! After all I did for him. Ten years! Ten years for nothing. That's enough to make anyone pack it in. What am I gonna do now, eh? What? Become a waitress at Kresge's like Lise? No thanks! Kresge's is fine for kids and old ladies, but not for me. I don't know what I'm gonna do. I just don't know. And here I've gotta pretend everything's great. But I can't tell Linda and Lise I'm washed up. (Silence.) Yeah … I guess there's nothing left but booze … Good thing I like that …

LISE: (interspersed throughout PIERRETTE's last speech) I'm scared, dear God, I'm scared! (She approaches PIERRETTE.) Are you sure this'll work, Pierrette? If you only knew how scared I am!

PIERRETTE: (laughing) 'Course it will. It'll be fine, kid. You'll see …

The lights come back up.

MARIE-ANGE: It's not even safe to go to the show anymore. I went to the Rex the other day to see Belmondo in something, I forget what. I went alone, 'cause my husband didn't wanna go. Well, all of a sudden, right in the middle of the show this smelly old bum sits down next to me and starts grabbing my knee. You can imagine how embarrassed I was but that didn't stop me. I stood up, took my purse and smashed him right in his ugly face.

DES-NEIGES: Good for you, Mme Brouillette! I always carry a hat pin when I go to the show. You never know what'll happen. And the first one who tries to get fresh with me … But I've never used it yet.

ROSE: Hey, Germaine, these Cokes are pretty warm.

GERMAINE: When are you gonna stop criticizing, eh? When?

LISE: Linda, you got a pencil and paper?

LINDA: I'm telling you, Lise, don't do it!

LISE: I know what I'm doing. I've made up my mind and nothing's gonna make me change it.

RHÉAUNA: (to THÉRÈSE) What are you doing there?

THÉRÈSE: Shh! Not so loud! You should take some, too. Two or three books, she'll never know.

RHÉAUNA: I'm not a thief!

THÉRÈSE: Come on, Mlle Bibeau, it's not a question of stealing. She got these stamps for nothing and there's a million of 'em. A million!

RHÉAUNA: Say what you will, she invited us here to paste her stamps and we've got no right to steal them!

GERMAINE: (to ROSE) What are those two talking about? I don't like all this whispering …

She goes over to RHÉAUNA and THÉRÈSE.

THÉRÈSE: (seeing her coming) Oh … Yeah … You add two cups of water and stir.

RHÉAUNA: What? (noticing GERMAINE) Oh! Yes! She was giving me a recipe.

GERMAINE: A recipe for what?

RHÉAUNA: Doughnuts!

THÉRÈSE: Chocolate pudding!

GERMAINE: Well, which is it? Doughnuts or chocolate pudding? (She comes back to ROSE.) Listen, Rose, there's something fishy going on around here.

ROSE: (who has just hidden a few books in her purse) Don't be silly … You're imagining things

GERMAINE: And I think Linda's spending too much time with Pierrette. Linda, get over here!

LINDA: In a minute, Ma …

GERMAINE: I said come here! That means now. Not tomorrow!

LINDA: Okay! Don't get in a flap ... So, what do you want?

GABRIELLE: Stay with us a bit ... You've been with your Aunt long enough.

LINDA: So what?

GERMAINE: What's going on between her and Lise there?

LINDA: Oh ... Nothing ...

GERMAINE: Answer when you're spoken to!

ROSE: Lise wrote something down a while ago.

LINDA: It was just an address ...

GERMAINE: Not Pierrette's, I hope! If I ever find out you've been to her place, you're gonna hear from me, got that?

LINDA: Will you lay off! I'm old enough to know what I'm doing! *(She goes back to PIERRETTE.)*

ROSE: Maybe it's none of my business, Germaine, but ...

GERMAINE: Why, what's the matter now?

ROSE: Your Linda's picking up some pretty bad habits ...

GERMAINE: You can say that again! But don't worry, Rose, I can handle her. She's gonna straighten out fast. And as for Pierrette, it's the last time she'll set foot in this house. I'll throw her down the goddamn stairs!

MARIE-ANGE: Have you noticed Mme Bergeron's daughter lately? Wouldn't you say she's been putting on weight?

LISETTE: Yes, I've noticed that ...

THÉRÈSE: *(insinuating)* Strange, isn't it? It's all in her middle.

ROSE: I guess the sap's running a bit early this year.

MARIE-ANGE: She tries to hide it, too. It's beginning to show, though.

THÉRÈSE: And how! I wonder who could have done it?

LISETTE: It's probably her step-father ...

GERMAINE: Wouldn't surprise me in the least. He's been after her ever since he married her mother.

THÉRÈSE: It must be awful in that house. I feel sorry for Monique. She's so young ...

ROSE: Maybe so, but you must admit, she's been looking for it, too. Look how she dresses. Last summer, I was embarrassed to look at her! And you know me, I'm no prude. Remember those red shorts she had on, those short shorts? Well, I said it then, and I'll say it again, "Monique Bergeron is gonna turn out bad." She's got the devil in her, that girl, a real demon. Besides, she's a redhead ... No, you can say what you like, those unwed mothers deserve what they get and I got no sympathy for 'em.

LISE starts to get up.

PIERRETTE: Take it easy, kid!

ROSE: It's true! It's their own damn fault! I'm not talking about the ones who get raped. That's different. But an ordinary girl who gets herself knocked up, uh! uh! ... She gets no sympathy from me. It's too goddamn bad! I tell you, if my Carmen ever came home like that, she'd go sailing right through the window! Not that I'm worried about her, mind you. She's not that kind of girl ... Nope, for me unwed mothers are all the same. A bunch of depraved sluts. You know what my husband calls 'em, eh? Cockteasers!

LISE: I'll kill her if she doesn't shut up!

GINETTE: Why? If you ask me, she's right.

LISE: You shut your trap and get out of here!

PIERRETTE: Isn't that a bit much, Rose?

ROSE: Listen, Pierrette, we know you're an expert on these matters. We know you can't be shocked. Maybe you think it's normal, but we don't. There's one way to prevent it ...

PIERRETTE: *(laughing)* There's lots of ways. Ever heard of the pill?

ROSE: It's no use talking to you! That's not what I meant! I'm against free love! I'm a Catholic! So leave us alone and stay where you belong, filthy whore!

LISETTE: I think perhaps you exaggerate, Mme Ouimet. There are occasions when girls can get themselves in trouble and it's not entirely their fault.

ROSE: You! You believe everything they tell you in those stupid French movies!

LISETTE: What have you got against French movies?

ROSE: Nothing. I like English ones better, that's all. French movies, they're too realistic, too far-fetched. You shouldn't believe what they say. They always make you feel sorry for the girl who gets pregnant. It's never anyone else's fault. Well, do you feel sorry for tramps like that? I don't! A movie's a movie and life's life!

LISE: I'll kill her, the bitch! Stupid fucking jerk! She goes around judging everyone—and she's got the brains of a ... And as for her Carmen. Well, I happen to know her Carmen and believe me, she does a lot more than tease! She oughta clean her own house before she shits on everyone else.

Spotlight on ROSE OUIMET.

ROSE: That's right. Life is life and no goddamn Frenchman ever made a movie about that! Sure, any old actress can make you feel sorry for her in a movie. Easy as pie! And when she's finished work, she can go home to her big fat mansion and climb into her big fat bed that's twice the size of my bedroom, for Chrissake! But the rest of us, when we get up in the morning ... When I wake up in the morning he's lying there staring at me ... Waiting. Every morning, I open my eyes and there he is, waiting! Every night, I get into bed and there he is, waiting! He's always there, always after me, always hanging over me like a vulture. Goddamn sex! It's never that way in the movies, is it? Oh no, in the movies it's always fun! Besides, who cares about a woman who's gotta spend her life with a pig just 'cause she said yes to him once? Well, I'm telling you, no fucking movie was ever this sad. Because movies don't last a lifetime! *(Silence.)* Why did I ever do it? Why? I should have said no. I should have yelled no at the top of my lungs and stayed an old maid. At least I'd have had some peace. I was so ignorant in those days. Christ, I didn't know what I was in for. All I could think of was "the Holy State of Matrimony!" You gotta be stupid to bring up your kids like that, knowing nothing. My Carmen won't get caught like that. Because I've been telling her for years what men are really worth. She won't be able to say I didn't warn her! *(on the verge of tears)* She won't end up like me, forty-four years old, with a two-year-old kid and another one on the way, with a stupid slob of a husband who can't understand a thing, who demands his "rights" at least twice a day, three hundred and sixty-five days a year. When you get to be forty and you realize you've got nothing behind you and nothing ahead of you, it makes you want to dump everything and start all over ... But women ... women can't do that ... They get grabbed by the throat, and they stay that way, right to the end!

The lights come back up.

GABRIELLE: Well, I like French movies. They sure know how to make 'em good and sad. They make me cry every time. And you must admit, Frenchmen are a lot better looking than Canadians. They're real men!

GERMAINE: Now wait just a minute! That's not true.

MARIE-ANGE: Come on! The little peckers don't even come up to my shoulder. And they act like girls! Of course, what do you expect? They're all queer!

GABRIELLE: I beg your pardon. Some of them are men! And I don't mean like our husbands.

MARIE-ANGE: After our husbands anything looks good.

LISETTE: You don't mix serviettes with paper napkins.

GERMAINE: Okay, so our husbands are rough, but our actors are just as good and just as good-looking as any one of those French fairies from France.

GABRIELLE: Well, I wouldn't say no to Jean Marais. Now there's a real man!

OLIVINE: Coke ... Coke ... More ... Coke ...

ROSE: Hey, can't you shut her up? It's impossible to work! Shove a Coke in her mouth, Germaine. That'll keep her quiet.

GERMAINE: I think I've run out.

ROSE: Jesus, you didn't buy much, did you? Talk about cheap!

RHÉAUNA: *(as she steals some stamps)* Oh, what the heck. Three more books and I can get my chrome dustpan.

ANGÉLINE comes in.

ANGÉLINE: Hello … *(to RHÉAUNA)* I've come back …

THE OTHERS: *(coldly)* Hello …

ANGÉLINE: I went to see Father Castelneau …

PIERRETTE: She didn't even look at me!

MARIE-ANGE: What does she want with Mlle Bibeau?

DES-NEIGES: I'm sure it's to ask forgiveness. After all, Mlle Sauvé is a good person and she knows what's right. It'll all work out for the best, you'll see.

GERMAINE: While we're waiting, I'm gonna see how many books we've filled.

The women sit up in their chairs. GABRIELLE hesitates, then speaks,

GABRIELLE: Oh, Germaine, I forgot to tell you. I found a corsetmaker. Her name's Angélina Giroux. Come over here, I'll tell you about her.

RHÉAUNA: I knew you'd come back to me, Angéline. I'm very happy. You'll see, we'll pray together and the Good Lord will forget all about it. God's not stupid, you know.

LISE: That's it, Pierrette, they've made up.

PIERRETTE: I'll be goddamned!

ANGÉLINE: I'll just say goodbye to Pierrette and explain …

RHÉAUNA: No, you'd best not say another word to her. Stay with me and leave her alone. That chapter's closed.

ANGÉLINE: Whatever you say.

PIERRETTE: Well, that's that. She's won. Makes me want to puke. Nothing left for me to do here. I'm getting out of here.

GERMAINE: Gaby, you're terrific. I'd almost given up hope. It's not everyone can make me a corset. I'll go see her next week. *(She goes over to the box that is supposed to hold the completed books. The women follow her with their eyes.)* My God, there isn't much here! Where are all the booklets? There's no more than a dozen in the box. Maybe they're … No, the table's empty! *(Silence. GERMAINE looks at all the women.)* What's going on here?

THE OTHERS: Well … Ah … I don't know … Really …

They pretend to search for the books. GERMAINE stations herself in front of the door.

GERMAINE: Where are my stamps?

ROSE: I don't know, Germaine. Let's look for them.

GERMAINE: They're not in the box and they're not on the table. I want to know what's happened to my stamps!

OLIVINE: *(pulling stamps out from under her clothes)* Stamps? Stamps … Stamps … *(She laughs.)*

THÉRÈSE: Mme Dubuc, hide that … Goddamn it, Mme Dubuc!

MARIE-ANGE: Holy Ste-Anne!

DES-NEIGES: Pray for us!

GERMAINE: But her clothes are full of them! What the … She's got them everywhere! Here … And here … . Thérèse … Don't tell me it's you.

THÉRÈSE: Heavens, no! I swear, I had no idea!

GERMAINE: Let me see your purse.

THÉRÈSE: Really, Germaine, if that's all the faith you have in me.

ROSE: Germaine, don't be ridiculous!

GERMAINE: You too, Rose. I want to see your purse. I want to see all your purses. Every one of them!

DES-NEIGES: I refuse! I've never been so insulted!

YVETTE: Me neither.

LISETTE: I'll never set foot in here again!

GERMAINE grabs THÉRÈSE's bag and opens it. She pulls out several books.

GERMAINE: Ahah! I knew it! I bet it's the same with all of you! You bastards! You won't get out of here alive! I'll knock you to kingdom come!

PIERRETTE: I'll help you, Germaine. Nothing but a pack of thieves! And they look down their noses at me!

GERMAINE: Show me your purses. *(She grabs ROSE's purse.)* Look at that … And that! *(She grabs another purse.)* More here. And look, still more! You too, Mlle Bibeau? There's only three, but even so!

ANGÉLINE: Oh, Rhéauna, you too!

GERMAINE: All of you, thieves! The whole bunch of you, you hear me? Thieves!

MARIE-ANGE: You don't deserve all those stamps.

DES-NEIGES: Why you more than anyone else?

ROSE: You've made us feel like shit with your million stamps!

GERMAINE: But those stamps are mine!

LISETTE: They ought to be for everyone!

THE OTHERS: Yeah, everyone!

GERMAINE: But they're mine! Give them back to me!

THE OTHERS: No way!

MARIE-ANGE: There's lots more in the boxes. Let's help ourselves.

DES-NEIGES: Good idea.

YVETTE: I'm filling my purse.

GERMAINE: Stop! Keep your hands off!

THÉRÈSE: Here, Mme Dubuc, take these! Here's some more.

MARIE-ANGE: Come on, Mlle Verrette. There's tons of them. Here. Give me a hand.

PIERRETTE: Let go of that!

GERMAINE: My stamps! My stamps!

ROSE: Help me, Gaby, I've got too many!

GERMAINE: My stamps! My stamps!

A huge battle ensues. The women steal all the stamps they can. PIERRETTE and GERMAINE try to stop them. LINDA and LISE stay seated in the corner and watch without moving. Screams are heard as some of the women begin fighting.

MARIE-ANGE: Give me those, they're mine!

ROSE: That's a lie, they're mine!

LISETTE: *(to GABRIELLE)* Will you let go of me! Let me go!

They start throwing stamps and books at one another. Everybody grabs all they can get their hands on, throwing stamps everywhere, out the door, even out the window. OLIVINE DUBUC starts cruising around in her wheelchair singing "O Canada." A few women go out with their loot of stamps. ROSE and GABRIELLE stay a bit longer than the others.

GERMAINE: My sisters! My own sisters!

GABRIELLE and ROSE go out. The only ones left in the kitchen are GERMAINE, LINDA and PIERRETTE. GERMAINE collapses into a chair.

GERMAINE: My stamps! My stamps!

PIERRETTE puts her arms around GERMAINE's shoulders.

PIERRETTE: Don't cry, Germaine.

GERMAINE: Don't talk to me. Get out! You're no better than the rest of them!

PIERRETTE: But …

GERMAINE: Get out! I never want to see you again!

PIERRETTE: But I tried to help you! I'm on your side, Germaine!

GERMAINE: Get out and leave me alone! Don't speak to me. I don't want to see anyone!

PIERRETTE goes out slowly. LINDA also heads towards the door.

LINDA: It'll be some job cleaning all that up!

GERMAINE: My God! My God! My stamps! There's nothing left! Nothing! Nothing! My beautiful new home! My lovely furniture! Gone! My stamps! My stamps!

She falls to her knees beside the chair, picking up the remaining stamps. She is crying very hard. We hear all the others outside singing "O Canada." As the song continues, GERMAINE regains her courage. She finishes "O Canada" with the others, standing at attention, with tears in her eyes. A rain of stamps falls slowly from the ceiling …

END

DAVID FRENCH

(b. 1939)

If a single playwright could be said to map the shape of Canadian drama in the 1970s and '80s, it would be David French. From his apprenticeship with the CBC and his early identification with alternate theatre in Toronto to the success of his plays as a mainstay of the regional theatres and a cultural export, his career coincided with the late twentieth century growth and maturation of Canadian theatrical art. French has written broadly popular, commercially appealing plays rooted in his own life and experience. His Mercer family saga and the backstage comedy *Jitters* are painful, funny, and affectionate examinations of conditions that are widely recognizable, yet at the same time distinctively local and emphatically Canadian.

French was born in Coley's Point, Newfoundland, but moved to Toronto with his parents and four brothers when he was six. After finishing high school in 1958 he studied acting for two years in Toronto and Pasadena, California, and from 1960–65 worked as an actor, mostly for CBC-TV. Meanwhile he was also writing. In 1962 CBC bought his first play, "Behold the Dark River," and over the next decade broadcast seven more of his half-hour television scripts. Through the late 1960s French supported his writing by working at a variety of jobs including a two-year stint in the Regina Post Office.

While summering on Prince Edward Island in 1971, he decided to try writing a stage play about his family's experience of adjusting to life outside Newfoundland in the late 1950s. By autumn he had a one-act called "Behold This House" which he offered to Bill Glassco after seeing Glassco's production of David Freeman's *Creeps* at the Tarragon. Retitled and expanded to full length, *Leaving Home* opened in May 1972 and immediately made French a star. The play has since enjoyed over a hundred productions. It also marked the start of a rich collaboration that has seen every one of French's plays premiere under Glassco's direction.

At the end of *Leaving Home*, young Ben Mercer sets out on his own after a terrible row with his father, Jacob, leaving the rift between them as unresolved as Jacob's own sense of manhood and feelings of cultural alienation. *Of the Fields, Lately* (1973) picks up two years later with Ben's temporary return to his parents' home in Toronto, ending with Jacob's death. The play is gentler and more elegiac, but also slighter than its predecessor. It won the Chalmers Award for 1973 and has been very successful in its own right with productions across Canada and the United States.

After a number of abortive attempts to write a third Mercer play, French altered his focus to the sleazy underworld of cheap hoods, hookers and con men, but *One Crack Out* (1975) was a disappointment. Glassco then suggested that he try translating Chekhov. French's version of *The Seagull* (1977) seemed to get him creatively on track again. (In 1992–93 it ran for two months on Broadway.) Now inspired to write a full-out comedy, he returned to a subject he knew well, this time the wonderful world of Canadian theatre itself. *Jitters* (1979), a self-referential backstage comedy set in a small, low-budget Toronto theatre, is both a conventional genre play—"an almost perfect comedy of its kind," the *New York Times* called it—and a hilarious rendering of Canadian cultural schizophrenia. To the standard insecurities and insanities common to show biz people everywhere are added those peculiar to a culture which continually looks across its border for approval and in which, at the same time, "success is like stepping out of line." *Jitters* was a smash hit in Toronto, then had productions in nearly every regional theatre across Canada and a successful run in New Haven prior to a planned Broadway opening in 1981. Ironically, like the play-within-the-play itself, *Jitters* never made it to that Promised Land. (*Of the Fields, Lately* did have a brief Broadway run in 1980.) Nevertheless, *Jitters* has been French's most popular play with well over a hundred productions.

The Riddle of the World (1981), a comedy of ideas about the sexual and spiritual lives of urban sophisticates, failed to catch fire with audiences or critics. But French found his way once again by returning to the Mercer family. *Salt-Water Moon* (1984), a "prequel" to his two earlier Mercer plays, chronicles the courtship of young Jacob and Mary in rural Newfoundland in 1926. A lyrical romantic comedy featuring only the two characters, it has proven as substantial a success as its predecessors. A Los Angeles production in 1985 earned it the Hollywood Drama-Logue Critics Award for best play, and the published text won the Canadian Authors Association Literary Award for drama the following year.

In 1989 the Mercer trilogy became a tetralogy with what French insists is the last play in the series, *1949*. For three days before Newfoundland officially joins Canada, Jacob and Mary host in their Toronto home a politically divided extended family of expatriate Newfoundlanders whose personal dramas unfold against the larger issue of cultural survival. By turns comedy and melodrama, *1949* brings onstage for the first time important out-characters from the earlier Mercer plays and provides rich subtext for the events, a decade later, of *Leaving Home*. In 1993 French shifted gears again with a mystery thriller, *The Silver Dagger*, produced in Toronto by Canadian Stage, the company that premiered *1949*. *That Summer*, a memory play about sisters in 1950s Ontario, opened at the Blyth Festival in 1999.

The Mercer plays are driven by archetypal energies: the difficult passage into manhood, the fierce protective love of one sister for another, the tangled dynamics of the family. What make the plays special are the cultural circumstances that shape those energies, especially the conflict between the characters who remain bound by the powerful pull of Newfoundland and those who make the perilous choice of "leaving home." Understood in the context of all four plays, that phrase resonates with emotional, psychological, political and cultural complexities in addition to its generational and geographical meanings. In *Leaving Home* Jacob asks Minnie about her boyfriend Harold: "What is he, Minnie? Newfie?" "No, boy—" she answers. "Canadian." After ten years of Confederation and even longer living in Toronto, Jacob and his expatriate contemporaries still think in terms of us and them.

Harold is a brilliant comic symbol of the "Canadian" Other as the Newfies see him: the gray, humourless undertaker who speaks not at all but carries a very big stick. Harold's comic potency serves as foil for Jacob's sense of impotence, of patriarchal failure. His own sons, after all, are colourless, fully assimilated Canadians for whom Newfoundland exists not even in memory but only in their father's embarrassing prejudices and oft-told tall tales. As Chris Johnson has argued, Jacob's cultural identity is closely tied to his patriarchal self-image. In order to sustain the legend on which his own sense of self is based ("I was out fishing on the Labrador when I was ten years old"), he must perpetuate it in his sons. So he tests Ben's manhood by demanding that Ben drink not Canadian whiskey but Newfie "screech." He tries desperately to keep Ben from going by showing him photos of the family back "home." Leaving home literally as they already have figuratively, the sons shatter Jacob's hope of sustaining and defending his cultural heritage within the garrison of the family.

Lacking the colourful language and theatrical vitality of Jacob, Mary and Minnie, the younger characters seem somewhat pale and conventional by comparison. French himself loses interest in the Bill-Kathy subplot, abruptly resolving it in a single stage direction. Ben's story is more compelling in its oedipal twists and turns and dramatic conclusion. In the context of the youth culture's ongoing generational battles and the nationalist impulse driving the new Canadian theatre in the early 1970s, Ben's thrust for independence made a powerful statement. But in the end the play's focus is fixed firmly on Jacob and on Mary, who gets the last word and makes the final adjustment to our emotional allegiance.

Leaving Home was first performed May 16, 1972 at the Tarragon Theatre, Toronto, with the following cast:

MARY MERCER	Maureen Fitzgerald
BEN MERCER	Frank Moore
BILLY MERCER	Mel Tuck
JACOB MERCER	Sean Sullivan
KATHY JACKSON	Lyn Griffin
MINNIE JACKSON	Liza Creighton
HAROLD	Les Carlson

Directed by Bill Glassco
Designed by Dan Yarhi and Stephen Katz
Costumes by Vicky Manthorpe

LEAVING HOME

CHARACTERS

MARY MERCER
JACOB MERCER
BEN MERCER
BILLY MERCER } *their sons*
KATHY JACKSON, *BILLY's fiancée*
MINNIE JACKSON, *her mother*
HAROLD, *MINNIE's boyfriend*

SCENE

The play is set in Toronto on an early November day in the late 1950s.

SET

The lights come up on a working-class house in Toronto. The stage is divided into three playing areas: kitchen, dining room and living room. In addition there is a hallway leading into the living room. Two bedroom doors lead off the hallway, as well as the front door which is offstage.

The kitchen contains a fridge, a stove, cupboards over the sink for everyday dishes, and a small drop-leaf table with two wooden chairs, one at either end. A plastic garbage receptacle stands beside the stove. A hockey calendar hangs on a wall, and a kitchen prayer.

The dining room is furnished simply with an oak table and chairs. There is an oak cabinet containing the good dishes and silverware. Perhaps a family portrait hangs on the wall—a photo taken when the sons were much younger.

The living room contains a chesterfield and an armchair, a TV, a record player and a fireplace. On the mantel rests a photo album and a silver-framed photo of the two sons—then small boys—astride a pinto pony. On one wall hangs a mirror. On another, a seascape. There is also a small table with a telephone on it.

ACT ONE

It is around five-thirty on a Friday afternoon, and MARY MERCER, aged fifty, stands before the mirror in the living room, admiring her brand new dress and fixed hair. As she preens, the front door opens and in walk her two sons, BEN, eighteen, and BILL, seventeen. Each carries a box from a formal rental shop and schoolbooks.

MARY: Did you bump into your father?

BEN: No, we just missed him, Mom. He's already picked up his tux. He's probably at the Oakwood. *(He opens the fridge and helps himself to a beer.)*

MARY: Get your big nose out of the fridge. And put down that beer. You'll spoil your appetite.

BEN: No, I won't. *(He searches for a bottle opener in a drawer.)*

MARY: And don't contradict me. What other bad habits you learned lately?

BEN: *(teasing)* Don't be such a grouch. You sound like Dad. *(He sits at the table and opens his beer.)*

MARY: Yes, well just because you're in university now, don't t'ink you can raid the fridge any time you likes.

BILL crosses the kitchen and throws his black binder and books in the garbage receptacle.

MARY: What's that for? *(BILL exits into his bedroom and she calls after him.)* It's not the end of the world, my son. *(pause)* Tell you the truth, Ben. We always figured you'd be the one to land in trouble, if anyone did. I don't mean that as an insult. You're more ... I don't know ... like your father.

BEN: I am?

Music from BILL's room.

MARY: *(calling, exasperated)* Billy, do you have to have that so loud? *(BILL turns down his record player. To BEN)* I'm glad your graduation went okay last night. How was Billy? Was he glad he went?

BEN: Well, he wasn't upset, if that's what you mean.

MARY: *(slight pause)* Ben, how come you not to ask your father?

BEN: What do you mean?

BILL: *(off)* Mom, will you pack my suitcase? I can't get everything in.

MARY: *(calling)* I can't now, Billy. Later.

BEN: I want to talk to you, Mom. It's important.

MARY: I want to talk to you, too.

BILL: *(comes out of the bedroom, crosses to kitchen)* Mom, here's the deposit on my locker. I cleaned it out and threw away all my old gym clothes. *(He helps himself to an apple from the fridge.)*

MARY: Didn't you just hear me tell your brother to stay out of there? I might as well talk to the sink. Well, you can t'row away your old school clothes—that's your affair—but take those books out of the garbage. Go on. You never knows. They might come in handy sometime.

BILL: How? *(He takes the books out, then sits at the table with BEN.)*

MARY: Well, you can always go to night school and get your senior matric, once the baby arrives and Kathy's back to work … Poor child. I talked to her on the phone this morning. She's still upset, and I don't blame her. I'd be hurt myself if my own mother was too drunk to show up to my shower.

BILL: *(a slight ray of hope)* Maybe she won't show up tonight.

MARY: *(glances anxiously at the kitchen clock and turns to check the fish and potatoes)* Look at the time. I just wish to goodness he had more t'ought, your father. The supper'll dry up if he don't hurry. He might pick up a phone and mention when he'll be home. Not a grain of t'ought in his head. And I wouldn't put it past him to forget his tux in the beer parlour. *(Finally she turns and looks at her two sons, disappointed.)* And look at the two of you. Too busy with your mouths to give your mother a second glance. I could stand here till my legs dropped off before either of you would notice my dress.

BEN: It's beautiful, Mom.

MARY: That the truth?

BILL: Would we lie to you, Mom?

MARY: Just so long as I don't look foolish next to Minnie. She can afford to dress up—Willard left her well off when he died.

BEN: Don't worry about the money. Dad won't mind.

MARY: Well, it's not every day your own son gets married, is it? *(to BILL as she puts on a large apron)* It's just that I don't want Minnie Jackson looking all decked out like the *Queen Mary* and me the tug that dragged her in. You understands, don't you, Ben?

BEN: Sure.

BILL: I understand too, Mom.

MARY: I know you do, Billy. I know you do. *(She opens a tin of peaches and fills five dessert dishes.)* Minnie used to go with your father. Did you know that, Billy? Years and years ago.

BILL: No kidding?

BEN: *(at the same time)* Really?

MARY: True as God is in Heaven. Minnie was awful sweet on Dad, too. She t'ought the world of him.

BILL: *(incredulously)* Dad?

MARY: Don't act so surprised. Your father was quite a one with the girls.

BEN: No kidding?

MARY: He could have had his pick of any number of girls. *(to BILL)* You ask Minnie sometime. Of course, in those days I was going with Jerome McKenzie, who later became a Queen's Counsel in St. John's. I must have mentioned him.

The boys exchange smiles.

BEN: I think you have, Mom.

BILL: A hundred times.

MARY: *(gently indignant—to BILL)* And that I haven't!

BILL: She has too. Hasn't she, Ben?

MARY: Never you mind, Ben. *(to BILL)* And instead of sitting around gabbing so much you'd better go change your clothes. Kathy'll soon be here. *(as BILL crosses to his bedroom)* Is the rehearsal still at eight?

BILL: We're supposed to meet Father Douglas at the church at five to. I just hope Dad's not too drunk. *(He exits.)*

MARY: *(studies BEN a moment)* Look at yourself. A cigarette in one hand, a bottle of beer in the other, at your age! You didn't learn any of your bad habits from me, I can tell you. *(pause)* Ben, don't be in such a hurry to grow up. *(She sits across from him.)* Whatever you do, don't be in such a hurry. Look at your poor young brother. His whole life ruined. Oh, I could weep a bellyful when I t'inks of it. Just seventeen, not old enough to sprout whiskers on his chin, and already the burdens of a man on his t'in little shoulders. Your poor father hasn't slept a full night since this happened. Did you know that? He had such high hopes for Billy. He wanted you both to go to college and not have to work as hard as he's had to all his life. And now look. You have more sense than that, Ben. Don't let life trap you.

BILL enters. He has changed his pants and is buttoning a clean white shirt. MARY goes into the dining room and begins to remove the tablecloth from the dining room table.

BILL: Mom, what about Dad? He won't start picking on the priest, will he? You know how he likes to argue.

MARY: He won't say a word, my son. You needn't worry. Worry more about Minnie showing up.

BILL: What if he's drunk?

MARY: He won't be. Your father knows better than to sound off in church. Oh, and another t'ing—he wants you to polish his shoes for tonight. They're in the bedroom. The polish is on your dresser. You needn't be too fussy.

BEN: I'll do his shoes, Mom. Billy's all dressed.

MARY: No, no, Ben, that's all right. He asked Billy to.

BILL: What did Ben do this time?

MARY: He didn't do anyt'ing.

BILL: He must have.

MARY: Is it too much trouble to polish your father's shoes, after all he does for you? If you won't do it, I'll do it myself.

BILL: *(indignantly)* How come when Dad's mad at Ben, I get all the dirty jobs? Jeez! Will I be glad to get out of here! *(Rolling up his shirt sleeves he exits into his bedroom.)*

MARY takes a clean white linen tablecloth from a drawer in the cabinet and covers the table. During the following scene she sets five places with her good glasses, silverware and plates.

BEN: *(slight pause)* Billy's right, isn't he? What'd I do, Mom?

MARY: Take it up with your father. I'm tired of being the middle man.

BEN: Is it because of last night? *(slight pause)* It is, isn't it?

MARY: He t'inks you didn't want him there, Ben. He t'inks you're ashamed of him.

BEN: He wouldn't have gone, Mom. That's the only reason I never invited him.

MARY: He would have went, last night.

BEN: *(angrily)* He's never even been to one lousy Parents' Night in thirteen years. Not one! And he calls *me* contrary!

MARY: You listen to me. Your father never got past Grade T'ree. He was yanked out of school and made to work. In those days, back home, he was lucky to get that much and don't kid yourself.

BEN: Yeah? So?

MARY: So? So he's afraid to. He's afraid of sticking out. Is that so hard to understand? Is it?

BEN: What're you getting angry about? All I said was—

MARY: You say he don't take an interest, but he was proud enough to show off your report cards all those years. I suppose with you that don't count for much.

BEN: All right. But he never goes anywhere without you, Mom, and last night you were here at the shower.

MARY: Last night was different, Ben, and you ought to know that. It was your high school graduation. He would have went with me or without me. If you'd only asked him. *(A truck horn blasts twice.)* There he is now in the driveway. Whatever happens, don't fall for his old tricks. He'll be looking for a fight, and doing his best to find any excuse. *(calling)* Billy, you hear that? Don't complain about the shoes, once your father comes!

BEN: *(urgently)* Mom, there's something I want to tell you before Dad comes in.

MARY: Sure, my son. Go ahead. I'm listening. What's on your mind?

BEN: Well …

MARY: *(smiling)* Come on. It can't be that bad.

BEN: *(slight pause)* I want to move out, Mom.

MARY: *(almost inaudibly)* … What?

BEN: I said I want to move out.

MARY: *(softly, as she sets the cutlery)* I heard you. *(pause)* What for?

BEN: I just think it's time. I'll be nineteen soon. *(pause)* I'm moving in with Billy and Kathy and I'll help pay the rent. *(pause)* I won't be far away. I'll see you on weekends. *(MARY nods.)* Mom?

MARY: *(absently)* What?

BEN: Will you tell Dad? *(slight pause)* Mom? Did you hear me?

MARY: I heard you. He'll be upset, I can tell you. By rights you ought to tell him yourself.

BEN: If I do, we'll just get into a big fight and you know it. He'll take it better, coming from you.

The front door opens and JACOB MERCER enters whistling "I's the B'y." He is fifty, though he looks older. He is dressed in a peaked cap, carpenter's overalls, thick-soled workboots and a lumberjack shirt over a T-shirt. Under one arm he carries his black lunchpail.

MARY: Your suit! I knowed it!

JACOB: Don't get in an uproar, now. I left it sitting on the front seat of the truck. *(He looks at BEN, then back to MARY.)* Is Billy home?

MARY: He's in the bedroom, polishing your shoes.

JACOB: *(crosses to the bedroom door)* Billy, my son, come out a moment. *(BILL enters, carrying a*

shoe brush.) Put down the brush and go out in my truck and bring back the tux on the seat.

BILL: What's wrong with Ben? He's not doing anything.

JACOB: Don't ask questions. That's a good boy. I'd ask your brother, but he always has a good excuse.

BEN: I'll go get it. *(He starts for the front door.)*

JACOB: *(calling after BEN)* Oh, it's too late to make up now. The damage is done.

MARY: Don't talk nonsense, Jacob.

JACOB: *(a last thrust)* And aside from that—I wouldn't want you dirtying your nice clean hands in your father's dirty old truck!

The front door closes on his last words. BILL returns to his room. JACOB sets his lunchpail and his cap on the dining room table.

JACOB: Did he get his diploma?

MARY: Yes. It's in the bedroom.

JACOB: *(breaks into a smile and lifts his cap)* And will you gaze on Mary over there. When I stepped in the door, I t'ought the Queen had dropped in for tea.

MARY: You didn't even notice.

JACOB: Come here, my dear, and give Jacob a kiss.

MARY: *(She darts behind the table, laughing.)* I'll give Jacob a swift boot in the rear end with my pointed toe. *(JACOB grabs her, rubs his rough cheek against hers.)* You'll take the skin off! Jake! You're far too rough! And watch my new dress! Don't rip it.

JACOB: *(releases her and breaks into a little jig as he sings)*
I's the b'y that builds the boat
And I's the b'y that sails her,
I's the b'y that catches the fish
And takes 'em home to Lizer.

Sods and rinds to cover your flake
Cake and tea for supper
Codfish in the spring of the year
Fried in maggoty butter.

I don't want your maggoty fish
Cake and tea for winter
I could buy as good as that
Down in Bona Vista.

I took Lizer to a dance
And faith but she could travel
And every step that she did take
Was up to her ass in gravel.

JACOB ends the song with a little step or flourish.

MARY: There's no mistakin' where you've been to, and it's not to church.

JACOB: All right, now, I had one little glass, and don't you start.

MARY: *(as she re-enters the kitchen)* How many?

JACOB: I can't lie, Mary. *(He puts his hand on his heart.)* As God is my witness—two. Two glasses to celebrate the wedding of my youngest son. *(He follows her into the kitchen.)*

MARY: Half a dozen's more like it, unless you expects God to perjure Himself for the likes of you. Well, no odds: you're just in time. Kathy'll soon be here, so get cleaned up.

JACOB: I washed up on the job.

MARY: Well, change your clothes. You're not sitting down with the likes of that on. *(She returns to the dining room with bread and butter for the dining room table.)*

JACOB: I suppose it's fish with Kathy coming and him now a bloody Mick. Next t'ing you knows he'll be expecting me to chant grace in Latin.

MARY: And I'll crown you if you opens your yap like that around Kathy. Don't you dare.

JACOB: *(following MARY, he sits at the dining room table)* 'Course we could have the priest drop by and bless the table himself. *(He makes the sign of the cross.)*

MARY: Jacob!

JACOB: Though I doubts he could get his Cadillac in the driveway.

MARY: *(back to kitchen)* If you comes out with the likes of that tonight, I'll never speak to you again. You hear?

JACOB: Ah, go on with you. What do you know? If you had nothing in your pockets but holes, a priest wouldn't give you t'read to sew it with.

BEN: *(enters with the box)* I put your toolbox down in the basement while I was at it, Dad. And rolled up the windows in your truck, in case it rains tonight.

JACOB: Did you, now? And I'm supposed to forget all about last night, is that it? Pretend it never occurred? Your brother's good enough for you but not your own father. *(as BEN crosses to kitchen)* Well, it would take more time than that to stitch up the hurt, I can assure you. And a long time before it heals. Don't be looking to your mother for support.

BEN: I wasn't. *(He sits at the kitchen table.)*

JACOB: Or for sympathy, either.

MARY: Jacob, it don't serve no purpose to look for a fight.

JACOB: *(to MARY)* You keep your two cents worth out of it. Nobody asked you. You got too much to say.

BILL: *(enters, carrying the shined shoes, which he gives to his father)* Hey, Dad, do me a favour? When Kathy gets here, no cracks about the Pope's nose and stuff like that. And just for once don't do that Squid-Jiggin' thing and take your teeth out. Okay? *(He sits at table across from his father and reads the evening paper.)*

JACOB: Well, listen to him, now. *(to MARY)* Who put him up to that? You? Imagine. Telling me what I can say and do in my own house.

MARY: *(returning to dining room)* Billy, my son, I got a feeling you just walked into it. *(She takes a polishing cloth from a cabinet and rubs her good silverware, including a large fish-knife.)*

JACOB: *(to BILL)* If you only knowed what my poor father went t'rough with the Catholics. Oh, if you only knowed, you wouldn't be doing this. My own son a turncoat. And back home, when we was growing up, you wouldn't dare go where the Catholics lived after dark. You'd be murdered, and many's the poor boy was. Knocked over the head and drownded, and all they done was let night catch them on a Catholic road. My father's brother was one. Poor Isaac. He was just fifteen, that summer. Tied with his arms behind him and tossed in the pond like a stone. My poor father never forgot that to his dying day. *(The family wait out the harangue.)* And here you is j'ining their ranks! T'ree weeks of instructions. By the jumping Jesus Christ you don't come from my side of the family. I'm glad my poor father never lived to see this day, I can tell you. The loyalest Orangeman that ever marched in a church parade, my father. He'd turn over in his grave if he saw a grandson of his kissing the Pope's ass. Promising to bring up your poor innocent babies Roman Catholics and them as ignorant of Rome as earthworms.

Oh, it's a good t'ing for you, my son, that he ain't around to see it, because sure as you'm there he'd march into that church tomorrow with his belt in his hand, and take that smirk off your face! Billy, my son, I never expected this of you, of all people. No, I didn't. Not you. If it was your brother, now, I could understand it. He'd do it just for spite ...

MARY: Hold your tongue, boy. Don't you ever run down? I just hope to goodness Ben don't call on you at the wedding to toast the bride and groom. We'll all be old before it's over. *(slight pause)* Did you try on your tux?

JACOB: No, boy, it was too crowded.

MARY: Then try it on. You're worse than the kids. *(She hands him the box.)* Go on.

JACOB: *(to BILL, referring to the shoes)* T'anks. *(He exits into his bedroom.)*

MARY: Ben, do your mother a favour? Fill up the glasses. I left the jug in the kitchen. *(She sits at the dining room table, checks and folds five linen napkins.)* Look at him, Ben. The little fart. My baby. *(to herself)* How quick it all goes ... I can still see us to this day ... the t'ree of us ... coming up from Newfoundland ... July of 1945 ... the war not yet over ... Father gone ahead to look for work on construction ... that old train packed with soldiers, and do you t'ink a single one would rise off his big fat backside to offer up his seat? Not on your life. There we was, huddled together out on the brakes, a couple, t'ree hours ... with the wind and the soot from the engine blowing back ... until a lady come out and saw us. "Well, the likes of this I've never seen," she says. "I've got four sons in the war, and if one of mine was in that carriage, I'd disown 'im!"

We've never had anyt'ing to be ashamed of, my sons. We've been poor ... but we've always stuck together. *(to BILL)* Is you frightened, my son?

BILL: No. Why should I be?

MARY: Don't be ashamed of it. Tomorrow you'll most likely wish you was back with your mother and father in your own soft bed.

BEN: He's scared shitless, Mom. *(to BILL)* Tell the truth.

MARY: Ben, is that nice talk?

BILL: *(to BEN)* I'll trade places.

MARY: Well, as long as you loves her, that's all that matters. Without that there's nothing, and with it what you don't have can wait. But a word of warning, Billy—don't come running to us with your squabbles, because we won't stick our noses into it. And before I forgets—you'd better not say a word to your father about moving out. I'll tell him myself after the wedding.

JACOB: *(off)* Mary!

MARY: *(calling)* What is it, boy?

JACOB: *(off)* Come here! I can't get this goddamn button fast!

MARY: *(shaking her head)* It's one of those mysteries how he made it t'rough life this far. If he didn't have me, he wouldn't know which leg of his pants was which. *(She exits.)*

BILL: *(slight pause)* You told her, huh? She doesn't seem to mind.

BEN: Keep your voice down. You want Dad to hear?

BILL: What did she say? Is she going to tell him?

BEN: Yeah, but do you think I ought to let her?

BILL: What do you mean?

BEN: Well, maybe I should tell him myself.

BILL: Are you crazy?

BEN: If I don't, you know what'll happen. Mom'll get all the shit.

BILL: *(pause)* Ben, you really want to do this? Are you sure?

BEN: Look—my books and tuition're paid for. All I got to worry about is the rent. I can handle that, waiting on tables. I'll make out. Listen, whose idea was it anyhow? Mine or yours? I wouldn't do it if I didn't want to.

BILL: Okay.

BEN: I need to, Billy. Christ, you know that. Either Dad goes, or I do.

BILL: I wish I felt that way. I don't want to move out. I don't want to get married. I don't know the first thing about girls. I mean, Kathy's the first girl I ever did it with. No kidding. The very first. We've only done it four or five times. The first time was in a cemetery, for Chrissake!

BEN: Well, at least you've been laid, Billy. I never.

BILL: Really? *(He laughs. Pause.)* I like Kathy. I like her a lot. But I don't know what else. What do you think Dad would do, if he was in my shoes? I think if Kathy was Mom he'd marry her, don't you?

MARY: *(enters)* Listen to me, you two. I don't want either one of you to say one word or snicker even when your father comes out. Is that understood?

BEN: What's wrong?

MARY: They gave him the wrong coat. I suppose he was in such a rush to get to the Oakwood he didn't bother trying it on.

JACOB enters singing, now dressed in the rental tux and polished shoes. The sleeves are miles too short for him, the back hiked up. He looks like a caricature of discomfort.

Here comes the bride,
All fat and wide,
See how she wobbles
From side to side.

The boys glance at one another and try to keep from breaking up.

JACOB: Well, boys, am I a fit match for your mother?

BEN: Dad, I wish I had a camera.

JACOB: Is you making fun?

MARY: No, he's not. The sleeves are a sight, but— *(giving BEN a censorious look)* —aside from that it's a perfect fit. Couldn't be better. Could it, Billy?

BILL: Made to measure, Dad.

JACOB: I t'ink I'll kick up my heels. I'm in the right mood. *(as he crosses to the record player)* What do you say, Mary? Feel up to it? *(He selects a record.)*

MARY: I'm willing, if you is, Jake.

JACOB: All right, boys, give us room. *(The record starts to play—a rousing tune with lots of fiddles.)* Your mother loves to twirl her skirt and show off her drawers! *(He seizes his wife and they whirl around the room, twirling and stomping with enjoyment and abandon.)*

BEN: Go, Mom! *(He whistles. BILL and BEN clap their hands to the music.)* Give her hell, Dad!

MARY: Not so fast, Jacob, you'll make me dizzy!

JACOB stops after a few turns. He is slightly dizzy. He sits.

JACOB: *(to BILL)* Dance with your mother. I galled my heel at work. *(BILL does.)* You ought to have seen your mother in her day, Ben. She'd turn the head of a statue. There wasn't a man from Bareneed to Bay Roberts didn't blink when she passed by.

MARY: Come on, Ben. Before it's over. *(She takes BEN, and they dance around the room.)*

JACOB: That's one t'ing about Ben, Mary. He won't ever leave you. The day he gets married himself he'll move in next door.

Finally MARY collapses laughing on the chesterfield. The music plays on.

JACOB: *(expansively)* I t'ink a drink's in order. What do you say, boys? To whet the appetite. *(He searches in the bottom of the cabinet. To MARY)* Where's all the whiskey to? You didn't t'row it out, did you?

MARY: You t'rowed it down your t'roat, that's where it was t'rowed.

JACOB: Well, boys, looks like there's no whiskey. *(He holds up a bottle.)* How does a little "screech" sound?

BEN: Not for me, Dad.

JACOB: Why not?

BEN: I just don't like it.

JACOB: *(sarcastically)* No, you wouldn't. I suppose it's too strong for you. Well, Billy'll have some, won't you, my son? *(He turns down the music.)*

BILL: *(surprised)* I will?

JACOB: Get two glasses out, then, and let's have a quick drink. *(BILL does and hands a glass to his father.)* Don't suppose you'd have a little drop, Mary, my love? *(He winks at BILL.)*

MARY: Go on with you. You ought to have better sense, teaching the boys all your bad habits. And after you promised your poor mother on her death-bed you'd warn them off alcohol …

JACOB: Don't talk foolishness. A drop of this won't harm a soul. Might even do some good, all you know.

MARY: Yes, some good it's done you.

JACOB: At least I'd take a drink with my own father, if he was alive. I'd do that much, my lady.

MARY: *(quickly)* Pay no attention, Ben. *(to JACOB)* And listen, I don't want you getting tight and making a disgrace of yourself at the rehearsal tonight. You hear?

JACOB: Oh, I'll be just as sober as the priest, rest assured of that. And you just study his fingers, if they'm not as brown as a new potato from nicotine. I dare say if he didn't swallow Sen-Sen, you'd know where all that communion wine goes to. *(to BILL)* How many drunks you suppose is wearing Roman collars? More than the Pope would dare admit. And all those t'ousands of babies they keep digging up in the basements of convents. It's shocking.

BEN: That's a lot of bull, Dad.

JACOB: It is, is it? Who told you that? is that more of the stuff you learns at university? Your trouble is you've been brainwashed.

BEN: You just want to believe all that.

MARY: And you'd better not come out with that tonight, if you knows what's good for you.

JACOB: *(to BILL)* Mind—I'm giving you fair warning. I won't sprinkle my face with holy water or make the sign of the cross. And nothing in this world or the next can persuade me.

BILL: You don't have to, Dad. Relax.

JACOB: Just so you knows.

BEN: All you got to do, Dad, is sit there in the front row and look sweet.

JACOB: All right, there's no need to get saucy. I wasn't talking to you! *(He pours a little "screech" in the two glasses. To BILL)* Here's to you, boy. You got the makings of a man. That's more than I can say for your older brother. *(JACOB downs his drink. BILL glances helplessly at BEN. He doesn't drink.)* Go on. *(BILL hesitates, then downs it, grimacing and coughing.)* You see that, Mary? *(his anger rising)* It's your fault the one's the way he is. It's high time, my lady, you let go and weaned him away from the tit!

MARY: *(angrily)* You shut your mouth. There's no call for that kind of talk!

JACOB: He needs more in his veins than mother's milk, goddamn it!

BEN: *(shouting at JACOB)* What're you screaming at her for? She didn't do anything?

JACOB: *(a semblance of sudden calm)* Well, listen to him, now. Look at the murder in his face. One harsh word to his mother and up comes his fists. I'll bet you wouldn't be so quick to defend your father.

MARY: Be still, Jacob. You don't know what you're saying.

JACOB: He t'inks he's too good to drink with me!

BEN: All right, I will, if it's that important. Only let's not fight.

MARY: He's just taunting you into it, Ben. Don't let him.

JACOB: *(sarcastically)* No, my son, your mother's right. I wouldn't wish for your downfall on my account. To hear her tell it I'm the devil tempting Saul on the road to Damascus.

MARY: Well, the devil better learn his scripture, if he wants to quote it. The devil tempted our Lord in the wilderness, and Saul had a revelation on the road to Damascus.

JACOB: A revelation! *(He turns off the record.)* I'll give you a revelation! I'm just a piece of shit around here! Who is it wears himself out year after year to give him a roof over his head and food in his mouth? Who buys his clothes and keeps him in university?

MARY: He buys his own clothes, and he's got a scholarship.

JACOB: *(furious)* Oh, butt out! You'd stick up for him if it meant your life, and never once put in a good word for me.

MARY: I'm only giving credit where's credit due.

JACOB: Liar.

MARY: Ah, go on. You're a fine one to talk. You'd call the ace of spades white and not bat an eye.

JACOB: *(enraged)* It never fails. I can't get my own son to do the simplest goddamn t'ing without a row. No matter what.

BEN: It's never simple, Dad. You never let it be simple or I might. It's always a test.

JACOB: Test!

MARY: Ben, don't get drawn into it.

JACOB: *(to BEN)* The sooner you learns to get along with others, the sooner you'll grow up. Test!

BEN: Do you ever hear yourself? "Ben, get up that ladder. You want people to think you're a sissy?" "Have a drink, Ben. It'll make a man out of you!"

JACOB: I said no such t'ing, now. Liar.

BEN: It's what you meant. "Cut your hair, Ben. You look like a girl." The same shit over and over, and it never stops!

JACOB: Now it all comes out. You listening to this, Mary?

BEN: No, you listen, Dad. You don't really expect me to climb that ladder or take that drink. You want me to refuse, don't you?

JACOB: Well, listen to him. The faster you gets out into the real world the better for you. *(He turns away.)*

BEN: Dad, you don't want me to be a man, you just want to impress me with how much less of a man I am than you. *(He snatches the bottle from his father and takes a swig.)* All right. Look. *(He rips open his shirt.)* I still haven't got hair on my chest, and I'm still not a threat to you.

JACOB: No, and you'm not likely ever to be, either, until you grows up and gets out from under your mother's skirts.

BEN: No, Dad—until I get out from under yours.

The doorbell rings.

MARY: That's Kathy. All right, that's more than enough for one night. Let's have no more bickering. Jake, get dressed. And not another word out of anyone. The poor girl will t'ink she's fallen in with a pack of wild savages.

JACOB: *(getting in the last word)* And there's no bloody mistakin' who the wild savage is. *(With that he exits into his bedroom.)*

MARY: Billy, answer the door. *(to BEN)* And you—change your shirt. You look a fright.

BEN exits. BILL opens the front door, and KATHY enters. She is sixteen, very pretty, but at the moment her face is pale and emotionless.

KATHY: Hello, Mrs. Mercer.

MARY: You're just in time, Kathy. *(MARY gives her a kiss.)* Take her coat, Billy. I'll be right out, dear. *(She exits.)*

KATHY: Where is everyone?

BILL: *(taking her coat)* Getting dressed. *(As he tries to kiss her, she pulls away her cheek.)* What's wrong? *(He hangs up her coat.)*

KATHY: Nothing. I don't feel well.

BILL: Why not? Did you drink too much at the party?

KATHY: What party?

BILL: Didn't the girls at work throw a party for you this afternoon?

KATHY: I didn't go to the office this afternoon.

BILL: You didn't go? What do you mean?

KATHY: Just what I said.

BILL: What did you say?

KATHY: Will you get off my back!

BILL: What did I say? *(slight pause)* Are you mad at me?

KATHY: *(looks at him)* Billy, do you love me? Do you? I need to know.

BILL: What's happened, Kathy?

KATHY: I'm asking you a simple question.

BILL: And I want to know what's happened.

KATHY: If I hadn't been pregnant, you'd never have wanted to get married, would you?

BILL: So?

KATHY: I hate you.

BILL: For Chrissake, Kathy, what's happened?

KATHY: *(sits on the chesterfield)* I lost the baby ...

BILL: What?

KATHY: Isn't that good news?

BILL: What the hell happened?

KATHY: I started bleeding in the ladies' room this morning.

BILL: Bleeding? What do you mean?

KATHY: Haemorrhaging. I screamed, and one of the girls rushed me to the hospital. I think the people at work thought I'd done something to myself.

BILL: Had you?

KATHY: Of course not. You know I wouldn't.

BILL: What did the doctor say?

KATHY: I had a miscarriage. *(She looks up at him.)* You're not even sorry, are you?

BILL: I am, really. What else did the doctor say?

KATHY: I lost a lot of blood. I'm supposed to eat lots of liver and milk, to build it up. You should have seen me, Billy. I was white and shaky. I'm a little better now. I've been sleeping all afternoon.

BILL: *(slight pause)* What was it?

KATHY: What was what?

BILL: The baby.

KATHY: Do you really want to know?

BILL doesn't answer.

BILL: What'll we do?

KATHY: Tell our folks, I guess. My mother doesn't know yet. She's been at the track all day with her boyfriend. *(slight pause)* I haven't told anyone else, Billy. Just you.

Enter JACOB and MARY. He is dressed in a pair of slacks and a white shirt. He carries a necktie in his hand. MARY wears a blouse and skirt.

JACOB: Billy, my son, tie me a Windsor knot. That's a good boy. *(He hands BILL the necktie and BILL proceeds to make the knot. Shyly, to KATHY)* Hello, my dear. *(KATHY nods.)* Lovely old day.

MARY: Come on. We may as well sit right down before it colds off. I'll serve up the fish and potatoes. *(She transfers the fish and potatoes into serving dishes.)*

JACOB: *(calling)* Ben! *(to KATHY, referring to the tie)* I'm all t'umbs or I'd do it myself.

BEN: *(enters, his shirt changed)* Hi, Kathy.

KATHY: Hi, Ben. Congratulations.

BEN: For what?

KATHY: Didn't you graduate last night?

BEN: Oh. Yeah.

JACOB: I suppose if Ben ever becomes Prime Minister, I'll be the last to know unless I reads it in the newspapers.

MARY: Kathy, you sit right down there, dear. Billy, you sit next to her. And Ben's right here. *(BILL hands his father the tie. Jacob slips it on as he approaches the table.)* Father, why don't you say grace?

JACOB: Maybe Kathy would like to.

KATHY: We never say grace at our house.

JACOB: Is that a fact? Imagine.

BILL: *(jumping in)* "Bless this food that now we take, and feed our souls for Jesus' sake. Amen."

ALL: Amen. *(They dig in.)*

JACOB: Have an eye to the bones, Kathy. *(slight pause)* You was born in Toronto, wasn't you? Someday you'll have to take a trip home, you and Billy, and see how they dries the cod on the beaches. He don't remember any more than you. He was just little when he come up here.

MARY: That was a long time ago, Kathy. 1945.

KATHY: *(slight pause)* Have you been home since, Mr. Mercer?

JACOB: No, my dear, and I don't know if I wants to. A different generation growing up now. *(glancing at BEN)* A different brand of Newfie altogether. And once the oldtimers die off, that'll be the end of it. Newfoundland'll never be the same after that, I can tell you. *(slight pause)* Do you know what flakes is?

KATHY: No.

JACOB: Well, they'm spread over the shore— these wooden stages they dries the codfish on. Sometimes—and this is no word of a lie, is it, Mary?—the fishflies'll buzz around that codfish as t'ick as the hairs on your arm. *(slight pause)* T'icker. T'ick as tarpaper.

MARY: Jacob, we're eating. *(to KATHY)* He's just like his poor mother, Jacob is. She'd start on about the tapeworm as you was lifting the pork to your mouth. *(to JACOB)* Let the poor girl eat in peace, Father. *(to KATHY)* You've hardly touched your food, dear. Has he spoiled your appetite? It wouldn't be the first time.

KATHY: I'm just not too hungry, Mrs. Mercer.

MARY: I understands. Big day tomorrow. I was the same way, my wedding day. It's a wonder I didn't faint.

JACOB: *(slight pause—to KATHY)* You notice Ben don't look my way? He's sore. *(KATHY glances at BEN, who goes on eating, oblivious.)* Oh, he knows how to dish it out with the best, but he can't take it. You can joke with Billy, he likes a bit of fun, but with the other one you don't dare open your mouth.

BEN: Will you shut up, Dad?

JACOB: *(to KATHY)* I'll bet you didn't get sore with your poor father and talk back all the time when he was alive, did you, my dear? No, that's what you didn't. You had more respect. And I bet now you don't regret it.

MARY: Don't ask the child to choose sides, Jacob. You've got no right to do that. Anyhow, Kathy's got more sense than to get mixed up in it. Don't you, Kathy?

JACOB: The Bible says to honour thy father and thy mother …

MARY: *(exasperated)* Oh, hold your tongue, for goodness sake. Don't your jaw ever get tired?

JACOB: *(to KATHY)* Well, you can see for yourself what happens, my dear. Anyone in this room is free to say what they likes about the old man, but just let him criticize back and you'd

t'ink a fox had burst into the chicken coop, the way Mother Mercer here gathers her first-born under her wing. *(slight pause—to KATHY, but meant for his wife)* I suppose by now you've heard your mother and me once went together? I suppose Minnie's mentioned it often enough? Fine figure of a woman, Minnie. Still looks as good as ever.

BILL: I hear you used to be a real woman's man, Dad.

JACOB: Who told you that?

BILL: Mom.

MARY: *(quickly)* Liar. I told you no such t'ing.

BILL: You did so. Didn't she, Ben?

BEN smiles at his mother.

JACOB: Well, contrary to what your mother tells, that particular year I had only one sweetheart, and that was Minnie Jackson. Wasn't it, Mary?

MARY: *(nodding)* She was still a Fraser then. That was the same year I was going with Jerome McKenzie. Wasn't it, Jacob?

JACOB: Oh, don't forget the most important part, Mary, the Q.C., the Queen's Counsel. Jerome McKenzie, Q.C. *(to KATHY)* Jerome's a well-known barrister in St. John's, and Mrs. Mercer's all the time t'rowing him up in my face. Ain't you Mary? Never lets me forget it, will you? *(to KATHY)* You see, my dear, she might have married Jerome McKenzie, Q.C., and never had a single worry in the world, if it wasn't for me. Ain't that so, Mary?

MARY: If you insists, Jacob.

BILL and KATHY stare silently at their plates, embarrassed. BEN looks from his father to his mother and then to BILL.

BEN: Did you get the boutonnieres and the cuff links for the ushers?

MARY: It's all taken care of, my son. *(pause)* What kind of flowers did your mother order, Kathy?

KATHY: Red roses.

MARY: How nice.

KATHY: I like yellow roses better, but— *(She stops abruptly.)*

BILL: But what?

KATHY: Nothing.

MARY: Yellow roses mean tears, my son.

KATHY: Did you carry roses, Mrs. Mercer?

MARY: I did. Red butterfly roses. And I wore a gown of white satin, with a lace veil. I even had a crown of orange blossoms.

KATHY: I'll bet you were beautiful.

JACOB: My dear, she lit up that little Anglican church like the Second Coming. I suppose I told you all about the wedding ring?

MARY: No, you didn't, and she don't want to hear tell of it, and neither do the rest of us. Don't listen to his big fibs, Kathy.

JACOB: I still remembers that day. I had on my gaberdine suit, with a white carnation in the lapel. In those days Mary t'ought I was handsome.

MARY: Get to the point, Father.

JACOB: We was that poor I couldn't afford a ring, so when the Reverend Mr. Price got t'rough with the dearly beloveds and asked for the ring, I reached into my pocket and give him all I had— an old bent nail.

MARY: Last time it was cigar band.

JACOB: (still to KATHY) And if you was to ask me today, twenty years later, if it's been worth it—my dear, my answer would still be the same, for all her many faults—that old rusty nail has brung me more joy and happiness than you can ever imagine. And I wouldn't trade the old woman here, nor a blessed hair of her head, not for all the gold bullion in the Vatican.

BILL: Dad.

JACOB: And my name's not Jerome McKenzie, Q.C., either. And the likes of Ben here may t'ink me just an old fool, not worth a second t'ought— (BEN shoves back his plate, holding back his temper.) —and run me down to my face the first chance he gets—

BEN: Ah, shut up.

JACOB: —and treat me with no more respect and consideration than you would your own worst enemy!—

BEN: Will you grow up! (He knocks over his chair and exits into his bedroom.)

JACOB: (shouting after him) —but I've always done what I seen fit, and no man can do more! (The door slams—slight pause.) I won't say another word.

MARY: You've said enough, brother. (slight pause) What Kathy must t'ink of us! (slight pause) And then you wonders why he's the way he is, when you sits there brazen-faced and makes him feel like two cents in front of company. You haven't a grain of sense, you haven't!

JACOB: Did I say a word of a lie? Did I?

MARY: No, you always speaks the gospel truth, you do.

JACOB: I never could say two words in a row to that one, without he takes offence. Not two bloody words! (MARY collects the supper plates. BILL and KATHY remain seated.) Look. He didn't finish half his plate. (calling) Come out and eat the rest of your supper, Ben. There's no food wasted in this house. (slight pause) Take it to him, Mary.

MARY: (picking up BEN's chair) You—you're the cause of it. You're enough to spoil anyone's appetite.

JACOB: Ah, for Christ's sake, he's too damn soft, and you don't help any. I was out fishing on the Labrador when I was ten years old, six months of the year for ten dollars, and out of that ten dollars had to come my rubber boots. (to KATHY) Ten years old, and I had to stand up and take it like a man. (to MARY) That's a lot tougher than a few harsh words from his father!

MARY: (as she serves the dessert) And you'll make him hard, is that it, Jacob? Hard and tough like yourself? Blame him for all you've suffered. Make him pay for all you never had.

JACOB: Oh, shut up, Mary, you don't understand these matters. He won't have you or me to fall back on once he gets out into the world. He'll need to be strong or— (He winks at BILL.) —he'll end up like your cousin Israel.

MARY: And don't tell that story, Jacob. You're at the table.

JACOB: (to KATHY) Israel Parsons was Mrs. Mercer's first cousin.

MARY: Might as well talk to a log.

JACOB: He was a law student at the time, and he worked summers at the pulp and paper mill at Corner Brook, cleaning the machines. Well, one noon hour he crawled inside a machine to clean the big sharp blades, and someone flicked on the switch. Poor young Israel was ground up into pulp. They didn't find a trace of him, did they Mary? Not even a hair. Mary's poor mother always joked that he was the only one of her relatives ever to make the headlines—if you knows what I mean.

MARY: She knows. And just what has Israel Parsons got to do with Ben, pray tell?

JACOB: Because that's what the world will do to Ben, Mary, if he's not strong. Chew him up alive and swallow him down without a trace. Mark my words. *(He lifts the bowl to his mouth and drinks the peach juice.)*

The front door bursts open.

MINNIE: *(off)* Anybody home?

JACOB: Minnie! *(He glances at MARY, then rises.)*

MINNIE enters. She is in her late forties, boisterous and voluptuous, a little flashily dressed.

MINNIE: Is you still eating?

JACOB: No, come in, come in.

MINNIE: If you is—guess what?—I brung along me new boyfriend to spoil your appetites ... Where's he to? Can't keep track of the bugger! *(She returns to the hallway, and shouts offstage.)* For Christ's sake, you dirty t'ing, you! You might have waited till you got inside!

KATHY: *(to BILL)* What's she doing here?

MINNIE: *(off)* Come on. There's no need to be shy.

HAROLD enters with MINNIE. He is conservatively dressed but sports a white carnation.

MINNIE: *(to HAROLD)* That's Jacob and Mary. This here's Harold. *(They shake hands.)*

JACOB: Here give me your coats. *(He takes the coats.)*

MINNIE: T'anks, boy. *(to KATHY)* Hello, sister! Still mad at me? *(KATHY doesn't answer. To MARY.)* Harold works in a funeral parlour. He's an embalmer. Imagine. We met when poor Willard died. He worked on his corpse.

MARY: *(incredulously)* You made that up, Minnie. Confess.

MINNIE: As God is my witness, maid!

JACOB: Just as long as you'm not drumming up business, Harold.

HAROLD doesn't crack a smile.

MINNIE: He ain't got an ounce of humour in his body, Harold. *(looking at JACOB)* But he's got two or t'ree pounds of what counts. Don't you, Lazarus?

KATHY: *(sharply)* Mother!

MINNIE: "Mother" yourself. *(sitting on arm of chesterfield next to HAROLD)* I calls him Lazarus because he comes to life at night. And what a resurrection. Ah, I'm so wicked, Mary. To tell you the truth, I haven't been exactly mourning since Willard died, as sister over there can testify. And I'll tell you why. I took a good solid look at Willard—God rest his soul!—stretched out in his casket the t'ree days of his wake, all powdered and rouged and made up like a total stranger, and I says to myself, Minnie, live it up, maid. This is all there is, this life. You're dead a good long time. *(to JACOB)* And I for one wouldn't bet a t'in dime on the hereafter, and God knows I've t'rowed hundreds of dollars away on long shots in my day.

JACOB: Now, Minnie, enough of the religion. Would you both care for a whiskey? *(MARY reacts.)*

MINNIE: *(meaning HAROLD)* Look at his ears pick up. Sure, Jake. That's one of the reasons we come early. *(JACOB crosses to the cabinet during MINNIE's speech and brings out a bottle of whiskey. He pours three drinks.)* And Mary, I got to apologize for last night. I suppose I'll never live it down. I don't know what happened, maid. I laid down with a drink in me hand after supper and the next t'ing I know it's this morning and I'm in the doghouse.

MARY: That's okay, Minnie. *(She sits.)*

JACOB: Billy, my son, bring me the ginger ale. That's a good boy. *(During the dialogue BILL fetches the ginger ale from the fridge and returns to the dining room table.)* How do you like your drink, Minnie?

MINNIE: A little mix in mine, and not'ing in Harold's. The ginger ale tickles his nose and gets him all excited.

JACOB: What is he, Minnie? Newfie?

MINNIE: No, boy—Canadian.

JACOB: Harold, there's only two kinds of people in this world—Newfies and them that wishes they was.

MINNIE: That's what I tells him, boy.

JACOB: Why else would Canada have j'ined us in '49? Right, Minnie? *(JACOB crosses to chesterfield with the drinks.)*

MARY: I t'ought you didn't have no whiskey? I t'ought all you had in the house was "screech"? Do you mean to tell me that was deliberate, what you put Ben t'rough?

JACOB: *(quickly changing the subject)* Minnie, don't you want to see the shower gifts?

MINNIE: Sure, boy. Where's they to?

JACOB: They're in the bedroom. Show her, Mary. Now's a good time.

MARY rises and crosses to the bedroom door. MINNIE follows.

MINNIE: *(indicating HAROLD)* Don't give him any more to drink, Jacob, till I gets back. The bugger likes to get a head start.

They exit.

MINNIE: *(off)* Maid, will you look! A gift shop! Jesus!

JACOB: *(slight pause—to HAROLD, embarrassed)* Well.

HAROLD nods. They drink.

MINNIE: *(off)* Even a rolling pin! *(She pokes out her head.)* My Jesus, Harold, I finally found somet'ing that compares!

JACOB glances at HAROLD. HAROLD glances at JACOB. They drink.

JACOB: *(after a moment)* Grand old day.

HAROLD nods. Silence.

JACOB: *(after a moment)* Couldn't ask for better.

HAROLD nods. Silence.

JACOB: *(after a moment)* Another grand day tomorrow.

HAROLD clears his throat.

JACOB: Pardon?

HAROLD shakes his head. Silence.

JACOB: *(embarrassed)* Well, why don't we see what mischief the women are up to?

HAROLD nods. With visible relief both men exit together.

BILL: Tomorrow's off! We've got to tell them, Kathy! And right now!

KATHY: We don't have to call it off.

BILL: What do you mean?

KATHY: You know what I mean.

BILL: You mean you'd get married without having to?

KATHY: I work, you know. I'll be getting a raise in two months, and another six months after that. I'll be making good money by the time you get into university. I could help put you through. *(slight pause)* I wouldn't be in the way. *(slight pause)* Billy? Don't you even care for me?

BILL: Sure.

KATHY: How much?

Enter HAROLD. During the dialogue he helps himself to another drink from the dining room and crosses to the chesterfield.

BILL: A lot. But I still don't want to get married. I'm not ready. We're too young. Christ, you can't even cook!

KATHY: And you're just a mama's boy!

HAROLD is now seated. KATHY stares at him a moment. Then she smiles.

KATHY: Well, Harold wants me, even if you don't. Don't you, Harold? *(She rises and crosses to the chesterfield, flaunting herself.)*

BILL: Kathy!

KATHY: *(to HAROLD)* I've seen the way you look at me. *(She drops on the chesterfield beside HAROLD.)* You'd like to hop in the sack with me, wouldn't you? Tell the truth.

BILL: Why are you doing this?

KATHY: You think he's any different than you?

BILL: What do you mean?

KATHY: This makes you jealous, Billy? *(She caresses the inside of HAROLD's thigh.)*

BILL: *(grabbing her by the wrist)* I don't understand you, Kathy.

KATHY: I understand you, Billy. Only too well. Poor trapped Billy.

BILL: I'm not trapped.

KATHY: Aren't you?

BILL: No! I'll call it off!

KATHY: Yes! Why don't you?

BILL: I will!

KATHY: I wouldn't want you to waste your life. I'll bet now you wished you'd never met me, don't you? You wish you'd never touched me. All this trouble because you didn't have the nerve to go to the drugstore!

BILL: Well, why did you let me do it if it wasn't a safe time? Answer me that?

Enter MINNIE, JACOB, and MARY.

MINNIE: Well, kids, you're well off now. More than we got when we started out, heh, Mary? Willard and me didn't have a pot to piss in or a window to t'row it out. *(to JACOB, as she sits)* Where's your eldest? I ain't met him yet.

JACOB: Ben? Oh, he's in his bedroom— *(He glances at MARY who is now sitting in the armchair.)* —studying. He's in university, Minnie. *(He calls to BEN's door.)* Ben, come out. *(slight pause)* And bring your diploma. *(He glances sheepishly at MARY and looks away. MARY shakes her head, amused.)*

Enter BEN, dressed in a sport jacket. He carries his rolled-up diploma tied with a ribbon.

JACOB: Graduated from Grade T'irteen last night, Minnie. That's Ben. Ben, this is Mrs. Jackson, and that's Harold.

They all nod hello.

MINNIE: *(appraising BEN with obvious delight)* So this is the best man, heh? Well. Well, well, well. What a fine-looking boy, Jacob. He'll be tall.

JACOB: A little too t'in, Minnie. And not much colour to his face.

MINNIE: What odds? You was a skeleton yourself at his age. Tell you what, Ben. Be over some Saturday night and give you a scrubbing down in the tub. We'll send your father and mother to the pictures. *(to MARY)* Oh, how wicked, maid. Don't mind me, I've got the dirtiest tongue. The t'ings I comes out with. That's what comes of hanging around racetracks and taverns with the likes of the Formaldehyde Kid here. *(slight pause)* You looks like your mother's side of the family, Ben.

JACOB: I kind of t'ought he looked like my side. *(to BEN)* Show Minnie your diploma.

BEN hands the diploma to MINNIE.

MINNIE: *(to BEN)* Proud father.

BEN: *(to JACOB)* I thought you didn't have any whiskey?

JACOB: *(ignoring BEN and glancing over MINNIE's shoulder as she reads the diploma)* He got honours all the way t'rough high school, Minnie. He got a scholarship.

MINNIE: Where'd he get his brains to? *(embarrassed silence—to BEN)* Told you you look like your mother's side. *(She hands back the diploma, rises, and hands her glass to JACOB.)* Next round less ginger ale, Jacob. Gives me gas. *(crossing to the record player)* And I'd hate to start cracking off around Father Douglas. *(She puts on a record—"Moonglow" theme from* Picnic.*)* What a face he's on him, already, the priest. Pinched little mouth. You'd t'ink he just opened the Song of Solomon and found a fart pressed between the pages like a rose. *(She starts to move slowly to the music.)*

KATHY: Mother, do you have to?

MINNIE: Do I have to what, sister?

KATHY: Make a fool of yourself.

MINNIE: Listen to who's talking! *(slight pause)* I'd dance with Harold except the only tune he knows is the Death March. And the only step he knows is the foxtrot. Imagine foxtrotting to the Death March. *(to JACOB)* Jacob, you was a one for dancing years ago. Wasn't he, Mary?

MARY: He still is, Minnie.

MINNIE: Did he ever tell you how I first got to go out with him?

MARY: I don't believe he did.

MINNIE: He didn't? Well, remember Georgie Bishop? He took me out one night—to the Salvation Army dance at Bay Roberts. It was in the wintertime, and cold as a nun's tit. I saw Jacob there, hanging about, and now and then he'd look my way and I'd wink. Oh, I was some brazen.

JACOB: I t'ought you had somet'ing in your eye, Minnie.

MINNIE: Yes, boy, the same as was in yours—the devil! ... To make a long story short, Mary, when it come time to go home, Georgie and me went outside where his horse and sled was hitched to the post. He'd tied it fast with a knot, and do you know what this bugger had gone and done?

JACOB: Now don't tell that, Minnie.

MINNIE: Pissed on the knot! He had, maid. A ball of ice as big as me fist. And who do you suppose walks up large as life and offers to drive me home in his sled? *(pause)* Poor Georgie. The last I remembers of him he was cursing the dirty son-of-a-bitch that had done it and was stabbing away at the knot with his jack-knife! *(She notices BEN's amused reaction to her story.)* Come dance with me, Ben. Don't be shy. Come on. If I'm not mistaken, you've got the devil in your eye, too. Just like your father. *(She puts BEN's arm around her waist and they dance.)* Look, Harold. You might learn a t'ing or two. *(She presses close against BEN.)* Mmm. You know, Jacob, this is no longer a little boy. He's coming of age.

KATHY: Mother, you're dirty.

MINNIE: How fast you've grown, Ben. How tall and straight. Do you want to hear a funny one? I could have been your mother. Imagine. But your grandfather—Jacob's father—put his foot down. I was a Catholic, and that was that in no uncertain terms. Wasn't it, Jacob? *(slight pause)* So I married Willard ... *(They break apart. To JACOB, as she sits)* Ah, well, boy, I suppose it all worked out for the best. Just t'ink, Jacob—if you had married me it might have been you Harold pumped full of fluids.

JACOB: That it might, Minnie. That it might.

MINNIE: But you can't help marvel at the way t'ings work out. Makes you wonder sometimes.

JACOB: *(turns off music)* What's that, Minnie?

MINNIE: Your son marrying my daughter and turning Catholic in the bargain. Serves you right you old bugger. The last laugh's on you. And your poor old father.

JACOB: You'm not still carrying that grudge around inside you, is you? I'm getting a fine girl in the family. That's the way I looks at it.

MINNIE: *(rising to help herself to another drink)* I don't mind telling you, Jacob, I've had my hands full with *that* one. Not a moment's peace since the day poor Willard died. She was kind of stuck on her father, you know. Jesus, boy, she won't even speak to Harold. Won't let him give her away tomorrow, will you, sister? Her uncle's doing that. Oh, she snaps me head off if I as much as makes a suggestion. T'inks she knows it all. And now look. All I can say is I'm glad her father ain't alive, this night.

JACOB: Now, Minnie, you knows you don't mean all that. Own up to it.

MINNIE: Oh, I means it, boy, and more. T'ank God it's only the second month. At least she don't show yet. If she's anyt'ing like me, she'll have a bad time. Well, a little pain'll teach her a good lesson.

KATHY: I wish you wouldn't talk about me like that, Mother.

MINNIE: Like what?

KATHY: Like I was invisible. I don't like it; I've told you before.

JACOB: Now, now, Kathy.

MINNIE: Listen to her, will you? Invisible. Sister, you may soon wish you *was* invisible, when the girls from work start counting back on the office calendar.

KATHY: Let them count!

MINNIE: See, Jacob? See what I'm up against? No shame!

JACOB: Minnie, let's not have any hard feelings. It's most time for church. I'll get the coats.

MARY: Yes, do.

JACOB gets MINNIE's and MARY's coats.

MINNIE: *(crossing to BEN)* You don't know, Mary, how fortunate you is having sons. That's the biggest letdown of me life, not having a boy ... We couldn't have any but the one ... *(bitterly)* and that had to be the bitch of the litter. How I curse the day. A boy like this must be a constant joy, Mary.

MARY: And a tribulation, maid.

MINNIE: Yes, but look at all the worry a daughter brings. *(as JACOB helps her into her coat)* This is the kind of fix she can get herself into.

KATHY: Mother, I just asked you not to.

BILL: Tell her, Kathy.

MINNIE: And then to top it off who gets the bill for the wedding? Oh, it's just dandy having a daughter, just dandy. I could wring her neck.

BILL: Kathy.

KATHY: *(to BILL)* You tell her.

MINNIE: If I had my own way I know what I'd do with all the bitches at birth. I'd do with them exactly what we did back home with the kittens—

KATHY: I'm not pregnant!

MINNIE: What?

KATHY: *(bitterly)* You heard me. I'm not pregnant.

MINNIE: What do you mean you're not? You are so, unless you've done somet'ing to yourself ...

KATHY: I didn't.

MARY: Kathy.

MINNIE: I took you to the doctor myself. I was in his office. Why in hell do you suppose you're getting married tomorrow, if it's not because you're having a baby?

KATHY: *(turning to MARY)* Mrs. Mercer, I had a miscarriage ...

MINNIE: A miscarriage ...

MARY: When, Kathy? *(She puts her arms around KATHY.)*

KATHY: This morning. I went to the doctor. There's no mistake. And I didn't do anything to myself, Mother.

MINNIE: *(quietly)* Did I say you did, sister?

MARY: Sit down, dear. *(She helps KATHY sit—long pause.)* This may not be the right moment to mention it, Minnie, but ... well, it seems to me t'ings have altered somewhat. *(She looks at BEN.)* T'ings are back to the way they used to be. The youngsters don't need to get married. There's no reason to, now.

Pause. No one moves except HAROLD who raises his glass to drink.

Blackout.

ACT TWO

A moment later. As the lights come up, the actors are in the exact positions and attitudes they were in at the end of Act One. The tableau dissolves into action.

JACOB: Sit down, Minnie. We've got to talk this out. *(to KATHY)* Can I get you anyt'ing, my dear?

KATHY shakes her head. MINNIE sits.

MINNIE: *(slight pause)* What time is it getting to be?

BEN: Seven-fifteen.

MINNIE: The priest expects us there sharp at eight. He's got a mass to say at half-past.

MARY: Now wait just a minute. I t'ink you're being hasty, Minnie. The children can please themselves, now, what they wants to do. Maybe they don't want to get married.

JACOB: Mary's right, Minnie. Ask them.

MINNIE: For someone who don't like to butt in, maid, you got a lot to say sometimes. Stay out of it or I might say somet'ing I'm sorry for.

MARY: I can't stay out of it. I wouldn't advise my worst enemy to jump into marriage that young, and neither would you, Minnie. They'd be far better off waiting till Billy finishes university ...

MINNIE: Well, maybe *they* can afford to put it off, but *I* sure as hell can't. The invitations are out … the cake's bought, and the dress … the flowers arranged for … the photographer … the priest and organist hired … the church and banquet hall rented … the food—

KATHY: *(jumping up)* I don't want to get married!

MARY: What?

MINNIE: What? Don't believe her, Mary. She do so. She's got a stack of love comics a mile high. *(to KATHY)* Now you shut your mouth, sister, or I'll shut it for you.

KATHY: I won't.

MINNIE: You knows what'll happen if you backs out now? I'll be made a laughing stock. Is that what you wants, you little bitch?

KATHY: Don't call me a bitch, you old slut!

MARY: Kathy.

MINNIE: *(to JACOB)* Did you hear that? Why, I'll slap the face right off her! *(She goes after KATHY.)*

JACOB: *(keeping MINNIE away from her daughter)* All right, now. This is no way to behave. Tonight of all nights!

KATHY: That's what you are, an old cow! He only wants you for your money. *(indicating HAROLD)*

MINNIE: That's a lie.

KATHY: Is it?

MINNIE: That's a lie. Let me at her, Jacob. I'll knock her to kingdom come.

JACOB: Enough, goddamn it! Both of you! *(Silence.)* That's better. Let's all ca'm down. We could all learn a lesson from Harold here. He's civilized. *(slight pause)* What we need's a drink.

MINNIE: *(as JACOB refills the glasses)* Imagine. My own flesh and blood, and she's got it in for me. She's never had much use for me, and even less since I took up with Harold here. She'll say anyt'ing to get back at me. Anyt'ing!

JACOB: Kathy's had a bad time of it, Minnie. No doubt she's upset. *(to MARY)* Remember how you was, when we lost our first? Didn't care if she lived or died. Didn't care if she ever laid eyes on me again, she was that down in the dumps. And

I'm surprised, Billy. Not once have you come to her defence or spoken a word of comfort. You've got to be more of a man than that.

BEN: Why can't they get married and Billy still go to school?

MARY: *(to BEN)* Mind your business.

MINNIE: You hear that, Jacob? That's the one with all the brains.

BEN: *(to MARY)* I'm just trying to help.

MARY: Who? Yourself?

KATHY: I want him to, Mrs. Mercer. He doesn't have to quit school. I like to work. Honest.

MARY: Well, Billy, you're the only one we haven't heard from. What do you say?

JACOB: Ah, what's it matter if he gets married now or after university? He won't do much better than Kathy.

MINNIE: She's a good girl, in spite of what I said about her. A hard worker. She always pays her board sharp. And clean as a whistle.

JACOB: That's settled, then.

MARY: Is it, Billy?

JACOB: For God's sake, Mary.

MARY: He's got a tongue of his own. Let him answer. The poor child can't get a word in edgewise.

JACOB: Stop smothering him. He's a man now. Let him act like one. *(amused)* Besides, he's just getting cold feet. Ain't you, my son?

BEN: Did you get cold feet, Dad?

JACOB: All men do. *(MARY glances at JACOB who nudges her.)* Even the best of us. He'll be fine after tomorrow.

MINNIE: T'anks, Jacob. I could kiss you. Now, Harold, wait your turn, and don't be jealous. *(She crosses to the record player and selects a record.)* The mother of the bride and the father of the groom will now have the next dance. With your permission, Mary?

MARY: With my blessing, maid.

JACOB: *(glancing at MARY)* I don't know whether I'm up to it, Minnie.

MINNIE: Go on, Jacob. You'll be dancing a jig at your own wake.

Music: "Isle of Newfoundland." JACOB takes MINNIE in his arms and they dance. BILL goes to KATHY, takes her hand and leads her into the darkened kitchen. They make up.

MINNIE: Ah, Jacob, remember when we'd hug and smooch in the darkest places on the dance floor? The way he stuck to the shadows, Mary, you'd swear he was a bat. Dance with her, Harold. *(indicating MARY)* He's some wonderful dancer, boy. Went to Arthur Murray's. He's awful shy, though.

MARY and HAROLD exchange glances. HAROLD clears his throat.

MINNIE: Ah, boy, Jacob, I'd better give Harold a turn. He'd sit there all night looking anxious. He likes a good foxtrot. Fancies himself Valentino. Come on, Lazarus.

MINNIE and HAROLD dance. JACOB crosses to MARY who is sitting behind the dining room table.

JACOB: Dance, Mary?

MARY: You'll make a good match, the two of you.

JACOB: Mary, I t'ink you'm jealous.

MARY: Don't be foolish. And don't start showing off. That's the next step.

JACOB: "How beautiful are thy feet with shoes, O prince's daughter! The j'ints of thy t'ighs are like jewels, the work of the hands of a cunning workman. Thy navel is like a round goblet, which wanteth not liquor: thy belly is like—"

MARY: *(sharply)* Jacob!

JACOB: "—an heap of wheat set about with lilies. Thy two breasts—"

MARY: All right, boy—enough!

JACOB: *(sitting)* Do you remember, Mary, when you was just a piss-tail maid picking blueberries on the cliffs behind your father's house, your poor knees tattooed from kneeling? Did you ever t'ink for a single minute that one day you'd be the mother of grown-up sons and one of 'em about to start a life of his own?

MARY: No, and that I didn't. In those days I couldn't see no further ahead than you charging down Country Road on your old white horse to whisk me away to the mainland.

JACOB: Any regrets?

MARY: What does you t'ink?

JACOB: Ah, go on with you. *(pause)* The old house seems smaller already, don't it?

MARY: Empty.

MINNIE: *(still dancing)* Tomorrow's a landmark for us all, Jacob. I lose me only daughter and you lose your two sons. *(JACOB reacts.)* Somehow I don't envy you, boy. I t'ink it'll be harder on you. If I had sons ...

JACOB crosses quickly to the record player and switches it off.

JACOB: What was that you just said, Minnie? Did I hear you correct? Whose sons?

MINNIE: Yours.

JACOB: Mine? Only one's going.

MINNIE: Didn't anybody tell you?

JACOB: Tell me what? I'm lucky to get the time of day. *(to MARY)* Tell me what?

MARY: Ben's moving in with Bill and Kathy. Taking their spare room.

JACOB: He is like hell!

BEN: I am!

JACOB: You'm not!

BEN: I am!

JACOB: Don't be foolish!

MINNIE: I t'ought he knowed, Mary. I t'ought the kids had told him.

JACOB: No, Minnie, they neglected to mention it. I'm not surprised!

MINNIE: I wouldn't have put me big foot in me mouth otherwise.

JACOB: Why should I know any more what goes on in my own house than the stranger on the street? I'm only his father. I'm not the one they all confides in around this house, I can tell you. I'm just the goddamn old fool. That's all! The goddamn fool.

BEN: I wanted to tell you after the wedding.

JACOB: Yes, you did so.

BEN: I would have sooner, but this is what happens.

JACOB: Oh, so now it's all my fault?

BEN: I didn't say that. Stop twisting what I say.

JACOB: How quick you is to shift the blame, my son. *(to MARY)* How come you to know? He was quick enough to run to you with the news, wasn't he?

MARY: I can't help that.

JACOB: Yes, you can. I'm always the last to find out, and you'm the reason, Mary. You'm the ringleader. The t'ree of you against the one of me.

MARY: And you talks about shifting the blame.

JACOB: Wasn't I the last to find out Billy was getting married? He told you first, but did you come and confide in me? That you didn't. If I hadn't found that bill from Ostranders for Kathy's engagement ring … !

BILL: We would have told you …

JACOB: A lot of respect you show for your father. A lot of respect. You'm no better than your brother.

MARY: Ca'm down, boy. You're just getting yourself all worked up.

JACOB: I won't ca'm down. Ca'm down. All I ever does is break my back for their good and comfort, and how is it they repays me? A slap in the face! *(to BEN)* What did you have in mind to do, my son? Sneak off with all your belongings, like a thief, while your father was at work?

BEN: Go to hell.

JACOB: What did you say?

BEN: You heard me. I don't have to take shit like that from anyone. And I don't care who's here!

JACOB takes a threatening step toward his son. MARY steps between.

JACOB: I'll knock your goddamn block off!

MARY: Now just stop it, the both of you! Stop it!

MINNIE: I'd never have gotten away with that from my father. He'd have tanned me good.

MARY: And Minnie—mind your own business. This is none of your concern.

JACOB: Talking like that to his own father …

BEN: And if you ever hit me again … !

JACOB: I'll hit you in two seconds flat, if you carries on. Just keep it up. Don't t'ink for one minute you'm too old yet!

BEN: Come on. Hit me. I'm not scared. Hit me. You'd never see me again!

MARY: *(slapping BEN)* Shut right up. You're just as bad as he is!

MINNIE: Two of a kind, maid. Two peas in a pod. That's why they don't get on.

JACOB: Why the hell do you suppose we slaved to buy this house, if it wasn't for you two? And now you won't stick around long enough to help pay back a red cent. You'd rather pay rent to a stranger!

BILL: Dad, I'm leaving to get married, in case you forgot.

JACOB: You don't need to. Put it off. Listen to your mother!

BILL: A minute ago you said—

JACOB: Forget a minute ago! This is now!

BEN: He'll have converted for nothing, if he does!

JACOB: You shut your bloody mouth! *(to BILL)* Put it off, my son. There's no hurry. Don't be swayed by Minnie. She's just t'inking of herself. Getting revenge for old hurts.

MINNIE: And you're full of shit, Jacob.

JACOB: You goddamn Catholics, you don't even believe in birth control. Holy jumping Jesus Christ. The poor young boy'll be saddled with a gang of little ones before he knows it! And all because my poor father hated the Micks!

MINNIE: Come on, sister, we don't need that. Get your coat. You, too, Harold. Let's go, Billy. The priest can't wait on the likes of us.

BILL and KATHY move to go.

JACOB: Don't go, Billy. There's no need!

BILL: First you say one thing, Dad, and then you say something else. Will you please make up your mind! *(to BEN)* Ben, what should I do? Tell me.

BEN: I can't help you, Billy.

KATHY looks at BILL, then runs out, slamming the door.

MARY: *(to BILL)* Go after her, my son. Now's the time she needs you. We'll see you in church. Go on, now.

BILL: Ben?

BEN: In a minute. I'll see you there.

BILL: Dad? *(JACOB turns away. BILL runs out.)*

MINNIE: I'll take the two kids with me, Mary. See you in a few minutes.

JACOB: You won't see me there tonight, Minnie, and you can count on that. And not tomorrow, either.

MINNIE: That's up to you, Jacob, though I hope you changes your mind for Billy's sake. *(slight pause)* We oughtn't to let our differences interfere with the children. *(slight pause)* Come along, Lazarus. It's time we dragged our backsides to the church.

They exit. Silence. MARY removes her coat, then slowly begins to clear the table. BEN looks over at his father. Finally he speaks.

BEN: Dad …

JACOB: What?

BEN: I want to explain. Will you let me?

JACOB: I should t'ink you'd be ashamed to even look at me, let alone open your mouth. *(slight pause)* Well? What is it? I suppose we'm not good enough for you?

BEN: Oh, come on.

JACOB: *(to MARY)* If you's going to the church, you'd better be off.

BEN: We still have a few minutes.

JACOB: *(to MARY)* And no odds what, I won't go to church. They can do without me.

MARY: Suit yourself. But I'm going. Just don't come back on me afterwards for not coaxing you to.

JACOB: You can walk in that church tonight, feeling the way you does? Oh, you'm some two-faced, Mary.

MARY: Don't you talk. You was quite willing to see Billy go, till it slipped out that Ben was going, too.

JACOB: That's a lie!

MARY: Is it?

JACOB: That's a damn lie!

MARY: I'll call a cab. *(She crosses to the phone, picks up the receiver, To JACOB.)* We can't always have it our way. *(She dials and ad libs softly while dialogue continues between father and son.)*

JACOB: A lifetime spent in this house, and he gives us less notice than you would a landlord! And me about to wallpaper his room like a goddamn fool! *(slight pause)* And don't come back broke and starving in a week or two and expect a handout, 'cause the only way you'll get t'rough that door is to break it in! *(slight pause)* You'll never last on your own. You never had to provide for yourself.

BEN: I'll learn.

JACOB: You'll starve.

BEN: All right, I'll starve. And then you can have the satisfaction of being right. *(slight pause)* You're always telling me it's time I got out on my own and grew up.

JACOB: Sure, t'row up in my face what I said in the past!

BEN: Dad, will you listen to me for once? It's not because home's bad, or because I hate you. It's not that. I just want to be independent, that's all. Can't you understand that? *(slight pause)* I had to move out sometime.

JACOB: Was it somet'ing I said? What was it? Tell me. I must have said somet'ing!

BEN: No, it was nothing you said. Will you come off it?

JACOB: Can you imagine what our relatives will say, once they hears? They'll say you left home on account of me.

BEN: Well, who the hell cares?

JACOB: And you any idea what this'll do to your mother? You'm her favourite. *(The last syllable rhymes with "night.")*

MARY: Jacob! That's not fair!

JACOB: What odds? It's true, and don't deny it. *(to BEN)* Your mother's always been most fond of you. She even delivered you herself. Did you know that?

MARY: There's no time for family history, Father.

JACOB moves quickly to the mantel and takes the photo album. He is slightly desperate now. He flicks open the album.

JACOB: *(intimately, to BEN)* Look. Look at that one. You could scarcely walk. Clinging for dear life to your mother's knee. *(turning the page)* And look at this. The four of us. Harry Saunders took that of us with my old box camera the day the Germans marched into Paris. *(turns the photo over)* There. You'm good with dates. June 14, 1940. Look how lovely your mother looks, my son. No more than ninety pounds when she had you.

MARY: Ninety-one.

JACOB: She was that t'in, you'd swear the wind would carry her off. We never believed we'd have another, after the first died. He was premature. Seven months, and he only lived a few hours.

MARY: Enough of the past, boy.

JACOB: That was some night, the night you was born. Blizzarding to beat hell. The doctor lived in Bay Roberts, and I had to hitch up the sled—

MARY: He's heard all that.

JACOB: Some woman, your mother. Cut and tied the cord herself. Had you scrubbed to a shine and was washed herself and back in bed, sound asleep, before we showed up.

MARY: Took all the good out of me, too.

JACOB: And wasn't she a picture? She could have passed for her namesake in the stained glass of a Catholic window, she was that radiant.

MARY: Get on with you.

JACOB: Your mother'd never let on, but you can imagine the state she'll be in if you goes. You'm all that's left now, Ben. The last son. *(a whisper)* I t'ink she wishes you'd stay.

MARY: I heard that. Look, you speak for yourself. I've interfered enough for one night.

JACOB: Your mother has always lived just for the two of you.

MARY: *(pained)* Oh, Jacob.

JACOB: Always.

BEN: Come on, Dad, that's not true.

JACOB: It is so, now. It is so.

MARY: Well it's not, and don't you say it is. The Likes of that!

JACOB: Confess, Mary. I don't count, I've never counted. Not since the day they was born.

BEN: If that's true, Dad, you should be glad to get rid of both of us. Have Mom all to yourself again.

JACOB: Don't be smart.

MARY: Who's the one making all the fuss? Me or you? Answer me that.

JACOB: No, you'd sit by silent and let me do it for you and take all the shit that comes with it. I'm wise to your little games.

MARY: I can't stop him, if he wants to go. I don't like it any more than you do. I can't imagine this house without our two sons. But if what Ben wants is to go, he's got my blessing. I won't stand in his way because I'm scared. And if you can't speak for yourself, don't speak for me. I'm out of it.

JACOB: If he's so dead set on going, he can march out the door this very minute.

MARY: He will not! Don't be foolish!

JACOB: He will so, if I say so! *(He charges into BEN's bedroom and returns with a suitcase which he sets on the floor.)* There! Pack your belongings right this second, if we'm not good enough for you.

MARY: Ben, don't pay him no mind.

JACOB: I don't want you in this house another minute, if you'm that anxious to be elsewhere. Ingrate!

MARY: If you don't shut your big yap, he just might, and then you'd be in some state.

JACOB: Oh, I would, would I? Well, we'll just see about that. I'll help him pack, if he likes! *(He charges into BEN's bedroom.)*

MARY: Ben, don't talk back to him when he's mad. It only makes it worse, you knows that.

JACOB: *(comes out with a stack of record albums which he hurls violently to the floor)* There. Enough of that goddamn squealing and squawking. Now I can get some peace and quiet after a hard day's work.

BEN: Dad, I think I ought to …

JACOB: Don't open your mouth. I don't want to hear another word!

BEN: All right, make a fool of yourself!

JACOB: *(to MARY)* And that goes for you too! *(He charges back into the bedroom.)*

BEN: What'll we do, Mom? We got to get out of here. Can't you stop him?

MARY: All you can do, when he gets like this, is let him run down and tire himself out. His poor father was the same. He'd hurl you t'rough the window one minute and brush the glass off you the next.

JACOB: *(comes out with a stack of new shirts still in the cellophane)* And look at this, will you? Talk about a sin. I walks around with my ass out, and here's six new shirts never even opened. *(He hurls the shirts on the pile of records.)*

BEN: I don't want to spoil your fun, Dad, but so far all that stuff belongs to Billy. *(JACOB stares at the scattered records and shirts, alarmed.)*

MARY: Now you've done it, boy. Will you sit down now? You're just making a bigger fool of yourself the longer you stands.

JACOB: *(Her reproach is all he needs to get back in stride.)* Sure, mock me when I'm down. Well, I'll show you who the fool is. We'll just see who has the last laugh! *(He charges into his own bedroom. MARY picks up the records and shirts.)*

BEN: *(pause)* I wanted to tell him, Mom, a week ago. I kept putting it off.

MARY: I wish you had, Ben. This mightn't have happened.

BEN: It's all our fault, anyhow.

MARY: What do you mean?

BEN: We've made him feel like an outsider all these years. The three of us. You, me, Billy. It's always been him and us. Always. As long as I can remember.

MARY: Blame your father's temper. He's always had a bad temper. All we done was try our best to avoid it.

BEN: Yeah, but we make it worse. We feed it. We shouldn't shut him out the way we do.

MARY: And what is it you're not saying, that's it's my fault somehow? Is that what you t'inks? Say it.

BEN: I didn't say that.

MARY: Your father believes it. He calls me the ringleader.

BEN: Well, you set the example, Mom, a long time ago. When we were little.

MARY: Don't you talk, Ben. You're some one to point fingers. *(slight pause)* Perhaps I did. Perhaps your father's right all along. But you're no little child any longer, and you haven't been for years. You're a man now, and you never followed anyone's example for too long unless you had a mind to. So don't use that excuse.

BEN: I'm not. I'm just as much to blame as anybody. I know that.

MARY: I always tried to keep the peace. And that wasn't always easy in this family, with you and your father at each other's t'roats night and day. And to keep the peace I had to sometimes keep a good many unpleasant facts from your father. Small, simple t'ings, mostly.

BEN: You were just sparing yourself.

MARY: I was doing what I considered the most good! And don't tell me I wasn't. Oh, Ben, you knows yourself what he's like. If you lost five dollars down the sewer, you didn't dare let on. If you did, he'd dance around the room like one leg was on fire and the other had a bee up it. It was just easier that way, not to tell him. Easier on the whole family. Yes, and easier on myself.

BEN: But it wasn't easier when he found out. On him or us.

MARY: He didn't always, Ben.

BEN: No, but when he does, like tonight—it's worse!

JACOB enters the room from the bedroom, slowly, carrying a small cardboard box. He removes the contents of the box—a neatly folded silk dressing gown—and throws the box to one side.

JACOB: I won't be needing the likes of this. Take it with you. I've got enough old junk cluttering up my closet.

BEN: I don't want it, either.

MARY: He gave you that for your birthday. You've never even worn it.

JACOB: Take it! *(He hurls it violently in BEN's face. Then he notices the diploma lying on the table. He grabs it.)*

MARY: Not the diploma, Jacob! No!

BEN says nothing. He just stares at his father, who stares back the whole time he removes the ribbon, unfolds the diploma, and tears it into two pieces, then four, then eight. He drops the pieces to the floor.

MARY: God help you. This time you've gone too far.

Pause. Then BEN crosses to the suitcase. He picks it up.

BEN: I'll pack. *(He exits into his bedroom.)*

MARY: All right. You satisfied? You've made me feel deeply ashamed tonight, Jacob, the way you treats Ben. I only hopes he forgives you. I don't know if I would, if it was me.

JACOB: I always knowed it would come to this one day. He's always hated me, and don't say he hasn't. Did you see him tonight? I can't so much as lay a hand on his shoulder. He pulls away. His own father, and I can't touch him. All his life long he's done nothing but mock and defy me, and now he's made me turn him out in anger, my own son. *(to MARY, angrily)* And you can bugger off, too, if you don't like it. Don't let me keep you. Just pack your bag and take him with you. Dare say you'd be happier off. I don't give a good goddamn if the whole lot of you deserts me.

MARY: You don't know when to stop, do you? You just don't know when to call a halt. What must I do? Knock you senseless? You'd go on and

on until you brought your whole house tumbling down. I suppose it's late in the day to be expecting miracles, but for God's sake, Jacob, control yourself. For once in your life would you just t'ink before you speaks? Please! *(slight pause)* I have no sympathy for you. You brought this all on yourself. You wouldn't listen. Well, listen now. Have you ever in your whole life took two minutes out to try and understand him? Have you? Instead of galloping off in all directions? Dredging up old hurts? Why, not five minutes ago he stood on that exact spot and stuck up for you!

JACOB: *(surprised, slightly incredulous)* Ben did … ?

MARY: Yes, Ben did, and don't look so surprised. Now it may be too late, but there are some t'ings that just have to be said, right now, in the open. Sit down and listen. Sit down. *(JACOB sits.)* For twenty years now I've handled the purse strings in this family, and only because you shoved it off on me. I don't like to do it any more than you do. I'm just as bad at it, except you're better with the excuses. *(JACOB rises.)* I'm not finished. Sit down. *(He does—slight pause.)* Last fall you tumbled off our garage roof and sprained your back. You was laid up for six months all told— November to May—without a red cent of Workmen's Compensation, because the accident didn't happen on the job. And I made all the payments as usual—the mortgages, your truck, the groceries, life insurance, the hydro and oilman, your union dues. All that, and more. I took care of it all. And where, Jacob, do you suppose the money came from? You never once asked. Did you ever wonder?

JACOB: Where? From the bank.

MARY: The bank! We didn't have a nickel in the bank. Not after the second month.

JACOB: What is you getting at, Mary?

MARY: Just this. *(She lowers her voice.)* If Ben hadn't got a scholarship, he wouldn't have went to college this fall. He couldn't have afforded to. It was his money that took us over the winter. All those years of working part-time and summers. All of it gone.

JACOB: Ben did that?

MARY: And you says he hates you!

JACOB: I don't want no handouts from him. I'll pay him back every cent of it.

MARY: Shut up. He'll hear you! He never wanted you to know, so don't you dare let on that I told you, you hear? He knowed how proud you is, and he knowed you wouldn't want to t'ink you wasn't supporting your family. *(slight pause)* Now, boy, who's got the last laugh? *(MARY takes her coat and puts it on as she crosses to BEN's door.)* Hurry up, Ben. The taxi ought to be here any second. *(She turns and looks at JACOB. There is anguish in her face. When she speaks her voice is drained.)* I'm tired, Jacob. And you ought to be, too, by all rights. It's time to quit it. A lifetime of this is enough, you and Ben. Declare it an even match for your own sake, boy, if for nothing else. I don't want to see you keep getting the worst of it. You always did and you still do.

Enter BEN, carrying his suitcase.

BEN: *(to MARY)* Isn't the cab here yet? It's almost eight.

MARY: He'll beep his horn. *(slight pause)* You don't need to take that now, my son. Pick it up Later.

BEN: That's okay, Mom. I've got all I want. The rest you can throw out. *(He sits on his suitcase.)*

JACOB: Your mother told me what you done last winter. I—

MARY: *(sharply)* Jacob!

JACOB: I wants to t'ank you. I'll pay you back.

MARY: You promised you— *(She stops, shakes her head in exasperation.)*

JACOB: *(slight pause)* I'm sorry what happened here tonight. I wants you to know that. I'll make it up to you. I will.

BEN: *(meaning it)* It's nothing. Forget it.

MARY: Let him say he's sorry, Ben. He needs to.

JACOB: Maybe I've been wrong. I suppose I ain't been the best of fathers. I couldn't give you all I'd like to. But I've been the best I could under the circumstances.

BEN: Dad.

JACOB: Hear me out, now. We never seen eye to eye in most cases, but we'm still a family. We've got to stick together. All we got in this world is the family— *(He rises.)* —and it's breaking up, Ben. *(slight pause)* Stay for a while longer. For a few more years.

BEN: I can't.

JACOB: You can. Why not?

BEN: I just can't.

JACOB: Spite! You'm just doing this out of spite! *(BEN shakes his head.)* Then reconsider ... like a good boy. Let your brother rent his room to a stranger, if he's that hard up. Don't let him break us up.

The taxi sounds its horn.

MARY: There's the taxi now.

JACOB: *(desperately)* You don't have to go, my son. You knows I never meant what I said before. You'm welcome to stay as long as you likes, and you won't have to pay a cent of rent. *(even more desperately)* Come back afterwards!

BEN: No, Dad.

JACOB: Yes, come back. Like a good boy. I never had a choice in my day, Ben. You do.

BEN: I don't!

JACOB: You do so! Don't contradict me!

BEN: What do you know? You don't know the first thing about me, and you don't want to. You don't know how I feel, and you don't give a shit!

JACOB: In my day we had a duty to—

BEN: In your day! I'm sick of hearing about your fucking day! This is *my* day, and we're strangers. You know the men you work with better than you do me! Isn't that right? Isn't it?

JACOB: And you treats your friends better than you do me! I know that much, I can tell you. A whole lot better! And with more respect. Using language like that in front of your mother!

The taxi honks impatiently. BEN moves to go. JACOB grabs the suitcase.

MARY: Jacob! The taxi's waiting!

JACOB: *(to BEN)* You're not taking that suitcase out of this house! Not this blessed day! *(He puts the suitcase down at a distance.)*

MARY: That's okay, Ben. Leave it. You can come back some other time. *(MARY exits.)*

JACOB: He will like hell. Once he goes, that's it. He came with nothing, he'll go with nothing!

BEN: *(slight pause)* Do you know why I want to be on my own? The real reason?

JACOB: To whore around!

BEN: Because you're not going to stop until there's nothing left of me. It's not the world that wants to devour me, Dad—it's you!

JACOB whips off his belt.

JACOB: *(as he brings it down hard on BEN's back)* Then go!

BEN instinctively covers his head, crouching a little, unprotesting.

JACOB: *(sobbing, as he brings the belt down again and again)* Go! Go! Go! Go! Go!

Finally as JACOB swings again for the sixth time, BEN whirls and grabs the belt from his father's hand. Then with a violent motion he flings it aside.

BEN: You shouldn't have done that, Dad. You shouldn't. *(He exits.)*

Silence. JACOB retrieves his belt. A slight pause.

JACOB: *(fiercely striking the chesterfield with his belt)* Holy Jumping Jesus Christ!

Silence. MARY enters from the hallway. JACOB begins to put on his belt. He notices MARY.

JACOB: What's you doing here? Isn't you going? *(He crosses into the dining room and sits at the table.)*

Slowly MARY puts down her purse and enters the dining room, crossing behind JACOB and sitting at the table beside him. She says nothing.

JACOB: *(anguished)* In the name of Jesus, Mary, whatever possessed you to marry the likes of me over Jerome McKenzie? *(MARY says nothing. Pause.)* I've never asked you before, but I've always wondered.

Pause.

MARY: It was that day you, me, and Jerome McKenzie was all sitting around my mother's kitchen and in walked my brother Clifford. He was teaching Grade Six in St. John's that year, and he told of a story that occurred that very morning at school. You've most likely forgotten. A little girl had come into his class with a note from her teacher. She was told to carry the note around to every class in the school and wait till every teacher read it. Clifford did, with the child standing next to him. The note had t'ree words on it: *Don't she smell?* Well, Jacob, boy, when you heard that, you brought your fist down so hard on the tabletop it cracked one of Mother's good saucers, and that's when I knowed Jerome McKenzie hadn't a hope in hell. *(slight pause)* Q.C. or no Q.C.!

Slowly MARY lifts one foot then the other onto the chair in front of her. The lights slowly dim into darkness.

END

RICK SALUTIN and THEATRE PASSE MURAILLE

In his production diary of *1837*, the original version of *1837: The Farmers' Revolt*, Rick Salutin remarks how the opening night audience in Toronto laughed at the mention of Bay and Adelaide, a downtown intersection. That reaction brought into sharp focus for Salutin the reasons for having created the play in the first place, the bizarre attitudes typically held by Canadians towards their own history. "We are so imbued with self-denial," he concluded, "so colonized, that the very thought of something historic happening here, at Bay and Adelaide, draws laughs." His ongoing project and that of Theatre Passe Muraille under Paul Thompson was to get Canadian audiences to laugh at themselves in the *right* places, presenting the everyday life and history of Canadians in theatrically playful and often brilliantly comical ways while at the same time insisting that they are subjects worthy of serious dramatic treatment.

Ironically, the man *Maclean's* once called "the country's foremost nationalist playwright" was educated almost entirely in the United States. Between 1960 and 1970 Salutin earned a B.A. in Near Eastern and Judaic Studies at Brandeis University, an M.A. in religion from Columbia, and was doing a Ph.D. in philosophy at New York's New School when he decided to return home to Toronto in 1970 after reading Harold Innis' *The Fur Trade in Canada*, an economic history that Salutin says "made sense of the present by making sense of the past." While working as a journalist and trade union organizer, he wrote his first play, *Fanshen*, produced in 1972 by Toronto Workshop Productions. An adaptation of William Hinton's classic study of the effects of the Chinese Revolution on the life of a small village, the play epitomizes Salutin's concern with the way history and politics are enacted in the daily lives of ordinary people. That concern would be at the heart of his next project, *1837*.

While Salutin was studying in the United States, Paul Thompson was getting an eclectic education in Canada and abroad: a B.A. in English and French from the University of Western Ontario in 1963 followed by a year at the Sorbonne; an M.A. in history at the University of Toronto in 1965 followed by two years' theatrical apprenticeship with Roger Planchon in Lyons. Thompson returned to Canada in 1967 and finally planted himself in Toronto with Theatre Passe Muraille just about the time Salutin came home. By the fall of 1972 when Thompson, Salutin and six Passe Muraille actors set to work creating *1837*, Thompson had been artistic director for a year and had already put his strong personal stamp on the company with innovative productions of Carol Bolt's *Buffalo Jump* and the collectively created *Doukhobors* and *The Farm Show*. The essence of Thompson's dramaturgy, as Brian Arnott has pointed out, "was a conscientious effort to give theatrical validity to sounds, rhythms and myths that were distinctively Canadian." The political and theatrical interests of Salutin and Thompson meshed perfectly with the skills of the Passe Muraille company on *1837* and a year later on *1837: The Farmers' Revolt*, which became one of the most popular plays in the Canadian repertoire.

Thompson stayed on as artistic director until succeeded by Clarke Rogers in 1982, after which he pursued freelance projects including *Jessica* (1982) with Linda Griffiths and Maria Campbell. He served as Director-General of the National Theatre School, 1987–91, then returned to Passe Muraille in 1993 to direct a new collective called *Urban Donnellys*. Since then he has continued his work as director, co-author, and what he calls "scenarist" both with collectives and individual playwrights such as Griffiths. Theatre Passe Muraille itself underwent a series of artistic and financial crises, and gradually dissociated itself from the collective process, but remained a major force in the development of new Canadian plays throughout the 1980s and into the '90s under Rogers and his successors. In 1997 the company celebrated its thirtieth anniversary with a new production of *1837: The Farmers' Revolt*.

Rick Salutin collaborated with Passe Muraille again on the collective *Adventures of an Immigrant* (1974) and on his own plays *The False Messiah* (1975) and *Nathan Cohen: A Review* (1981). He also pursued the collective form with two Newfoundland companies in theatrical examinations of that province's history, *I.W.A.* with the Mummers Troupe (1976) and *Joey* with Rising Tide (1982). His play about hockey and nationalism in Quebec, *Les Canadiens*, first produced at the Centaur in 1977, won the Chalmers Award and has been widely performed across Canada. He collaborated with Ian Adams on the stage version of *S: Portrait of a Spy* (1984) for Ottawa's Great Canadian Theatre Company and wrote *Grierson and Gouzenko* (1986), a CBC-TV drama. He also wrote *The Reluctant Patriot* (1987), a ten-part radio drama for CBC's *Morningside*, commemorating the 150th anniversary of the 1837 rebellion.

In addition to playwriting, Salutin has written books on Canadian trade unionism (*Kent Rowley: The Organizer*, 1980) and the federal election and free trade debate of 1988 (*Waiting for Democracy: A Citizen's Journal*, 1989). *Marginal Notes* (1984) and *Living in a Dark Age* (1991) are lively collections of his award-winning journalism for a variety of newspapers and magazines, including *This Magazine* for which he was a long-time editor. His novels include *A Man of Little Faith*, winner of the *Books in Canada* First Novel Award for 1988, and *The Age of Improv* (1994), a futuristic look at Canadian politics. He currently writes a column for the *Globe and Mail*.

The politics of *1837: The Farmers' Revolt* are very much Salutin's own. The play presents a Canada lacking independence and subservient to British imperialism, finding its revolutionary impulse in the ordinary people of the time. Created during the heyday of Canadian nationalism, it was meant to speak to the contemporary sense of American imperial domination and economic, political and cultural colonialism many Canadians still feel. Salutin also intended the play as a corrective to what he called in a 1973 *Maclean's* article "The Great Canadian History Robbery": the textbook view of Canadian history in which "we learned that all our problems were resolved 'peaceably' long ago; that there is nothing in our history to get excited over; that Canadians don't *get* excited; that they never fight back against things as they've always been."

Ideology, however, was probably less crucial to the play's success than its theatricality, a product of the unique collective chemistry brought to bear in its creation. Salutin's diary reveals how he would bring in Mackenzie's newspaper article on the Family Compact or Robert Davis' book *The Canadian Farmer's Travels in the U.S.A.*, and Thompson would lead the actors on improvisational forays through it. The wittiest scenes in Act One, including "The Head" and "The Lady in the Coach," grew out of improvisations based on documentary material. The actors were also asked to improvise 1837 objects and do 1837 "anger exercises," the latter shaped by Salutin into the final scene of Act One. When necessary Salutin would script a scene (like "Doel's Brewery" opening Act Two), but as much as possible the emphasis was on the actors' imaginative reconstructions of the 1837 world, coaxed out of them by Thompson's sympathetic direction.

Salutin's final role was to shape the resulting material into a coherent, dramatically effective whole, and his success in that regard can be seen most clearly in Act One. Its non-linear arrangement of scenes masks a clever and deceptively rigorous dialectical structure. The farmers' struggle with the stump in "Clearing" and Mackenzie's with the mud in "Hat" are both amplified and clarified in "The Tavern" where the people learn that the system itself is the obstacle: the swamp that can only be cleared through collective action. The ensuing scene, "The Family Compact," further illuminates the system by individualizing the forces of oppression. Then the lovely "Mary Macdonald" introduces a wholly different kind of family compact, what Mackenzie will later call "the real nobility of Upper Canada." As Edward exits with Mary he warns, "there's ruts," and "The Lady in the Coach" bogs down in them. That scene provides a wonderful comic illustration of the imperialist approach to problem-solving—let the colonials pull us out of the mud while we give the orders—a view reaffirmed by Sir Francis' speech in "The Head" promising "paternal care" of his subjects. The self-fulfilling nature of such colonialist attitudes is vividly shown in "The Election of '36." Obviously the farmers haven't learned how to take care of themselves politically. Their only solution will be to develop a revolutionary consciousness.

The play's imaginative energy flags a little in the second act. Both Salutin and Thompson have acknowledged feeling "handcuffed by history" into presenting a more or less chronological narrative of the events of the rebellion ending with its defeat. Still, the historical narrative is leavened and humanized by the reintroduction of the non-historical characters we've met in Act One. The farmers, the collective hero, become almost as individualized as their catalyst, Mackenzie himself. And while history dictates that they must fail in the end, Salutin has taken mild dramatic license to ensure that defeat doesn't mean despair; we haven't really lost, we just haven't won ... yet. Salutin's preface, which follows, illuminates this distinction along with many of the other agonies and ecstasies involved in the making of the play.

1837: The Farmers' Revolt opened June 7, 1974, on tour in southwestern Ontario with the following cast:

Doris Cowan
David Fox
Eric Peterson
Miles Potter
Terry Tweed

Directed by Paul Thompson
Designed by Paul Williams

1837: THE FARMERS' REVOLT

PREFACE

1837 was first produced at Theatre Passe Muraille in Toronto in January, 1973. Here is a "diary" of that production.

Fall, 1972

Last year, while I was in rehearsal with a play called *Fanshen*, about the Chinese Revolution, the director said, "Now what we ought to do *next* year is—Quebec!"

Oh no, I thought. No more getting off on these exotic foreign revolutions. Next year if we do a revolution it will be right here in Ontario.

Sunday, Dec. 3

Drove out to the Niagara Peninsula with Paul (director) and Williams (designer). On a winding narrow road that once was the thoroughfare between Hamilton and the frontier we found a neglected monument, high as my waist and shaped like a gravestone. Divided into crescents, it read:

Up the hill 50 feet stood the home of Samuel Chandler Patriot

He guided Mackenzie to Buffalo

And here they had supper

Dec. 10, 1837

It is encouraging. With all the denigration spattered on the rebellion during our schooldays and since, I was beginning to ponder whether we were the first who had ever thought to treat it as a serious national event.

Wednesday, Dec. 6

Rehearsals begin tomorrow, the 7th, the anniversary of the Battle of Montgomery's Tavern. The 7th was also a Thursday in 1837. Odd how those things fuel you. We have no script yet, only general ideas of why and how we want to do it. I've tried too. In September, I sketched out scenes, then showed it to L. "Looks just the way we learned it in school," she said. Back to the drawing board. Paul is delighted. He said all along we're better off without a script, that it makes the actors lazy. Even if we had one, he'd be for hiding it. Fine—but what do they need me for?

Thursday, Dec. 7

We have six actors. Three men and three women. Two I know from *Fanshen*. The rest are strangers. I brought in a few goodies: maps and pictures of Old Toronto. Great stir at finding the *history* of places we've all lived around. We're starting very far back: other countries may have to relive or reinterpret their past, but they know they *have* a past. In Quebec they may hate it, but it's sure as hell there. English Canadians, at least around here, must be convinced there *is* a past that is all their own.

We paraded to Mackenzie House on Bond St. in midafternoon where little WASP women in period dress served us tea and apple butter. I nearly choked on it, and the rest of what they've wreaked on our only militant independantiste. Our work is cut out.

Before splitting up, we asked each of the actors to present an 1837 object. The best was Clare. She set herself before us and said:

I'm William Lyon Mackenzie's house. My feet are spread wide apart and are firmly planted. My hands are on my hips and I look straight ahead. I have *lots* of windows and any questions you ask me, I'm not afraid to answer.

It's already apparent that Paul is right. The absence of a script is drawing material out of the actors. After all, they have more theatre experience than anyone, and they're almost never asked to draw on it.

Friday, Dec. 8

We gave the actors anger exercises today. Each had to simulate anger around 1837. For some it was agony—or constipation. Neil was superb. "Nobody," he roared, "is going to make me speak with an English accent." That is a true Canadian actor's anti-imperialism. Theatre is one of the few areas left in Canada where the main imperial oppressor remains England and not the U.S. They run every regional theatre in the country; Englishmen waft over and drown in role offers. Stratford—our *national* theatre—gobbling public money to become an acknowledged *second* best in *another* country's national playwright. Neil was one of Stratford's golden boys—an apprentice—in its early years. Then he rebelled by going to act for twelve years in New York, instead of London. He's been back about two years now.

Last spring, when Paul and I first talked about this play, I said it was to be an anti-imperialist piece. He leaped joyfully and cried, "Right—we'll really smash the Brits"—making me wince, but in theatre he was right.

Monday, Dec. 11

First resistance. From Clare. She looked to me and said, "*There's* all the research—bottled up in your head—and we can't get at it."

Actors have been so infantilized. Writers tell them what to say and directors tell them where to stand and no one asks them to think for themselves. They come to work with Paul because they want to break that pattern, but then they freeze up. I remember my first horrified encounter with actors, during *Fanshen*. They were treating this play exactly as they would any other; it might have been *Barefoot in the Park*. Like the mailman, they'd deliver anything. It shocked me that they were like any other group in the country, politically, that is. But the actors are also the real proletariat of the theatre; that too was clear from the first rehearsal. They are the bottom rung. They take shit from everyone else, and *their* labour holds it all up: reproduces it all, night after night.

This matter of research: the material on 1837 is endless, to my surprise. The collective method takes the pressure off me for digesting all of it. Everyone reads like crazy. Mornings, before we start, the rehearsal room looks like a library.

Tuesday, Dec. 12

We're still concentrating on texture, and haven't begun to build scenes.

The woman problem remains completely unsolved, although we are ignoring it at this point. Paul originally wanted only one woman. I insisted on at least two and claimed we could show the class conflict through two women. He went along, and since Suzette became available, we now have three, in addition to the three men. But what will we do with them, given the paucity of the sources on women? I've ransacked the records, talked with historians, writers, feminists. All we find are interminable journals by the *gentle*women of the time, who complain of their hard life in the Bush, and how tough it is to get servants. Women didn't fight, and they didn't legislate. Clearly they worked. But what they did, and how they felt, in specifics … ? Every time I go back over it, I end up nowhere. In *Fanshen*, the woman issue was so *clear*.

Wednesday, Dec. 13

Williams brought in the set—that is, a mockup in a shoebox. What a triumph. A series of four platforms ranging from 2 to 8 feet off the floor connected by ramps which will be corduroyed. Plus five enormous trees set throughout the theatre that will tower up through the roof.

The effect of the platforms will be to give us the possibility of isolation and concentration—*plus* the possibility of movement (between the platforms); it is the best of all possible worlds, in terms of design. Instantly all our thinking about the play is transformed. I keep wandering by it and conjuring miniature people on the ramps.

Thursday, Dec. 14

We tried Mackenzie's newspaper piece on the Family Compact today. It's a fine hatchet job. He numbers them from one to thirty, and cross references them by number. We did it with five people taking all the roles—switching—and Neil reading. It will, I hope, become the definitive version of the Family Compact. I suppose I like it because I have been writing political satire for radio three years now and see Mackenzie's piece as the start of a Canadian tradition.

I gave Miles *The Canadian Farmer's Travels in the U.S.A.* to read. Written by an Upper Canadian farmer named Davis in 1836. I discovered it in the rare book room of the public library. Heartsick at the election of '36, he went travelling to the U.S., was thrilled by the abundance he saw everywhere and the efficacy of the democratic system, and resolved to return home and struggle for improvement here. He published the book, and died in the fighting in 1838. It's a very naive book—he's so overwhelmed by what he saw, that he loves *everything*—slavery, Indians—all of it. It's a trip scene and should work well, especially with the kind of energy Miles can give it.

More texturing: we've given everyone a minor character to do from the time. Someone who's barely mentioned in the records. Sally Jordan, who worked for Anne Langton, who wrote a journal. Ira Anderson, innkeeper, who's on the arrest record. A name mentioned in Mackenzie's paper as seconding a motion at a meeting. They must build their character according to what they know of the time. We'll quiz the actors in coming days on what may come out of it, but more important is the *thickness*—to pour into and onto whatever and whoever we end up using. We have to build the reality of the ordinary people of the time. They are the core of our past we have to get through to; they must be the centre of the play—not any of the "great" individuals who hog most of the records.

Friday, Dec. 15

Blizzard. After the break Janet said, "Can I go home?" and Paul said, "If you walk all the way up Yonge St. and do it in character." Upshot was we bundled up and trekked through Old Toronto. Down to the site of the hangings on King St., along King to Berkeley, up Parliament and over to the cemetery where Mackenzie, Lount and Matthews are buried. It was locked when we arrived. One thing we concluded: December was a hell of a time to make a revolution here.

Monday, Dec. 18

A row at the end of the day. "I'm sick of our Canadian politeness," Paul complained. We'd been doing break-ins by loyalists at the homes of rebels after the battle. The traditional Canadian knock at the door. Our intruders had tied themselves in knots trying not to be too, too nasty.

It is a crux: the ability to *really* identify with the main struggles and passions of the people at the time; else it will be just play-acting, better or worse. Clare dealt it back the strongest. "One of the nicest things about Canadians is that they *don't* get angry," she yelled.

I argued—academically I fear—that this "typical" Canadian reserve is not genetically rooted; that Canadians did fight and shout in 1837; and that our esteemed diffidence is the result of the failure and repression of such moments of resistance and assertion. If it is that historically based, we're not going to shake it loose by doing a passionate play; still, we may gain an inch or two.

Wednesday, Dec. 20

Pictures: we give the actors five minutes to rummage through books, choose an image, and give it back.

David plunged: "Now sir, when we moved onto that plot, there was nothing there. All I'm asking is … " Suzette hauled a table and chair in front of him, and leaned back like a contemptuous land agent. As he stammered on, about how he and his family had worked, the others filled in behind, chopping and clearing. Hewers of wood and drawers of water. Very strong. David is our staunchest, in a way. Our oak— (and we have Miles chop him down in a scene). He grew up in Kirkland Lake, taught high school ten years in Brantford, and did his first professional acting this past summer.

Janet did a brilliant picture. Back to us, passed her palm above her head, saying, "A smooth broad forehead." Then she stood Suzette and Neil side by side facing us as, "Two piercing eyes." Drew their inner arms forward together as, "A classic nose." Got Clare in to make a mouth; and announced it was John Beverley Robinson, one of the leading members of the Compact. Now to find a way of integrating it into the production so that it becomes more than a *tour de force* of theatricality.

(The "Head" developed this way: Paul felt we had to make it the head of Lieutenant-Governor Francis Bond Head, not Robinson, since Mackenzie had been so fond of punning on Head's name. Neil found a speech by Bond Head that was the quintessence of the Imperial attitude; as one of the eyes he also delivered it. It fit perfectly as the prelude to the Canadian Farmer's Travels to the U.S. The whole didn't come together until weeks after Janet had given us the original image.)

Friday, Dec. 22

There was no point trying to rehearse today. Everyone is gripped with job insecurity, because Actors' Equity is about to shut down Factory Theatre Lab, and is preparing an offensive against the other small Canadian theatres like ourselves. Ostensibly the issue is kickbacks. Equity actors who work at the small theatres must sign contracts at Equity rates, but since these are unrealistic for the small theatres, they often return a part of what they are paid. We have four Equity actors and they've all received threatening letters from *their* union. (They can't seem to get the incongruity of this through their heads.) They fear they'll be expelled. We talked all day, mostly about American unions and how typical this is of the way they operate in Canada—and about other forms of imperialism, especially American. I am the only one with a thoroughly paranoid interpretation: that Equity's real purpose is to shut down the small Canadian theatres because they provide increasing competition and audience drain from the downtown mausoleums that house touring Broadway shows, American-mounted productions, to which Equity gives its main allegiance. I was alone in deeming it a conspiracy, but various forms of fear and indignation reign among the rest. They're tired of yearly questionnaires from Equity asking how many hours they've worked on-Broadway, off-Broadway, etc. There is certainly no way of avoiding this discussion in the context of the play we are making.

Boxing Day

Finally tried Ventriloquism. Inspired by a handbill for an 1830's travelling show (" ... and featuring—VENTRILOQUISM"). It's a perfect metaphor for colonialism—maybe too perfect? Divided our actors into teams of dummy and master; David and Clare were far the best technically. Now to work on the problem of what they're to say.

Thursday, Dec. 28

We had our good day today, as Janet said.

For his anger homework, David came in with a team stuck in the mud. Got off his wagon, stuffed his shoulder against a wheel, shoved and cursed. Others moved in as horses etc., and Janet sang "God Save the Queen." *Finally* we got behind the academicism of the "roads" issue. Each time someone uses it, it sounds plucked from the section of the textbook called *Causes of the Rebellion.* We've taken to barking "Cause Three" when they mention roads, and "Cause Four" to the Clergy Reserves. But this was real and *felt.*

Neil began musing about the secret meeting at Doel's Brewery in Toronto before the rebellion— the night when the city was unguarded and Mackenzie urged his fellow reformers to seize it and the four thousand arms that were there. I've yearned to do it from the start. It was the time to act, but they stalled till they could bring down the farmers to take the risks for them. Had they acted there is no doubt our history would have been different. The British would have been forced to return half their forces from Quebec, where fighting had already begun; the French just might then have succeeded; in Ontario there'd have been arms and impetus ... Still, dreams aside, the point of the scene is not to show what might have been, but the unreliability and timidity of bourgeois leadership in a struggle for Canadian independence. Then as now, Paul felt it was too programmatic to get out of the actors, but Neil was so keen on it that we both gulped, "Let's try it." It went not badly, broad lines emerged, and in this one case, I am going to write it up as a scene, based on the improvised work. My first chance to be a playwright. Now they get a chance to judge my work.

We finally got the Davis scene, the Canadian farmer travelling in the U.S. Miles had had an anxiety attack each time he moved into it. Today we literally sat on him, holding him down, and by the time he finally escaped he'd gathered so much energy it carried him right through the trip.

The key is to satirize the farmer's enthusiasm for all things American. To put through our eyes what we saw through his. On one side lethargic Windsor (yawns) and then—Industrious Detroit—everyone pumping and rushing and HAPPY. He adores it all; Neil ran up and said, "Excuse me sir, I'm a runaway slave, which way is Canada?" and he said—"No, don't go, it'll get better here." Got quite wild, snatches of Aquarius, etc. Very exciting. I'm still excited about it.

Friday, Dec. 29

I've got a last line. Talking with Suzette about Canadian plays and what downers they are—always about losers. Yet what to do? Our past is negative. The country has remained a colony; the struggle in 1837 did not succeed. I've thought of changing the ending, having the rebels win (Stop that Hanging!); or cutting off before the battle and the defeat, at, say, the high point in October '37. But finally we have to wrestle with what actually happened and wring something positive out of that. Losing, I argued, does not have to make you a "Loser"; there are winners who lose. It is the difference between saying, "We lost," and saying, "No, we just haven't won yet." There it is.

Saturday, Dec. 30

The Family Compact is turning into a hell, more demoralizing each time we run it. The novelty of the numbering has worn off, they are reaching for ever more corn to cover their changes. We're down to staging number 21-25 as a bloody cricket match. Paul can't get it. Damn. Paul's strength—his genius—is working with people and eliciting their creativity. I try to help—but I'm no director. Christ what a loss it would be—it's right there!

Sunday, Dec. 31

They showed me a scene Suzette had improvised yesterday while I was out. An English gentlewoman doing the tour of the colonies gets stuck in her coach on the road from Toronto to Niagara, blusters at the driver, fidgets about her manservant, yammers endlessly, but together they push free and suddenly she is ecstatic about the "adventure" they've just had. ("My cousin Stephanie was one experience up on me, you know.") I loathed her—extolling "Nature's cathedral" which only she and not the gruff coachman could appreciate, bidding "Goodbye Brave Bush," before she'd climb back in the coach. I grabbed for one of our stage rifles and would gladly have plugged her through her "jaded, civilized eyes." But she is so right and brilliant and hilarious—I suppose there will be no way of keeping it out of the play.

We are starting to think about how to shape these things. About time. It is New Year's Eve. We open on the 17th.

Tuesday, Jan. 2

Working with Mackenzie's newspaper again. Divided them, as usual, into an upper class and a dirt poor family, each reacting to the same articles differently. Today though, they fell into interrupting each other's readings and emerged in fullblown battle. All the good arguments were with the reactionaries. And all the articulateness. "My dear man, you can't expect illiterate farmers to actually *govern?*" "What do *you* know about economics?" "Are you admitting then that you are *disloyal?*" On and on, Neil and his gathering steam; David and his, being ground down. Miles (for the rich) made some patronizing analogy, to which David tried pathetically to respond. Janet got closer to the class reality, barging in with, "That's a stupid argument!" Suzette cooed, "Why can't we all get *along?*" in a perfect Rosedale tone. Janet tore through the paper looking for counter-arguments, looking to us—what she really felt was—if only Mac was here, he'd tell them. We suddenly saw Mackenzie's real importance for these people. The oppressed never control the ideological apparatus; it is always used by the ruling classes to confuse and demoralize them. Mackenzie took the ideological skills he possessed and put them at the disposal of the oppressed instead of the oppressors, doing for them what they had not been given the resources to do for themselves. He really served the people. What nonsense the way we learned it—as if it was Mackenzie against the Family Compact in personal combat. It was the working people against the Empire. They were the centre, but they needed him.

Wednesday, Jan. 3

I distributed the script for the brewery scene today; reaction was astounding. They blinked and wouldn't believe—a real script—went berserk with gratitude and joy. Much feigned, of course, but it came from somewhere. The pressure and demands on them in this method of work are vast. That we knew; but not quite how *much*.

Most striking was how the presence of a script shot everyone into an instant role. They became actors, underlining their speeches and saying bitchy things like, "Let me feel my way into this, will you?" Paul became a director urging interpretations and line readings on them ("Let me coach you"). And I became a writer, skulking in back, gritting my teeth at what they were doing to "my" lines, nodding when they "got it," and not intervening except to occasionally whisper to Paul. Till now, roles have been loose; everyone was writing, directing and acting, though of course not all to the same extent. With the script, compartmentalization sets in like terminal cancer. I'm glad we did it—just this one scene—to watch it happen.

Toward the end of the day, with everyone tired and loath to take on a bummer like the Compact, Paul spied a length of rope in the corner, looped it six times, put it over their heads and told them they were prisoners being returned to Toronto after the rebellion. They trudged and told us what they felt and saw. Too much self-pity at the moment, but a strong image and one that will work on our set. Where did that come from? I asked Paul. Desperation, he said.

Friday, Jan. 5

Last night I read through seven or eight accounts of the Siege of Toronto between Dec. 4 and 7, culminating with the Battle, and typed a composite account, very long and detailed. Then I cut it up with scissors into thirty different pieces, numbered, and this morning gave five pieces to each actor. Each has to say his section as they come up in sequence, though everyone acts out the events. It will take lots of choreography and coordination, and we will be at it once a day till we open— like taking vitamins, says Paul. I think our audiences will be captivated—all those warlike events up and down Yonge St.

I feel less guilt about my contribution, now that I've done some scripting. And I think I can see the shape of Act II. From Doel's, through the Battle, the march of the prisoners, the hangings. We'll be leaping right into the maw of the defeat, and see what kind of victory we can bring from it. But as for Act I, God only knows …

Monday, Jan. 8

Awful. Just awful. I can't say how bad. There is nothing there. And they will not work, will not give. The Family Compact is a horror; we haven't dared touch it in five days. Miles is stumped on his Farmer's Travels. We all see what a good scene it is; we've seen him do it brilliantly; but he's clogged up, he makes excuses and accuses Paul of not directing him. Paul fires back that Miles won't commit himself. I stalk around the theatre—we moved in today out of the rehearsal room— wanting to rip Miles into bits for his stingy withholding. I know that's false, but it's what I feel. Paul and I confer hostilely, and they pick it up and sulk or fling back angry glares—Janet is doing that more and more. We are at a dead halt—no, we are careening backwards. There is no giving, no expansiveness—and no script to fall back on!

Christ, I said to Paul, is it this way every time?

I don't know, he sighed. I can't remember. I guess so.

How do you stand it?

I must forget. If I remembered, I would never do it again.

Tuesday, Jan. 9

Today it was Clare. She has no lines in the Doel's scene, but is a brewery hand who sets it up and works away in the background while the leaders of the rebellion are conspiring below. She is the lurking presence of the ordinary working people who will have to take all the chances while most of their "leaders" sit tight. But she's been a lump. I challenged her on it and she maintained that since she knows nothing about brewing beer, she can't act it. I said she should figure out something that seemed to her like brewing and do that. She pouted that she'd take off the rest of the day and go research brewing in the library. More tight-assed withholding—I stormed off. Paul? I don't know where he gets the patience. Like a shrink fighting through layers of resistance, he patiently counters argument after argument of hers till she admits she just doesn't want to take a chance. Then she went ahead and did it—beautifully. I don't know what the hell *she* thought she was doing, but at the least it didn't look like *not* brewing beer.

Wednesday, Jan. 10

The Ventriloquism is in trouble. We haven't figured out how to use it—is it metaphor, is it to the audience, is it within the play itself? David and Clare are balking, say it's no fun, no point. I'll try and script it as a two minute skit—as if I were writing for radio.

We did get the Family Compact. We'd written it off regretfully but I was looking at the set today—ramps running down from platform to platform—and said, Why don't we try it on the ramps, unwinding the Compact from top to bottom? So we did, and we have a scene.

Thursday, Jan. 11

Came up with an Act I closing. Our anger exercises. Spread our people over the set, doing bursts of anger one after another. They made them up on the spot; some were extraordinary.

> MILES: *(climbing off the floor onto the set)* I don't care who you are and what your name is. From now on you can clean the muck out from under your own damned English footbridge.

> NEIL: See this cabinet. Took me six months. Know why I can't sell it? Because it was made in *(an awful angry whine)* Torrrrooonnntttoooo—

> JANET: So I sez to her—Milk your *own* cow!

And finally a chance to use Suzette's Quebec half: Moé-la, j'aimais plus je'n chant'rai pour les Anglais!

It is the boiling point of 1837, where grievances and resentments are irrepressible and have to burst into the action of the rebellion itself—in Act II.

Friday, Jan. 12

Just what we'd considered our strongest suit—the pictures—just won't work down here in the theatre. They were grand in the little rehearsal room with the low ceiling but—ah well, they served their purpose: got us into the texture of the time.

Saturday, Jan. 13

Worked with David on his (Lount's) gallows speech. He's been to the provincial archives mornings this week, reading accounts of the trial of Lount and Matthews.

Finally found a use for those lists I like so much—the names of those arrested or charged in the aftermath of the rebellion. 885 men, their homes, and occupations. Fine names—Caleb Kipp, Josiah Dent, Joshua Doan: yeoman, labourer, tanner, etc. When I have been stymied by this work both before and then during rehearsals, I've taken to reading through those names. I've wanted to employ them as a sort of litany. They work well into the rope scene, the march of the prisoners. Each gives his name and when they've gone round once, they go round again, and then again, creating with the six an endless line of captured revolutionaries. I gave a page of names to each actor; they can choose the ones they'll use each night.

The final form is now clear. Act I will be fairly diffuse, a view of the life of the times—our blessed texture—though building to the inevitability of the outbreak. It should end high, with the feeling, This Can't Miss. After intermission we change pace completely.

Act II drives right through with the line of the rebellion, defeat and aftermath. It will have the guts of our politics, what we make of this event and why we are returning to it now.

Monday, Jan. 15

We hit the crunch today with the Farmer's Travels. Miles capsized again midway. He tried to get Paul to call it off, cut the scene, give it to someone else—do *something*. I could see Paul struggling with the offer; then he leapt up on the set and refused. Said he would not become the paternalistic director at this point. If Miles really wanted to do the scene, Paul would stand by him no matter how much it seemed to lack—and he was sure the audience would accept it. Or—if Miles really didn't want to do it, *he* would have to say so. It was a trap for Paul and he was magnificent in avoiding it. Suzette, bless her, said, "I vote to have it in," not pressing but making the point that, if not Miles, then someone else should do it. Miles wrestled with it, started the trip again, stalled, slumped down, and said, "I don't want to do it like this." "O.K.," said Paul, "Janet—will you try it?"

Janet looked to Miles, he nodded generously, she launched it, and was fine. When we tried it again later, Miles came in as the wife, urging the farmer not to leave for the States. It works, and I think it also means we've solved the women problem as far as we can. Clare argued with me the other day that one of the men on the scaffold should be played by a woman, and I argued back that it would be so obtrusive that we would end up with a scene about the equality of women, not about 1837. It might be right politically, but if it doesn't work as theatre there is no point in doing it in a play. Janet plays a man because it has become dramatically necessary in the travel scene. We have women playing men in the battle and the brewery scene for the same reason and it is unobtrusive there. We've failed to find a centrality for women in 1837 terms. But we are *doing* the play in *our* terms—with an equal cast, fair distribution of parts, etc. It is an attempt to portray an oppressive reality in a liberated way.

Tuesday, Jan. 16

We've put the Ventriloquism unit as the introduction to the meeting Mackenzie addresses before the rebellion. As a skit presented by two farmers for their friends at the rally. Agitprop of '37. Allows the other actors to react to it as *its* audience, drains off the heavy symbolism, and clarifies that Clare is playing a real person who is *playing* a dummy.

Great consternation about the newspaper scene with which we'd wanted to open. It is important for me 1) to open a play about Canadian history with a scene of class conflict, and 2) to show the centrality of Mackenzie's paper—its propaganda and education—for the movement. Paul's retort was—it's not doing either of those things as it is now. I had to agree. We put it to them and—wonder of wonders—they say they want to do it as we have it and are sure they can pull it off tomorrow night, though they'd like me to settle on four or five articles and choose an order for them. Instead of suggesting another cut, they propose an inclusion—a good, good sign.

The programs came today, and I like them. They are of a piece with the rest of this work: single sheets with a map of Old Toronto and an alphabetical list of the people who made the play.

I think I see now Paul's vision of theatre and the value he places on improvisation. Without a script, there is real tension and the possibility of creative breakthrough on stage at any moment. It is not set. People come to plays thinking of them as movies or TV gone live, perfect realizations of a script or theme, and frozen at that point of perfect realization. But a play is made live each night, and its possibility is not frozen perfection but ongoing re-creation. The edge for an audience should not be awe at a perfect performance, but anxiety about something new and possibly better at any moment.

Opening Night

Two instructive things happened. When Clare started Act II with "Bay and Adelaide, the north-west corner," the audience laughed. If an actor said, "Montmartre, 4 a.m.," or "Piccadilly Circus, twelve noon," no audience anywhere would laugh. But we are so imbued with self-denial, so colonized, that the very thought of something historic happening *here*, at Bay and Adelaide, draws laughs.

Again, during the Battle, in the nighttime skirmish when both inexperienced sides broke ranks and fled, Miles lost his line for a moment, and the audience laughed. Miles—American Miles—said that moment made clear to him for the first time what I'd been saying about the problem of Canadian history for a Canadian audience. There was nothing funny about the moment. It was terrifying or should have been.

Three Weeks Later

The actors have come to take it as a challenge to deliver those lines so that the audience cannot laugh at them. At the same time, Janet says the response to *1837* is different from any play she's ever appeared in. It's not just appreciation. It's something warmer.

It is, I think, identification. Beyond the identification you get in any good theatre. It is a meeting with ourselves.

Over a year later, the play was reworked. The result—amounting to a new play—was called *1837: The Farmers' Revolt*. It was produced in the spring, summer and fall of 1974—first in the auction barns of southwestern Ontario, then in Victoria Playhouse in Petrolia, Ontario, and then in Toronto. It has since had many productions throughout the country. It is the script of this latter production which is included below.

1837: The Farmers' Revolt was developed in exactly the same way as the first version of the play. But it was meant for a tour of farming communities instead of an urban theatre audience and it differed from the earlier play in the following ways.

It was not Toronto-centred. In the first *1837* we had made hay of the events and locales of early Toronto. We de-emphasized these in the country, and looked for elements that reflected what had happened out there, where we were planning to tour the show.

So, for instance, we cleared a larger space for Anthony van Egmond, the old colonel who led the revolutionary force at Montgomery's Tavern. Van Egmond had lived just outside Seaforth—in the village now called Egmondville. The family home is still standing, and local people are restoring it.

Instead of showing the entire four days of fighting around Toronto, we showed only the final battle there. For the first three days, we went out to the country, and followed Van Egmond, as he marched from his home down to Toronto, to take command of the forces there.

Numerous such changes in the script occurred. Another change which took place was, in a way, political.

The earlier play—beamed into the Toronto milieu—could assume a somewhat left-of-liberal politics on the part of the audience; more or less of a sympathy, or at least tolerance, for the revolutionary sentiments of the play. But the farming community is, at least in its explicit attitudes, far more conservative. So some of the rhetoric—what Miles called the "bombast"—came out. And more justification of the movement for change went in. For instance, we had two scenes, instead of one, depicting the bitterness of the farmers over the land policies of the 1830s.

The play also changed dramatically, or artistically.

It became much tighter than the earlier version. In the first version, for example, we served the battle up whole. In the second, by concentrating on the experience of Van Egmond, we gave the scene a dramatic focus it had lacked. In the end, I would say version two (the one included here) is a far better play.

This is largely so because on the first time round we were intent on getting clear *what* we were going to say about 1837. By round two, that most crucial of matters was basically settled; we could concentrate on how to say it more effectively, refining scenes, characters, etc. The resulting script proves, I think, that the collective process can produce a play as dramatically tight as the more typical scripting approach.

In some ways though, I preferred the earlier version. It would not make as good reading, and it did not play as well. Yet it had a rawness and a timeliness. It felt to me, when we first put this show up in January of 1973, that we were expressing something of what was happening in the country at the time: a determination to throw off colonial submissiveness in all areas. *1837* was a theatrical expression of that feeling, making it more of a political event, and not just, or even primarily, a theatrical one.

By the second time round, a mere year and a half later, things seemed to have changed, have slowed. The movement for Canadianization of trade unions had *not* yet taken off; the universities were more dominated than ever by Americans; the Waffle had been expelled from the NDP, largely for its nationalism; the cries for economic control had muted. The nationalist, anti-imperialist impetus was still present, and *more* necessary than ever; but it was less fresh, was in a bit of a withdrawal.

And so the play became more of a theatrical, and less of a political, event. That is why I preferred version one, though version two is no doubt superior "theatre."

1837: The Farmers' Revolt had an original cast of five: three men and two women. Men played women, and women played men, or animals or objects or parts of the body—depending on the needs of the scene. There were very few props. I mention this because anyone reading the script will be tempted to imagine a well-equipped cast of thousands.

The actors who worked on the various productions were Janet Amos, Clare Coulter, Suzette Couture, Doris Cowan, David Fox, Eric Peterson, Miles Potter, Terry Tweed, and Neil Vipond. I had a notion of including a list with this script indicating which actors were primarily responsible for which scenes—but when it comes to the doing it is terrifically difficult to assign such credit. So I will just reiterate that the play is *entirely* a creation of the company in rehearsals and performance. The present script is an after-the-fact, somewhat composite, effort, assembled *following* the close of the fall 1974 run.

The director of *1837* was Paul Thompson. The designer was Paul Williams. I was the writer on—but not of—*1837*.

Rick Salutin

1837: THE FARMERS' REVOLT

ACT ONE

WALKING

A man is walking on the set. He carries an axe and a sack. He walks and walks, seeing the forests and the occasional cleared farm of Upper Canada pass by him as he goes. The audience are still entering. They are asking each other, Who is he? Where's he going? What's he got with him? He keeps walking. This is a play about a time when people in Canada walked to get anywhere and do anything. Eventually two FARMERS enter, one stage left and one stage right. They are taking a rest. They watch him go by their field.

FIRST FARMER: Who is that fellow?

SECOND: Name's Thomas Campbell.

FIRST: Where's he from?

SECOND: Glasgow.

He walks. Enter two more FARMERS.

THIRD FARMER: Where's he going?

FOURTH: He's bought a plot of land near Coldwater.

They watch him awhile. They are all tired from hard work.

SECOND: How much did it cost him?

FIRST: Twenty dollars down—he'll work the rest out.

FOURTH: How long has he been walking?

THIRD: Four and a half days.

FIRST: *(feeling his own feet)* Ouch.

SECOND: Does he have any family?

FOURTH: Wife. Son. Three daughters. Younger brother. All back in Scotland. They'll be over later.

THIRD: What's he got with him?

FIRST: Everything he owns.

SECOND: Think he knows how to use that axe?

THIRD: If he doesn't, he'll learn.

FIRST: What does he see?

THIRD: Trees.

SECOND: Trees.

FOURTH: Trees.

FIRST: Trees and trees and trees and trees—

They all fill in the word "trees" as he speaks. They are planting a forest of trees with their voices. It mounts, then recedes and dies.

THIRD: What's he going to do when he gets there?

He gets there. He puts down his load, very weary. Looks around at the trees, up at the trees, tries to see through to the sky. He decides not to rest, raises his axe, and begins clearing his land.

Blackout.

CLEARING

Grunts and sounds of straining in the dark. Lights up slowly. Four people working around a great (imaginary) stump, hacking it and hauling it. With one mighty heave it comes loose and they fall away from it, spent.

VOICE: *(offstage)* Hallooooo—

STEADMAN: *(panting)* Hallooo—

VOICE: *(offstage)* Is there a Peter Steadman there?

They lie there, too exhausted to respond. Enter MAGISTRATE THOMPSON, obviously an official. He approaches one of them.

MAGISTRATE: Peter Steadman?

He is motioned toward STEADMAN.

MAGISTRATE: Magistrate Thompson, from Richmond Hill.

STEADMAN: Magistrate, how do you do? *(With distaste, the MAGISTRATE shakes STEADMAN's sweaty hand.)* It's a long ride from Richmond Hill. Will you take something to drink? Sit down?

MAGISTRATE: Thank you, no.

STEADMAN'S WIFE: Can I get you anything?

MAGISTRATE: No. I was told I would find you here.

STEADMAN: We've been here a long time.

MAGISTRATE: How long, exactly?

STEADMAN: Close to two years.

MAGISTRATE: This is fine land. How much have you cleared?

STEADMAN: Eighteen acres.

STEADMAN'S BROTHER: Eighteen acres in two years!

STEADMAN'S WIFE: We've been working hard.

MAGISTRATE: Yes. Congratulations. That's a fine home.

STEADMAN'S WIFE: First one I've ever had that was my own.

STEADMAN: We were going to come up to Toronto to see you people pretty soon.

MAGISTRATE: Good, black, fertile soil.

STEADMAN: Yes, it's a good farm.

MAGISTRATE: Could I see your deed please, Mr. Steadman?

STEADMAN: I don't have a deed.

MAGISTRATE: Then your letter of license.

STEADMAN: Now I wouldn't have one of those without a deed, would I?

MAGISTRATE: Mr. Steadman, don't presume to tell me my business. (He unrolls a survey map, which looks to us like a Union Jack.) Your lot is number seventeen. On this government survey map, lot seventeen, here in the corner—I see no record whatever of the name Steadman. But it *is* part of a parcel of one thousand acres which was granted three weeks ago to Colonel Sparling of the Forty-Eighth Highlanders.

STEADMAN: Granted!

MAGISTRATE: By the Lieutenant-Governor.

STEADMAN'S SISTER-IN-LAW: This farm is not for sale!

STEADMAN'S BROTHER: You listen—we homesteaded this land.

MAGISTRATE: I choose to call it squatting.

STEADMAN'S BROTHER: Call it what you want. It's what everybody does when they don't have any money to start.

MAGISTRATE: And everybody who does it accepts the risk that something of this sort will happen.

STEADMAN: (trying to be reasonable) I'll be glad to go down to Toronto and talk to this Colonel and buy the land from him.

MAGISTRATE: Mr. Steadman, I know with certainty that he simply does not want you on his land. He is not however an ungenerous man, and if you approach him on the right footing, he might be willing to recompense you for your labour on his land.

STEADMAN'S BROTHER: How's he going to pay us for two years of clearing?

MAGISTRATE: He wants you off the land. You have one week, Steadman.

STEADMAN: (burning) You have one minute, Magistrate—to get off my farm.

STEADMAN'S BROTHER picks up his axe. The MAGISTRATE beats a retreat.

MAGISTRATE: (as he goes) One week, Steadman—

STEADMAN: (calling after him) We'll be here a week from now, Magistrate. We'll be here long after you're dead—

Now that they are left alone again, the anger quickly drops away and doubt sets in.

STEADMAN'S WIFE: What do we do now?

STEADMAN: (ponders, then—) Go back to work. Come on—

They set in around the stump again, straining and grunting. Lights down slowly to black.

HAT

Lights up on MACKENZIE.

MACKENZIE: My name is William Lyon Mackenzie. I run a small newspaper here in Toronto—it's called *The Advocate*. Used to be *The Colonial Advocate*, but I decided it was high time to get rid of the "Colonial" part. It's a good paper, pick one up if you get the chance. Now I was on my way down King Street to the office the other day—and it had rained just the night before. Well, any time it rains here the roads turn into quagmires, and the only way you can use them is to pick your way from one high, dry spot to another. So I was picking my way along King— just outside here—when I noticed this hat lying in the mud in the middle of the road. Well, it looked like a good hat and I decided it was worth muddying my boots to get it, so I picked my way over … *(He is doing it.)* … best I could, and I picked up the hat.

As he lifts the hat he uncovers a MAN's head. The MAN spits out a mouthful of mud.

MACKENZIE: There was a man under it! *(to MAN)* It looks like you're in trouble.

MAN: Yes, I certainly am.

MACKENZIE: *(bending down to hoist him)* Here, let me give you a hand.

MAN: You're quite a little fellow. I think you'd better go for some help.

MACKENZIE: Oh I'm pretty tough. I think I can pull you out myself.

MAN: But it's not just me I'm worrying about. It's the wagon and the two oxen!

Blackout.

THE TAVERN

Onstage right: ISAAC CASSELMAN, Tavernkeeper; EMMA, his wife; RUTH, a friend and customer; and JAMEY, local drunk and part-time help at the tavern.

ISAAC: *(singing)*
When I got up in the morning,
My heart did give a wrench,
For lying on the table
Was the captain and a wench—

Freeze. Enter FRED BENCH, stage left. Addresses audience.

FRED: That's why you cut your roots and come thousands of miles across the ocean—to buy your own land, be your own boss. I just got back from Toronto about that very thing—

Tavern action resumes.

ISAAC: *(singing)*
And then one fine spring morning,
I did a dancing jig—

Freeze.

FRED: This is Isaac Casselman's Inn. When I'm not working in the bush I spend most of my time right here.

Tavern resumes.

ISAAC: For lying on the table was the captain and—

Enter FRED.

ISAAC: Fred Bench! You're back—

EMMA: Fred—welcome home.

FRED: Hello Emma. Jamey! Hasn't Isaac fired you yet?

JAMEY: He can't fire me Fred.

FRED: Why not?

JAMEY: *(tottering into cellar)* I'm the only one who knows the inventory—

FRED: Ruth—

They embrace. RUTH is so excited she can't talk. Enter JAMEY, carrying a keg.

JAMEY: In your honour Fred. The best keg of rum in Isaac's cellar.

FRED: How do you know that Jamey?

JAMEY: Because I tested four others before I found it. It's the best.

EMMA: Fred—come on and tell us some good stories about Toronto.

RUTH: And show us what you've got!

ISAAC: Now first things first. In honour of the traveller's return—a toast!

ALL: Hear hear; a toast; etc.

They all take mugs.

ISAAC: To Fred Bench—and his new land.

ALL BUT FRED: To Fred Bench and—

FRED: Hold it. That's not quite right. To Fred Bench—and his *almost* land.

ISAAC: Wha—?

EMMA: Have you been drinking Fred?

JAMEY: *(undaunted)* To Fred Bench and the almost land. *(down the hatch)*

RUTH: What do you mean?

FRED: Haven't touched a drop Emma. At least not yet. But now I'll tell you that story. Do you want to hear it?

ALL: Yes; *etc.*

FRED: It's a story about Toronto. What a city! For three days I walked through the bush. It was dark. Trees blocking out almost all the light. But when you get to the top of Yonge St., that bush just sweeps away. And there's Toronto. Morning fog coming in off the lake. Spires poking through here and there. It was like a dream. And I knew that day the city belonged to Fred Bench! Down into it I went—why, do you know they've got it built up all the way to Queen St.? *(disbelief)* I walked right in alongside the gentlemen and ladies. Isaac—you should see the taverns they've got now. And the traffic. Right along the flagstone sidewalks of King Street to the Courthouse—that's where the Land Office is. Up the steps—just a whiff of fish coming in from the wharf—inside are pillars that lay the fear of God in you. And there's the Land Office. And behind its thick oak door sits the Commissioner of Crown Lands. *(He is seized with an idea.)* Jamey—c'mere. You want to help me show these fine people some of the facts of life?

JAMEY: *(stumbling to FRED's side)* Facts of life? You've come to the right man for the facts of life.

FRED: Stand over here Jamey. Peter Robinson, Commissioner of Crown Lands. *(JAMEY looks around.)* No. That's you. Straight and tall. Fine satin shirt. Stiff collar. *(JAMEY begins to assume the role.)* Velvet trousers. And boots that you can see your face in.

JAMEY: *(He has become the Lands Commissioner.)* Shine my boots Fred!

FRED: Oh yes sir! Because you see, you control all the government land in the province.

JAMEY: All the land in the province? Mine?

FRED: Lord Jamey!

JAMEY: That's me—Lord Jamey!

FRED moves away from JAMEY.

FRED: Now on the other side of this oak door is the waiting room, three times the size of your tavern Isaac. And it's packed with people like me—all wanting land.

RUTH: Come on, let's help him out.

They all join FRED in the waiting room.

FRED: And we're packed in so tight—fifty or sixty of us—that we can't even sit down. Hey, Jamey, we got no land, you got it all. What do you think of us?

JAMEY: *(swaggering)* I think you're all—pieces of dirt!

FRED: We just couldn't get past the door. We waited one, two, three, four days, and never saw the Commissioner. Then, on the fifth day, in walks a private land agent—a Mr. Bronlyn. *(ISAAC assumes the role as FRED talks.)* A rich man, in a grey suit, with a bit of a paunch and cold grey eyes that look right through anything and anyone they—

BRONLYN barges right through the waiting room, slapping people out of his way. The COMMISSIONER opens the door to him.

ISAAC: *(as BRONLYN)* Ah, Mr. Commissioner—

JAMEY: Mr. Bronlyn, come in. *(to the others)* Slam!

EMMA: Fred—you mean he just walked in there—nice as you please!

FRED: Just like that.

EMMA: What'd you do?

FRED: What would you do?

EMMA stalks up to the door and knocks.

EMMA: Mr. Commissioner! I want to talk to you. We were promised land. We've been waiting here for five days. Some of us are hungry. You've got to—

JAMEY: *(without opening door)* My dear woman—who do you think you're talking to? The Commissioner of Crown Lands—that's who you're talking to. Now can't you see I'm busy? Go away. I've got important business to discuss with my friend, Mr. Bronlyn. If you want, you can leave your names with my clerk.

FRED: So we left our names with the clerk, walked out of the waiting room, and stood around Toronto for another two days. And then, in comes Mr. Bronlyn.

ISAAC: Is there a Mr. Bench here? A Mr. Fred Bench?

FRED: Yeah?

ISAAC: Mr. Bench, I understand that you wish to purchase some land.

FRED: Oh yes, yes sir—you bet I do.

ISAAC: Well I have just the land for you. One hundred acres of good, fertile—

FRED: And I have the twenty dollars here to buy it.

ISAAC: You don't understand Mr. Bench. This land sells for two hundred dollars an acre.

RUTH: What?

EMMA: But that's two hundred dollars—

ISAAC: That's correct, Madam. Well Mr. Bench—

FRED: Now hold on. I got the newspaper that says I can get one hundred acres of government land for twenty dollars.

ISAAC: That might be, Mr. Bench—though I rather doubt it. But I do not represent the government. I am a private land agent. I sell land for a profit.

FRED: (to EMMA and RUTH) Now where did he get my name?

JAMEY: (still in his "office") I gave it to him, Fred. I gave him all your names—for a little ... consideration.

FRED: A little consideration. You see, they're in it together. Two crooks working hand in glove.

ISAAC: Well Mr. Bench? Do you or do you not want to buy the land? (reverting to himself) What'd you do, Fred?

FRED: I laughed in his face, grabbed him by his fancy shirt, and threw him out—because nobody makes a fool of Fred Bench!

EMMA: Good for you, Fred!

JAMEY: You really did, did you Fred?

RUTH: You mean ... you didn't get the land ... there's nothing ...

FRED: (keeping up the bravado) Well—no. But I've still got twenty dollars, and if it's not going for land, it's going for the biggest party we've ever had around here! Jamey—come on—

JAMEY: I'm with you Fred—

FRED: Isaac, more drinks—

All but RUTH cheer and raise their glasses. Freeze. Lights down on them. RUTH, alone on the other side of the stage, wails her disappointment.

Blackout.

THE FAMILY COMPACT

MACKENZIE: Ladies and gentlemen, this evening for your entertainment, and with the help of my charming assistant ... (enter charming ASSISTANT) ... I would like to demonstrate for you a magical trick. Now the thing that interests me about magic is not so much the phenomenon of the trick itself, as how it is actually accomplished, and I shall try to perform this trick in such a way that you can share its secret with me. (to ASSISTANT) We need the volunteers onstage. (to audience) I would have got volunteers from the audience, but you're all far too respectable for that.

Enter the three VOLUNTEERS. They are a sullen, brutish lot.

MACKENZIE: Now this trick will go down in the annals of conjuring history as one of the most remarkable ever performed anywhere in the world, for you are about to see this gang of thieves, rogues, villains and fools transformed before your very eyes into the ruling class of this province. Yes indeed—this band of criminals, by magical transformation, will become the government of Upper Canada. Now I've said I was going to do this trick slowly, so that you'll be able to see the positions they hold in the government, as well as the bonds that tie them together: bonds of blood, marriage, or greed—and in most cases it's all three. Anyway, on with the trick. Number one—

The ASSISTANT covers up the first VOLUNTEER with her cape.

MACKENZIE: Presto—Darcy Boulton Sr.

The cape is whisked away, revealing VOLUNTEER transformed into member of the Family Compact.

MACKENZIE: Retired pensioner, at a pension of five hundred pounds a year, paid by the people of Upper Canada. Number two—Presto—Henry Boulton, son to number one. *(So on with the cape. After three she begins again with one.)* Now Henry is the Attorney-General for Upper Canada as well as being bank solicitor. Number three—Presto!—Darcy Boulton Jr., Auditor-General for Upper Canada as well as being Master in Chancery and a commissioner in the police. Numbers four and five—William and George Boulton—Presto!—also sons to number one, brothers to two and three, and holding various positions in the government. Number six—Presto!—John Beverley Robinson. Now Robinson is a brother-in-law to the Boultons there. He is the Chief Justice for Upper Canada. He's a member of the Legislative Council and the Speaker of the Legislative Council. Number seven—Peter Robinson, brother to number six. He's a member of the Executive Council, he's a member of the Legislative Council, he's the Commissioner of Crown Lands and Commissioner of the Clergy Reserves, as well as being the Surveyor-General of Woods. Number eight—William Robinson, brother to number six and seven. He's the Postmaster for Newmarket, he's a member of the Assembly for Simcoe, he's a government contractor, a colonel in the militia, and a Justice of the Peace.

MACKENZIE claps his hands twice. This brings the VOLUNTEERS out of their trance. They are dumbfounded.

MACKENZIE: We'll skip over nine, ten, eleven, twelve, thirteen, fourteen, and fifteen. They're just more of the same: they're all related to each other and they all hold various positions in the government. Which brings us to sixteen.

He claps again, thrusting VOLUNTEERS back into character. The ASSISTANT can barely keep the blistering pace.

MACKENZIE: —James B. Macaulay. Macaulay is a justice of the court of King's Bench. Number seventeen—Christopher Alexander Hagerman— presto!—Now Hagerman is a brother-in-law to Macaulay—

The cape is still in place, and a struggle is evidently taking place behind it. MACKENZIE rushes across, and snatches it away to reveal HAGERMAN in an unseemly clinch with the ASSISTANT.

MACKENZIE: This man is the Solicitor-General of Upper Canada! Now we won't do eighteen to twenty-two for the same reason we skipped the earlier batch, which brings us to twenty-three, twenty-four and twenty-five—the Jarvis family: Samuel Peter Jarvis, Grant Jarvis—his son—and William Jarvis, his brother. They hold such varied positions between them as clerk of the Crown in Chancery, Secretary of the Province, bank solicitor, clerk of the Legislative Council, police justice, judge, Commissioner of Customs, and two high sheriffs. And that brings us to twenty-six, the biggest fish in this small pond of Upper Canada—Archdeacon John Strachan, family tutor and political schoolmaster to this mob. This man is the archdeacon and rector of York. He's a member of the Executive Council, he's a member of the Legislative Council, he's President of the University, President of the Board of Education, and twenty other situations. *(MACKENZIE and STRACHAN glare at each other.)* Oh I almost forgot—twenty-seven—Thomas Mercer Jones. He's the son-in-law to Strachan and he's the agent and director for the Canada Company land monopoly here in Upper Canada. And there you have it—the government of this fair colony. *(They take a bow.)*

Now this family connection rules Upper Canada according to its own good pleasure. It has no effective check from the country to guard the people against its acts of tyranny and oppression. It includes the whole of the judges of the supreme civil and criminal tribunals; it includes the agents and directors for the Canada Company land monopoly; it includes the president and solicitor and members of the board of the Bank of Upper Canada; it includes half of the Executive Council and all of the Legislative Council. *(They are chortling with self-satisfaction.)* Now this is pretty impressive, I'd say—criminals into government. But there's one piece of magic even more mind-boggling than that you've already seen—and that is how this Family Compact of villainy stays in power in Upper Canada!

They laugh him off the stage.

MARY MACDONALD

EDWARD PETERS, a farmer, is stage left. He is waiting for someone to arrive. Enter MARY MACDONALD, stage right. She is expecting to be met. She does not notice him. He approaches her nervously.

EDWARD: Excuse me, are you Miss Mary Macdonald?

MARY: I am. *(She is very Scottish.)*

EDWARD: Oh. I'm Edward Peters.

They are both horribly awkward.

MARY: I'm very pleased to make your acquaintance Mr. Peters.

EDWARD: I'm very pleased to meet you. *(a painful silence)* You must be tired after such a long trip.

MARY: Yes, I am—a bit.

EDWARD: They have benches here for people if you'd care to—um—

MARY: Oh, thank you.

They cross and sit down.

EDWARD: *(plunging)* I wrote you a letter, Miss Macdonald. I don't know if you received it, proposing a date for the—um—for our wedding.

MARY: *(nearly choking with nervousness)* Yes. I got it.

EDWARD: Ah. Well. Would two weeks be satisfactory then?

MARY: Yes. That would be just fine. I wouldn't want to put you to any trouble.

EDWARD: No. It's no trouble.

They sit in awful silence. He leans over and away from her, to spit. He notices her watching him and swallows it instead.

MARY: Oh feel free.

EDWARD: Ah, no. I didn't really feel like it.

MARY: It's quite hot, is it not?

EDWARD: Yes. It's usually quite hot here in August. It's going to get a lot colder though.

MARY: What kind of farm do you have Mr. Peters?

EDWARD: It's a *good* farm. I raise wheat, built most of a barn, got a good frame house. I think you'll be very comfortable there. Nice furniture. Rough, but it's usable. I built it myself. I'm good with my hands.

MARY: *(trying hopelessly to relax him and herself)* Yes—

EDWARD: And I don't drink.

MARY: *(not really happy about it)* Oh.

EDWARD: I bought a cow.

MARY: You did—

EDWARD: Yes. I thought you'd be used to fresh milk so I went and bought a cow.

MARY: *(pleased)* And what's her name?

EDWARD: *(embarrassed again)* Cow.

MARY: Cow?

EDWARD: Well when you only have one, you just ... call it ... cow ...

MARY: *(feeling their lack of success in communicating)* Oh—

EDWARD: But you could go ahead and give her a nice name.

MARY: I could?

EDWARD: Sure. You'll be milking her and looking after her. You could go ahead and name her.

MARY: Thank you.

EDWARD: You're welcome.

With great relief he spots someone coming up the street.

EDWARD: That's George. See that big fellow on the wagon there? That's my brother George. He's come down to take us back to the farm.

MARY: Now?

EDWARD: Yes.

They start across the stage. MARY is in front of EDWARD. MARY stumbles and almost falls. EDWARD catches her by the arm. It is the first time they've touched. They smile.

EDWARD: You've got to watch where you're walking, Mary. There's ruts.

MARY: Yes.

They go off together.

THE LADY IN THE COACH

Enter LADY BACKWASH, an English gentle-woman of the memoir-writing ilk. (Note: This role has been played by both male and female actors.)

LADY B.: Ladies, I should like to talk to you this evening about my adventures in Upper Canada. I call this lecture—Roughing It In The Bush. The Bush is a term which these quaint Canadians use when describing the vast trackless forests which cover nine-tenths of the colony; dark impenetrable woods much like a jungle, complete with insects, but not the heat. I was on my way to visit a very old and dear friend, Colonel Stockton, in Niagara-on-the-Lake.

As she speaks, the COACH DRIVER appears, brings in and harnesses his horse to the coach and settles in for the ride.

LADY B.: We were to have a sumptuous meal and then witness the spectacular beauty of Niagara Falls by moonlight, which I shall describe later in this evening's talk. Our transportation from Toronto to Niagara was to be accomplished by coach. Now I use this word in the broadest sense of the term, for the vehicle which was produced for our conveyance, if 'twere in England, would not be called a coach. It would be called a great many things, but certainly not a coach. However, despite this hardship, it was with the greatest anticipation that I set out, with my man Johnson … *(Enter JOHNSON, with a discreet bow toward the audience. JOHNSON is a young lad, notably Cockney.)* … to travel from Toronto to Niagara.

They enter and are seated in the coach. The DRIVER lets out a "hyaaah" to his horse and they are off with much bumping.

DRIVER: Giddup Winnifred—whoa—hyaah—giddup …

LADY B.: Johnson, have they never heard of springs in this country?

JOHNSON: I don't believe so madam—

They hit an enormous bump, they bounce, stop, and the coach rocks from side to side. The LADY

and her man are discomfitted. The DRIVER has leapt from his seat down to the side of the coach and is straining to push it out of the hole in which it is stuck.

LADY B.: Johnson—the driver has jumped off!

JOHNSON: I don't blame him. I'd get off too if I could.

LADY B.: Driver. *(The DRIVER does not respond.)* Driver! We've stopped.

DRIVER: *(hoping she'll go away)* That's right, ma'am.

LADY B.: Why have we stopped?

DRIVER: Well ma'am—it's the mud.

LADY B.: Mud? You hear that Johnson—mud! My dear man, I have a very important dinner engagement in Niagara-on-the-Lake this evening, and with some candor I might tell you that if I am forced to go without my dinner tonight, you shall be obliged to do without your job tomorrow. Mud or no mud!

DRIVER: Ma'am—if you think this is bad, why we've got bogs up the way ahead of us that'll make this look like a puddle. Now we'll be able to get on our way in a minute if you'll just step out of the coach.

LADY B.: Out? Get out? My dear man, your impertinence is only matched by your incompetence as a driver. It is my duty to ride in this coach from Toronto to Niagara. It is yours to get me there. Now I am doing my duty. Kindly do yours.

DRIVER: *(patience, patience)* Ma'am—if you won't get out of the coach, to lighten the load, so that I can push her out of this hole, we'll never get to Niagara.

JOHNSON: *(aping his mistress' tone)* Absolutely not. We paid good money to ride in this coach and we're not getting out of it. *(turning to LADY B., pleased with himself)* Got to be firm with his type.

LADY B.: *(interrupting)* Johnson, you and I shall get out of this coach.

JOHNSON: *(stung)* Wot—

LADY B.: *(firmly)* —thereby lightening the load, thereby facilitating this nincompoop in getting us out of here.

DRIVER: Thank you ma'am. There's a dry spot here—

JOHNSON: I don't see a dry spot—

The DRIVER tries to help JOHNSON down. JOHNSON tries to avoid being dropped in the mud. The upshot is, the DRIVER is holding JOHNSON aloft. LADY B. stands up grandly and strides out of the other door of the coach onto the side of the road. She notices the confusion with JOHNSON and upbraids him.

LADY B.: Johnson, come over here. Don't worry about a little mud. Where would the glorious Empire be today if it weren't above mud?

JOHNSON crosses here and stands beside her. The DRIVER puts his shoulder to the wheel.

DRIVER: Now pull Winnifred. Pull girl—

LADY B.: *(to DRIVER)* Oh you'll not do it that way. You're not strong enough.

DRIVER: *(straining)* Hyaah, hyaah—

JOHNSON: He's not smart enough either.

LADY B.: He's not smart enough to know he's not strong enough.

DRIVER: *(giving up)* Whoa Winnifred—

LADY B.: Told you so. No, Johnson shall have to help you push from behind.

JOHNSON: *(stung)* Wot?

LADY B.: Yes, Johnson shall have to get in the mud and help you push from behind.

JOHNSON: Wot—me get in the mud and push that thing. Not likely—

LADY B.: *(cutting him off with great master-servant authority)* Johnson!

JOHNSON breaks off his tirade and assumes instant humility. He has remembered his place.

LADY B.: This colony is having a most disturbing effect on your personality. Now into the mud and push! (JOHNSON jumps obediently into the mud.) That's British pluck.

DRIVER: Alright Mr. Johnson. You just put your back into it, right about there, and give it what you've got—

JOHNSON wrinkles his nose at the DRIVER.

LADY B.: Johnson, push with a will—the eyes of England are upon you.

DRIVER: Alright, Winnifred, pull girl, hyaah—

They strain away. Enter, rear of LADY BACKWASH, an INDIAN carrying an axe. He is amused by the sight and wanders up. LADY B. hears his laughs, turns to see him and emits a shriek.

LADY B.: Eeek. Johnson, I'm being attacked by a savage!

JOHNSON: *(springing to the rescue)* Savage is it? That's my job. *(running up to confront the savage)* Alright Savage—put 'em up. I studied with the Marquess of Queensbury, I did—Omygawd, he's got an axe!

He flees to the other side of the stage and climbs a tree.

DRIVER: *(to INDIAN)* Hello Bart. How are you today?

INDIAN: *(moving over to LADY B.)* Fine. Hello ma'am, Wells is the name.

He offers his hand which she shakes, her mind already grinding away about how she can use this new arrival.

INDIAN: *(moving on to DRIVER)* Where did you find that one?

LADY B.: Johnson, come down from that tree. You're not a monkey. (JOHNSON obeys.) Johnson, it *(referring to the INDIAN)* speaks English. And if it speaks English, it can take orders. Johnson, you shall take the savage in hand and push from behind. Driver—Johnson and the savage shall push from behind. While they push, you shall lift from the middle, and I myself shall take Winnifred by the head, and encourage her to greater effort. Right Winnifred?

WINNIFRED whinnies. They assume their appointed positions.

LADY B.: Altogether now—push, pull, come on Winnifred, it's coming—

They are straining, pushing, lifting. Suddenly, with a lurch, the coach comes free. They are all—except for LADY B.—panting from the effort. She is babbling more than ever.

LADY B.: *(elated)* There! We did it! What did I tell you? Just needed a little leadership.

Johnson—you were superb. Driver—you were tremendous. Savage—you were alright. And Winnifred—you pulled with a will.

INDIAN: *(to DRIVER)* You sure it's safe for me to leave you alone with her?

LADY B.: Johnson, I haven't felt so good since I arrived at this wretched colony. *(a sudden inspiration)* Johnson—quickly, my diary.

JOHNSON fetches it and takes down her dictation. She addresses posterity.

LADY B.: We had fought the good fight and won. We had been faced with insurmountable obstacles and we had overcome them. And now we took the rest of the victorious, and what better place than here, in Nature's Cathedral.

JOHNSON: *(copying)* Oh, I like that.

LADY B.: I looked up at the tall trees, like giant columns supporting the vast infinite blue of the sky above. The birds sang, the bees—um, the bees— *(She searches.)*

JOHNSON: Might I suggest "buzzed"?

LADY B.: *(accepting with alacrity)* Buzzed. Of course—buzzed. Very good, Johnson. And everywhere was peace, tranquillity and beauty.

WINNIFRED whinnies impatiently.

DRIVER: Ma'am can I suggest you get back into the coach. Once Winnifred gets us out of one bog, she just can't wait to get us into the next one.

JOHNSON: Huh?

LADY B.: An example of Canadian humour, I believe, Johnson. *(They chuckle.)* That's enough, Johnson.

They get back into the coach. The DRIVER is about to crack the whip. LADY BACKWASH takes one final look at the site of this enchanted event.

LADY B.: Farewell, brave bush!

DRIVER: Hyaah!

The coach bounces into motion. They are bouncing with it.

Blackout.

THE HEAD

Note: Sir Francis Bond Head was Lieutenant-Governor of Upper Canada in 1837. Mackenzie could rarely resist punning on his name. In this scene four actors comprise themselves as Head's head. Two of their heads are his eyes, two arms his arching eyebrows, two other arms his nose. So on for his mouth, dimple, etc. The scene begins with the narrated, piece by piece construction of the head, after which the "head" talks.

VOICE: Two piercing blue eyes ... *(Enter the eyes.)* ... arching eyebrows, a long aristocratic nose, a firm mouth—and a dimple on the chin. Sir Francis Bond Head, Lieutenant-Governor of Upper Canada, addresses an assembly of voters before the election of 1836.

HEAD: *(sniffing, scowling, smiling, etc., as the speech proceeds)* Gentlemen, as your district now has the important duty to perform of electing representatives for the new Parliament, I think it might practically assist if I clearly lay before you the conduct I intend inflexibly to pursue. If you choose to dispute with me and live on bad terms with the Mother Country, you will—to use a homely phrase—only quarrel with your own bread and butter. If you choose to try this experiment by again electing members who will oppose me, do so. On the other hand, if you choose to embark your interests with my character, I will take paternal care of them both. Men—women and money are what you want. And if you send to Parliament members who will assist me, you can depend upon it, you will gain more than you possibly can by trying to insult me. But—let your conduct be what it may—I am quite determined, so long as I occupy this station, neither to give offense, nor to take it. Gentlemen, you may now cast your ballots.

Blackout.

Further note: The above is a quotation from an actual speech by Sir Francis at the time.

THE ELECTION OF '36

A TORY and a REFORMER

TORY: Hey!

REFORMER: Yeah?

TORY: How're you voting?

REFORMER: Me? Reform.

TORY: Oh yeah? *(Ploughs him one.)*

ANOTHER REFORMER: Well—you're obviously voting Tory.

TORY: That's right.

REFORMER: Uh-huh. *(Ploughs the TORY. Then loudly proclaims:)* Reform!

ANOTHER TORY: Didn't hear that. All votes have to be heard to be recorded.

REFORMER: I said—Reform!

TORY: That's what I thought you said. *(Wham.)*

ROBERT DAVIS: *(This character has, for some reason, been played by a woman in all productions of 1837 so far.)* Hey don't hit him like that. This is no way to carry on an election—

All then turn on this poor peacemaker and attack him, screaming their political slogans as they flail away at each other and particularly at ROBERT DAVIS. The cry of "Tory" rings above the others. The Tories are obviously most proficient at this political bullying. The mayhem concludes with the brutal cry, "God—Save—The—Queen!" Freeze.

THE CANADIAN FARMER'S TRAVELS IN THE U.S.A.

ROBERT DAVIS, Upper Canadian farmer, drags himself out from the bottom of the brawl during the election of 1836.

DAVIS: Would you believe that was an election? I would! Lost two teeth in it—and that proves it's an election around here. My name's Robert Davis. I have a small farm here in Nissouri Township. Lived here all my life. Got two fine kids. Taught myself to read and write. But this election was just about the end for me. Why we've been working for reform for fifteen years— and now things in Upper Canada are worse than ever. I'd about lost hope. And I needed to get my hope back somehow. So I decided I'd take a trip to the United States. I'd heard things were different down there, and I thought—if I can see that someone else has succeeded, maybe I can keep on trying myself. So I started out.

He walks.

DAVIS: Now the first place I came to on my way to the border was the little town of Chatham. Beautiful little place for a town, but very sleepy …

The Town Council of Chatham comes to order.

MAYOR: My friends, as members of the Town Council of Chatham I think we should establish what is going to be happening here for the next twenty years.

DAVIS: Good. I'd like to see that. What have you got in mind?

The members of the Council yawn, fall flat on their backs, and snore.

DAVIS: See that! That's despair—I'm not going to stay around here. *(Walks.)* So I kept on, till I came to the town of Sandwich, that's right across the river from Detroit. Look around. There's nothing happening here.

BOATMAN: All aboard for Detroit.

DAVIS: Can you take me to Detroit?

BOATMAN: Yup. Get aboard fast. Miss the boat and there isn't another one for a week.

DAVIS: That's ridiculous—one boat a week!

They start across the river.

DAVIS: And as we left Sandwich snoozing in the sunshine, I could see a kind of stir on the other side of the river. And sounds—sounds like I'd never heard before—

The bustling sounds of Detroit begin to come up.

DAVIS: And suddenly we were surrounded by boats, big and little, carrying grain, and goods, and *people*—

BOATMAN: *(yelling)* Detroit! Gateway to the American Dream—

The sounds of industry and trade explode around poor DAVIS. People rush back and forth past him, happy, productive—

AMERICAN: Howdy stranger, I'd like to stay and shoot the breeze, but I'm too busy getting rich.

DAVIS: Look at all these people—and this *industry*, and—and—two thousand immigrants a day—most of them from Upper Canada!

IMMIGRANT: *(kissing the ground)* America! America!

RUNAWAY SLAVE: *(to DAVIS)* Excuse me sir, I'm a runaway slave. Which way is Canada?

DAVIS: No, no. Don't go there. It's terrible. Stay here. I'm sure things will get better for you. *(turning)* Oh—look. A four-storey brick building! *(Someone plays it.)* Isn't it wonderful?

WRECKER: 'Scuse me fella. Gotta tear down this four-storey building.

DAVIS: *(horrified)* Why?

WRECKER: *(knocking it down)* 'Cause we're gonna put up a six-storey one in its place! There— *(Whoosht—up it goes.)*

DAVIS: Oh—and look at what it says on it— Museum!

MUSEUM: Sure. Come on in

DAVIS enters, sees statues of American heroes— "We got more than we know what to do with"— Whistler's Mother, or some such nonsense. (By the way, this scene has never been "set." DAVIS has seen different things nearly every time he has taken his trip.)

DAVIS: This is all fine, but you know I'm a farmer, and I'll really know what to make of your country when I see what's happening outside the cities. So can you tell me how I can get to the country?

AMERICAN: Sure. How'd you like to go?

DAVIS: How? I thought I'd walk—

AMERICAN: Pshaw—nobody walks down here. Now you can go by coach, or canal—

DAVIS: Don't talk to me about canals! Did you ever hear of the Welland Canal? They've been building it for twelve years! It's only twelve miles long. It's cost us millions of dollars and you *still* have to dig your way through!

AMERICAN: No kidding. Well we've got the Erie Canal. Five hundred miles and clear straight through—

DAVIS: *(stunned)* Five hundred miles …

AMERICAN: But if you don't like that, you can always take the train.

DAVIS: Train? What was that word you just said?

Zip. He is suddenly in the country.

DAVIS: So I went to the country. Acre after acre of cleared, fertile land—

FARMER: Excuse me friend, would you mind moving your foot?

DAVIS: My foot? Why?

FARMER: Well, do you feel something moving under it?

DAVIS: Moving? Why yes—I do!

FARMER: Just move it aside—there.

They both watch as a crop of wheat grows from the floor to the ceiling.

FARMER: Crop of wheat I planted this morning. A little small this year. Well, watch yourself while I harvest it. *(with his axe)* Timber!

DAVIS: Wheat—and apple orchards—and thousands of head of cattle—and sixty pound cheeses!

These appear—or fail to do so—at the whim of the other actors onstage. The most fun occurs when someone introduces into the scene something DAVIS and the others have not expected.

DAVIS: And then I went to one of the hundreds of thriving country towns—

SCHOOLHOUSE: Bong! Bong! Come on kiddies—everybody into school for your free universal education.

DAVIS: Free? Universal? You mean your schools aren't just for your aristocracy?

SCHOOLHOUSE: You watch your language down here. We don't use words like that!

DAVIS: Everyone can go to school! Does it work?

SCHOOLHOUSE: Hah! Where's that dumb kid. C'mere kid, get inside.

The DUMB KID walks through one door of the schoolhouse and emerges from the other.

FORMERLY DUMB KID: $E=mc^2$

CHURCH: Ding Dong—Methodist.

ANOTHER: Ding Dong—Lutheran.

ANOTHER: Ding Dong—Quaker.

Somebody has not declared himself.

DAVIS: What are you?

TOWNSMAN: I'm an atheist.

DAVIS: You allow atheists down here too?

CHURCH: We don't like them but we allow them.

DAVIS: But which one is your established church, you know, the official church?

They all laugh.

TOWNSMAN: Say—you must be a Canadian.

DAVIS: *(delighted)* I am. How'd you know?

TOWNSMAN: Say house.

DAVIS: House.

TOWNSMAN: Say about.

DAVIS: About.

TOWNSMAN: I knew it. Now excuse us, we're going to have an election.

DAVIS: *(panicking)* An election? Let me out of here—I'm going to hide—I've lost enough teeth.

He watches from a distance.

FIRST VOTER: Having searched my conscience, I have decided to cast my vote as a Democrat.

The next VOTER steps up. DAVIS winces in expectation of the clash.

SECOND VOTER: Well, in that case, I'm going to vote Republican.

THIRD VOTER: Then I vote Democrat.

FOURTH VOTER: Let's see—the Republicans won last time, so I'll vote Democrat too.

ALL: Hurray!

They all commiserate with the lone Republican.

DAVIS: Hey—wait a minute. When does the fight start?

VOTER: Fight? What do you mean? This is an election. Now come here, uh, what's your name?

DAVIS: Davis.

VOTER: No, I mean your first name. We all use first names here.

DAVIS: Bob.

VOTER: Well Bob, I'd like you to meet the new governor of our state. This is Ole. Ole, this is Bob, from Canada—

OLE: *(a very slow speaking farmer)* Well, how do you do. You wouldn't like to buy a pig would you?

DAVIS: Pig? You mean you're the governor of this state and you still work as a farmer.

OLE: Well, gotta make some money somehow—

DAVIS: You know, you've all given me new hope. You've proven to me it can be done. This is what we've been working for for years, and I can go home now and—

VOTER: Home? Wait a minute Bob. Why don't you stay right here with us and make this your new home?

DAVIS: Here? But why should I?

ANOTHER VOTER: Because it's the best darned country in the world. That's why.

DAVIS: But—but I've got my family back there.

ANOTHER: Bring 'em down here. Bring your whole country.

DAVIS: But—but there's my farm.

ANOTHER: Tell you what we'll do Bob. We'll give you a four hundred acre cleared farm right here. Just for you.

DAVIS: *(getting excited)* Cleared? *(suspicious)* How much?

ANOTHER: Nothing. Just take good care of it.

DAVIS: I can have that farm?

ANOTHER: Sure. We'll just sweep those Indians off it and—

DAVIS: Why that's wonderful! You're all so generous! This must be the finest—

ANOTHER: See. He's starting to act like an American already. Being happy and talking loud—

DAVIS: No. No, I can't do it.

ANOTHER: Those words don't exist in America.

DAVIS: I can't stay. You see—it's not my home. I can't just leave Canada. It's up to us to do there what you've done here. But you've given me hope. Now I know it can be done— (*He is leaving.*) So I went home.

Lethargic, snoring, apathetic Canadians surround him.

DAVIS: And I said—Don't lie around. Get up. Help each other. You can do it.

He drags them to their feet. They are rubbery-legged. They cling to each other and anything they can find.

DAVIS: I've seen it now. I know it can be done. We can do it too, if we stay together. Now is not the time for Reformers to fawn and crouch. Now is the time to unite and fight!

Blackout.

THE DUMMY

A political rally in rural Upper Canada attended by angry Reform farmers.

FARMER: He's here, he's here alright. The great man is here. I saw him just out back.

They cheer.

FARMER: He's come down here to talk to all of us—now you put that jug away, this is a dry meeting—but before the great man talks to us, a couple of the folks have worked up one of their little skits to do for us. So come on up here and get it over with, so we can all get on with hearing the great man's speech. (*Two farmers come up front.*) And don't forget your lines this time.

The two stand in front of the rally. One assumes the role of the VENTRILOQUIST. The other plays his DUMMY.

VENTRILOQUIST: Ladies and gentlemen. Presenting for your enjoyment, straight from England, John Bull—your Imperial ventriloquist—and his companion, Peter Stump—the Canadian axeman. Say hello to the people, Peter.

PETER: (*The VENTRILOQUIST is throwing his voice.*) Hello.

JOHN: Aren't you forgetting to add something, Peter?

PETER: God Save The Queen.

JOHN: Good, Peter. Very loyal. I say—what is that in your hand?

PETER: My axe.

JOHN: What do you do with your axe, Peter?

PETER: Chop down trees. (*He chops.*) Timber!

JOHN: And what do you do with the wood you cut?

PETER: Send it to you in England, John.

JOHN: Very fine Peter. Say, what else do you have there?

PETER: My rifle.

JOHN: Aha—and who are you going to shoot?

PETER: Yankees.

JOHN: Good. And quickly too— (*He hides behind PETER.*)

PETER: Bang, bang, bang, bang—

JOHN: (*emerging*) Whew! Well done, lad. Now could you loan me twenty of your dollars?

PETER: (*protesting*) John, I'm short myself—

JOHN: (*picking his pocket*) There. I knew you wouldn't mind. Now is there anything else I can do for you?

PETER: Yes.

JOHN: What's that?

PETER: Please take your hand away from my neck.

JOHN: (*surprised*) I beg your pardon?

PETER: Take your hand away from me.

JOHN: If I do that, you will be helpless. Do you understand?

PETER: I want to try.

CROWD: Let him go. Give him a chance.

JOHN: Very well, Peter—

He yanks his hand out. PETER stands stock still. JOHN moves away from him.

JOHN: Now Peter, now let's hear you speak. Ha! Chop down trees Peter! Shoot Yankees! Can't do a thing can you?

CROWD: Come on, Peter. You can do it.

JOHN: Without me, John Bull, you are nothing. Pathetic isn't he, ladies and gentlemen? A pitiable, colonial—

PETER: *(with his own voice, for the first time)* Mm—

JOHN: *(stunned)* What? What was that?

PETER: *(louder)* Mm—mm—I—I—

JOHN: Peter, Peter—what are you up to?

PETER: *(slowly finding his voice)* I want to say: *(more confidently)* Thank God for the man who is giving me a voice— *(shouting, no longer a dummy at all)* William Lyon Mackenzie!

The CROWD cheers. Enter MACKENZIE and bounds onto the rostrum.

THE SPEECH

MACKENZIE: Thank you, ladies and gentlemen, thank you. Now let's start off this meeting by giving three cheers for the men who made it possible, or rather I should say necessary. Let's have three cheers for Archdeacon John Strachan. Hip hip hurray! Hip hip hurray!—

CROWD: Booo—

MACKENZIE: Come now my friends, you won't cheer John Strachan? I didn't realize feelings ran that high. Now I was talking to someone the other day who said about Strachan—if that man's godliness were gunpowder, he couldn't blow his own nose. Alright then, if you won't cheer Strachan, let's have three cheers for Christopher Alexander Hagerman. Hip hip hurray—

CROWD: Booo—

MACKENZIE: My friends, these people tell us over and over that they are the nobility of this colony so we should cheer them. Come on now—

CROWD: No!

MACKENZIE: Alright then, let's give three cheers for the real nobility of Upper Canada. Three cheers for the farmers!

CROWD: Hip hip hurray! Hip hip hurray! Hip hip hurray!

MACKENZIE: Alright now, I'm going to tell you a story. It's an old story, but there's no stories like old stories. It concerns a little Reformer who goes to the Assembly to see what he can do to rectify the wrongs in this colony. So he puts forward all those bills he feels are for the general good and he opposes all those bills he feels are against the general good, please or offend whom it might. And it seemed to offend some people. For Bolton called him a reptile and Hagerman called him a spaniel dog. Now that shows you one thing about Hagerman, and that is—that his knowledge of dogs is only equalled by his knowledge of decent government. For anybody who knew anything about dogs could tell you that this Reformer was not a spaniel dog—but a Scots terrier hot on the trail of a rat!

The CROWD cheers.

MACKENZIE: But these men didn't stop at calling him names. They thought that more forceful action was necessary. So they grabbed him by the seat of the pants and the collar of the coat, and they threw him out of the Assembly! *(MACKENZIE leaps into the CROWD.)* But what did the people do?

CROWD: We put you back. *(They hoist him back onto the platform.)*

MACKENZIE: And they threw him out again! *(He leaps out.)*

CROWD: And we put you back—

MACKENZIE: And out again—

CROWD: And back again—

MACKENZIE: And a fourth time—

CROWD: And back a fourth time—

MACKENZIE: Yes, four times they threw him out, and four times the people sent him back. And that's round one for the people. For try as they might, these men cannot oppose the will of the people to send to the Assembly who they want. So the little Reformer finds himself securely in the Assembly. But what can he do? His hands are tied. So he says to himself, I've got to go above the heads of these people, above Strachan and Bolton, and Hagerman. I've got to go to the top— to the King of England! So the little Reformer goes to England, and he's armed with a petition of grievances that's half a mile long. And the signatures on that petition aren't one, two, three, or four names. Oh no no no—there's twenty-five thousand names on that petition. And the King of England looks at it, and he goes—Oh my my my my! And he calls for the Colonial Secretary, and the Colonial Secretary gets the Colonial Office moving, and the Colonial Office gets our government over here moving, so everybody's moving hither-thither, helter-skelter, but out of all this government activity what real good comes? What happens here in this colony?

CROWD: Nothing!

MACKENZIE: Nothing? Not quite. For the Pharaoh of England in his wisdom sends us a saviour—a new Lieutenant-Governor, Sir Francis *Bone* Head. Now what are Sir Francis' credentials for holding this very important office?

CROWD: None! He hasn't got any!

MACKENZIE: Oh yes he does. It's a long and impressive list and I'm going to tell you what they are, Number one. He's a damn fool. Number two. He's English. Number three. He's arrogant. And number four. He's very good with a lasso.

CROWD: What?

MACKENZIE: The lasso. Sir Francis' specialty is the lasso—a skill he picked up in Argentina, used there for herding cattle. So the first thing Sir Francis does when he gets to our colony is he gets out his lasso, and he circles it above his head once, twice, three times—and he lets it go! And who does he catch? You! He catches the people of Upper Canada, and there we all are in Sir Francis' lasso. And he pulls it a little tighter and he says—alright, now it's time for an election; all those in favour of Reform, stand up! And he pulls very hard and he pulls all of us off our feet. Now how did one man pull all of us off our feet? I'll tell you how he did it. We're all in that lasso and we're pushing this way and pulling that way in our frustration and despair. But I tell you that, if as one man we took hold of that rope and turned to Sir Francis then with one mighty tug, we could pull him off his high horse and send him back to England on his ass!

The CROWD cheers.

MACKENZIE: And that's what I want to talk to you about today. Pulling as one man—Union! For the power of the people is as nothing without union and union is nothing without confidence and discipline. Now the Tories have been following me around to these various meetings, taking what I say back to Toronto, and I'm flattered by the attention. But I don't want to get

in trouble with the authorities—treason or anything of that sort, so I'm going to talk to you now in a roundabout manner. Now first of all I think we have to form ourselves into small groups—say fourteen to forty people—just to talk. There's no law against talking. And each of those groups is in contact with other such groups around the province, so we know who our friends are in case of an emergency. But I think the time for talking is past. It's gone by. And I think now it's time for us to work on our muscle power, develop our strength—and I think the best way to do that is through turkey shoots.

CROWD: Turkey shoots?

MACKENZIE: Yes—

CROWD: We know how to shoot turkeys!

MACKENZIE: But don't you think a turkey shoot would be more fun if there was a little drilling beforehand? And don't you think you could shoot turkeys a bit better if everyone shot at once— bang bang bang bang. Because you see, the thing about a Tory—I mean a turkey—the thing about a turkey is you can shoot it with a rifle, you can cut its head off with an axe, a pike is an excellent tool for getting turkeys out of high places—and if worse comes to worst, you can always grab a turkey in your own bare hands and wring its bloody neck!

The CROWD cheers.

MACKENZIE: Now once we get very good at killing turkeys, we go down to that turkey parliament, and we say—this is what we want! And this is what we intend to get! And if they refuse—

CROWD: Yes! What then?

MACKENZIE: We declare open season on turkeys and you'll all have one on your plate this year for Christmas!

The CROWD cheers.

MACKENZIE: Now who's going to be the first to come up here and sign the paper and pledge themselves to shooting turkeys?

CROWD: Me! I will!

MACKENZIE: That's the spirit!

Freeze. Blackout.

LOUNT'S FORGE

SAMUEL LOUNT's blacksmith shop at Holland Landing. LOUNT is at stage centre, hammer in hand, standing over his anvil. Around him are various voices of discontent. All lines are spoken to the audience.

LOUNT: Oh yes! I'm back—doing what I know how to do. I've been a farmer, a surveyor, mostly a blacksmith—but the most useless job I ever tried was politics!

MAN: It took me twelve years to drain the swamp off my land. Then, last summer, the Canada Company dams up the river and floods all the low lands. You look now—you've never seen such a bog!

LOUNT: Samuel Lount for the Assembly! Sam— you've got to run. Sam—we need you.

WOMAN: I can work in her kitchen, but she doesn't want me in the rest of her house. Well I know all about it anyway—because my husband built it!

LOUNT: So off I go to the Assembly. Every man's vote behind me. And went to sleep for two years.

WOMAN: Sure it's a nice farm. And the town's over there, two miles. But there's no road between our farm and the town—because all the land in between belongs to John Strachan and his accursed Church of England!

LOUNT: I'd no sooner stand up to propose a bill, than some Tory would call for a recess.

MAN: Here's a road. Fine road too. Except for the river that runs across it. Now they won't build the bridge. Now what the hell good is a road without a bridge?

LOUNT: Tories got you scared Sam? That why you're not going back? Yes I'm scared. Scared if we waste two more years with this government, there won't be anything left in this country worth saving!

MAN: Now I don't know anything about politics. But there must be *something* wrong in this province. Because there ain't no women!

LOUNT: So Mackenzie comes to me. "Sam, it's time. We need you." I've heard that one before.

MAN: See this cabinet? Took me four months to make. Know why I can't sell it? Because it was made in Toronto!

WOMAN: Yes, I took in travellers for the night. And maybe I did a few favours for men in return for money. But what else can a woman alone with six children do? So they put me in jail and took away my children. Well watch out Mister— because your turn is coming and it's coming soon!

LOUNT: Mac—I said—I'm a blacksmith, not a politician. "Fine, Sam—that's just what we need. A blacksmith."

MAN: I voted Reform in the last election so the Colonel foreclosed on my mortgage. Now that's four years work all gone. But that's all right. Because now I've got nothing to lose!

LOUNT: So I'm back. But I'm not making horseshoes. And I'm not making laws. I'm making pikes—

He raises the redhot pike he has had on the anvil and lowers it into a bucket of water.

ALL: Sssssssssss—

Blackout.

ACT TWO

DOEL'S BREWERY

MACKENZIE sets the scene. Onstage with him are three of his Reform associates, and a BREWERY WORKER.

MACKENZIE: November 11, 1837. Doel's Brewery, at the corner of Bay and Adelaide Streets, in Toronto. I've called an emergency meeting of the leading Reformers of this city: John Doel—he owns this brewery; lawyer Parsons; Dr. Rolph. These gentlemen are all leading and respected citizens. And this man over here—he's one of Doel's workers—and a good man he is too. We don't seem to have any influence with the government of this country. We have none at all with the King of England. But to my surprise and delight, I find we have some influence with someone up there *(skyward)* for the opportunity which has been presented to us can only be described as heaven-sent. The brave French patriots under Papineau in Lower Canada have struck for their own freedom. Now that means two things to us. First—it indicates to us in Upper Canada the route we too must take to achieve our ends. Second—and even more important—it means there isn't one English soldier left here in Toronto tonight. They've all marched off to Lower Canada. But our blessings don't stop there. No no no no—for in City Hall are four thousand muskets, still in their crates, not even unpacked yet. Guarded by only two men! Now anyone who would leave four thousand muskets guarded by only two men cannot be averse to them being used. At Government House, Sir Francis Bond Head has just come in from his ride; he sits before his fire, feet up on the fender, sipping a glass of expensive French brandy, and imagines he presides over the most contented colony in the entire Empire. He is guarded by only one sentry. At Kingston, Fort Henry lies open and deserted. A steamer only has to sail up to the wharf and it's ours. *(turning to his colleagues)* Now here's the plan—we seize Sir Francis, we take him to City Hall and seize the arms, which we distribute to our friends here and in the country. We then declare a Provisional Government and demand of Sir Francis a Legislative Council responsible to a new and fairly elected Assembly. If he refuses—

DOEL: Yes? If he refuses?

MACKENZIE: We go at once for Independence and take whatever steps are necessary to secure it! *(He grabs DOEL and pilots him across the stage.)* Doel, it's so easy, all you have to do is come along here, pick up those muskets, and we've won!

DOEL: *(pulling away)* Shhh. Now we all want the same things Mac—but we don't want to cause trouble.

MACKENZIE: Right! And if we do it this way it'll be no trouble at all—

PARSONS: *(trying to settle him down)* Now Mackenzie—you're our leader, we all agree to that. But why don't you just sit down for a moment and—

MACKENZIE: *(springing back up)* This is no time to sit down! It's time to rise up and act!

ROLPH: *(authoritatively)* Mackenzie! What if we fail?

MACKENZIE: Rolph, with this much nerve—this much courage—we cannot fail.

DOEL: Now Mac—don't rush like this. We've put four months of careful organization and preparation into this.

MACKENZIE: Doel, what in God's name have we been organizing *for*?

PARSONS: Mac, I want to go with you, but I just don't know how to make the jump— *(He mimes it.)*

MACKENZIE: If you want to jump—you jump. *(He leaps across the stage.)*

ROLPH: We don't have the men.

MACKENZIE: We do! We've got Doel's own workers. We've got Armstrong's axemakers. Dutcher's foundrymen—they're strong, dependable, and they're ready to *act*—

The WORKER starts moving determinedly toward the stand of muskets (indicated by one or two guns). The three REFORMERS scurry to interpose themselves before the weapons actually are seized. They head off the WORKER by a whisker.

ROLPH: Mackenzie—we have pledged ourselves to Reform—not Revolution.

MACKENZIE: It doesn't matter what you call it, Rolph. The question is, what are you going to do about it?

DOEL: Well, if it's force we want, I move we bring down our friends from the country.

MACKENZIE: That's the way is it, Doel? Bring down the farmers to do your dirty work? Besides—it will take four weeks to get the farmers down here.

PARSONS: Well alright then—four weeks. That makes it what?—December seventh.

DOEL: Yes. Agreed. December seventh.

ROLPH: December seventh.

DOEL: Mackenzie?

MACKENZIE: *(with a helpless look at the WORKER, and a gesture of disgust toward his colleagues)* Alright—December seventh!

Blackout.

DRILLING

A FARMER is alone onstage, with a pitchfork, drilling with it as one would with a rifle.

FARMER: Present ... Attack! Present ... Attack! Present ... Attack!

Enter another FARMER, who sees the drill and starts to chuckle about it. FIRST continues drilling, but is irked by the derision.

SECOND: Come on. Come on now.

FIRST: Present ... Attack! ...

SECOND: You're not going to march to Toronto with that?

FIRST: Present ...

SECOND: What are you going to do with it? Feed hay to the British?

FIRST wheels on SECOND and presses the very menacing point of the pitchfork against his throat. (In fact, this scene has always been played by two women.)

SECOND: Wait—what're you doing?

FIRST: Go on. Laugh some more.

SECOND: Alright. Stop.

FIRST continues pressing. It is quite ominous. That is a real pitchfork up there onstage.

FIRST: Say it—

SECOND: Alright, alright

FIRST: Say It!

SECOND: Say what?

FIRST: Present—

SECOND: *(practically a whimper)* Present—

FIRST: *(whirling and stabbing the fork directly out toward the audience)* Attack!

TIGER DUNLOP

DUNLOP: The date is November 19. The place—Gairbraid, near Goderich, home of William "Tiger" Dunlop—raconteur, wit, doctor of medicine, and arch-Tory.

Enter MACKENZIE and COLONEL ANTHONY VAN EGMOND, an older man. They join

DUNLOP and all three participate in a hearty after-dinner laugh.

DUNLOP: Yes—I believe that was the same evening we were dining at your home, Van Egmond, and your housekeeper said to me— *(imitating the housekeeper)* Doctor, why is it, sir, we never see you in church? And I said, Because, Madam, I have an abiding distrust of any place where one man does all the talking, you're liable to meet your wife, and people sing without drinking!

They all laugh.

VAN EGMOND: An amazing likeness, Tiger, and I must tell you that she still anxiously awaits your return. Tiger here is one of the most eligible bachelors in the tract.

DUNLOP: And intending to remain so. But—that was a long time ago. Strange, isn't it, what time does—to men like Van Egmond and myself, who spent so much time in the same camp in the bush—yet now find ourselves in such separate camps.

VAN EGMOND: Perhaps.

DUNLOP: But, times being what they are, I'm sure you gentlemen haven't come here to hear my old stories. Not with having brought this screaming Reformer with you. I imagine you've come for something—so tell me—What can Tiger Dunlop do for you?

MACKENZIE: Tiger Dunlop can let us help him.

DUNLOP: I beg your pardon.

MACKENZIE: Let us help you.

DUNLOP: What could you possibly do to help me?

MACKENZIE: What do you think of John Strachan?

DUNLOP: I hate the bastard.

MACKENZIE: And Thomas Mercer Jones?

DUNLOP: Jones. Well, anyone who would marry Strachan's daughter can't be all good.

MACKENZIE: Dunlop, you and I seem to concur in our opinions of these people.

DUNLOP: Yes. I believe we do.

MACKENZIE: Every time we turn around in this colony, we see its wealth being carted off someplace else. And what about the honest, hardworking people—the farmers and the labourers? The fruits of their effort are being scooped up to support the idle dandies in Toronto or London—

DUNLOP: Just a moment, Mr. Mackenzie. When you start in about the honest, hardworking people, it's obvious you're about to launch one of your famous political speeches. Now don't let my reputation fool you. I'm still a man who likes plain speaking. I beg you—speak to me plainly.

MACKENZIE: Alright. I'll speak to you plainly. There's going to be some changes in this colony, Dunlop. Big changes. It's going to be out with the old and in with the new. Now the question is, Tiger—are you going to be part of the new or are you going out with the old?

DUNLOP: You talk about changes. Now I have always stood for change in this colony. Isn't that true, Colonel?

VAN EGMOND: Yes. Yes, Tiger—that's the man I remember. Long ago, before this part of the country was even opened up, Tiger here, John Galt—remember him, Tiger?—and myself, we used to go up on a rise by the lake, look about us and talk of the tremendous potential of the country. And Tiger had the most vivid dreams of all. Eighty thousand families, I believe you said, could be supported by the Huron Tract alone. And we set about to make that a reality. We built roads—remember, Tiger?—pushing the roads through the bush to bring in the settlers—built mills, provided for schools, and churches, shipped in supplies—anything that would bring in the settlers. And the towns. That you founded.

But look about you, Tiger. Where are the eighty thousand? For every one settler there should be a hundred more. The roads that were built to bring people in are leading them out. By the thousands. Land value is where it was five, ten years ago. Why? What has happened? I think you have let go of your dream, Tiger. Given it up to men like Jones, Strachan, Hagerman. Fops and dandies. Mushroom aristocrats. Bladders of pride and arrogance—who care not a damn for the country—but only for their own fiefdoms—filling their pockets. I don't think you are the kind of man to let this abuse continue. John Galt could

not tolerate such leadership and he resigned his post with the Canada Company. I rather think you are cast in the same mould as Galt.

DUNLOP: Time brings changes, Colonel, and might I say—compromise?

MACKENZIE: Compromise! Dunlop, I've been from one end of this colony to the other. Now there is discontent, vengeance, rage—in men's minds. But not compromise! I've seen it at over two hundred public meetings. Thousands of signatures, names of men pledging themselves to use force of arms if necessary to alleviate their suffering. This colony wants cheap, efficient responsible government and it's going to have it, and there's nothing that the Lieutenant-Governor, or the King of England, or the whole British army can do to stop it.

VAN EGMOND: Tiger, you know what the people want, what they think. You talk to them, high and low alike. They admire you. You are a brilliant man—I don't flatter—you have ideas, and you have the energy to put those ideas into effect.

MACKENZIE: An independent country. A new nation. Think of it, Tiger. Think what this country could be with its natural bounty, under the leadership which men like yourself could provide—it could be one of the greatest in the world. It's a tremendous responsibility staring you right in the face. Now are you man enough to meet that responsibility, Dunlop?

DUNLOP: *(He deliberates a long while, then chuckles.)* Excuse me, gentlemen, but you remind me of a couple of Yankee schoolboys who just read the Declaration of Independence. Now I'm a political realist. Change is one thing, but I call what you're talking about rebellion.

MACKENZIE: Call it revolution if you want, Tiger.

DUNLOP: Well, I don't think you're the man to lead it. My God, man, you can't even buy a cow without offending the herdsman. Colonel, you're a dear and old friend, but it is the truth sir—you are old. Waterloo was long ago. Now if you gentlemen will permit me, I believe I have a responsibility to history. Dr. William Dunlop does not join in insurrection against the rightful government of—

MACKENZIE: I take it all this pomposity is leading up to a "no."

DUNLOP: Yes—I mean, no.

MACKENZIE: Well, it's a long ride back to Toronto, Dunlop. Goodbye.

He exits.

VAN EGMOND: Tiger, do you know that you are twice as old as I am?

VAN EGMOND starts out. DUNLOP calls to him as he is almost out the door.

DUNLOP: Van Egmond—

VAN EGMOND: Goodnight.

He exits. Light on TIGER alone. Fade to black.

LEAVING

The following six scenes concern people leaving for the battle. Each is introduced by a verse from the song "Across Toronto Bay."

ALL:
Up now and shoulder arms, and join this free men's march boys,
It's time to show the Tories that this country's no man's toy.
So it's march, march, march to Toronto town today,
And we'll use that fork to pitch Bond Head— across Toronto Bay.

A MERCHANT and the man who does his chores. The EMPLOYEE is carrying an armful of wood. He drops it with a crash.

MERCHANT: Rather sloppy of you Thomas.

THOMAS: That's just my way of saying goodbye sir.

MERCHANT: Goodbye?

THOMAS: Yes sir. I'm going to be leaving your employ.

MERCHANT: You've never mentioned anything of this before.

THOMAS: Well, you see the way I figure it sir, I think there's going to be a fight and I have just the merest suspicion that you and me are going to be on different sides.

MERCHANT: Thomas, I would not become embroiled in this if I were you.

THOMAS: I just don't think it would be fair, sir, for me to keep taking your wages, in case we met on the battlefield—and I had to shoot you dead. *(chortling)* So I'll just be off now sir. Goodbye— and good luck. *(A hearty laugh as he goes out.)*

ALL:
It's time to do a different job and take a different stand,
They said we're good for chopping wood and clearing off the land.
So it's march, march, march to Toronto town today,
And we'll use that fork to pitch Bond Head— across Toronto Bay.

HAROLD, a farmer, holding a pistol.

HAROLD: I just can't do it. I never thought I'd have to really shoot somebody when we were drilling. I—I'll tell them I can't go. No, that's no good. I know—I'll say I can't go tonight. I'll meet them tomorrow.

Enter his friend TOM.

TOM: Ready, Harold?

HAROLD: Tom—uh, yeah, I'm ready.

TOM: Good!

HAROLD: Uh, look—I even stole a pistol.

TOM: A pistol! Well then—you're in charge!

They exit together.

ALL:
So let those Tories have their fun and slop up all that tea.
I'd just as soon I killed myself a Tory as a tree.
So it's march, march, march to Toronto town today,
And we'll use that fork to pitch Bond Head— across Toronto Bay.

FRED BENCH and his new wife RUTH, both of whom we met in the tavern scene in Act One. They are in bed.

RUTH: Fred—I heard awful stories in town today. People were talking about the Rebels. They say that they're going to burn Toronto.

FRED: Some people have just cause Ruth.

RUTH: Fred Bench, don't you talk that way. Oh Fred! You wouldn't yourself—don't tell me that you'd—

FRED: Now Ruth—I'll do what I think is best for you.

RUTH: Well that's better. Don't let me even think that you'd … oh well, I'm sure the Governor will soon put a stop to all this.

FRED: Uh-huh.

RUTH: Goodnight.

FRED: Goodnight Ruth.

She falls asleep. He feigns sleep, then rolls out of bed, grabs his boots and rifle, and steals toward the door.

ALL:
A war will bring some death, boys, it's sure to bring you sorrow.
But if we stand back to back today, we'll own this land tomorrow.
So it's march, march, march to Toronto town today,
And we'll use that fork to pitch Bond Head—across Toronto Bay.

A BOY sneaking through the woods. His younger BROTHER and SISTER intercept him.

BOY: How'd you two get in front of me?

SISTER: We followed you.

BOY: Well, you're not supposed to. Go home.

BROTHER: You're supposed to be looking after us.

BOY: I can't for now. So get on home.

SISTER: We know where you're going.

BOY: I don't care if you know. You're not coming with me.

BROTHER: We'll tell.

BOY: Don't you dare tell! Just take your sister and get on home.

They whine.

BOY: Get going. I'll be back.

He exits. His BROTHER darts after him. The SISTER looks around, lost, and cries.

ALL:

Now Old Mac says we've got a cause to load our rifles for,
So leave that stove and woman home and march right out the door.
For it's march, march, march to Toronto town today,
And we'll use that fork to pitch Bond Head—across Toronto Bay.

ISAAC CASSELMAN's Tavern, as in Act One. EMMA and JAMEY are cleaning around. Enter ISAAC, carrying his rifle and pistol.

ISAAC: Emma, put out the fire. Jamey, you lock the tavern. This tavern is closed.

EMMA: What's going on?

ISAAC: There's a war on, by God, and Isaac Casselman is going off to fight.

JAMEY: Isaac—gimme your pistol.

He grabs it and points it into his mouth.

ISAAC: Jamey—what're you doing?

JAMEY: I'm going to kill myself.

ISAAC: *(grabbing the pistol back)* Why?

JAMEY: Well if you're closing the tavern, I've got no reason to go on living.

ISAAC: Jamey—why don't you come along?

JAMEY: *(scornful)* Naaa—

ISAAC: Maybe there'll be a rum ration.

JAMEY: Rum? *(He grabs the pistol and leads the way.)* Forward—

ALL:
Now all across the country, you can hear the Rebel yell,
We'll follow you Mackenzie, to Toronto or to hell.
So it's march, march, march to Toronto town today,
And we'll use that fork to pitch Bond Head—across Toronto Bay.

MARY MACDONALD, whom we met in Act One, fresh from Scotland, is sitting in her farmhouse doing some chore. She is singing to herself.

MARY: Speed, bonnie boat, like a bird on the wing. Onward the sailors cry—

Enter her husband EDWARD.

MARY: Edward, you're home early.

EDWARD: *(kissing her)* Mary—

MARY: Is anything wrong? *(EDWARD sits down uncomfortably.)* What is it, Edward?

EDWARD: You remember when we first met— and we didn't know each other at all—and we were afraid things wouldn't work out—

MARY: Yes, I remember—

EDWARD: I know I've never said very much. That's just my way. But I want you to know that it's been ... Hell—I've got to go fight.

MARY: *(accepting it with difficulty)* Yes. Of course.

EDWARD: *(relieved)* Of course? Do you think it's wrong—us being married such a short time?

MARY: No. I don't. Of course you must go.

EDWARD is immensely grateful that she accepts it.

MARY: When do you have to go?

EDWARD: They said they'd come by about daybreak.

MARY: Oh. We have some time then.

EDWARD: Yes. *(getting her drift)* Oh. You mean ...

He takes her hand and leads her upstairs. There is a knock at the door.

EDWARD: Who's there?

FLETCHER: *(outside)* It's Fletcher, Edward. There's been a change in plans. We have to go meet Lount at the crossroads right now.

EDWARD: But they said tomorrow—

FLETCHER: I don't care what they said. We have to leave right away.

EDWARD: I'll be right out.

FLETCHER: Right now!

EDWARD: *(angrily)* I *said* I was coming!

MARY: I'll get your things.

She hands him his coat and his rifle. They embrace. He starts toward the door, stops, returns to her.

EDWARD: I love you. By God I do. I love you.

He rushes out.

MARY: *(sobbing)* Oh no. No. He never said that to me before. No. No—

Fade to black.

VAN EGMOND'S MARCH

During this scene, the focus is on COLONEL ANTHONY VAN EGMOND as he travels toward Toronto. But around him many things take place: the daily work of the people he passes; events occurring in Toronto; encounters with people on the road. A small table serves as VAN EGMOND's horse.

VAN EGMOND: Colonel Anthony Van Egmond— age sixty-seven, veteran of the Napoleonic Wars, owner of a parcel of fourteen thousand acres in the Huron Tract near Goderich—is appointed commander-in-chief of the Patriot forces. December 3, 1837, he sets out from his farm on horseback, to meet with his troops at Montgomery's Tavern, north of Toronto, on December 7—the date set for the advance on the city.

He mounts his horse and begins his march.

VAN EGMOND: Day one. There is a light snow falling, muffling the sound. I shall travel alone to avoid suspicion. If we are to get the advantage of the enemy, we must take them by surprise. *(Notes as he goes.)* St. Columban—

MESSENGER: *(rushing from the opposite direction)* Colonel! Colonel!—I'm glad I caught you sir. There's been a change—

VAN EGMOND: Change?

MESSENGER: Yes sir—they've changed the date. From the seventh to the fourth.

VAN EGMOND: Who issued this change?

MESSENGER: It's a message sir—from that Dr. Rolph.

VAN EGMOND: Dr. Rolph does not have the power to make such changes. Only Mackenzie does.

MESSENGER: Yes he does. He said—

VAN EGMOND: There has been no change! December 7 is the date for the advance on the city!

MESSENGER: Yes sir. No change.

He exits.

VAN EGMOND: *(continuing his march)* We could not possibly muster enough men before December 7. *(noting his progress)* Mitchell. Ah— another homesteader. He shall see such changes made!

A TORY PICKET IN TORONTO: Anderson!

He fires a shot. ANTHONY ANDERSON, a Rebel, is hit, lurches across the stage, and falls dead at the feet of VAN EGMOND.

A FARMER: *(to VAN EGMOND)* You—you hear the news?

VAN EGMOND: News?

FARMER: Yup. Seems a man named Anderson— Anthony Anderson—and another fellow named Moodie—both shot outside of Toronto. Don't know any more about it.

VAN EGMOND: *(dismounting for the night)* Seebach's Inn. Sebringville. *(to the INNKEEPER)* What do you know of events in Toronto?

INNKEEPER: I heard that a government man named Moodie'd been shot. And a Rebel name of Anderson.

VAN EGMOND: Confirmed.

INNKEEPER: No, no—that's just talk as far as I know.

VAN EGMOND: Anthony Anderson was the only other Rebel leader with military experience.

Freeze.

VAN EGMOND: Day two. *(He remounts his horse.)* Stratford. There's much more activity on the roads today.

A TRAVELLER: Where are you going sir?

VAN EGMOND: Toronto.

TRAVELLER: You can't go there. The Americans have attacked. They're going to burn the city—

VAN EGMOND: The Americans have not attacked.

TRAVELLER: Yes they have. I heard it from somebody who heard it from someone who was there—

VAN EGMOND: Nonsense.

TRAVELLER: I'm warning you. I wouldn't go on—

He exits, blathering.

VAN EGMOND: Mackenzie, you must hold fast for more forces!

A MOUNTED HORSEMAN enters, dismounts and posts a handbill advertising a reward for MACKENZIE. (This was done using the actor who played MACKENZIE and, as it were, nailing him to the wall as though he were the poster.)

HORSEMAN: By authority of the Lieutenant-Governor, a reward of one thousand pounds is hereby offered to anyone who will apprehend and deliver up to justice William Lyon Mackenzie. God Save the Queen.

VAN EGMOND: *(dismounting)* Helmer's Inn. Waterloo.

He approaches the "handbill" and addresses it, with MACKENZIE's own call to arms.

VAN EGMOND: Canadians, do you love freedom?

MACKENZIE: *(i.e., the MACKENZIE in the handbill)* I know you do. Do you hate oppression? Who would deny it. Then buckle on your armour and drive out these villains who enslave and oppress our country.

VAN EGMOND: *(responding)* Long after we are dead, free men shall salute us.

They embrace. Freeze. VAN EGMOND remounts.

VAN EGMOND: Day three. Breslau.

OLD MAN: Sir—have you heard the news from Toronto?

As he tells this news to VAN EGMOND, someone else recounts it directly to the audience.

A REBEL: Well I can tell you exactly how it happened because I was there. It was a hell of a battle and it was right there at the corner of Yonge and College. You see, Sheriff Jarvis stationed his men behind a fence, just waiting for the Rebels to come marching down. Well, we came alright—in the dead of night. We moved out of the tavern, formed up at the tollgate at Bloor Street and then marched down Yonge, proud as peacocks, five abreast. They waited till we got really close, and then they let loose. Well they cut some of us down, but we fired back. And then we dropped down to let the men behind us fire. But the men behind—they were green—they thought we'd dropped because we were all dead. So they turned around and ran back to the tavern. Sheriff Jarvis' men—they were even greener than that—they threw away their guns and ran back to Toronto.

Great confusion onstage. People milling and fleeing. VAN EGMOND tries to stem the tide.

VAN EGMOND: Wait! If you want something you stay and fight for it!

They push past him, leaving him alone and dejected. He dismounts and sits down despairingly.

VAN EGMOND: What is happening in Toronto? Why didn't they wait? Fools—so much at stake— if only I knew! I am an old man; there is still honour in retreat. I shall return home—

Enter a REBEL, overhears VAN EGMOND.

REBEL: Yah, you go home, go back to your farm. Whatever you do, don't go to Toronto.

VAN EGMOND: Have you come from Toronto?

REBEL: I *ran* from Toronto. I'm going home.

VAN EGMOND: What is happening there?

REBEL: Macnab's in the city. He's brought four hundred armed militiamen. They're barricading the city. They're going to shoot us like rats—

VAN EGMOND: Macnab? I'd like to fight Macnab.

REBEL: You're welcome to him.

VAN EGMOND: What is the condition of the patriot forces?

REBEL: Bad.

VAN EGMOND: Are they still coming in?

REBEL: Yah, they're coming in—

VAN EGMOND: They are—

REBEL: But they're leaving just as fast as they come in.

VAN EGMOND: Why?

REBEL: Because there's no leadership there. Nobody knows what they're doing. Someone orders this. Another one orders that—

VAN EGMOND: If there had been a leader there—whom you trusted—would you have fled?

REBEL: I'm no coward. I'd have stayed.

VAN EGMOND: *(extending his hand)* Colonel Anthony Van Egmond, son—

REBEL: Colonel—

VAN EGMOND: Will you march back to Toronto with me?

REBEL: Yes sir.

A chorus of "yes sir" begins to build in the background.

VAN EGMOND: You see Macnab is no soldier. He is a bully but he has no strategy. Help me up. *(He mounts.)* Have you ever been in a real battle, boy?

REBEL: Only on Yonge Street, sir.

VAN EGMOND: That was no battle. It was a skirmish. Do you know—I was fifteen years in the Napoleonic Wars. Wounded fourteen times and never once in the back.

The chorus of "yes sir" builds and transforms into the "Marseillaise."

A REBEL: Remember Moscow!

VAN EGMOND: Macnab, you'll rue the day—

REBEL: Remember Waterloo!

VAN EGMOND: Mackenzie, hold fast now—

REBEL: Think of Montgomery's Tavern!

VAN EGMOND: Lancers ho—

A SENTRY: Halt!

Silence.

A SENTRY: Who goes there?

VAN EGMOND: Colonel Van Egmond.

SENTRY: Hot damn general—are we glad to see you!

VAN EGMOND: Where is Mackenzie?

SENTRY: He's inside, sir. I'll show you. We didn't know if you were coming at all. Some said you weren't.

VAN EGMOND: Well I'm here aren't I?

SENTRY: Yes sir. You are. He's right in there. Don't tell him I forgot to salute—

VAN EGMOND: Mackenzie—

He storms in.

THE BATTLE

This scene continues directly from the previous scene.

VAN EGMOND: Mackenzie, what in hell is going on here?

MACKENZIE: Colonel, thank God you're here. Rolph changed the date. Everything's in a mess. Macnab's in the city with four hundred men.

VAN EGMOND: How many do we have?

MACKENZIE: Two hundred and fifty.

VAN EGMOND: Not enough. When do we expect more?

MACKENZIE: Tonight. December 7. They'll be down tonight.

VAN EGMOND: Then we wait till they arrive.

MACKENZIE: Colonel, we can't wait to be attacked.

VAN EGMOND: You cannot go against Macnab with a handful of men.

MACKENZIE: We've got to do something—

REBEL SOLDIER: *(to audience)* It is finally decided to send a diversionary force under Peter Matthews to the east to burn the Don Valley Bridge and draw off the main Loyalist force. The rest wait at Montgomery's for reinforcements. Meanwhile, back in Toronto, the Loyalist army is drawn up in front of Archdeacon Strachan's residence—known as The Palace—on Front Street.

The Loyalist army forms up.

BOND HEAD: I am Sir Francis Bond Head. I have a double-barrelled pistol in my bandolier, a rifle leaning against my thigh, and a brace of pistols in my belt. So good to see so many respected citizens standing in the ranks today.

THE RANKS: Pip pip—Hear hear—

BOND HEAD: We march at noon. Forward—march!

They set out.

REBEL SOLDIER: Meanwhile to the east, Matthews and his men have crossed the bridge and moved west on King Street. They meet a contingent of militia and retreat back across the bridge, attempting to burn it as they go. In the exchange of fire, one man is fatally shot through the throat. *(This all is acted out.)* The bridge itself is saved.

A LOYALIST: But the main Loyalist force is already moving north toward Montgomery's. *(Shouts)* Bugler—strike up a tune!

The Loyalist army marches to "Yankee Doodle"—an old British parody of Americans and Americanizers.

LOYALIST: Six hundred men remain in the centre with Bond Head. One hundred fifty off to the right flank. Two hundred on the left.

A REBEL SENTRY: Hey wake up—

HIS FRIEND: What? *(looking out at the approaching army)* Good God!

SENTRY: There must be thousands of them—

FRIEND: I'll stay and watch them. You go tell Mackenzie—

SENTRY: *(riding off)* Mackenzie! They're coming this way—you'd better go see—

MACKENZIE: Form up the men! *(The Rebels form up.)* There is the enemy! They outnumber us. They are better armed. And they have artillery—but they are the men we came to fight. Will you fight them?

A hearty Rebel cheer.

MACKENZIE: Forward—

A REBEL: A force of two hundred and fifty under Van Egmond and Samuel Lount advance into the woods to the south of the tavern. Another sixty position themselves behind rail fences on the other side of the road. Two hundred yet unarmed men remain in the tavern.

The battle is staged. The Rebel soldiers talk frantically among themselves as they watch the overwhelming force of the Loyalists moving toward them. The battle itself is bitter and very brief. The two nine-pound cannons of the Loyalists decimate the Rebel formations. The Rebels are crushed. In the end the Loyalists are totally triumphant. The bodies and weapons of the Rebels litter the field. The Loyalists clean up. All of this with much screaming, swearing and writhing.

MACKENZIE: *(as he escapes)* Mackenzie is the last man to leave the field. Together with Van Egmond he goes to a nearby farmhouse. The farmer's wife diverts soldiers while Mackenzie escapes, but Van Egmond, exhausted, is captured. Mackenzie heads west toward the Niagara border. Rewards are offered for him everywhere, but not a soul who sees him reports him. Within days he has established the provisional government of the State of Upper Canada on Navy Island in the Niagara River. He arrives with twenty-six men but soon has hundreds more. Macnab encamps on the opposite shore with a government force of five thousand. Mackenzie gathers the arms and provisions which will enable him to return and join Dr. Charles Duncombe, who has raised a Rebel army near London. He waits for his chance to move. *(stepping into character)* And while I wait, I fire my four cannons here at Macnab across the river—just to let him know I'm still here!

Boom. Boom. Boom. Boom.

Blackout.

KNOCK ON THE DOOR

An old Canadian tradition. The following three scenes depict break-ins by government forces at the homes of suspected Rebels. Knock, knock, knock in the dark. Lights up as a SOLDIER breaks through the door and in on a WOMAN alone.

SOLDIER: Get the hell out of here. We're burning this house down!

She screams. He shoves her out. Blackout.

Knock, knock, knock in the dark.

SOLDIER: Open up in the name of the Queen!

Lights up. A WOMAN opens. He barges in.

SOLDIER: Where's your husband, Mrs. Polk?

WOMAN: I have no husband.

SOLDIER: No? Then who's that ugly man you've been living with for the last seven years.

WOMAN: Go away—

SOLDIER: *(searching)* Where is he?

WOMAN: He's dead. There's nothing here for you, so please leave my house—

SOLDIER: He's been seen Mrs. Polk. He's gone too far this time—

He is bashing away at her belongings with his rifle butt. She leaps on him furiously from behind. He wrestles her to the ground, pins her there. She struggles futilely.

SOLDIER: We're going to get him, and we're going to hang him, but before we do, I'm going to punch his face off. And then, Mrs. Polk, what're you going to do for a man—

She spits in his face. He raises a fist.

ANOTHER SOLDIER: *(from outside)* Come on George. There's no one here.

SOLDIER: I'll be back.

He exits.

Blackout.

Knock, knock, knock in the dark.

Lights up. Enter HAROLD, the fellow from the earlier scene who was afraid to go off to fight. He rushes in and hides under a stair, floorboard or the like. Enter TOM, the friend with whom he'd left to fight the rebellion. TOM is carrying a rifle and clearly searching for Rebels. (Because of all the doubling in this play, it is not immediately evident to the audience that these are HAROLD and TOM from an earlier scene. This works to the advantage of this brief scene as it develops.)

TOM: *(nervously)* Now I seen you come in here. So come on out.

HAROLD coughs.

TOM: If you don't come out by the time I count three, I'll shoot— *(He aims at the place HAROLD is hiding.)* One, two, three— *(He shoots, but his gun misfires.)* Goldarn gun—

HAROLD leaps out of his hiding place and jumps on TOM; the two struggle for several seconds before they recognize each other.

TOM: Harold!

HAROLD: Tom!

TOM: What're you doing here?

HAROLD: I'm hiding! What're you doing? You were with me at Montgomery's Tavern!

TOM: I doubled back through the woods and joined up. Otherwise they'd have arrested me. They're making everyone search. Harold, they know who you are—

HAROLD: I know. They nearly got me twice today. Tom, you gotta help me. I haven't even got a—gimme your gun.

TOM: I can't do that. They'll ask me where it went.

HAROLD: *(grabbing it)* Tell them—tell them you were searching down a well and it fell in. Thanks Tom—

He rushes off.

TOM: *(calling after)* You hide good next time, Harold— *(looking down at his hands, realizing he's stuck without a gun)* What in hell am I—

Blackout.

THE ROPE

Captured Rebels being led to jail in Toronto. A rope is looped over each of their necks. Their hands are tied behind their backs. They march single file. They state their names in turn. When they have gone round once, they go round again.

REBELS: Jacob Beemer, farmer. Taken January 3, 1838, near Stratford.
Richard Thorpe, labourer. Taken December 7, at Montgomery's Tavern.
Caleb Kipp, yeoman. Taken on the road to Buffalo.
John Bradley, teacher. I'm no Rebel. I voted Reform but I'm no Rebel.
Absalom Slade, farmer.
Elijah Rowe, tinker. Taken December 7, at Montgomery's. But it took six of them.
They're burning. Look at that smoke—
I can't feel my toes.

William Stockdale, farmer.
Jonathan Grimes, ropemaker.
Damn the Tories! What're you looking at, lady?

They reach their destination

Hey, lookit who's here!
There's thousands of us!
Hey, anybody here from Newmarket?
Hell, the whole country's in here—
Newmarket?—

A rising babble of greetings etc.

Blackout.

EMIGRATING

A REBEL WOMAN. She is packing, and talking to a neighbour.

REBEL WOMAN: Now the coach is coming at four, got to be ready. And my brother is picking that up, and this is for you. You always admired it and I want you to have it now. We won't need no winter coats where we're going. Yes, I finally convinced my Dan, I just sat down the other day, had the kids all around—they've been getting an awful time from the other kids—and I said, Now Dan, we've tried. We voted Reform, we did what we thought was best, we lost, it's time to face facts. And I just got this letter from my sister. She's got a farm and a fine husband and she said we could go down and stay with them as long as we want, and oh the kids were yelling and screaming and—well what can he say? So we're going.

You know, this place, it's my home, the kids were both born here, but times have changed and we're going to change with them. I wouldn't stay in Stouffville one more day, I'll tell you. But I want you to know you're welcome to come down and visit us any time you want. Oh, it's going to be so fine down there, we'll have a big house, and the kids will go to school— *(calling out the window)* Hey, Mrs. Phipps, you know those two plates you borrowed from me two years ago? You can keep them. She never did like me. What are you people staring at? Anything else in here you can come and take when we're gone. We're leaving it behind. We're going to have five times better. You know why? Because we're going to the Yew-Nited States!

Blackout.

THE HANGINGS

Toronto City Jail.

VAN EGMOND: April 12, 1838. Government forces have scattered Dr. Duncombe's army in the west. Mackenzie himself has fled Navy Island for the United States. Toronto City Jail. Near King and Church Streets. The cells are cold, dark, wet, filled for the most part with patriots awaiting trial and sentencing on charges of high treason. Today they press against the bars of their cells to witness the executions of two of the patriot leaders, Peter Matthews and Samuel Lount. It is the laws, and not their crimes, that condemn them. Anthony Van Egmond might also have been witness to this spectacle but he died, untried, in his cell, December 30, 1837.

MATTHEWS and LOUNT advance to the gallows.

LOUNT: My friends, I address as friends all those in the jail behind me, in all the jails across this province, in the ships bound for Van Diemen's Land, in exile in the United States—there are over eight hundred of us. I am proud to be one of you. John Beverley Robinson—Chief Justice Robinson—you seem to fear we will become martyrs to our countrymen. Well still your fears.

This country will not have time to mourn a farmer and a blacksmith. It will be free, I am certain, long before our deaths have time to become symbols. It cannot remain long under the hell of such merciless wretches that they murder its inhabitants for their love of liberty.

As for us, I do not know exactly how we came to this. Except by a series of steps, each of which seemed to require the next. But if I were to leave my home in Holland Landing again, and march down Yonge Street, I would go by the same route, only hoping that the journey's end would differ. And there will be others coming down that road you know, and others after them, until it does end differently. But for us, the only way on now is by the rope.

MATTHEWS laughs bitterly.

LOUNT: What Peter? What?

MATTHEWS: Sam, we lost—

LOUNT: No! We haven't won yet.

The trap falls. They dangle by the ropes.

Blackout.

END

JAMES REANEY   (b. 1926)

Observing how "life reflected art" in Stratford, Ontario, near where he was born and grew up, James Reaney wrote in a 1962 poem, "Let us make a form out of this: documentary on one side and myth on the other." Perhaps no other Canadian dramatist or poet has so successfully transmuted the local into the universal, the stuff of documentary into the stuff of myth. Avoiding politics for the most part, Reaney makes of the life and history of Souwesto—the small towns and farms of southwestern Ontario—a rich poetic brew steeped in Blake and the Brontës, Walt Disney and the Bible, and leavened with a childlike propensity to treat everything as creative play. In his hands the story of the Donnellys, local history and legend, emerges as an experience of extraordinary theatrical scope and complexity, a trilogy of plays that many people considered the finest achievement of the Canadian theatre in the 1970s.

Reaney was well established as a poet and academic before attempting to write for the stage. He enrolled at the University of Toronto in 1944, and in 1949 earned an M.A. in English and a Governor General's Award for his first book of poetry, *The Red Heart*. After teaching at the University of Manitoba for seven years, he returned to Toronto to pick up his Ph.D. in 1958 along with another Governor General's Award for his second book of verse, *A Suit of Nettles*. In 1960 Reaney began teaching English at the University of Western Ontario, a position he held for thirty years, and founded the innovative journal *Alphabet* which he published and edited until 1971. He also made his remarkable debut in the theatre that year with *The Killdeer*. Mavor Moore hailed it as "the first Canadian play of real consequence, and the first demonstration of genius among us." It won five awards at the 1960 Dominion Drama Festival and a third Governor General's Award for Reaney on its publication in 1962. The play's eclectic symbolist style, melodramatic plot and archetypal struggle between the forces of innocence and corruption signalled the shape of much of Reaney's work to come, including *The Donnellys*.

Reaney kept writing poetry—*Twelve Letters to a Small Town* (1962) and *The Dance of Death at London, Ontario* (1963) —but most of his subsequent work would be in the theatre. *The Killdeer* was followed by *Night-blooming Cereus* and *One-man Masque* (1960), *The Easter Egg* (1962) and a series of fantastical plays for children commencing with the Manitoba Theatre Centre's 1963 production of *Names and Nicknames*.

With *The Sun and the Moon* (1965) at the London Summer Theatre, Reaney began his long association with Keith Turnbull, a key development in the evolution of his stagecraft. In *Listen to the Wind* (1966), produced by Keith Turnbull and directed by Reaney himself, the young protagonist "dreams out" a play-within-a-play from his sickbed. The complex action unfolds on a bare stage with a props table, a few actors, and a chorus of children providing visual metaphors and sound effects. The presentational style reminds us that acting is merely formalized play, a revelation of the power of imagination to transform reality. Out of *Listen to the Wind* developed the Listeners' Workshop. Once a week for two years Reaney led groups of twenty-five or more local children and adults through elaborate play exercises designed to stretch their imaginations by, for example, improvising the Book of Genesis. From these workshops grew what he called the "embryonics" of *Colours in the Dark*, commissioned by the Stratford Festival in 1967. A Joycean epic revealing the macrocosm of all human history in the microcosm of an individual life, the play is described by Reaney as a theatrical experience "designed to give you that mosaic—that all-things-happening-at-the-same-time-higgledy-piggledy feeling that rummaging through a play box can give you."

The embryonics of *The Donnellys* also arose out of the Listeners' Workshop, though Reaney had been fascinated since childhood by this story that had occurred only twenty miles from where he was born. He began researching the project in 1967; and except for a major revision of *The Killdeer* in 1968, *The Donnellys* remained his sole dramatic concern for the next eight years. In 1973 Reaney took what was by then a massive script to Halifax where Keith Turnbull and a group of actors that included Jerry Franken and Patricia Ludwick (the future Mr. and Mrs. Donnelly) put it through a series of workshops from which three separate plays emerged. Bill Glassco agreed to produce them at the Tarragon with Turnbull directing, and in November 1973, *Sticks and Stones: The Donnellys, Part One* opened in Toronto. *Part Two, The St Nicholas Hotel, Wm Donnelly Prop.,* premiered in November 1974 and won the Chalmers Award. *Handcuffs: The Donnellys, Part Three* opened in March 1975. Later that year the newly christened NDWT Company—Reaney, Turnbull, et al.—toured all three plays across Canada. *Fourteen Barrels from Sea to Sea* (1977) is Reaney's highly personal account of the tour. The trilogy had a notable revival at Banff in 1996–97.

Reaney continued to use the workshop-preparation method with the NDWT Company for his next series of plays, all based on local Ontario history or pseudo-history: *Baldoon* (1976), written with C.H. Gervais; *The Dismissal* (1977), featuring Mackenzie King as a scheming undergraduate; *Wacousta!* (1978) and its sequel *The Canadian Brothers* (1983), products of nearly two years' intensive workshops (some of them led by Tomson Highway); *King Whistle* (1979); and *Antler River* (1980). In *Gyroscope* (1981) Reaney returned to more personal dramatic material. With his libretto for John Beckwith's opera *The Shivaree*, first performed in 1982, he was reunited with the composer for whose music he had written *Night-blooming Cereus* twenty years earlier. In 1989 Reaney and Beckwith collaborated on another opera, *Crazy To Kill*, for the Guelph Spring Festival, and the following year Reaney's historical opera *Serinette* (music by Harry Somers) premiered at the Sharon (Ont.) Music Festival. The 1990s saw the publication of a short story collection, *The Box Social* (1996), and a stage adaptation of Lewis Carroll's *Alice through the Looking Glass*, produced at Stratford in 1994 and again in 1996. *Performance Poems* (1990) includes a poem for two voices, "Imprecations," which celebrates the arts of cursing and name-calling, a fitting celebration for a writer who has always held names to be as tangible as sticks and stones, only more powerful.

The Donnelly story as Reaney tells it is very much about the power of names. To carry the Donnelly name is both a curse and a blessing, a sacrament and a doom. In *The St Nicholas Hotel*, Will Donnelly looks into the future and sees how his enemies "smeared our name for all time so that when children are naughty their mothers still say to them be quiet, or the Black Donnellys will get you." Historically, the Donnellys were Irish Catholic immigrants who settled in Biddulph Township near Lucan, Ontario, in 1844. James and Johannah and their seven sons and a daughter almost immediately became embroiled in conflict with their neighbours, and much of the violence that wracked the region—barn burnings, assaults, mutilations of farm animals—was attributed to the Donnellys. In 1857 James Donnelly killed a man in a fight and went to prison for seven years. In 1879 Mike Donnelly was stabbed to death in a hotel bar-room, his assailant imprisoned for only two years. Finally, on the night of February 3, 1880, a mob of vigilantes burst into the Donnelly home and murdered Mr. and Mrs. Donnelly, son Tom and niece Bridget, and later that night son John. Though an eyewitness identified many of the killers, no one ever went to prison for the crimes.

In researching the plays, Reaney discovered that his source material embodied two opposing views of the principals. First there were the evil Donnellys of popular history and local lore, incarnated in Thomas P. Kelley's 1954 best-seller, *The Black Donnellys*, a potboiler that presented the family as "the most vicious and heartless bunch of devils that ever drew the breath of human life." In Kelley's version, the depraved family, led by the monstrous Johannah, terrorize the district for the sheer malicious joy of it and get only what they deserve in the end. A more objective and sympathetic treatment was Orlo Miller's book *The Donnellys Must Die* (1962). Miller argued that the Donnellys were essentially victims of a nasty feud that had carried over from Ireland where they had refused to join the secret anti-Protestant society of Whiteboys (or Whitefeet). As a result, in the largely Irish settlement of Biddulph they were branded with the hated name "Blackfeet," persecuted and made scapegoats for a great deal of local violence which was not of their doing. Reaney ultimately followed Miller's lead, but he went further than just exonerating the Donnellys. He celebrates them.

Part One, *Sticks and Stones*, covers the period 1857–67, opening with an expository flashback showing the Donnellys' stubborn refusal to bend to Whitefoot pressures in Ireland. We see them struggling to make a place for themselves in Biddulph, caught between the Roman (Catholic) and Protestant Lines of settlers, uncomfortable with both. They lose half their farm in a bitter dispute with the Fat Woman and her husband, and Mr. Donnelly is goaded into fighting with the Fat Woman's brother, Pat Farl, who won't stop calling him "Blackfoot." When Mr. Donnelly kills Farl, only a heroic effort by Mrs. Donnelly gets her husband's sentence commuted to seven years in prison. At the end the Biddulph Whitefeet burn the Donnellys' barn and try to intimidate them into leaving the township, but Mr. Donnelly refuses, reiterating what he told them in Ireland: "Donnellys don't kneel." "It was at this time," Reaney writes, "that the Donnellys decided to be Donnellys."

To be a Donnelly in Reaney's portrayal is to be strong, proud, heroic, stubborn, forthright. It is to choose to be true to your own values no matter how much pain that may cause you. It is to stand up against the mob, the community, the church, even the law if they pressure you to be what you are not. It is to be intensely loyal to your own family and to be generous as a family to others whose own have rejected or betrayed them. To be a Donnelly, in short, is to have an integrity lacking in almost every character or institution that opposes them throughout the trilogy, from the corrupt magistrates George Stub and Tom Cassleigh in Part One to the churchmen who organize the vigilantes in Part Three, *Handcuffs*, and the jury that finds mob leader Jim Carroll not guilty of their murder. *Handcuffs*, focusing on the massacre itself and the few months in 1879–80 immediately preceding and following it, really just fills in the details of what Parts One and Two have already told us will happen. The Donnellys *must* die; their pride and stubbornness cannot be endured. They are tragic.

Whereas *Sticks and Stones* introduces the circumstances of the Donnellys' tragedy and *Handcuffs* presents its dénouement, the second play, *The St Nicholas Hotel*, poses the trilogy's key question: "Why did they all hate you so much?" Rev. Donaldson asks it of Will Donnelly in 1891 on the twelfth anniversary of Mike's murder, and Reaney gives us the events of 1873–79 as an answer. Superficially it is Mike's story. The play opens with intimations of his death and closes with his murder, his ghost, and his bloodstain that will never come out. But Mike doesn't die for anything that he as an individual has done; he dies because he is a Donnelly. The events that build inexorably to his death are part of the larger conspiracy that will culminate in the 1880 massacre.

One reason the Donnellys are so hated is their sheer zest for life which makes *The St Nicholas Hotel*, despite its tragic undertones, the most joyful and exhilarating of the three plays, full of stagecoach races, whirling tops, rousing music and dancing. Brimming with positive energy, the Donnellys provide a constant, unwelcome challenge to the negativity and complacency of their neighbours. Will and Maggie's romantic courtship in Act One is set against the calculated bargaining of Stub and Miss Maguire, and the loveless marriage bed of Bill and Mary Donovan. In Act Two young Tom Ryan tells how he ran away from his own brutal home to the Donnellys— making his humiliated father another of their lifelong enemies—"because they're brave" and "they're handsome," and because "there's love there." The Donnellys themselves understand the double-edged nature of their condition. Mr. Donnelly acknowledges that they deserve the way they are treated: "for we're Donnellys." Like the spinning tops that symbolize their vitality, they are caught up in a momentum over which they have little control. They can't help being what they are. "Yes. It would be nice to stop, but we can't oh no we must keep on spinning and spinning," Mrs. Donnelly says. The context is Stub's proposal that they compromise their support of the Liberal candidate and back his Conservative opponent in exchange for a cessation of hostilities. Their rejection of this deal and the subsequent defeat of the Tory candidate add significantly to the enemies who will destroy them in Part Three.

The St Nicholas Hotel is by no means simply a whitewash of the Donnellys. Having exploded the myth of "the Black Donnellys" in Part One, Reaney seems willing in this play to admit to shades of grey. In Acts One and Two we see at times how pride and strength can turn to arrogance and bullying, playfulness to maliciousness, and energy to destruction. Will and Mike never hesitate to employ unfair business practices in running their Opposition Stage Line, even to the point of putting the competition's drivers in danger. Reaney intentionally leaves ambiguous their role in Ned Brooks' fatal accident, but there is little doubt about the responsibility of James Jr. for a variety of atrocities. By the third act, though, the balance of sympathy has swung back wholly in the Donnellys' favour as a result of the pettiness and cowardice of their enemies in the mob scene as well as in Mike's murder. When Will, Norah and Mrs. Donnelly face down the mob, we understand both the awe and the blind hatred this family could inspire. As Reaney's stage direction notes, "We should feel ashamed ourselves that we did not make a better showing against a lame man & two women."

The lame man, and really the central figure in the play, is Will, often called "Cripple" because of his club foot. He and Mrs. Donnelly are the two strongest characters in the trilogy and the ones at whom the most venom is directed. Will is also the most sensitive Donnelly, an artist of sorts, riding a horse called Lord Byron and opposing Jim Carroll with his handwriting and the music of his fiddle. But most of all he is a function of his name, very much the offspring of his father who is described in Part One as "a small square chunk of will"—the essence of Donnelly. The title of the play, The St Nicholas Hotel, Wm Donnelly Prop., locates Will outside Biddulph in a future beyond the massacre, a survivor, proprietor of his own fate and chief prop of a family name that endures as a curse, a legend, a stain on a bar-room floor, and now as a classic of Canadian theatre.

The St Nicholas Hotel, Wm Donnelly Prop.: The Donnellys, Part II was first performed at the Tarragon Theatre on November 16, 1974, with the following cast:

Ken Anderson	Miriam Greene
Nancy Beatty	Michael Hogan
Jay Bowen	Patricia Ludwick
Tom Carew	Don MacQuarrie
Peter Elliott	Keith McNair
David Ferry	Gord Stobbe
Jerry Franken	Suzanne Turnbull
Rick Gorrie	

Directed by Keith Turnbull
Designed by Rosalyn Mina

Note: The punctuation of The St Nicholas Hotel—eccentric, inconsistent and often technically incorrect—has been left as Reaney intended it, to reflect the rhythms of his characters' speech. "Publishers beware: you rob the performers when you change Reaney's punctuation." (Patricia Ludwick, "One Actor's Journey with James Reaney," in Approaches to the Work of James Reaney [1983].) —Ed.

THE ST NICHOLAS HOTEL, WM DONNELLY PROP.
THE DONNELLYS, PART II

CHARACTERS

MR DONNELLY (James)
MRS DONNELLY (Johannah)
MIKE
WILL
JAMES JR
TOM   } *their sons*
JOHN
BOB
PATRICK
JENNY, *their daughter*
BRIDGET, *their niece*
NELLIE, *Mike's wife*
NORAH (née Macdonald), *Will's wife*

JOHN MACDONALD, *Norah's brother*
MOTHER

BARTENDER (Frank Walker)
NED BROOKS, *a stage driver*
PATRICK FINNEGAN, *a stageowner*

REV. DONALDSON, *a traveller*

MISS MERCILLA MAGUIRE (*later Mrs George Stub*)
REV. DR MAGUIRE, *her father*
GEORGE STUB, *a merchant*

FAT LADY
JIM CARROLL, *her son*
BRIDGET, *her daughter (the Stubs' parlourmaid)*
WILL FARL, *her nephew*

MAGGIE DONOVAN, *her niece*
FATHER
AUNT THERESA
BILL DONOVAN, *Maggie's brother*
MARY DONOVAN, *his wife*
MOTHER SUPERIOR
NUNS

TOM RYAN
NED RYAN, *his father*
MRS RYAN

BAKER
BAKER'S APPRENTICE
McKELLAR, *a stage driver*
MR SCANDRETT, *a tollman*

MRS SCANDRETT
CHILD
CESSMAN

SQUIRE FERGUSON, *a Justice of the Peace*
CONSTABLE BERRYHILL
HUGH McCRIMMON, *a detective*
BAILIFFS
CONSTABLES
PRIEST
FIDDLER

TIMOTHY CORCORAN, *a Tory candidate*
ELECTIONS CLERK

CHAIRMAN (of the "Peace Society")
O'HALLORAN
DAN QUIGLEY, *a farmer*
SCHOOLMASTER

SID SKINNER (aka "Bill Lewis")
BILL LEWIS, *a trainer*
GREENWOOD
JIM MORRISON, *Mike Donnelly's workmate*

2 MAIDS

STAGE DRIVERS
STAGE PASSENGERS
TOLLGATE KEEPERS
TRAVELLERS
FARMERS
BOYS AND GIRLS
MOB
CHORUS

AUTHOR'S NOTE

The story of this play concerns a race, a race between the Donnelly boys and their enemies. The road the race takes place on has tollgates with signs on them saying: NO DONNELLYS ARE TO ... run a stage line, marry my daughter, &c., &c. "Helped" by their brothers, William & Michael Donnelly smash through most of the tollgates, but their victories only drive their enemies to build stronger & stronger barriers until, at last, Michael is suddenly & brutally murdered.

It is a tale of barrooms, wheels, horses, nuns, tops, convent yards, derailed trains, homeless boys, tavern brawls, refinements, squalors, wedding cakes, drunkards—and ghosts. In a certain hotel deserted for thirty years there is a stain on the floor no ordinary scrubbing brush can ever wash away.

James Reaney

ACT ONE

The barroom of the City Hotel, London; later on it will be the barroom of the Royal Hotel in Exeter, the St Nicholas Hotel (Wm Donnelly, prop.) in Appin, and Slaght's Hotel in Waterford. The barman seems always there; his somewhat skullish face and presence will remind us later on before we go to sleep that—this is the man who eventually killed Mike Donnelly. Behind the bar is a picture of Wm Donnelly's black stallion, Lord Byron. Passengers to the stages to the north slowly fill the benches at the sides of the room we too are waiting in; we see actors spinning tops (each one seems to have one) and hear them singing songs from the play. Like a cloud shadow the stage picture is slowly invaded now by the story of a road; the actors stop being actors and become fighters for the ownership of that road, a map of which goes all around the walls of the theatre from Crediton to Exeter to Clandeboye down to Lucan to Elginfield to London to St Thomas to Waterford, and advancing towards us comes the

STAGEDRIVER (NED BROOKS): *(belching)* Are there any passengers for Masonville, St John's, Bobtown, Ryan's Corners, Lucan, Flanagan's Corners, Mooretown, Exeter? Now loading at the front door please.

MIKE DONNELLY: Are there any more ladies and gentlemen for Calamity Corners as tis sometimes called, St John's, Birr—my old friend Ned here calls it Bobtown, the more elegant name is Birr. Elginfield known to some as Ryan's Corners, Lucan that classic spot if it's not all burnt down, Clandeboye, Mooretown, Exeter and Crediton. If Ned here hasn't sawn it to pieces the coach is waiting for you at the front door and it pleases you.

STAGEDRIVER: What does it matter if it's Bobtown or Birr; elegance be damned, Mike Donnelly, it's my team will get you there faster.

LADY: *(coming back in)* Which stage is yours then? Louisa, there are no less than four stages out there all with different names. Sir wh—

STAGEDRIVER:
The Favourite Line
Hawkshaw's Stage
Good Horses, Comfortable Stages & Fast Time. Leaves the City Hotel for all points north at two o'clock p.m.

WILLIAM & MIKE DONNELLY pass out announcement cards.

ANCIENT STAGEDRIVER: *(entering & flourishing a ragged whip)* Come on everybody, Ho! for the North Uriah Jennings here, fifty years on the road, *(coughing)*

YET ANOTHER STAGEDRIVER: Anybody here want a lift up north. You'll have to share the accommodation a little with

LADY TWO: Martha, he's got six young pigs, two geese and a sack of flour in there already.

CHORUS: *(reading cards)*
Notice
Exeter, Lucan & London Daily Stage: Change of Time.

WILL: Leaves City Hotel at 2 p.m. and arrives Maclean's Hotel, Lucan at half past four

MIKE: Twenty minutes ahead of all other stages.

Both halves begin together, but the first half pauses so the names are spoken after the second half has completed its speech:

HALF CHORUS	HALF CHORUS
Drivers	calling all places along the route for passengers
William and Michael Donnelly	

Into the bar comes a hard-driving Irishman who has as much force as the Donnellys but all as hard as grindstone.

FINNEGAN: Just a minute there, Donnelly—whoa!! You boys aren't going to Lucan today.

WILL: *(with whip)* It's Patrick Finnegan says we won't get to Lucan?

FINNEGAN: Ah, yes, Will, because *(to audience)* good evening—don't you know my brother John Finnegan and myself, Pat, have bought out your boss and all his horses and wagons, so it's the Finnegan Stage now. Come along now, these passengers are mine, the road is mine, and the wheels. Give your whip to my driver, Will. Mr. Brooks, here's—he's driving for me, Will. I don't need you Donnelly boys. *(trying to take whip)*

MIKE: Give that whip back to my brother. *(grabbing it)* No one ever lent us a whip.

WILL: No, my father bought me that whip with the very first money I ever earned, on St Nicholas day—five years ago and that's how long we've been driving our stage.

FINNEGAN: There you go, Will, it was never your stage. It belonged to Hugh McPhee and now it belongs to Pat Finnegan. We leave at two p.m. sharp, ladies and gentlemen, passengers to reach Lucan safely to connect with east and west trains to St Mary's and Sarnia.

MIKE: Do you want to know, Mr. Pat Finnegan, how Will and Mike Donnelly will still beat you to Lucan today by a good half hour?

FINNEGAN: It's my brother and myself here run a store and tavern up the road north of here— why the place is called after our father Finnegan's Corners, for God's sake, there were three hundred buggies at his funeral. Sure our father built the Proof Line Road these fellows say is theirs. So step up into my stage wagon and see whose road it is. Mike Donnelly, we'll run yous off it. Are there anymore passengers— *(exit)*

MIKE: Look, we're starting our own line with our own equipment. Mr. Jennings, how much do you want for your vehicle that's been fifty years on the road. Will, just take a look at his beasts.

WILL: We'll have to get new horses, fast ones, where we can get—

CHORUS: William Donnelly, Groom.

The actors "melt" into a scene at the London races. They are held back from the track by a long rope. The BARTENDER jumps up on the bar and interprets the race through a megaphone. We only hear the drumming of invisible hooves and see on human faces the effect of the race.

MIKE:
The horses for our stage line were bred from the winner of this race. We had the rights to a mare called Irish Girl whose mother you may recall was Billet Doux, grandmother to Sir Walter Scott. So, Will, is it let this race decide who'll sire the foal that is the nighhorse of our team on—what'll we call it.

Get a pool of extra silence around the naming of the line

WILL:
The Opposition Stage

BARTENDER:
The second day's meeting of The London Turf Club on the Newmarket race course attracted a large crowd yesterday afternoon. The weather was delightful and the track in good condition, except that it was a trifle dusty.

CHORUS:
(over & under) Words blown away by the wind, dust & words in the stream of the time we all lie dreaming in

CHORUS:
dreaming of horses and wagons going up the hill

This speech and the ones below go on simultaneously with WILL's "Opposition Stage" coming in just after the CHORUS's "dreaming in." The BARTENDER should blur his voice under and over the other levels so that we get the effect of a real racetrack where wind & distance play tricks with announcements; also it is a remembered racetrack where MIKE DONNELLY not only saw the horse they needed but also the first omen of his own death.

BARTENDER: Dash of 1 1/2 miles. Entries. Sleepy Jim, bay stallion & his colours are blue & yellow owned by Messrs Bookless & Thomas, Guelph. Florence Nightingale, grey mare. Scarlet & white.

CHORUS: Down the hill

BARTENDER: Lord Byron, full brother to Clear Grit out of Fleetwood the Second. He thus comes of good stock & will be heard of further.

CHORUS: Long white road

BARTENDER: Black & red, and *(an actor runs around as Lord Byron—sometimes disappearing from view, then reappearing and followed avidly by all of the spectators' eyes)* they're off! Although the delay in starting caused a good deal of impatience this, ladies and gentlemen, is an ex—citing dash. From the first it lies between Sleepy Jim, Nigger Baby & Lord Byron and, ladies & gents, as they first pass the string they are well abreast. On the turn, however, they're breaking up & now it's an open question. It's an open question, ladies & knights, which is going to win. It's Sleepy Jim, no it's Lord Byron—past the string slightly ahead of Finnegan who flashed up from behind with Nigger Baby third. Lord Byron, ran, ladies & gentlemen, without his regular *(gasp from the crowd who see the jockey's death before the barman does)* trainer & his victory here today is therefore a greater tribute to his speed. Sorry to report. There seems to have been an accident there to Lord Byron's jockey among the oak trees there at the edge of the grove. A low branch.

CHORUS: Words blown away by the wind, dust & words in the stream of

BARTENDER: Time. Two minutes forty-nine & a half seconds.

Two human runners in singlets appear—one of them is DETECTIVE McCRIMMON whom Finnegan will one day hire to pursue the Donnellys.

BARTENDER: Next ladies & gentlemen, it is calculated to have a foot race in addition, 100 yards, for a shake-purse. BANG!

The runners sweep toward us and then— whistles! and the actors all turn into a herd of horses in a Biddulph pasture; the Donnellys with their father have come to take out a team for evening training. Umbrella, fiddle.

MIKE: Our father and another old man helped us to train the horses. Ploughboy! Pilot!

MIKE & CHORUS: Farmer. Indian.

MIKE: You see our horses came running to their names!

MIKE & CHORUS: Manilla. Ginger.

A team comes up for training, umbrella thrown at them, horses shy, then calm. Slowly, all the horses grow used to umbrella & fiddle.

MR DONNELLY: Throw the frightening old floppy thing at him again, Mike. And again. There my beauty. Again. There. Whisper to you. The fiddle, Will. *(excruciating notes)* There my beauty, my dove.

We return from the horse pasture to the tavern; crowd is a crowd once more.

MIKE: Our brother Patrick had been apprenticed to a Carriage Works in town here. As a black-smith. He helped turn the rusty old vehicle we bought from Jennings into a pretty smart, smooth road bird with new wheels for wings.

anvil in distance

FINNEGAN: Are there any more passengers for London? Sure you'll want to see Mr. Barnum's Circus that's in town today, and we've put on an extra stage just to accommodate the crowd.

WILL & MIKE: On the sides of our stage what did we have painted?

CHORUS: *(with varying strength and texture)*
The Opposition Stage.
Between London & Crediton
Through Exeter daily at 4 a.m.
First Rate Accommodation
Prices Moderate
Proprietor, William Donnelly,
Driver, Michael Donnelly.
William Donnelly, Gentleman.

LADY: Prices moderate, Mr. Donnelly? How much is a ticket to Lucan on your conveyance?

WILL: Seventy cents, m'am.

TWO GIRLS: Mr Finnegan, does your stage go into Crediton?

FINNEGAN: Shure, and it can be induced to.

TWO GIRLS: Are you entirely sure because your advertisement notes your destination as Exeter which is just four miles short of where Uncle Dan Philip lives.

FINNEGAN: Girls, I'll get you there if I have to take yous on my back. *(to LADY)* Sixty cents.

A routine where she wavers between FINNEGAN & DONNELLY, running back & forth.

WILL: Fifty

FINNEGAN: Forty it is.

WILL & MIKE: Thirty it is.

FINNEGAN: Donnelly! Twenty, Madam.

WILL: Sure that's nothing at all. We'll take you for a kiss and a penny. Michael, take the fare.

LADY: *(held on MIKE's arms and another's as in a cart, after being kissed)* I prefer the Opposition Stage. A smooth ride with fast, evenly matched horses. Polite & skillful drivers. One hardly knows where the time has gone when—the diligence stops, the driver jumps down …

But cows are faintly mooing, as if we had reached her farm, and the actors giggling under her effusiveness have crept around to confront her as embarrassing cows …

with firm hand takes yours and helps you across to your very gate.

CHORUS: Her father's cows have come to meet her. *(laughter)*

FINNEGAN: Allaboard for the circus excursion. *(He or his driver blows a horn.)* Here comes Finnegan. Here comes Finnegan.

WILL DONNELLY walks behind the bar and lights a candle as we slide into the next scene. Most of the tavern crowd depart. We hear them getting into the stage & driving off. More horns blast & "Here comes Finnegan." "The Favourite Stage." Behind WILL DONNELLY there is a picture of a black horse. His wife NORAH brings in a tray of glasses and sets them behind the bar. The light changes. Fiddle. Wind.

CHORUS: *(a drifting voice)* Yes, Bill Donnelly ran the St Nicholas Hotel down here at Appin. Was still running it when he died in the nineties. My father bought me some ice cream there in 1924.

And now we are at the St Nicholas Hotel, years after what we have just been watching.

NORAH: Well, so our visitor will not stay the night, is that

WILL: He'll come back. I put something in his cutter

NORAH: It's too stormy a night for anyone to come out save the odd traveller like this reverend gentleman. But perhaps he's right. He should push on to Glencoe now rather than in the morning.

WILL: No. He's going to stay here tonight. You'll see.

NORAH: Are you that lonely, Will?

WILL: Well, if he does not come back maybe we should call up the children and have a game of dominoes. *(pause)* Norah, you know the sort of travellers we get at the St Nicholas Hotel—grain-buyers and sewing machine agents, but—and neighbours into the bar here, but—it's seldom anyone comes down this road from the past, from up there.

The candle wavers.

NORAH: Hsst! That blast came from Biddulph for sure. Sure there's water from there flows by here, in the river doesn't there. But the reverend gentleman did not seem Biddulphian to me, Will.

WILL: We'll find out. I've met him somewhere in the seventies when Mike and me drove stage.

NORAH: So that's why you've lit the candle. I'd forgotten, forgive me, tonight's

WILL: Tonight's the night they murdered Mike, Norah. In a bar not unlike this one

Enter MINISTER with a block of ice in his hands.

NORAH: Sir, you've come back to us out of the storm?

DONALDSON: Who put this block of ice to my feet in my cutter?

WILL: I did, now I'll ask my son to put up your horse. *(through a door)* Jack, we've a customer after all.

DONALDSON: I had to come back to find out why—

WILL: To keep your feet warm, you might as well stay with us, sir. What time is your appointment tomorrow in Glencoe?

DONALDSON: Sabbath School starts at nine. But how would that keep me warm?

WILL: By bringing you back to my St Nicholas Hotel instead of you driving seven miles on through a blizzard. It's warmer here than that.

He takes the ice block and puts it in a pail, all through the evening we watch it slowly melt till it is used by the scrubwomen at the end of the play to wipe MIKE DONNELLY's blood off the floor.

DONALDSON: Now, sir, I've met you somewhere before. The name of the hotel you are running is the St Nicholas Hotel, proprietor is—

WILL: My name is William Donnelly *(pause)* Perhaps you'll want to hitch up your cutter again.

DONALDSON: Now why would you say that, Mr Donnelly?

WILL: Aren't you afraid of me?

DONALDSON: No. Quite the contrary. I remember you and your brother when you ran the stage between London and Lucan, excuse me *one* of the stages. The Opposition Stage.

NORAH: That must be a good many years ago, sir. Twenty years?

DONALDSON: More than that. I started visiting the Presbyterian Church in Lucan on appointments which I would receive, oh let me see now—the fall of 1875. I preferred your stage although people at the church wanted me not to patronize your line. *(to us)* Once I happened to come down to Lucan from Parkhill by train—hence to Irishtown by your rival's stage—The Finnegan Line. The Finnegan Line. I asked the driver how the new railway had affected the stage route between London and Lucan. What has become of the Donnellys?

STAGEDRIVER: *(belching)* Ugh, the Donnellys've been run off the line at last.

DONALDSON: And what do they do now then?

STAGEDRIVER: Yes, what don't they do, sir. They're a bad lot and we're bound to get rid of them.

DONALDSON: Yes, Mr Donnelly. A small glass of wine would not go amiss. Thank you. Then I said *(to him)* It's strange that young men so good looking and so polite as I've always found the Donnelly boys to be, should be so much run down and set on by all parties, Romanists, Protestants and Secretists, when they are so very polite and strive so hard to live down all this opposition, by attention to business and kind treatment of all who favour them. He replied:

STAGEDRIVER: You do not know them, sir. They just put on appearances to deceive strangers. I once thrashed Mike and I will thrash him again.

DONALDSON: *(pause)* Which son is Mike?

STAGEDRIVER: The second from the youngest. No sir, the people are bound to get rid of that family some way or another and that too before too long.

DONALDSON: We had reached the railway station and I told him what I thought as a teacher of the Gospel. I said: "You surely do not mean what you say, or you would not speak so to a stranger: there's room enough for the Donnellys and their opponents also in the world. Why, man, competition is the life of trade; we are all the better of the opposition lines."

STAGEDRIVER: *(laughing)* You're too good yourself, sir, to understand what this family is like. We are bound to snuff out that family and we shall do it, so that it shall never be known how it was done.

DONALDSON: He turned on his heel and left. So, yes, I was never afraid of the Donnellys. William Donnelly. Mike Donnelly.

WILL: And when would that conversation be?

DONALDSON: In January of 1879. As early as that

WILL: As early as that then we were marked out for slaughter.

DONALDSON: Mike, what happened to Michael Donnelly?

WILL: Oh, they got him first at the end of that year—just before Christmas, December the 9th, 1879.

DONALDSON: This is the 12th Anniversary of his death then? *(pause)* I find it very pleasant to be sitting by such a warm fire after travelling through such a storm this afternoon. *(They listen to the gale outside for a few moments.)* You have settled here, Mr Donnelly, in this peaceful place after a stormy journey far worse. Far worse.

WILL: Yes, I keep the inn here, I travel about in the spring with my stallion—True Grit out of Lord Byron and this may astonish you, but people are saying that I am the best constable this village ever had.

NORAH: Sir, I am going upstairs with a warm brick for your bed. I promise you no more ice blocks. How soon do you wish to retire?

DONALDSON: I may never drive this way again. Midnight. Until then Mrs. Donnelly, I should like your husband to explain what lay behind the bloody statement of that young man at the railway station. Why did they all hate you so much?

NORAH: Oh sir, that would take till the dawn itself. *(passing out of the room)*

WILL: I'll tell you why the stage drivers for the other lines hated us so much. *(taking a scissors from Norah's sewing basket)* They blamed us for cutting the tongues out of their horses. Like this. *(laughing & illustrating!)* But at first it was something not quite so Sodom & Gomorrah we were blamed for.

Screams & curses offstage; some monumental collapse of Mr FINNEGAN's stage. Yes, a wheel has come off, for into the barroom it rolls. Passengers enter, shaken & muttering.

FINNEGAN: Who in the mother of Hell's name loosened the bolts and cut the nuts off my wheels. Oh funny it is, Cripple, and one of my wheels skated right into your hands, and funny it is, Mike. Well it wouldn't be so funny if I'd been going down Mother Brown's Hill and they'd come off; we'd been all killed. *(pause)* Ladies & gentlemen, be patient for the twenty-minute delay there'll be while we fix up the wheels. You see what they done, don't go in his stage, you see what they done to me. Oh, Alec *(to bartender)* give me anything you got, oh

MIKE: Now, are there any more passengers for St John's, Birr, Elginfield, Lucan, Finnegan's Corners, Mooretown, Exeter, and even Crediton.

He has been outside for a quarter of this; we hear his voice again outside and nearly the whole chorus eventually decide to follow the hypnotic elegance. Left now are only a maidservant (MAGGIE) and the FAT LADY.

MIKE: Now leaving the City Hotel—the Opposition Stage.

MAGGIE: Cousin Patrick, do me a pleasant thing and allow me to take the Opposition Stage out of town. They'll be put out with me I'm late to serve dinner.

In a necessary manoeuvre we can't see, the Donnelly Stage goes around the hotel, so that it circles the barroom and MAGGIE follows it inside in a circular, birdlike, trapped motion.

FINNEGAN: Your father says, Maggie, you're to have no truck with the Donnellys, shun them and if you get on with them I'll drag you off of—I'll tell your father, miss.

MAGGIE: No need to, Patrick Finnegan. I'll do that myself *(pause, wavering)* Some day. Well how long do I have to wait then, for the sake of heaven?

FINNEGAN: How do I know, the blacksmith made no—but I swear I'll get them, for it's only them would do a trick like that, loosen my wheels *(runs outside)* I'll snuff them …

FAT LADY: Maggie Donovan I'd wait a week, a year not to have to take that blackguard Donnelly's wagon. I'd walk up to Biddulph on my bare knees rather than use their coach.

MAGGIE: Would you now.

FAT LADY: Why girl, it's them and their mother cheated us out of half the farm that should've been ours. Don't you know how their old woman put a spell on my cows so they bear freemartens and my daughter is barren. Have you no ears?

FINNEGAN: The wheels are back on, Maggie. We'll catch up to them. At Holy Corners. Why yes, why won't we. He's got the weight of all my passengers—

MAGGIE: And you've got the weight of only one of his—Here comes Finnegan! Tootletee too!

FINNEGAN: Onto the stage, girl. Don't you dare make mock of me.

MAGGIE: I won't go. *(FAT LADY & FINNEGAN chase her all over the barroom until he picks her up in his arms and carries her out.)*

FINNEGAN: Well you will. You will even if I have to hitch you to the wagon and drag you to Lucan. *(horn)* The stage for Lucan, the Favourite Line. Here comes Finnegan. Aroint thee, ye jades, I'm after you, Donnelly.

Whip sounds &c., but also MAGGIE laughing. In the fading light the BARTENDER with his skullish face listens & thinks. He comes towards us and actors with tollgates mime the flow of the road against him.

BARTENDER: Finnegan's stage and Donnelly's stage goes north on the road that goes north from here through crossroads and tollgates and Lucan until the road is outside the parsonage of the English priest.

The barroom clock strikes six. A decisive lady at the top of her youth, MISS MAGUIRE enters & rings a servant bell. She has managed the parsonage for her father ever since her mother's death ten years ago.

MAGGIE: You rang, m'am.

MISS MAGUIRE: That chamberpot needs emptying. Yes, I did ring and I have been ringing to no avail until now why?

MAGGIE: Oh, Miss Maguire, the wheels fell off my cousin Patrick's stage.

MISS MAGUIRE: Very nice that must have been, was anybody hurt, were you?

MAGGIE: Not enough to mention, m'am.

MISS MAGUIRE: Your being so late puts me in half a mind to say you cannot go to vespers, but I suppose the priest would denounce me from the pulpit if I did so, could you finish up this room and be at the door till Mr Stub calls.

MAGGIE: Yes m'am.

MISS MAGUIRE: And did you leave the silk thread in your basket?

MAGGIE: Oh thank you, Miss Maguire, I was so afraid you'd keep me in for being late, just dump the basket out and you'll find the thread, never mind my things.

She goes out with the chamberpot; MISS MAGUIRE looks into the basket. Offstage we hear: "Good evening, Mr Stub. The upstairs drawing room, if you please sir." The REVEREND MAGUIRE enters first; an old, snowy vicar.

DR MAGUIRE: Daughter?

MISS MAGUIRE: Father? Mr Stub is coming to see me tonight.

DR MAGUIRE: Then I shall drop in later, Mercilla I've no intention of ruining your tête à tête with the foremost merchant of Main Street.

MISS MAGUIRE: Are you composing your sermon? I shall tell him that is why you are

absent. I suppose you are wondering what I am doing in the maidservant's basket.

DR MAGUIRE: Did she give you permission to rumple it out like that?

MISS MAGUIRE: Oh yes. You're always worrying about the servants, Father.

DR MAGUIRE: We are servants too, you know. Mercilla. *(He fades away.)*

MAGGIE: *(still with chamberpot)* Mr Stub to see you, m'am.

GEORGE STUB: *(with nosegay for MERCILLA)* Good evening, Mercilla.

MISS MAGUIRE: Thank you, Mr Stub. I'd ask Maggie here to put these in some water in a vase, but I'm terrified what she might do. So. Do please be seated, Father is busy in his study with next Sunday's sermon, I'm finding the silk thread for the banner you're having me mend and so—what else?

GEORGE: I've bought the land for a house on what the villagers call Quality Hill.

MISS MAGUIRE: Is it going to be what size of a house, George Stub?

GEORGE: I want you to decide how big it should be, Mercilla.

MISS MAGUIRE: Because I'm to be the mistress of it, is that it?

GEORGE: *(sweating)* Yes.

MISS MAGUIRE: And you're not married to someone else already?

GEORGE: I've been alone in my bed for a year & a half now, Mercilla.

MISS MAGUIRE: What a way you have of putting things. Why I've been alone in my bed ever since I was born. Well, seeing it's your second marriage and I'm older too than is usual, I feel that I ought to put some things in your way.

GEORGE: In my way?

MISS MAGUIRE: Yes, because I needn't get married. So—make it worth my while.

GEORGE: I've already mentioned the house I'm building.

MISS MAGUIRE: Glad you did because I'd not come to live above an old hardware store. Now, here are the rules. After all I'm mending your silly old Masonic banner for you, you do some promising for me.

GEORGE: Mercilla.

MISS MAGUIRE: Who are you anyway?

GEORGE: I've been a self made man. You know what a great thing I've made of the store, and I'm—

MISS MAGUIRE: One of the rules I might make tonight is that I expect the man I marry to be somebody, really somebody, like a Member of Parliament. What about that George?

GEORGE: It'll never come to pass. I'm far better behind the scenes. I get too excited in public.

MISS MAGUIRE: Didn't I hear you say once that you'd been promised a senatorship if you could get a Conservative candidate in this riding?

GEORGE: Yes.

MISS MAGUIRE: Then that's the rules. It's some day to be Senator Stub, or else. I have depths of meanness, George. Don't ruffle them.

GEORGE: If I promise to obey the rules, I want things to be clearer.

MISS MAGUIRE: You mean when? I'll think it over tonight after you'll be gone.

GEORGE: I'd like something on—all this.

MISS MAGUIRE: Something on account. Here take my hand.

GEORGE: No.

MISS MAGUIRE: Oh, my mouth. Here, stop me from talking so much.

Her father enters.

MISS MAGUIRE: Remember, sir, I am no widow. You may be a hot blooded widower, but my father has kept me in his parsonage, a chaste spinster, for many more years than Jacob served Laban for both Leah and Rachel. And I haven't minded that a bit.

GEORGE: Good evening, Doctor Maguire. It is a pleasure to see you looking so well.

DR MAGUIRE: Mr George Stub. How many faces of the poor did you grind in the main street of Lucan today?

GEORGE: Business is business, Doctor Maguire. I have to foreclose and get my money back sometimes twice in a month.

MISS MAGUIRE: Look what treasures I'm finding in the girl's basket. What are these strange lumps of metal, George, and here's a locket. *(a small bell rings)* Father, Maggie said I could "dump the basket out."

DR MAGUIRE: I don't think she meant you to open her locket.

MISS MAGUIRE: *(tempted and walking about the room)* It's the one she's always wearing and she's had the catch fixed by a jeweller in town, why not here in Lucan, ah—George, open it for me.

GEORGE: These are the nuts off the axles of a wagon. Her father must have given her a list of things to bring him home on the farm out there. And this—I hate to tell tales on your servant girl, Doctor Maguire, but this is a picture of William Donnelly, William Donnelly Cripple.

DR MAGUIRE: Is there no other name you can call him then?

GEORGE: No, sir. I'll never call him anything else but that. He and his gang of cutthroats are one of the reasons that this riding often does not return a Conservative candidate.

MISS MAGUIRE: But George, he's devilishly handsome.

DR MAGUIRE: Mr George Stub, if I may venture an opinion in the face of your prejudice, I think he has a very sharp intelligent face. So that is Maggie's secret. Do you know I was asked to officiate at his brother Patrick's wedding not so long ago.

GEORGE: You would have met the whole monstrous family then.

DR MAGUIRE: Monstrous, not at all. They were a very handsome, unusual family with a—as if there was something there they weren't telling you. I disagree with you totally, Mr. Stub, and here's the text for my sermon. Four wheels! *(picking up the nuts)* Now as I behold the living creatures, behold one wheel upon the earth by the living creatures, with his four faces. The appearance of the wheels and their work was like unto the colour of a beryl …

GEORGE: Mercilla, I must leave. Please show me down.

MISS MAGUIRE: Follow me, Mr Stub. Father, George Stub is leaving, oh it is no use when he starts quoting scripture, no use at all.

They leave. As he goes on quoting from the Bible (Ezekiel I) he juggles the four nuts.

DR MAGUIRE: And they four had one likeness; and their appearance & their work was as it were upon a wheel in the middle of a wheel. When they went, they went upon their four sides; and they turned not when they went.

MAGGIE enters with a cup of tea. She collects the nuts, the locket, and begins to work at the banner with the coloured thread.

MAGGIE: Miss Maguire suggests, sir, that you take a drink of this camomile tea to calm your nerves. I have fit the lamp in your bedroom and changed your pillow case.

DR MAGUIRE: Ah, I have frightened him away. The Bible is a great help in getting me rid of people I don't like.

MAGGIE: Mr Stub is no angel of mercy, sir, but your daughter has to have some sort of life. Surely you don't expect her to be cooped up here in the parsonage by the river on this lonely stretch of the road all her livelong days.

DR MAGUIRE: I know what I know. He's the worst of a whole set of flinty hearted shop-keepers, just because my daughter comes from what he knows as an old family he wants her to be the lady in his new big house. You mark my words he'll call it Castle Stub—

MERCILLA enters and calmly slides into her father's flow.

MISS MAGUIRE: George Stub is not going to call his new place Castle Stub, Father. He's going to call it after me—Castle Mercilla, that is, if I marry him. Take heart, Father, I've put so many obstacles in his way.

DR MAGUIRE: The best obstacle is a firm "No." You've no idea what his set, the five families that consider themselves the aristocracy of the village,

look like from the pulpit. I once dreamt their pale marble faces turned into sheep and I walked around with my crook— *(on his way to bed)* — until this exquisite pain around my ankles made me look down. There was George Stub, the biggest ram of them all, gnawing away at my leg. Blood.

MISS MAGUIRE: *(also retiring)* Good night, Father. Maggie, clear up the teacups. Goodnight, I shan't get up for breakfast, nervous exhaustion, nervous *(repeat this last phrase ad libato)*

CHORUS: *(singing)*
Oh St Patrick was a gentleman
Who came of decent people
He built a church in Dublin town
And on it put a steeple …
No wonder that those Irish Lads
Should be so gay and frisky
For sure St Pat he taught them that
As well as making whiskey …

MAGGIE clears the chairs of the previous scene, but leaves the Masonic banner MERCILLA has been mending in the centre of the floor; as members of the CHORUS light candies and kneel by their chairs we are changing from MAGGIE as a servant with a cap to MAGGIE remembering a world of power and love that might have been hers forever.

MAGGIE: As I go to my bed over the kitchen of the parsonage I think I see in the moonlight on the floor—a letter, an envelope coming up through the floor, but it is my sleepy brain remembering what many people would regard as a—the strange thing that happened to me in the church tonight at vespers. *(The Vespers service in the background. There are other kneelers.)* Will Donnelly crawls under the floor of the church, the old wooden frame church, and he as I kneel is pushing the letter up to me through the cracks in the floor. My father and brother are so against me seeing him that it is only by letter or accident we can meet.

WILL: *(lying down)* I sent her my picture which she had cut out to be placed in a locket.

MAGGIE: And I in turn pushed a letter down through the crack in the floor. *(A letter comes down from above into WILLIAM's hand.)* I address you with these few lines hoping they will find you in good health as they leave me enjoying the same blessing at present. I thank you for your picture. Until my next birthday you will understand why I cannot wear it in public. Dear William, I was a long time about getting this picture for you. You can keep it now in hopes you think as much of me as I do of you.

WILL: In my next letter which she burnt to save it from their attention I proposed marriage and on April the 30th, 1873, my girl replied

MAGGIE: I now wish to inform you that I have made up my mind to accept your kind offer, as there is no person in this world I sincerely love but you. This is my first & only secret, so I hope you will let no person know about it. But I cannot mention any certain time yet.

They start rolling on the floor towards each other; this ends up with their standing back to back or kneeling back to back or with the banner veil between them. The rolling might be right over each other, but never so that their bodies coincide.

WILL: In our dreams we did this & wore the lockets although she was afraid to wear hers in the daylight.

MAGGIE: At night I am your wife; in the daytime I drudge for a woman who does not know whether she wants to be married or no. But although my hair is bound up for you and you alone to let down, Will, make no mistake, there was always something between us that summer—a fence, a veil, a muzzle on him, a wall about me, a floor between us. But I cannot mention any certain time yet. You can acquaint my parents about it any time you wish after the first of November next.

WILL fiddles. Since his letters are lost, we hear him play chords & enharmonics instead.

MAGGIE: Do not think that I would say you are soft for writing so often, for there is nothing would give me greater pleasure than to hear from you, but no matter now. I think soft turns is very scarce about you.

WILL fiddles.

MAGGIE: No, Will. Those who told you that I said I could never marry a lame boy are liars. If you have ever heard anything of the kind after me and it has given you pain, ask yourself if I have ever wanted that for you. If it does not suit you to

wait so long, let me know about it, and I will make it all right.

WILL: You'll never know, Maggie, how much it's not like me to talk to a woman about that. Because my foot's deformed they think he's not a man. They'd laugh if they knew I write you a letter every day. But, Maggie, they'll come at you about the foot and what can you tell them? Why that he's not a cripple when he's on horseback, nor is he a thing soft when he has a pistol in his hand which makes all men equally tall; *(fiddles)* nor am I a Cripple when I'm driving or writing or riding I'm—our stage is a bird with wheels for wings and I'm free.

And the scene changes to early morning in Lucan with the two rival stages getting ready for the daily race to London. The convention for the stage wagons should involve at least one wheel each and a solid block of actors "inside" the coach; other actors are the sides of the road and move against the coaches to give the illusion of a journey; a sleepy TOLLGATE MAN with his gate is the first of a series of such gates which will keep stopping the stages as they gallop down to London. The drivers hitch up horses and check wheels and parcels; passengers.

CHORUS: The Opposition Stage

NED BROOKS: The Finnegan Stage. My name is Ed Brooks from Exeter. First carefully checking the wheels of my stage with a wrench I climb up determined to beat Donnelly this day, to beat him in the race to London even if it kills me.

A red haired boy makes his first appearance: TOM RYAN.

MIKE: Tom Ryan, you can't come with us today. You should be home in your father's house. Why you've been sleeping all night in Pilot's manger lad, are you stage struck?

TOM: Mike Donnelly, ask your brother if I can go with yous again today. My old man won't let any of us come near the place right now and I watched the stable for you all night, Mike?

WILL: Mike, where's the bridle for the off-horse—Ploughboy. Tom Ryan, they sneaked that away on you when you were sleeping—sure you can come, but go up the street and get us a new bridle. Knock on the shutters till they open up. You don't want him along, do you Mike, is that it?

MIKE: It's his father I'm thinking of. "The Donnellys've stolen my only son away from me, work him to death on their stage line."

WILL: Pilot's shoe is loose, Manilla then. I'll let you drive her then, see if you can control her, my arms were out of their sockets the last time she's such a puller. *(Horn sounds. TOM runs up with the new bridle.)*

MIKE: Ah, but we're having a race today I see so maybe I won't hold him in. *(The Finnegan horn blows.)* Here comes Finnegan. Put those packages with me, Will. Haw, Ploughboy. Easy does it, Manilla, there girl, there …

CHORUS:
Out from the yard of Levitt's Hotel
The Main Street of Lucan all quiet and still
Down the road between Goderich & London

The TOLLGATE KEEPER reaches up a cup on a stick, we hear seven pennies.

WILL: Down with that tollgate, Let us out of
  Lucan
Thank you, Mr. Kelly.

MIKE: Yes, we hope to surpass him
We'll win your wager,

CHORUS:
a spark in each window
people getting up

TOM: Mike Donnelly, I think the coach is a boat.

MIKE: Tom Ryan, it has wheels. Sit into the seat and you can feel the road coming up against our wheels. It's no boat you truant. Where's the sails?

TOM: I've heard Will call it a boat once and I see the sea all around us. Somehow I feel like jumping off into the water.

MIKE: Did you hear that, Will? On the way back we're putting you in a trunk for safety's sake and our own peace of mind. Where'd you buy the bridle, Tom?

TOM: At Mr Stub's store.

MIKE: Well, Will, do we turn back?

WILL: For a penny I would. That was a foolish thing to do, Tom. Don't you know who our enemies are yet? We'll take it off at Birr, the blacksmith will have one there and, Tom, tonight you must take it back to Mr Stub and tell him it was a mistake.

TOM: Why was it a mistake?

MIKE: Because we never buy anything from Mr Stub and as you charged the bridle that means he'll be after us for a debt.

CHORUS:
So early in the morning, shadows aren't yet and stars still out.
The big elm, St Patrick's, the taverns at Elginfield.

MIKE: Open up Mr. Scandrett, Let us out of Biddulph.

This chorus has several "tracks" and ribbons of sound and imagery rippling through it; there's an old doggerel song about the road; there's also a quiet voice naming the concession roads whose numbers get smaller as we get closer to London.

CHORUS:
concession 16
Proof Line Road straight down to London
Down the hill, whizzing down, down into the
  hollow
Rain in our faces, up the hill.

Two stages converge on one passenger.

FINNEGAN COACH: That's our passenger.

DONNELLY COACH: No, she's ours.

WOMAN: But I'm a Finnegan customer

MIKE: Too late now, ma'm, and we can't stop for we're in competition and—whree whurrah!! we're ahead of you now, Finnegan!

CHORUS:
concession 15
Proof Line Road straight down to London!
Sun's up. Travellers to where we come from
Gallop up to meet us. Up the hill down the hill
The four tavern corners. Holy Corners! (singing)
The taverns they lined each side of the way.
As thick as the milestones in Ireland today.
And then the farmers all thought it was fine
If they once got as far as the London Proof Line.
concession 14
Up to then any man that went for a load
concession 13
Generally spent two days on the road;
concession 12
And I hear that Sam Berryhill says to this day
That some took three—when he kept the Bluejay!
concession 11

MIKE: Gate, Mr. Walden, why so slow. Wait a minute, how'd he get through the check gate so fast

WILL: If he gets a pass, we get a pass. That's not fair.

CHORUS:
concession 8
Montgomery House, there, the bar goes east and west!
concession 6
Monoghan's, Talbot's—both bakes bread and brews beer.
concession 5
Up the hill, cross the creek, down the hill to the
concession 4
River valley: McMartin's and the last tollgate

TOM: Let us into London, Mr Murrow

CHORUS:
& over the river
concession 2
Past the mill, tree branch shadow, up Mount Hope
The Convent of the Sacred Heart

DONNELLY COACH:
concession 1
We're turning out to pass him, he's going faster, watch yourself, Brooks, your front wheel. He's
fallen down on his head. Horses run away.
On his head.
The front wheel came off.
At one end of our journey, we'll stop for a while
Watch your step, sir. Take my hand, m'am.
At the City Hotel. No, the Dead House for him.

In the conventions worked out for this accident, BROOKS should be held upside down so that his words come from an overturned face. CHORUS might try some upside down speech too.

MIKE: Oh, for God's sake, Will, he's dying. Don't try to talk, Ned, we'll put you in our stage and take you to a physician. *(pause)* He wants to talk to you, Will.

BROOKS: I got the other one to come over just when life comes to the edge-place where you can see for ever and ever because you're neither alive nor are you dead. I said, Bill Donnelly, you done this to me and my wife and little ones will curse you and I'll tell you how your brother Mike's going to die. Fair play, neighbour. They'll never finish scrubbing up his blood. My God, neighbour. I'm gone. They'll never finish scrubbing up his blood.

His body is carried away and laid on the bar.

MIKE: What did he tell you, Will.

WILL: Nothing. Nothing that matters, Mike.

MIKE: Look at them looking at us. They all think we killed him.

WILL: Yes, Mike. Now how did we kill him? He tightened his wheel at Lucan, but still we managed. Maybe at Swartz's Hotel, or maybe at the Montgomery House at the eighth concession?

MIKE: Will. I don't want to drive stage anymore.

WILL: Why?

MIKE: Odd how there is always something happening when we're by. *(pause)* So how did his wheel come off then?

WILL: Get your head up, my brother. My brother what does it matter whether we killed him or Fortune did. We might just as well have, for they blame us anyhow. Get your head up and we'll turn and face them.

MIKE: The boy, did you get him to do it?

WILL: *(with irony)* Oh Yes! And Mike. I also got our father to train our horses so well that when Brooks' passenger that was riding beside him fell directly in front of us you were able to stop those horses on a penny, or he'd been cut to pieces instead of standing over there gawping at the Donnelly brothers whose same father failed to train one of his sons still to hold up his head though all the world is thinking you should crawl.

MIKE's face clears; he holds up his head and they turn to face a crowd that is growling at them.

CHORUS: We the undersigned jurymen summoned upon the inquest held upon the body of Edward Brooks do hereby agree that deceased came to his death from injuries received by being thrown from the Exeter Stage which was caused by the forewheel of said stage coming off and that the deceased came by his death

accidentally

This scene dissolves into a bakeshop where a BAKER proudly shows off a wedding cake to an APPRENTICE.

BAKER: Isn't that the lovely object now?

APPRENTICE: Who ordered this cake, Pa?

BAKER: Why it's for John Finnegan owns the store up at Irishtown, he sent down for it as there is some farmer getting his daughter married in the vicinity. Now what did you find out about delivery?

APPRENTICE: Went to the Western Hotel. They say there'll be no Finnegan Stage today, the driver fell off this morning and got himself killed. So they said to send it with the Donnelly Line—it's the best anyhow for moving a cake and they leave the City Hotel at 2 o'clock.

BAKER: By golly, we'll start packing it right away then. Get me some straw. You know I sort of hate to see it get wrapped up in a mere brown paper box.

A city bell rings twelve; a street fiddler plays "Buffalo Gals"; distant sounds. A penny in his cup. The CHORUS illustrate the shadows changing of the buildings near the City Hotel.

CHORUS:
Shadows of the building and the trees along the white road
Disappear at noon.
Sun, you golden stage, make our shadows
Passengers again to night, now longer and longer in
the stream
We all lie dreaming in

BAKER: What can I do for you, sir.

McKELLAR: I'm the new stage driver for Finnegan's stage and I've come to collect the cake his brother ordered here.

BAKER: Well, golly, now, we were led to believe that The Finnegan Stage wasn't running today. But we found a way to send the cake.

McKELLAR: What way?

BAKER: The Opposition Stage. They're real good at carrying cakes. I've had good reports from customers whereas you people seem to sit on them or—it's too late. They'll have left town by now. With the cake.

McKELLAR: Look you old gossoon, do you not know there's a war on between them and us? I'll catch up to them and I'll get that cake back. *(The*

BAKER and his BOY run out of the shop after the STAGE DRIVER in protest.)

Already simply set up: MAGGIE'S FATHER washing feet in the coal scuttle containing the block of ice; his sister & MAGGIE. Plus another aunt waiting to take MAGGIE away.

FAT LADY: Ever since you came home, Maggie, from service at the English priest's you're so slow in doing things. You was two hours I swear looking for these eggs. Take this switch and keep the flies off your father while I finish packing your trunk.

MAGGIE: Packing my trunk, is it. Where am I going then?

AUNT THERESA: Maggie, you're welcome to come back with me to Limerick and stay as long as you like where that fellow won't be bothering you.

MAGGIE: What fellow won't be bothering me?

FATHER: Cripple. Whoever was playing that fiddle under your window last night till all hours, whoever wrote me a lawyer's letter asking for your hand, who came to my door and took me by the beard to tell me how old you are.

MAGGIE: And how old am I? Am I not of age All Souls' Day, Father?

FATHER: I don't know, maybe you'd better call Father Brennan to look it up, in the baptismal register, have you? *(pause)* But All Souls' Day doesn't change the spots on Cripple, he's a Donnelly and no girl of mine's of age who's thinking of marrying that Cripple. I'd rather see you going to your grave.

MAGGIE: Father, if only you'd speak a little faster. Faster! What have you got against Will Donnelly, tell me now, Father, you've never told me. Is it the father killing the man at the bee?

FATHER: Keep switching the flies off of me, will you? It's evidence not fit for the ears of either a young girl or an old one. He's been the mastermind of a gang in this neighbourhood and fleeces of wool, post offices, derailing a train have been some of that gang's amusements for the last four years until now high and mighty he starts his own stage line.

FAT LADY: Brother, this girl'll never understand I'm afraid and it's a secret place we'll have to put such a girl. Her brother is getting married to the proper sort, but no she has to cross battle lines. Have you no gratitude for your upbringing, girl?

MAGGIE: All the money I've ever earned as a servant girl you've received, Father. I emptied chamberpots so you could buy two new cows. Yes, look at what my brother's marrying. All Mary Egan talks about is cows. Will Donnelly's the only young man around here with brains in his head who didn't go into the priesthood, and no girl is to take a look at him, is it?

AUNT THERESA: A fine priest that lame devil would have made.

FATHER: Theresa, see if Martin's got the cart hitched up. Maggie, you're right. Will is a clever boy. Clever at getting the forewheel of a stage to roll off so the driver gets killed. Yes. But he is a Donnelly and they are to be left alone. They don't dig with the right foot. They always are digging with the wrong foot. Since Cripple's threatening to come and kidnap her—yes Maggie—Theresa, tell Martin to drive over to Finnegan's Corners, but when it gets dark to turn & take her down to Gallagher's. That's right by the Donnellys and they'll never think of looking there.

MAGGIE: I'll run to him now. Will! Will! Come and rescue me, take me away.

She is pursued; there is a struggle and we see her next taken away tied in a net. We are now moving closer to FINNEGAN's store at Irishtown; first to a tollgate house where a bag of pennies is poured out for counting. The counting of the money into a tin box goes under the dialogue like the road itself.

MOTHER: Come, children, help your father count the take at the tollgate today. The shadows are getting so long they're joining together anymore travellers up or down the road, Sam?

The privy cleaner or CESSMAN comes towards us; he is whistling "Buffalo Gals."

TOLLMAN: Just foot travellers. There's that old fellow makes a living cleaning out privies. Good night there, you look dusty.

CESSMAN: Oh I doesn't mind the dust, thank thee, Mr. Scandrett.

CHILD: He always whistles the same tune doesn't he.

MOTHER: Heading north down into Biddulph. What was all that racket today with the second stage that went through.

The tollgate scene begins to move forward and dissolve.

TOLLMAN: They were chasing the Donnelly Stage. The Donnellys got away on them with something. A cake. A wedding cake.

We are in FINNEGAN's store up at Finnegan's Corners.

FINNEGAN: No Donnellys are allowed on Finnegan premises ever again no, neither his store nor his tavern nor his very privy.

MIKE: Even so, Mr. Finnegan, an express parcel from the Forest City Confectionery on Horton Street. Where shall I set it down?

FINNEGAN: I said get out, Mike Donnelly.

MIKE: Now, now, Mr. Finnegan, I do believe it is a cake. I'll just set it down on the floor here and that will be Cash on Delivery two dollars, twenty-seven and a half cents.

FINNEGAN: Don't you dare tell me it had to be by your line that cake come, when I've got my own stage line, now get that bloody parcel out of here.

MIKE: Well, it is a puzzle but the upshot of it was that our Opposition Stage was preferred. Twenty-seven a half cents plus two dollars. Careful, Finnegan, it's a cake.

FINNEGAN: Is it now, well it's a *(He kicks it around the shop.)*

MIKE: I see how it is, Mr Finnegan. We have to pay for the cake, do we. You should know all about that, you're the bailiff of the Division Court up here, and another thing before I say Goodnight—don't take any more passengers to Crediton. We bought the rights there, you have not got them. Good evening, Mr. Finnegan.

FINNEGAN backs him out of the store with a gun. BILL & MARY DONOVAN come forward behind the dissolving FINNEGAN with a quilt which is their wedding bed.

BILL: Come to bed, Mary. I'm told it's our wedding night.

MARY: Well, you're the boss now, but it did just cross my mind.

BILL: What crossed your mind?

MAGGIE's FATHER is quietly washing his feet in the tub WILLIAM DONNELLY put the ice block in.

MARY: Did you never hear of the custom of leaving the bride alone for three nights.

BILL: Yes, I have, now why don't you get into the bed?

MARY: It did just cross my mind that—they'll come looking here for Maggie.

BILL: *(yawning)* Who'll come looking—

MARY: Bill Donnelly and his gang.

BILL: Well, they won't find her. She was in the cellar during the wedding, but she's crying in the garret at Gallagher's now. Father keeps moving her, and Will Donnelly just keeps missing her. You should of seen the letter he wrote Pa.

WILL: Dear friend, my sole business last night (yes, I was in the crowd myself) was to have satisfaction for some of your mean low talk to your daughter that never deserved it. I want you to understand, dear sir, that I will have my revenge. You or your son will be prepared to receive me and my Adventurers before long again, and if old friend I want it impressed on your mind that if the business must be done on the way to church I can get any amount of men to do it so you may just as well stop getting yourself into trouble first or last.

MARY: Sending his gang of scoundrels into your father's house and pretending it was a tavern and them constables was searching for a horse-thief when all the time it's Maggie they want.

BILL: So come on then.

MARY: Is she never to be married off then, or what is to be done with her?

BILL: She'll either marry one of the Gallagher boys who's soft on her by next Saturday, or then it's Lent and it's too late to get married so I think Father plans to let the Sisters take care of her. If I were her—

MARY: *(getting into bed)* Good, then this nonsense will be over. Galloping around the countryside trying to kidnap your lovely sister because he loves her. She doesn't really love that Cripple, does she?

BILL: Mary, she does love him, and I don't blame her for it. I do blame her for not making a run for it, but I suppose she can't.

MARY: Oh a woman can never do that. The man would never marry her then. How can you say she could really love him?

BILL: Mary, she does. If ever I saw love. Not like us. Your mother and my father put us together like a pair of cattle.

Shivaree* serenaders gather in the shadows.

MARY: Speaking of cows, Bill Donovan, what sort is your cows?

BILL: Don't you like my cows?

MARY: I never saw such miserable calves as them two you had in the yard today. Maybe it's late they were

BILL: Cows, Mary, always cows.

MARY: That's how the Egans and the Trehys got where they are now. Cows

BILL: And where might that be now?

MARY: Why I think one of them's in bed with a young bull, or is that not what you think you are sir?

BILL: Ah, Mary

MARY: Take it back then that your sister really loves Will Donnelly, that cripple and devil.

BILL: She never loves him, I was wrong, it's a lie.

MARY: That's better now— *(knocking)* Hark! There's somebody going to shivaree us.

VOICES: Shivaree!

MARY: Get them to go away. Give them some whiskey, Mother of God, it is the Donnellys, Bill.

MIKE: Tell us where Maggie is and we'll go away.

BILL: *(at window)* Boys, she's not here now and if she were she'd say to leave her alone.

---

* shivaree—a raucous mock-welcome for newlyweds

MIKE: Oh no you don't. We got a letter here from Maggie. She says she's being held against her will and to come and get her.

BILL: Mary, shall I tell them she's at Gallagher's and get them off our backs?

MARY: *(running and stopping his mouth at the window)* You tell them where your sister's hidden & I'll withhold bed privileges. I'll ask for my dower third of the farm back and my red cow with the white ear back.

BILL: She's not here you blackguards. Off with you, Bill Donnelly.

Silence. Husband & wife return to bed. Then a blast of sound. Choose from buzzsaw sounds, guns firing, drums, horns, fiddles, maskers, circle of dancers around a bonfire, maskers entering bridal chamber and lifting up MARY.

MASKER: We found Maggie, Bill. She was under her brother's bed all the time. Is this her, Bill? Quick, for God's sakes, we can hardly lift her off the floor.

WILL'S VOICE: No, that's not Maggie, that's too fat for Maggie. That's probably Mary.

BILL & MARY crouch as the sounds melt into the newspaper's account.

MARY: Mother of God, there goes the chimney.

CHORUS:
RURAL ROUGHS ON RAMPAGE
ATTEMPTED ABDUCTION IN BIDDULPH

MAGGIE: *(in lay sister's working costume, with attendant nun)* I wasn't there of course. I was too much in love to unravel their cunning, and so— we lost sight of each other.

CHORUS:
THE BIDDULPH   DISGRACEFUL
KU KLUX   CONDUCT OF
                      LOVE-SICK SWAIN

Newspaper boy, "extra, read all about it," bulletin readers in front of newspaper office, &c.

CHORUS:
HOW HE WENT ABOUT IT
AND HOW HE FAILED TO SUCCEED

MAGGIE: And a needless enemy was my brother who before had been our ally as much as he dared, but after the serenade

BILL: Except to say hello I don't speak to that man. Speak to Will Donnelly—no, and Mary and me have the very next farm to the Donnelly place now, no, William Donnelly, no. No.

CHORUS:
THE MIDDLE AGES REVIVED
LOVE'S LABOUR LOST EVIDENTLY

WILL: *(with whip)* Read that cheap newspaper heading again.

CHORUS: THE MIDDLE AGES REVIVED

WILL: That's enough, thank you. Middle Ages Revived by whom? Me or them? We were hauled up in court, but I got off I suppose because Maggie had asked us to take her away. My God, I was never to see her again. And I'm not in the least sorry I tried to steal her away if that's what you call a life for a woman. *(to MAGGIE'S FATHER who is in bare feet at the tub)* And I'm not in the least sorry for any thing that happens from now on in that happens to those who try the same trick on me as you pulled on that girl that was once my sweetheart. I'll switch the flies off you you old fool.

He has taken MAGGIE'S FATHER up & is about to whip him, but then throws him down & chases him out of the theatre or attacks his feet with a toy whip & spins him out of the room.

HALF CHORUS: Question. The Convent of the Sacred Heart *(Sung: "incense" music as before)* At Mount Hope on Richmond Street, why does the Opposition Stage always slow down?

HALF CHORUS: Answer. Oh I can answer that. When Will Donnelly is the driver.

MAGGIE: He senses that I am drudging here in the kitchen of the Sisters' house. And when he is not the driver he has told the others to slow down at the chestnut tree because he knows that I wait each day for the sound. In the morning, in the evening—down the hill, past the mill and over Brough's Bridge until you can't hear the wheels or the hooves anymore. You hear the other stage. You hear your own heart. I scrub the stones of the convent yard as close to the gate as I can, but it is no use—the gate is locked. Someday, in the middle of the night, there will come such a knocking at that gate and it will be smashed open, and the nuns will run hither and thither screeching because my husband has come for me and in my wedding dress I will enter his coach to drive up his road forever. I love William Donnelly.

As MAGGIE lies dead before them, the MOTHER SUPERIOR confers with the sisters as to where she should be buried.

NUN: Mother Superior Finnegan, Maggie Donovan is dead. What shall we do with her? *(They kneel.)*

MOTHER: What were the last words she said, Sister Feeny?

NUN: Her last words were

MAGGIE & NUN: I love William Donnelly.

MOTHER: Sister Feeny, where do you think she should be buried.

NUN: *(pause, then crisply and swiftly)* By William Donnelly's grave up in Biddulph.

MOTHER: Sister Gallagher?

NUN: In the convent yard where the rest of us lie.

MOTHER: Sister Egan?

NUN: In the convent yard, Mother Superior, but close by the gate.

MOTHER: And that is where Maggie Donovan lies buried.

MAGGIE: I love William Donnelly.

WILLIAM DONNELLY sings a verse of "Buffalo Gals. "

WILL:
I asked her if she'd be my wife
Be my wife, be my wife
She'd make me happy all my life
If she stood by my side.

CHORUS: End of Act One.

ACT TWO

Actors spin tops, dance, recite poems until this recitation of poems slowly fades into TOM RYAN standing up on the bar and letting us see the story from a new angle.

TOM RYAN: And I'll recite you a poem I learnt once at school while we're waiting for the two o'clock stage to Lucan which I may have the honour of driving, young though I am, since the Donnelly boys have to put in a appearance in court.

Waiting for Pa

Three little forms in the twilight grey
Scanning the shadows across the way:
Six little eyes, four black, two blue,
Brimful of love and happiness too,
Watching for Pa

Soon joyous shouts from the window-seat
And eager patter of childish feet
Gay musical chimes ring through the hall
A manly voice responds to the call
"Welcome papa!"

The actor playing NED RYAN, TOM's father, now proceeds to growl drunkenly.

TOM RYAN: Well ladies and gentlemen, my home life wasn't like that quite, and since I'm said to be one of the reasons for the Donnelly Tragedy, you don't understand me unless you understand what waiting for my Pa was like. Tom Ryan is my name, this is my Pa, here's my Ma and a couple of my sisters. What are we doing? We are all waiting one cold winter morning for Pa— to get his rump off a chest that contains bread, cheese, tea and other necessaries of life which he refuses to let us have

TOM RYAN starts to saw a rail.

NED RYAN: They might cook it and poison me.

TOM RYAN: It's a cold day outside, but there's no fire in the stove because—

NED: You're ruining me with all this wasting of my substance. Stop the sawing, Tom stop sawing that rail! Or I'll take this ax to you.

MRS RYAN: It isn't enough to be starving but we must freeze to death as well.

NED: Tell your son to stop sawing that rail and to clear out of here. *(starting to give chase)*

TOM: Oh I admit I was pert and I should have stopped sawing, but I couldn't sit there and see my sisters and my mother shivering much longer.

NED: Get out of the house you bastard brat, talking back to your pa.

TOM: Don't hit me Pa. I was only. I will go and I will never come back, and I stepped out onto the road and looked in the snow for somebody to take me in: Who will take in the barefoot Ryan Boy?

*The actors set up the Roman Line gamut of Part One as the road he will run up and down.**

Barry?	Trehy?	
Feeny?	O'Halloran?	*He is rejected by*
Cahill?	Cassleigh?	*everyone in*
McCann?	Flynn?	*various ways:*
Egan?	Marksy?	*backs turned,*
Quinn?	Farl?	*clubs, kicks &c.*
Gallagher?	Duffy?	
Clancy?	Donovan?	

Bell and jug sound for the tavern and the church; then MRS DONNELLY comes towards the rejected boy and accepts him.

MRS DONNELLY: Donnelly.

We see her at the end of a corridor of people. We renew her acquaintance now.

CHORUS: Yes, the Donnellys took him in.

JAMES DONNELLY, the Younger, sitting invalid in a chair by the stove should also register here. His mother has just finished giving him medicine.

MRS DONNELLY: Tom Ryan, climb up on the stove there and stop your shivering till I get these dry feet on you; here's a pair of Tom's pants to put on those you got on are drenched, what devil has your father got into that he drives you out barefoot in this weather or was there a reason, Tom?

TOM: I was only sawing a rail, Mrs Donnelly, to get a fire on so we would be warm.

MRS DONNELLY: Get behind the stove now and hide in the woodbox, your father I can see in the lid of my tea kettle coming in our gate. Can you not get the key to the pantry away from him while he's asleep?

TOM: He sleeps with it tied round his leg, Mrs Donnelly.

MRS DONNELLY: Well there are four of you and one of him, he's no giant, give him clout and get the key some fine day Good day to you, Ned Ryan?

TOM: But he's always got the ax.

NED: Good morning, Mrs Donnelly. Have you seen my madcap, scapegrace harum scarum son Tom about?

MRS DONNELLY: No madcap, scapegrace, harum scarum son of yours has run in here, Ned Ryan.

NED: Then I just heard your stove say something about an ax.

MRS DONNELLY: My stove talks a lot to itself, Ned Ryan, what with the kettle getting up steam and the wood crackling inside and the wind in the chimney. Do you not see my stove has a name? She's called Princess and she just saw the ax you're holding in your hand. I'd have said something myself at the strangeness of a father with an ax in his hand.

He backs up and slides off; MRS DONNELLY returns to sewing. TOM gets up on top of the stove (bar) and continues.

TOM: Pretty soon, he'd drag me back home again and say he'd try to be decent to us, but it didn't last and as I grew older if I could I helped the Donnelly boys with their stage, and if I couldn't I stayed home and caused trouble. Like—I set fire to the barn once with him—Pa— in it, he barely got out in time and he thought it was lightning, and I pissed in his whiskey after drinking half of it, oh my God was he mad at me. (*Violin screech—a poltergeist bottle flies through the air, disappears and we hear it smash.*) Yes, I can make things like that happen if I don't abuse myself for a month. It's like having a fit and I can will it that I'm going to have a fit. One day I asked my mother if it was true I had been born. And she said

MOTHER: Yes, Tom Ryan, you were born.

He starts to pack a carpet bag.

---

* *the Roman Line gamut of Part One—in Sticks & Stones Reaney frequently shows the Donnellys caught between the lines of their Catholic neighbours, two parallel rows of actors "like the line-up of a reel."*

NED: And where might you be going, great high and mighty one with your clothes barely covering your thin little parsnip of a rump and your hair like a snipe's nest on fire, oh little runt of mine.

TOM: My mother here tells me it's St Bridget's Eve and tomorrow I'm old enough so I'm leaving forever.

MRS RYAN: Oh son, where will you stay?

TOM: *(pause)* Donnellys.

MRS RYAN: Could you not pick a better place than that den of everything wicked.

TOM: If you want to know Mother, there's love there.

NED: Your poor father over here, Tom. Will you not give him a look, will you shame him before all our neighbours?

TOM: I'm not going to hang around here anymore and hear you say mean low things to my mother.

MRS RYAN: Would you live with people whose sons tried to carry a poor girl off, Tom?

TOM: Yes, because she wanted to be carried off from a house that was worse than this.

MRS RYAN: Could you not get a job in the town building the new lunatic hospital they're putting up?

TOM starts his speech now and walks into the GEORGE STUB scene.

NED: It's into the lunatic hospital he should be going. *(growling)*

TOM: But of course the first thing I did to the Donnellys was to bring them trouble in the shape of the bridle I bought for them on tick at Mr Stub's store.

STUB: Tom Ryan, lad, just ask your boss William Donnelly, gentleman, when in the name of Heaven is he going to pay for the bridle you tapped on my shutters for last summer?

TOM: Mr Stub, it was a mistake, and we brought it back.

STUB: I know that, lad, but I didn't accept the return, it's used and I want my money.

TOM: We paid for the use.

STUB: Not by agreement, that's not the way I do business but I tell you, lad, I'm suing William Donnelly, gentleman, in Division Court next Tuesday so be warned.

TOM: Aw, sue away. We'll never pay you for it, you old skinflint. But he kept summoning Mr Donnelly, sending summonses and we just wiped our ass with them. I used to ride up and down on the stage, they gave me a cap to wear. There was another lad hung around the Donnellys a lot— Will Farl. Some of the people were shocked that he got on with the Donnellys so well.

The two boys crouch by the Donnelly stove; MRS DONNELLY is sewing while JAMES DONNELLY JR sleeps in a rocking chair.

WILL FARL: Why aren't you sitting still, Tom, does your shirt itch you?

TOM: Old man beat me last night, my back's all welted up.

MRS DONNELLY: Tommy Ryan and Will Farl, what were we talking about just now—yes, you say that you'll help my sons against their enemies, what kind of help do my sons need against what kind of enemies?

TOM: Oh—help.

MRS DONNELLY: Wouldn't it be wise to consult us first before you go helping. *(train whistle)* What is the latest sample of your helping my sons, please tell their mother?

WILL FARL: We've just put a log across the railway down at Granton.

MRS DONNELLY: Now, just how does that help Will & Mike?

TOM: Why don't you know George Stub, your Will's arch enemy, is coming back from the fair at St Mary's tonight. Most women would have screamed here but

MRS DONNELLY: Is he coming back from the fair at St Mary's now, why Tom and Will Farl, my husband Mr Donnelly's at the fair too. You wouldn't want him to be train-wrecked, would you?

TOM: There's lots of time, we'll take the logs off, Mrs Donnelly. See the welts, Will Farl?

WILL FARL: You know I remember my father whaling me like that. And people ask me why I like to stay at the Donnellys' so much.

TOM: *(train whistle)* We'd better get a move on. Will Farl there's the train. So why is it you like to stay at the Donnellys' so much then?

WILL FARL: They killed my father.

They run off, train whistle; MRS DONNELLY turns to her patient and says:

MRS DONNELLY: Were you listening, James Donnelly the Younger, or are you still asleep from the medicine the doctor gave you.

JAMES JR: Oh mother, I'm still asleep from the medicine the doctor gave me.

MRS DONNELLY: Good, because it's time you had another dose of it.

JAMES: Mother, I won't take it. *(pause)* I won't take it unless

MRS DONNELLY: Unless what, high and mighty.

JAMES: Where's the saw? Let me hold it in my hand here. And I'll *(She gets the saw. Gives him medicine. Sleepily he continues.)* I'll pull his beard out.

An actor sitting on the side benches with his fingers drumming on wood suggests the rain pouring down outside.

MRS DONNELLY: Hsst. There's a whirlwind outside and the sky is dark. Your father's late home from the fair. Maybe he'll bring you something James though you're a trifle big and old for a bauble and did you pull his beard out in this big fight you had with him.

JAMES: Ah, *(in his sleep)* it fell out of him. By God, I'll knock your brains out, there's no constable in Lucan able to take me.

MRS DONNELLY: When I get you on your feet, my son, it's off to the priest and you're taking the pledge. It's either the water wagon or smash and when the smash comes your father and I won't be able to help you one little bit.

JAMES: Where's Will and where's Mike?

MRS DONNELLY: Where else would they be, but driving their stage up and down in this rain.

JAMES: Where's John and Bob and Tom?

MRS DONNELLY: Out plowing. Tom went up to the blacksmith's.

JAMES: Why isn't Pat home helping us fight Finnegan?

MRS DONNELLY: Why isn't he? Have you asked him sure enough and get him into trouble. Is that why you came back from Michigan to get us all into trouble?

JAMES: No. No. I came to help Will and Mike smash Finnegan. Where's Father

MRS DONNELLY: He's just coming into the yard this very minute and if you're not quiet and good I'll tell him on you. Mr Donnelly I'm surprised to see you home from the fair at all.

MR DONNELLY: I am myself. There was a log across the rails. How'd you know about that? *(pause)* How's our first one?

MRS DONNELLY: Mr Donnelly, Doctor Quarry says—and he knows this himself for he was told—that even if we get him to stop the drink he's got only two more years to live.

MR DONNELLY: It's his lungs. And they're bad. How is he now then?

JAMES: Never felt better in my life. I'm going into Lucan.

MR & MRS DONNELLY: No, you're not. *(They hold him down till he falls asleep.)*

MRS DONNELLY: And what's that you've brought us home from the fair to give to a little one perhaps some time. *(He gives her a top and she spins it. There is a whipstick that comes with it which she uses.)* I wonder how much longer they can all keep going, Jim?

MR DONNELLY: Stub was on the train.

MRS DONNELLY: And I knew that too. The things I've heard this afternoon, Mr Donnelly, and I was at no fair.

MR DONNELLY: Jim, says Stub, Jim—

STUB: *(train whistle)* Jim, thought I saw you back here coming back to see what in hell's holding up this train. Jim—if you and your boys get me Ward Three next election *(pause)* and you alone can do it—I don't care how, tell them not to vote or vote for my man who's going to be an Irish Catholic,

Jim, yes—if you can promise me that, Finnegan will stop running his stage wagons tomorrow.

MRS DONNELLY: Yes, and my husband said—

MR DONNELLY: Nothing. We're promised long ago to Mr Scatcherd.

MRS DONNELLY: And you are so promised

MR DONNELLY: And yet

MRS DONNELLY: *(whipping the top)* Yes. It would be nice to stop, but we can't oh no we must keep on spinning and spinning, Mr Donnelly, because if we stop spinning we'll fall down and over and we hit them and they hit us and we—one day—our whip-arm's broke off. Go back to him and say yes!

MR DONNELLY: Never!

TOM: Mother and Father, wake Jim up will you? There's a fight up town and Will and Mike can't get the stage past Levitt's.

MRS DONNELLY: Your brother's not fit to go out anymore, Tom. Hush …

JAMES: No, Mother. The medicine worked. I'm well. Father … . Get my horse Tom.

MR & MRS DONNELLY: Get back in that chair.

JAMES: *(escaping them)* You heard what Tom said. Every man's needed, my brother's in a fight!

MR DONNELLY: Take your coat, Jim. At least put something on your back.

MRS DONNELLY: Take your hat, it's rain—he took the saw.

MR DONNELLY: Come back here, Tom and Jim. What's he got the saw for? *(Exit)*

FINNEGAN: Now I can explain the saw. Exactly a year ago, Thursday, September the 20th, 1874, someone took my stage wagon after dark and sawed it to hundreds of small pieces. I built a new stage. 1875. Today, Friday, September 20th—someone took that new stage out of my stable, dragged it up the road a piece and sawed it into even more pieces. There are to be no stages on the road, but Donnelly stages, are there? The Donnelly tribe is getting to be a terror to the neighbourhood.

JOHN MACDONALD approaches the bartender and buys a stage ticket. His MOTHER and sister, NORAH, approach for the same reason.

MACDONALD: A ticket, one way to Lucan please.

BARTENDER: Which line will you go on …

NORAH: Two tickets the same to Lucan please, for myself, sir, and my mother here. The Donnelly Line.

MACDONALD: Not the Donnelly Line for your brother, Norah, nor for your son, Mother, but the Finnegan Line, please.

NORAH: Please yourself, brother John, if you want your bones shaken to a jelly by Mr Finnegan's drivers. We'll be in Lucan before you.

MACDONALD: I want the two of you to get your money back and come on the same coach as your brother and son is going on. The wagon you're going on carries away more than my mother and my sister, for it bears away sister's reputation and any love for her son my old mother has ever had.

MOTHER: Will you lower your voice in a public place, my son John Macdonald. Why you've palled around with Donnellys ever since you can remember, what have you suddenly determined against them?

MACDONALD: Mother, you know and I know what Norah's up to with their Cripple now he's lost the Thompson girl.

MOTHER: Don't you dare call him a cripple, or there's people here standing'll see me haul off and give you the clout you so long for. Let Norah decide the man she'll marry, one thing, it can't be you, you get such rages into yourself about your sisters, it's the land you're worried about isn't it, that father likes William Donnelly a lot, not just that Norah does, is that not so?

MACDONALD: Your husband and my father make me wonder sometimes if I am his wife's husband's son.

As the quarreling Macdonalds leave the barroom, the other actors form two coaches indicating that we have dissolved into the street outside the City Hotel, but just before this happens MRS MACDONALD raises her arms and says:

MOTHER: No wonder he likes Will Donnelly. At least Will Donnelly can talk straight when it comes to naming his relatives. I've even heard him call his mother his mother and his father his father, but with you John, your mother, why your mother is liable to be your grandfather's daughter and your sister, she's not your sister, she's your unborn grandchild's great aunt.

And out the Macdonalds go to immediately return as if we then saw them step out of the hotel and go to their respective coaches. We are getting ready for a decisive journey up the road, this time to some startling new developments.

MACDONALD: Mother, I'm sorry, but this wouldn't happen if Donnelly would just leave us and Norah alone.

They shout at each other through the windows of the stages, then the Finnegan horn, the tollgate and penny convention, the slight up and down movement of the two stages' passengers indicate that they're off!

NORAH: Brother, who's been at you? I'll tell you I'm proud he's in love with me, can you not remember the love you once felt for himself when you were always over there …

MOTHER: Mrs Donnelly had more to do with bringing you up than I did, now look at you. Sure, Father's given you one hundred acres already, he's not made of gold, leave him alone about his property.

MACDONALD: When I get home, Norah, I'm going to dig up all the potatoes in the front field you've been planting and I'll cut down the orchard mark my words if I see you talking to him when we get to Lucan, it's lucky it is there's no Cripple driving today I suppose I'd see you both up on the driver's seat with him. There go the Cripple lovers, folks, my mother and my sister.

NORAH: Oh, Mother, give me the parcels, which one is the iron we bought I'll crack him one on his skull.

MOTHER: Pay no heed to him, darling, I just hope and pray he doesn't get up his courage at the taverns and try to drag us off at a tollgate, but we're outdistancing him I see, here we are shut up in a box with four wheels and the window blinds down for the heat and you can hear the drivers cursing each other through the roof. You have to pretend not to hear.

NORAH: A ride to Lucan is a sentimental education I can tell you. You'd hear Finnegan's driver say— *(trumpet)* hold your ears. I guess only men would understand why they'd have to get down and fight about that, once a Donnelly said, "And your father wasn't married either, McKellar." To which came the reply: *(trumpet)* to which Mike Donnelly said:

NORAH & MIKE: "You'll not drive the stage another morning with your life, McKellar."

MOTHER: I don't mind hearing a good bout of swearing if they're really good at it, but it does slow up the journey which is somewhat more important, and that last remark by my future son-in-law.

NORAH: I think it was Mike said that, Mother.

MOTHER: Well, whoever it was, that would lead to both stage drivers putting in an appearance at a local Justice of the Peace along the road called Squire Ferguson.

WILL: Squire Ferguson, I wish to lay a complaint against Peter McKellar re perjury in the information he laid against me and Mike last July the third, 1875.

SQUIRE: Mr Donnelly, I don't think you can do that.

WILL: Oh yes you can. Victoria, 1859, Chapter 1, subsection 6. Give me your manual, sir, and I'll show

NORAH: When Finnegan's witnesses would try to go down to the courthouse, Will Donnelly would get them arrested somehow at Birr for disorderly conduct. I bought him a couple of old law books for a Christmas box, and it was what we called the game of information and complaint or Legal Amusements. And if two of the Donnelly boys got arrested why their mother had had the foresight to have seven sons, so it would be Tom or Bob or John would drive if they'd snared my Will or Mike into their clutches.

MOTHER: And they'd be at it again.

A brief horn and fiddle contest. Finnegan's horn taunts are returned with interest by Donnelly fiddle sounds.

MAN ON FINNEGAN'S STAGE: I used to ride both lines and turn about and you could see what was going to happen, sooner or later ... oh, there were happy times too I observed in my going back and forth. I can remember the whole Donnelly family going down the road on their way to Bothwell to get Jennie married off. Or the day Mike all dressed up went down to London to get married to Ellen Haines, her father kept the City Hotel there. Mike didn't show up for a week after that, too tired, still abed at two in the afternoon his brothers said, stage drivers make good husbands, all the jouncing up and down. God knows, but sooner or later ...

NORAH: Yes stage drivers do make good husbands. I was so proud of the way William drove and acted to his customers and I knew then that my life with him was like this journey. Through it all we would eventually come to the St Nicholas Hotel here off the road and out of the storm. My old mother's fallen asleep. Where does she dream she is?

LADY ON THE OTHER STAGE: Asleep! Not me, I keep thinking when the wheels will they come off, when will the wheels come off, oh Mother, when will the wheels come have those Donnellys loosened the wheels?

CHORUS: fur hats in winter, straw hats in summer

MAN: our collar limp, our hat crushed, our watch stopped, our brain dizzy with vertigo, the elastic band of our wig snapped, our false teeth displaced in their setting, curses not loud but deep,

MIKE: Gee Ploughboy Gee Pilot

CHORUS: were carriers of passengers upon a stage or covered wagon from the City of London to the Village of Lucan

FINNEGAN: Hrup hrup there you slow beasts, don't try to beat me at the bridge, Donnelly, there's not room for the both of us.

MIKE: There's two sides to a road, Finnegan.

CHORUS: the defendant, William Donnelly, did not safely & securely carried upon the said on the said

MIKE: Oil your wheels, Finnegan.

The "coaches" are getting closer to each other & are blurring in outline just as things do before they collide.

FINNEGAN: Your half of the road's the ditch, Donnelly, *(horn & fiddle)*

CHORUS:
August the 31st, 1875
maliciously ran races with other stage coaches

MAN: I think that Finnegan kept as close as he could to the Hotel side to keep Donnelly from getting to the Hotel before him.

MIKE: The ladies wanted a drink of water at the hotel. He made a quick turn as quick a turn as ever I seen. I had ten passengers three in the driver's seat besides myself seven inside

Using the whole team of actors, suggest the collision.

CHORUS: plaintiff was thereby wounded & injured in consequence on the said road and suffered great pain and expense in and about the cure of her wounds and injuries. And the plaintiffs—Mrs Louisa Lindsay & Miss Jennie Lindsay—claim five hundred dollars *(groaning)* damages.

MIKE: What did you do that for, Finnegan? *(whip)*

FINNEGAN: *(whip)* Mike Donnelly, I'd do it again like as not until and again till I've run you off this road.

The two stage drivers confront each other among a pile of coach fragments and accident victims slowly reassembling themselves; but the scene is darkening, a bell rings, MIKE DONNELLY's face grows red from some fire he is looking at.

FINNEGAN: I said to myself under my breath why in God's name is Mike Donnelly's face turning so red. *(turning around)* He's thinking he's looking at my stables going up in flames with five horses alive in them.

FINNEGAN runs out into a blazing stable door as the tollgate between Birr & Elginfield is set up with the money pouring out for counting of the day's take.

FINNEGAN: Mother of God help me save my poor beasts from Donnelly's fire.

TOLLGATER: Guess that's all for today, let's count her up, sunset's hanging on there quite a while. Good night to you, sir. You're our last traveller for the day.

TRAVELLER: That's not the sunset by the way.

As this scene develops there should be well-spaced red glares that build till the Donnelly Boys in a photograph scene are surrounded by Hell with a mob of farmers in front of them with sharp hayrakes.

SOLO: *(sings)* Patrick Finnegan's stables burning

CHORUS: Dies irae dies illa *(ecclesiastical)*

SOLO: Solvet Finnegan in favilla

WIFE: Sam and me's been seeing quite a few red glows in the sky north of here lately every night.

TRAVELLER: Oh it's them Donnellys, another barn they've set fire to if it's a friend of Finnegan, burned down Pat Finnegan's stable last week with six horses in it burnt up alive.

TOLLGATER: That's one step up from loosening wheels and having you up in court for assault and battery, isn't it.

TRAVELLER: A considerable step indeed. I guess you see the Donnelly boys every day?

TOLLGATER: Twice a day regular as clock-work—their coach, Finnegan's coach down to town; except one day last week when both the stages were awful late and then part of the Finnegan wagon limped by, and then two thirds of the Donnelly conveyance and then the rest of the Finnegan and then the handwheels of the it was a Armageddon of a road catastrophe I can tell you.

WIFE: That night we saw our first red glow.

Three or more FARMERS come up to listen with hayrakes, big wooden spikes on them: lanterns.

TOLLGATER: And I can tell you ladies and gentlemen, when the other Finnegan stable got burnt up in Clandeboye why there was people said—what next?

WIFE:
What next indeed, Sam. The Maclean's Hotel where Finnegan ties up his stage, someone got into their kitchen and broke every dish and cup and teapot and soup tureen Mrs Maclean had to her name.

SOLO:
William Donnelly's stables burn too

CHORUS:
Tuba Finnegan spargens sonum
Per sepulchram regionum
Coget Biddulph ante thronum

CHORUS:
Oh them Donnellys

FARMER ONE: Is it all the members of the family, the mother and the father?

TOLLGATER: There's some say as that they called the oldest of the boys back from where he's been hiding out in Michigan—James Donnelly the Younger—and he drinks you see, and they just sort of let him loose at night

FARMER TWO: There's others say after the outrage at Walker's Hotel where they cut the tongues out of the stage horses there …

ALL: Cut the tongues out of the horses!

FARMER TWO: God yes, have you not heard—Finnegan went to hitch up on Monday morning and his horses were all—hacked open, dying or dead, and they had to be shot; the farrier said—put them out of their misery and there was a whole bunch in the village said—lynch Tom Donnelly or Will or Mike or Jim, yes, Jim he's the one and it's Bob who sets the fires and it's Will who plans it all.

WILL & MIKE drive up to the gate.

TOLLGATER: Toll there, travellers. Oh—it's you

WILL: Good evening, Mr Scandrett. Mrs Scandrett. *(pause)* I said Mr Scandrett—Good evening. *(pause)* Mr Scandrett, there's a lady passenger felt under the weather at Swartz's Hotel coming up from London today and she asked us if we could come and pick her up down there later in the evening.

WIFE: Sam, don't let them through, Sam. They're lying. They're out for night mischief.

FARMERS: Sam, we'll help you keep the firebugs out of our township. Nobody's going to cut our horses' throats.

| MIKE: Gate, Mr Scandrett. | *A suspended moment in which we look at the Donnelly boys held back at the gate. They* |
| SOLO: *(sung)* Donnelly's new stage sawn to pieces | *look at us still as a photograph. Who are they? What are they?* |

CHORUS: Confutatis maledictis

SOLO: Sawn to pieces Watson's horses

CHORUS: Flammis acribus addictus

The penny slides into the TOLLGATER's cup, a Donnelly penny.

WIFE: I saw blood on his sleeve I could swear. I was going to be sick then—

ANOTHER TRAVELLER: *(from our side of the gate)* Good night, Scandrett. Whoa. Guess we don't need to go any farther, Lila. There's Will and Mike waiting for you and I'm glad you feel more like completing your journey than you did at three o'clock there. *(The gate finally comes down to let Mrs Shoebottom through.)* Good night, Bill, Mike. *(He turns around and goes back towards us.)*

LADY: Thank you, Will Donnelly. Thank you, Mike. You're kind gentlemen both of you to put yourselves out so for an old woman like me. *(They depart with her.)*

WIFE: But when their hands came down to help her up into their buggy the blood on their sleeves was gone.

Bar noise & scene. MIKE going through with trunk.

MIKE: I heard what you said, sir. If you ever say again that my brother Tom robbed Ned Ryan of eighty dollars I'll kill you. *(Exit)*

Voice of man who enters as MIKE leaves with trunk.

SOLO VOICE: The Donnellys are coming, they're walking over from Levitt's.

A knocking, then a door-rending.

Lock up your doors, close the bar; hide everybody.

JIM, TOM & BOB enter to face a lone bartender, FRANK.

FRANK: No Donnelly gets a drink at this bar; I'll not serve you, James.

JAMES: I see. And it's a good bar you used to have too, Frank Walker.

FRANK: Used to have!

JAMES: Because you'll get a scorching inside of six weeks as it's laid out for you now, but I don't intend to have anything to do with it.

FRANK: What'll it be, Jim Donnelly, what'll it be?

JIM: Three gingerbeers for us lads here and a big bowl of porridge.

FRANK: Don't you mean three bowls?

JAMES: No, it's not for us. One big bowl of porridge and hustle it.

CONSTABLE BERRYHILL enters swaggering with his warrants in pocket.

BERRYHILL: *(with beard)* I can lick any man in this tavern, I can lick any man in Biddulph. *(He backs away from JIM DONNELLY.)* Jim Donnelly I've got twelve warrants for your arrest.

Out of range we hear a scream from BERRYHILL & he returns in the power of JAMES DONNELLY, JR.

MIKE: He had followed my brothers to Walker's Hotel.

BERRYHILL: They tore half my beard out.

JAMES: Oh—the beard fell out of him

MIKE: By the time I got there my brothers and their pals were throwing stones at home.

BERRYHILL: Several of the stones weighed five pounds each.

MIKE: That's a lie. Frank, how much does that one weigh?

FRANK: Got a bit afraid when I saw the stones flying through the air. *(weighing a stone in a balanced scale on bar)* It's three pounds? *(MIKE smiles.)*

WILL: My brother Mike then hauled James and the others off and parted them.

BERRYHILL: But left me with them and you know what they made me do, that James Donnelly the Younger took the warrants out of my pocket and

They tear up the warrants, sprinkle them over the porridge and feed it to BERRYHILL.

FRANK: You're probably going to hit me, Jim, for asking you this, but why?

JAMES: I'm only feeding him the ones we didn't do, Frank. This one here—I'll eat myself, yes I did beat that grocer up and I couldn't stand the way he whined and whoever is doing all those terrible things on these warrants will stop doing them, Frank, when the powers that be let my brothers have half of the road again. I started eating the paper and then it tasted bitter, I took it out of my mouth and saw Dr Quarry's signature why it was my death certificate and it was getting time to take the saw back to my mother and father.

Facing us a change comes over him: he dissolves from the bully into someone coughing blood on his sleeve and crawling toward us, towards his mother who waits for him.

MRS DONNELLY:

Yes, my oldest son came home and after the doctor came it was time for the priest to come, but he did not come and we waited and he did not come so that it was I who had to lie down beside this grown man and lead him backwards and forwards through a life he had forgotten the deeds and maps to. As he whispered in my ear, yes, what do you want me to say, I could see life for him again some time. But for the first time I saw my own death. Just before he died I told him what I was to tell another son of mine not many years after.

Ritual walking confession, his back to us, she with her face as his life pours out. They are walking through are walking through his brutal life under some of the next scene, then he parts from her forever.

CHORUS:
Nominations for North Middlesex
One of the Donnellys is Dead!

(hilarious reaction)

The CHORUS divide into those watching the news bulletin board where several are chalking up headlines, and others reading newspapers.

SOLO:
Solvet Jacobus in favilla

CHORUS:
Another diabolical outrage—a horse disemboweled with a scythe. Flammis acribus addictus Fiendish outrage—a tree across the London, Huron & Bruce railway this morning. The trestles of the Grand Trunk Railway bridge at Lucan Crossing sawn through by some fiend in human form. There is work for some clever detective in Lucan. Voca me cum benedictus, Dies irae, dies illa Dona eis requiem. The Detective. Our serial for the month of December. "A Detective's Diary," or

MRS DONNELLY's arm cannot keep her oldest son here anymore; she lets it drop to her side and walks across the CHORUS gossipers.

McCRIMMON: *(disguised as an old beggar-woman)* How I brought the Donnelly Gang to heel. Gentlemen, are all the blinds down and the doors to Mr Stub's store room locked? Yes? Then I will resume my civilian garb. *(flinging off his disguise)* Mr Finnegan, I have been for some time engaged in ferreting out at your behest the perpetrators of certain crimes which have been committed in Lucan & its vicinity. Today is—I make this interim report to you Thursday, February the 24th, 1876. Sunday—5th of December, 1875—we met here as you recall in camera.

FINNEGAN: First of all, let me introduce you to Mr George Stub at the back of whose store we are hiding. Mr Stub, this is the private detective the town council gave permission to bring in. He's been here incognito already for about a month and I sure hope to hell he's going to tell us what we can do to prevent all our business affairs going bust. Gentlemen, Hugh McCrimmon.

CHORUS: A giant in size, he was gentle as a child. Shy as a woman, his heart was bold as a lion's. Modest as a maiden … And in first place in the five mile dash! Hugh McCrimmon!

McCRIMMON: Yes. For my athletic prowess in weight-lifting and foot running alone I have won over a thousand gold medals both here and in Uncle Sam's dominions. You may remember how I asked you each to tell me your story and to tell me all of the story. Because there is a great detective up in the sky (all glance up) who does know and He'll make it known if you don't so I want all of the truth. My notes. This family—seven of them have done all these terrible things and they've been charged, but the constables can't arrest them. Too bad the one died and got away on us. You say no witnesses will dare to testify for fear of reprisal, in short they're running this town with a reign of terror, you want to run it and I'm here to help you. Chapter One, sirs, is to

STUB: I'm having Will Donnelly arrested today if you must know—he's owed me a bill at the store in there for a bridle for over a year now and I'm having him arrested for that debt.

McCRIMMON: An arrest for a minor debt? Rather small potatoes, don't you think?

STUB: He won't pay, his bowels hate me so much he won't pay that debt even though today is his wedding day, he won't pay it to keep out of jail.

CHORUS: May the God of Israel join you together and may He be with you, who was merciful to two only children: and now, O Lord, make them bless Thee more fully. Alleluia, alleluia.

PRIEST: William Donnelly, wilt thou take Norah Macdonald here present for thy lawful wife according to the rite of our holy Mother the Church?

WILL: I will

PRIEST: Norah Macdonald, wilt thou take William Donnelly here present for thy lawful husband, according to the rite of our holy Mother the Church?

NORAH: I will (They hold right hands.)

PRIEST: Ego conjungo vos in matrimonium, in nomine Patris, et Filii et Spiritus Sancti, Amen

He sprinkles them with water. Then he blesses the ring, gold & silver coins. BAILIFFS appear at the back of the church with staves.

Let us pray. Bless, O Lord, this ring which we bless in Thy Name, that she who shall wear it, keeping true faith unto her husband may abide in Thy peace and will, and ever live in mutual charity. Through Christ our Lord, Amen.

He sprinkles the ring with holy water in the form of a cross. The bridegroom receives from the PRIEST the ring and places it on the fourth finger of his bride.

WILL: With this ring I thee wed and I plight unto thee my troth. (silent Lord's Prayer)

BAILIFF: Are you just about through. Because which one of you is William Donnelly; we've come with writ against him for debt.

PRIEST: Look, O Lord, we beseech Thee, upon these Thy servants, and graciously assist Thine own institutions, whereby Thou hast ordained the propagation of mankind, that they who are joined together by Thy authority may be preserved by Thy help. Through Christ our Lord. Amen. Mr & Mrs William Donnelly, who are these men?

WILL: Father Flannery, they are bailiffs for a debt I refuse to pay to a man you know well, Mother and Father, who used the ignorance of a child six months ago to snare me now on my wedding day. How many days?

BAILIFFS: It says here—ten days in the jug, Bill.

WILL: Norah. Meet me at Tom Ryder's wedding dance which is to be in ten days time at Fitzhenry's Tavern. Promise? We'll recommence there and no, Mother and Father, don't offer to pay, as a man I've decided not to. If George Stub wants me in jail he can have what he wants. And when I want him to lose this election that's coming up then I can have what I want. Got my fiddle there? I'll give you a tune as the bailiffs here march me off. Attention! March! (He goes off playing "Boney over the Alps." They listen to it dying away and then follow.)

NORAH: Mrs Donnelly, you gave Will that fiddle didn't you.

MRS DONNELLY: Are you thinking if I hadn't you might have your husband in your arms at this very moment, Norah, instead of his doing such a proud fool thing?

NORAH: No. I've never been so happy in my life to have married such a man.

McCRIMMON: Chapter One. January the twenty-second, I wrote to my sweetheart. Chapter Two. I visit the outlaw's nest—in disguise.

Our attention focuses on JOHN washing himself at the Donnelly farmhouse. MIKE drives into the yard.

MIKE: What are we going to do, Jack? There's a detective on the way out here.

JOHN: He's already here. The boys brought him home with them.

MIKE: Do they know who he is?

JOHN: They think he's a pal, he stood up for them in some dispute at the Dublin House and slapped a man down. You should see him, he's all muscle. Should we tell them?

MIKE: No. It'd be too much for their minds to bear. Is he disguised?

MRS DONNELLY enters, kisses MICHAEL, and shows him a baby shawl she has knit.

JOHN: *(whispering)* He's got an eye patch.

McCRIMMON enters & slouches around. BOB & TOM stand behind him.

MRS DONNELLY: Nellie was just showing me the baby, Mike, what shoulders he has already on him, and this is what I've knitted for Jenny's child and your father and me's off to the christening in St Thomas. Bob and Tom are you not going to say goodbye to your mother and father?

They come over to kiss her, she singles out the lounging pirate for a glance.

McCRIMMON: *(vulgar voice)* Well, look at who it is. This must be your mother, boys. Old Johannah Donnelly herself. *(He is hoping to provoke something.)*

MRS DONNELLY: I always thought that gentlemen stood up when a lady came into the room.

McCRIMMON: I'm no gentleman, and this is no room. *(laugh)*

MRS DONNELLY: The yard of any house I live in, sir, has a very high blue ceiling called a sky, and I call it a room particularly if I say so and I step out into it.

McCRIMMON: *(shambling & bowing)* Mrs Donnelly, I'm enchanted to meet you, met your two youngest ones while strolling through the village, and I gather you do not mind if they entertain a stranger at your high ceilinged residence. *(glances up)*

MRS DONNELLY: Strangers are always welcome here and I'm only sorry my husband and myself won't be here this weekend since we're going to St Thomas to visit my daughter and grand-daughter there. Tom and Bob, why don't you take your friend to help father catch the driving horse. It seems to me I caught a glimpse of you earlier on looking at one of my son's shirts on the clothesline. *(She comes over to him with a shirt & claps her hands together in front of his face.)* Well, if you're that interested in our laundry and linen out here, you can mend the big tear in that one yourself which was no doubt got in the sort of place my boys would meet you.

TOM: Mother, he stuck up for us. You and Will always do this to our friends.

MRS DONNELLY: Do what, this is the first one I ever caught pawing over my clothesline. Off to help with the horse now. *(They exit.)* Mike and John, who is that man? Of all the orphans and has beens and poor lost souls you've brought home for me to take the edge of hunger off them, this is the only one I cannot seem to stand. How in Heaven's name can Tom and Bob not see that he's a rascal.

JOHN: Mother, you don't know what a dreadful comment this is on your character.

MRS DONNELLY: How so, is he really a good man? *(The boys laugh as she leaves.)*

McCRIMMON: And with that she swept out. I took notes on all they said and done, but she breaks any pencil I have around me to describe. But I put them through their paces, and they never caught on. For instance, *(vulgar voice again)* Bob. Which would you rather see—it burn, or put it out and have it cool in your pocket—a nice green dollar bill?

He sets fire to a dollar bill & floats it. BOB watches in fascination and fails the test utterly, squiggling as it burns and obviously "interested" in fire.

TOM: You know, Jake, you're not the only clever person around here and this is all among friends now. *(He sticks a lead pipe in his trousers & drops a penny from his nose into the pipe.)* Mike?

MIKE: I haven't the skill, Tom, but I bet your new friend can't do it either.

McCRIMMON: *(taking the pipe & sticking it in his trousers)* Bender's the name, Mike, Jake Bender.

JOHN: Ladies are present, Mr. Bender.

After making sure they're not, McCRIMMON balances the penny, TOM pours a dipper of cold water down the pipe. He roars & chases after them.

JOHN: *(with head to ground)* What a runner he is, Mike. You can hear him pounding the earth like a giant. Where is he now?

MIKE: Where the creek runs through. He's caught up to them. He's bringing them back, one under each arm. Look at the front of his pants!

McCRIMMON enters & modestly turns his back to us; STUB, FINNEGAN et al. resume the back-room positions. The wedding party music strikes up.

McCRIMMON: Yes, I was the first man to bring the Donnelly gang to heel. She got a pair of pants I had to leave out there, but I got all the sons save Mike into the jails and prisons they belonged in. Thursday February the 24th, 1876, Gentlemen, my constables are ready. I hear the dance about to start over at Fitzhenry's Hotel over there and we'll soon see some more wildcat action.

STUB: Well, I hope so, the room we used to meet in got burnt down. What kind of a case have you made out against them?

McCRIMMON: *(going over to barrel)* They've got about thirty friends. I'm going to select the weakest and dance him on a rope till he tells us what he knows about the Donnellys' activities, starting right here with this redhaired lad in the barrel. It's Tom Ryan the little sneaking spy it is. Chapter Three!

He closes the barrel & they roll TOM off as the wedding sweeps in. A FIDDLER jumps out over the bar; someone collects money in a hat to pay him; the bar in full flow, someone ladling out the punch, girls sitting on boys' knees.

BOY: What will you dance?

GIRL: Your will is my pleasure, Dan.

FIDDLER: What'll you have?

BOY: Barney, put your wrist in it or Kitty here'll leave us both out of sight in no time. Whoo! Success! Clear the floor. Well done, Barney. That's the go.

The dance: Polka, Schottische, Reel if time. Play WILL's march "Boney over the Alps" when he & JOHN enter, NORAH, Mr & Mrs Tom Ryder—the new bride & groom whose party this is.

CONSTABLE(S): *(with staves)* John Donnelly, we've come to arrest you for assault & battery of Joseph Berryhill. Read the warrant if you like. Come along now, John.

JOHN: But it's dated a month ago, why have you waited till now when I'm at the dance?

CONSTABLE: Come along with us to the lock-up.

WILL: Come back here, John. Don't be dragged away by that fellow.

CONSTABLE: Come back here, Jack Donnelly.

WILL: Stay here, John. You're staying with me at this dance. I'm just out of jail and my brother's not going there and I'm not going back. Bob, where's Tom and Will Farl?

VOICE: Give it to him. Will

CONSTABLE: Hey you! Bring that man back here, he's my prisoner *(grabbing)*

JOHN: What's this about, Bawden? When you arrested me before I went with you like a man.

CONSTABLE: Yes, when you had to

He pulls at John, crowd pulls the other way.

VOICES: *(chanting)* We won't let John go ever from this party oh

WILL: Let him go, you son of a bitch. You couldn't have tried this at a more infuriating time I'll blow your heart out of you or any other man that'll try, just try to take him or any other of the family.

Melee, shots. All out save the hanging scene.

McCRIMMON: Chapter Four! Tom Ryan, the militia are rounding up your friends and herding them into the lock-up so there's no one to gallop by and see you hanging up in this tree, so just tell us the answers please like a good lad.

CONSTABLES enter with JOHN & put him behind a ladder.

CONSTABLE: The Queen versus John Donnelly. Assault and resisting arrest.

CHORUS: Three months in the Central Prison.

STUB: Three months! It should have been three years!

McCRIMMON: You won't tell. No? Pull him up. *(pause)* Now will you tell on the Donnellys?

CONSTABLES: The Queen versus Tom Donnelly. Misdemeanor.

CHORUS: Nine months in the Central Prison. The Queen versus Bob Donnelly

Again the two are brought in & placed behind ladders with clanking sounds.

CONSTABLES: Shooting with intent, two years in the penitentiary

McCRIMMON: Do you know anything about the burning & cutting up of those stage wagons? Do you know anything about the meat that's been stolen?

TOM: Listen, mister, if you'd let me see who you are I'd tell you everything. *(McCRIMMON motions to have his eye bandage removed.)* Ready? *(pause)* I done them things. I stole the meat because I was hungry, I broke the dishes in the hotel. The Donnelly boys themselves would like to know who does half the things— *(He is pulled up.)*

McCRIMMON: The young liar. If he wants to go to prison with those he loves so let him go.

CHORUS: The Queen versus William Donnelly.

RYAN comes to his ladder cell about the same time as WILL.

CONSTABLES: Shooting with intent. Nine months in the county jail.

McCRIMMON: Gentlemen, I'm ashamed of the brevity of their sentences, but we could not break the boy. I wish you'd warned me that he was subject to fits. Chapter Five!

TOM: Will, I'm so proud to be in jail with you. I love the jail.

WILL: Oh God, Tom Ryan. I hate the jail. Did Norah send anything along with you when you left Lucan now?

TOM: A bar of soap. Here. *(throws)* Has it got a saw in it, Will, you're eating it?

WILL: I know I am, Tom, and it's going to make me terribly ill.

McCRIMMON: But despite all that, gentlemen, I have rid your township of the vermin for some time and you Finnegan are again the King of the Road and you Squire Stub—can look forward to an election campaign where your candidate will meet only fair opposition, not the shears, clippers and torch he very well might have. Gentlemen, my pay. *(Just as they give him a bag—)*

VOICE: *(lady reading newspaper)* Well it says here that William Donnelly is very sick of a low fever in the jail and is not expected to live much longer—his wife is petitioning the Attorney-General to let him off his sentence.

McCRIMMON: Chapter Six! Thank you. Thursday, August 22nd. Today I proposed to my beloved and was accepted. She will marry a man who has just been appointed Chief of Police for Belleville.

He exits into the audience with the quilt that is MIKE & NELLIE's bed held behind him.

CHORUS: Like a flower, Eunice found herself and her pink frilly dress swept into the powerful arms of the brave Detective, winner of many athletic events.

MIKE & NELLIE in bed.

NELLIE: Always seem to wake up before Mike. Listen for the children. Take a look at the newspaper. Think. The village has been quiet since they're all gone off to jail. Didn't get Mike though. In his dreams he's finally got off the stage, you can tell from his breathing. When he first wakes up there's a minute before he tenses up for the day on the road which goes by our window and in that moment you can tell him things that might get him too excited later on, apt to rush off and hit somebody. But there's something I've got to tell him before it's too late. When we first met at the dance—I broke off my engagement with a lad called Sid Skinner because I fell so in love with Mike. Sid and me'd been courting for a year, but I could not help it, Mike was the man for me, but Sid's been coming to my mother's house on Horton Street lately, tipsy from his work at the hotel and saying he's going to kill you, Mike. Wake up, Mike, so I can put this to you. I've never told you but the man who tends bar at the City Hotel used to be in love with me. Mike?

MIKE: What time is it? Five o'clock by the light. Nellie?

NELLIE: Mike.

MIKE: Do you want to spend the rest of your life here in this house on Main Street of Lucan? Don't be afraid to tell me.

NELLIE: You know how happy I've been with you, Mike, wherever you are and whatever happens.

MIKE: I don't mean that, I know that, but have you ever thought you'd like to live another place?

NELLIE: Yes, oh God yes, Mike. *(Finnegan's stage horn)* Mike, there's Finnegan's stage—it's later than I thought, you'll be late for work.

MIKE: Nellie, I don't know why I've been ashamed to tell you, but yesterday was the last day I'll ever drive the Opposition Stage. They've won. Without my brothers beside me I can't go on. So I've got a job as a brakeman on the Canada Southern and we'll leave today for St Thomas. Do you feel ashamed of me?

NELLIE: God no, Mike. There was something else I wanted to tell you, but it's all right now we're moving so far away, what's the matter.

Stage passes with horn and shout.

MIKE: *(shaking fist out window)* I'll drive over your grave yet, McKellar. Oh God, I loved driving that road. *(pause)* Nellie, there's smoke coming out of our kitchen window downstairs, they've set fire to our house, quick get the babies. Mother of God save us from Finnegan's Fire.

A red glare we have seen before. Viewpoint: roll on floor with baby dolls; scream from wife.

CHORUS:
The Election of 1878

Then shout John A. forever boys,
That is the heading cry;
Every election we will win,
The time is drawing nigh,
The scheming Grits may bag their heads
That is if they've a mind,
Or go and dig up taters
With their shirts hung out behind.

STUB: Gentlemen of Ward Three, it gives me great pleasure to see the Conservative Meeting at the Donnelly Schoolhouse so crowded tonight. As I see some of our Grit friends here I trust and hope that you will give our speaker a fair hearing. May I give a particularly warm welcome to Mr William Donnelly whom the Grit government of our fair province has seen fit to release from his chamber at the Queen's boarding house where he was reportedly deathly ill. Although looking quite recovered from his fever, I would ask as a special favour that he not overtax himself or it might bring on another—attack. As you all know the Conservative Candidate for this riding is an Irish Catholic nominated by his Irish Protestant brothers. Gentlemen, I have been requested to perform a very pleasing duty this evening and it is to introduce to you the next member for the riding of North Middlesex—Mr Timothy Corcoran. *(applause)*

CORCORAN: *(manipulating a puppet version of himself)* Gintlemen farmers of Biddulph, yees are ruined by Mr McKinsey and his free trade. Ivery market in the country is filled with Yankee horses, cattle and hogs. Yees are losing fifteen cints on ivery bushell of barley ye sell, and yees can't get over half price for yees pays and oats, bekase millions uv bushels uv Yankee corn comes into the country not paying a cint of duty. You farmers have to pay tin cints more for yare tay and two cints more for yare sugar—Mr Chairman, I see a hand up at the back of the room.

MRS DONNELLY: *(who has been following the speech in a newspaper and has been reading along with the speaker for a bit)* This is the same speech as he gave in Ailsa Craig a week ago. It's all printed down here in the *Advertiser.*

STUB: Don't heed that hand, on and louder, Tim.

COCORAN: —two cints more for yare sugar, yes, Will Donnelly what did you want to ask?

WILL: If, Mr Corcoran, you were elected to parliament next Tuesday and say in a year's time—say your party got in, Macdonald's party— and again there was a scandal about money and there came up a vote of confidence in the government how, Mr Corcoran, would you vote?

CORCORAN: I don't know. When the time comes, Bill, I'd know by that time because I'd have studied it up you see.

WILL: Although you are a Catholic the Orange Lodge supports your candidacy, Mr Corcoran. What is your vote likely to be when their Grand Master tries to ram a bill through Parliament for the incorporation of the Orange Lodge?

CORCORAN: Oh, Will Donnelly, never fear I'd vote for such a thing.

WILL: But Mr Corcoran, you would have to as a member of the Conservative Party.

CORCORAN: Yes, I suppose I would. Mr Stub—

VOICE: It's Mr Stub should be telling us instead of Tim

VOICE: Sure, it's well known George Stub here gets a senatorship if Tim gets in

VOICE: Sure, send him to parliament by voting for Tim. I say three cheers for the Grit Candidate Mr Colin Scatcherd who has one face under one hat. Hip Hip Hurrah.

In the cheers, objects fly at the speakers who withdraw. The newsclerk chalks up results on the bulletin board; a feeling of tension, torches, election night fever, close arithmetic.

CLERK: Mr Scatcherd … the North Middlesex Riding has been won by the Grit Candidate in a tight race. Mr Scatcherd has won the seat by seven votes. *(Cheers for Scatcherd led by WILL DONNELLY.)*

STUB: *(in the drawing room)* Seven votes. We lost by seven votes. We were supposed to win by four hundred! Where's my wife, Bridget?

BRIDGET: *(parlourmaid)* Master Stub, your wife has gone back to live with your father-in-law. She said to tell you it might look like a Senator's house, but she read about the election results in the paper and you had not kept her promise to her.

STUB: She's nervous and overwrought with the baby coming on. Bridget, what's your family's theory about why we lost. Is it not just the Donnellys?

BRIDGET: Sir, my brother says, sir, it is the Donnellys. Without them and we'd have a Catholic gentleman in parliament this evening and maybe in Sir John A.'s cabinet, but no—it's the Donnellys don't want that.

STUB: Could I speak to your brother some time, Bridget. How long has it been since he's back from the States?

BRIDGET: Please, sir, not very long. He just arrived on the Finnegan Stage from town a good hour ago and sure I'm giving him a bit of supper in your kitchen.

STUB: Tell him to come in here. *(pause)* What's your name?

CARROLL: *(wiping mouth)* I told him what my name was.

STUB: James Carroll. Did you leave here for the States because you were in any kind of trouble, Jim?

CARROLL: No, sir. My father married again and I could not get along with my stepmother, after he died, she got his land away from us and I've come back to see about that and—

STUB: Your mother was a Farl, was she not, Jim?

CARROLL: How'd you know that?

STUB: Donnellys killed her brother, didn't they?

CARROLL: Yes. *(to audience)* What this man was asking me to do was what my mother on her deathbed made me promise to do. To kill the Donnellys. But at first no one had the courage, no one except my poor dead mother, to say that. At first it was drive them out of the township, they were all out of prison more or less and all back on top of us so I was made a constable in Lucan and my aim was to find one victim of the Donnellys brave enough to stick to his story and fight it out in the courts and keep after them again and again until we had these Donnellys behind bars or out of the township or—out!

NED RYAN: *(falling flat)* I've been robbed! Tom Donnelly robbed me of, he and Jim Feeney, robbed me of 85 dollars!

CARROLL: When did the robbery take place, Mr Ryan?

NED: Wednesday night, whatever night that was. About a year ago.

WILL: Mr Ryan, what did you have to drink at Walker's Hotel?

NED: Well, I do not get drunk often. I treated Tom and Jim to some whiskey, but I myself had some sherry wine and some ginger wine.

WILL: Is it true you were come into town that day for a spree, that you had been at the following hotels first: the Dublin House, the Queen's, the Royal, Fitzhenry's, the Western, Levitt's—

NED: Never at Levitt's, never darken his door, haven't got to Fitzhenry's, still haven't got there!

WILL: Is it true that you have several times lately entered my father's house and my own house in search of your son who has run away from you?

NED: My son! Waiting for his pa to come home with some food for the table and the Donnellys have stolen all his money away from him and I'm at home waiting for my son and he does not come to his pa and you want to know why— because the Donnellys've stolen him away from his dear pa and ma like the fairies used to steal little children away when you weren't watching.

WILL: Is it not true also that although you say that my brother choked you when you fell down, the inmates of the house who took you in could find no marks on your throat?

SQUIRE: I dismiss this case, Ned Ryan. I think one of the constables summed it all up when he said that you were so drunk that night you couldn't have known your mouth from your arsehole.

CARROLL: Your honour, may I as a friend of Ned Ryan's here and as a—may I say that I am not satisfied with the way my friend's case has been handled. We will bring it up before another magistrate.

WILL: Your honour, in view of Mr Carroll's statements, I would like the fact that the charges against my brother, Thomas Donnelly, have been dismissed, I would like a certificate made out to that effect.

CARROLL: Yes, and I could make you out a certificate about the way justice has been administered in this village so that his family and their ruffian friends can bully and terrify a township of three thousand inhabitants. You Donnellys say you're persecuted; ask the horses and cattle and the barns and the stables and the women and the men here like Ned Ryan who's lost his boy to you who is being persecuted. Is there anybody in this room who'll stick up for this gang of mad Donnelly dogs—look at his foot!—whom some of you think of as being so wonderful. And I hear one or two of yous thinking of renting my father's farm from my stepmother and there's some of you stopping at the Donnellys' for a drink of water at their well. There's a whole lot of you still doing that and if we hear of any such, or of any man or woman offering Mrs Donnelly a ride in their cart on the way to mass or

He menaces the whole theatre; we are afraid of him.

WILL: *(lightly and suddenly entering)* Now is that you, Jim Carroll, sitting on that horse of yours, under the tree talking to yourself about us give me that whip of yours before you hurt yourself with it and come out of the shadow so we can get a look at you. Yes, you won. You smeared our name for all time so that when children are naughty their mothers still say to them

WILL & CHORUS: Be quiet, or the Black Donnellys will get you.

WILL: Isn't that what most of you in this room think of us as being? Because of him my mother was turned into a witch who rode around burning down sheds and barns, because of him ... but there's one thing, Jim, that some people coming after will remark on. And that is—the difference between our handwritings. There is my signature. There is his. Choose. You can't destroy the way my handwriting looks, just as you can never change the blot that appears in every one of your autographs and the cloud and the smudge and the clot and the fume of your jealousy. There! the living must obey the dead! Dance the handwriting that comes out of your arm. Show us what you're like. Very well, I'll dance mine.

First WILL (fiddle) then CARROLL (trumpet) dance; the latter falls down in a fit. Placards displaying their signatures are held up for us to see.

WILL: Oh now Jim, I didn't mean you were to fall down in one of those fits you have now and again. Is it your heart sometimes, is it your mind sometimes, is it your great big feet sometimes, Jim, is it that you couldn't stand the way the Donnellys dressed, the way they looked right through you, the way my mother looked down at you. So you clubbed her to kneel at your feet, but you forget that our eyes don't kneel at your feet, but you forget that our eyes don't kneel and that her eyes will look down and through you until dies irae and beyond. Down and through the clown with blood on his sleeves they call James Carroll. *(Exit)*

CARROLL: It's true. I couldn't club down their eyes. After it was over I had to leave Biddulph. I never went back there. You people here'd used me like a piece of dirty paper to wipe the Donnellys off your backsides. I died out West alone. Grave whereabouts unknown. I hate William Donnelly. I hate William Donnelly.

CHORUS: End of Act Two.

ACT THREE

A gravel train with MIKE DONNELLY as brakeman backs into the audience. Three whistles for stop after MIKE has signalled this with his lantern. Switch light and the two red lanterns on the back of the train move accordingly. Song over and NELLIE to one side as commentary.

MIKE & CHORUS:
I want to be a brakeman
And with the brakeman stand
A badge upon my forehead
A tail rope in my hand

With links & pins & bell cord
And signals red & white
I'd make a freight train back up
Or slack ahead all right.

When ere a train I shunted
At St Thomas so fair
I'd not forget my darling wife
But keep the crossing clear

NELLIE: My husband, Michael Donnelly, was a brakeman on a gravel train out of Waterford on the Canada Southern Line, division point St Thomas where I live with our children in a house on Mill Street—two nights he spends alone boarding at Waterford; tomorrow is his day off and he'll be home with us for four nights. But this is Wednesday, December 9th 1879. There's no snow yet. About four o'clock it begins to rain. His mate afterwards told me this is the way it went with Michael and the train, I wanted to know every crossing they came to before when their work was over they walked into the barroom at Slaght's Hotel.

Two blasts. The journey establishes itself then goes under her speech.

That means the engineer is ready to go. From the hind end of the train Mike gives him the highball so he whistles two short blasts meaning "I understand." Yes, I understand—that in the months before my husband was murdered in that barroom at Slaght's Hotel—there was a train, there was another sort of train that started out just after that election of 1878 and every crossing it blew its whistle for was a crossing that was closer to my husband's death and I wish I could be clear in my own mind what that First Crossing was but I think I can see you there in cold blood talking about how you'll kill him and I run towards you to stop you but I meet the glass of mystery and time and trickery. I fall down and only know that I must listen for all the other four crossings Mike's train whistled for before the last time he walked out of the rain.

The barroom of the City Hotel fades in: CARROLL, SID SKINNER & a TRAINER (BILL LEWIS).

CARROLL: Well, shall we get started? We've got the job set up for you, Sid.

SID: That's good of you. And then what do I do?

CARROLL: What's the matter?

SID: It's a great thing I'm to do, kill a man and go to prison for God knows how long. All today, all tonight at this bar I've been thinking about it and I have to pinch myself to wake up—this is happening to me, this is happening to you, Sid. Sid is getting out of here.

CARROLL: Suit yourself, Sid Skinner. Maybe, and Bill here would agree with me, it'd just prove what Mike Donnelly said about you as he boasted about the girl he took away from you.

SID: I don't want to know what he said. Just the last few days I realized what a duck I was going to her mother and saying I was going to kill Mike Donnelly. I'm not a fighting man.

CARROLL: Then what kind of man was it who handled the bar in here tonight, eh Bill? That was a fighting man, but a fighting man that's not all just fight, but some brains in his head as well, eh? If Mike had seen you tonight he'd have had to eat his words—

SID: What words?

CARROLL: That you were a man of no prick. Yes, them's the dirty words he used about you, auh, he's a little fellow with no prick on him at all— *that* little fellow.

SID: Teach me how to kill him then. What dirt do I have to go through to wipe that off his mouth, yes, what's the false name you're giving me?

CARROLL: After the lesson tonight, Sid, if you learn it well, you'll have a new name. Now, you're lucky you don't have to deal with the whole tribe the way I have to up in Biddulph. I wish I just had the one desperate character to clean up, but I've got six or seven of Mike's relatives to deal with every day and do you know who's the worst?

SID: You're afraid of them?

CARROLL: The mother, she's the one I'm

SID: You're afraid of an old woman?

CARROLL: Well, what would you have done? if you can do it, maybe I can Sid, I don't know. On Monday morning last, Bill here saw me just after in Gallagher's yard and I was shaking like a leaf, for not an hour ago, I'd took my life in my hands and dared to walk down the road past the Donnellys' place—was going to get some notes from a man I'd sold a fanning mill, Jack Donnelly was out plowing. Mrs Donnelly was milking a cow by the gate and Tom had just cursed me— Jack said—

JOHN: Now there's that fighting man, Mr Jim Carroll. Jim—I want to talk to you. What were

you saying about Bob and our family at the sale last night?

CARROLL: I don't want to talk to you, Jack Donnelly. I've got too much respect for myself. Meet me this afternoon at Whalen's Corners.

JOHN: Let's have no mobbing at Whalen's Corners, Jim. I'll fight you, right now, I'll make your big head soft right there on that road. What business is it of yours how light a sentence Bob got?

CARROLL: Don't want much to fight, but if you'll meet me at Whalen's Corners I'll fight you. I'll lick all the Donnellys. Well, Jack drops his plow and he strode at me. I'm an inoffensive man. You come at me and I'll shoot you. Keep off

TOM throws a stone.

JOHN: Tom—get out on the road and thrash him—the coward, the thief.

CARROLL: Now listen to what she said.

MRS DONNELLY: You son of a bitch, you thief, you rogue. Give it to him, Tom, on his big head. Point a gun at an old woman milking a cow, would you, you bastard, you should be arrested, Jim Carroll, and when they arrest you they should put you back down into the devil with thirty tails you belong to.

CARROLL: Oh—the dirty names she called, calling my mother a dog and saying my father never married her, she made me feel so jumpy I just walked on, oh—I need someone to show me the way, I wouldn't dare shoot any of them now or ever. It's her, Sid, do you understand me, she's a witch and we'll never get rid of any of them unless there's someone brave enough to just— But there isn't. The mad dogs have won.

SID: No, they haven't.

CARROLL: Oh, well then, Bill to the bar please and just let on that you're Michael Donnelly taking a drink. Now, Sid—

SID goes up to the TRAINER, hauls him around by the shoulder; they fight, but the TRAINER soon pins SID to the ground.

BILL: It's no use, Jim, all we've taught him doesn't put the weight on him Donnelly has and I'm doing just the things Donnelly does.

CARROLL: Let's add something. Sid, watch me. Bill. Stop shooting off your big mouth, Mike Donnelly.

BILL is stationed by the bar again. CARROLL draws a jackknife which he holds in his left hand; he hits BILL from behind and draws BILL into chasing him behind the bar. In the clinch, BILL has hold of CARROLL's shoulders but CARROLL holds him by the vest and with the other knife hand stabs him below the belt.

BILL: Do you want something from me. Holy name of God, Jim Carroll, go easy with that open knife. Do you want to try that now, Sid? And I think, Jim, the first few times with Sid here we'll have the knife closed.

SID: Stop shooting off your big mouth, Mike Donnelly.

BILL: Do you want something from me?

SID & BILL go through the new business. Exhausted but livened up & confident once more, SID leans back against the bar while CARROLL unlocks the bar and pours them all a drink ... even for the privy cleaner who now comes forward with shaving mug & lather.

CARROLL: The mad dogs have lost.

SID: Who's he? He's been watching all this.

CARROLL: He's Mr Nobody, Sid, a retired barber, well semi-retired, he'd like to start shaving you just to rearrange your face whiskers a bit as well as your topknot.

SID: He smells!

CARROLL: Well, when you enter the world where you have two faces under the one hat, Sid, you can't be too choosy about your barber any more. Cleans out privies for a living now because the razor hand got rather unsteady there one famous time, oh nothing to fear, Sid, by the way we've got to start calling you by your new name.

SID: What's my new name.

CARROLL: You've got a new name with the new job you're going to take tonight—you'll be a navvy for the Canada Southern near Waterford where your friend from Biddulph is a brakeman on their gravel train right now and everything is fixed up, don't worry, remember borrow the jack-knife a few days before from some chum at your rooming house, let's go back in here to shave him.

SID: What's my name.

BILL: Same as my name, Bill Lewis.

SID: But that's your name. I'm not a bit like you

BILL: Sure it is. Sure you're not, but look here don't start wanting some other name. Jim, he doesn't like my name. I'm getting sore.

CARROLL: Ah, darling, you like his name really don't you at heart. It's a stout little plain name for a stout little plain little—you'll be like St Patrick, "Bill Lewis."

Laughing they both sing the St Patrick song as they escort him out behind the bar.

BOTH:
When blind worms crawling in the grass
Disgusted all the nation,
He gave them a rise which opened their eyes
To a sense of their situation.

So, success attend St Patrick's fist
For he's a saint so clever;
Oh! he gave the snakes and toads a twist
And bothered them forever ...

The toads went pop, the frogs went hop,
Slap-dash into the water;
And the snakes committed suicide
To save themselves from slaughter.

So, success &c.

The clock in the St Nicholas Hotel strikes eleven: wind—establish this well before the other scene quite fades and we are back with the MINISTER & WILL.

WILL: Mr Donaldson, the next time the clock strikes, I know that I will have come to that part in my story I promised you—my brother Michael's death.

DONALDSON: You were telling me, Mr Donnelly, that the new priest formed a society against your family from among your fellow parishioners.

WILL: Oh he turned them against us. But the man who really worked at turning people against us, and you see we were not to be trusted because we had led the parish in not voting the way that Bishop and Sir John A would have had us vote—the man who really worked at it was a drifter named James Carroll. I'll show you, sir, how our family first met him. We became an obsession with him, I think he was hungry for land, our land, our eyes, our clothes, our mother. They'd just lost the election, we'd won and down the road he came and my mother was milking a cow by the gate.

JOHN: Oh I was on speaking terms with him. But he was a queer fellow.

CARROLL: Jack, what's this you were saying about me.

JOHN: Nothing yesterday, Jim Carroll, but what I could say today.

CARROLL: I wish you'd come out of that field and do it. You meet me at Whalen's Corners at two o'clock and we'll fight there.

JOHN: There's none here but the two of us. We'll have it out here, Jim Carroll, and have no mobbing about it.

CARROLL: *(drawing a revolver)* You son of a bitch. If you come one foot further, I'll blow your brains out.

TOM comes with stones.

WILL: Tom—throw the stones down, he wants law, not fight.

MRS DONNELLY: Go back, John, don't mind the blackguard or he'll shoot you.

CARROLL: I'd as leave shoot you as him.

MRS DONNELLY: *(She rises, looks at him & turns her back on him.)* Go away and mind your own business. I don't want anything to do with you.

CHORUS: The Queen against Julia Donnelly

CARROLL: Using abusive and insulting, grossly insulting language.

MRS DONNELLY: And I was convicted of doing so and fined one dollar and costs. He dragged me into court and into one of the newspapers where it was printed that I had thrown stones at him. Why, sir, are you hunting me down. Yes, I must be a beast if you can draw a revolver and aim it at me and no one says no

CHORUS: The Queen against James Carroll

MRS DONNELLY: Making threats to use revolver with intent. *(pause)* Well, I see that we get nowhere with that charge so that next time he walks by our house it may be with a mob who will—Jim Carroll, when I looked into your eyes I could see your mother's eyes *(FAT LADY's ghost crosses to her chair.)* and I could see you hating me long ago because you were fat and we'd killed your brother, on your deathbed you must have sharpened his teeth for me. And if you have got some mud on the mother, the next crossing is to bring a mob to their father and mother's door, but first we have come to the *(train journey up with crossing signal)*

CHORUS: Third Crossing.

Actors form Roman Line leaving their chairs unguarded. TOM RYAN, TOM DONNELLY, JAMES CARROLL with cheesecloth over their faces play tricks, steal props from chairs, spin tops illegally, pick pockets, gallop up & down the road after they've gone asleep, snoring—whole Puck episode, ladies on their bums from chamberpots sort of thing.

WILL: *(after a silent build)* Soon after this there began in the neighbourhood a whole parade of little mischievous things—Little, they began to get bigger and bigger and they told stories that my brother Tom took out horses, their horses at night and rode them up and down.

CHORUS: From tollgate to tollgate.

FARMER: Until they're nigh dead and you know what Tom Donnelly's tied to her tail.

He holds up a placard saying "Vote Grit & Vote Right."

FAT LADY: *(a scream of rage at this)* That's Cripple's beautiful handwriting.

WILL: There were stories that Tom Ryan in the middle of the night let people's cattle out of their fields and drove them up into Blanshard township.

VOICES IN SUCCESSION: Who stole my disk? Who stole my pig? My tea chest is gone. Who done that? I know who done that. Who shaved my horses' tails? Who put stones in my threshing machine and iron pins? We know who done that

WILL: Do you now and who done that?

CHORUS:

Who? stole my disk and stole my pig
rode my horses and drove my cows
cut out their tongues and cut off their ears?

(repeat softly)

The three mystery faces whip them like tops humming: Donnelly!

WILL: Until my father said one day: If a stone fell from heaven they'd say

WILL & CHORUS: Donnelly done it.

WILL: We were blamed for everything and people shunned us, *would* not talk to us. Three times Carroll arrested my brother Tom on the charge of stealing

NED: One hundred dollars from me—Ned Ryan—and three times the case fell through

WILL: But one fall night Carroll got a new warrant from the Grand Jury and he was out at our house at dawn to serve it.

MRS DONNELLY: Yes, you should look behind the stove, Mr Carroll, and why not look right in the stove while you're at it.

CARROLL: I could not find him. I went over as far as Skinner's in Usborne and where Will lived at Whalen's Corners before I turned back.

MARY DONOVAN: I was spinning opposite the doorway in the house that day—could see the concession from where I was working. Saw Thomas Donnelly in his father's potato field picking potatoes. I went upstairs for yarn rolls and I saw William Donnelly drive into his father's place and signal to Tom in the field

CARROLL: I went over the fence into Mr Donnelly's field—went across a fall wheat field expecting to get in his tracks to follow him

MARY: When I saw Carroll & Thomas Donnelly running they were both near the stable. Saw John Donnelly come out with a horse. Tom Donnelly came up running, got on the horse and ran away.

CARROLL: If you'll stay away out of the country it's not particular if I catch you, Tom Donnelly. *(to JOHN)* I'll make it hot for you when I get to Lucan, John Donnelly. You'd no business giving him that horse to escape with.

JOHN: Jim, you never told me you had a new warrant for Tom.

CARROLL: What do you think I was running all over that wheat field for?

JOHN: Jim, Tom's not running away on you, sure he hardly seen you, he's going up to Kenny's blacksmith shop to get us some

CARROLL: I went over to Quigley's and stopped the thrashing. They got their horses and we chased Tom Donnelly into the bush all around the township from tollgate to tollgate all that night, but by the holy name of God could we *(helter skelter pursuit of TOM DONNELLY)*

CHORUS:
We've got him who stole my disk and stole my pig
rode my horses and drove my cows
cut out their tongues and cut off their ears

NED RYAN: It's my son, Tom, dressed up in Tom Donnelly's clothes. Tom, why would you play such a trick on us? Why would you side with the family that won't let the thrashing machine come to thrash at your father's farm and the crops are rotting in the field, why

TOM: You old ruffian—I'll tell you why I side with the Donnellys. And you clodhoppers and you drifter—trying to pull them down. Three reasons. Because they're brave. They're not afraid. They're so little afraid of living here among you that this morning they started sowing their fall wheat. Two. They're handsome. Look at your faces—your faces'd fit into the hoofprints of forty old cows hopelessly lost in a bog. Yes, high & mighty one with your dirty linen scarce covering your hippopotamus rump and your hair like—Third. When pa here took the ax to mother and Bridget and Sarah & me who was the only family on the whole road with enough sand to take us in? *(pause)* So that's why I side with them, Pa, and if you want to know who's doing all the mischief on this road it's him over there—Jim Carroll.

CARROLL: Is it Jim Carroll for sure now, Tom Ryan?

NED RYAN: Stand back from him all of you, let a father deal with his begetting. Come here my darling. I want you to be my boy again and not the Donnellys' boy.

TOM: You're going to beat me, aren't you, Pa.

NED: No. (*pulling open his shirt*) Look at my heart in my chest now beating with love for you. Come to my heart—don't the rest of you lay a hand on him. Tom.

His arms are extended although we do see the club in his back pocket ready. TOM pauses, then runs at his belly with his head down and knocks him down, escapes. Everyone feels out of fuel, gawk listlessly, even CARROLL. All at wits' end then cowbell and spinning sound before it, leading up to

MARY: (*ear-shattering*) My cow! The Donnellys have stolen my cow. On Sunday evening my cattle were all at my gate when I came home. On Monday morning I went to look for her. I cannot get a trace of her. Who's man enough here to come and help me look for my cow? My cow! They're skinning and eating and cooking my cow right this very minute now and you just sit on your backsides and gawp at me, you gomerils. My cow's hidden somewhere at the Donleys.

CHAIRMAN: Mary Donovan, Magistrate Stub says we can't have a warrant now because it's night time, but we are to keep watch and at dawn we can search. Will all members of the Peace Society who plan to visit the Donnelly homestead tomorrow come into the schoolhouse and take turns watching for dawn?

MARY: (*whispering as she exits with the others*) It'll be too late by daybreak, they'll have eaten my cow all up, my cow! I had good reason to suspect the Donleys of taking my cow. The reason I suspected the Donleys is I had heard things spoke against them.

Silence as the night passes; crickets of early September, a bell rings matins, a wagon passes, train whistle, a clock strikes an early hour in the Donnelly house.

MRS DONNELLY: The air was hollow so that you could hear things far away that night. Or did I dream it that first I was on a coach and then a train and I was taking an empty coffin to a tavern where they were going to kill one of my sons. Their leaving the school and tramping down the roads towards our place must have wakened me, but as I lit the stove and went to wake up my niece Bridget they were quiet enough.

CHORUS: There's smoke coming up now from their chimney.

Whispers offstage under the audience. We are part of the mob.

MRS DONNELLY: The sun comes up, there's my shadow line—getting shorter already, turn earth another morning and noon and night I wish I could stop it Bridget take out the pail and pump us a fresh pail of water, yesterday I could hear Mary Donovan spinning in her doorway, watching us, I wonder

BRIDGET screams and runs in.

BRIDGET: Aunt Judith, where shall we hide, there's a mob in the yard with sticks in their hands.

JOHN sleeps behind the stove.

MRS DONNELLY: Augh! what has possessed them now. Go tell Mr Donnelly. John, get dressed. I stood behind the door and looked through the crack at them. Why is it getting so dark in our house. Because the light of each window is shut out by the people there.

BRIDGET: Uncle Jim, the yard is full of men with clubs. Johnny, you'd best get up.

MR DONNELLY, hitching up trousers, goes to the door and addresses a mob whose presence we feel rather than see.

MR DONNELLY: Good morning, boys, what's up with you?

CARROLL: We want nothing but to tell you Donnellys that we're not afraid of you

MRS DONNELLY: Look at the dark bunch of them and he alone, what is it, it's

VOICE: We're not afraid of you anymore, Donnelly.

MARY: I have lost a cow

MRS DONNELLY: A cow they say has been stolen from Mary Donovan's farm and we are suspected

VOICE: We're through being scared of the Donnellys.

MRS DONNELLY: Why 'tis only right the cow should be found. If you think the cow is here, Jim Carroll, don't leave one straw on top of another

JOHN: Turn the strawstack upside down. There's no stolen cow here, but I see the man who stole your cow in your crowd

Searching sounds, pails getting kicked, doors slammed &c.

VOICE: We'll make you keep quiet, Jack Donnelly.

JOHN: If you go up to the priest he'll curse the man who stole the cow and you'll find the cow before night.

CARROLL: How'd you like a good stiff kick in the ribs?

MR DONNELLY: And you can all kiss my backside. And I was a man, Jim Carroll, when you were not able to wipe your backside.

CARROLL: We could break your bones at your door and you won't be able to help yourself.

MR DONNELLY: I'll be here if the devil would burn the whole of you. I'm not in the least afraid of you. *(He comes into the house.)*

MRS DONNELLY: They're kicking over hen-coops and looking down the well, yes, fall down if you can, John Macdonald, what is it I hear him begging them to do, they're putting forks through the strawstacks we thrashed yesterday, he's saying—

MR DONNELLY: I wish John would stay in closer to the house, do you see that?

MRS DONNELLY: Yes, they've circled him and they're saying things like

CHORUS: Who stole my disk

JOHN: I don't know who stole your disk

CHORUS: Who stole my pig

JOHN: How the hell would I know

CHORUS:
who stole my disk and stole my pig
rode my horses and drove my cows
cut out their tongues and cut off their ears
who shaved off my horses' tails

JOHN: I don't know anything at all about your horses' tails, all I know is that you're trespassing and my father's farm has a fence, my father's land is enclosed, by the way you're acting you'd think it was a public path

MARY: I have lost a cow.

CHORUS: Don't you tell us to get out Jack Donnelly. We're not afraid of you I'll get satisfaction if it's for twenty years. This work'll be put down and it'll be put down by us.

A roar as they find TOM RYAN. They rush on stage with him & now we & the Donnellys look out at the mob.

CHORUS: Here's one thing found.

CARROLL: Sit up there in the wagon and don't you move

CHORUS: Harbouring this young horserider and cattle driver, eh Donnelly.

MR DONNELLY: I'd harbour your father's son, O'Halloran, if all the world said no

O'HALLORAN: Little do you care Donnelly for my father's sons. Tie his hands, it's off to jail with this one.

TOM RYAN: Mr Donnelly wasn't harbouring me, I slept in their strawstack last night, they didn't know I was there. *(pause)* And I sat up there on the wagon. She came out. I was handcuffed. She came out and looked across at me. Between me and her was them with their clubs. What have I brought down on you, or would it have happened anyhow? Mrs Donnelly she was tall. If I could have I would have died for her. The wagon took me off to jail. I never saw her again.

Carrying TOM RYAN on their shoulders the mob circle and depart.

MRS DONNELLY: Yes, I stood there and I watched them tie up that lad and cuff him and knock him about. They were leaving, they hadn't found Mary Donovan's cow, but I was so glad they were leaving that I didn't dare try to help the boy because for the first time in my life I felt old and small & afraid. There were so many of them. Is this not a pretty way we are treated Mr Donnelly?

MR DONNELLY: But we deserve it, Mrs Donnelly.

MRS DONNELLY: In the name of Heaven how?

MR DONNELLY: For we're Donnellys.

MRS DONNELLY: Yes, and I also heard Will's brother-in-law say they were going to his place at

Whalen's Corners next. John, hitch up the driving horse for me, please.

There is a slight tug of war over the whip with MR DONNELLY.

MRS DONNELLY: Haven't they gone up the road by Keefe's, Mr Donnelly?

MR DONNELLY: Yes. If you must go, Mrs Donnelly, then you can cut over on the sideroad.

MRS DONNELLY: *(pause)* I must go.

What we have now is a bare stage with the bar as a place where MRS DONNELLY can coast up & down & around. A blacksmith should enter and stand near the bar which is going to be WILL DONNELLY's house. MARY DONOVAN should be sitting getting ready to spin & we need a girl who can simply fill in the choral replies to MRS DONNELLY, spin about perhaps supported by offstage voices. I'm in favour of a "Listen to the Wind" wheel & horse with MRS DONNELLY running behind. Simple & light.

JOHN: Mother, what are you listening for? *(triangle sounds)*

MRS DONNELLY:
I can hear the blacksmith who lives over at the village where Will & Norah live
Closer and louder the sound of his hammer
Wheels take me Hooves draw me
Out of the yard of his father's house

GIRL:
In the stream that I lie dreaming in I hear
A humming sound that fills me up with fear

MRS DONNELLY:
My neighbour, Mary Donovan, cow lady,
I leave you behind me.

And MRS DONNELLY has done one circuit of the stage & vanished.

MARY: I heard a cow bawling over on Donley's place that sounded like my cow. I honestly believed the Donleys had my cow. The Donleys had my cow shut up. A great deal of pork & cattle stealing has been taking place in our neighbourhood. *(A FARMER enters with two pails, which he sets down.)* Dan Quigley, did you hear I've lost my cow? The Donleys've stolen my cow.

FARMER: Mary Donovan, I just seen your cow.

MARY: Seen my cow? Impossible. Where?

FARMER: She's in our yard. I keep telling you the fence is down by McLaughlin's bush there and she strayed up to our yard with our cattle last night.

MARY kicks the pails & hits him off with either stick or spinning wheel or spindle.

MARY: Who the hell's side do you think you're on, Dan Quigley. Are you telling me I didn't hear her bawling over at Donley's?

anvil

MRS DONNELLY:
Closer and louder the sound of his hammer
Wheels take me
Hooves draw me
Gee Pilot! round the corner of Marksey's farm
Down this road grown over with grass

Mob humming the tune of the St Patrick song & just about to burst out from beneath bar crossing down to us & meet SCHOOLMASTER.

GIRL:
In the spinning I lie dreaming in I hear
A humming sound that fills me up with fear

MRS DONNELLY:
Look not this way, Jim Carroll, my enemy.
I leave you behind me

Circuit ends & she disappears.

MOB:
When blind worms crawling in the grass
Disgusted all the nation
He gave them a rise which opened their eyes
To a sense of their situation

SCHOOLMASTER: I was the schoolmaster at the Donnelly School. On the morning of September 3rd, 1879, I met 40 to 50 men at half past eight in the morning. They had clubs and bludgeons in their hands in the name of God, where are you all going to?

CHORUS: We are going away for a heifer that was lost.

SCHOOLMASTER: Did every one of you lose a heifer?

CHORUS: No, no.

SCHOOLMASTER: Then it's time to bid the devil good morning when you meet him.

CHORUS: Oh, we're a long time seeking him.

SCHOOLMASTER: Would you know the old lad when you meet him?

CHORUS: Would we know him, sure he's a cripple and lives near a forge. (anvil)

MRS DONNELLY:
Closer and louder the sound of his hammer
Wheels take me Hooves draw me
Haw Pilot! turn north on the Cedar Swamp Line!
What is the matter with that field of grain?

GIRL: In the humming I lie dreaming in I wake and hear

MRS RYAN: Mrs Donnelly, have mercy on my children, tell your sons to please let the thrashing machine come harvest our wheat and barley. We'll starve this year if it rots away.

MRS DONNELLY: (the anvil gets louder & louder) No! There's no time for the wife of Ned Ryan (and louder as she enters Whalen's Corners)
The first house, a shed, the second
A ditch, picket fence, gateway, a path, my
    journey is over
Will, Norah (she knocks) at my son's door.

But she has no sooner entered WILL's house than we hear the mob already at the blacksmith's; the anvil stops and there are sounds of hammers and forges being tossed down.

MOB: (offstage) We'll visit you at all hours of the night when you least expect it.

Now WILL, NORAH & MRS DONNELLY come out. WILL can use either a fiddle or a gun—both are hanging behind the bar that represents his house.

WILL: Mother, Norah—I'll ask them for their authority to search either my house or its premises. Did they show Father any warrant to search?

MRS DONNELLY: Nothing but their shadows

WILL: Well then, if they can't show me a warrant, I'll shoot the first man who comes in the gate.

MOB:
Nine hundred thousand reptiles blue
He charmed with sweet discourses,
And dined on them at Killaloe
In soups and second courses

The mob now slowly come towards the backs of the Donnellys. They are afraid. It's not the same as at the other house. WILL's hand reaches up for his fiddle, he turns, tunes & then plays "Boney over the Alps" laughing at them. Some of them get into the audience by mistake. We should feel ashamed of ourselves that we did not make a better showing against a lame man & two women.

MRS DONNELLY: Are you looking for your mother Dennis Trehy? That you left to starve in the workhouse at Ballysheenan though you're rich here in Canada?

WILL: My mother's taken the hunger off a great many of you days gone by when your parents sent you to our school with no lunch.

MRS DONNELLY: And I wonder at Martin O'Halloran being with such a gang as his father's the decentest man in Biddulph.

WILL: Give them another, they're in full flight down the road. (She turns sharply away.) James Carroll fell down and there's others tripping about the proud Napoleons they are. Mother, Norah, do you remember I told you how mother gave me this fiddle? (sings)

Then they sold me to the brewer
And he brewed me on the pan,
But when I got into the jug
I was the strongest man.*

And it's right what you told me then. If you're afraid you should be. If you're not you'll live. Today I thank you. One fiddle you gave me, a lame boy of twelve, has been worth forty men with rifles and clubs.

MRS DONNELLY: Yes, I've marked you with all my foolish words

WILL: Not foolish. You've been dreaming of a train. This fiddle stopped that train.

MRS DONNELLY: Yes. But only in the daylight. The night, Will and Norah, may have—the dark has shoulders they can stand upon. To reach our eyes and our minds at last. Hush!

---

* *Then they sold me to the brewer … I was the strongest man*—a verse from the Barley Corn Ballad which opens and closes *Sticks & Stones* and runs through the play as the Donnellys' theme.

They stand again with their backs to the vigilantes who enter with a sick CARROLL. It is as if MRS DONNELLY can hear them for she half turns. They stagger about as before. CARROLL is stretched on floor.

VOICE: What's the matter with him?

NED RYAN: They've made him ill. *(tends him with some restorative)*

VOICE: He's having a fit if you ask me and I don't want to have anything more to do with this. I'm leaving.

They are all sitting down on their haunches.

CARROLL: How's your old mother, Dennis, back in the workhouse at Ballysheenan?

NED RYAN: How'd she get there ahead of us so fast?

CARROLL: She's a witch, that's why. And she shall be burnt for a witch. *(relapses)*

VOICE: Ned Ryan, I think he wants something. Bend over him and—

NED RYAN: *(pause)* He wants you to bring him the Holy Bible out of the school cupboard.

It is brought & CARROLL uses it for a pillow.

CARROLL: Yes, Dennis, I ran like the rest of you. Now that's better. I ran like the rest of you—but there wasn't one of you behind me and there wasn't one of you I could keep up to—tell me, how many of yous are willing to draw lots *(They all shy away.)* to see who will sue Jack Donnelly for perjuring himself when he says that we trespassed on his father's farm today. Because, you'll note the old man did tell us "if you think the cow is here, Jim Carroll, don't leave one straw on top of another."

They raise hands & come closer.

Well, who wouldn't dare to do that, but here's one more thing, and we'll just see who's man enough to raise their hands to this proposition. In this Bible someone has placed eight slips of paper each with the name of a Donnelly written thereon. Who is brave enough to come up and draw one of those slips of paper out?

VOICE: Jim, what does it mean if we do draw the piece of paper out?

CARROLL: It means that that Donnelly will be executed before the year is out. If it can be shown that one can be killed and the executioner get away with it how many of you are then willing to go on with me at your head against the rest of the family and I promise you there will be no risk involved.

VOICE: Sure if this one is killed and no one is punished, sure.

CARROLL: Let's take a vote then. Ned, take the vote will you?

NED: Yeas? *(hands are raised)* Nays? *(some hands go up)* Forty-one to seven, Jim.

CARROLL: The seven nays are to leave this room forever, and I dare them to speak. When the execution takes place remember—you must help or join the Blackfeets. Come up and swear.

VOICE: But, Jim, nobody's drawn the lot yet and I'm not.

NED: I'll draw it. She took away my son, I'll take back one of hers.

CARROLL: Remember what you're about to promise because yes a brave man has been found, not afraid of them, and he'll show us the way, the way I could not show you this shameful morning.

VOICE: Who's he going to kill then?

NED RYAN: Michael Donnelly.

MRS DONNELLY says the name too, screams "My son," train whistle, the train proceeds to the

CHORUS: Fourth crossing!

The BARTENDER at Slaght's Hotel slides a glass down the bar as MIKE & MORRISON, his mate, enter. "WILLIAM LEWIS" is waiting, an old man named GREENWOOD is standing at the bar, sometimes bending down to spin a top.

BARTENDER: Mike, Jim. You're off early tonight. Still raining outside?

MIKE: We both ordered hot whiskeys because we were cold & wet still. I could feel the heat of the drink coming through the glass into the flesh of my hand. There's that old fellow always in here spinning his top and going to make the same joke he always does about fighting dogs. My top against your top, Greenwood. You've been waiting for this all day, haven't you?

They both spin tops which fight each other.

GREENWOOD: How's your big bulldog you got, Mike Donnelly.

MIKE: Back home in St Thomas I've got a bull-dog that can lick anything its weight in Ontario

GREENWOOD: I ain't got no dog, just this top, but I can whip any dog myself, I'll strip off my clothes and commence anytime.

MIKE: Ah, you couldn't beat my bulldog, you can't even beat my top with your old top it's got more than a few holes gnawed out of it, where do you keep it, old fellow, there's been rats biting away at this one.

GREENWOOD: Here, don't you insult my top. Those holes are for balance.

LEWIS: You don't want to hop on that man, Donnelly.

MIKE: No one is touching him, and it's none of your business if there was.

LEWIS: You are always shooting off your mouth, aren't you Donnelly. *(taking off his coat)*

MIKE: Do you want anything of me.

MORRISON: Now look, you two, quit it. All he said, Bill Lewis, was that his top had holes in it. Turn around away from each other. Greenwood if that's your name, see if Mike'll do you a favour and have a return match with his top meanwhile where's the washroom around here?

A clock strikes six.

MIKE: You do want something from me.

"LEWIS" strikes DONNELLY from behind; as MIKE tries to pin him he leads him back behind the bar with the knife open & ready. Just as MORRISON returns from the washroom, MIKE is stabbed below the belt. LEWIS glides away; MORRISON catches MIKE just as he falls. Train whistle.

MIKE: My God, Neighbour, I'm gone stabbed. Jim, that's our train!

The CHORUS comes—at the wake for MICHAEL at the Donnelly farm—with four poles which represent the fourposter bed he was laid on.

Candles. People kneel by the bier, then retire to the sides of the room.

MRS DONNELLY: Yes, his bed is ready. Bring Michael in here boys. Bridget, bring me the clean shirt I've got ready for him.

She takes off his old shirt, washes him & puts on a white shirt.

MORRISON: We carried Mike to the washroom. I held his head for a while and saw him die.

CHORUS: He was under bonds to keep the peace, and he was considered a desperate character.

MORRISON: We were brakemen on that train together. I think he would fight if he was set upon, but as a bully I never saw him have a row.

CHORUS: The first named testified that the deceased was a quarrelsome bully and started the row, but the others testified that he was not a disorderly character—

MORRISON: I caught hold of Donnelly for the purpose of assisting him. I never heard anybody say anything against Donnelly, and I never saw him engaged in a row.

MRS DONNELLY: I then read in the newspaper that the respective lawyers and the judge then addressed the jury, after which they retired and returned in a short time with a verdict of manslaughter. Since there was no defence offered at all, one supposes that if the lawyer for this William Lewis had offered a defence why my son's murderer might have got off completely scot free, but as it was the judge sentenced this man whom Michael had never even met before that night, whom none of us knows—two years in prison. In this forest there is now a proclamation that the hunting season on my sons is open now. There are only five of them left, the breed is rare, but do not let that limit your greed for their hearts' blood.

Michael. I wish that as I spoke with your oldest brother as he lay dying last summer I could have been there with you this winter. I told him what I tell you now—to look straight ahead past this stupid life and death they've fastened on you— just as long ago your father and me and our first-born walked up over the last hill in Ireland and saw, what you will see now—for the first time in our lives we saw freedom, we saw the sea.

MR DONNELLY: Mrs Donnelly, the sleighs have come to take our son to the church.

Candles, fourposter, all sweep out of the room. We are in a barroom again. Slaght's years after; two CHAMBERMAIDS have just been assigned to clean out the barroom; outside the sun is just getting up. The old tramp is whistling "Buffalo Gals" as he walks up the empty Main Street of Waterford; train whistle. The one MAID throws the pail of water over the floor and starts scrubbing. A clock strikes twelve. The ghost of MIKE DONNELLY stands behind the bar.

MAID ONE: Ugh, clean the hotel from top to bottom would you. We won't be done in here till midnight, the old muck from their feet and mouths. What're you looking so pale for, it's only an old barroom, been closed up for thirty years till this fool thinks he can run it for a profit again.

MAID TWO: I thought I saw someone standing by the end of the bar over there.

MAID ONE: There's no one there I can see, Mary.

MAID TWO: You don't know Waterford, this place, too well do you.

MAID ONE: What's there to know? There's that old man sloping off into the dawn, I wish I were free to walk the roads, not tied down like this to a scrubbing brush.

MAID TWO: I wish you wouldn't pick that place by the bar to scrub so, Sarah.

MAID ONE: There you go with your ghosts again. I don't believe them.

MAID TWO: Would you please stop your damn scrubbing at the same spot, Sarah.

MAID ONE: Are you against clean floors or something? There's something on the floor here that won't come out.

MAID TWO: He's looking right down at you

MAID ONE: I'll wet his feet for him then. Give me that soap, I'll …

MAID TWO: Don't you know there was a murder in this barroom about thirty years ago, one of the brakemen on the Canada Southern, was stabbed right there where you're scrubbing. That's the blood from his wound you're trying to wash out and my mother says …

MAID ONE: Mary, go up and start the sitting room if this is too … what did your mother say?

MAID TWO: That's the blood of Michael Donnelly on the floor there. No matter how hard you try it never comes out.

A top spins across the floor. Scrubbing of the remaining woman; Ghost still there. Whistling dies away. "Buffalo Gals."

CHORUS:
The St Nicholas Hotel
    William Donnelly Proprietor
        The Donnellys, Part Two

END

THREE SONGS USED IN THE PLAY

ST PATRICK
(to the tune of *Pop Goes the Weasel*)

Oh! St Patrick was a gentleman,
  Who came of decent people;
He built a church in Dublin town,
  And on it put a steeple.
His father was a Gallagher;
  His mother was a Brady;
His aunt was an O'Shaughnessy,
  His uncle an O'Grady.

(Chorus)
So, success attend St Patrick's fist,
  For he's a saint so clever;
Oh! he gave the snakes and toads a twist,
  And bothered them forever.

The Wicklow hills are very high
  And so's the Hill of Howth, sir;
But there's a hill much bigger still,
  Much higher nor them both, sir.
'Twas on the top of this high hill
  St Patrick preached his sarmint
That drove the frogs into the bogs,
  And banished all the varmint.

So, success attend St Patrick's fist, &c.

There's not a mile in Ireland's isle
  Where dirty varmin musters
But there he put his dear fore-foot,
  And murdered them in clusters.
The toads went pop, the frogs went hop,
  Slap-dash into the water;
And the snakes committed suicide
  To save themselves from slaughter.

So, success attend St Patrick's fist, &c.

Nine hundred thousand reptiles blue
  He charmed with sweet discourses,
And dined on them at Killaloe
  In soups and second courses.
When blind worms crawling in the grass
  Disgusted all the nation,
He gave them a rise which opened their eyes
  To a sense of their situation.

So, success attend St Patrick's fist, &c.

No wonder that those Irish lads
  Should be so gay and frisky,
For sure St Pat he taught them that,
  As well as making whiskey;
No wonder that the saint himself
  Should understand distilling,
Since his mother kept a shebeen shop
  In the town of Enniskillen.

So, success attend St Patrick's fist, &c.

Oh! was I but so fortunate
  As to be back in Munster,
'Tis I'd be bound that from the ground
  I never more would once stir.
For there St Patrick planted turf,
  And plenty of the praties,
With pigs galore, ma gramma's store,
  And cabbages … and ladies!

Then my blessings on St Patrick's fist,
  For he's a darling saint, oh!
Oh! he gave the snakes and toads a twist;
  He's a beauty without paint, oh!

HECTOR O'HARA'S JUBILEE SONG
(to the tune of *Perhaps She's on the Railway*)

Hark! the trumpets sounding
Proclaim this is the day,
With hearts so bright and bounding,
Thousands haste away;
To have a look on Salter's Grove,
The lads and lasses true
All thro' the day will shout hurrah,
For the Dominion's bonny blue.

(Chorus)
Perhaps you've come to London
Upon this glorious day,
To Salter's Grove to have a lark,
You're sure to take your way.
The blues so true will stick to you,
So boldly they will stand,
The Grittish crew will never do,
No longer in the land.

The lads and lasses in their best,
Will ramble thro' the grounds—
The bands will play throughout the day,
In music's sweetest sounds;
The pleasant strains goes thro' the brains
Of each unhappy Grit,
It gives them all the belly ache,
And sends them home to—

From here and there and everywhere,
The folks have come today,
Darby and Joan have come from home
To see the grand display.
From east and west from north and south
There's people without end,
With frills and bows and furbelows,
They'll do the Grecian Bend.

Elgin girls and Biddulph swells,
Each other try to please,
By doing the lardy dardy dum,
All among the trees,
From Westminster the pretty girls
Are rolling in the hay.
Their mothers say they mustn't,
But their fathers say they may.

There's little Popsy Wopsy here,
From Ingersoll she has come—
She's doing the double shuffle
With the chap that beats the drum;
There's Bob and Jack, Sal and Pat
And Polly coming on,
Upon her head she carries a bed
And calls it her chignon.

Strathroy girls are here today,
So nicely dress'd in blue—
With chaps that come from Exeter,
The grand they mean to do.
Polly Strong, couldn't come on
For a nasty old tom cat,
Has got a lot of kittens in
Her Dolly Varden bat.

Then shout John A. forever boys,
That is the heading cry;
Every election we will win,
The time is drawing nigh,
The scheming Grits may bag their heads
That is if they've a mind,
Or go and dig up taters
With their shirts hung out behind.

BUFFALO GALS

(Chorus)
Buffalo gals won't you come out tonight
Come out tonight, come out tonight
Buffalo gals won't you come out tonight
And dance by the light of the moon.

1.
As I was tramping down the street
Down the street, down the street
I chanced a pretty girl to meet
Oh, she was fair to view

2.
I asked her if she'd have some talk
Have some talk, have some talk
Her feet covered the whole sidewalk
As she stood close to me

3.
I asked her if she'd be my wife
Be my wife, be my wife
She'd make me happy all my life
If she stood by my side.

GEORGE F. WALKER   (b. 1947)

In the 1970s when so many playwrights were busy examining the Canadian character and family, regional and national history, the experiences and meanings of being Canadian, George F. Walker's gaze was elsewhere. Avoiding the subjects and styles that came to characterize the Canadian theatrical mainstream, Walker staked out his own distinctive territory somewhere between satire and parody. He drew from the generic fringes of popular culture both present (cartoons, *film noir*) and past (revenge tragedy, gothic melodrama). Even as his plays have grown steadily more naturalistic and domestic from the mid-1980s on, they remain peopled with obsessive characters living in extremity and given to philosophical musings about such things as the need to wrench order out of chaos. His work exists, Walker has said, along "that fine line between the serious and the comic." No play of his occupies that black comic territory with greater stylishness or command than *Zastrozzi*.

Walker's personal turf was east end, working-class Toronto. He was driving taxi in 1970 when he read a flyer on a lamppost soliciting scripts for Ken Gass' new Factory Theatre Lab. The play he submitted, *Prince of Naples*, was not only his first attempt at writing drama, but when he attended its opening in 1971 it was only the second play he had ever seen. Despite Walker's inexperience, Gass made him resident playwright from 1971–76, an invaluable apprenticeship and the start of an enduring association that has seen the majority of Walker's plays premiere at the Factory.

Prince of Naples and *Ambush at Tether's End* (1971) were basically absurdist exercises, more derivative of Ionesco and Beckett than original. With *Sacktown Rag* (1972) and *Bagdad Saloon* (1973) Walker began to find his own voice, planting increasingly exotic landscapes of the mind with pop icons like Gary Cooper and Gertrude Stein. This phase of his work climaxed with *Beyond Mozambique* (1974) and *Ramona and the White Slaves* (1976). The former features a B-movie jungle locale populated by a drug-addicted, pederastic priest, a disgraced Mountie, a porn-film starlet and a demonic ex-Nazi doctor whose wife thinks she is Olga in Chekhov's *Three Sisters*. *Ramona*, a murder-mystery-cum-opium-dream that marked Walker's directing debut, takes place in a Hong Kong brothel in 1919, opening with the heroine's rape by a poisonous lizard.

Walker took his next three plays to Toronto Free Theatre. *Gossip* (1977), *Zastrozzi* (1977), and *Filthy Rich* (1979) were all less obscure, more accessible and consequently more popular than his previous work. *Gossip* and *Filthy Rich*, heavily indebted to Humphrey Bogart and Raymond Chandler, were the first of his plays in *film noir* style. Along with *The Art of War* (1983) they comprise a trilogy, published under the title *The Power Plays* (1986). All feature a character named Tyrone Power as either investigative reporter or private eye, equally cynical and shabby in both incarnations, reluctantly involved in sorting out political intrigue and murder. Related in theme and mood is the Chalmers Award-winning *Theatre of the Film Noir* (1981), a bizarre murder mystery set in wartime Paris.

Exotic locales still feature prominently in *Rumours of Our Death* (1980), an anti-war parable directed by Walker as a rock musical, and *Science and Madness* (1982), a turn-of-the-century gothic melodrama. But the modern city explored by Walker in the first two Power plays became increasingly the focus of his attention. *Criminals in Love* (1984), winner of the Governor General's Award, *Better Living* (1986), a Chalmers Award winner, and *Beautiful City* (1987) were published as *The East End Plays* (1988), this time transparently the east end of Toronto itself. The nihilism of Walker's earlier work gives way in these political comedies to tenuous hope for a life of simple happiness in a city salvaged from the powerful and greedy.

Love and Anger (1989) and *Escape from Happiness* (1991), a sequel to *Better Living*, continue Walker's championing of women, the oppressed and the marginal against the patriarchal centre. These two comedies, both Chalmers Award winners, have had critical and popular success across the United States as well as Canada. But the play that really made Walker's reputation outside Canada was *Nothing Sacred* (1988), his adaptation of Turgenev's novel *Fathers and Sons*, set in pre-revolutionary Russia. Winner of the Governor General's, Chalmers, and a variety of other Canadian awards, it became so popular among American regional theatres that the *Los Angeles Times* called it "the play of the year." In 1993 Walker wrote *Tough!* for Vancouver's Green Thumb Theatre, a comedy about sex and gender relations among three young people.[1]

After taking some time off from the theatre, writing for television and moving to Vancouver, Walker returned in triumph to his first theatrical home. Toronto's Factory Theatre had suffered through difficult times and nearly folded but was now once more under the direction of Ken Gass who premiered the six new one-act plays Walker had written, all set in the same shabby motel room. Running the gamut from bitter drama to wacky comedy, *Suburban Motel* (1997–98) was presented in repertory format, two plays a night. It was a huge success, winning multiple Chalmers and Dora awards and acclaimed for subsequent productions in Montreal, Vancouver and elsewhere. Walker rang in the millennium with another hit, *Heaven* (2000), an ethical revenge comedy whose characters come back from the dead, premiered by Toronto's Canadian Stage.

Zastrozzi has been produced across the United States and Canada, in London, Australia and New Zealand, as well as in French translation in Montreal and it remains one of Walker's most popular plays. Walker himself directed a highly acclaimed revival in Toronto in 1987. It was also seen under the auspices of Joseph Papp at the New York Shakespeare Festival's Public Theater in 1982 at the end of Walker's year as playwright-in-residence there. In 1991 he became the first resident playwright at the National Theatre School of Canada.

Zastrozzi epitomizes the kind of play Walker wrote for the first decade of his career. Typically trying to assert order or impose meaning in the face of chaos, his early protagonists come in three basic kinds. First is the artist who dreams up his own reality, but without much success, as in the "cartoon" plays *Sacktown Rag* and *Bagdad Saloon*. Verezzi is Walker's portrait of the artist as narcissist, a genuinely silly man who believes he is the messenger of God. Second there is the justicer: the detective-heroes of *Ramona* and the *film noir* plays who specialize in making things clear and putting them right. Victor, like them, is "an ordinary man" obsessed with symmetry and balance and committed to justice, playing superego to Verezzi's ego. (In Walker's later plays "ordinary" men and women will increasingly occupy centre stage.) But in *Zastrozzi* he is merely a foil for the much more potent forces of darkness embodied in the third of Walker's protagonists, the arch-criminal atheist. Assuming a metaphysical void in which, according to Zastrozzi, "life is a series of totally arbitrary and often meaningless events," he fills it with the unfettered self ("I am the absence of God," proclaims Rocco in *Beyond Mozambique*). Unlike the reformist protagonists of the later plays, Zastrozzi does not try to oppose the fundamental disorder he sees at the heart of things. Rather, he makes himself its agent. For in a world defined by what Zastrozzi calls "negative spirituality," chaos is the natural condition, evil the most powerful motive force and crime the only meaningful action. As Rocco says, "there's something about committing crimes against humanity that puts you in touch with the purpose of the universe."

Zastrozzi is unique among Walker's protagonists in that he is not only the master criminal but also the justicer himself. Utilizing all the baroque conventions of Jacobean tragedy, Walker makes him the revenger, a man in obsessive pursuit of Verrezzi for the murder of his mother. But revenge turns out to be only a secondary matter. Zastrozzi's real vocation is "making everyone answerable" to his own dark truth. As the self-appointed "Master of Discipline" he is both judge and executioner. Verezzi is singled out for special attention because of his facile religious optimism, his artistic impressionism, his smile—the incarnation of everything "pleasantly vague" that Zastrozzi abhors about the modern age relentlessly dawning in 1893.

Though Zastrozzi is a monster, the play asks that we feel sympathy for this diabolical Don Quixote who suffers the fate of all anachronisms caught in a time of transition and unwilling to adapt. A giant among pygmies, he is also a dying breed without a successor. Just compare his "student" Bernardo—a mere thug without artistry or imagination. Weary, preoccupied and dogged by nightmares in which he is overwhelmed by goodness and weakness, Zastrozzi begins to show more and more cracks in his façade of invincibility, losing interest in his satanic soul-mate Matilda and falling in love with the purity and innocence of Julia. At the end, surveying his victories, he knows that he is only marking time. He has won another battle but will surely lose the war.

All this may sound solemn, but it isn't. Like all good comedy *Zastrozzi* is at heart a serious play, but at the same time its inflated Grand Guignol style lovingly sends up a broad array of literary and theatrical sources: Shelley's overheated gothic romance; Nietzsche's philosophy; the stark dichotomies of melodrama; Artaud's theatre of cruelty. What these have in common is a dramatic excessiveness that tends toward self-parody. *Zastrozzi* celebrates their excesses—and its own—with elegant deadpan humour and a self-conscious inversion of values that rings of Oscar Wilde and Joe Orton, but ultimately can only be called Walkeresque.

NOTES

1. In the late 1990s after Coach House Press went bankrupt, nearly all of Walker's plays were repackaged by his new publisher, Talonbooks. Walker took the opportunity to revise many of them, and to redefine and rearrange his East End Plays in two volumes. *The East End Plays, Part 1* comprises *Criminals in Love, Better Living* and *Escape from Happiness*. Included in *Part 2* are *Beautiful City, Love and Anger* and *Tough!*.

Zastrozzi opened on November 2, 1977, at Toronto Free Theatre with the following cast:

ZASTROZZI	Stephen Markle
BERNARDO	George Buza
VEREZZI	Geoffrey Bowes
VICTOR	David Bolt
MATILDA	Diane D'Aquila
JULIA	Valerie Warburton

Directed by William Lane
Designed by Doug Robinson
Lighting by Gerry Brown
Sound by Wes Wraggett
Fights arranged by Patrick Crean

ZASTROZZI:
THE MASTER OF DISCIPLINE
A MELODRAMA

AUTHOR'S NOTE

This play is not an adaptation of Shelley's *Zastrozzi*. The playwright read a brief description of this novella in a biography of Shelley and that provided the inspiration for *Zastrozzi: The Master of Discipline*, something quite different from Shelley's work.

CHARACTERS

ZASTROZZI, *a master criminal, German*
BERNARDO, *his friend*
VEREZZI, *an Italian, an artist, a dreamer*
VICTOR, *his tutor*
MATILDA, *a gypsy, a raven-haired beauty*
JULIA, *an aristocrat, a fair-haired beauty*

SCENE

Europe. Probably Italy. The 1890s.

SET

It should combine a simplified version of a Piranesi prison drawing with the ruins of an ancient city. There are interesting and varied chambers within and the walls are crumbling. The tops of several trees are visible and weeds are growing out of the stones.

PROLOGUE

Just before the storm. BERNARDO is looking up at the sky.

BERNARDO: It is not a passion. Passion will eventually reward the soul. It is not an obsession. Obsession will sustain you for a lifetime. It is not an idea. An idea is the product of an ordinary mind. It is not an emotion. It cannot be purged. It is not greed or lust or hate or fear. It is none of those things. It is worse. The sky is swelling. And all those with timid natures had better go hide. It will conspire with the sky, and the air will explode, and the world will break apart and get thrown around like dust. But it is not the end of the world. It is easily worse. It is revenge.

Blackout followed by a loud sustained volley of thunder. Deadly calm. ZASTROZZI lights an oil lamp and stands rigidly. His face is twisted with hatred.

ZASTROZZI: You are looking at Zastrozzi. But that means very little. What means much more is that Zastrozzi is looking at you. Don't make a sound. Breathe quietly. He is easily annoyed. And when he is annoyed he strikes. Look at his right arm. *(holding it up)* It wields the sword that has killed two hundred men. Watch the right arm constantly. Be very careful not to let it catch you unprepared. But while watching the right arm *(suddenly producing a dagger with his left hand)* do not forget the left arm. Because this man Zastrozzi has no weaknesses. No weakness at all. Remember that. Or he will have you. He will have you any way he wants you.

Lightning. A long pause. ZASTROZZI's face and body relax. He looks around almost peacefully. He smiles.

I am Zastrozzi. The master criminal of all Europe. This is not a boast. It is information. I am to be feared for countless reasons. The obvious ones of strength and skill with any weapon. The less obvious ones because of the quality of my mind. It is superb. It works in unique ways. And it is always working because I do not sleep. I do not sleep because if I do I have nightmares and when you have a mind like mine you have nightmares that could petrify the devil. Sometimes because my mind is so powerful I even have nightmares when I am awake and because my mind is so powerful I am able to split my consciousness in two and observe myself having my nightmare. This is not a trick. It is a phenomenon. I am having one now. I have this one often. In it, I am what I am. The force of darkness. The clear, sane voice of negative spirituality. Making everyone answerable to the only constant truth I understand. Mankind is weak. The world is ugly. The only way to save them from each other is to destroy them both. In this nightmare I am accomplishing this with great efficiency. I am destroying cities. I am destroying countries. I am disturbing social patterns and upsetting established cultures. I am causing people such unspeakable misery that many of them are actually saving me the trouble by doing away with themselves. And, even better, I am actually making them understand that this is, in fact, the way things should proceed. I am at the height of my power. I am lucid, calm, organized and energetic. Then it happens. A group of people come out of the darkness with sickly smiles on their faces. They walk up to me and tell me they have discovered my weakness, a flaw in my power, and that I am finished as a force to be reckoned with. Then one of them reaches out and tickles me affectionately under my chin. I am furious. I pick him up and crack his spine on my knee then throw him to the ground. He dies immediately. And after he dies he turns his head to me and says, "Misery loves chaos. And chaos loves company." I look at him and even though I know that the dead cannot speak, let alone make sense, I feel my brain turn to burning ashes and all my control run out of my body like mud and I scream at him like a maniac, *(whispering)* "What does that mean."

Blackout.

Scene One

A vicious series of lightning bolts flash, illuminating the entire stage. A bed chamber. ZASTROZZI is reeling about violently.

ZASTROZZI: Where is the Italian Verezzi. Tell him I have come to send him to hell. Tell him that Zastrozzi is here. Tell him I am waiting. He can hide no more. He can run no farther. I am here. And I am staying. *(grabbing a flask of wine and drinking)* Ah, Jesus, this wine tastes like it was made by amateurs. I hate amateurs. Death to all of them. Remember that.

BERNARDO bursts into the chamber. ZASTROZZI throws a sabre at him like a spear. BERNARDO ducks. The two men look at each other.

BERNARDO: It's Bernardo.

ZASTROZZI: Step closer. The light is tricky.

BERNARDO: It *is* Bernardo, sir.

ZASTROZZI: Ah, Jesus! *(turning and violently ripping all the coverings from the bed)* I thought I saw an Italian to be killed.

BERNARDO: Not this one I hope. Please be more careful.

ZASTROZZI: Don't worry, Bernardo. Of all the Italians worthy of killing I am interested in only one. *(sitting on the bed)* But my mind is becoming clearer by the minute and unless I get some satisfaction I may come to the inevitable conclusion that all Italians are worthy of killing for one reason or another.

BERNARDO: Yes, I like your threats. They keep me alert.

ZASTROZZI: Learn to smile when you are being ironic. It might save your life some day.

BERNARDO: *(smiling)* The best advice is that of the best advised.

ZASTROZZI: Remind me to order you to say that again when I'm not preoccupied.

BERNARDO: It doesn't—

ZASTROZZI: Have you found him.

BERNARDO: He is here.

ZASTROZZI: Where.

BERNARDO: At least he was here. He has gone off into the countryside. But he is expected back.

ZASTROZZI: How soon.

BERNARDO: Eventually.

ZASTROZZI advances on BERNARDO.

BERNARDO: That is what I was told. And that is what I am reporting.

ZASTROZZI: Told by whom.

BERNARDO: The innkeeper where he stays.

ZASTROZZI: Then you were at his rooms?

BERNARDO: Yes.

ZASTROZZI: How do they smell. What do they look like. Describe them to me. No, wait, first, are you sure it is the same man. Verezzi the poet.

BERNARDO: Now Verezzi the painter.

ZASTROZZI: Yes, yes. And before that Verezzi the dramatist. And before that Verezzi the dancer. His vocation makes no difference. Always changing. Always pleasantly artistic. But the man himself, Bernardo. A description.

BERNARDO: The innkeeper described the same man.

ZASTROZZI: Even so. Possibly a coincidence. But the important things.

BERNARDO: Those as well.

ZASTROZZI: A religious man?

BERNARDO: Very.

ZASTROZZI: Always praying?

BERNARDO: Before and after every meal. Often during the meal. Occasionally throughout the meal.

ZASTROZZI: And the ladies. Does he have a way with them.

BERNARDO: Many ladies have visited him in his room. Most come back again.

ZASTROZZI: What about the smile. The smile that I see clearly in my head even though I have never met the man who wears it. That smile is an unnatural thing, Bernardo. Empty.

BERNARDO: "He smiles an annoying much of the time." I quote the innkeeper directly.

ZASTROZZI: Then it is him. It is Verezzi the artiste. The Christian. The great lover. The optimist. I will have him soon. Are you happy for me, my friend.

BERNARDO: I have watched you wanting him for a long time. I have grown fond of the force behind the search for revenge. I think I'll miss it.

ZASTROZZI: At first I wanted him just for myself. For what he did to my mother. But what I have learned of this man, Verezzi, makes me want him for another reason. That smile, Bernardo, I will remove it from the earth. It is a dangerous thing. It raises a bigger issue than revenge. (repeating this last sentence in German)

BERNARDO: Is this a new development.

ZASTROZZI: Actually, it is still revenge. But in a larger sense. In fact it is revenge in its true and original meaning. And, therefore, some other

word is probably necessary. It is 1893 and language, like everything else, has become pleasantly vague.

BERNARDO: I'm not sure I understand.

ZASTROZZI: Naturally. Because if you did then there would be two of us and there is only need for one. No. Call it revenge, Bernardo. Tell everyone else to call it revenge. If it will make you happy I'll even call it revenge.

Blackout.

Scene Two

The countryside, a light rain is falling. VEREZZI is sitting behind an easel, paintbrush in hand. VICTOR holds an umbrella over VEREZZI's head and examines the painting in silence for a while.

VICTOR: Always tell the truth. Except when under pressure.

VEREZZI: What does that mean.

VICTOR: How can you paint a German landscape when you have never been to Germany.

VEREZZI: My father was in Germany. He told me all about it.

VICTOR: That's silly. You present a false image.

VEREZZI: Perhaps. But my heart is in the right place.

VICTOR: Unsuspecting people will look at your art and think they see the truth.

VEREZZI: Perhaps my Germany is the real Germany. And if not, then perhaps it is what the real Germany should be.

VICTOR: What is that supposed to mean.

VEREZZI: I'm not quite sure. Yes, I am. Perhaps Germany is ugly. Or perhaps Germany is bland. What is the point of creating bland or ugly art.

VICTOR: To illustrate the truth.

VEREZZI: Art has nothing to do with truth.

VICTOR: Then what is its purpose.

VEREZZI: To enlighten.

VICTOR: How can you enlighten if you don't serve the truth.

VEREZZI: You enlighten by serving God.

VICTOR: Then God is not serving the truth.

VEREZZI: Is that a question or a statement.

VICTOR: Both.

VEREZZI: Then you are a heretic.

VICTOR: And you are a liar.

VEREZZI: A dreamer, Victor. A dreamer.

VICTOR: The same thing.

VEREZZI: Enough. I don't even remember asking your opinion.

VICTOR: If I waited to be asked you would never receive my criticism and, therefore, no education.

VEREZZI: You weren't hired as a tutor. You were hired as a servant.

VICTOR: That was before either of us realized how monumentally ignorant you are.

VEREZZI: Enough. What colours do you mix to make ochre.

VICTOR: Ochre is unnecessary.

VEREZZI: That hill should be shaded with ochre.

VICTOR: On some other planet perhaps. On earth it's green.

VEREZZI: Earth is boring.

VICTOR: Why don't you ask God to move you.

VEREZZI: Don't make fun of God.

VICTOR: I was making fun of Verezzi.

VEREZZI: The two are interchangeable.

VICTOR: That sounds slightly narcissistic to me.

VEREZZI: I am His messenger on earth.

VICTOR: What.

VEREZZI: *(a revelation)* I *am* His messenger on earth.

VICTOR: This is a new development. Until recently you were His servant.

VEREZZI: Through devotion and regular prayer, I have attained a new position.

VICTOR: Then God encourages linear growth.

VEREZZI: I beg your pardon.

VICTOR: When will you be made Messiah.

VEREZZI: Atheist. How do you sleep without fear.

VICTOR: A secret. Besides, I am not an atheist. I just have a more pragmatic relationship with God than you do.

VEREZZI: What is it.

VICTOR: It is based on reality, Verezzi. You wouldn't comprehend it.

VEREZZI: I should dismiss you. I think you mean to corrupt me.

VICTOR: Can I ask you a question.

VEREZZI: No.

VICTOR: Not even a sincere one?

VEREZZI: In all the time I've known you, you've never once been sincere on the subject of my religious experiences.

VICTOR: Be patient. At least I don't laugh in your face anymore.

VEREZZI: Ask your question.

VICTOR: How do you reconcile being God's messenger on earth with the fact that you find earth boring.

VEREZZI: That is my cross. I bear it.

VICTOR: *(sadly)* Yes. Of course you do. You probably do.

VEREZZI: Besides, I am an artist. Even if I was not a religious artist I would be dissatisfied. That is the nature of an artist.

VICTOR: That is the opinion of a very silly man.

VEREZZI: Enough. I have to finish.

VICTOR: When are we going back to the village.

VEREZZI: When I have completed my painting.

VICTOR: And what will you do with the painting.

VEREZZI: It contains His message. I'll give it to someone.

VICTOR: Not sell it?

VEREZZI: His message should not be sold. It's a gift. Besides I have no need of money.

VICTOR: That's because your father was very rich.

VEREZZI: Yes. So what.

VICTOR: I was just wondering how a messenger of God would get by if he weren't independently wealthy.

VEREZZI: You are a subversive.

VICTOR: And you are a saint.

VEREZZI: Oh. Thank you.

VICTOR: No. It wasn't a compliment.

Blackout.

Scene Three

A dining chamber. Occasional thunder, lightning, and rain outside. MATILDA and ZASTROZZI are some distance apart preparing to fight. They cut the air with their sabres. On the table are the remnants of a meal. BERNARDO sits in a chair, munching a chicken leg, his legs on the table. He describes VEREZZI's room.

BERNARDO: The room smelled of lilacs, incense and mint tea. This Verezzi is an orderly fellow for sure. Nothing about the room was haphazard. Everything was neat and clean. In fact, the place appeared to have been arranged by a geometrist, for all objects were placed at perfectly right angles to each other. And between the two halves of the room—one used for work and the other for play—there was a perfect symmetry.

ZASTROZZI: Then he has someone with him. A man like Verezzi is not capable of symmetry. *(pause)* Balance. A dangerous opponent in regulated combat. But get him in an alley or a dark street and you have him disoriented. Nevertheless, out of respect for his inclination, I'll cut him up into thirty-two pieces of equal size. Are you ready, Matilda.

MATILDA: First I want to make one thing clear. I do not suffer from rapier envy. I just like to fight.

MATILDA and ZASTROZZI cross swords and begin to fight. As they progress it becomes clear that MATILDA is very good even though ZASTROZZI is not trying very hard.

BERNARDO: There were several of his paintings in the room. For the most part he is a mediocre artist but occasionally he exhibits a certain flair. It's naive but it's there. One painting in particular caught my eye. An informal unrecognizable series of swirls and circles in white, off-white and beige. He seems very fond of it himself. He has given it a title.

ZASTROZZI: What does he call it then.

BERNARDO: *God's Stomach.*

MATILDA: The man is a fool.

BERNARDO: I would tend to agree.

ZASTROZZI: Then how has he evaded us for three years.

BERNARDO: I've been thinking about that.

ZASTROZZI: Thinking?

BERNARDO: Perhaps he doesn't know we've been chasing him.

ZASTROZZI: Nonsense. He's a clever man.

BERNARDO: But surely there are none more clever than the guileless.

ZASTROZZI: Stop thinking, Bernardo. It causes you to have absurd poetic fantasies. I am clever. I am the most accomplished criminal in Europe. Matilda is clever. She is the most accomplished seductress in Europe. Do either of us seem guileless to you.

BERNARDO: No. But you, sir, are motivated by a strange and powerful external force and Matilda has certain physical assets which allow her activities a certain ease.

MATILDA: I also have a first-class mind, Bernardo, and it gives me self-confidence. But if I didn't and I heard that patronizing comment about my body I would take off your head.

BERNARDO: If I ever have my head taken off I hope you'll be the one who does it. But not with your sword. I would like you to use your teeth.

MATILDA: Are comments like that what you use to show sexual interest in someone.

BERNARDO: Excuse me. *(standing and starting off)*

MATILDA: Don't be shy, Bernardo. Are you being shy, Bernardo.

BERNARDO: If you wish.

MATILDA: Actually all I wish is that men in general could perform with the same intensity that they lust with.

BERNARDO: I might surprise you.

MATILDA: You might. But I think we both doubt that.

BERNARDO: Excuse me. I think I'll go visit the inn again. *(starting off again)* Oh, I forgot. Here is one of his drawings. I took it from his room.

ZASTROZZI: You stole it.

BERNARDO: Yes.

ZASTROZZI: Why.

BERNARDO: Zastrozzi asks why someone steals something. Zastrozzi, who has stolen more than any man alive.

ZASTROZZI: Put it back.

BERNARDO: Why.

ZASTROZZI: We are not thieves anymore.

BERNARDO: Then what are we.

ZASTROZZI: We are not thieves.

BERNARDO leaves.

MATILDA: I don't want to do this anymore. *(throwing down her sabre)* Let's make love.

ZASTROZZI: I'm preoccupied.

MATILDA: With what.

ZASTROZZI: The image of Verezzi's painting.

MATILDA: You didn't even look at it.

ZASTROZZI: I saw it in my head. It is a colourful pastoral. An impression of a landscape. Impressionism. Distortion.

MATILDA: Very interesting. Great material for preoccupation, I'm sure. But you were pre-occupied the last time I came to you. And the time before that as well. We haven't made love in over a year.

ZASTROZZI: Then go somewhere else. Making love is not an accurate description of what we do anyway.

MATILDA: I realize that. I know what we do. We ravage each other. Nevertheless I miss it. Don't you?

ZASTROZZI: No.

MATILDA: Zastrozzi is hollow. I have come three hundred miles just to be reminded once again that Zastrozzi is hollow.

ZASTROZZI: Drink. *(picking up a flask and drinking)*

MATILDA: Don't you ever get physically aroused anymore.

ZASTROZZI: No. All sexual desire left me the moment I realized I had a purpose in life.

MATILDA: So now you have a purpose. I thought you just wanted to make people suffer.

ZASTROZZI: Can't that be a purpose.

MATILDA: I don't know. But I do know it can't stop you from desiring me. There's something you're not telling me.

ZASTROZZI: Very well. I swore a vow of chastity.

MATILDA: To whom.

ZASTROZZI: The Emperor of Spain's mistress.

MATILDA: Nonsense. When would you have met her.

ZASTROZZI: When I robbed the Emperor's country estate. His mistress was there alone. One thing led to another and I raped her. Just as I was leaving she looked up and said, "I can live with this if you vow never to be intimate with another woman." I shrugged my shoulders, said "all right," and left.

MATILDA laughs.

I knew you would understand.

MATILDA: I'm the only woman alive who could. We belong together. It would be delicious while it lasted. There's no one alive we couldn't victimize in one way or another. And when we're finally caught we can go to hell together.

ZASTROZZI: No, not hell. Some place less specific. Atheists don't go to hell. They don't know where it is. The Christians invented it and the only decent thing they've done is to keep its whereabouts a secret to outsiders.

MATILDA: Then forget hell. Let's go to Africa instead.

ZASTROZZI: Later. I have things to do.

MATILDA: Ah, yes. This search for revenge on some God-obsessed Italian. You are letting it change your personality.

ZASTROZZI: He murdered my mother.

MATILDA: So find him. Then kill him. It's a simple matter. It should not be your purpose in life. Revenge is an interesting obsession but it isn't worthy of the powers of Zastrozzi.

ZASTROZZI: I know. But Verezzi represents something which must be destroyed. He gives people gifts and tells them they are from God. Do you realize the damage that someone like that can do.

MATILDA: Damage to what.

ZASTROZZI makes a dismissive gesture.

I don't understand.

ZASTROZZI: I don't need your understanding.

MATILDA: Yes. I know that. I haven't been coming to you all these years because I think you need anything from me. It's that I need something from you.

ZASTROZZI: Really. What.

MATILDA: The whore sleeps with the devil so she can feel like a virgin?

ZASTROZZI: Something like that. Yes. What a comfortable little solution to guilt. Except that your devil is unpredictable. *(hits MATILDA and knocks her down)* Get out.

MATILDA: Let me stay.

ZASTROZZI: Get out. Or your devil might slit your throat just to show the flaw in your argument.

MATILDA: If I crawl across to you and beg, will you let me stay.

ZASTROZZI: *(looks at her silently for a moment)* First, let's see how you crawl.

MATILDA crawls slowly over to him, wraps her arms around his legs and rests her head on his boot.

MATILDA: Let me stay. Do what you have to. Go send this Italian Verezzi to hell and then let me stay forever.

ZASTROZZI: Shush. *(thinking, breaking away from her and pacing slowly)* Send this Verezzi to hell. *(chuckling)* Yes.

ZASTROZZI paces some more, stops and looks at MATILDA.

I will. He is a Christian. He can go to hell. Or at least he thinks he can. And the pain. Such excruciating pain. Much, much more than if I were to merely kill him. He must be made to send himself in his mind to hell. By killing himself. The most direct route to hell is by suicide. Over a woman. The most desirable woman in the world. She will entrap him then destroy him. And his destruction will be exquisitely painful and it will appear to everyone to have happened naturally as if it were meant to be.

Pause.

You will do this for me, won't you, Matilda.

MATILDA looks at him. Stands. Straightens her clothes.

MATILDA: First, let's see how you crawl.

They stare at each other. Finally ZASTROZZI gets down and slowly crawls over to her. He wraps his arms around her legs.

ZASTROZZI: Entrap him. Then destroy him.

BERNARDO walks in, sees them, smiles.

BERNARDO: He's back.

Blackout.

Scene Four

Street scene. A light rain is falling. JULIA is sitting on some steps, holding an umbrella above her head. VEREZZI is standing centre stage, looking up, smiling, hitting himself on the head with both his hands and moving about delicately.

VEREZZI: I'm so happy. Life has once again given me the giggles. What a surprise. In the ruins of an ancient city, on a foul, damp day in spring, the soggy young artist, walking aimlessly about in search of something to draw, meets the most beautiful and sensitive woman alive.

JULIA: You are kind. But you flatter me.

VEREZZI: Not yet. But I will. I am growing silly with delight. *(reeling around a few times)*

JULIA: Good heavens. What's wrong with you. Why can't you just come sit down and have a pleasant conversation.

VEREZZI: You want me to be sober.

JULIA: If you'd just stay still for a moment. We only met a minute ago. All we said to each other was hello. And you started prancing about and giggling.

VEREZZI: Yes. A less perceptive person would think I was insane.

JULIA: Well, you might be insane for all I know. Can't you even introduce yourself.

VEREZZI sobers.

VEREZZI: Yes. Of course. *(walking over)* I am Verezzi.

JULIA: My name is Julia.

VEREZZI: *(spinning around)* Of course it is! Could it be anything else. You are spectacular and your name is a song.

JULIA: Sir. You will sit down. You will stop talking like a frenzied poetic moron and will make rational conversation. It can be pleasant conversation. It can even be romantic conversation. But it will be rational or I am leaving.

VEREZZI: *(sitting)* I am Verezzi.

JULIA: Yes, you've said that.

VEREZZI: And you are Julia.

JULIA: And I have said that.

VEREZZI: Will you marry me.

JULIA: No.

VEREZZI: I am depressed.

JULIA: How old are you.

VEREZZI: Twenty-five.

JULIA: You have the emotions of a ten-year-old.

VEREZZI: That is often the case with a visionary.

JULIA: So you have visions.

VEREZZI: *(a revelation)* I *am* a visionary.

JULIA: So you … have visions.

VEREZZI: Yes. But don't tell anyone. I'm not ready to meet my followers yet.

JULIA: Visions of what nature.

VEREZZI: Religious.

JULIA: Visions of God?

VEREZZI: Of God. By God. For God. Through God.

VEREZZI smiles. JULIA just stares silently at him for a while.

JULIA: You are the first visionary I have met. At least the first one who has told me that he was one.

VEREZZI: I hope you're not thinking I'm bragging.

JULIA: No, that's not what I'm thinking.

VEREZZI: Good. Because I worked hard to be what I am. At first I was just a person, then a religious person, then a servant of God, then a messenger of God.

JULIA: And now a visionary.

VEREZZI: Yes.

JULIA: When did you have your first vision.

VEREZZI: I haven't had one yet.

JULIA: I don't understand.

VEREZZI: Neither do I. I suppose I'll just have to be patient.

Pause.

JULIA: But you told me you had visions. Of God. By God. For God etcetera.

VEREZZI: Yes. I was speaking hypothetically.

JULIA: I'm sorry. But I don't think that makes any sense.

VEREZZI: No. Then I was speaking meta-phorically.

JULIA: That neither.

VEREZZI: Symbolically.

JULIA: No.

VEREZZI: Will you marry me.

JULIA: No. *(standing)*

VEREZZI: Where are you going.

JULIA: Home.

VEREZZI: May I call on you.

JULIA: No. *(exiting)*

VEREZZI: I love her. She is just the right kind of woman for me. She has no imagination and she takes her religion very seriously. God is creating a balance.

VICTOR enters.

VICTOR: Who was that woman.

VEREZZI: Her name is Julia. She lives here. She is very bright. She is an aristocrat. She thinks I'm insane. I gave her that impression intentionally by making fun of religious states of mind. It was a test. She passed. I'm going to marry her.

VICTOR: Shut up.

VEREZZI: I won't shut up. You are my servant. You shut up.

VICTOR: You're getting worse daily. You're almost insensate. There is danger here and you can't appreciate it.

VEREZZI: There is no danger here. There is only love here.

VICTOR: You are insane.

VEREZZI: Who says so.

VICTOR: I do.

VEREZZI: You are my servant. You are not to say I am insane. I say you are insane. Yes, Victor, you are insane. So there.

VICTOR: Shut up.

VEREZZI: You shut up.

VICTOR grabs VEREZZI by the throat and shakes him.

VICTOR: Shut up, shut up, shut up.

VEREZZI raises a hand and VICTOR lets him go.

VICTOR: Now are you ready to listen to me.

VEREZZI: You hurt me.

VICTOR: I'm sorry. You were in a daze.

VEREZZI: I was?

VICTOR: Yes. How do you feel now.

VEREZZI: My throat hurts.

VICTOR: But are you sensible.

VEREZZI: Of course.

VICTOR: I found out from the innkeeper that someone has been making enquiries about you. Do you know what that means.

VEREZZI: Yes. My followers are beginning to gather.

VICTOR: Shut up. You don't have any followers.

VEREZZI: As of last count my followers numbered 454. I can describe each of them to you in detail.

VICTOR: You've hallucinated every one of them. The man making enquiries about you was probably a friend of that man Zastrozzi.

VEREZZI: Zastrozzi. Zastrozzi, the German? The master criminal? The man who seeks revenge upon me?

VICTOR: Yes.

VEREZZI: He does not exist! He is a phantom of your mind. For three years you have been telling me I have been hunted by Zastrozzi and yet I have never seen him.

VICTOR: Because I have kept us ahead of him. I have evaded him.

VEREZZI: As only you could. Because he is a phantom of *your* mind.

VICTOR: He was making enquiries about you.

VEREZZI: That was one of my followers.

VICTOR: Your followers do not exist. It was Zastrozzi.

VEREZZI: Zastrozzi does not exist! I have 454 followers. Follower number one is short and bald. Follower number two is tall with a beard. Follower number three is …

VICTOR: Shut up. You are insane. And you grow worse every day. But I promised your father I would take care of you so I will.

VEREZZI: You didn't know my father. I hired you. As a servant. You must be feverish in your brain. But I will save you. You are a challenge.

VICTOR: Very well. But let's move on. You can save me at some other place.

VEREZZI: I can't. The birds are here.

VICTOR: I beg your pardon.

VEREZZI: Look up. What do you see.

VICTOR: A flock of birds.

VEREZZI: Yes. They are the sign.

VICTOR: What sign.

VEREZZI: The one my followers will be able to see in order to know where I am.

VICTOR: I don't believe this.

VEREZZI: Try. Please.

VICTOR: I will not.

VEREZZI: Very well. But when my followers arrive you're going to feel very out of place. They all believe it.

VICTOR gestures in disgust and leaves. VEREZZI drifts off in his mind.

Follower number 54 is of medium height but he limps. Follower number 101 is blind. Follower number 262 is ... a Persian immigrant.

BERNARDO comes on dragging MATILDA by the hair. He is carrying a whip.

BERNARDO: Here's a nice quiet place for a beating. Strip to the waist.

MATILDA: No, sit. Please forgive me. I won't do it again.

BERNARDO: For sure you won't. Not after this.

MATILDA tries to run away. He intercepts and throws her down. VEREZZI raises his hand.

VEREZZI: Excuse me.

BERNARDO: What do you want.

VEREZZI: A little human kindness, sir.

BERNARDO: Mind your own business.

BERNARDO raises the whip. VEREZZI approaches them.

VEREZZI: Leave her alone.

BERNARDO: You have been warned. *(drawing his sabre)* Defend yourself.

VEREZZI: Do I look like an angel of God, sir.

BERNARDO: No.

VEREZZI: Then you are in for a big surprise.

VEREZZI draws his sabre. Swishes it about. Trying to impress BERNARDO with his style. BERNARDO laughs. They fight. BERNARDO allows himself to be disarmed. VEREZZI has his sabre at BERNARDO's chest. Suddenly VEREZZI drifts off in his mind.

No. This is violence, isn't it. I shouldn't be doing this. This is wrong. I am an artist. I am in touch with Him.

BERNARDO slips away. MATILDA goes to VEREZZI and seductively runs her fingers through his hair.

MATILDA: Thank you.

VEREZZI looks up.

VEREZZI: You're welcome.

MATILDA: No. Thank you very, very much.

MATILDA smiles. VEREZZI smiles.

Blackout.

Scene Five

Evening. A secluded place. ZASTROZZI is sitting inert. JULIA comes on with a picnic basket.

JULIA: Excuse me, sir. But do you mind if I sit here.

ZASTROZZI slowly turns towards her and looks at her impassively for a moment.

ZASTROZZI: It would be best if you did not.

JULIA: But I always come here at this time on this particular day of the week to have my picnic.

ZASTROZZI: Without fail?

JULIA: Yes.

ZASTROZZI: Well, today you have been broken of a very silly habit. Move on.

JULIA: Why should I.

ZASTROZZI: I want to be alone.

JULIA: Then you move on.

ZASTROZZI: I want to be alone. And I want to be alone exactly where I am.

JULIA: Well, today you are not going to get what you want. I am sitting and I am eating.

JULIA eats and ZASTROZZI watches her for a moment.

ZASTROZZI: You are an only child from a very wealthy family.

JULIA: Perhaps.

ZASTROZZI: You don't have a worry in the world.

JULIA: Perhaps not.

ZASTROZZI: You don't have a thought in your head.

JULIA: I have one or two.

ZASTROZZI: And you are a virgin. *(pause)* Well, are you or are you not a virgin.

JULIA: Why. Are you looking for one.

ZASTROZZI: Go away.

JULIA: In good time. Perhaps when I'm finished eating this piece of cheese. Perhaps after I eat my apple. In good time.

Pause.

ZASTROZZI: Do you know who I am.

JULIA: No. Who are you.

ZASTROZZI: I am the man who is going to take away your virginity.

JULIA: Many have tried. All have failed. It will never be taken away. It will be given. In good time.

ZASTROZZI: Yes. Before you eat your apple to be exact.

JULIA: I'll scream.

ZASTROZZI: If you scream it will be the last sound you ever hear.

JULIA: Then I'll go limp. You won't enjoy it.

ZASTROZZI: It's not important that I enjoy it. It's important that you enjoy it.

JULIA: Impossible.

ZASTROZZI: Look at me.

JULIA: No. I don't think I will.

ZASTROZZI: Why not. Don't you find me attractive.

JULIA: That's not the point. You've threatened to rape me.

ZASTROZZI: Surely you knew I was joking.

JULIA: You didn't sound like you were joking.

ZASTROZZI: I was only trying to hide the embarrassing truth.

JULIA: And what might that be.

ZASTROZZI: That, like so many other men, I have admired you from a distance and could never gather the courage to approach you.

JULIA: So you waited here knowing I was coming on this particular day.

ZASTROZZI: Yes.

JULIA: And you adopted an aggressive attitude to disguise your true and romantic feelings for me.

ZASTROZZI: Yes.

JULIA: Yes. I can believe that. Men have done sillier things for me. Do you still want me to look at you.

ZASTROZZI: No. I'm too embarrassed.

JULIA: I understand.

ZASTROZZI: Just look ahead.

JULIA: If you wish.

Pause.

ZASTROZZI: I hope you don't mind that I'm doing this.

JULIA: What.

ZASTROZZI: Running my hand through your hair.

ZASTROZZI does nothing. He will do nothing.

JULIA: Oh. I don't feel anything.

ZASTROZZI: I am running my hand through your hair. Very softly.

JULIA: Well, I guess it's all right.

ZASTROZZI: You have a very soft neck.

JULIA: Are you touching my neck. *(looking at him)*

ZASTROZZI: Please just look ahead. *(looking at her)* Please.

JULIA: All right. *(turning away)*

ZASTROZZI: Very soft neck. Very soft shoulders too. And if I may just lower my hand a little.

JULIA: Please, sir.

ZASTROZZI: I'm sorry you spoke too late. Yes, your breast is also soft. But firm.

JULIA: Please. No one has ever—

ZASTROZZI: Both breasts so wonderfully firm. And my face so nice against your neck. If I could just reach down.

JULIA: No, sir—

ZASTROZZI: You should have said so earlier. Your stomach. My God. This is such a wonderful feeling, isn't it.

JULIA: I'm not quite—

ZASTROZZI: That's it. Lean back a little.

JULIA: I shouldn't be doing this.

JULIA does nothing. She will do nothing.

ZASTROZZI: Back a little farther. Lie down.

JULIA: All the way?

ZASTROZZI: Yes.

JULIA: But—

ZASTROZZI: Lie down.

JULIA: Like this?

ZASTROZZI: Yes.

JULIA: What are you doing now.

ZASTROZZI: Kissing you on your mouth.

Pause.

JULIA: Yes. And now?

Pause.

ZASTROZZI: Your breasts.

Pause.

JULIA: Yes. And now?

Pause.

ZASTROZZI: Relax.

Pause.

JULIA: Yes.

Blackout.

Scene Six

The sky is rumbling again. ZASTROZZI is drunk. He is at the doorway of his bed chamber. He drinks the last of the wine in his flask and throws it on the floor.

ZASTROZZI: Where is my wine. I called for that wine an hour ago. I warn you it is in your best interest to keep me drunk. I am at my mellowest when drunk. Innkeeper!

A VOICE: Coming, sir.

ZASTROZZI grunts. He goes and sits in a chair near the bed, picks up a book, reads, grunts, grunts louder, throws the book across the room.

ZASTROZZI: Liar! *(standing, pacing)* They're all liars. Why do I read books. What is this new age of optimism they're all talking about. It's a lie sponsored by the Church and the government to give the people false hope. The people. I care less about the people than I do about the Church or the government. Then what do you care about sin. I care that I should not ask myself questions like that. I care to be dumb and without care. I care that I should not ask myself questions like that ever again. *(sitting, pausing)* Sad. *(standing)* Wine! *(sitting)* Sad.

VICTOR comes in with the wine.

ZASTROZZI: Who are you.

VICTOR: I own this inn.

ZASTROZZI: No. I've met the owner.

VICTOR: The former owner. I won it from him in a card game last night.

ZASTROZZI: Congratulations. Put the wine down and get out.

VICTOR puts the wine down.

VICTOR: You are the Great Zastrozzi, aren't you.

ZASTROZZI: I am a lodger in your inn.

VICTOR: Are you ashamed of being Zastrozzi.

ZASTROZZI: If you were to die in the near future would many people attend your funeral.

VICTOR: No.

ZASTROZZI: Then save yourself the embarrassment. Get out.

VICTOR: I heard that Zastrozzi once passed through Paris like the plague. Leaving the aristocracy nearly bankrupt, their daughters all defiled and diseased, the police in chaos and the museums ransacked. And all because, it is said, he took a dislike to the popular French taste in art.

ZASTROZZI: A slight exaggeration. He took a dislike to a certain aristocratic artist who happened to have a very willing daughter and one painting in one museum.

VICTOR: And did Zastrozzi kill the artist, rape his daughter and destroy the painting.

ZASTROZZI: The daughter was not touched. She had syphilis. Probably given to her by the father. The painting was not worth destroying. It was just removed from the illustrious company it had no right to be with. *(taking a drink)*

VICTOR: But the artist was killed.

ZASTROZZI: Yes. Certainly.

VICTOR: Why.

ZASTROZZI: To prove that even artists must answer to somebody.

VICTOR: And what has Zastrozzi come to this obscure place to prove.

ZASTROZZI: Zastrozzi is starting some new endeavour. He is going to murder only innkeepers for a year.

VICTOR: I am not afraid of you.

ZASTROZZI: Then you are stupid. *(pause)* And you are not an innkeeper.

VICTOR: They say that all Europe has no more cause to fear Zastrozzi. They say that for three years he has been single-minded in a search for revenge on one man and that all the rest of Europe has been untouched.

ZASTROZZI: They think and say only what Zastrozzi wants them to think and say.

VICTOR: They also say that any man can cross him, that any woman can use him. Because the master criminal, the Great Zastrozzi, is in a trance.

ZASTROZZI: Ah. But then there are trances … *(He draws his sword and does four or five amazing things with it.)* … and there are trances.

He puts the sword to VICTOR's throat.

Now, who are you.

VICTOR steps back. Afraid.

VICTOR: Your revenge upon Verezzi will be empty.

ZASTROZZI: Who is he to you.

VICTOR: I'm his tutor.

ZASTROZZI: His what.

VICTOR: Tutor. I teach him things.

ZASTROZZI: Is that so. And what, for example, do you teach him.

VICTOR: How to evade the man who wants to destroy him.

ZASTROZZI: You are the one responsible for stretching my search to three years.

VICTOR: Yes.

ZASTROZZI: Interesting. You don't look capable of having done it. You look ordinary.

VICTOR: I am.

ZASTROZZI: No. In your case the look might actually be deceiving. But we'll soon find out. Where is your weapon.

VICTOR: I don't have one.

ZASTROZZI: Then why the innkeeper disguise. You must be here to intervene for your student.

VICTOR: Intervention doesn't have to be violent.

ZASTROZZI: I'm afraid it does. Haven't you been reading the latest books. The world is in desperate need of action. The most decisive action is always violent. *(repeating this last sentence in German)*

VICTOR: Interesting. But all I'm saying is that I didn't think killing you would necessarily have to be the only way to stop you. I thought I could try common sense with you.

ZASTROZZI: You were wrong. Try something else.

VICTOR: Verezzi is insane.

ZASTROZZI: I don't care.

VICTOR: But revenge on an insane man can't mean anything.

ZASTROZZI: Wrong. I don't share the belief that the insane have left this world. They're still here. They're just hiding.

VICTOR: But he thinks he is a visionary.

ZASTROZZI: Well, perhaps he is. I don't care about that either. That's between him and his God. This matter is between him and me.

Pause.

VICTOR: I know why you seek revenge on Verezzi.

ZASTROZZI: No one knows!

VICTOR: I know of the crime that he and his father committed upon your mother.

ZASTROZZI: Ah, yes. The crime. What version have you heard.

VICTOR: The real one.

ZASTROZZI: Is that so.

VICTOR: I was a friend of his father. I was away studying. Hadn't seen him for years. Had never even met his son. A letter arrived. He said he was dying. And asked if I would protect his son who would probably be in danger.

ZASTROZZI: And the letter described what they had done?

VICTOR: Yes.

ZASTROZZI: What did you think.

VICTOR: It was horrible, of course.

ZASTROZZI: Describe exactly what you mean by horrible.

VICTOR: Bloody. Vicious. Unforgivable.

ZASTROZZI: Wrong. Not even close. Horrible is when things proceed unnaturally. When people remain unanswerable for their actions.

VICTOR: But the letter also told me why they had done it. This woman's son had killed my friend's daughter. Verezzi's sister.

ZASTROZZI: No. It wasn't me.

VICTOR: Then who was it.

ZASTROZZI: Never mind. But even if I had killed her then the quarrel would be with me. Not my mother. That is usually the way with revenge, isn't it.

VICTOR: You couldn't be found.

ZASTROZZI: I was away. Studying. I was called back to examine my mother's corpse. And the father's letter actually did describe what they had done to her?

VICTOR: Yes.

ZASTROZZI: Imagine that. How could he bring himself to tell anyone. I thought he was a Christian.

VICTOR: It was a confession, I think.

ZASTROZZI: Are you a priest.

VICTOR: I was at the time.

ZASTROZZI: And you left the Church just to protect Verezzi?

VICTOR: It doesn't matter why I left the Church.

ZASTROZZI: Yes. That's correct. Only two things should matter to you. That Verezzi killed my mother in a horrible manner. And that I, her son, have a legitimate claim to vengeance.

VICTOR: But he has no memory of the crime. He never has had. He must have blocked it out almost immediately.

ZASTROZZI: I don't care. I seek revenge. Revenge is a simple matter. You shouldn't have turned it into such an issue by hiding him from me for all this time.

VICTOR: But there's something else, isn't there.

ZASTROZZI: I beg your pardon.

VICTOR: I think there's another reason altogether why you want to destroy Verezzi.

ZASTROZZI: What is your name.

VICTOR: Victor.

ZASTROZZI: No. You are not an ordinary man, Victor. But you would be wise to become one within the next few hours.

VICTOR: When are you coming to take him.

ZASTROZZI: I am here now. Are you going to run off again.

VICTOR: No. He won't leave. He's waiting for his followers. Listen. I don't care much for violence. But to get to him you will have to go around me.

ZASTROZZI: I have already done that. And I didn't even know you existed.

VICTOR: How.

ZASTROZZI: Never mind. Concern yourself with this. If what I plan doesn't work I will not be going around you or anyone or anything else. I will be coming directly at him. And if you are in the way you will be killed. Now go away. I'm tired. Tired of the chase. The explanation of the chase. Of everything. Of you specifically at this moment.

ZASTROZZI turns around. VICTOR pulls a knife from inside his shirt, raises it to ZASTROZZI's back, and holds it there. Finally VICTOR lowers it.

Go away.

VICTOR exits, passing BERNARDO coming in.

BERNARDO: He had a knife about six inches away from your back.

ZASTROZZI: Why didn't you stop him. He could have killed me.

BERNARDO: I doubt it.

ZASTROZZI: Did you arrange for the introduction.

BERNARDO: Yes.

ZASTROZZI: I wonder now if it is a good enough plan.

BERNARDO: Probably not. *(starting off)*

ZASTROZZI: It doesn't matter. It's almost over. I sense it. One way or the other I have him. This way would be less violent but more satisfying. Where are you going.

BERNARDO: A young woman in the village smiled at me. She's very pretty. And obviously well-off. I think I'll seduce her and rob her blind.

ZASTROZZI: You know, Bernardo, that you don't have to do these things just to impress me.

BERNARDO: Thank you.

ZASTROZZI: You could try to become the nice young man you were before your one little mistake.

BERNARDO: And what was that.

ZASTROZZI: You murdered Verezzi's sister. Don't tell me you had forgotten.

BERNARDO: Yes, I had. I've murdered so many others since then.

ZASTROZZI: You really are a seedy little butcher, aren't you.

BERNARDO: Once you make your one little mistake, sir, you must continue or be destroyed. The insulation of evil is the only thing that makes you survive. I learned that from watching you.

ZASTROZZI: But sometimes your crimes are heartless enough to shock even me. Who is the dark personality here after all.

BERNARDO: You, sir. But I strive hard to be your shadow.

ZASTROZZI: Good. That man with the knife to my back. His name is Victor. He is Verezzi's tutor. He looks harmless, doesn't he.

BERNARDO: Yes.

ZASTROZZI: He isn't. I give him to you. He'll probably present a challenge.

BERNARDO: Thank you. *(starting off)*

ZASTROZZI: Oh, Bernardo.

BERNARDO: Yes.

ZASTROZZI: I don't expect you to understand why you are killing him. But I do expect you to do it with some imagination!

BERNARDO leaves. ZASTROZZI takes a long drink.

Blackout.

Intermission.

Scene Seven

VEREZZI's room. VEREZZI and MATILDA are making love. He is delirious. We know they are finished when he makes an absurdly loud and sustained groaning sound. MATILDA gets out of bed and looks at him in disbelief. She is clothed. He is naked.

VEREZZI: I am in love.

MATILDA: So soon?

VEREZZI: I am enthralled. You were wonderful. What a new treat. Usually I am the one who is wonderful and the women are enthralled. Where did you get this strange power.

MATILDA: It's something I was born with.

VEREZZI: How do you know.

MATILDA: What else could it be. It's not something you get from practice. I'm not a whore.

VEREZZI: No. But you're not a saint either. I'd know if you were. Because … *(a revelation) I'm* a saint.

MATILDA: Of course you are.

VEREZZI: Don't be intimidated. Saints are human.

MATILDA: Why should I be intimidated. Saint or no saint. You are the one who loves me.

VEREZZI: You mean you don't love me?

MATILDA: No. Of course not.

VEREZZI: I don't understand. Explain. But be kind about it.

MATILDA: I love someone else.

VEREZZI: Who.

MATILDA: You saw him earlier.

VEREZZI: That man who was going to beat you?

MATILDA: Yes. Bernardo.

VEREZZI: That's disgusting. How can you love someone who beats you.

MATILDA: It's not *that* he beats me. It's *how* he beats me.

VEREZZI: I don't understand. Explain. But be kind.

MATILDA: He beats me like he could kill me. And I love him for that.

VEREZZI: You should love me instead. I'm gentle. I'm an artist. I'm a saint. And I love you.

MATILDA: Could you kill me. If you could kill me I might love you.

VEREZZI: You're very strange. And you're very exciting. But I don't think you're very healthy. That's a challenge. I can help you. Stay with me.

MATILDA: I can't! I love someone else.

VEREZZI: Then why did you make love to me.

MATILDA: A part of me is gentle. It wanted to thank you. But a larger part of me is something else. It wants to be beaten. *(starting off)*

VEREZZI: Stay. I could beat you. A little.

MATILDA: If you really loved me you could do better.

VEREZZI: But I'm a saint. I love things. I can't hurt things. How could I face my followers. They're coming soon. Some of them are very vulnerable. Some of them are swans. Some of them are tiny little caterpillars who have been crawling for weeks to get here. I can't disappoint them. How can I preach love and human kindness to all my followers then go into the privacy of my bedroom and beat a woman unconscious.

MATILDA: If you are a saint you can take certain liberties. People will understand.

VEREZZI: But will the caterpillars. They are dumb. I love them. Honestly I do. But they are dumb. Crawl, crawl. That's all they do. Crawl. Life's dilemmas are multiplied for a saint. He has to deal with too many things at once. One of my followers is a Turk. I don't even speak his language. When he comes, how am I going to give him the message. I keep waiting for the gift of tongues but it never comes. God is handicapping me. And now you want me to beat you. I abhor violence. It makes me retch. But I love you. I'll die if you leave me.

MATILDA starts off, VEREZZI crawls out of the bed and over to her.

VEREZZI: Please don't go. I know. You can beat me instead.

MATILDA: That just won't do.

VEREZZI: But won't you even try.

VICTOR comes in.

VICTOR: What's this. Get up.

VEREZZI stands.

VICTOR: *(to MATILDA)* Who are you.

VEREZZI: She is the woman I love.

VICTOR: And why were you grovelling on the floor.

VEREZZI: Because she doesn't love me. What can I do, Victor. She's breaking my heart.

VICTOR: It seems to me that I met the woman you love earlier. That virgin God sent for you.

VICTOR starts to pack.

VEREZZI: Yes. Julia. That's right. I love her. I'd forgotten. Oh, thank God. For a moment there I didn't know what I was going to do. It's all right, Matilda. You can go now.

MATILDA: So you don't love me after all.

VEREZZI: But I do. It's just that I also love Julia. And she's less of a challenge. She just thinks I'm insane. I can deal with that. But I don't know if I can ever deal with you, Matilda. You want me to want to kill you. That's unique. But it's not healthy. But I do love you. And if it weren't for Julia I would probably destroy myself over you. Or something to that effect.

MATILDA: *(with clenched teeth)* Or something to that effect. *(starting off)*

VEREZZI: Oh. Say hello to Bernardo for me. I think he likes me.

MATILDA looks at him oddly, shakes her head and leaves.

VICTOR: What was that all about.

VEREZZI: One of the tests of sainthood, I imagine.

VICTOR: Did you pass.

VEREZZI: I don't know. Tell me, Victor, how do you suppose I can find out.

VICTOR: Oh, shut up. Get packed. We're leaving.

VEREZZI: Why.

VICTOR: Zastrozzi is here.

VEREZZI: Who.

VICTOR: Zastrozzi. Zastrozzi!

VEREZZI: Oh, yes. The phantom of your brain. You've dreamt him up again have you.

VICTOR: I've seen him. I was at his rooms.

VEREZZI: Oh, really. And what does he look like. Does he have fangs. Does he have horns. Does he have eyes dripping blood.

VICTOR: No. He's a man. Just a man. Calm. Purposeful. And very experienced. Just a man. But a very dangerous one.

VEREZZI: Well then bring him along and I'll deal with him. A little human understanding should get him to leave you alone.

VICTOR: You're no match for him.

VEREZZI: Why not.

VICTOR: Because he's perfectly sane. And you're a delirious lunatic.

VEREZZI: And if I am, is it good and right for you to be telling me so. Would it not be more good and more right for you to be more understanding. That's an hypothesis of a religious nature. I have decided that your degeneration has gone far enough. And I am commencing spiritual guidance with you immediately. *(sitting on the bed)* Now come sit at my feet.

VICTOR: Get packed.

VEREZZI: Lesson number one. When the Messiah speaks, listen.

VICTOR: When did you become the Messiah.

VEREZZI: Did I say Messiah. No.

VICTOR: I heard you.

VEREZZI: No. Not me. God. God said Messiah.

VICTOR: I don't understand. Are you God or are you the Messiah.

VEREZZI: I am Verezzi. I am whoever He wants me to be.

VICTOR: You are exploring new dimensions of the human mind, Verezzi. But I don't think the world is ready for you yet. Get packed. We're leaving.

VEREZZI: No.

VICTOR: Please! I promised your father. It's the only promise in my life I've ever kept. It keeps me sane. Please get packed!

VEREZZI: No. I have to go find Julia. I have to tell her that God is talking to me. I know she'll marry me now.

VICTOR: Let me try to explain it to you in a way you will understand.

VICTOR drops to his knees.

VEREZZI: Don't patronize me, Victor. I am not a moron. I am just a good and lovely man.

VICTOR: Well, that could be a matter of opinion. But let us suppose you are in fact just a good man.

VEREZZI: And lovely.

VICTOR: Yes.

VEREZZI: And very tidy as well.

VICTOR: Yes. All those things. A good lovely tidy man. Who is gentle to all things living and dead, et cetera, and wishes only to carry about the positive uplifting spirit of God. Then doesn't it make sense that in order to do that you should become aware of the obstacles that lie naturally in your path. The forces of evil that wish to stop you. In effect, doesn't it make sense that a good man should also be a cunning man.

VEREZZI: No.

VEREZZI leaves. VICTOR sits on the bed. Shakes his head.

VICTOR: I give up. Zastrozzi will get his revenge on the lunatic Verezzi. After three years he will finally destroy a vegetable. I don't know who to pity more. Zastrozzi, the poor vegetable, or whatever it was that created them both. Sad. *(shrugging)* No. I can't give up. I promised. I must save him. Even if I must hurt him a little.

VICTOR stands and searches the room for something heavy. He finds something, takes it, and runs out.

Blackout.

Scene Eight

A lull in the storm. VICTOR is walking through a dark alley. Suddenly a torch is lit. It is held by BERNARDO. He is standing with sword drawn in VICTOR's way.

VICTOR: Excuse me. Did a man pass by here recently. A young man.

BERNARDO: Forget him. His time is almost here. You have business with me.

VICTOR: What do you want.

BERNARDO: I am from Zastrozzi.

VICTOR: And what does Zastrozzi want from me.

BERNARDO: Your life.

VICTOR: A bizarre request. Do you understand the reason for it.

BERNARDO: No. I am a more simple man than Zastrozzi. I can only understand simple reasons for killing a man. And very simple ways of going about it.

VICTOR: Interesting. What, for example, are the simple reasons for killing a man.

BERNARDO: To get his money.

VICTOR: I have none.

BERNARDO: If he has done some wrong to me.

VICTOR: I don't even know you.

BERNARDO: Or if he presents some kind of threat.

VICTOR: Surely you can tell just by looking at me that I'm harmless.

BERNARDO: Zastrozzi says you are not.

VICTOR: Zastrozzi flatters me.

BERNARDO: Zastrozzi sees things that others cannot.

VICTOR: Perhaps that is because he is insane.

BERNARDO: He is not the least bit insane.

VICTOR: Are you absolutely sure of that.

BERNARDO: Yes.

VICTOR: Oh.

BERNARDO: In fact, he is the sanest man I have ever met. He is also the most perverse. The combination makes him very dangerous. You do not upset a man like this. When he tells you to kill someone, you do it. Even though you personally have nothing to gain from it. When he tells you to do it with imagination you try to do so. Even though you do not know why or even how to go about it.

VICTOR: Poor fellow. You're in quite a fix.

BERNARDO: While you on the other hand are not, is that it.

VICTOR: I am probably going to die. That I can understand. You are going to spend the rest of your life fulfilling someone else's wishes that you do not understand. That, sir, is a state of mental chaos usually associated with purgatory. I pity you.

BERNARDO: Shut up.

VICTOR: I pity you like I would a diseased dog.

BERNARDO: I said shut up.

VICTOR: You are out of your element. Zastrozzi is the master of evil and you are just a thug.

BERNARDO: I am more than that, I know.

VICTOR: A thug. And a murderer. You cannot think of an imaginative way to kill me because you have no imagination. You stand there with a sword and threaten a man who is unarmed. That is the posture of a cheap murderer.

BERNARDO: I could use my hands. Would you feel better about that.

VICTOR: I am only thinking of you.

BERNARDO: (throwing down the sword) It will take a little longer this way.

He approaches VICTOR.

I'm going to have to strangle you.

VICTOR: Well, it's not exactly inspired. But it's better than just cutting me down with a sword. Congratulations.

BERNARDO: Thank you.

VICTOR: But before you start, I have a confession to make.

VICTOR quickly takes out the heavy object he has taken from the room in the previous scene and hits BERNARDO over the head. BERNARDO falls unconscious to the ground.

I lied about not being armed.

VEREZZI comes on in a daze.

VEREZZI: Victor. I'm glad you're here. I can't find any of my followers. They must have gotten lost.

VICTOR: (pointing off) No. There's one now.

VEREZZI turns and VICTOR hits him over the head with his object. VEREZZI falls unconscious. VICTOR picks him up under the arms.

A place to hide. Some place quiet. I have to think about what is happening to me. That vacant prison I saw this morning. (dragging VEREZZI away) What's this. He's smiling. Even in pain he smiles.

Blackout.

Scene Nine

ZASTROZZI's room. ZASTROZZI is standing in the middle of the room, a blanket wrapped around him, shivering.

ZASTROZZI: I am having a nightmare. It involves the final battle over control of the world between the forces of good and evil. It is the most terrifying nightmare I have ever had. Something so extremely unusual has happened that my mind in all its power cannot even begin to comprehend it. I am in charge of the forces of good. And I am winning. I think there is just the slightest possibility that there might be something wrong with my mind after all. The nightmare continues. I lead the forces of good with their toothy, God-obsessed smiles into the fortress of the commander of the forces of evil. We easily over-come the fortress and become gracious victors—not raping or murdering or even taking prisoners. We just smile and wish goodness and mercy to rain down on everyone. And I am smiling and wishing out loud for goodness and mercy as well except that inside I am deeply ill and feel like throwing up. And then we are taken to meet the commander of the forces of evil and he walks through a large wooden door and I see that he looks familiar. And he should. Because it is Zastrozzi. And even though I know that I am

Zastrozzi I cannot help but feel extremely confused. And he reinforces this confusion when he opens his mouth and says, "I am Zastrozzi." At which point I feel myself smile even wider, so wide that I feel my skin tighten and I know that my face will become stuck forever like this in the widest, stupidest, most merciful and good smile ever worn by a human being. Then I die. But before I die I remember thinking—they are going to make me a saint. They are going to make me a Christian saint. The patron saint of smiles. The nightmare ends. I need a drink. I need to sit down. I need more than anything to stop having nightmares. They're getting worse every day. There might be something wrong with my mind. *(shivering)* The nightmare continues. Again. *(smiling)*

MATILDA comes on dragging a whip along the floor. She is furious.

MATILDA: Zastrozzi! *(swinging the whip around above her head, cracking it)* Zastrozzi! I'm going to whip you. I'm going to whip you for making a fool out of me. For sending me to entrap a man who is an idiot and feels nothing except idiotic things.

Pause.

The nightmares. *(sighing and starting off, seeing him shaking)* No. *(turning back)* Zastrozzi, I have failed. Whip me.

ZASTROZZI: I can't be bothered. *(turning to her, smiling stupidly)*

MATILDA: Zastrozzi, you have a stupid empty smile on your face. Just like the one the idiot wears. You are standing there shivering under a blanket like a sick old man. You don't look like Zastrozzi. You look like an ass.

ZASTROZZI: *(trying to concentrate)* And now.

MATILDA: You are still shivering.

ZASTROZZI: *(closing his eyes and concentrating)* And now.

MATILDA: You are still smiling like an idiot.

ZASTROZZI: *(closing his eyes and concentrating)* Now? *(approaching her slowly)* Now?!

MATILDA: Now I feel like whipping you for threatening me.

MATILDA begins to whip him. He doesn't move.

Don't ever make a fool of me again. Don't ever threaten me again. Who do you think I am. I am not one of those who quiver when they hear your name. I am your match, sir. I am every bit your match.

MATILDA throws the whip down.

ZASTROZZI: Are you.

MATILDA: In every way.

ZASTROZZI: In every way?

MATILDA: Yes.

ZASTROZZI: Ah, well. You must know. And if you know then I must agree. Correct?

MATILDA: Yes. So you will let me stay? We'll be together?

ZASTROZZI: I'm afraid that's impossible.

MATILDA: Why.

ZASTROZZI: We're too much alike. You've just said so. I am in love with someone else.

MATILDA: Impossible.

ZASTROZZI: Life is strange, isn't it. I met her just a short while ago. She is quite different from me. That is probably why I love her. She is pure and innocent and possesses a marvellous gentle sensuality that I have never experienced before. In fact, just thinking about her arouses me. I am thinking about her now and I am getting aroused now.

ZASTROZZI grabs MATILDA.

MATILDA: What are you doing.

ZASTROZZI: I am going to make love to you. Haven't you wanted me to for a long time.

MATILDA: Not while you are thinking about another woman.

ZASTROZZI: I'm sorry. But that is the way it must be.

MATILDA: I couldn't bear it.

ZASTROZZI: But you are a match for me in all ways. And I could bear it. I could even enjoy it. In fact that is the way people like us should enjoy it. Try to enjoy it.

MATILDA: I can't.

ZASTROZZI: Try.

MATILDA: No.

ZASTROZZI: Are you crying.

MATILDA: No.

ZASTROZZI: You are crying, aren't you.

MATILDA: No.

ZASTROZZI: Are you sure.

MATILDA: Yes.

ZASTROZZI: Are you crying.

MATILDA: Yes.

ZASTROZZI hits her and she is propelled across the room and falls.

MATILDA: What are you doing.

ZASTROZZI: Making a point.

MATILDA: You treat me this way because I am a woman.

ZASTROZZI: Nonsense. Women, men, children, goats. I treat them all the same. I ask them to be answerable.

BERNARDO walks on, his head bandaged.

(to MATILDA) Here. I'll show you what I mean.

ZASTROZZI walks over to BERNARDO.

I take it from your wound that you have failed.

BERNARDO: Yes, I'm sorry.

ZASTROZZI: That's not necessary. I don't want you to feel sorry. I don't want you to feel anything. Do you understand.

BERNARDO: I think so.

ZASTROZZI: Try to understand. Try to feel nothing. Are you feeling nothing now.

BERNARDO: I'm not sure.

ZASTROZZI: Try. Feel nothing. Are you feeling nothing.

BERNARDO: Yes.

ZASTROZZI: Good.

ZASTROZZI hits BERNARDO's face viciously with the back of his hand. BERNARDO staggers back, but doesn't fall.

Fall down when I hit you, Bernardo.

BERNARDO: Why.

ZASTROZZI: Because it makes it appear that you are resisting when you don't. And you have nothing to gain from resisting.

ZASTROZZI hits BERNARDO again. BERNARDO staggers back but doesn't fall. He looks at ZASTROZZI and drops to his knees.

Some advice for both of you. Get to know your limitations. Then remember that as you go through life there are only two things worth knowing. The first is too complex for you to understand. The second is that life is a series of totally arbitrary and often meaningless events and the only way to make sense of life is to forget that you know that. In other words, occupy yourselves. Matilda, go seduce Verezzi and if he is preoccupied remove his preoccupations. The plan to drive him to suicide is not the most inspired I have ever thought of but it will do to keep us occupied for a while. After you have done that, come looking for me and if I am in the mood we can play your silly whipping games. And as for you, Bernardo, go do something you at least understand. Commit some foul, meaningless crime. That village girl you mentioned earlier. Go abuse her and steal everything she values. And enjoy it as much as possible because eventually you will be made accountable. And now if you will excuse me, I am going to visit the local prison. It hasn't been used in years. But I'm sure it is still full of wondrous sensations. I do some of my best thinking in prisons. Did you know that.

MATILDA: Yes.

BERNARDO: No.

ZASTROZZI: It's true though. I've visited some of the best prisons in Europe. I find it invigorating. It helps to confirm my sanity. Only a sane person could function in those places as well as I do. Does that make sense.

BERNARDO: Yes.

MATILDA: No.

ZASTROZZI: You see I must visit these prisons. It is the only way to make myself answerable. I have never been apprehended and I never will be. So I have to voluntarily submit to a prison in order to make myself experience judgement. When I have experienced enough, I escape. Do you understand.

BERNARDO: Yes.

MATILDA: Yes.

ZASTROZZI: No, you don't.

ZASTROZZI smiles and leaves.

BERNARDO: He *is* crazy.

MATILDA: Of course he is. He has always been crazy.

BERNARDO: Not always.

MATILDA: How would you know. You are crazy yourself. For that matter so am I. For wanting him the way I do. I should find a more simple man.

BERNARDO stands and goes to MATILDA.

BERNARDO: I am a more simple man.

MATILDA: That's the problem. It is men like you who make me want men like him.

BERNARDO: I could surprise you.

MATILDA: You would have to.

BERNARDO: I would like to make love to you.

MATILDA: I know.

BERNARDO: May I.

MATILDA: I will be thinking of Zastrozzi.

BERNARDO: I might surprise you.

MATILDA: Well, you can try at least.

BERNARDO grabs her and kisses her.

Harder.

She grabs him savagely and kisses him.

Blackout.

Scene Ten

For the first time the focus is on the full set. Stripped of all furnishings, it should appear like an old dungeon. BERNARDO comes on pulling JULIA, whom he has chained at the wrists. He takes her into one of the chambers.

JULIA: What are you doing this for.

BERNARDO: You smiled at me.

JULIA: It was just an invitation for polite conversation.

BERNARDO: What would that mean to me. What was I supposed to do after the conversation. Marry you? Settle into a wonderful, lawful, domestic life?

JULIA: I really had no plans beyond conversation, sir.

BERNARDO: You wouldn't. You spend too much time with civilized men. This will teach you never to smile at strangers.

JULIA: Have I offended you.

BERNARDO: No. I'm just accepting your invitation and using it in the only way I can.

JULIA: What are you going to do with me.

BERNARDO: Anything I please.

JULIA: What is this place. I've never been here.

BERNARDO: No, you wouldn't have. It's an old prison. It used to house the criminally deranged but now it's vacant. More or less. A friend of mine found it. He has a way of finding places like these. What do you think of it.

JULIA: It's horrible.

BERNARDO: Yes. It is, isn't it. It will do very nicely.

JULIA: For what.

BERNARDO: For whatever I please.

JULIA: You're going to rape me, aren't you. You're going to rape me and murder me.

BERNARDO: Not necessarily in that order, though.

JULIA: You appeared to be such a nice young man.

BERNARDO grabs her hair.

BERNARDO: Nice? What would I do if I was nice. If a pretty woman smiled at me and we had a polite conversation could I marry her and be lawful and decent? No, I wouldn't do that now. My mind would explode. Yet I am a man. When a woman smiles, I must do something. So I do what I am doing.

JULIA: You don't have to do this. Let me go. We'll start again from the beginning. We'll meet in the fresh air on a sunny day. Talk about healthy things. Develop a respectful attitude towards each other. Eventually fall in love on just the right terms.

BERNARDO: Impossible. You're not the woman I could be in love with.

JULIA: I could try.

BERNARDO: Impossible. I can tell from your smile. There is a woman I love, though, who could love me on the right terms. But she loves someone else. His name is Zastrozzi. Have you heard of him.

JULIA: I ... I think so.

BERNARDO: He is the one they talk about in whispers in your circles. I am the one who follows him around like a dog. *(starting off)*

JULIA: Where are you going.

BERNARDO: Back to your house. To rob it of everything of any value at all. And to kill your parents.

JULIA: Please don't.

BERNARDO: Why not. And give me a reason I can understand.

JULIA: They're dreadful people. You would only be putting them out of their misery.

BERNARDO: Not bad. That's interesting. So there is something else behind that civilized smile. I'll be back.

JULIA: If you leave me alone I'll scream until someone finds me.

BERNARDO: *(walking to her)* You shouldn't have said that. That was a mistake.

BERNARDO hits JULIA. She falls, unconscious. He unlocks the chain.

She doesn't need these now. And I might have to use them. *(sadly)* I might want to use them. I might love to use them.

He leaves. In another corner of the set VICTOR comes on carrying the unconscious VEREZZI on his shoulders. He takes him into a chamber, puts him down and examines his head.

VICTOR: Perhaps I hit you too hard. You're barely breathing. Well, you were doomed anyway. At least this way you have a chance. *(looking around)* This place is horrible. But he'll be safe here I suppose. *(sitting)* Now what am I to

do. The only way I can get him to run is to keep him unconscious and that's just not practical. I could leave him here and forget the whole matter. That's practical. Leave him here! Forget the whole matter! That's practical! But I did make that promise. And it's the only promise I've ever kept. I certainly didn't keep my promise to God. But I don't feel so bad about that, having met this Zastrozzi. If he is one of God's creatures then God must be used to disappointment. On the other hand, I just don't like the man. Everything he does, everything he represents unsettles me to the bone. Zastrozzi decides that an artist must be judged by someone so he kills him. Zastrozzi is to blame for his own mother's death in a crime of passion but hounds a poor lunatic because he cannot accept the blame himself. Zastrozzi steals, violates and murders on a regular basis, and remains perfectly sane. Verezzi commits one crime of passion then goes on a binge of mindless religious love and becomes moronic. Something is wrong. Something is unbalanced. I abhor violence. But I also abhor a lack of balance. It shows that the truth is missing somewhere. And it makes me feel very, very uneasy. Uneasy in a way I have not felt since I was ... Yes, Verezzi, I will restore a truth to your lunatic mind and your lunatic world. *(taking VEREZZI's sword)* Zastrozzi.

VICTOR exits. JULIA groans, she slowly regains consciousness and gets up. She makes her way around the dungeon, sees VEREZZI and goes to him. She kneels down and takes his pulse.

JULIA: What's happening to me. I go for a series of walks in the street. Smile at two young men. One of them tells me he is a visionary. The other one abducts me and tells me he is going to rape and murder me, not necessarily in that order. Then he hits me like he would a man and knocks me unconscious. I wake up and find the young man who thinks he is a visionary lying on the ground bleeding to death from a head wound. What's happening to me.

MATILDA enters.

MATILDA: You must be the virgin. The one with the marvellous, gentle sensuality.

JULIA: Who are you.

MATILDA: My name is Matilda. I am your competition. I have a sensuality which is not the least bit gentle.

JULIA: Really. What do you want.

MATILDA: I want to kill all the virgins in the world.

JULIA: Oh no. What's happening to me.

MATILDA: Unfortunately for you, we are both in love with the same man.

JULIA: *(pointing to VEREZZI)* Him? I don't love him. I don't even like him.

MATILDA: Not him. Zastrozzi.

JULIA: I've heard of him. He's the one who is whispered about in polite society.

MATILDA: He is the evil genius of all Europe. A criminal. And I am a criminal too. We belong together. So we must fight and I must kill you.

JULIA: Why can't I just leave.

MATILDA: That won't do. Besides, I will enjoy killing you. It is women like you who make me look like a tart.

JULIA: Nonsense. It's the way you dress.

MATILDA: Stand up, you mindless virgin.

JULIA: *(standing)* Madame, I am neither mindless nor a virgin. I am merely a victim of bizarre circumstance. A product of healthy civilization thrown into a jungle of the deranged.

MATILDA: Yes, get angry. You are better when you are angry. If I were a man I would seduce you on the spot.

JULIA: That's perverse!

MATILDA takes a knife from under her skirts.

MATILDA: Yes, get indignant. You are quite provocative when you are upset. Take off your clothes.

JULIA: Why.

MATILDA: We are going to make love.

JULIA: Oh no, we are not.

MATILDA: Yes, get confused. You are quite ridiculous when you are confused. And it is exactly the way someone like you should die. *(advances)*

JULIA: What are you doing.

MATILDA: We are going to fight. And we are only going to stop fighting when one of us is dead.

JULIA: I would rather not. I would rather discuss some other possibility. I'm only seventeen years old. People tell me I have so much to live for.

MATILDA: Oh. Name something worth living for and I might spare your life.

JULIA: But how could I. A woman like you could never appreciate what I think is worth living for. No offence. But take your dress for example. I would live to dress much better than that.

MATILDA: You mindless, coy, disgusting virgin!

MATILDA attacks and they struggle. The knife falls and JULIA scrambles after it. MATILDA leaps on her and somehow MATILDA is stabbed. She falls over dead. JULIA feels her pulse.

JULIA: Dead. Oh my God. *(standing)* What is happening to me. First a victim. Now a murderer! And I don't even know her. This is grossly unfair. I'm young. I've had the proper education. My future was a pleasant rosy colour. I could see it in my head. It was a rosy colour. Very pretty. This is truly grossly unfair.

BERNARDO comes in. He sees MATILDA's body and rushes to it.

BERNARDO: You killed her.

JULIA: I had no choice. She attacked me.

BERNARDO: She was the only woman I could have been in love with on the right terms. You have blocked out my future.

JULIA: I'm sorry. But she didn't love you anyway. She loved that Zastrozzi.

BERNARDO: You have closed off my life from my brain. It is exploding!

JULIA: Well, if you'll pardon me expressing an opinion, I think she was not entirely a rational person. Not at all the kind of person you need. You are not a rational person either and you would be better off with someone who could tame your tendency towards violence. If you'll pardon my opinion, I mean.

BERNARDO approaches her.

JULIA: What are you going to do.

BERNARDO: Stay still.

JULIA: *(backing away)* No. This isn't fair. I shouldn't be involved in any of this. I didn't love him. I didn't hate her. I've only a strange and vague recollection of this Zastrozzi. And all I did was smile at you.

BERNARDO: Stay very still.

JULIA: Please.

BERNARDO strangles her. ZASTROZZI appears out of the darkness.

ZASTROZZI: Bernardo.

BERNARDO drops JULIA, who falls to the floor lifeless. He turns to face ZASTROZZI.

Another victim, Bernardo?

BERNARDO: She murdered Matilda.

ZASTROZZI: She was merely defending herself.

BERNARDO: You saw?

ZASTROZZI: I have been here for hours.

BERNARDO: Why didn't you do something.

ZASTROZZI: I was preoccupied.

BERNARDO: Matilda is dead.

ZASTROZZI: I didn't know you had such deep feelings for her.

BERNARDO: It wouldn't have mattered to you. You only have one thought. Well, there he is. Verezzi the Italian. Take him. I am going to bury Matilda.

ZASTROZZI: Verezzi will wait. You are not going anywhere. You have to face your judgement.

BERNARDO: It will come.

ZASTROZZI: It has.

BERNARDO: From you?

ZASTROZZI: Is there anyone better at it.

BERNARDO: Judgement for what exactly.

ZASTROZZI: For all your crimes. All the people you have murdered have spoken to me in my nightmares and asked that you be made answerable.

BERNARDO: I am just a student to the master.

ZASTROZZI: And only the master is qualified to judge. Draw your sword, Bernardo. Let us have the formality of a contest. But know now that you are dead.

BERNARDO: Sir. Let me go.

ZASTROZZI: No.

ZASTROZZI draws his sword. BERNARDO draws his. They fight. Viciously. Expertly. BERNARDO is good. ZASTROZZI is the master though, and eventually he pierces BERNARDO's chest. BERNARDO drops to his knees.

BERNARDO: Sir.

ZASTROZZI: You are dead.

ZASTROZZI knocks BERNARDO over with his foot. BERNARDO is dead. ZASTROZZI walks over to VEREZZI and stands silently looking down at him for a while, then sits down and cradles VEREZZI's head.

Verezzi. Finally. Not dying at all. It's just a flesh wound. Your breathing becomes stronger. Soon you will wake up. I want you to be awake for this. It would have been more satisfying to have you destroy yourself. But you are too clever for that. Everyone thinks you are out of your mind. But I know you have just been hiding. Hiding from your crimes, Verezzi. Hiding from the crime of telling people you are giving them gifts from God. The crime of letting them think there is happiness in that stupid smile of yours. The crime of making language pleasantly vague and painting with distorted imagination. The crime of disturbing the natural condition in which the dark side prevails. Wake up, Verezzi. Zastrozzi is here to prove that you must be judged. You can hide no more.

A VOICE : And what is Zastrozzi hiding from.

ZASTROZZI stands.

ZASTROZZI: What do you want.

VICTOR comes out of the darkness carrying VEREZZI's sabre.

VICTOR: Sir. Tell me. What is this about. *(looking around)* All this death.

ZASTROZZI: It is a continuing process of simplification. I am simplifying my life. These people came here to be judged.

VICTOR: By you?

ZASTROZZI: Is there anyone better at it.

VICTOR: Apparently not. Well then, I too want to be judged by Zastrozzi, who judges for a profession.

ZASTROZZI: Then step closer.

VICTOR: Is there a fee.

ZASTROZZI: Yes. But I take it from you quickly. You'll never even know it's gone.

VICTOR: I have another idea. I think a man who enjoys his profession as much as you should be the one to pay the fee.

ZASTROZZI: Perhaps. But I have never met anyone who would collect from me.

VICTOR: You have now, sir.

ZASTROZZI: I doubt it very much. You don't even hold your weapon properly.

VICTOR: I have an unorthodox style. But it serves.

ZASTROZZI: Let's see.

He draws his sword. VICTOR begins a short prayer in Latin which ZASTROZZI finishes for him. VICTOR looks at ZASTROZZI. Pause.

ZASTROZZI: *(in German)* Did you not know that I could see into your heart.

VICTOR: *(in any Romance language)* Yes. But I can see into your heart as well.

ZASTROZZI: *(in the same Romance language)* Then it will be an interesting battle.

Pause.

VICTOR: So.

ZASTROZZI: So.

They approach each other, cross swords and begin to fight. The fight will continue and move across the entire stage at least once.

ZASTROZZI tests VICTOR. He responds well but his moves are very unusual. VICTOR will gradually get better by observing ZASTROZZI's moves.

ZASTROZZI: What are all these strange things you are doing designed for.

VICTOR: To keep me alive.

ZASTROZZI: Eventually I will find a way to penetrate your unorthodox style.

VICTOR: That might be difficult. Since I am making it up as I go along.

ZASTROZZI: You look silly.

VICTOR: But I am alive.

ZASTROZZI: Perhaps more alive than you have ever been. That is sometimes the way a person faces death.

VICTOR: I intend to live.

ZASTROZZI: Then you should have taken my advice and become an ordinary man.

VICTOR: Sir. The point is that I *am* an ordinary man.

ZASTROZZI: An ordinary man does not challenge Zastrozzi.

ZASTROZZI attacks him viciously. VICTOR defends himself well.

VICTOR: I am still alive. I am still waiting to be judged.

ZASTROZZI: And growing arrogant as well.

VICTOR: You talk about arrogance. The man who kills on a whim. Who kills an artist simply because he is mediocre. Who commits crimes against people because he believes he is the thing to which they must be answerable.

ZASTROZZI: They must be answerable to something.

VICTOR: There is always God, you know.

ZASTROZZI: I am an atheist. If a man who is an atheist believes that people must be answerable, he has a duty to make them answerable to something.

VICTOR: Answerable to your own demented personality.

ZASTROZZI: I am what they are. They answer to themselves.

VICTOR: All right, forget God. A man is responsible to humanity.

ZASTROZZI: And I am part of humanity.

VICTOR: The irresponsible part.

ZASTROZZI: No. It is my responsibility to spread out like a disease and purge. And by destroying everything make everything safe.

VICTOR: Explain exactly what you mean by safe.

ZASTROZZI: Alive. Untouched by expectation. Free of history. Free of religion. Free of everything. And soon to be free of you.

ZASTROZZI attacks and VICTOR defends himself very well.

VICTOR: I am still alive.

ZASTROZZI: But you are totally on the defensive.

VICTOR: I don't have to kill you. I only have to survive. By merely surviving I neutralize you.

ZASTROZZI: You cannot neutralize something you do not understand.

VICTOR: We are approaching a new century, and with it a new world. There will be no place in it for your attitude, your behaviour.

ZASTROZZI: This new world, what do you suppose it will be like.

VICTOR: Better.

ZASTROZZI: Describe what you mean by better.

VICTOR: More humane. More civilized.

ZASTROZZI: Wrong. Better is when the truth is understood. Understanding the truth is understanding that the force of darkness is constant.

VICTOR: No, it is not. Your time is over.

ZASTROZZI: Wrong again.

ZASTROZZI attacks him viciously. VICTOR defends himself and is ebullient.

VICTOR: I am alive! Everything I said was true. You are neutralized. I am the emissary of goodness in the battle between good and evil. I have found God again.

VICTOR lunges forward wildly.

ZASTROZZI plunges his sabre through VICTOR's heart.

VICTOR: I am alive.

VICTOR falls down and dies.

ZASTROZZI: Ah, Victor. You understood what was in your heart. But you did not know your limitations.

ZASTROZZI throws down his sabre. VEREZZI groans and slowly wakes up. He sits, then stands, while ZASTROZZI watches him. VEREZZI staggers around looking at the bodies and slowly regaining his equilibrium.

VEREZZI: Look at all these dead people. What happened.

ZASTROZZI: A series of unfortunate accidents.

VEREZZI: Who are you.

ZASTROZZI: Zastrozzi.

VEREZZI freezes.

VEREZZI: I thought you didn't exist.

ZASTROZZI: Nonsense. You know me well.

VEREZZI: Are you responsible for all these dead people.

ZASTROZZI: No. You are.

VEREZZI: That's quite impossible. I am a servant of God.

ZASTROZZI: You are dead.

ZASTROZZI has drawn a knife.

VEREZZI: What are you going to do.

ZASTROZZI: Cut open your stomach.

VEREZZI: You can't. I'm immune. I am in touch with Him. Protected by Him. Loved by Him.

VEREZZI closes his eyes. ZASTROZZI approaches him.

VEREZZI: You can't hurt me. I'll just wait here. Nothing will happen.

ZASTROZZI: Do you feel anything.

VEREZZI: Yes.

ZASTROZZI: Do you feel fear.

VEREZZI: Yes.

ZASTROZZI: Now who am I.

VEREZZI: Zastrozzi.

ZASTROZZI: And what is Zastrozzi.

VEREZZI: The devil.

ZASTROZZI: Nonsense. What is he.

VEREZZI: A man.

ZASTROZZI: What kind of man.

VEREZZI: I don't know.

ZASTROZZI: A sane man. What kind of man.

VEREZZI: A sane man.

ZASTROZZI: And what kind of man are you.

VEREZZI: I don't know.

ZASTROZZI: You feel fear when you are about to be murdered. And you are no longer smiling. You are a sane man too. From this moment on and forever. Do you understand. Perfectly sane and very, very afraid.

VEREZZI: Yes.

ZASTROZZI: Now get going.

VEREZZI: Where.

ZASTROZZI: You have to hide. I am giving you a day and I am coming after you. And do you know why I am coming after you.

VEREZZI: No.

ZASTROZZI: Because it will keep me preoccupied. Now leave. And hide well. I wish to be preoccupied for a long time.

VEREZZI slowly leaves. ZASTROZZI looks at all the corpses.

(smiling) I like it here. Sad. No. I like it here. *(He takes a cape off one of the corpses and wraps himself with it.)* I think I'll visit here again. It will help me stay sane.

Pause.

Yes. I like it here.

Blackout.

End

JOHN GRAY
(b. 1946)
with ERIC PETERSON
(b. 1946)

In a theatrical context the term "musical" has traditionally evoked visions of Broadway extravaganzas like *Oklahoma* or *Annie*. In the 1980s and '90s the "megamusical" gained ascendancy—*Les Miserables, The Phantom of the Opera*—big-budget spectacles mass-marketed on an international scale. But with the exception of hybrid megamusicals like *Kiss of the Spider Woman*, the musical tradition in Canadian theatre has been more modest and generally more off-beat, encompassing *Anne of Green Gables*, the satirical *Spring Thaw*, the sociological *Ten Lost Years*, and *Cruel Tears*, Ken Mitchell's country and western adaptation of *Othello* set in Saskatchewan. One of the dominant figures in Canadian musical drama has been John Gray. As writer, composer, director and performer, Gray has created literate and immensely entertaining plays that bridge the gap between "legitimate" theatre and the musical. By any criteria *Billy Bishop Goes to War* is one of the most successful Canadian plays ever written.

Gray was born in Ottawa and grew up in Truro, Nova Scotia, one of three brothers who all became professional musicians. From 1965–68 while attending Mount Allison University, he played organ and trumpet with The Lincolns, a local rock'n'roll band. After graduating in 1968 with a B.A. in English, Gray headed for Vancouver where he studied directing at the University of British Columbia, emerging in 1971 with an M.A. in theatre. Over the next four years, as a founding member of Tamahnous Theatre, he directed eight of the plays that established Tamahnous as one of the most exciting experimental companies in the country. Gray moved to Toronto in 1975, joining Theatre Passe Muraille as a composer and sometime director. From 1975–77 he wrote music for a half dozen Passe Muraille shows including *1837: The Farmers' Revolt*.

Gray's first play, *18 Wheels*, was produced by Passe Muraille and then Tamahnous in 1977 under his own direction. Its all-night truckers and truck-stop waitress tell their stories in country and western song. With its simple set, witty lyrics, affection for the ordinary guy, and keen sense of Canadian identity, *18 Wheels* established Gray's musical and dramatic signature, including its dark existential streak. The trucker, like Billy Bishop, rides out alone, "Where the night is all around, as thick as clay,/ And death is riding shotgun all the way."

Billy Bishop Goes to War made its first appearance in November 1978, co-produced by the Vancouver East Cultural Centre (VECC) and Tamahnous, after a workshop earlier in the year at Passe Muraille. Its genesis goes back to 1971 when Gray and Eric Peterson first met. Peterson, Saskatchewan-born, had spent two years in British repertory theatre before arriving on the West Coast. After two years with Tamahnous he preceded Gray to Toronto in 1973 and quickly gained a reputation as one of Passe Muraille's most imaginative actors, playing, among other parts, Mackenzie and Lady Backwash in *1837*. It was Peterson who discovered Bishop's autobiography, *Winged Warfare*, in 1976, and co-researched the show with Gray over the next two years. Though Gray is the writer of record, Peterson's skilled character development and virtuoso acting have been essential ingredients in the play's success (and in his own subsequent success, most publically as one of the lead characters in the long-running CBC-TV series *Street Legal*).

After their initial Vancouver run, Gray and Peterson took *Billy Bishop Goes to War* on a sixteen-month Canadian tour. Then in 1980, with Mike Nichols as co-producer, they opened in Washington as a prelude to four months on and off Broadway where Peterson won the Clarence Derwent Award for Most Promising Actor in the New York theatre. Later that year the show went to the Edinburgh Festival, then to Los Angeles where it won both Best Play and Best Actor awards. The published play won the 1982 Governor General's Award for Drama. In 1998 Gray and Peterson, both just having turned 50, toured Canada in a highly acclaimed twentieth anniversary production, revised to frame the original play as the now 50-year-old Bishop's retrospective look at his own story. (The revised version is published in the single-play Talonbooks edition. This anthology retains the original script.)

Gray's third consecutive hit musical, *Rock and Roll*, opened under his own direction in 1981, co-produced by the VECC and National Arts Centre. In this semi-autobiographical play about a '60s Nova Scotia dance band, Gray once again tells an exuberant comic tale of small-town Canadian boys who look back slightly disillusioned and nostalgic at their coming of age. The play won the 1988 Canadian Authors' Association Literary Award for Drama. Two children's plays followed *Rock and Roll*: *Bongo from the Congo* (with Eric Peterson) and *Balthazar and the Mojo Star*. Halifax's Neptune Theatre has since premiered Gray's only non-musical, *Better Watch Out, Better Not Die* (1983), a farcical thriller, and *Don Messer's Jubilee* (1985), Gray's homage to the legendary Maritime folk band and his fourth successive musical smash. *18 Wheels*, *Rock and Roll* and *Don Messer's Jubilee* were published together in 1987 under the title *Local Boy Makes Good*. A paean to the pains and lusts of the middle-aged male body, *Health, The Musical* (1989) premiered at the Vancouver Playhouse, starring Eric Peterson. Gray returned to the skies in 1993 with *Amelia!*, a musical about Amelia Earhart, co-produced by Vancouver's Carousel Theatre and the National Arts Centre. CBC Radio produced *The Tree, the Tower, the Flood*, a musical about the Creation, in 1997.

In 1984, Gray scripted and co-directed a prize-winning television version of *Rock and Roll* titled *The King of Friday Night*, and published his first novel, *Dazzled*, a comic saga about growing up absurd in the '70s. He wrote and performed satirical music videos for CBC-TV's *The Journal* from 1987 to 1990, and wrote the screenplay for the feature film *Kootenay Brown* (1990). His eclectic publications include an irreverent history of tattooing titled *I Love Mom* (1995) and a collection of essays on Canadian culture, *Lost in North America* (1995). His second novel, *A Gift for the Little Master*, was published in 2000. Gray's columns for *West* Magazine won a number of awards. A resident of Vancouver, he has also written weekly newspaper columns for the *Vancouver Sun* and the *Globe and Mail*.

Billy Bishop Goes to War is first and foremost a *tour de force* for one actor. Apart from the Narrator/Pianist who provides mostly musical support, the actor playing Bishop is alone on stage telling his story, doing all the other characters without changes of costume or makeup, and nearly all the sound effects (the Pianist does the rest). He works on a bare set except for the piano, and is equipped with a minimum of props. Perhaps the essence of the play is to be found in the extraordinary scene where Bishop describes his first solo flight, accompanying his narrative with his own vocal effects and (in the original production) only a hand-held model airplane for illustration. This is theatre pared down to its essentials: a skilled actor on a bare stage creating a world before our eyes. As always, *reading* the play demands an imaginative reconstruction on the reader's part.

Hearing *Billy Bishop Goes to War* makes one aware of the subtle modulations of tone effected by Gray's music and songs. Most of the criticism directed at the play concerns Bishop's attitude towards war and his own part in it, as well as the play's attitude towards Bishop. Does Gray celebrate war by glamourizing Bishop and his bloodlust, or trivialize war by showing it as a game? Does Bishop have any doubts about his own cold-bloodedness? Gray insists in his preface that the play "does not address itself to the issue of whether or not war is a good thing or a bad thing." But colouring Bishop's ascendancy to the status of war hero is the terrific melancholy of the opening song in Act One, "We Were Off to Fight the Hun," which resonates through the play, belying his naive idea that war would be "lots of fun." Many of the songs share that tone. The play's most beautiful song, "In the Sky," is as much a poignant lament as a romantic celebration of aerial warfare; and "Friends Ain't S'posed to Die" makes blatant, in melody and lyrics, the shame Bishop felt in surviving when "most of us never got old."

Of course there are also the spirited anthems that reflect Bishop's joy in his work. He did love flying and he makes us share in his exhilaration. But he came to love killing, too. We watch the comic innocent of Act One develop into the icy professional of Act Two who stays "as calm as the ocean" and goes up even on his days off because he likes it so much. Gray never allows Bishop to be totally unconscious of the ironies in his situation. The fact that the "Survival" song at the top of Act Two is sung by Bishop in the voice of a French chanteuse, "the Lovely Hélène," gives it an edge of self-mockery; maybe Bishop is even a little embarrassed about his new-found cynicism. "The Dying of Albert Ball" is Bishop's indirect response to his manipulation by Lady St. Helier and the rest of the British ruling class who "like their heroes / Cold and dead." Finally, the rousing "Empire Soirée" provides a bitter counterpoint to the celebrations of victory. The personal heroism and sacrifice of the brave men dancing and dying in the sky is superceded by the pointless and impersonal "dance of history" as one war is followed by another.

"Makes you wonder what it was all for," Bishop mutters in 1941. Though he is not a very introspective man, he is far from blind to the insanity of war. His visions of No Man's Land and of the two German flyers falling out of their plane are among the most chilling moments in the Canadian theatre. But ultimately, Billy Bishop's reminiscence is not so much about his experience of horror and death as it is about being young and the most intensely alive he ever felt. "One thing's for sure," he sings. "We'll never be that young again." He sings not only for himself but for a world that would never be the same.

Billy Bishop Goes to War opened on November 3, 1978, at the Vancouver East Cultural Centre, produced by the Vancouver East Cultural Centre in association with Tamahnous Theatre.

BILLY BISHOP	Eric Peterson
NARRATOR/PIANIST	John Gray

Directed by John Gray
Set and Lighting Design by Paul Williams
Music and Lyrics by John Gray

BILLY BISHOP GOES TO WAR

PREFACE

Billy Bishop Goes to War was born out of a nasty case of the Three B's of Canadian Theatre—Broke, Bored and Branded. Broke, because it was 1976 and there was not much work. Beating a trail from one one-hundred seat theatre to another is the usual lot of the Canadian theatre artist. Consequently, he is always broke. Bored, because our leaders, the Old Warriors of Canadian Nationalism, were in a rut. Audiences were getting ugly and scarce. But being Broke and Bored did not prevent us from being Branded as Canadian Nationalists, and therefore unfit for the more cosmopolitan world of the Regional Theatres. And so, we came full circle again, back to Broke—and the landlord turns off the heat.

It was at this time that Eric Peterson lent me a book called *Winged Warfare*. We were in Ottawa at the time, performing for Theatre Passe Muraille. Ottawa is one of the few Canadian cities in which the all-Canadian bookstore is a major entertainment resource. *Winged Warfare* was written by a twenty-one-year-old pilot named Billy Bishop and it contained a cool account of his first six kills during World War I. A little research indicated that before the war was over, he had upped his total to seventy-two. As representatives of a generation of Canadians who had never been anywhere near a war, we regarded the man with apprehension and curiosity. Was he a homicidal maniac? What was going on in that war? What was it like to be a Canadian then? Why were more top aces Canadian than any other nationality? As citizens of a relatively pacifist country, what was it about our nature that made us bold and daring whenever we became involved in a foreign war? What did all this have to do with our colonial heritage, our sense of inadequacy when it comes to our position in the English-speaking world? What was the experience of two generations before us whose lives were defined and shaped by war? Eric and I talked about these things for about a year in our favourite snooker halls and beer parlours—in between trips to the Military Archives to do research.

In January, 1978, I started writing and by March, I had a draft of a play that was almost as long as the war itself. Eric read it and approved. The Old Warriors of Canadian Nationalism read it. They approved. Theatre Passe Muraille gave us some workshop money, and Tamahnous Theatre got a commitment from the Vancouver East Cultural Centre for a production in the fall. With dreams of steady employment to inspire us, we set to work.

One choice we made: *Billy Bishop* would take its narrative form from a phenomenon I noticed while playing the barn circuit of Southwestern Ontario. Playing on stages where you had to kick the cowpies aside while crossing the boards, I noticed that Canadians don't much like listening in on other people's conversations. They think it's impolite. This plays havoc with the basic convention of theatre itself, so what do you do? Well, you drop the fourth wall and you simply talk to the audience. They tend to relax a bit because they are in an arena whose aesthetics they understand: the arena of the storyteller. A dogfight can be a tricky number to stage, and the sky is a hard thing to evoke with a roof over your head. But to a good storyteller anything is possible, and Eric is a wonderful storyteller.

Another choice: only two of us would do it. Eric would play all the parts and I would play the music; Eric would be the mouth and I would be the hands. That way, we got to keep all the money. Besides, one-man shows were all the rage in those days, times being what they were.

Billy Bishop Goes to War opened in Vancouver around Remembrance Day in 1978. The fact that there was a newspaper and a postal strike on didn't make November the best month for a premiere, but response was good and we were held over for two weeks. We seemed to have tapped a well of experience that had been hidden for years. Veterans from both wars came backstage to tell us stories, to talk about the ironic position of being a colonial in a British war; to express their ambivalence about their own survival in a war where so many of their friends died. This response was a source of tremendous relief to Eric and me. Our one fear was that someone would come backstage and say to us, "You're wrong. You got it all wrong. That's not the way it was at all."

Sometime during the holdover in Vancouver, a tall stranger came backstage. He was an American and he was smoking a cigar. He wore a sheepskin coat, had grey hair and the smile of a country doctor. His name was Lewis Allen. He was a producer; then, the co-producer of *Annie*. *Annie* was making the profit of an oil sheikdom at the time and he said that he thought *Billy Bishop* deserved to go to Broadway too. He would get his partner Mike Nichols to look at it. That's a good one, we thought. We entertained the fantasy for a few minutes, then left for the bar and forgot all about it.

We were feeling good. The Cultural Centre had arranged a two-week run in Saskatoon, a tour of Southwestern Ontario and a run at Theatre Passe Muraille. Even the Regional Theatres were beginning to nibble. We might work until the spring. Maybe buy a car. We were as happy in December of 1978 as any Canadian theatre artist can be. We had work, we had a show that didn't bore us; we had audiences who wanted to see our play, who gave us standing ovations. We were being paid.

Touring Canada in mid-winter, one encounters a lot of snow. A lot of snow and a lot of viruses. Every acting school in the country should teach a course entitled "Performing While Sick" because their students are going to be doing a lot of that. In Saskatoon, we learned how to perform with a bad cold. In Owen Sound, it was the flu. In Listowel, Ontario, it all came together in a kind of winter fugue. Eric had the flu; I had a cold—and there was a blizzard so bad that traffic from Kitchener had been stopped. This meant that the risers which the audience were to sit on didn't arrive, nor did the stage. And we were performing in an old railway station. We looked bad. That is, we looked bad if you could see us at all. Watching the show was like trying to get a peek at the scene of an accident. Those who did get a glimpse recoiled at the sight of two broken men croaking their way through a play, accompanied by a piano with six important keys missing. It was an evening to remember. But we got through the show. Once you're out there, it seems there's no alternative, so you go on. The audience applauded sympathetically and left. We collapsed backstage, calling for the antibiotics we had come to know and love.

In walked Mike Nichols. How he had got from New York to Listowel in a blinding snowstorm was a mystery to us. Perhaps he hired a personal snowplough. But there he was, looking just like he did on the cover of *Time*. He said that he liked the show. He said that he intended to bring it to New York. When he left, the snow swirled around his Vicuna coat like fog around a genie. We stared after him, wondering if the fever was worse than we thought. But Mike left something behind with us: the idea that we might become rich and famous. It was winter. It was Canada. What were the odds?

In theory, we all belittle the coarser rewards of life, but it's usually sour grapes. When the prospects of riches and fame are actually dangled in front of us, we are in there like rats up a drainpipe. I've seen New York or Hollywood bring on many a pair of sunglasses in my life. We were no exception. Visions of limousines, handsome West Side suites, Piaget watches, dinners at Elaine's and smart Italian suits came to mind. Before you pass judgement, let's face it, most of us get into theatre for childish, silly reasons. You start out thinking that being in the theatre will make you an interesting person. I myself got interested in the theatre in the belief that women there would be looser than the general female populace. But after you have been working for a while, you find yourself just as boring as ever and your chances of scoring remain the same. So you replace an improbability with a complete absurdity: you dream about becoming a star. It is a rare person who knows that working in the theatre will not make you anything other than what you already are. And so you plod on, hoping against hope that one morning you'll wake up, read the reviews and realize that you've become glamorous and witty and cosmopolitan and rich. And you accomplish little, because when a dream of *being* takes hold, there is little room for thoughts of *doing*.

By the time we hit Toronto, we had become Top of the Pops. It's really amazing the extent to which Yankee acceptance affects Canadian prestige. Suddenly, *Billy Bishop* had become the show that Mike Nichols liked. This was the Canadian show that was going to Broadway. Overnight, a modest little work by and for Canadians had become a Hot Property. Newspaper articles, reviews, interviews all centred around the fact that we were going to Broadway. Were we excited? Would our play be a hit? Would it fail? How would we feel if it failed? There was never a word about the show itself; no interest in what it meant, what it was trying to say about war, about heroes, about Canada, about life. All that mattered was that we were going to Broadway. Would it make us rich and famous? It was as if we'd suddenly switched careers. We were no longer Canadian performers. We were athletes on our way to the Olympics. Would we win or lose? Would we cure or confirm the National Inferiority Complex?

Canadians have long existed with the suspicion that we have something missing in our chromosomal make-up when it comes to art; that there is some wishy-washy component in our gene structure that makes us incapable of strong artistic statement. This is our colonial heritage at work. We export natural resources and we import culture. This is our lot in life. When a Canadian work goes abroad, it is a little like an Indian running for Prime Minister. Our cultural inadequacy makes the odds for success rather long.

Still, I must say, the whole thing was very good for business. Interest from the Regional Theatres blossomed. Neither Eric nor I had worked in a Regional Theatre before. A tour of Regional Theatres was arranged for the following fall and winter. You see, government cutbacks and the demand for more Canadian plays had come at the same time. And what could be cheaper than a Canadian play with two actors? Then we were to go to Washington, D.C., for a tryout at the Arena Stage. Then we were to go to Broadway. Over a year's worth of work for us; we who had never run a show for more than six weeks of our lives. And a carrot on the end of the stick as well: New York.

I don't want to appear ungrateful for the opportunities that were presented to us, but we really weren't ready for this. We had barely got used to the idea of steady work when suddenly we were an international property with Canada's theatrical self-esteem in our care. For us, the future was full of peril. Terrible images came to mind: an anvil suspended above our heads ready to fall at any moment. We were like straight men in some monstrous slapstick comedy, for if there is such a thing as success, then there must be the opposite. Would we be heroes—or would we be bums? In the world in which we found ourselves, there was no middle ground, for Canadians reserve their greatest contempt for artists who fail abroad.

However, one adapts. One evolves. Some new plumage; an extra toe, but you cope. And cope we did—on a six months tour of the Regionals where we were to find what we had been missing all those years: the audience that goes to a hit show because it's the thing to do. It's a souvenir hunt. The fact that you saw such and such will make wonderful dinner conversation for days to come. "I saw *Billy Bishop Goes to War*. It's going to Broadway, you know."

The winter went by. We played Ottawa, Montreal, Halifax, Kingston, Hamilton, Kitchener, London, St. Catharines, Edmonton and Calgary. More snow fell on our heads; more viruses passed through our systems. Perhaps human beings were invented to transport viruses from one place to the next? Then there were the interviews. How does it feel to be a success? What's it like to be finally working in the big time? We never told them the truth. It wasn't newsworthy. We were being educated and education is expensive. We were learning that there was no such thing as easy money; we were learning just what kind of a meatgrinder you had to go through to get your sausage.

In March, 1980, we headed for the Arena Stage in Washington, D.C. Mike Nichols filled us in on the difference between the Canadian and the American aesthetic. To begin with, our little set with its roll drop and miniature plane simply would not do. For Canadians, this set gave the play a comic and human perspective in keeping with the hero. For Americans, the set was puny. When your American spectator pays upwards of twenty bucks a ticket, he wants to see equally conspicuous consumption on the part of the play. Our toy plane became a full-sized plane. The roll drop went and was replaced by a hydraulic lift, a smoke machine and triple the number of lighting instruments. Instead of forty thousand dollars, the budget was now three hundred thousand dollars. But we were still a modest little show.

We opened well. We received raves from the Baltimore and Washington papers, and, wonder of wonders, from *The New York Times*. Success seemed near at hand. However, we wondered just what it was audiences were seeing when they saw the show. I mean, these were Americans we were playing to, not Canadians. The difference between the two audiences was never so apparent as the night we were sitting in our underwear after the show when in walked the heads of the F.B.I., the C.I.A., the Joint Chiefs of Staff, the Air Force, along with Hodding Carter, the President's Press Secretary. These guys can make you feel real small, particularly when you're half naked. In any case, they pumped our hands, slapped our backs and said that they loved the show—without reservation. This gave us pause. We had been hoping for a little more appreciation of irony, but Americans, it seems, aren't into irony. In America, when you address a subject such as War, you're either for it or agin it. And when your hero is a military man, he is either a good guy or a bad guy. So when it came to *Billy Bishop*, which does not address itself to the issue of whether or not war is a good thing or a bad thing, we became pro-war by default. As a result, to the liberal press, we were bad guys, a disturbing harbinger of violent things to come. And to the conservative press, we were good guys, reassessing the military man without simplistic sixties judgements. Because popular mythology at the time had it that America was turning right, it was thought that we had hit just the right note for the times. For us, we were never sure whether or not we had hit the note that we wanted to hit. This was our first encounter with the American penchant for obscuring an issue by simplifying it beyond belief. As Canadians who tend to be paralyzed by the complications of life, we found all this a little strange.

But then again, who really cares about the content? How many people leave a play asking what it meant? Isn't it more important whether or not it was fun, whether or not it was skillfully produced, whether or not it was a hit, whether or not it was going to make its participants rich and famous? With no serious discussion of content among either audiences or press, an artist finds himself in a vacuum where ideas have no power. In a society where ideas are effectively robbed of their power, either by disinterest, greed, ignorance or decadence, an artist abandons the pursuit of an idea in favour of the pursuit of money. He is woven into the fabric of the capitalist system. By the time we reached New York, our little play, despite its original meaning, had become an expression of our desire to become rich and famous. *Billy Bishop Goes to War* had become an expression of the American Dream.

A Canadian never feels more Canadian than when he is in the United States. These two Canadians were beginning to weary of the American Dream. In fact, we had taken to flying to Canada for a few days now and then, like divers coming up for air. And, to continue the metaphor, it seemed we were in a whirlpool that began to spin faster and faster. We were introduced to a great many rich and famous people in those months and we learned something about them. First of all, rich and famous people tend to come in pairs. The only way a rich and famous person can *feel* rich and famous is by hanging around with other rich and famous people. Rich and famous people tend to be very frightened of *not* being rich and famous. They are constantly looking over their shoulders to see if their riches and fame have decreased any. Another thing: only a certain number of people can be rich and famous. Somebody has to fail. The whole thing is now in perspective. In the search for riches and fame, you will either succeed or fail. If you fail, you will be disappointed. If you succeed, you will be frightened. Take your pick.

Billy Bishop Goes to War opened at the Morosco Theatre on May 29, 1980. It received a standing ovation and rave reviews from eighty percent of the critics. The party at Sardi's was a huge success, with glittering people everywhere, and Andy Warhol, the Samuel Pepys of Gotham, snapping Polaroids of everyone for posterity. When we walked back to our hotel at four o'clock in the morning, New York wasn't a city of filth, decay, bag ladies, derelicts and junkies. It was a magic city—a magic city where childish and greedy dreams come true.

The next morning, our producers were talking about closing the show. Nobody was buying tickets. "What happened?" the anguished Canadian press wanted to know. Was it a muddy review from the *Times?* Was it that the show was too small for the Broadway stage? Was the show not as good as we had thought? Was there really something missing from the Canadian chromosomal make-up? Were Canadians really inferior? Canadians take failure on Broadway much more seriously than Americans do. Americans know that hardly anything ever succeeds on Broadway— maybe about one show in a hundred. And we Canadians have put far less than one hundred shows on Broadway. It's a tremendous longshot. But this explanation is far too simplistic and pragmatic for the Canadian press. It doesn't address itself to the National Inferiority Complex. We still have interviewers asking, "What happened?" as though we were two runners who had failed to post their best times at the Olympics, and so had let their country down.

What had happened was that our American producers had made a miscalculation. They were betting that rave reviews and the name of Mike Nichols, tastemaker to Broadway, would be enough to draw the huge grosses that were necessary to survive on a Broadway stage. They had thought that if they loved a play, Americans would love a play—even a Canadian play. They were wrong. Of course, if *Billy Bishop* were a British play, the job of selling it would have been tough, but possible. America has long had a love-hate relationship with Britain. Britain is the country it fought to achieve its independence; it was the country it eventually replaced as muscleman of the Western World. And Americans have a National Inferiority Complex too. They are afraid that even with all their technological, financial and military achievements, they have still not become a civilized country. Americans are afraid they are Rome to Britain's Greece. And admiration, envy and fear can combine to make a British success in America possible.

But a Canadian play? Forget it! Americans don't want to see two unknown Canadians perform a play about an unknown Canadian war hero who fought in a war that America did not win. Not with *Barnum* across the street. How good the play was was irrelevant, as were the reviews and the awards. Americans simply weren't buying it. It took our producers a few months and an unprecedented move to off-Broadway, where we should probably have been to begin with, before they admitted defeat. Rich and Famous, those two sirens, were finally silent.

When we left New York in August for the Edinburgh Festival, which was another story entirely, our parting was amicable. We have friends in New York and Mike Nichols jokingly offers to misproduce anything I write. I sometimes think that education has more to do with the loss of illusions than with the acquisition of knowledge. If that is true, we received more education in four months in New York than in seven years at university. The tuition was high, but the school gave good value. Our experience in New York has given me the suspicion that, in fact, it may be better to give than to receive; that perhaps it is more difficult for a rich man to enter the kingdom of heaven. It seems that the greater our so-called international success became, the more we longed for audiences like those first few thousand souls who braved strikes, snow, viruses and lousy sightlines to see our little play about Billy Bishop. Perhaps theatre is a very simple activity in which a group of people get together to focus on what is best about ourselves …

Billy Bishop Goes to War is dedicated to all those who didn't come back from the war, and to those who did and wondered why.

John Gray

(1981)

BILLY BISHOP GOES TO WAR

CHARACTERS

NARRATOR/PIANIST

BILLY BISHOP, *who also plays*
    AN UPPERCLASSMAN
    ADJUTANT PERRAULT
    AN OFFICER
    SIR HUGH CECIL
    LADY ST. HELIER
    CEDRIC, *her butler*
    A DOCTOR
    GENERAL JOHN HIGGINS, *Brigade*
        Commander
    A TOMMY
    THE LOVELY HÉLÈNE
    ALBERT BALL
    WALTER BOURNE, *Bishop's mechanic*
    A GERMAN
    GENERAL HUGH M. TRENCHARD
    AN ADJUTANT
    SECOND OFFICER
    KING GEORGE V

ACT ONE

The lights come up slowly on BILLY BISHOP and the PIANO PLAYER, who sits at the piano. They are in an Officers' Mess.

BISHOP and PIANO PLAYER: *(singing)*
We were off to fight the Hun,
We would shoot him with a gun.
Our medals would shine
Like a sabre in the sun.
We were off to fight the Hun
And it looked like lots of fun,
Somehow it didn't seem like war
At all, at all, at all.
Somehow it didn't seem like war at all.

BILLY BISHOP speaks to the audience. He is a young man from Owen Sound, Ontario. His speech pattern is that of a small town Canadian boy who could well be squealing his tires down the main street of some town at this very moment.

BISHOP: *(to the audience)* I think when you haven't been in a war for a while, you've got to take what you can get. I mean, Canada, 1914?

They must have been pretty desperate. Take me, for instance. Twenty years old, a convicted liar and cheat. I mean, I'm on record as the worst student R.M.C. ... Royal Military College in Kingston, Ontario ... I'm on record as the worst student they ever had. I join up, they made me an officer, a lieutenant in the Mississauga Horse. All I can say is they must have been scraping the bottom of the barrel.

BISHOP and PIANO PLAYER: *(singing)*
We were off to fight the Hun,
Though hardly anyone
Had ever read about a battle,
Much less seen a Lewis gun.
We were off to fight the Hun
And it looked like lots of fun,
Somehow it didn't seem like war
At all, at all, at all.
Somehow it didn't seem like war at all.

BISHOP: *(to the audience)* Yeah, it looked like it was going to be a great war. I mean, all my friends were very keen to join up, they were. Not me. Royal Military College had been enough for me. Now the reason I went to R.M.C. is, well ... I could ride a horse. And I was a great shot. I mean, I am a really good shot. I've got these tremendous eyes, you see. And R.M.C. had an entrance exam and that was good because my previous scholastic record wasn't that hot. In fact, when I suggested to my principal that, indeed, I was going to R.M.C., he said, "Bishop, you don't have the brains." But I studied real hard, sat for the exams and got in.

He imitates an R.M.C. Officer.

Recruits! Recruits will march at all times. They will not loiter, they will not window shop. Recruits! Recruits will run at all times when in the parade square. Recruits! Recruits will be soundly trounced every Friday night, whether they deserve it or not.

As himself.

I mean, those guys were nuts! They were going to make leaders out of us, the theory being that before you could learn to lead, you had to learn to obey. So, because of this, we're all assigned to an upperclassman as a kind of, well … slave. And I was assigned to this real sadistic S.O.B., this guy named Vivian Bishop. That's right, the same surname as me, and because of that, I had to tuck him into bed at night, kiss him on the forehead and say, "Goodnight, Daddy"! I mean, it's pretty hard to take some of that stuff seriously. One of my punishments: I'm supposed to clean out this old Martello Tower by the edge of the lake. I mean, it's filthy, hasn't been used for years. Now I do a real great job. I clean it up real well. This upperclassman comes along to inspect it.

UPPERCLASSMAN: What's this in the corner, Bishop?

BISHOP: That? *(He has another look.)* That's a spider, Sir.

UPPERCLASSMAN: That's right, Bishop. That's a spider. Now you had orders to clean this place up. You haven't done that. You get down on your hands and knees and eat that spider.

BISHOP: *(to the audience)* I had to eat that spider in front of all my classmates. You ever have to eat a spider? In public? I doubt it. Nuts! Now, whenever I'm not happy, I mean, whenever I'm not having a really good time, I do one of three things: I get sick, I get injured or I get in an awful lot of trouble. My third year at R.M.C., I got into an awful lot of trouble. This friend of mine, Townsend, one night, we got a bottle of gin, eh? And we stole a canoe. Well, we'd arranged to meet these girls on Cedar Island out in Dead Man's Bay. Well, of course, the canoe tips over. Now, it's early spring, really cold. We get back to shore somehow and we're shivering and Townsend says to me, "Bish, Bish, I'm going to the infirmary. I think I got pneumonia." And I'm sitting there saying, "Well, whatever you do, you silly bugger, change into some dry clothes." Because we couldn't let anybody know what we'd been doing. I mean, we were absent without leave, in possession of alcohol and we'd stolen a canoe. What I didn't know was the officer on duty had witnessed this whole thing. Townsend goes to the infirmary and is confronted with these charges and he admits everything. I didn't know that. I'm rudely awakened out of my sleep and hauled up before old Adjutant Perrault.

At attention, addressing ADJUTANT PERRAULT.

Sir! I've been in my bed all night. I really don't know what you're talking about, Sir.

PERRAULT: Come on. Come on now, Bishop. We have the testimony of the officer on duty. We also have the full confession of your accomplice implicating you fully in this. Now, what is your story, Bishop?

BISHOP: *(to the audience)* Well, I figured I was in too deep now to change my story. *(to PERRAULT)* Sir, I still maintain …

PERRAULT: Bishop! I'm going to say the worst thing that I can say to a gentleman cadet. You are a liar, Bishop!

BISHOP is sobered briefly by the memory, but he quickly recovers.

BISHOP: *(to the audience)* I got twenty-eight days restricted leave for that. It's like house arrest. Then they caught me cheating on my final exams. Well, I handed in the crib notes with the exam paper! And that's when they called me the worst student R.M.C. ever had. They weren't going to tell me what my punishment was until the next fall, so I could stew about it all summer, but I knew what it was going to be. Expulsion! With full honours! But then the war broke out and I enlisted and was made an officer. I mean, for me, it was the lesser of two evils. But everyone else was very keen on the whole thing. They were.

BISHOP and PIANO PLAYER: *(singing)*
We were off to fight the Hun,
Though hardly anyone
Had ever seen a Hun,
Wouldn't know one if we saw one.
We were off to fight the Hun
And it looked like lots of fun,
Somehow it didn't seem like war
At all, at all, at all.
Somehow it didn't seem like war at all.

The PIANO PLAYER raps out a military rhythm.

BISHOP: *(to the audience)* October 1st, 1914, the First Contingent of the Canadian Expeditionary Forces left for England. I wasn't with them. I was in the hospital. Thinking of Margaret …

The PIANO PLAYER plays the appropriate "Dear Margaret" music under the following speech.

BISHOP: *(as if writing a letter)* Dear ... Dearest Margaret. I am in the hospital with pneumonia. I also have an allergy, but the doctors don't know what I am allergic to. Maybe it's horses. Maybe it's the Army. The hospital is nice, so I am in good spirits. Thinking of you constantly, I remain ...

The PIANO PLAYER raps out a military rhythm once again.

BISHOP: *(to the audience)* March, 1915, the Second, Third, Fourth, Fifth and Sixth Contingents of the Canadian Expeditionary Forces left for England. I wasn't with them either. I was back in the hospital ... thinking of Margaret.

As if writing a letter.

Sweetheart. Please excuse my writing, as I have a badly sprained wrist. Yesterday, my horse reared up and fell over backwards on me. It was awful, I could have been killed. My head was completely buried in the mud. My nose is, of course, broken and quite swollen, and I can't see out of one eye. I have two broken ribs and am pretty badly bruised, but the doctor figures I'll be up and around by Monday. The hospital is nice, so I am in fine spirits. Thinking of you constantly, I remain ...

The PIANO PLAYER raps out a military rhythm once again.

BISHOP: *(to the audience)* June, 1915. The Seventh Contingent of the Canadian Expeditionary Forces left for England. I was with them. Now, this was aboard a cattle boat called the *Caledonia*, in Montreal. There was this big crowd came down to the pier to see us off. I mean, hundreds and hundreds of people, and for a while there, I felt like the whole thing was worth doing. It's pretty impressive when you look out there and you see several hundred people cheering and waving ... at you. I mean, when you're from a small town, the numbers get to you. And you're looking out at them and they're looking back at you, and you think, "Boy, I must be doing something right!"

The PIANO PLAYER strikes up "God Save the King."

And they play "God Save the King," and everybody is crying and waving and cheering, and the boat starts to pull out, and they start to yell like you've never heard anybody yell before. I mean, you feel good. You really do! And we're all praying, "Please God, don't let the fighting be over before I can get over there and take part ..."

He becomes carried away and starts yelling.

"On the edge of destiny, you must test your strength!"

He is suddenly self-conscious.

What the hell am I talking about?

The music changes from heroic to the monotonous roll of a ship.

The good ship *Caledonia* soon changed its name to the good ship Vomit. It was never meant to hold people. Even the horses didn't like it. Up, down, up, down. And they're siphoning brandy down our throats to keep us from puking our guts up on deck. It was a big joke. Whenever anyone would puke, which was every minute or so, everyone would point to him and laugh like it was the funniest thing they had ever seen. I mean, puke swishing around on the deck, two inches deep, har, har, har! You couldn't sleep, even if it was calm, because every time you closed your eyes, you had a nightmare about being torpedoed.

He demonstrates a torpedo hitting the ship.

Every time I closed my eyes, I could see this torpedo coming up through the water, through the hull of the ship and ... BOOM! And we were attacked, too, just off the coast of Ireland. I was scared shitless. All you could do was stand at the rail and watch the other ships get hit and go down. Bodies floating around like driftwood. But we made it through. The Good Ship *Caledonia*, latrine of the Atlantic, finally made it through to Portsmouth, full of dead horses and sick Canadians. When we got off, they thought we were a boat load of Balkan refugees.

BISHOP and PIANO PLAYER: *(singing)*
We were off to fight the Hun,
We would shoot him with a gun.
Our medals would shine
Like a sabre in the sun.
We were off to fight the Hun
And it looked like lots of fun,
Somehow it didn't seem like war
At all, at all, at all.
Somehow it didn't seem like war at all.

BISHOP: *(to the audience)* A few days later, we marched into Shorncliffe Military Camp, right on the Channel. You know, on a clear night, you could see the artillery flashes from France. I took it as a sign of better things to come … It wasn't.

As if writing a letter.

Dearest Margaret … Shorncliffe Military Camp is the worst yet! The cold wind brings two kinds of weather. Either it rains or it doesn't. When it rains, you've got mud like I've never seen before. Your horse gets stuck in a foot and a half of mud. You get off and you're knee deep. The rain falls in sheets and you're wet to the skin. You are never dry. Then the rain stops and the ground dries out. What a relief, you say? Then the wind gets the dust going and you have dust storms for days. The sand is like needles hitting you, and a lot of the men are bleeding from the eyes. I don't know which is worse, going blind or going crazy. The sand gets in your food, your clothes, your tent, in your … body orifices. A lot of the guys have something called desert madness, which is really serious. As I write this letter, the sand is drifting across the page. Thinking of you constantly, I remain …

To the audience.

Being buried alive in the mud … I was seriously considering this proposition one day when a funny thing happened.

He demonstrates with a chair.

I got my horse stuck in the middle of the parade ground. The horse is up to its fetlocks; I'm up to my knees. Mud, sweat and horse shit from head to toe.

The music becomes ethereal and gentle.

Then, suddenly, out of the clouds comes this little single-seater scout. You know, this little fighter plane? It circles a couple of times. I guess the pilot had lost his way and was going to come down and ask directions. He does this turn, then lands on an open space, like a dragonfly on a rock. The pilot jumps out. He's in this long sheepskin coat, helmet, goggles … warm and dry. He gets his directions, then jumps back into the machine, up in the air, with the mist blowing off him. All by himself. No superior officer, no horse, no sand, no mud. What a beautiful picture! I

don't know how long I just stood there watching until he was long gone. Out of sight.

He breaks the mood abruptly.

I mean, this war was going on a lot longer than anyone expected. A lot more people were getting killed than anyone expected. Now I wasn't going to spend the rest of the war in the mud. And I sure as hell wasn't going to die in the mud.

The PIANO PLAYER strikes up a new tune. BISHOP drunkenly joins in.

BISHOP and PIANO PLAYER: *(singing)*
Thinking of December nights
In the clear Canadian cold,
Where the winter air don't smell bad,
And the wind don't make you old.
Where the rain don't wash your heart out,
And the nights ain't filled with fear.
Oh, those old familiar voices
Whisper in my ears.

(Chorus)

Oh, Canada,
Sing a song for me.
Sing one for your lonely son,
So far across the sea.

The piano continues with a popular dance tune of the period. BISHOP's reverie is interrupted by a Cockney OFFICER, who is also drunk and who is slightly mad.

OFFICER: You don't fancy the Cavalry then, eh?

BISHOP: What?!

OFFICER: I say, you don't fancy the Cavalry then, eh? It's going to be worse at the front, mate. There, you got blokes shooting at you, right? … With machine guns. *(He imitates a machine gun.)* DakDakDakDakakaka. Har, har, har. It's a bloody shooting gallery. They still think they're fighting the Boer War! Cavalry charges against machine guns. DakDakDakak. Har, har! It's a bloody shooting gallery with you in the middle of it, mate.

BISHOP: This is awful. Something's got to be done. Jeez, I was a casualty in training.

OFFICER: Take a word of advice from me, mate. The only way out is up.

BISHOP: Up?

OFFICER: Up. Join the Royal Flying Corps. I did. I used to be in the Cavalry, but I joined the R.F.C. I like it. It's good clean work. Mind you, the bleeding machines barely stay in the air and the life expectancy of the new lads is about eleven days. But I like it. It's good clean work.

BISHOP: Just a minute. How can I get into the Royal Flying Corps? I'm a Canadian. I'm cannon fodder. You practically have to own your own plane to get into the R.F.C.

OFFICER: Au contraire, mate. Au contraire. The upper classes are depressed by the present statistics, so they aren't joining with their usual alacrity. Now, anyone who wants to can get blown out of the air. Even Canadians.

BISHOP: Well, what do I have to do?

OFFICER: You go down to see them at the War Office, daft bunch of twits, but they're all right. Now … you act real eager, see? Like you want to be a pilot. You crave the excitement, any old rubbish like that. Then, they're not going to know what to ask, because they don't know a bleeding thing about it. So, they'll ask you whatever comes into their heads, which isn't much, then they'll say you can't be a pilot, you've got to be an observer.

BISHOP: What's an observer?

OFFICER: He's the fellow who goes along for the ride, you know? Looks about.

BISHOP: Ohhh …

OFFICER: So, you act real disappointed, like your Mum wanted you to be a pilot, and then, you get your transfer …

BISHOP: Just a minute. So, I'm an observer. I'm the fellow that goes along for the ride, looks about. So what? How do I get to be a pilot?

OFFICER: I don't know. Sooner or later, you just get to be a pilot. Plenty of vacancies these days. Check the casualty lists, wait for a bad one. You've got to go in by the back door, you know what I mean? Nobody gets to be a pilot right away, for Christ's sake. Especially not bleeding Canadians!

BISHOP: *(to the audience)* Did you ever trust your future to a drunken conversation in a bar? Two days later, I went down to see them at the War Office.

The PIANO PLAYER plays some going to war music. In the following scene, SIR HUGH CECIL interviews BISHOP at the War Office. He is getting on in years and the new technology of warfare has confused him deeply.

SIR HUGH: So … you wish to transfer to the Royal Flying Corps? Am I right? Am I correct?

BISHOP: Yes, Sir. I want to become a fighter pilot, Sir. It's what my mother always wanted, Sir.

SIR HUGH: Oh … I see. Well, the situation is this, Bishop. We need good men in the R.F.C., but they must have the correct … er … qualifications. Now, while the War Office has not yet ascertained what qualifications are indeed necessary to fly an … er … aeroplane, we must see to it that all candidates possess the necessary qualifications, should the War Office ever decide what those qualifications are. Do you understand, Bishop?

BISHOP: Perfectly, Sir.

SIR HUGH: That's very good. Jolly good. More than I can say. Well, shall we begin then?

BISHOP: Ready when you are, Sir.

SIR HUGH: That's good, shows keenness, you see … And good luck, Bishop. *(to himself)* What on earth shall I ask him? *(There is a long pause while he collects his thoughts.)* Do you ski?

BISHOP: Ski, sir?

SIR HUGH: Yes … do you ski?

BISHOP: *(to the audience)* Here was an Englishman asking a Canadian whether or not he skied. Now, if the Canadian said he didn't ski, the Englishman might find that somewhat suspicious. *(to SIR HUGH)* Ski? Yes, Sir. *(to the audience)* Never skied in my life.

SIR HUGH: Fine, well done … thought you might. *(pause)* Do you ride a horse?

BISHOP: I'm an officer in the Cavalry, Sir.

SIR HUGH: Doesn't necessarily follow, but we'll put down that you ride, shall we? *(pause)* What about sports, Bishop? Run, jump, throw the ball? Play the game, eh? What?

BISHOP: Sports, Sir? All sports.

SIR HUGH: I see. Well done, Bishop. I'm most impressed.

BISHOP: Does this mean I can become a fighter pilot, Sir?

SIR HUGH: Who knows, Bishop? Who knows? All full up with fighter pilots at the moment, I'm afraid. Take six months, a year to get in. Terribly sorry. Nothing I can do, old man.

BISHOP: I see, Sir.

SIR HUGH: However! We have an immediate need for observers. You know, the fellow who goes along for the ride, looks about. What do you say, Bishop?

BISHOP: *(to the audience)* I thought about it. I wanted to be a pilot. I couldn't. So, in the fall of 1915, I joined the Twenty-First Squadron as an observer. That's what they were using planes for at that time. Observation. You could take pictures of enemy troop formations, direct artillery fire, stuff like that. It seemed like nice quiet work at the time and I was really good at the aerial photography. I've got these great eyes, remember? And to fly! You're in this old Farnham trainer, sounds like a tractor. It coughs, wheezes, chugs its way up to one thousand feet. You're in a kite with a motor that can barely get off the ground. But even so, you're in the air … You're not on the ground … You're above everything.

The PIANO PLAYER plays some mess hall music.

It was a different world up there. A different war and a different breed of men fighting that war … Flyers! During training, we heard all the stories. If you went down behind enemy lines and were killed, they'd come over, the Germans, that is … they'd come over under a flag of truce and drop a photograph of your grave. Nice. If you were taken prisoner, it was the champagne razzle in the mess. Talking and drinking all night. It was a different war they were fighting up there. And from where I stood, it looked pretty darn good.

PIANO PLAYER: Can you be a bit more specific, please?

BISHOP and the PIANO PLAYER sing a song of champagne and vermouth.

BISHOP and PIANO PLAYER: *(singing)*
I see two planes in the air,
A fight that's fair and square,
With dips and loops and rolls
That would scare you (I'm scared already).
We will force the German down

And arrest him on the ground,
A patriotic lad from Bavaria (Poor bloody sod).

But he'll surrender willingly
And salute our chivalry,
For this war is not of our creation.
But before it's prison camp
And a bed that's cold and damp,
We'll all have a little celebration.

(Chorus)

Oh, we'll toast our youth
On champagne and vermouth,
For all of us know what it's like to fly.
Oh, the fortunes of war
Can't erase esprit de corps
And we'll all of us be friends
'Til we die.

PIANO PLAYER: Can you go on a bit, please!

BISHOP and PIANO PLAYER: *(singing)*
Oh, we'll drink the night away,
And when the Bosch is led away,
We'll load him down with cigarettes and wine.
We'll drink a final toast goodbye,
But for the grace of God go I,
And we'll vow that we'll be friends (Cheers—ping!)
Another time.

(Chorus)

Oh, we'll toast our youth
On champagne and vermouth,
For all of us know what it's like to fly.
Oh, the fortunes of war
Can't erase esprit de corps
And we'll all of us be friends
'Til we die.

BISHOP: You want chivalry? You want gallantry? You want nice guys? That's your flyer. And Jeez, I was going to be one! January 1st, 1916, I crossed the channel to France as a flyer. Well, an observer anyway. That's when I found out that Twenty-First Squadron was known as the "suicide squadron." I mean, that awful nickname used to prey on my mind, you know? And the Archies? The anti-aircraft guns? Not tonight, Archibald! I mean, you're tooling around over the line, doing your observation work, a sitting duck, when suddenly you are surrounded by these little black puffs of smoke. Then … wham-whizz! Shrapnel whizzes all around you. I was hit on the head by a piece of flak, just a bruise, but a couple of inches lower and I would have been killed. And we were all scared stiff of this new German machine, the Fokker. It had this interrupter gear, so the pilot could shoot straight at you through the propeller without actually shooting the propeller off. All he had to do was aim his plane at you! And casualties? Lots and lots and lots of casualties. It was a grim situation. But we didn't know how grim it could get until we saw the RE-7 ... the Reconnaissance Experimental Number Seven. Our new plane. What you saw was this mound of cables and wires, with a thousand pounds of equipment hanging off it. Four machine guns, a five hundred pound bomb, for God's sake. Reconnaissance equipment, cameras ... Roger Neville (that's my pilot), he and I are ordered into the thing to take it up. Of course, it doesn't get off the ground. Anyone could see that. We thought, fine, good riddance. But the officers go into a huddle.

Imitating the Officers.

Mmmmum? What do you think we should do? Take the bomb off? Take the bomb off!

As himself.

So we take the bomb off and try again. This time, the thing sort of flops down the runway like a crippled duck. Finally, by taking everything off but one machine gun, the thing sort of flopped itself into the air and chugged along. It was a pig! We were all scared stiff of it. So they put us on active duty ... as *bombers!* They gave us two bombs each, told us to fly over Hunland and drop them on somebody. But in order to accommodate for the weight of the bombs, they took our machine guns away!

As if writing a letter.

Dearest Margaret. We are dropping bombs on the enemy from unarmed machines. It is exciting work. It's hard to keep your confidence in a war when you don't have a gun. Somehow we get back in one piece and we start joking around and inspecting the machine for bullet and shrapnel damage. You're so thankful not to be dead. Then I go back to the barracks and lie down. A kind of terrible loneliness comes over me. It's like waiting for the firing squad. It makes you want to cry, you feel so frightened and so alone. I think all

of us who aren't dead think these things. Thinking of you constantly, I remain ...

PIANO PLAYER: *(singing)*
Nobody shoots no one in Canada,
At least nobody they don't know.
Nobody shoots no one in Canada,
Last battle was a long, long time ago.

Nobody picks no fights in Canada,
Not with nobody they ain't met.
Nobody starts no wars in Canada,
Folks tend to work for what they get.

Take me under
That big blue sky,
Where the deer and the black bear play.
May not be heaven,
But heaven knows we try,
Wish I was in Canada today.

Nobody drop no bombs on Canada,
Wouldn't want to send no one to hell.
Nobody start no wars on Canada,
Where folks tend to wish each other well.

The music continues as BISHOP speaks.

BISHOP: Of course in this situation, it wasn't too long before the accidents started happening again. It's kind of spooky, but I think being accident prone actually saved my life. I'm driving a truck load of parts a couple of miles from the aerodrome and I run into another truck. I'm inspecting the undercarriage of my machine when a cable snaps and hits me on the head. I was unconscious for two days ... I had a tooth pulled, it got infected and I was in the hospital for two weeks ... Then Roger does this really bad landing. I hit my knee on a metal brace inside the plane so hard I could barely walk ... Then I got three weeks leave in London. None too soon. On the boat going back to England, we all got into the champagne and cognac pretty heavy, and, by the time we arrived, we were all pretty tight and this game developed to see who would actually be the first guy to touch foot on English soil. I'm leading the race down the gangplank. I trip and fall! Everyone else falls on top of me, right on the knee I hurt in the crash! Gawd, the pain was awful! But I was damned if I'd spent my leave in the hospital, so I'd just pour down the brandy until the thing was pretty well numb. I had a hell of a time! If the pain got to me in the night and I couldn't sleep, I'd just pour down the brandy. But around my last day of leave, I started thinking about the bombing runs, the Archies, the Fokkers, and I thought, Jeez, maybe I better have someone look at this knee. The doctor found I had a cracked kneecap, which meant I'd be in the hospital for a couple of weeks. They also found I had a badly strained heart, which meant I would be in the hospital for an indefinite period. As far as I was concerned, I was out of the war.

BISHOP and PIANO PLAYER: *(singing)*
Take me under
That big blue sky,
Where the deer and the black bear play.
May not be heaven,
But heaven knows we try,
Wish I was in Canada today.

I'm dreaming of the trees in Canada,
Northern Lights are dancing in my head.
If I die, then let me die in Canada,
Where there's a chance I'll die in bed.

BISHOP: The hospital is nice. People don't shoot at you and people don't drop things on you. I thought it would be a nice place to spend the rest of the war. I went to sleep for three days.

Distorted marching music is heard.

I had this nightmare. A terrible dream. I am in the lobby of the Grand Hotel in London. The band is playing military music and the lobby is full of English and German officers. They're dancing together and their medals jingle like sleighbells in the snow. The sound is deafening. I've got to get out of there. I start to run, but my knee gives out underneath me. As I get up, I get kicked in the stomach by a Prussian boot. As I turn to run, I get kicked in the rear by an English boot. Then I turn around and all the officers have formed a chorus line, like the Follies, and they are heading for me, kicking. I scream as a hundred black boots kick me high in the air, as I turn over and over, shouting, "Help me! Help me! They are trying to kill me!"

He wakes up abruptly.

LADY ST. HELIER: My goodness, Bishop, you'll not get any rest screaming at the top of your lungs like that.

BISHOP: *(to the audience)* In front of me was a face I'd never seen before. Very old, female, with long white hair pulled back tightly in a bun, exposing two of the largest ears I had ever seen.

LADY ST. HELIER: You'd be the son of Will Bishop of Owen Sound, Canada, would you not? Of course you are, the resemblance is quite startling. Your father was a loyal supporter of a very dear friend of mine, Sir Wilfred Laurier. It was in that connection I met your father in Ottawa. *(She zeros in on BISHOP.)* A gaping mouth is most impolite, Bishop. No, I am not clairvoyant. I am Lady St. Helier. Reform alderman, poetess, friend of Churchill, and the woman who shall save your life.

BISHOP: *(speechless)* Ahh ... oh ... mmmm Ahhh ...

LADY ST. HELIER: Enough of this gay banter, Bishop. Time runs apace and my life is not without its limits. You have been making rather a mess of it, haven't you? You are a rude young man behaving like cannon fodder. Perfectly acceptable characteristics in a Canadian, but you are different. You are a gifted Canadian and that gift belongs to a much older and deeper tradition than Canada can ever hope to provide. Quite against your own wishes, you will be released from this wretched hospital in two weeks' time. Promptly, at three o'clock on that afternoon, you will present yourself before my door at Portland Place, dressed for tea and in a positive frame of mind. Do I make myself clear? Good. Please be punctual, Mr. Bishop.

BISHOP: *(to the audience)* Well, Jeez, that old girl must have known something I didn't, because, two weeks later, I'm released from hospital. Promptly, at three o'clock, I find myself in front of her door at Portland Place, in my best uniform, shining my shoes on my pants. The door is opened by the biggest butler I have ever seen. *(He looks up and speaks to the butler.)* Hi!

The butler looks down at him with distaste, turns away and calls to LADY ST. HELIER.

CEDRIC: *(calling)* Madam, the Canadian is here. Shall I show him in?

LADY ST. HELIER: *(from a distance)* Yes, Cedric, please. Show him in.

CEDRIC: *(turning his back to BISHOP)* Get in!

BISHOP: *(to the audience)* I'm shown into the largest room I've ever seen. I mean, a fireplace eight feet wide and a staircase that must have had a hundred steps in it. I'm not used to dealing with nobility. Servants, grand ballrooms, pheasant hunting on the heath, fifty-year-old brandy over billiards, breakfast in bed ... shit, what a life!

CEDRIC: Madam is in the study. Get in!

BISHOP: The study. Books, books ... more books than I'll ever read. Persian rug. Tiger's head over the mantle. African spears in the corner. "Rule Britannia, Britannia rules the ... " I stood at the door. I was on edge. Out of my element. Lady St. Helier was sitting at this little writing desk, writing.

LADY ST. HELIER: Very punctual, Bishop. Please sit down.

BISHOP: I sat in this chair that was all carved lions. One of the lions stuck in my back.

CEDRIC: Would our visitor from Canada care for tea, madam?

LADY ST. HELIER: Would you care for something to drink, Bishop?

BISHOP: Tea? Ahhh, yeah ... Tea would be fine.

LADY ST. HELIER: A tea for Bishop, Cedric. And I'll have a gin.

CEDRIC: Lemon?

BISHOP: (disappointed) Gin! I wonder if I could change ... No, no. Tea will be fine. (to the audience) Tea was served. I sip my tea. Lady St. Helier sips her gin. And Cedric loomed over me, afraid I was going to drool on the carpet or some-thing. Lady St. Helier stared at me through her thick spectacles. Suddenly, her ears twitched, like she was honing in on something.

LADY ST. HELIER: I have written a poem in your honour, Bishop. I can but hope that your rustic mind will appreciate its significance. (She signals to the PIANO PLAYER.) Cedric!

LADY ST. HELIER: (spoken to music)
You're a typical Canadian,
You're modesty itself,
And you really wouldn't want to hurt a flea.
But you're just about to go
The way of the buffalo.
You'd do well to take this good advice from me.

I'm awfully sick and tired
Being constantly required

To stand by and watch Canadians make the best
   of it,
For the Colonial mentality
Defies all rationality.
You seem to go to lengths to make a mess of it.

Why don't you grow up,
Before I throw up?
Do you expect somebody else to do it for you?
Before you're dead out,
Get the lead out
And seize what little life still lies before you.

Do you really expect Empire
To settle back, retire,
And say "Colonials, go on your merry way"?
I'm very tired of your whining
And your infantile maligning.
Your own weakness simply won't be whined
   away.

So don't be so naïve,
And take that heart off your sleeve,
For a fool and his life will soon be parted.
War's a fact of life today
And it will not be wished away.
Forget that fact and you'll be dead before
   you've started.

So, Bishop, grow up,
Before I throw up.
Your worst enemy is yourself, as you well know.
Before you're dead out,
Get the lead out.
You have your own naïveté to overthrow.

LADY ST. HELIER: (to the PIANO PLAYER) Thank you Cedric. (to BISHOP) Do I make myself clear, Bishop? You will cease this mediocrity your record only too clearly reveals. You will become the pilot you wished to be but were lamentably content to settle for less. Now this will take time, for you must recover the health you have so seriously undermined. To that end, you will remain here, a lodger at Portland Place, top of the stairs, third floor, seventh room on the left. Cedric, be kind to Bishop and ignore his bad manners. For cultivation exacts its price. The loss of a certain ... vitality. Beneath this rude Canadian exterior, there is a power that you will never know. Properly harnessed, that power will win wars for you. Churchill knows it and I know it too. Good day, Bishop.

BISHOP: *(to the audience)* Now there are one or two Canadians who would have taken offence at that. Not me. Staying at Portland Place, I found out some things right away. For example, life goes much smoother when you've got influence. Take this pilot business, for example. Lady St. Helier was on the phone to Churchill himself, and, the next day, I was called down to the War Office. The atmosphere was much different.

Going to war music is heard once again.

SIR HUGH: Bishop, my boy. Good to see you, good to see you. Well, well, well, your mother's wish is finally going to come true.

BISHOP: Really, Sir?

SIR HUGH: Yes, yes. You are going to become a pilot. No problem, pas de problème. Medical examination in two days time, then report for training.

BISHOP: *(to the audience)* Medical examination! What about my weak heart? What about the fact that three weeks ago I was on the verge of a medical discharge?

DOCTOR: *(addressing BISHOP, but seldom ever looking up from his desk)* Strip to the waist, Bishop. Hmnmnmnm? Stick out your tongue and say ninety-nine ... Good ... Cough twice ... That's good, too ... Turn around ten times ... Eight, nine, ten ... Attention! Still on your feet, Bishop? You're fit as a fiddle and ready to fly!

BISHOP: *(singing)*
Gonna fly ...
Gonna fly so high,
Like a bird in the sky,
With the wind in my hair,
And the sun burning in my eyes.
Flying Canadian,
Machine gun in my hand,
First Hun I see is the first Hun to die.

Gonna fly ...
In my machine,
Gonna shoot so clean,
Gonna hear them scream
When I hit them between the eyes.
Flying Canadian,
Machine gun in my hand,
First Hun I see is the first Hun to die.

(Chorus)

Flying ...
What have I been waiting for?
What a way to fight a war!
Flying Canadian,
Machine gun in my hand,
First Hun I see is the first Hun to die.

Gonna fly ...
Gonna shoot them down
'Til they hit the ground
And they burn with the sound
Of bacon on the fry.
Flying Canadian,
Machine gun in my hand,
First Hun I see is the first Hun to die.

(Chorus)

Flying ...
What have I been waiting for?
What a way to fight a war!
Flying Canadian,
Machine gun in my hand,
First Hun I see is the first Hun to die.

The song ends abruptly.

BISHOP: I'll never forget my first solo flight. Lonely? Jeeezus! You're sitting at the controls all by yourself, trying to remember what they're all for. Everyone has stopped doing what they're doing to watch you. An ambulance is parked at the edge of the field with the engines running. You know why. You also know that there's a surgical team in the hospital, just ready to rip.

The PIANO PLAYER calls out the following. BISHOP repeats after him.

PIANO PLAYER: Switch off.

BISHOP: Switch off.

PIANO PLAYER: Petrol on.

BISHOP: Petrol on.

PIANO PLAYER: Suck in.

BISHOP: Suck in.

PIANO PLAYER: Switch on.

BISHOP: Switch on.

PIANO PLAYER: Contact!

BISHOP: Contact!

During the above, BISHOP does all the sound effects vocally, much as a small boy would do during a demonstration.

The propeller is given a sharp swing over and the engine starts with a roar ... coughs twice, but soon starts hitting on all cylinders. You signal for them to take away the chocks. Then you start bounding across the field under your own power and head her up into the wind.

He checks the equipment.

Rudder.

Click, click.

Elevator.

Click, click.

Ailerons.

Click, click.

Heart.

Boom-boom! Boom-boom!

I open the throttle all the way ... and you're off! Pull back on the stick, easy, easy.

He demonstrates the plane bumping along, then rising up into the air.

Once I was in the air, I felt a lot better. In fact, I felt like a king! Mind you, I wasn't fooling around. I'm flying straight as I can, climbing steadily. All alone! What a feeling!

He looks about.

I've got to turn. I execute a gentle turn, skidding like crazy, but what the hell. I try another turn. This time, I bank it a little more. Too much. Too much! ... All in all, I'm having a hell of a time up there until I remember I have to land ... . What do I do now? Keep your head, that's what you do. Pull back on the throttle.

The engine coughs.

Too much! I put the nose down into a steep dive. Too steep. Bring it up again, down again, up, down ... and in a series of steps, kind of descend to the earth. Then I execute everything I remember I have to do to make a perfect landing. Forty feet off the ground! I put the nose down again and do another perfect landing. This time, I'm only eight feet off the ground, but now I don't have room left to do another nose down

manoeuvre. The rumpty takes things into her own hands and just pancakes the rest of the way to the ground. First solo flight! Greatest day in a man's life!

PIANO PLAYER and BISHOP: *(singing)*
Flying ...
What have I been waiting for?
What a way to fight a war!
Flying Canadian,
Machine gun in my hand,
First Hun I see is the first Hun to die,
First Hun I see is the first Hun to die.

BISHOP: In the early part of 1916, I was posted back to France as a fighter pilot. Sixtieth Squadron, Third British Brigade. I worked like a Trojan for these wings and I just about lost them before I really began. I was returning from my first O.P., Operational Patrol, and I crashed my Nieuport on landing. I wasn't hurt, but the aircraft was pretty well pranged, and that was bad because General John Higgins, the Brigade Commander, saw me do it. Well, he couldn't help but see me do it. I just about crashed at his feet!

HIGGINS: I watched you yesterday, Bishop. You destroyed a machine. A very expensive, a very nice machine. Doing a simple landing on a clear day. That machine was more valuable than you'll ever be, buck-o.

BISHOP: Sir, there was a gust of wind from the hangar. I mean, ask Major Scott, our patrol leader. It could have happened to anyone.

HIGGINS: I was on the field, Bishop.

BISHOP: Yes, Sir.

HIGGINS: There was no wind.

BISHOP: No wind? Yes, Sir.

HIGGINS: I have your record here on my desk, Bishop, and it isn't a very impressive document. On the positive side, you were wounded. And you score well in target practice, although you have never actually fired upon the enemy. The list of your negative accomplishments is longer, isn't it, much longer? Conduct unbecoming an officer. Breaches of discipline. A lot of silly accidents, suspicious accidents, if I might say so. A trail of wrecked machinery in your wake. You are a terrible pilot, Bishop. In short, you are a liability to the R.F.C. and I wish to God you were back in Canada where you belong, or failing that, digging a trench in some unstrategic valley. In short, you are finished, Bishop, finished. When your replacement arrives, he will replace you. That is all.

BISHOP: That was the lowest point of my career. Then came March 25, 1917.

The following is performed on microphone with BISHOP creating the sound effects. The PIANO PLAYER joins him. The mike should be used as a joy stick and the aggression implied in the story should be transferred to the microphone.

March 25, 1917. Four Nieuport scouts in diamond formation climb to nine thousand feet crossing the line somewhere between Arras and St. Léger. Our patrol is to crisscross the lines noting Heinie's positions and troop movements.

The sound of an airplane engine is heard.

RRrrr. I'm the last man in that patrol, tough place to be, because if you fall too far behind, the headhunters are waiting for you. It starts out cloudy, then suddenly clears up. We fly for half an hour and don't see anything, just miles and miles of nothing. RRrrr. Suddenly, I see four specks above and behind us. A perfect place for an enemy attack. I watch as the specks get larger. I can make out the black crosses on them. Huns! It's hard to believe that they are real, alive and hostile. I want to circle around and have a better look at them. Albatross "V" strutters, beautiful, with their swept back planes, powerful and quick. RRrrr. We keep on flying straight. Jack Scott, our leader, either hasn't seen them or he wants them to think he hasn't seen them. They are getting closer and closer. We keep on flying straight. They are two hundred yards behind us, getting closer and closer. Suddenly, RRrrr! Jack Scott opens out into a sharp climbing turn to get above and behind them. The rest of us follow. Rrrr! RRrrr! RRrrrr! I'm slower than the rest and come out about forty yards behind. In front of me, a dogfight is happening, right in front of my very eyes. Real pandemonium, planes turning every which way. RRRrrr! Machine gun fire. Suddenly, Jack Scott sweeps below me with an Albatross on his tail raking his fuselage and wing tips with gunfire! For a moment, I'm just frozen there, not knowing what to do, my whole body just shaking! Then I throw the stick forward and dive on the Hun. I keep him in my Aldis sight 'til he completely fills the lens. AKAKAkak! What a

feeling, as he flips over on his back and falls out of control! But wait, wait ... Grid Caldwell warned me about this. He's not out of control, he's faking it. He's going to level out at two thousand feet and escape. Bastard! I dive after him with my engine full on. Sure enough, when he comes out of it, I'm right there AKAkakaka! Again, my tracers smash into his engine. Gawd, I've got to be hitting him! He flips over on his back and is gone again. This time, I stay right with him. EEEeeeeee! The wires on my machine howl in protest. Nieuports have had their wings come off at 150 miles per hour. I must be doing 180. I just don't give a shit! I keep firing into the tumbling Hun. AKAKaka! He just crashes into the earth and explodes in flames. BAA-WHOOSH! I pull back on the stick, level out, screaming at the top of my lungs, I win, I WIN, I WIN!

The sound of wind is heard—no engine, no nothing.

Jeezus, my engine's stopped! it must have filled with oil on the dive. I try every trick in the book to get it going again. Nothing. Oh God, I'm going to go in! Down, down.

The sound of gunfire is heard.

Gunfire! I must still be over Hunland. Just my luck to do something right and end up being taken a prisoner. Lower and lower. I pick out what seems to be a level patch in the rough terrain and I put her down.

The sound of a bouncing crash is heard.

I got out of the plane into what must have been a shell hole. I took my Very Lite pistol with me. I wasn't exactly sure what I was going to do with it.

TOMMY: *(in a "Canadian" accent)* Well you're just in time for a cup of tea, lad.

BISHOP: *(surprised)* ARrghgh ... you spoke English! Hey, look, where am I?

TOMMY: You're at the corner of Portage and Main in downtown Winnipeg. You want to keep down, lad. Heinie is sitting right over there. Well, goll, that was a nice bit of flying you did there! Yep, you're a hundred yards our side of the line.

BISHOP: OOhhh, look ... can you do me a favour? I'd like to try and get the plane up again.

TOMMY: Not tonight, lad, nope … You're going to have to take the Montcalm Suite here at the Chateau.

BISHOP: I spent the night in the trench in six inches of water! The soldiers seemed to be able to sleep. I couldn't.

The sound of shelling gets progressively louder.

Next morning at first light, I crawled out to see how my plane was. Miraculously, it hadn't been hit. And that's when I got my first real look at "No Man's Land." Jeezus, what a mess! Hardly a tree left standing. And the smell! It was hard to believe you were still on earth. I saw a couple of Tommys sleeping in a trench nearby.

He goes over to the Tommys.

Hey, you guys, I wonder if you could give me a hand with … ?

He takes a closer look. The Tommys aren't asleep. He backs off with a shudder.

The PIANO PLAYER sings and BISHOP joins him.

BISHOP and PIANO PLAYER: *(singing)*
Oh, the bloody earth is littered
With the fighters and the quitters.
Oh, what could be more bitter
Than a nameless death below.
See the trenches, long and winding,
See the battle slowly grinding,
Don't you wonder how good men can live so
    low.

Up above, the clouds are turning,
Up above, the sun is burning,
You can hear those soldiers yearning:
"Oh, if only I could fly!"
From the burning sun, I'll sight you,
In the burning sun, I'll fight you.
Oh, let us dance together in the sky.

(Chorus)

In the sky,
In the sky,
Just you and I up there together,
Who knows why?
One the hunter, one the hunted;
A life to live, a death confronted.
Oh, let us dance together in the sky.

And for you, the bell is ringing,
And for you, the bullets stinging.
My Lewis gun is singing:
"Oh, my friend, it's you or I."
And I'll watch your last returning
To the earth, the fires burning.
Look up and you will see me wave goodbye.

(Chorus)

In the sky,
In the sky,
Just you and I up there together,
Who knows why?
One the hunter, one the hunted;
A life to live, a death confronted.
Oh, let us dance together in the sky.

ACT TWO

The lights come up, as in Act One, with the PIANO PLAYER and BILLY BISHOP at the piano.

BISHOP and PIANO PLAYER: *(singing)*
Oh, the bold Aviator lay dying,
As 'neath the wreckage he lay (he lay),
To the sobbing mechanics beside him,
These last parting words he did say:

Two valves you'll find in my stomach,
Three sparkplugs are safe in my lung (my lung).
The prop is in splinters inside me,
To my fingers, the joystick has clung.

Then get you six brandies and soda,
And lay them all out in a row (a row),
And get you six other good airmen,
To drink to this pilot below.

Take the cylinders out of my kidneys,
The connecting rod out of my brain (my brain),
From the small of my back take the crankshaft,
And assemble the engines again!

The music changes to a theme reminiscent of a French café. Time has gone by and BISHOP has changed.

BISHOP: Survival. That's the important thing. And the only way to learn survival is to survive. Success depends on accuracy and surprise. How well you shoot, how you get into the fight and how well you fly. In *that* order. I can't fly worth shit compared to someone like Barker or Ball, but I don't care. If I get a kill, it's usually in the first few seconds of the fight. Any longer than that and you might as well get the hell out. You've got to be good enough to get him in the first few bursts, so practice your shooting as much as you can. After patrols, between patrols, on your day off. If I get a clear shot at a guy, he's dead. You ever heard of "flamers"? That's when you bounce a machine and it just bursts into flames. Now, I don't want to sound bloodthirsty or anything, but when that happens, it is very satisfying. But it's almost always pure luck. You hit a gas line or something like that. If you want the machine to go down every time, you aim for one thing: the man. I always go for the man.

The music stops. The PIANO PLAYER becomes a French announcer.

ANNOUNCER: Ladies and Gentlemen … Madames et Messieurs … Charlie's Bar, Amiens, proudly presents: The Lovely Hélène!

BISHOP: *(as the LOVELY HÉLÈNE, singing)*
Johnny was a Christian,
He was humble and humane.
His conscience was clear,
And his soul without a stain.
He was contemplating heaven,
When the wings fell off his plane.
And he never got out alive,
He didn't survive.

George was patriotic,
His country he adored.
He was the first to volunteer,
When his land took up the sword,
And a half a dozen medals
Were his posthumous reward.
And he never got out alive,
He didn't survive.

(Chorus)

So when you fight, stay as calm as the ocean,
And watch what's going on behind your shoulder.
Remember, war's not the place for deep emotion,
And maybe you'll get a little older.

BISHOP: *(as himself)* Come into a fight with an advantage: height, speed, surprise. Come at him out of the sun, he'll never see you. Get on his tail, his blind spot, so you can shoot him without too much risk to yourself. Generally, patrols don't watch behind them as much, so sneak up on the last man. He'll never know what hit him. Then you get out in the confusion. Hunt them. Like

Hell's Handmaiden. If it's one on one, you come at the bugger, head on, guns blazing. He chickens out and you get him as he comes across your sights. If you both veer the same way, you're dead, so it's tricky. You have to keep your nerve.

BISHOP: *(as the LOVELY HÉLÈNE, singing)*
Geoffrey made a virtue
Out of cowardice and fear.
He was the first to go on sick leave,
And the last to volunteer.
He was running from a fight,
When they attacked him from the rear.
And he never got out alive, (no),
He didn't survive.

BISHOP: *(as himself)* Another thing is your mental attitude. It's not like the infantry where a bunch of guys work themselves up into a screaming rage and tear off over the top, yelling and waving their bayonets. It's not like that. You're part of a machine, so you have to stay very calm and cold. You and your machine work together to bring the other fellow down. You get so you don't feel anything after a while … until the moment you start firing, and then that old dry throat, heartthrobbing thrill comes back. It's a great feeling!

BISHOP: *(as the LOVELY HÉLÈNE, singing)*
Jimmy hated Germans
With a passion cold and deep.
He cursed them when he saw them,
He cursed them in his sleep.
He was cursing when his plane went down
And landed in a heap.
And he never got out alive, (no),
He didn't survive.

(Chorus)

So when you fight, stay as calm as the ocean,
And watch what's going on behind your shoulder.
Remember, war is not the place for deep emotion,
And maybe you'll get a little older.

BISHOP: Bloody April? We lost just about everyone I started with. Knowles, Hall, Williams, Townsend, Chapman. Steadman, shot down the day he joined the squadron. You see, the Hun has better machines and some of their pilots are very good. But practice makes perfect, if you can stay alive long enough to practice. But it gets easier and easier to stay alive because hardly anyone else has the same experience as you. Oh yeah, another thing. You take your fun where you can find it.

The music and mood change.

He has noticed the Lovely Hélène. She has noticed him. They meet outside. Without a word, she signals him to follow. Silently, they walk down an alley, through an archway, and up a darkened stairway. They are in her room. He closes the door. He watches her light a candle. She turns to him and says: "I should not be doing this. My lover is a Colonel at the front. But you are so beautiful and so, so young." An hour later, they kiss in the darkened doorway. She says: "If you see me, you do not know me." She's gone. He meets his friends who have all enjoyed the same good luck. It's late, they've missed the last bus to the aerodrome. Arm in arm, they walk in the moonlight, silently sharing a flask of brandy, breathing in that warm spring air. As they approach Filescamp, they begin to sing, loudly: "Mademoiselle from Armentières, parley-vous. Mademoiselle from Armentières, parley-vous" … as if to leave behind the feelings they have had that night. In an hour, they will be on patrol. They go to bed. They sleep.

There is an abrupt change of mood. BISHOP is flying and shooting once again.

As if writing a letter.

Dearest Margaret. It is the merry month of May, and today, I sent another merry Hun to his merry death. I'm not sure you'd appreciate the blood-thirsty streak that has come over me in the past months. How I hate the Hun. He has killed so many of my friends. I enjoy killing him now. I go up as much as I can, even on my day off. My score is getting higher and higher because I like it. Yesterday, I had a narrow escape. A bullet came through the windshield and creased my helmet. But a miss is as good as a mile and if I am for it, I am for it. But I do not believe I am for it. My superiors are pleased. Not only have I been made Captain, they are recommending me for the Military Cross. Thinking of you constantly, I remain …

BISHOP and PIANO PLAYER: *(singing)*
You may think you've something special
That will get you through this war,
But the odds aren't in your favour,
That's a fact you can't ignore.

The chances are, the man will come
A-knocking at your door.
And you'll never get out alive,
And you won't survive.

(Chorus)

So when you fight, stay as calm as the ocean,
And watch what's going on behind your shoulder.
Remember, war's not the place for deep emotion,
And maybe you'll get a little older.

The music stops. There is a blackout.

BISHOP talks to ALBERT BALL.

BISHOP: Albert Ball, Britain's highest scoring pilot, sat before me. His black eyes gleamed at me, very pale, very intense. Back home, we would have said he had eyes like two pissholes in the snow. But that's not very romantic. And Albert Ball was romantic, if anybody was.

BALL: Compatriots in Glory! Oh, Bishop, I have an absolutely ripping idea. I want you to try and picture this. Two pilots cross the line in the dim, early dawn. It is dark, a slight fog. They fly straight for the German aerodrome at Douai, ghosts in the night. The Hun, unsuspecting, sleeps cosily in his lair. The sentries are sleeping. Perhaps the Baron von Richthofen himself is there, sleeping, dreaming of eagles and … wiener schnitzel. It is the moment of silence, just before dawn. Suddenly, he is awakened from his sleep by the sound of machine gun fire. He rushes to his window to see four, maybe five, of his best machines in flames. He watches as the frantic pilots try to take off and one by one are shot down. The two unknown raiders strike a devastating blow. Bishop, you and I are those two unknown raiders.

BISHOP: Jeez, I like it. It's a good plan. How do we get out?

BALL: Get out?

BISHOP: Yeah. Get out? You know, escape!

BALL: I don't think you get the picture, Bishop. It's a grand gesture. Getting out has nothing to do with it.

BISHOP: Oh! Well, it's a good plan. It's got a few holes I'd like to see plugged. I'd like to think about it.

BALL: All right, Bishop, you think about it. But remember this: Compatriots in Glory!

BISHOP: Quite a fellow.

He turns to the audience and announces.

"The Dying of Albert Ball"

The following is performed like a Robert Service poem.

He was only eighteen
When he downed his first machine,
And any chance of living through this war was
    small;
He was nineteen when I met him,
And I never will forget him,
The pilot by the name of Albert Ball.

No matter what the odds,
He left his fate up to the gods,
Laughing as the bullets brushed his skin.
Like a medieval knight,
He would charge into the fight
And trust that one more time his pluck would let
    him win.

So he courted the reaper,
Like the woman of his dreams,
And the reaper smiled each time he came to call;
But the British like their heroes
Cold and dead, or so it seems,
And their hero in the sky was Albert Ball.

But long after the fight,
Way into the night,
Cold thoughts, as dark as night, would fill his
    brain,
For bloodstains never fade,
And there are debts to be repaid
For the souls of all those men who died in vain.

So when the night was dark and deep,
And the men lay fast asleep,
An eerie sound would filter through the night.
It was a violin,
A sound as soft as skin.
Someone was playing in the dim moonlight.

There he stood, dark and thin,
And on his violin
Played a song that spoke of loneliness and pain.
It mourned his victories;
It mourned dead enemies
And friends that he would never see again.

Yes, he courted the reaper,
Like the woman of his dreams,
And the reaper smiled each time he came to call;
But the British like their heroes
Cold and dead, or so it seems,
And their hero in the sky was Albert Ball.

It's an ironic twist of fate
That brings a hero to the gate,
And Ball was no exception to that rule;
Fate puts out the spark
In a way as if to mark
The fine line between a hero and a fool.

Each time he crossed the line,
Albert Ball would check the time
By an old church clock reminding him of home.
The Huns came to know
The man who flew so low
On his way back to the aerodrome.

It was the sixth of May,
He'd done bloody well that day;
For the forty-fourth time, he'd won the game.
As he flew low to check the hour,
A hail of bullets from the tower—
And Albert Ball lay dying in the flames.

But through his clouded eyes,
Maybe he realized,
This was the moment he'd been waiting for.
For the moment that he died,
He was a hero, bonafide.
There are to be no living heroes in this war.

For when a country goes insane,
Obsessed with blood and pain,
Just to be alive is something of a sin.
A war's not satisfied
Until all the best have died,
And the devil take the man who saves his skin.

But sometimes late at night,
When the moon is cold and bright,
I sometimes think I hear that violin.
Death is waiting just outside,
And my eyes are open wide,
As I lie and wait for morning to begin.

Now I am courting the reaper,
Like the woman of my dreams,
And the reaper smiles each time I come to call;
But the British like their heroes
Cold and dead, or so it seems,
And my name will take the place of Albert Ball.

The PIANO PLAYER sings a sad song. BISHOP joins in.

BISHOP and PIANO PLAYER: *(singing)*
Look at the names on the statues
Everywhere you go.
Someone was killed
A long time ago.
I remember the faces;
I remember the time.
Those were the names of friends of mine.

The statues are old now
And they're fading fast.
Something big must have happened
Way in the past.
The names are so faded
You can hardly see,
But the faces are always young to me.

(Chorus)

Friends ain't s'posed to die
'Til they're old.
And friends ain't s'posed to die
In pain.
No one should die alone
When he is twenty-one,
And living shouldn't make you feel ashamed.

I can't believe
How young we were back then.
One thing's for sure,
We'll never be that young again.
We were daring young men,
With hearts of gold,
And most of us never got old.

In an abrupt change of mood, a loud pounding is heard. CEDRIC is knocking on BISHOP's door.

CEDRIC: Wakey, wakey, Bishop. Rise, man! Rise and shine!

BISHOP: *(hung over)* Ohhhh, Cedric. What's the idea of waking me up in the middle of the night?

CEDRIC: It's bloody well eleven o'clock and Madam has a bone to pick with you.

BISHOP: All right, all right, I'll be right there. *(pause)* Good morning, Granny.

LADY ST. HELIER: Bishop! Sit down. I have a bone to pick with you. Cedric, the colonial is under the weather. Bring tea and Epsom salts. Where were you last night, Bishop!

BISHOP: I was out.

LADY ST. HELIER: Good. Very specific. Well, I have my own sources and the picture that was painted for me is not fit for public viewing. Disgusting, unmannered and informal practices in company which is unworthy, even of you, Bishop. But what concerns me is not where you were, but where you were not. To wit, you were not at a party which I personally arranged, at which you were to meet Bonar Law, Chancellor of the Exchequer. What do you have to say in your defence?

BISHOP: Look, Granny …

LADY ST. HELIER: I'll thank you not to call me Granny. The quaintness quite turns my stomach.

BISHOP: Look, that was the fourth darn formal dinner this week! First, it's General Haigh, then what's-his-name, the Parliamentary Secretary … I want to have some fun!

LADY ST. HELIER: Bishop, I'm only going to say this once. It is not for you to be interested, amused or entertained. You are no longer a rather short Canadian with bad taste and a poor service record. You are a figurehead, unlikely as that may seem. A dignitary. The people of Canada, England, the Empire, indeed, the world, look to you as a symbol of victory and you will act the part. You will shine your shoes and press your trousers. You will refrain from spitting, swearing, gambling and public drunkenness, and you will, and I say this with emphasis, you will keep your appointments with your betters. Now, tonight you are having dinner with Lord Beaverbrook, and tomorrow night, with Attorney-General F.E. Smith. Need I say more?

BISHOP: No, no. I'll be there.

LADY ST. HELIER: Good. Oh, and Bishop, I had the occasion to pass the upstairs bathroom this morning and I took the liberty of inspecting your toilet kit. There is what I can only describe as moss growing on your hairbrush and your after-shave lotion has the odour of cat urine. I believe the implications are clear. *(addressing CEDRIC)* Cedric, a difficult road lies before us. Empire must rely for its defences upon an assemblage of Canadians, Australians and Blacks. And now, the Americans. Our way of life is in peril!

BISHOP: *(slightly drunk and writing a letter)* Dearest Margaret. I'm not sure I can get through this evening. In the next room is Princess Marie-Louise and four or five Lords and Ladies whose names I can't even remember. I drank a little bit too much champagne at supper tonight and told the Princess a lot of lies. Now I'm afraid to go back in there because I can't remember what the lies are and I'm afraid I'll contradict myself and look like an idiot. Being rich, you've got a lot more class than me. They'd like you. Maybe we ought to get married. Thinking of you constantly, I remain ...

The PIANO PLAYER and BISHOP break into song.

BISHOP and PIANO PLAYER: *(singing)*
Breakfasting
With Queens and Kings,
Dining with Lords and Earls;
Drink champagne,
It flows like rain,
Making time with high class girls.
Just a Canadian boy,
England's pride and joy,
My fantasies fulfilled;
Ain't no one
Asks me where I'm from,
They're happy for the men I killed.

(Chorus)

Number One is a hero,
Number One's the hottest thing in town!
While I'm in my home
Away from home,
Nobody's gonna shoot me down.

I'm a hired gun,
Gonna shoot someone,
But England's gonna stand by me;
And if I die
You can't deny
They're gonna call it a tragedy.
I'm quaint company,
From the Colonies;
Their love is so sincere.
And when the war is done
And the battle won,
I've got friends as long as I stay here.

(Chorus)

Number One is a hero,
Number One's the hottest thing in town!

While I'm in my home
Away from home,
Nobody's gonna shoot me down.

The music changes to a more sinister note. The following story is half-told, half-acted out, the overall effect being of an adventure story being told in the present tense, It is done as a boy might tell a story, full of his own sound effects.

BISHOP: I woke up at three o'clock in the morning. Jeez, was I scared! Very tense, you know? I mean, Ball said you couldn't do it with just one guy and Ball was a maniac. But I figure it's no more dangerous than what we do every day, so what the hell. I mean, it's no worse. I don't think. The trouble is, no one has ever attacked a German aerodrome single-handedly before, so it's chancy, you know what I mean? I put my flying suit on over my pyjamas, grab a cup of tea and out I go. It's raining. Lousy weather for it, but what can you do? Walter Bourne, my mechanic, is the only other man up. He has the engine running and waiting for me.

BOURNE: Bloody stupid idea if you ask me, Sir. I would put thumbs down on the whole thing and go back to bed if I was you, Sir.

BISHOP: Thanks a lot, Walter. That's really encouraging.

BOURNE: It's pissing rain, Sir. Bleeding pity to die in the pissing rain. I can see it all now. Clear as crystal before me very eyes. First, Albert Ball snuffs it. Then, Captain Bishop snuffs it. It's a bleeding pity if you ask me, Sir. I mean, it's a balls-up from beginning to end. Why don't you take my advice and go back to bed like a good lad, Sir?

BISHOP: Why don't you shut up, Walter? Ready?

BOURNE: Ready, Sir!

The plane takes off.

BISHOP: God, it's awful up here! Pale grey light, cold, lonely as hell. My stomach's bothering me. Nerves? Naw, forgot to eat breakfast. Shit, just something else to put up with. RRRrrrr. I climb to just inside the clouds as I go over the line. No trouble? Good. Everybody is asleep. Let's find that German aerodrome. RRrrr. Where is it? Should be right around here. RRRrrr. *(He spots something.)* All right, a quick pass, a few bursts inside those sheds, just to wake them up, and then pick them off one by one as they try to come up. Wait a minute, wait a minute. There's no planes. There's no people. The bloody place is deserted. Well, shit, that's that, isn't it? I mean, I can't shoot anyone if there is nobody here to shoot. Bloody stupid embarrassment, that's what it is. RRrrr. Feeling really miserable now, I cruise now looking for some troops to shoot them. RRrrrr. Nobody! What the hell is going on around here? Is everybody on vacation? Suddenly, I see the sheds of another German aerodrome ahead and slightly to the left. Dandy. Trouble is, it's a little far behind the lines and I'm not exactly sure where I am. But, it's either that or go back. My stomach is really bothering me now. Why didn't I eat breakfast? And why didn't I change out of my pyjamas? That's going to be great, isn't it, if I'm taken prisoner, real dignified? Spend the rest of the bloody war in my bloody pyjamas. RRRrrrrrr. Over the aerodrome at about three hundred feet. Jeezus, we got lots of planes here, lots and lots of planes. What have we got … six scouts and a two-seater? Jeez, I hope that two seater doesn't come up for me. I'll have a hell of a time getting him from the rear. It's a little late to think about it now. RRRRrrrrrr.

Machine gun fire opens up.

AKAKAKakakakak, RRRRRRRRRrrr. AKAKAK-akaka.

On the ground, GERMANS are heard yelling.

GERMANS: Ach Himmel! In's Gelände! In's Gelände! Hier sind wir alle tot!

BISHOP: I don't know how many guys I got on that first pass. A lot of guys went down; a lot of guys stayed down. I shot up a couple of their planes pretty bad.

The sound of ground fire is heard.

I forgot about the machine gun guarding the aerodrome, bullets all around me, tearing up the canvas on my machine. Just so long as they don't hit a wire. Keep dodging. RRrrr. RRRrrr. I can't get too far away or I'll never pick them off as they try to come up. Come on, you guys, come on! One of them is starting to taxi now. I come right down on the deck about fifteen feet behind him. AKAKAkakaka. He gets six feet off the ground, side slips, does this weird somersault and smashes into the end of the field. I put a few rounds into him and pull back on the stick.

RRRrrrrrr. I'm feeling great now. I don't feel scared, I don't feel nothing. Just ready to fight. Come on, you bastards, come on! Wait a minute, wait a minute. This is what Ball was worried about. Two of them are taking off in opposite directions at the same time. Now I feel scared. What do I do now? Get the hell out, that's what you do! One of them is close enough behind me to start firing. Where's the other one? Still on the ground. All right, you want to fight? We'll fight! I put it into a tight turn, he stays right with me, but not quite tight enough. As he comes in for his second firing pass, I evade him with a lateral loop, rudder down off the top and drop on his tail … AKAKAKAKAKAKAKAKAK … I hit the man. The plane goes down and crashes in flames on the field. Beautiful! The second man is closing with me. I have just enough time to put on my last drum of ammunition. I fly straight for him, the old chicken game. I use up all my ammunition … AKAKAKAka … I miss him, but he doesn't want to fight. Probably thinks I'm crazy. I got to get out of here. They will have telephoned every aerodrome in the area. There will be hundreds of planes after me. I climb and head for home. RRRrrrrr. All by myself again, at last. Am I going the right way? Yeah. Jeezus, my stomach! Sharp pains, like I've been shot. Nope, no blood. Good, I haven't been shot, it's just all that excitement on an empty stomach. Being frightened. Jeez, I think I'm going to pass out. No, don't pass out! *(He looks up.)* And then I look up and my heart stops dead then and there. I'm not kidding. One thousand feet above me, six Albatross scouts, and me, with no ammunition. I think I'm going to puke. No, don't puke! Fly underneath them, maybe they won't see you. RRRrrrrr. I try to keep up … For a mile, I fly underneath them, just trying to keep up. RRRrrrr. I got to get away. They're faster than me and if they see me, they got me. But I got to get away! I dive and head for the line … RRRRRRRRRR! … I can feel the bullets smashing into my back at any second, into my arms, into my legs, into my … *(He looks up again.)* Nothing! Jeez, they didn't see me. RRRRrrrr. Filescamp. Home. Just land it, take it easy. RRRR. I land. Walter Bourne is waiting with a group of others.

BOURNE: I'm standing around, waiting for him to be phoned in missing, when there he comes. Like he's been out sightseeing. He lands with his usual skill, cracking both wheels, then comes to a halt, just like usual, except there is nothing left of his bloody machine. It's in pieces, bits of canvas flopping around like laundry in the breeze. Beats me how it stayed together. Captain Bishop sits there, quiet-like, then he turns to me and he says: "Walter," he says, "Walter, I did it. I DID IT! Never had so much fun in me whole life!"

BISHOP: That was the best fight I ever had. Everyone made a very big deal of it, but I just kept fighting all summer. My score kept getting higher and higher and I was feeling good. By the middle of August, I had forty-three, just one less than Albert Ball. And that's when the generals and colonels started treating me funny.

Going to war music is heard once again.

TRENCHARD: Bishop! Yes, we have lots of medals for you, eh? Lots and lots of medals. And that's not all, no, no, no. You will receive your medals, then you'll go on extended Canada leave and you won't fight again.

BISHOP: What did you say, Sir?

TRENCHARD: Do I have a speech impediment, Bishop? I said you won't fight again.

BISHOP: Not fight again? But I've got to fight again. I've got forty-three; Ball had forty-four. All I need is one more of those sons of …

TRENCHARD: Bishop! You have done very well. You will receive the Victoria Cross, the Distinguished Service Order, the Military Cross. No British pilot has done that, not even Albert Ball, God rest his soul. Leave it at that, Bishop. You have done England a great service. Thank you very much. Now you don't have to fight any more. I should think you'd be delighted.

BISHOP: You don't understand, Sir. I like it.

TRENCHARD: Oh, I know you like it. But it's becoming something of a problem. You see, you have become a colonial figurehead.

BISHOP: I know, a dignitary.

TRENCHARD: A colonial dignitary, Bishop. There is a difference. You see, Bishop, the problem with your colonial is that he has a morbid enthusiasm for life. You might call it a Life-Wish. Now, what happens when your colonial figurehead gets killed? I'll tell you what happens. Colonial morale plummets. Despair is in the air. Fatalism rears its ugly head. But a living

colonial figurehead is a different cup of tea. The men are inspired. They say: "He did it and he lived. I can do it too." Do you get the picture, Bishop?

BISHOP: I believe I do, Sir.

TRENCHARD: Good lad. You shall leave Squadron Sixty, never to return, on the morning of August 17th. That is all.

BISHOP: Well, that still gives me a week. A lot can be done in a week.

To the audience.

In the next six days, I shot down five planes. I really was Number One now. And the squadron, they gave me a big piss-up on my last night. But something happened in that last week that made me fairly glad to get out of it for a while. It was number forty-six.

Music is heard.

It's dusk. Around eight o'clock. I'm returning to Filescamp pretty leisurely because I figure this is my last bit of flying for a bit. It's a nice clear evening and when it's clear up there in the evening, it's really very pretty. Suddenly, I see this German Aviatic two-seater heading right for me. It's a gift. I don't even have to think about this one. I put the plane down into a steep dive and come up underneath him and just rake his belly with bullets. Well, I don't know how they built those planes, but the whole thing just fell apart right before my very eyes. The wings came off, bits of the fuselage just collapsed, and the pilot and the gunner, they fall free. Now I'm pretty sure I didn't hit them, so they are alive and there is nothing I can do to help them or shoot them or anything. All I can do is just sit there and watch those two men fall, wide awake … to die! It's awful. I know I've killed lots of them, but this is different. I can watch them falling down, down. One minute, two minutes, three minutes. It's almost like I can feel them looking at me.

He stops for a moment, perplexed by unfamiliar qualms, shrugs and then goes on.

So when I leave for London the next day, I'm pretty glad to be going after all.

The scene changes to London.

LADY ST. HELIER: Bishop, today you will meet the King. This represents a high water mark for us all and you must see to it that you do not make a balls-up of it. I understand the King is particularly excited today. It seems this is his first opportunity of presenting three medals to the same gentleman. Furthermore, the King is amused that that gentleman is from the colonies. The King, therefore, may speak to you. Should you be so honoured, you will respond politely, in grammatically cogent phrases, with neither cloying sentimentality nor rude familiarity. You will speak to the King with dignity and restraint. Do you think you can manage that, Bishop? Is it possible that the safest course would be for you to keep your mouth shut?

Music is heard.

BISHOP: I arrived at Buckingham Palace, late. It is very confusing.

ADJUTANT: Excuse me, Sir, but where do you think you're going?

BISHOP: Oh, look, I'm supposed to get a medal or something around here.

ADJUTANT: Oh, you're way off, you are, Sir. This is His Majesty's personal reception area. You just about stumbled into the royal loo!!!

2ND OFFICER: What seems to be the trouble around here?

ADJUTANT: Good Lord! Well, the colonial here wants a medal, but his sense of direction seems to have failed him.

2ND OFFICER: Come along, Bishop. We've been looking all over for you. Now, the procedure is this: ten paces to the centre, turn, bow.

The music strikes up "Land of Hope and Glory."

It's started already, Bishop. You're just going to have to wing it!

The music continues as a processional. BISHOP enters stiffly into the presence of the King.

BISHOP: Here comes the King with his retinue, Order of St. Michael, Order of St. George, and here I am. The King pins three medals on my chest. Then he says …

The King's voice is booming, echoing. It is spoken by the PIANO PLAYER and mimed by BISHOP.

KING GEORGE: Well, Captain Bishop. You've been a busy bugger!

BISHOP: I'm not kidding. I'm standing here and the King is standing here. The King talks to me for fifteen minutes! I can't say a word. I've lost my voice. But after the investiture comes the parties, the balls, the photographers, the newspaper reporters, the Lords and Ladies, the champagne, the filet mignon and the fifty-year-old brandy. And here's me, Billy Bishop, from Owen Sound, Canada, and I know one thing: this is my day! There will never be a day like it! I think of this as we dance far into the night, as we dance to the music of … the Empire Soirée.

The PIANO PLAYER and BISHOP sing sotto and sinister.

BISHOP and PIANO PLAYER: *(singing)*
Civilizations come and go (don't you know),
Dancing on to oblivion (oblivion).
The birth and death of nations,
Of civilizations,
Can be viewed down the barrel of a gun.

Nobody knows who calls the tune (calls the tune),
It's been on the Hit Parade for many years (can't you hear).
You and I must join the chorus,
Like ancestors before us,
And like them, we're going to disappear.

(Chorus)

You're all invited to the Empire Soirée,
We'll see each other there, just wait and see;
Attendance is required at the Empire Soirée,
We'll all dance the dance of history.

Revolutions come and go (don't you know).
New empires will take the others' place (take their place).
The song may be fun,
But a new dance has begun,
When someone points a gun at someone's face.

Alexander and Julius had their dance (had their chance),
'Til somebody said: "May I cut in?" (with a grin).
All you and I can do,
Is put on our dancing shoes,
And wait for the next one to begin.

(Chorus)

You're all invited to the Empire Soirée,
We'll see each other there, just wait and see;
Attendance is required at the Empire Soirée,
We'll all dance the dance of history.

*At the end of "The Empire Soirée," BISHOP does
a little dance of victory for the audience, ending
with a final salute.*

Blackout.

*A spotlight hits the PIANO PLAYER, who sings a
narration summing up BISHOP's career and
building to a reprise of "We Were Off to Fight the
Hun." The song has a bitter edge now, for it is
World War II we are talking about.*

PIANO PLAYER: *(singing)*
Billy went back home again,
But still, he was not done;
Seventy-two planes did their dance,
To the rhythm of his guns.
And in twenty years, he was back again,
A new war to be won;
And the hero calls to new recruits in 1941.
The hero calls to new recruits in 1941.

And they were off to fight the Hun,
They would shoot him with a gun.
Their medals would shine,
Like a sabre in the sun.
They were off to fight the Hun
And it looked like lots of fun,
Somehow it didn't seem like war
At all, at all, at all.
Somehow it didn't seem like war at all.

*The lights come up slowly on BISHOP. Twenty
years have gone by and he is much older and
very tired. He is wearing an astonishing array of
medals and they seem to weigh him down a bit.
BISHOP addresses the audience as though they
were fresh World War II recruits. His voice has
the tone and melody of war rhetoric.*

The PIANO PLAYER plays "God Save the King."

BISHOP: I have seen you go and my heart is very
proud. Once again, in the brief space of twenty
years, our brave young men rush to the defence
of the Mother Country. Once again, you must go
forward with all the courage and vigour of youth
to wrest mankind from the grip of the Iron Cross
and the Swastika. Once again, on the edge of
destiny, you must test your strength. I know you
of old, I think. God speed you. God speed you,
the Army, on feet and on wheels, a member of

which I was for so many happy years of my life.
God speed you the Air Force, where in the
crucible of battle, I grew from youth to manhood.
God speed you and God bless you. For, once
again, the freedom of mankind rests in you: in the
courage, the skill, the strength and the blood of
our indomitable youth.

*BISHOP's recruitment speech ends on a grand
note. He stops and stares at the audience for a
while with a certain amount of bewilderment.
The PIANO PLAYER plays a haunting and
discordant "In the Sky." BISHOP speaks, but this
time it is quiet and personal.*

You know, I pinned the wings on my own son this
week. Margaret and I are very proud of him. And
of our daughter. Three Bishops in uniform fighting
the same war. Well, I guess I'm on the sidelines
cheering them on. It comes as a bit of a surprise
to me that there is another war on. We didn't
think there was going to be another one back in
1918. Makes you wonder what it was all for? But
then, we're not in control of any of these things,
are we? And all in all I would have to say, it was
a hell of a time!

BILLY BISHOP sings a cappella.

BISHOP: *(singing)*
Oh, the bloody earth is littered
With the fighters and the quitters.
You can hear the soldiers yearning:
"Oh, if only I could fly!"
From the burning sun, I'll sight you,
In the burning sun, I'll fight you,
Oh, let us dance together in the sky.

The PIANO PLAYER joins him in the chorus.

BISHOP AND PIANO PLAYER: *(singing)*
In the sky,
In the sky,
Just you and I up there together,
Who knows why?
One the hunter, one the hunted;
A life to live, a death confronted.
Oh, let us dance together in the sky.

BISHOP: Goodnight   ladies.   Goodnight,
gentlemen. Goodnight.

Blackout.

END

DAVID FENNARIO (b. 1947)

One of the distinguishing features of modern Canadian drama has been its tendency to give a stage voice to the dispossessed, those living outside or on the fringes of the Canadian mainstream. In the 1960s and '70s, plays like *The Ecstasy of Rita Joe*, *Fortune and Men's Eyes*, and *Creeps* drew their protagonists from worlds only marginal to the lives of the middle class majority. George F. Walker, Judith Thompson, Tomson Highway and others have continued to write plays dramatizing the "other Canada." But no Canadian playwright has focused on a single group as consistently as David Fennario. Fennario's world is "the Pointe," the primarily anglophone working-class district of Pointe St. Charles in Montreal. His characters are a politically disenfranchised urban proletariat doomed to a culture of poverty by socio-economic circumstances and their own sense of futility. Fennario's plays show them coping with the daily indignities at work and at home. And they show us what happens when these people are pushed beyond the point at which apathy, jokes or another beer are sufficient painkiller. In *Balconville* Fennario presents a vision of working-class Quebec in microcosm, a sharply etched, richly human portrait of French and English divided by language though joined in every other significant way, still seemingly unable to recognize their common cause. In the process he has given us Canada's first truly bilingual play.

Fennario himself comes from the world he writes about. Born David Wiper in the Pointe, he was raised, as he explains in *The Work*, to be stupid: "That's about survival; if I think I'm stupid I'll be able to last forty years working at Northern Electric ... That was basic Pointe training." He dropped out of school at seventeen, took the name Fennario from a Bob Dylan song, and temporarily became a part of the hippie sub-culture. In 1968 he went to work in a Montreal dress factory and then in a Simpson's warehouse—experiences he would use in his first two plays—meanwhile becoming an active member of the Socialist Labour Party.

Hoping to avoid the dead-end he seemed destined for, Fennario enrolled at Montreal's Dawson College in 1970. His English teacher recognized the astonishing raw talent shown in a journal he had been keeping, and she helped him have it published in 1972. *Without a Parachute*, Fennario's impressions of life in the Pointe from 1969–71, came to the attention of Maurice Podbrey, artistic director of the Centaur Theatre, and he commissioned Fennario to write a play. Like George F. Walker, Fennario had seen only one play before. So Podbrey helped get him a Canada Council grant to spend two years sitting in on rehearsals and learning theatre from the inside as writer-in-residence at the Centaur. He remained the Centaur's resident playwright for nearly a decade.

On the Job (1975), his powerful first play, brought Fennario theatrical success and personal notoriety. Gary, the young worker from the Pointe whose revolutionary politics initiate the wildcat strike in the dress factory shipping room, was obviously the playwright himself. Fennario became a media darling, the Canadian theatre's own angry young man, the artist as working-class hero. That had an effect on his next play, *Nothing to Lose* (1976), which is better in many ways than *On the Job* but suffers from the gross intrusion of autobiography. This time the workers are on a lunch break at a tavern. Job action is brewing when in walks Jerry, once a fellow worker but now a celebrity writer, back with tales from that other world. He's back yet again in *Toronto* (1978), Fennario's most self-indulgent and least successful play.

Balconville distilled the best of all Fennario's work. He wrote himself into the play only peripherally in aspects of young Tom; brought Jackie, the crazy worker and Pointe legend from the two early plays, into the foreground as Johnny Regan; increased the role of the francophone characters, an important but subordinate element in the earlier plays; and moved his setting from the workplace to the home, giving women a central role in his drama for the first time. But the real *coup de théâtre* was writing nearly a third of the dialogue in French. More than 50,000 Montrealers saw *Balconville* during its two runs in January 1979 and a year later. A revised version with a new ending broke attendance records at the St. Lawrence Centre in the fall of 1979, toured Canada, and won the Chalmers Award. In 1981 the Centaur took its production to Belfast, Bath and London, the first Canadian company ever to play the Old Vic. In 1992 the play had a major Montreal revival at the Centaur, directed by Paul Thompson.

Following *Balconville*, Theatre Passe Muraille produced an adaptation of *Without a Parachute* (1979), and from that developed *Changes* (1980), an autobiographical one-man show. Fennario was back at the Centaur for his next major play, *Moving* (1983), in which a single family becomes the battleground on which are fought the social and political wars of contemporary Quebec. Fennario walked away from middle-class, professional theatre in the mid-1980s to devote himself to working with the Black Rock project, a cultural organization in Pointe St. Charles, where he still lives. For it he wrote and directed a series of plays examining Montreal's ruling elite and their victimization of the city's working classes: the historical satires *Joe Beef* (1984) and *Neill Cream: The Mysteries of McGill* (1985) —retitled *Doctor Thomas Neill Cream (Mystery at McGill)* upon its 1993 publication—and *The Murder of Susan Parr* (1989). He returned to the Centaur in 1991 with *The Death of René Lévesque*, a highly controversial play condemning the Parti Québécois leader for betraying his social democratic principles. In 1994 he wrote and performed *Banana Boots* for Toronto's Annex Theatre and subsequently for television. In this one-man show Fennario describes his changing feelings about his own role in the theatre while on tour with *Balconville* in Belfast. "I mean, I'm supposed to be writing shows about the working class for the working class, right? So what am I doing sitting in the Hotel Europa looking at myself in the mirror?"

In the plays leading up to *Balconville*, the politics are mostly a veneer behind which the young workers act out their frustration and rage against the repressive system with wild releases of anarchic energy. *On the Job* and especially *Nothing to Lose* show us the last hurrahs of sixties rebelliousness. With *Balconville* everyone has grown older. Elvis is dead and the sixties are just a dim memory. Johnny was a "rebel, a real teen angel," but he's grown up to be a drunk. The Parti Québécois is in power but nothing has really changed for the Montreal poor except that now the *maudits anglais* are in the same boat as the French. "That's one good thing now," Paquette tells Tom. "We're all equal. Nobody's got a chance." This kind of bitter fatalism (the psychology of the poor, Fennario calls it) seems borne out in the play not only by Paquette's losing his job, but by the future apparently in store for the young people, Tom and Diane. Tom tries unsuccessfully to escape but can't get across the border. By the end he's on the treadmill, working at an unskilled job he already hates. Diane will help out her family by going to work as a waitress. But we see from Irene's life where that is likely to lead her: through the same bleak cycle of futility and despair.

Fennario dismisses "the myth of the happy poor," and indeed except for simple-minded Thibault his characters are not very happy. But they are funny and resilient in the tradition of what might be called "tenement naturalism" shared by playwrights like Michel Tremblay and Sean O'Casey. Like them Fennario finds great strength in his women. Although they all have desperate moments, they are not easily fazed. Cécile persists in feeding her "air force" and cultivating her plants no matter how often the cats piss on them. Irene never stops trying to rally her neighbours to political activism no matter how great their apathy.

And towards the end there are real signs of hope. Despite the heat making everyone irritable, despite the strong sense of two solitudes evoked by separate flags, separate languages, separate TV sets side by side, some progress is made. Johnny stops drinking and commiserates with Paquette *in French*. The broken step, the play's most conspicuous symbol of the disrepair in these people's lives, gets fixed. It can only happen one small step at a time, Fennario seems to be saying in this revised version of the play. The ending of the original production was a contrivance of wishful thinking: "the characters suddenly fall misty-eyed into each other's arms, ready to enter some nebulous franglophone workers' paradise," Fred Blazer reported in his *Globe and Mail* review. In rethinking the ending Fennario replaced his Marxist answer with a Brechtian question which the characters ask in their own separate languages. "I think maybe the other ending is more enjoyable," Fennario has said, "but this one seems more true."

A note on the text: Because the French dialogue is such an essential component of this play, the text has been presented here just as it was in production, intact and untranslated. Bilingualism is at the very heart of *Balconville*. The anglophone audience member who is unilingual or has only minimal French is in the same relationship to the play as an anglophone working-class Quebecker like Johnny Regan is to the francophone culture that surrounds him. He has to struggle to make sense of French speech. Thus the audience's experience of *Balconville* reiterates one of the things the play is about: language differences are a serious obstacle to communication, but can be overcome with effort. With its French passages translated it would be a different play. Of course a theatre audience has access to vocal inflection, gesture, facial expression and body language which can communicate eloquently even where words are not understood. The reader of a play, on the other hand, has only stage directions and his own imagination to help fill in the blanks. So the reader who knows little or no French will have to work even harder for a full understanding of *Balconville*. But the rewards are well worth the effort.—Ed.

Balconville was first performed at the Centaur Theatre in Montreal on January 2, 1979, with the following cast:

CLAUDE PAQUETTE	Marc Gélinas
CÉCILE PAQUETTE	Cécile St-Denis
DIANE PAQUETTE	Manon Bourgeois
MURIEL WILLIAMS	Terry Tweed
TOM WILLIAMS	Robert Parson
JOHNNY REGAN	Peter MacNeill
IRENE REGAN	Lynn Deragon
THIBAULT	Jean Archambault
GAËTAN BOLDUC	Gilles Tordjman

Directed by Guy Sprung
Set and Costume Design by Barbara Matis
Lighting Design by Steven Hawkins
Sound Design by Peter Smith

BALCONVILLE

CHARACTERS

CLAUDE PAQUETTE
CÉCILE PAQUETTE, *his wife*
DIANE PAQUETTE, *their daughter*
MURIEL WILLIAMS
TOM WILLIAMS, *her son*
JOHNNY REGAN
IRENE REGAN, *his wife*
THIBAULT
GAËTAN BOLDUC, *a politician*

SET

The back of a tenement in the Pointe Saint-Charles district of Montreal. We see a flight of stairs leading up to two balconies which are side by side, the Regans' and the Paquettes'. Directly below the Paquettes' balcony is the ground floor balcony of the Williams'.—Ed.

ACT ONE

Scene One

It is night. TOM is sitting on his back balcony trying to play "Mona" on his guitar. The sound of a car screeching around a corner is heard. The car beeps its horn. DIANE enters.

VOICE: Diane, Diane …

DIANE: J'savais que t'avais une autre blonde.

VOICE: Mais non, Diane, c'était ma soeur.

DIANE: Oui, ta soeur. Mange d'la merde. Fuck you!

CÉCILE comes out of her house and stands on her balcony.

CÉCILE: C'est-tu, Jean-Guy? Diane?

DIANE: Oh, achale-moi pas.

The car screeches away

MURIEL: *(from the screen door behind TOM)* Goddam teenagers, they don't stop until they kill someone. Tommy, what are you doing there?

The sound of the car screeching is heard on the other side of the stage.

VOICE: Hey, Diane. Diane …

DIANE: Maudit crisse, va-t'en, hostie.

CÉCILE: Diane, c'est Jean-Guy.

VOICE: Hey, Diane. Viens-t'en faire un tour avec moi. Diane?

The car beeps its horn.

DIANE: Jamais, jamais. J't'haïs, j't'haïs.

VOICE: Hey, Diane.

The car beeps its horn again.

PAQUETTE: *(from inside his house)* Qu'est-ce qu'y a? Qu'est-ce tu veux, hostie?

VOICE: Diane, viens ici.

PAQUETTE: *(yelling from the upstairs window)* Si tu t'en vas pas, j'appelle la police.

MURIEL comes out of her house, goes down the alley and yells after the car.

MURIEL: Get the hell out of here, you goddamn little creep!

The car screeches away. MURIEL returns to her house.

MURIEL: Tom you gotta get up tomorrow.

TOM: Yeah, yeah.

MURIEL goes into her house.

PAQUETTE: Maudit crisse, j'te dis que t'en as des amis toi. C'est la dernière fois que j'te préviens. Cécile, viens-tu t'coucher?

CÉCILE: Oui, oui, Claude, j'arrive. Diane, Jean-Guy devrait pas venir si tard.

DIANE: Ah, parle-moi pu d'lui.

CÉCILE: Son char fait bien trop de train, y devrait faire réparer son muffler.

CÉCILE goes into her house with DIANE. JOHNNY enters. He is drunk and singing "Heartbreak Hotel." He finds that the door to his house is locked.

JOHNNY: Hey, Irene ... Irene, open the fuckin' door.

IRENE opens the door.

PAQUETTE: *(from inside his house)* Hey! Ferme ta gueule, toi-là.

JOHNNY: Fuck you!

He goes into his house and slams the door shut.

Blackout.

Scene Two

The next day. It is morning. THIBAULT enters wheeling his Chez Momo's delivery bike down the lane. TOM comes out of the house with toast, coffee, cigarettes and his guitar. When he is finished his toast and coffee, he begins to practise his guitar.

MURIEL: *(from inside her house)* Tom, you left the goddamn toaster on again.

TOM: Yeah?

MURIEL: Yeah, well, I'm the one who pays the electric bills.

THIBAULT: *(looking at the tire on his delivery bike)* Câlice, how did that happen? The tire, c'est fini.

TOM: A flat.

THIBAULT: Eh?

TOM: A flat tire.

THIBAULT: Ben oui, un flat tire. The other one, she's okay ... That's funny, eh? Very funny, that.

TOM: Don't worry, Thibault, it's only flat on the bottom.

THIBAULT: You think so? Well, I got to phone the boss.

He goes up the stairs and steps over the broken step.

TOM: Hey, watch the step!

THIBAULT: *(knocking on PAQUETTE's door)* Paquette, Paquette ...

PAQUETTE: *(from inside his house)* Tabarnac, c'est quoi?

THIBAULT: C'est moi, Paquette. J'ai un flat tire.

PAQUETTE: Cécile, la porte ...

CÉCILE: *(from inside the house)* Oui, oui ... Une minute ...

THIBAULT: C'est moi, Paquette.

CÉCILE: *(at the screen door)* Allô, Thibault. Comment ça va?

THIBAULT: J'ai un flat tire sur mon bicycle.

CÉCILE: Oh, un flat tire.

PAQUETTE: Que c'est qu'y a?

CÉCILE: C'est Thibault, Claude.

PAQUETTE: Thibault? Thibault?

THIBAULT: Oui. Bonjour.

PAQUETTE: Es-tu tombé sur la tête, tabarnac? Il est sept heures et demie du matin, hostie de ciboire.

CÉCILE: Claude a travaillé tard hier soir.

THIBAULT: That's not so good, eh?

PAQUETTE: Que c'est qu'y veut?

CÉCILE: Y veux savoir c'que tu veux.

THIBAULT: *(yelling at PAQUETTE through the window)* J'ai un flat tire. Je voudrais téléphoner à mon boss.

PAQUETTE: Cris pas si fort, j'suis pas sourd. Cecile, dis-lui rentrer.

JOHNNY: *(from inside his house)* What the fuck's going on?

THIBAULT: C'est-tu, okay?

CÉCILE: Oui, oui. Entre.

THIBAULT goes into PAQUETTE's house. JOHNNY comes out on his balcony.

JOHNNY: What's going on?

TOM: *(from below)* Thibault's got a flat tire.

JOHNNY: Flat tire? Big fuckin' production!

He goes back into his house.

THIBAULT: *(inside PAQUETTE's house)* Allô, Paquette. J'vas téléphoner a mon boss. C'est-tu, okay? C'est-tu, okay?

PAQUETTE: *(from inside his house)* Ferme ta gueule! Tu m'as reveille asteur. Fais ce que t'as à faire.

THIBAULT: *(on the telephone)* Oui, allô, Monsieur Kryshinsky … This is the right number? This is Monsieur Kryshinsky? … Bon. C'est moi, Thibault … Oui … Quoi? … Yes, I'm not there. I'm here …

CÉCILE: *(from inside the house)* Veux-tu ton déjeuner, Claude?

PAQUETTE: Non, fais-moi un café. Ça va faire.

THIBAULT: Un flat tire, oui … Okay. Yes sir. I'll be there … Oui. I'll be there tout de suite … Okay, boss. Bye … Allô? Bye. *(He hangs up the telephone.)* Faut que j'm'en aille. C'était mon boss. Tu le connais, "I don't like it when you're late. When I get to the store, I want you there at the door. Right there at the door."

PAQUETTE: *(at the door, pushing THIBAULT outside)* Salut, Thibault. Salut, Thibault.

THIBAULT: Okay, salut.

Coming down the stairs, THIBAULT trips on the broken step and loses his cap.

TOM: *(from below)* Watch the step!

THIBAULT: Hey, that was a close one. Very close, that one.

THIBAULT exits on his bike.

PAQUETTE: *(on his balcony)* Cécile, est-ce que Diane veut un lift pour aller à l'école?

CÉCILE: *(at the screen door)* Diane?

DIANE: *(from inside the house)* Non.

PAQUETTE: Pourquoi faire?

DIANE: Parce que j'aime pas la manière qu'y chauffe son char.

CÉCILE: Elle a dit que …

PAQUETTE: J'suis pas sourd. Qu'elle s'arrange pas pour manquer ses cours, c'est moi qui les paye cet été.

DIANE: Inquiète-toi pas avec ça.

JOHNNY comes out on his balcony.

PAQUETTE: *(to JOHNNY)* Hey, people gotta sleep at night, eh?

JOHNNY: You talking to me?

PAQUETTE: *(pointing to the wall)* No, him. Hostie.

CÉCILE: Claude, j'pense que ce soir, je vais te faire des bonnes tourtières. Tu sais celles que t'aimes, celles du Lac St-Jean.

PAQUETTE: Encore des tourtières.

CÉCILE: Claude, t'aimes ça des tourtières.

PAQUETTE: Oui, j'aime ça des tourtières, mais pas tous les jours.

DIANE: *(from inside the house)* Maman, où sont mes souliers … mes talons hauts?

CÉCILE: J'sais pas. Où est-ce que tu les as mis hier soir?

She disappears into the house.

PAQUETTE: Cécile, j'm'en vas.

JOHNNY: Watch the step!

PAQUETTE: *(coming down the stairs)* C'est qui a encore laissé les vidanges en dessous des escaliers?

TOM: *(from below)* Not me.

PAQUETTE: It's me who got the trouble with the landlord, eh?

CÉCILE comes running out on the balcony with PAQUETTE's lunchbucket.

CÉCILE: Claude, Claude … T'as oublié ton lunch.

PAQUETTE: C'est l'affaire de Thibault … Pitch moi-la.

CÉCILE tosses him his lunch.

JOHNNY: Baloney sandwiches again, eh Porky?

PAQUETTE exits. IRENE comes out on her balcony to take the underwear off the clothesline.

JOHNNY: What time is it, Irene?

IRENE: *(looking at him)* You look a wreck.

JOHNNY: You don't look so hot yourself.

IRENE: You're beginning to look like a boozer. Ya know that?

JOHNNY: Hey, all I want is the time.

DIANE comes out on the balcony carrying her school books.

DIANE: J'perds mon temps avec ce maudit cours stupide, surtout l'été.

CÉCILE: Diane, est-ce que tu vas venir souper?

DIANE: Peut-être.

CÉCILE goes back into her house. DIANE comes down the stairs. She is wearing shorts and high heels. JOHNNY and TOM both look at her.

JOHNNY: Hey, Diane, ya look like a flamingo in those things.

DIANE makes a face at him and exits down the lane.

IRENE: You like that, eh?

JOHNNY: Just looking.

IRENE: Well, no more meat and potatoes for you.

JOHNNY: Eh?

IRENE: You know what I mean.

JOHNNY: What?

IRENE goes back into the house.

JOHNNY: Fuck!

TOM: She's mad, eh?

JOHNNY: Ya ask her for the time and she tells you how to make a watch.

He listens to TOM practising his guitar.

Hey, softer on the strings. Strum them, don't bang them.

TOM: *(trying to strum)* Like that?

JOHNNY: Yeah, sort of …

TOM: You used to play, eh?

JOHNNY: Yeah. Ever heard of "J.R. and the Falling Stars"?

TOM: No.

JOHNNY: You're looking at "J.R."

MURIEL comes out of her house carrying a bag of garbage.

MURIEL: *(to TOM)* What are you doing?

TOM: The U.I.C. don't open till nine o'clock.

MURIEL: Yeah, but there's gonna be a line-up.

TOM: It's a waste of time. They never get ya jobs anyhow.

MURIEL: Well, don't think you're gonna hang around here doing nothing.

TOM: Okay, okay. Ma, I need some bus fare and some money for lunch.

MURIEL: You can come home for lunch.

TOM: Ma …

MURIEL: I'm not giving you any money to bum around with.

TOM goes into the house with his guitar.

MURIEL: And you leave my purse alone in there too.

TOM: *(coming back out with her purse)* Ma, I want my allowance.

MURIEL: What allowance? You don't go to school no more.

TOM: I want my money.

MURIEL: Gimme that purse. Gimme that goddamn purse.

She snatches her purse away from TOM, opens it and gives him some bus tickets.

That's it … that's all you get.

TOM: Fuck!

MURIEL: Don't you swear at me. Don't you ever swear at me.

TOM exits.

JOHNNY: *(singing)* "Hi-ho, hi-ho, it's off to work we go."

MURIEL: *(to JOHNNY)* You're not funny.

JOHNNY: You're a little hard on the kid, aren't ya, Muriel?

MURIEL: Yeah, well, look what happened to you.

JOHNNY: Fuck! What's with everybody today? Is it the heat or what?

He goes into his house. CÉCILE comes out on her balcony. She notices MURIEL's wash hanging from the clothesline.

CÉCILE: It's so nice to see that, madame.

MURIEL: See what?

CÉCILE: To see you put up the washing the right way. First the white clothes, then the dark ones. The young girls, they don't care anymore.

MURIEL: Yeah, well, why should they?

CÉCILE: Having children is not easy today? Eh?

MURIEL: Ah, they don't know what's good for them.

CÉCILE: Oui, I suppose.

MURIEL: When I was a kid, you just did what you were told and that was it.

CÉCILE: Yes, I remember that too.

MURIEL: Everybody got along alright. Now, nobody knows their ass from their elbow.

CÉCILE: Elbow? … Yes …

THIBAULT enters on his bike again. He is looking for his cap.

CÉCILE: Allô, Thibault. Comment ça va?

THIBAULT: Ma casquette …

CÉCILE: Ta casquette?

THIBAULT: Ben oui, j'ai perdu ma casquette. Oh, elle est en bas.

He looks under the stairs and finds his cap.

J'veux pas la perde. J'ai payé quatre dollars chez Kresge.

CÉCILE: Eh, Thibault, ton boss était pas trop fâché?

THIBAULT: Il a sacré un peu après moi, but so what, eh? Il est jamais content anyway. Qu'tu fasses n'importe quoi.

CÉCILE: C'est la vie, hein ça?

THIBAULT: Oh, oui. C'est la vie. (He checks his transistor radio.) Hey, thirty-two degrees. That used to be cold. Now, it's hot.

CÉCILE: Comment va ta mère? Est-ce qu'elle va toujours à Notre-Dame-des-Sept-Douleurs?

THIBAULT: Oh, oui. Tous le jours. Mes frères sont tous partis, mais moi, j'suis toujours avec.

CÉCILE: C'est bien ça. Ta mère doit être contente.

THIBAULT: J'fais toute pour elle. Toute. Dans un an, elle va recevoir sa old age pension et puis on va pouvoir s'payer un plus grand logement. On va déménager à Verdun.

CÉCILE: À Verdun. Ça va être bien ça. Thibault, ton boss.

THIBAULT: Oh, oui. Mon boss. I better go now.

THIBAULT exits. MURIEL's phone rings. She goes into her house to answer it. CÉCILE goes into her house.

MURIEL: (on the telephone) Yeah, hello … Who? … Bill, where the hell are ya? … On the docks … shipping out to Sault Ste. Marie … Are you coming back or what? … Don't give me that crap. What's her name, eh? … Yeah, I'm getting the cheques … Tom? No, he's not here … Yeah … Yeah … Look, I'm busy … Bye. (She hangs up the telephone.) Christ, I wish I knew for sure.

IRENE and JOHNNY come out on their balcony. JOHNNY is sipping a cup of coffee. IRENE is wearing her waitress uniform. She is on her way to work.

IRENE: I want to talk to you when I get back, Johnny.

JOHNNY: Yeah, yeah. (sipping his coffee) Agh! What are you trying to do, poison me?

IRENE: I used brown sugar instead of white.

JOHNNY: Shit.

IRENE: It's healthier for you … You going down to the U.I.C.?

JOHNNY: Yeah.

IRENE: Today?

JOHNNY: Yeah, today.

IRENE starts to come down the stairs.

JOHNNY: Irene, what shift are you on?

IRENE: Ten to six this week.

JOHNNY: Why don't you quit that fucking job? Get something else.

IRENE: (stopping) Like what?

JOHNNY: Like anything except a waitress.

IRENE continues down the stairs and exits down the lane.

JOHNNY: *(shouting after her)* Pick me up a carton of smokes, I'm sick of these rollies.

Blackout.

Scene Three

TOM and JOHNNY enter from the alley. JOHNNY is carrying a case of beer.

JOHNNY: I'm telling ya, they're all fucking separatists at the U.I.C. If you're English, you're fucked.

TOM: The phones are always ringing and nobody ever answers them. Ever notice that?

JOHNNY: Too busy having coffee breaks. *(He hands TOM a beer.)* Unenjoyment disappointment office.

JOHNNY sits at the foot of the stairs. TOM leans on the railing.

TOM: Hey, I went down to Northern Electric. I figured I've been breathing in their smoke all my life, so the least they could do is give me a job. Didn't get one ... They're automating.

MURIEL comes out of her house.

JOHNNY: Hi, Muriel.

MURIEL: *(to TOM)* What are you doing?

TOM: Standing up.

JOHNNY: Wanna brew, Muriel?

MURIEL: I told you to keep your goddamn beer to yourself. Tom, come here.

TOM: What?

MURIEL: Never mind what. Just come here. *(TOM moves toward her.)* So, did you go to that job interview?

TOM: Yeah.

MURIEL: So?

TOM: So the guy didn't like me.

MURIEL: He didn't like you? How come?

TOM: I dunno.

MURIEL: What do you mean, you dunno?

TOM: He wanted to send me to some stupid joe job way out in Park Extension. Minimum wage.

MURIEL: Since when can you afford to be fussy?

TOM: I'd have to get up at five in the morning.

MURIEL: There's a lot of things I don't like either, but I do them.

TOM: Well, I don't.

MURIEL: Anyhow, your father phoned. He's not coming home.

TOM: I don't blame him.

MURIEL: What's that?

TOM: Forget it.

MURIEL: Don't you get into one of your moods, mister, 'cause I'll give it to you right back.

MURIEL goes into her house,

TOM: Fuckin' bitch!

JOHNNY: Hey, don't worry about it.

TOM: Just 'cause she's frustrated, don't mean she's gotta take it out on me.

JOHNNY: Let them scream, that's what I do.

JOHNNY leaves TOM and starts up the stairs for his balcony. TOM goes into his house to get his guitar. CÉCILE comes out on her balcony with a handful of breadcrumbs. She starts to feed the birds.

CÉCILE: Hi, Johnny.

JOHNNY: Hi, Cécile.

CÉCILE: Nice day, eh?

JOHNNY: Yeah, but it's too hot.

CÉCILE: Oh yes, too hot.

She continues to feed the birds.

JOHNNY: Feeding your Air Force?

CÉCILE: My what?

JOHNNY: Your Air Force ... Cécile's Air Force.

CÉCILE: Ah, oui. Air Force.

JOHNNY: Just kidding ya, Cécile.

He sits on his balcony with his beer.

CÉCILE: You just kidding me, eh, Johnny?

She throws some more breadcrumbs over the railing. They fall on MURIEL as she comes out of her house carrying a basket of washing.

MURIEL: Jesus Murphy!

CÉCILE: Oh, excuse me, madame. Excuse me. Hello!

MURIEL: Yeah, hello ...

CÉCILE: Aw, it's so nice, eh?

MURIEL: What?

CÉCILE: The sun. It's so nice.

MURIEL: Yeah, I guess it is.

CÉCILE: It's so good for my plants.

JOHNNY: How are your tomatoes?

CÉCILE: My tomatoes? Very good. This year, I think I get some big ones. Last year, I don't know what happened to them.

JOHNNY: The cat pissed on them.

CÉCILE: The what?

JOHNNY: The big tomcat that's always hanging around with Muriel. He pissed on them.

CÉCILE: You think so?

JOHNNY: Sure.

CÉCILE sits on her balcony. TOM comes out of the house again and sits practising his guitar.

JOHNNY: *(to TOM)* Too heavy on the strings ...

PAQUETTE enters carrying his lunchbucket. He is coming home from work.

JOHNNY: Hey, the working man!

PAQUETTE: Somebody has to work, eh?

He starts to climb the stairs. JOHNNY stops him.

JOHNNY: Have a brew here.

PAQUETTE: Okay.

He takes a pint from JOHNNY and sits down on JOHNNY's balcony.

PAQUETTE: Hey, my car, it's not working again. That goddamn carburetor ... *(to CÉCILE, on her balcony)* Cécile ... Hey, Cécile.

CÉCILE: Oui.

PAQUETTE: J'vas manger plus tard.

CÉCILE: Quoi?

PAQUETTE: *(shouting at her)* J'vas manger plus tard.

CÉCILE: Tu vas manger plus tard?

PAQUETTE: Oui, tabarnac!

CÉCILE: T'as pas besoin de sacrer, Claude.

PAQUETTE: C'est correct. As-tu appelé Chez Momo pour faire venir de la bière?

CÉCILE: Oui, Claude.

JOHNNY: Hot, eh? Can't breathe in the fuckin' house ... Can't sleep.

PAQUETTE: Hey, don't talk about it. Today in work one guy, he faints.

JOHNNY: Oh yeah?

PAQUETTE: No, the bosses say there's some energy crisis or something, so they stop the air conditioning in the factory, eh? Not in the office, of course.

JOHNNY: Tell the union.

PAQUETTE: Hey, the union. It's too hot to laugh, câlice.

JOHNNY: Another fire last night, eh?

PAQUETTE: Ah, oui. What street?

JOHNNY: On Liverpool.

PAQUETTE: Liverpool encore. Tabarnac.

JOHNNY: Fuckin' firebugs, man. This block is gonna go up for sure.

PAQUETTE: Oui, that's for sure.

JOHNNY: Soon as I get my cheque, I'm gonna pull off a midnight move. Fuck this shit!

PAQUETTE: Oui, midnight move, for sure. Hey, just like the Arsenaults en bas. Fuck the landlords! It's the best way.

JOHNNY: Yeah ... Whew, hot. Going anywhere this summer?

PAQUETTE: Moi? Balconville.

JOHNNY: Yeah. Miami Bench.

THIBAULT drives in on his Chez Momo's delivery bike.

THIBAULT: Chez Momo's is here.

JOHNNY: Hey, Thibault T-bone.

TOM: Hey, ya fixed the flat?

THIBAULT gets off his bike. He takes a case of beer from the bike.

THIBAULT: Oui. Hey, me, I know the bike, eh? I know what to do.

JOHNNY: Hey, T-bone.

THIBAULT: Chez Momo's is here.

Coming up the stairs, he trips on the broken step.

JOHNNY: Watch the step!

PAQUETTE: Watch the beer!

JOHNNY: You okay?

THIBAULT: Me? I'm okay. But my leg, I don't know.

PAQUETTE: Why don't you read the sign?

THIBAULT: Eh?

PAQUETTE: The sign ...

THIBAULT reads the sign on the balcony. It reads: "Prenez garde."

THIBAULT: Prenez garde. Okay, prenez garde. So what? Tiens, ta bière.

He puts the case of beer down next to PAQUETTE. PAQUETTE gives him some money for the beer.

PAQUETTE: As-tu fini pour à soir?

THIBAULT: Oui, fini. C'est mon dernier voyage. *(shaking the change in his pocket)* Hey, des tips.

JOHNNY: Had a good day, eh?

THIBAULT: Hey, Johnny. Johnny B. Good. Long time no see, like they say.

JOHNNY: Yeah.

THIBAULT: Bye-bye, Johnny B. Good. You remember that?

JOHNNY: Remember what?

THIBAULT: Hey, there in the park, when they used to have the dances. You used to sing all the time like Elvis. *(He does an imitation of Elvis.)* Tutti-frutti, bop-bop-aloo, bop-a-bop, bam-boom. Like that, in the park.

JOHNNY: Yeah, yeah.

THIBAULT: C'était le fun. Me, I like that, but the girls grew up. They got old. You too. Paquette too. He's so fat now. Very fat.

PAQUETTE: Hey, hey.

JOHNNY: You remember all that shit?

THIBAULT: Me? Sure. I remember everything. Everything. Everybody forgets but me. I don't. It's funny, that, eh?

JOHNNY: Yeah.

THIBAULT: But you, you don't sing no more.

JOHNNY: No, I don't sing no more.

THIBAULT: Well, everybody gets old. It's funny, I watch it all change, but it's still the same thing ... I don't know. So what, eh?

PAQUETTE takes THIBAULT's nude magazine out of his back pocket and flips through it.

PAQUETTE: Hey, Thibault. You have a girlfriend?

THIBAULT: Me? Sure. I got two of them. Deux.

PAQUETTE: Deux?

THIBAULT: *(taking back his magazine)* Sure. I got one on Coleraine and the other one, she lives on Hibernia. Two girls. It's tough. *(He comes down the stairs.)* English too. That surprise me. English, they do it too.

THIBAULT exits on his bike. PAQUETTE takes his beer and moves over to his balcony.

JOHNNY: *(pointing to his head, referring to THIBAULT)* The lights are on, but nobody's home.

PAQUETTE: He might as well be crazy, eh? it helps.

JOHNNY: Thinking's no good, man. I wish I could have half my brain removed. Boom! No more troubles. Just like Thibault.

CÉCILE: Pauvre homme. He was such a good boy when he was young. Remember?

PAQUETTE: It's easy to be good when you're young.

CÉCILE: He should have become a priest.

PAQUETTE: Cécile, nobody becomes a priest anymore.

He bumps into one of CÉCILE's plants.

CÉCILE: Claude, fais attention à mes plantes!

PAQUETTE: Toi, pis tes câlices de plantes. Y'en a partout sur le balcon.

IRENE enters. She is wearing her waitress uniform, coming home from work. She stops at MURIEL's house.

IRENE: Hi, Tommy. Your mother home?

TOM: Yeah.

IRENE: *(knocking on MURIEL's door)* Yoo-hoo, Muriel. It's me ... Pointe Action Committee meeting tonight at seven-thirty, eh?

MURIEL: *(at the screen door)* I don't think I'll be going, Irene.

IRENE: It's an important meeting, Muriel. We're going down to the City Hall to demand more stop signs on the streets. Kids are getting hurt.

MURIEL: Yeah, I know.

IRENE: The more of us there, the better.

MURIEL: Yeah. I'm just not in the mood.

IRENE: You okay?

MURIEL: Yeah.

IRENE: Well, okay.

MURIEL goes back into her house. IRENE goes up the stairs, avoiding the broken step.

IRENE: Shit, why doesn't somebody fix that goddamn step?

JOHNNY: I didn't break it.

PAQUETTE: Hey, if I fix it, the landlord will raise the rent.

IRENE: *(at the top of the stairs, looking at JOHNNY and his beer)* Having fun?

JOHNNY: Just having a couple of brews, Irene.

IRENE: Yeah, sure.

JOHNNY: *(offering her a beer)* Here, have one.

She pushes his arm out of the way.

Hey, don't get self-righteous, okay? I get bored, alright? Bored!

IRENE: *(giving him his carton of cigarettes)* Did you go down to the U.I.C.?

JOHNNY: "The cheque's in the mail," unquote.

IRENE: They said that last week.

JOHNNY: They'll say it again next week, too ... Irene, relax. Have a brew.

IRENE: Let me by.

She goes into the house.

PAQUETTE: *(from his balcony)* Hey, there's always trouble when a woman gets a job, eh?

JOHNNY: Yeah, fuckin' U.I.C. slave market, people lined up like sheep. I hate lines.

PAQUETTE: Me, I don't know what's worse, working or not working. Sometimes I wish they'd lay me off for maybe a month.

JOHNNY: Factory getting to ya?

PAQUETTE: Hey, I even dream of it at night, hostie. Click, clack, bing bang. It's bad enough being there in the day, but I see it at night too, hostie.

JOHNNY: Twelve weeks I've been waiting for that cheque ... Four weeks penalty for getting fired, four weeks for filing the claim late, and another four weeks for them to put the cheque in the fuckin' mail.

PAQUETTE: Hey, if they treat a dog like that, the S.P.C.A. would sue them.

DIANE enters, prancing along in her shorts and high heels.

JOHNNY: Love that walk, Diane.

DIANE: Fuck you!

PAQUETTE: Hey, watch ton langage, toi.

DIANE climbs the stairs. When she has passed PAQUETTE, she turns and mouths the words, "Fuck you too." She goes into the house.

JOHNNY: *(shouting after her)* Hey, you're gonna break a leg in those things.

PAQUETTE: Maudit.

JOHNNY: She's starting to look good.

PAQUETTE: Oui. Too good.

JOHNNY: Lots of nice young pussy around the neighbourhood, man. Breaks my heart to see it all.

PAQUETTE: *(reaching for his wallet)* Johnny, I have something ...

He comes over and shows JOHNNY a photograph from his wallet.

PAQUETTE: Hey. Look at that …

JOHNNY: Who's that? Cécile?

PAQUETTE: Oui … She was nice, eh?

JOHNNY: Yeah. *(looking at the photograph again)* Who's that?

PAQUETTE: That? That's me. Moi.

JOHNNY: You're not serious?

PAQUETTE: Hey. Okay, okay.

He snatches back his wallet and returns to his balcony. From DIANE's room, the record "Hot Child in the City" can be heard.

PAQUETTE: Hey, Cécile … Cécile, dis à Diane de baisser sa musique de tuns.

CÉCILE: *(shouting into the house)* Diane, baisse la musique juste un peu.

The volume goes down. The music fades away. IRENE comes out on her balcony to hang up her waitress uniform. JOHNNY goes over to her and starts to hug her.

IRENE: Stop it.

JOHNNY: Honey, don't be mad.

IRENE: I'm not mad, Johnny. Stop it. You smell of beer.

JOHNNY: Okay. I'll hold my breath, Irene.

IRENE: Johnny, you've got to do something … anything … Keep yourself busy.

JOHNNY: Yeah, I'm gonna call up some people, try to get something together, as soon as I get my first cheque.

IRENE: That goddamn cheque!

JOHNNY: Well, I don't want to give up now. Those bastards owe me that money, Irene.

IRENE: Well, why don't you come down to our Unemployment Committee meetings?

JOHNNY: You know that I don't like meetings.

IRENE: Yeah, yeah. Ya'd rather watch *Charlie's Angels.*

JOHNNY: Irene, it's gonna be alright, okay? Say "okay." Say "okay."

IRENE: Okay.

JOHNNY: Alright.

IRENE: I don't know why I have to nag. I don't want to nag. Don't want to sound like my mother.

JOHNNY: Hey, what's the matter? *(tickling her)* You sensitive, eh? You sensitive?

IRENE: Johnny.

JOHNNY: Come on, a Québec quickie.

PAQUETTE: *(from his balcony)* Hey, Jean. It's too hot for that, eh?

JOHNNY: Aw, the heat makes me horny …

An election campaign truck passes by playing Elvis Presley music and broadcasting in French and English.

VOICE: Vote for Gaëtan Bolduc. Gaëtan Bolduc's the man for you. The man of the people. Bolduc is on your side.

JOHNNY: Fuck you, Bolduc!

IRENE: Bolduc is on *his* side.

VOICE: Remember, on the 6th, vote for progress, vote for change, vote for a winner. Vote for Bolduc, the man for you … available and dynamic …

The sound fades away.

JOHNNY: Circus is starting early this year. A month away from the election and he's already doing his fuckin' number.

IRENE: Bolduc, the boss. Did ya see the size of his new house?

JOHNNY: Once a year, he buys hot dogs for the kids on the Boardwalk. Big fuckin' deal!

TOM: Yeah … stale hot dogs.

PAQUETTE: Those guys are all the same crooks.

IRENE: I don't know what's worse, Joe Who or René Quoi?

She goes and gets the mail.

PAQUETTE: Bolduc, he was okay … until he got the power. Then, that's it. He forgets us.

JOHNNY: Any mail for me?

IRENE: *(looking through the mail)* No. Aw, shit. La merde.

JOHNNY: What?

IRENE: Water tax. Eighty-four dollars for water. Christ, it tastes like turpentine and they charge us like it's champagne.

JOHNNY: Hey, all the bills are in French anyhow, separatist bastards. Tell them we're paying in English.

PAQUETTE: Hey, I don't like that.

JOHNNY: What?

PAQUETTE: There's a lot of English bastards around too, eh?

JOHNNY: Yeah, but they're not forcing ya out of the province.

PAQUETTE: Learn how to speak French, that's all.

CÉCILE: You know, Irene, there was another fire last night.

IRENE: Another one?

CÉCILE: Oui. Last night. A big one.

IRENE: The Pointe Action Group thinks the landlords are setting the fires themselves.

PAQUETTE: The landlords? Burning down their own houses?

IRENE: For the insurance.

JOHNNY: Yeah, I believe that.

PAQUETTE: It's the punk kids that do it. They got no father. The mother, she drinks in the taverns. What do they care, eh? They should make them work. Stop all the welfare.

IRENE: There is no work.

PAQUETTE: There's jobs, if they want them. They don't try hard enough.

JOHNNY: Yeah, there's jobs, but who wants to be a busboy all their lives?

PAQUETTE: It's a job.

JOHNNY: Yeah, well, I'm no fuckin' immigrant. I was born here.

PAQUETTE: That's the trouble … too many people. Overpopulation, they call it. We need another war or something. Stop all the welfare and make the lazy bums work.

IRENE: How come people always blame the poor? They never blame the rich.

PAQUETTE: Hey you, tell me, who's got the money, eh? Who's got all the money?

JOHNNY: Not me.

PAQUETTE: It's the English and the Jews.

IRENE: Hey!

PAQUETTE: They control everything, the goddamn Jews. That's the trouble.

IRENE: Hey, my mother was Jewish, so don't give me that shit, okay?

PAQUETTE: Hey, I don't talk about the good Jews …

JOHNNY: What the fuck's going on?

PAQUETTE: Hey, me, I work all my life. All my life, me. Since I was ten years old.

JOHNNY: Yeah, so why cry about it?

PAQUETTE: Hey, John, that's not what I'm talking about.

JOHNNY: Hey, fuck the politics!

CÉCILE: Who knows what is true, eh? What is the truth?

PAQUETTE: You, you go light candles in the church. Me, I know what is the truth. A piece of shit, câlice.

CÉCILE: Claude.

PAQUETTE: Ah, oui, Claude.

IRENE: Anyhow, forget it.

JOHNNY: Yeah, fuck the politics. Nobody has fun in the Pointe anymore. We should have a party or something.

IRENE: A party, on what?

JOHNNY: Next week, I get my cheque, right? We'll have a party, just like the old days. Invite everybody on the block. We'll have a ball.

IRENE: You'll have a ball. I'll clean up the mess.

IRENE goes into the house.

JOHNNY: Irene, fuck!

He exits after her.

MURIEL: *(from inside her house)* Tom, your supper's on the table.

TOM: Yeah, yeah.

MURIEL: *(coming out of the house carrying a pot of spaghetti)* Tommy, I'm not going to tell you again.

TOM: What is it? Spaghetti?

MURIEL: Yeah, spaghetti.

TOM: I'm not hungry. I don't want any.

MURIEL: You don't want it? You don't want it? Well here, take it!

She dumps the spaghetti on TOM's head.

TOM: Ma! Shit!

He exits down the alley.

PAQUETTE: That woman, she's a little bit crazy, I think.

CÉCILE: T'as pas faim, Claude?

PAQUETTE: Y fait trop chaud. Fais-moi une limonade.

CÉCILE goes to get him a lemonade. DIANE comes out on the balcony and sits in the rocking chair. She is reading a magazine. PAQUETTE starts in on her.

PAQUETTE: Où est-ce que t'étais hier soir?

DIANE: Dehors.

PAQUETTE: Où ça dehors?

DIANE: Dehors. J't'ai dit dehors.

PAQUETTE: Dehors avec Jean-Guy pis toute la gang. Vous avez fumé, vous avez bu, vous avez fourré, vous avez en du fun, hein?

DIANE: Oui, on a eu ben de fun.

PAQUETTE: Il est même pas pusher. Qu'est-ce qu'y fait pour vivre d'abord?

DIANE: Il travaille des fois. J'sais pas. Demande-lui si tu veux savoir.

PAQUETTE: Diane, tu vois pas que c'est un hostie de pas-bon.

DIANE: Parce que toi tu sais ce qui est bon pour moi. Tu t'es pas regardé.

PAQUETTE: Pis tu t'penses smart. Tu penses que t'as inventé le monde. Eh. Diane, regarde les femmes dans la rue. C'est ça que tu veux? Te marier, avoir un petit par année, devenir large de même, t'écraser devant la télévision, manger des chips et pis attendre le welfare et le mari. C'est ça que tu veux avec Jean-Guy?

DIANE: Tant qu'à ça pourquoi pas?

PAQUETTE: Bon. Ben tant que tu vas rester ici, tu vas rentrer à minuit. Tu vas à l'école. C'est pour te sortir de cette câlice de merde-là.

DIANE: Tu vas à l'école, pis y a même pas de job en sortant.

PAQUETTE: Diane, pense. Sers-toi de ta tête, pas de ton cul, crisse.

CÉCILE: *(returning with the lemonade)* Claude.

PAQUETTE: Comment, Claude? Tabarnac, t'es sa mère, parles-y.

CÉCILE: Mais elle est jeune.

PAQUETTE: Oh. Oh, elle est jeune. Parce qu'est jeune, elle a droit de tout faire, pis quand elle va nous arriver en ballon.

DIANE: Fais-toi en pas, parce que j'prends la pillule.

She shows him her pill dispenser.

PAQUETTE: Maudit crisse. *(He comes down the stairs and exits into the shed.)* Va chez-toi.

CÉCILE: Tu l'as fait fâcher.

DIANE: Il est stupide.

CÉCILE: Mais, c'est ton père, Diane.

DIANE: Il est stupide pareil.

CÉCILE: Il essaye de t'aider. Y s'inquiète pour toi.

DIANE: Ça, Cécile, c'est ton problème. C'est pas le mien. J'suis pas obligée de l'endurer.

CÉCILE: C'est la job qui fait qu'y est fatigué. Y voudrait être fin avec toi des fois, mais il en peut plus, il est trop fatigué.

DIANE: Tu le gâtes trop, Cécile. C'est de ta faute. Tu le gâtes trop.

CÉCILE: Faut bien vivre.

DIANE: Dis-y donc non des fois, peut-être qu'il serait plus fin avec toi.

They hear a hammering noise coming from the shed. PAQUETTE is in there working on his car.

DIANE: Regarde, y passe plus d'temps avec son maudit Buick qu'il passe avec toi.

CÉCILE: Mon erreur moi-là, ç'a été d'avoir juste un enfant. Si tu te maries, Diane, arrange-toi pas pour avoir juste un enfant parce que tu vas te sentir bien toute seule.

DIANE: Maman, t'aurais dû rester au Lac St-Jean à la campagne avec ta famille. C'était là ta place, pas ici. C'est vrai, ça.

IRENE and JOHNNY come out of their house. IRENE is on her way to her Pointe Action Committee meeting.

IRENE: You wanna come to the meeting?

JOHNNY: No.

IRENE: Why not?

JOHNNY: 'Cause they're boring.

IRENE: Boring?

JOHNNY: Yeah, everybody's sitting around with a long face … Boring!

IRENE: We're planning our next action.

JOHNNY: Yeah, sure. Another demonstration. Big fuckin' deal!

IRENE: We gotta start somewhere.

JOHNNY: Yeah, well, they got a long fuckin' ways to go.

IRENE: *(coming down the stairs)* If you're waiting for Superman, you're gonna wait a long, long time.

JOHNNY: If you wanna fight politicians, go out and shoot a couple of them. All this talking drives me nuts.

He goes back into the house.

IRENE: *(starting after him)* I'll be back at ten. There's some supper in the fridge.

IRENE sees MURIEL crying as she cleans up the spaghetti.

IRENE: Muriel, you okay? You alright, girl?

MURIEL: Oh, go away.

IRENE: What's wrong? … What's right? Guess that's an easier question, eh?

MURIEL: Oh, I feel stupid.

IRENE: Here, I got a kleenex.

MURIEL: Thanks.

IRENE: You're not pregnant, are you?

MURIEL: Don't be crazy.

IRENE: Got the blues?

MURIEL: I'm worried about my stomach. It's acting up again.

IRENE: Maybe it's ulcers.

MURIEL: I don't know.

IRENE: Go to the hospital.

MURIEL: I'm afraid.

IRENE: You're afraid of what the doctor might say?

MURIEL: Yeah.

IRENE: Well, at least you'll know what you've got … You'll feel better once you do.

MURIEL: I dunno.

IRENE: I'll go with ya.

MURIEL: Irene, you don't have to.

IRENE: Listen, I wouldn't want to go alone either. So, how about, uh, Tuesday?

MURIEL: I don't know. All they do is give ya pills, dope ya up and send ya back home again.

IRENE: Well, let them take a look at ya anyhow.

MURIEL: Tuesday?

IRENE: Yeah.

MURIEL: Sick or not, what's the difference?

IRENE: When is your old man due back from the boats?

MURIEL: Him? Oh, he's taking his time. Don't worry, he's in no hurry to come back. It's the perfect life for him. He can drink all he wants, screw around … and he gets paid for it.

IRENE: Well, still it'll be nice to have him back.

MURIEL: Come off it! And your old man isn't much better. I'd dump him so quick, it wouldn't be funny. You're too good for him, Irene.

IRENE: Oh well, ya know how it is? Ya marry a prince and he turns into a frog.

MURIEL: Yeah, Bill was always great for a good time. But he was no good for nothing else.

IRENE: He still sends the cheques?

MURIEL: Yeah. Aw, it's nobody's fault ... everybody's fault ... Ever think about what we'll be doing in ten years?

IRENE: Ten years? Ugh, I don't think about it. Maybe we'll win the Super Loto or something ... You know, you gotta get out of the house more. Ya make a lousy housewife. Try something else.

MURIEL: Like what?

IRENE: I don't know. School?

MURIEL: Jesus Christ, they threw me out of Grade 8 for punching out the teacher.

IRENE: Yeah, I remember that.

MURIEL: Yeah. Old man Breslin with the wandering hands.

IRENE: Pow, pow! Love it!

MURIEL: He had it coming.

IRENE: He sure did and you gave it to him. People still talk about it, eh? Sure.

MURIEL: Yeah, eh?

IRENE: Yeah ... Tuesday?

MURIEL: Yeah, Tuesday ... Thanks, Irene.

IRENE: Aw, us girls got to stick together, eh?

CÉCILE starts to water her plants. The water drips down on IRENE and MURIEL below.

IRENE: Aw, shit. When she's not feeding her Air Force, she's watering her jungle ... Bye.

IRENE exits. The broadcast VOICE is heard again.

VOICE: Gaëtan Bolduc, the man for you. The man of today, the man of the people, the man who cares. Vote for action, vote for a winner, vote for Bolduc. Gaëtan Bolduc ... available and dynamic ... the man for you.

FIRST VOICE: *(from the truck)* Yeah, yeah. Bolduc, Bolduc, Bolduc. Câlice, how many more times do we have to drive around the block?

SECOND VOICE: *(from the truck)* We got three more hours, hostie.

FIRST VOICE: *(from the truck)* That shithead. Bolduc. Bolduc. Me, I'm so sick of his fuckin' name. Bolduc. Bolduc. Fuck you, Bolduc! You cheap son of a bitch.

SECOND VOICE: *(from the truck)* Next time, we'll ask for forty bucks a day.

FIRST VOICE: *(from the truck)* Hey, fifty. Fifty bucks a day.

SECOND VOICE: *(from the truck)* Oui, fifty.

FIRST VOICE: *(from the truck)* Crisse, François. The speaker is still on. They can hear us.

SECOND VOICE: *(from the truck)* The speaker? What? The speaker!? Câlice.

The voices stop. Elvis Presley music comes on.

Blackout.

Scene Four

It is night. The sound of a record playing rock music is heard. DIANE, CÉCILE, IRENE, MURIEL, THIBAULT, and TOM are dancing in the street.

THIBAULT: Hey, look. I got one. The mashed potato duck.

IRENE: Hey, come on everybody, make a circle. Take turns in the middle. Come on.

DIANE steps into the circle and does a dance, then TOM takes his turn.

MURIEL: Move your feet. Move your feet,

THIBAULT: *(stepping into the circle)* Hey, the duck. Look, I got one. The mashed potato duck.

They push him out of the circle.

IRENE: Hey, Cécile. Come on.

They push Cécile into the circle. She moves a bit. They applaud.

IRENE: Hey, shake that thing. Alright, Muriel. Come on, your turn. Come on.

MURIEL: Aw, that's kids' stuff.

IRENE: Come on.

Just as MURIEL starts to dance, the record ends.

MURIEL: Well, that's it.

THIBAULT: It's hot, eh? Hot … whew.

TOM: Hey, where's Johnny?

IRENE: Him? He's always late. He's the star, right?

MURIEL: That's one word for him.

IRENE: Hey, Muriel. Tell that joke. The one you told me this morning.

MURIEL: Naw, naw. You tell it.

IRENE: Come on.

MURIEL: No. You tell it better.

IRENE: Okay. You ready? Okay, this guy is going to bed with a girl for the first time …

THIBAULT: Oh, dirty joke! Hey!

MURIEL: Don't worry, Thibault. You'll never get it.

IRENE: Yeah, and he takes off his socks and shoes, and his feet are deformed, and she says, "What's wrong with your feet?" And he says, "Well, when I was a kid, I had toelio."

TOM: "Toelio."

IRENE: And she says, "You mean, polio." "No, toelio." And well, then, he takes off his pants …

THIBAULT whistles.

MURIEL: Down, Thibault. Down.

IRENE: And … and his knees are all, you know, bulgy.

DIANE: C'est quoi ça, "bulgy"?

IRENE: Tout enflé … And the girl says, "What's wrong with your knees?" "Well, when I was a kid, I had the kneasles." "You mean, measles." "No, kneasles." Then, he takes off his underwear …

THIBAULT whistles again.

IRENE: And she says, "Oh, no, don't tell me you had smallcocks too." Small cocks.

They all laugh.

MURIEL: Thibault, ya got it now?

CÉCILE: Diane. "Smallcocks," c'est quoi?

DIANE: P'tite bizoune.

CÉCILE: Oh, bizoune. Oui.

MURIEL: Shit, it's been so long I forgot what they look like.

The girls all laugh.

THIBAULT: Hey, that's funny, that, eh?

TOM: Hey, ya wanna see my Elvis Presley imitation? Eh?

DIANE: Oui.

TOM: Ya wanna see it?

MURIEL: No.

IRENE: Sure.

TOM: Okay? Ya ready?

IRENE: Ready.

TOM: Elvis!

He bends his head back and crosses his arms like a laid-out corpse. They all groan.

DIANE: I like that. *(She copies his Elvis imitation.)* Elvis!

THIBAULT: That's all?

TOM: Yeah.

DIANE puts another record on. It is "Hot Child in the City." THIBAULT grabs her and begins to dance.

THIBAULT: Cha-cha-cha, hostie.

DIANE: Hey, not so close, okay? Not so close. J'vas te puncher.

THIBAULT: Hey, let's dance. Dansons.

IRENE: *(cutting in)* Here, Diane. You take Tom.

She grabs THIBAULT. TOM and DIANE dance.

IRENE: Come on, Thibault, you sexy thing.

THIBAULT: Cha-cha-cha, hostie.

IRENE and THIBAULT dance

IRENE: *(turning to MURIEL)* Christ, hey Muriel, look. *(referring to her and THIBAULT)* The last tango in the Pointe.

MURIEL: Careful. You'll get him so excited, he'll piss himself.

PAQUETTE and JOHNNY enter with their arms around one another's shoulders. They are drunk and singing.

PAQUETTE and JOHNNY: *(singing)*
Jesus saves his money at
    the Bank of Montréal.
Jesus saves his money at
    the Bank of Montréal.
Jesus saves his money at
    the Bank of Montréal.
Jesus saves, Jesus saves—
Jesus saves.

IRENE: Shit, he's drunk already.

PAQUETTE: Hey, les femmes. Nous sommes ici.

DIANE mimics him.

THIBAULT: Hey, Paquette. Watch me dance.

JOHNNY: *(singing with PAQUETTE)*
Irene, goodnight,
Irene, goodnight,
Goodnight, Irene,
Goodnight, Irene,
I'll see you in my dreams.

PAQUETTE: Hey, les femmes. C'est moi.

JOHNNY: Hey, Irene. I'm a little late. Had a few drinks with what's his name.

PAQUETTE: Paquette.

JOHNNY: Pole-quette.

PAQUETTE: Naw. Paw-quette.

JOHNNY: Okay, tell the people your name *(together)* ... Paquette.

THIBAULT: Thibault. My name, Thibault.

PAQUETTE and JOHNNY start to climb the stairs. JOHNNY stumbles on the broken step.

PAQUETTE: Eh, Johnny? Un autre p'tit step. La bière est en haut.

IRENE: Fais attention à sa tête.

She goes to help JOHNNY up the stairs. She is followed by MURIEL, THIBAULT, DIANE and TOM.

PAQUETTE: C'est sa tête carrée. C'est les coins qui accrochent.

When JOHNNY gets up the stairs, he grabs IRENE.

JOHNNY: Irene, I love ya, love ya, love ya ...

THIBAULT: We have fun, eh? Watch me dance.

JOHNNY: Yeah, we're gonna rock this joint. Where's the beer?

MURIEL: You've had enough.

PAQUETTE: Hey, Johnny. Dansons, dansons.

He does a dance step.

JOHNNY: Where *is* everybody?

IRENE: This is it. We're all here.

JOHNNY: What do ya mean? Where are they? Danny? Jerry?

IRENE: Guess they couldn't make it.

JOHNNY: I knew the fuckers wouldn't come.

IRENE: Maybe they'll come later.

JOHNNY bangs into his house.

IRENE: Johnny ...

PAQUETTE: Put on some music. Hey, what's wrong? Put on some music. We'll have a good time.

He goes into his house and puts on the record "Hot Child in the City."

THIBAULT: Tutti-frutti, hostie. Let's twist some more.

JOHNNY: *(inside his house)* What's Jerry's number? What's his fuckin' number?

IRENE: I dunno.

PAQUETTE: Hey, Diane. C'est ta tune. *(to MURIEL)* Hey, let's dance ... Why not?

MURIEL: Ask your wife.

PAQUETTE: Come on. I don't bite.

MURIEL: You're drunk.

They dance on the balcony.

PAQUETTE: Eh? Not bad, eh? I dance good, eh?

MURIEL: Yeah, sure. Terrific.

PAQUETTE: Not bad for a peasoup, eh?

JOHNNY: *(inside the house, on the phone)* Jerry, that you? What are ya doing at home? You're supposed to be here … What? … Hey, turn that fuckin' music down … What? … Fuck that shit, man. This is supposed to be a get together and nobody's here. Nobody! Just the Pepsi's next door … What? … What? … I don't want to hear that shit, Jerry. You coming? You coming? … Maybe later? Fuck you!

He slams down the receiver and bangs his way out onto the balcony.

IRENE: Johnny, Johnny …

JOHNNY: The party's over. Fuck off! Everybody, fuck off!

PAQUETTE: Hey, Jacques. We'll have a good time, eh?

JOHNNY: *(pushing PAQUETTE)* Get on your own fuckin' side.

PAQUETTE: Hey. Hey.

JOHNNY: Fuckin' gorf. Pepper. Get on your own side.

PAQUETTE: Hey, watch that, eh? Fais attention, okay?

JOHNNY: We were here first, ya fuckin' farmer. Go back to the sticks.

PAQUETTE: Hey, reste tranquille, eh?

JOHNNY: You wanna fight? Wanna fight?

JOHNNY swings at PAQUETTE, but misses him. He falls down. IRENE and MURIEL push him towards the door of his house.

PAQUETTE: Keep your garbage on your side.

JOHNNY: *(stumbling)* The party's over. No more parties. No more.

IRENE: Get him into the house.

MURIEL: Stupid men.

They carry him into his house.

JOHNNY: Jerry. Where's Jerry? Jerry?

MURIEL: Good old days … Never was any good old days.

They exit into the house.

THIBAULT: Johnny, he gets a little drunk tonight, eh?

TOM: Hey, a little.

DIANE: It's fun for them. That's the way they have fun.

CÉCILE: It's a full moon. That's why everyone is so crazy.

PAQUETTE: What's wrong? Hey, what's wrong?

He puts the record back on. It is "Hot Child in the City" once again.

THIBAULT: Away, Paquette. Let's twist some more.

TOM: *(to MURIEL, as she comes out of JOHNNY's house)* Is he okay?

MURIEL: He's okay. You wanna end up just like him? That's the way you're going.

TOM: Yeah, yeah.

PAQUETTE goes over to MURIEL, who isn't interested in dancing, so he starts dancing with DIANE. He begins to slobber all over her. She pushes him away, goes down the stairs and exits down the lane.

CÉCILE: Diane. Diane.

PAQUETTE: Who wants to dance? Hey.

He heads towards MURIEL.

MURIEL: *(pushing him aside)* Get lost. Beat it.

PAQUETTE: Quoi?

MURIEL: Ya make me sick.

PAQUETTE: Hey, parle-moi en français, eh? Parle-moi en français.

MURIEL: Go on. Hit me. Hit me. Try it.

PAQUETTE: Maudits anglais. Throw them all out. Toute le gang. On est au Québec. On est chez-nous.

MURIEL: I was born here too, ya bigmouth Frenchman.

PAQUETTE: It's our turn now, eh? Our turn. And Ottawa, Ottawa can kiss my Pepsi ass.

MURIEL: Ferme ta guele, toi.

THIBAULT: Fuck the Queen!

MURIEL: Fuck Lévesque!

MURIEL goes back into IRENE's house. PAQUETTE knocks over one of CÉCILE's plants by accident.

CÉCILE: Claude, fais attention à mes plantes. Claude.

PAQUETTE picks up one of her plants and throws it over the railing.

PAQUETTE: Tiens, ta câlice de plante.

CÉCILE runs into the house crying.

PAQUETTE: *(opening another beer)* It's crying time again, eh? Crying time again.

THIBAULT: Me, I don't hate the English. I just don't like them, that's all.

PAQUETTE: Maudits anglais!

THIBAULT: They got funny heads. Square heads.

PAQUETTE: *(to TOM)* You. Hey, you. Think maybe you got a chance, eh? No more. That's one good thing now. We're all the same now, eh? We're all equal. Nobody's got a chance. Nobody.

THIBAULT: Fuck the Queen!

PAQUETTE: Maybe you got dreams, eh? Me too. I had dreams. Thibault too. He had dreams.

THIBAULT: Oui, me too.

PAQUETTE: If you knew what I know, you'd go jump in the river right now. Tonight.

THIBAULT: Oui, tonight. The river. No joke, that.

PAQUETTE: *(hugging THIBAULT)* Thibault, you're a bum ... a bum and a drunk.

THIBAULT: Oui, a bum.

PAQUETTE: You know what? Me, I work all my life. All my life.

THIBAULT: That's too bad.

PAQUETTE: When I was young, I was going to do this and that, but the job, the fuckin' job, it took my life away. What can you do? Everybody says, "what can you do?" That's the way it goes.

THIBAULT: That's the way it goes.

PAQUETTE: You get old and ugly and you die ... and that's all.

THIBAULT: That's all.

PAQUETTE: I try, but it don't help. No matter what you do.

TOM comes down the stairs and goes into his house to get his guitar.

PAQUETTE: No matter what you do.

THIBAULT: So what? That's what I say. So what?

PAQUETTE: So what? Maudits anglais.

THIBAULT: Oui. So what? *(looking into the case of beer)* Hey, no more beer.

IRENE and MURIEL come out on the balcony.

THIBAULT: Eh, y a plus de bière?

PAQUETTE: On va aller en chercher en ville.

THIBAULT: Comment?

PAQUETTE: Ben ... avec mon char.

THIBAULT: Ton char?

PAQUETTE: Ben oui. Mon char, hostie.

They come down the stairs.

THIBAULT: Ah, oui. Ton char dans le garage. Prenez garde. Watch the step.

They pick up some tools and exit for the shed to fix the car.

IRENE: They're gonna get themselves killed.

MURIEL: Don't worry, they'll never get that car to start.

IRENE: Well, Johnny's out for the night. He'll wake up tomorrow, drink a bottle of Coke and ask me what he did.

MURIEL: He needs a kick in the ass ... and fast.

IRENE: He told me he wants me to find another man ... Yeah ... Here I am, thirty-four years old, and he wants me to go find another man. Fat chance.

MURIEL: I dunno. You're still in pretty good shape.

IRENE: Aw, I'm no spring chicken anymore ... I'm a broiler.

MURIEL: You're better off without a man. Who needs them?

IRENE: Aw, I guess I love the creep.

MURIEL: Love? Love never got through the Wellington Tunnel.

IRENE: I had this guy who was nuts about me … always phoning me up, calling on me. He's a teacher now in N.D.G. … But I fell for Johnny. He was a rebel. A real teen angel, ya know what I mean?

MURIEL: Yeah, so they grow up to be drunks.

IRENE: I can't blame him. He's been trying.

MURIEL: No, guess you can't blame the poor ignorant stupid bastards.

IRENE: I'm scared for him.

MURIEL: It never pays to be too nice, Irene. I used to be nice, but it never got me nowhere.

IRENE: Yeah … But why, Muriel? Why? How do you change it?

MURIEL: They're all the same, Irene … all of them.

IRENE: The doctor's still taking tests?

MURIEL: Yeah … you know doctors. They never tell ya nothing. All they do is poke your stomach, take your blood, give ya some pills and tell ya to come in next week. Makes ya feel like a goddamn guinea pig.

IRENE: Yeah, well, meanwhile there's the late movie, eh? What's on anyhow?

MURIEL: I dunno.

IRENE: See ya …

MURIEL: Yeah, Irene … don't let him walk on you. That's what I'm trying to say anyhow.

IRENE: 'Night.

MURIEL: Yeah.

IRENE goes into her house. MURIEL comes down the stairs. She sees TOM sitting on her balcony with his guitar.

MURIEL: I'm locking the door at twelve o'clock.

TOM: Yeah.

MURIEL: I mean it.

TOM: Yeah, yeah.

MURIEL goes into her house.

PAQUETTE: *(yelling at THIBAULT in the shed)* Non, non. Le wrench. Donne-moi le wrench qui est sur la valise.

THIBAULT: La valise.

PAQUETTE: Oui, tabarnac.

THIBAULT: Y fait noir. Ouch!

PAQUETTE: Le hood. Fais attention au hood. Ta tête.

A slamming sound is heard.

Maudit, tabarnac de câlice de Sainte Vierge. Hostie, que t'es cave! Tiens la lumière.

THIBAULT: La lumière. Okay.

TOM: *(playing his guitar and singing)*
Tell you, Mona, what I'm gonna do,
Build a house next door to you,
Then I can see you in the summertime,
We can blow kisses through the blinds.
Come on, Mona, out in the front,
Listen to my heart go bumpetity-bump.

DIANE enters. When TOM has finished playing, she applauds.

TOM: Uh, hi … Want some beer? … Go ahead, I got an extra bottle. *(DIANE takes a sip.)* The party's over, eh?

DIANE: The party. Oui.

TOM: Uh … everybody got drunk and crazy, eh?

DIANE: Quoi?

TOM: Drunk, crazy … like that …

He mimes "drunk."

DIANE: Drunk? Ah, oui … Mon anglais est pas tellement bon.

TOM: My French is, uh … comme ci, comme ça … Like that … So, uh … what's new?

DIANE: What's new?

TOM: Yeah, what's new?

DIANE: You tell me? … Bon? … Well?

She moves towards the stairs.

TOM: Hey, uh … where ya going?

DIANE: I don't speak the good English.

TOM: Look, finish your beer. I mean, uh … why not?

DIANE: *(stopping at the foot of the stairs)* I don't want to go home.

TOM: Yeah. I know the feeling. You, uh … never look too happy.

DIANE: Happy? What's that? … Something on TV?

TOM: Yeah, well, I dunno … You're so pretty. Ya should be happy. *(DIANE groans.)* That's a dumb thing to say, eh? Yeah … So, uh … what do you do?

DIANE: Me? I still go to school … I write poems sometimes.

TOM; Yeah, that figures … Uh … what kind of poems?

DIANE: Sad ones.

TOM: I'm asking 'cause, well … ya look like a girl who writes poems. Guess I could do it too, but I wouldn't know why. I flunked English. French too … Babysitting, that's all school is …

DIANE: Do you like films? … Me, I like films. But they make me feel bad too. I don't want them to stop.

TOM: Hey, cinemascope. In living colour. Diane Paquette.

DIANE: No, I'll never use that name. Not Paquette.

TOM: Okay, Diane, uh …

DIANE: Diane Desmarchais. Why not Diane Desmarchais?

TOM: Yeah. Okay. Boulevard Desmarchais. Sounds good …

DIANE: So, you don't go to school no more?

TOM: Naw. I mean, I know my ABCs … most of them … Looking for work … I dunno, it's crazy. I mean, if someone wanted me to work for them, why don't they ask me. I mean, I don't know why I've got to go looking for work when I don't even want it.

DIANE: No job, no money. No money, no nothing.

TOM: Yeah, money … Hey, uh … don't you ever blink?

DIANE: Never.

TOM: Once a year or what? …

DIANE: Your hair, it makes you look funny.

TOM: Funny? What do you mean?

DIANE: I think it's too short.

TOM: Oui, too short.

DIANE: I think you have to grow it longer …

TOM: Yeah, well, I'm getting out. I'm leaving … Ever think of doing that? Goodbye Pointe Saint-Charles.

DIANE: Where will you go?

TOM: I dunno … anywhere. New York City.

DIANE: New York City?

TOM: Yeah, sure.

DIANE: They got jobs down there?

TOM: I dunno … It's a big place. Ya never know. I might find a job as a musician, ya know? Once I learn about, uh, major chords, minor chords. Shit like that …

DIANE: Well, salut. Bonne chance.

She starts up the stairs.

TOM: Hey, Diane. Wait. Attends peu … You wanna come with me?

DIANE: Avec toi? Pourquoi?

TOM: Well, I figure you wanna get out too … Anyhow, forget it. It's stupid. Ya don't even know me … I'm a bit stoned … Well, see ya.

DIANE: Bye … Write me a letter, okay?

She goes into her house.

TOM: Aw, forget it. It's stupid … stupid.

TOM exits with his guitar. PAQUETTE and THIBAULT are heard banging away in the shed.

PAQUETTE: Verrat de tabarnac de crisse de ciboire.

THIBAULT: J'pense que c'est pas le spark plug, eh?

PAQUETTE: Fuck you. Où est le pipe wrench?

THIBAULT: Le pipe wrench?

PAQUETTE: Oui, le pipe wrench. Je pense que j'l'ai laissé sur le balcon.

THIBAULT: Le balcon. Okay, okay, okay, okay. Okay, so what?

He comes in from the shed and goes up the stairs. While he is looking for the pipe wrench, he drinks some beer from some discarded beer bottles.

Le pipe wrench, le pipe wrench. So what? On se rendra jamais en ville.

PAQUETTE: Thibault … Hostie …

THIBAULT: Oui, j'cherche. J'cherche. *(He takes a slug of beer from one of the beer bottles and gags on a cigarette butt.)* Agh. Touf. Une cigarette, hostie.

PAQUETTE gets the car started, guns the engine, then chokes it.

PAQUETTE: Tu veux pas partir. Tu veux pas partir. Ben. J'vas t'arranger ça.

PAQUETTE takes a hammer to the car. The sound of smashing is heard. CÉCILE comes out on her balcony.

CÉCILE: Mais, qu'est-ce qui se passe? Claude? …

PAQUETTE comes out of the shed carrying a hammer. He throws the hammer to the ground and climbs the stairs.

THIBAULT: *(to PAQUETTE)* You fix it?

PAQUETTE: *(to CÉCILE)* Pas un mot s'a game. Pas un mot.

PAQUETTE and CÉCILE exit into their house, leaving THIBAULT standing alone on the balcony.

THIBAULT: Okay, on ira jamais en ville. So what? Thibault, he's okay. I go find my own beer. So what?

He comes down the stairs and exits. MURIEL comes out on her balcony.

MURIEL: Tommy, I'm gonna lock this door. Tommy? … Alright.

She shuts the door and bolts it closed.

Blackout.

ACT TWO

Scene One

It is night. JOHNNY and THIBAULT enter singing. Both of them are drunk. JOHNNY is riding THIBAULT's delivery bike.

JOHNNY and THIBAULT: *(singing)*
We don't care about
All the rest of Canada,
All the rest of Canada,
All the rest of Canada.
We don't care for
All the rest of Canada,
We're from Pointe Saint-Charles.

MURIEL: *(from inside her house)* Shut up out there!

JOHNNY: Fuck you!

THIBAULT: So what, eh? Get off my bike, you … Away.

JOHNNY: *(getting off THIBAULT's bike)* Hey, Thibault, you're not a separatist, are ya?

THIBAULT: FLQ, moi. Boom! I blow everything up. *(He kicks a garbage can.)* Boom!

MURIEL: *(from inside her house)* Jesus Murphy.

THIBAULT: *(taking a magazine out of his back pocket)* We have a good time, eh? Good time. Look, big tits.

He sits down on a bench. JOHNNY sits down beside him.

JOHNNY: You're my friend, eh, Thibault?

THIBAULT: Sure, if that's what you say.

JOHNNY: You're my only, only friend.

THIBAULT: I'm your only friend … and I'm not even your friend.

JOHNNY: So whose friend are ya?

THIBAULT: I don't know.

JOHNNY: You wanna know whose friend you are? You're my friend.

THIBAULT: Sure … My mother, once she takes me to the Oratoire, because I got the polio. So, she takes me there. She prays to Saint Joseph, but the polio, it don't go away …

JOHNNY: Fuck off.

THIBAULT: Eh, so what?

JOHNNY: What, so what?

THIBAULT: What so what?

JOHNNY: Yeah, you say, "So what?" and I say, "What so what?"

THIBAULT: You crazy, you.

JOHNNY: Fuckin' right, I'm crazy. *(yelling)* I'm trying Irene. I'm trying … I'm dying.

THIBAULT: Hey, Johnny. Do Elvis. Do Elvis … "I'm all shook up."

JOHNNY: *(snapping into an Elvis imitation)* "I'm all shook up."

IRENE comes out on her balcony.

IRENE: Johnny.

JOHNNY: Irene, remember me when I was eighteen? *(He does his Elvis imitation.)* "Bebop-a-lula."

IRENE: Come on up to bed, Johnny. I've got to work tomorrow.

JOHNNY: Tomorrow? Fuck tomorrow! Everybody's worried about tomorrow. I'm worried about right now.

THIBAULT: Hey, do Elvis. Do some more Elvis … "You ain't nothing but a hound dog."

JOHNNY: Elvis is dead, ya dumb Pepsi. He's dead. Don't ya understand that? He's dead.

He goes to the stairs and starts to climb them. He collapses.

IRENE: Come on, Johnny.

She comes down and tries to get him up the stairs. He grunts.

IRENE: Shit. La merde … Muriel? Muriel?

MURIEL: *(from inside her house)* Leave him there, it'll do him good.

CÉCILE: *(coming out on her balcony)* Madame, you need some help?

IRENE: Thanks.

CÉCILE comes down the stairs. Together, she and IRENE carry JOHNNY up the stairs and into his house.

JOHNNY: Irene, I love you … Gonna buy ya a house, Irene.

CÉCILE comes back out. She sees THIBAULT sitting on the steps looking at one of his magazines.

THIBAULT: Paquette, Paquette, tu t'souviens? Toi et moi à la Rodéo? Big Fat Babette … "Please Help Me I'm Falling in Love with You." Big tits … big tits.

CÉCILE: Shhhhhh, Thibault. Claude dort.

THIBAULT: *(looking at his magazine)* Tits … big tits.

He rips a page out of the magazine. He goes and sits on his bike. IRENE comes out on the balcony carrying two Cokes.

IRENE: Veux-tu un Coke, Cécile?

CÉCILE: Yes, that would be nice.

CÉCILE sits down on her rocking chair. IRENE comes and sits down beside her.

CÉCILE: It's so quiet, eh? This is my favorite time, when it's quiet.

IRENE: Yeah.

CÉCILE: Look, there's the Big Dipper.

IRENE: Oh yeah?

CÉCILE: Right there. Right next to that shed.

IRENE: You know, I haven't looked at the sky in years.

CÉCILE: When I was a little girl in Lac St-Jean, I knew the names of all the stars … the Great Bear, the Swan, the Hunter …

IRENE: They've got names, eh?

CÉCILE: Of course. Everything has a name.

IRENE: How did you meet Paquette? Uh … Claude?

CÉCILE: He had a truck. He was a truck driver … So handsome … At first, we thought he would marry one of my older sisters, but she didn't want him because he was too loud … And my mother too, she didn't like him. But …

IRENE: You liked him.

CÉCILE: I was a young girl …

IRENE: So was I ... I had a dream last night

CÉCILE: A dream? Tell me. I love dreams.

IRENE: I ... I dreamed I saw Jacob wrestling the angel. Imagine that.

CÉCILE: Jacob?

IRENE: Yeah, you know? Jacob ... in the Bible.

CÉCILE: Jacob. Ah, oui.

IRENE: Anyhow, I woke up feeling good ... Well, it's been one of those years, eh?

CÉCILE: Johnny and Claude, right now ... they not getting along so good?

IRENE: Well, they're both being stupid. But Johnny started it. He's such a goddamn redneck sometimes.

CÉCILE: It's strange ... Before, Claude, he wants to be like the English ... and now, he puts everything on them.

DIANE enters.

CÉCILE: Diane, il est passé minuit. Ton père va être fâché.

DIANE: *(coming up the stairs)* Irene, I have something ...

IRENE: Oh?

DIANE: Une lettre de Tom.

IRENE: Tom. He wrote you?

DIANE: Oui, but I can't understand all the words.

IRENE: Let me see it. *(She takes the letter and looks at the postmark.)* Ormstown? What's the silly bugger doing in Ormstown? ... You want me to read it?

DIANE: Oui.

IRENE: "Hi, Diane ... Took me a day hitchhiking to get this far so far. Tomorrow, guess I'll reach the border and cross over into the land of Jimmy Carter and Mickey Mouse."

DIANE: *(laughing)* Mickey Mouse.

IRENE: "I can feel New York City down there, pulling me like a magnet." Tu comprends? Magnet?

IRENE mimes "magnet," banging the fist of one hand into her other hand.

DIANE: Oui.

IRENE: "Pull at him." Shit, it's gonna hit him on the head.

DIANE: Quoi?

IRENE: Uh ... okay. "I don't have no money, but a faggot bought me a meal." Faggot? C'est un tapette.

DIANE: Oui.

IRENE: "I'm glad we had that talk, even if I did sound kind of crazy ... I think you're beautiful. I mean, how do you say something like that? But it's true." Wow! Hot stuff!

DIANE: *(taking back the letter)* It's okay ... I understand the rest.

IRENE: Hey, sounds like Tom really likes ya, girl.

DIANE: Hey, I know what he wants.

IRENE: Yeah, so is he gonna get some?

DIANE: He's cute ... a bit.

IRENE: New York City.

DIANE: Me, I want to go there.

IRENE: Yeah?

DIANE: Sure. Go there and live like in the movies. It would be fun, eh?

IRENE: Yeah ... like the movies. Poor Muriel.

DIANE: His mother? ... What for? ... She was going to throw him out anyhow.

IRENE: Well, I've got to work tomorrow. Bye.

DIANE: Bye.

CÉCILE: Goodnight, Irene.

IRENE exits into her house.

CÉCILE: Diane, viens-tu coucher?

DIANE: Non.

CÉCILE exits into her house. DIANE sits at the top of the stairs. THIBAULT is still sitting on his bike at the bottom of the stairs.

THIBAULT: Diane. Diane.

DIANE: Va-t'en chez-vous, Thibault.

THIBAULT: Eh, Diane? J'vas m'acheter une Honda 750. C'est vrai, Diane. Brammmmm, brammmmm. Honda. J'vas m'en acheter une.

DIANE: Oui, oui.

THIBAULT: J'vas t'faire des rides, eh?

DIANE: Va-t'en chez-vous, Thibault.

THIBAULT: C'est vrai, Diane. Une 750. Brammmmmm, brammmmm.

He exits on his bike. DIANE remains at the top of the stairs looking at her letter.

Blackout.

Scene Two

The next day. It is a very hot Sunday afternoon. JOHNNY, PAQUETTE and DIANE are on the balcony watching the ball game on TV—on separate TVs. MURIEL is sweeping her balcony.

JOHNNY: *(watching TV)* Aw, shit … bunch of bums!

PAQUETTE: *(watching TV)* Maudits Expos!

IRENE enters yawning. She is coming home from work, wearing her waitress uniform. She sees MURIEL sweeping her balcony.

IRENE: Boy, this heat …

MURIEL: Couple more days of this and we'll be having riots.

IRENE: Yeah.

MURIEL: Sorry about last night … I was in one of my moods.

IRENE: Aw, forget it. Hey, Diane got a letter from Tom, eh? … Yeah.

MURIEL: He writes to her, but he doesn't write to his mother?

IRENE: He's in Ormstown.

MURIEL: Ormstown? Where's that?

IRENE: Somewhere in the bush.

MURIEL: Well, as soon as he gets hungry, he'll come home … just let him try to get through the door.

IRENE: Aw, don't worry. Young guys are like tomcats. They always land on their feet.

MURIEL: Who says I'm worried?

IRENE: Okay.

PAQUETTE: *(watching TV)* Away, away … câlice.

JOHNNY: *(watching TV)* Aw, shit! Le merde! Move your ass! Move your ass!

PAQUETTE: *(watching TV)* Il est temps, tabarnac!

JOHNNY: *(seeing IRENE coming up the stairs)* Hey, did you pick me up some smokes?

IRENE dumps a pack of smokes in his lap and goes on into the house. CÉCILE enters. She is wearing her church clothes. She comes up behind MURIEL.

CÉCILE: Bonjour, Madame Williams.

MURIEL: *(jumping in fright)* Oh, God, don't creep up on me like that.

CÉCILE: How are you? … Nice day, eh?

MURIEL: Too hot.

CÉCILE: Ah, yes, too hot … It's so nice to see people together in the church. Being together makes people feel so good.

PAQUETTE and JOHNNY: *(together)* Grimsley, ya bum! … Aux douches!

MURIEL: Yeah … *(looking at where CÉCILE is standing)* Move …

CÉCILE moves and MURIEL continues sweeping. CÉCILE goes up the stairs. DIANE notices her hat.

DIANE: Maman, les femmes n'ont plus besoin de porter de chapeau pour aller à la messe.

CÉCILE: Je sais, Diane, mais je suis habituée de même.

PAQUETTE and JOHNNY both react to something on the baseball game on TV.

CÉCILE: Diane, tu devrais venir avec moi dimanche prochain.

DIANE: C'est toujours le même show. Quand ils changeront le programme, peut-être que j'irai.

PAQUETTE: *(to CÉCILE and DIANE)* Tabarnac, y a tu moyen d'écouter ma game tranquille? Ça fait une semaine que j'attends après ça. Cécile, va me chercher une bière.

CÉCILE: Oui, Claude ...

She goes to get him a beer.

JOHNNY: Hey, Irene? ... Irene? ...

IRENE: *(at the screen door)* Yeah?

JOHNNY: Get me a Coke.

IRENE: What's the matter, you break your leg?

JOHNNY: It's too hot to move.

IRENE: I'm moving.

PAQUETTE: *(watching TV)* Merde!

JOHNNY: *(watching TV)* Shit!

PAQUETTE: Un autre foul ball, hostie!

CÉCILE: *(bringing PAQUETTE a beer)* Claude, veux-tu un sandwich?

PAQUETTE: Quoi?

CÉCILE: Un sandwich?

PAQUETTE: *(watching TV)* Away ... away là!

She goes to get him a sandwich.

JOHNNY: *(watching TV)* Faster! Get under it! Get under it! ... No, fuck!

PAQUETTE: *(watching TV)* Shit! La merde!

CÉCILE comes back and puts a sandwich in one of PAQUETTE's hands and a beer in his other hand.

DIANE: Paquette est assez grand pour se mouvoir tout seul, Cécile.

PAQUETTE: Cécile ... c'est ta mère que t'appelles Cécile. Tu vas me faire le plaisir de l'appeler Maman.

DIANE: *(to PAQUETTE)* You are a piece of shit.

She throws a bag of potato chips at him and stomps off into the house.

PAQUETTE: Voyons. Qu'est-ce qu'y lui prend?

CÉCILE: J'sais pas. J'pense qu'elle s'est chicané avec sa chum.

JOHNNY: *(watching TV)* Go, go, go!

PAQUETTE: *(watching TV)* Vite, vite, vite! ... Bonne. That's it ... Oui.

JOHNNY: *(watching TV)* About time ...

Inside the house, DIANE puts on a record. It is "Hot Child in the City."

PAQUETTE: Cécile, dis-lui de baisser sa câlice de musique de hot child in the city, hostie.

CÉCILE goes into the house. The music fades away. IRENE comes out and hands JOHNNY a Coke.

IRENE: Johnny, I want to talk to you.

JOHNNY: Yeah, yeah.

IRENE: What happened last night?

JOHNNY: Last night? ... Hey, I'm watching the game.

IRENE: When does it end?

JOHNNY: Eh? ... Ten minutes.

IRENE: I want to talk to you before I go out.

JOHNNY: Yeah, yeah ... talk. Okay.

IRENE: I mean it.

JOHNNY: Don't do the martyr, okay? Not the martyr, please.

IRENE exits into the house. THIBAULT enters on his bike. He starts putting "Gaëtan Bolduc ... available and dynamic" campaign posters all over the walls.

MURIEL: *(watching THIBAULT)* What's this?

THIBAULT: Dix piastres pour la journée ... Me and four other guys are putting them up all over. Bolduc, he wants to win this time, eh?

MURIEL: *(ripping down one of the posters)* Not on my wall ...

THIBAULT: Eh? Not on your wall?

MURIEL: No.

THIBAULT: No?

MURIEL: No, you stupid little jerk.

She crumples up the poster and throws it at him.

THIBAULT: No? ... Okay, no.

He goes up the stairs with his posters and sees PAQUETTE and JOHNNY watching TV. He sits beside PAQUETTE.

THIBAULT: Hey, c'est quoi l'score? What's the score?

PAQUETTE: Huit à cinq.

JOHNNY: *(shouting across at them)* The Expos got five.

THIBAULT: Hey. Good game, eh? ... Hot, eh? Hot ... very hot. Très chaud ... Agh ... hard to breathe. *(He coughs.)* Agh, my throat ... Hot ...

PAQUETTE: *(calling to CÉCILE)* Cécile, apporte-moi deux autres bières.

CÉCILE: *(at the screen door)* Deux?

PAQUETTE: Oui.

THIBAULT: Ah, oui ... Good game, eh?

PAQUETTE: Ferme ta gueule, toi. Okay?

THIBAULT: Hey, regarde.

He shows PAQUETTE a poster.

PAQUETTE: Ote-toi d'là. C'est quoi ça? Bolduc?

THIBAULT: Oui. Prends-en une.

PAQUETTE: Tu vas laisser tes cochonneries ailleurs.

He crumples up the poster and throws it over the balcony.

THIBAULT: Eh, tu votes pas Libéral cette année?

MURIEL: *(from downstairs)* Hey ... watch the garbage, okay?

CÉCILE: *(bringing out two beer)* Ah, bonjour, Thibault. Comment va ta mère?

THIBAULT: Oui, ça va bien.

JOHNNY: *(watching TV)* Slide, for fuck's sake! Slide!

PAQUETTE: *(watching TV)* C'est pas un coursier, c'est un cheval de labo!

CÉCILE: Claude, j'aurais besoin de cinq piastres.

PAQUETTE: Cinq piastres, pourquoi? Diane? Dis-y de venir les demander à sa piece of shit, okay?

CÉCILE exits into the house.

THIBAULT: *(looking at both TVs)* Hey, hey, it's the same game! The same game!

The broadcast VOICE is heard again.

VOICE: N'oubliez pas dans deux semaines, votez Gaëtan Bolduc. Bolduc est sur votre côté, toujours disposible et dynamique ... Bolduc ...

The broadcast truck plays Elvis Presley music. The music fades away.

THIBAULT: *(referring to the broadcast VOICE)* Oui, that's him right there.

PAQUETTE: *(watching TV)* Maudit, même pas capable de regarder sa game tranquille.

THIBAULT: *(watching TV)* Trois hommes sur les buts.

PAQUETTE: *(watching TV)* Y sont capables, si y veulent.

IRENE comes out on the balcony.

IRENE: Can we talk now?

JOHNNY: Shit, it bugs me when goofs like Bolduc use good Elvis music.

IRENE: Johnny, you got drunk again last night.

JOHNNY: Yeah ...

IRENE: Four nights in a row ... You said you were gonna stop. I thought we had all that settled.

JOHNNY: Listen ... this is not the right time.

IRENE: It's never the right time. I'm tired of waiting for the right time. Let's talk now ... Let's try to talk.

JOHNNY: Talk ... Look, I just need one more night to straighten out.

IRENE: Straighten out what?

JOHNNY: I'm not working, so you think you can pick on me, is that it? Is that it?

IRENE: This is not a contest.

JOHNNY: I got a hangover ... I'm in a bad mood.

IRENE: So, you're gonna go out tonight too?

JOHNNY: Yeah, that's right ... Yeah.

IRENE: Well, don't count on me being here to wipe up your puke forever.

JOHNNY: Nobody's asking you to.

IRENE: I'm tired of being the wife in your life, Johnny. I'm not gonna hang around here and watch you wreck yourself ... No thanks.

JOHNNY: I don't want to hear this.

IRENE: From now on, every time you get drunk, that's one more step towards goodbye ... Not tomorrow or next week, but soon, because it's not doing either of us any good.

JOHNNY: Irene, it's too hot to get mad.

IRENE: Wish I was mad. Can't even cry about it anymore.

JOHNNY: Look, I'm going up to the hospital next week. There's a pill they got, it makes ya sick every time ya take a drink.

IRENE: Johnny, you got to do it yourself.

JOHNNY: Okay, that's it for now. Okay? ... You're right, but it's the wrong time, okay? Okay?

IRENE goes into the house.

JOHNNY: *(shouting after her)* Hey, Irene, is there any more Coke in the fridge? Irene? ... Fuck!

CÉCILE comes out to water her plants.

CÉCILE: Mes plantes. They get thirsty too.

JOHNNY: Eh?

CÉCILE: *(holding up a plant)* See? ... They're smiling.

JOHNNY shrugs and gets up and turns off the TV. CÉCILE goes back into her house,

JOHNNY: Goddamn bums don't know how to win ...

THIBAULT: *(to JOHNNY)* They're losing in French too.

PAQUETTE: *(watching TV)* Nos champions! L'ont encore dans le cul, hostie.

JOHNNY: *(to PAQUETTE)* So, Paquette, what do ya think of the game? Eh?

THIBAULT: He don't speak the English no more.

JOHNNY: Oh yeah?

THIBAULT: Oui, and me too. I don't speak the English since last week. Maybe a few times, but that's all.

JOHNNY: Yeah, well, fuck the both of yas!

He goes into his house and comes out with a Canadian flag which he starts nailing up above his window.

THIBAULT: *(looking at JOHNNY's flag)* As-tu vu ça, Paquette?

PAQUETTE: Tu t'as pompé là, hostie!

PAQUETTE dashes into his house and comes out with a huge Québec flag, which THIBAULT staples to the wall.

PAQUETTE: Tabarnac! Tu m'en spotteras pas avec ça. Thibault, viens m'aider, prends ton bord.

THIBAULT goes over to help JOHNNY staple his flag above the window. When JOHNNY turns around, he sees PAQUETTE's huge Québec flag.

JOHNNY: Fuck!

He exits into his house. PAQUETTE and THIBAULT laugh. They turn off their TV set and exit into PAQUETTE's house. The broadcast VOICE is heard again.

VOICE: Gaëtan Bolduc, the man for you ... available and dynamic ... Gaëtan Bolduc, the man for you ... available and dynamic ...

The sound fades away. GAËTAN BOLDUC enters and knocks on MURIEL's door.

MURIEL: *(coming to the door)* Yeah, yeah. Hold your horses. (She opens the door and sees BOLDUC.) Holy shit!

BOLDUC: Ah, bonjour ... Tu parles anglais? English?

MURIEL: Yeah.

BOLDUC: Ah ... I'm Gaëtan Bolduc, your Member of Parliament. We all know that something is wrong with Québec right now, eh?

MURIEL: You're goddamn right.

BOLDUC: Well, I would like to help fix it ... Bon. Here's my card with information ... Don't be afraid to call, eh?

MURIEL: Yeah, yeah.

BOLDUC: Don't forget me on the 6th.

MURIEL: Don't worry, I will.

She slams the door shut in his face. He goes up the stairs and knocks on JOHNNY's door.

IRENE: *(inside the house)* Johnny ... there's someone at the door, Johnny. I'm in the tub.

JOHNNY: *(inside the house)* Shit! *(He opens the door.)* You!

BOLDUC: Ah, bonjour … Tu parles anglais? English?

JOHNNY: Yeah.

BOLDUC: Ah, I'm Gaëtan Bolduc, your Member of Parliament …

JOHNNY: Oh, "Gaëtan Bolduc, the man for you … available and dynamic." So what can I do for you?

BOLDUC: No … What can *I* do for you?

JOHNNY: You mean, what can I do *to* you?

BOLDUC: Bon. Here is my card with information. Don't forget, a vote for Gaëtan Bolduc is a vote for me … Bonjour.

JOHNNY: Hey! Wait a minute … I'm not finished yet. I only get to see you once every four years.

BOLDUC: Is there something you'd like to know?

JOHNNY: Yeah … Houses are still burning down, there's no jobs … What happened to all them promises?

BOLDUC: It takes time … We're working on it …

JOHNNY: Yeah? Eh, well, you got a lot of nerve walking around here … and quit using Elvis music, okay? What's the matter, you got no respect for the dead?

JOHNNY exits into his house.

IRENE: *(from inside the house)* Johnny, what's that all about?

JOHNNY: *(from inside the house)* It's fuckface, Bolduc.

IRENE: *(from inside the house)* Bolduc?

BOLDUC knocks on PAQUETTE's door. DIANE answers the door.

DIANE: Oui?

BOLDUC: Êtes-vous la femme de la maison?

DIANE: Moi? Jamais … Paquette? Paquette, c'est Bolduc.

PAQUETTE: Quoi?

THIBAULT sneaks out the window and goes downstairs where he starts putting up more Bolduc posters. PAQUETTE comes to the door.

BOLDUC: Bonjour. Je suis Gaëtan Bolduc, votre député au parlement.

PAQUETTE: Salut, Gaëtan.

BOLDUC: Allô?

PAQUETTE: Tu me reconnais? Claude Paquette? … École de Notre-Dame-des-Sept-Douleurs?

BOLDUC: Ah, oui … Oui …

PAQUETTE: Claude Paquette …

BOLDUC: Claude Paquette? … Oui, c'est ça …

PAQUETTE: Tu sais que t'as l'air de pas t'arranger, mon Bolduc.

BOLDUC: Je travaille fort, tu sais … On fait ce qu'on peut …

PAQUETTE: Moi aussi … J'travaille fort. Tu sais qu'j'ai jamais été sur le welfare. Moi, jamais. Les jeunes y se câlicent de ça, mais y faut que quelqu'un paye les taxes. Ces crisses de jeunes-là, y devraient toutes les câlicer dans l'armée. Comme ça y travailleraient.

BOLDUC: Alors, tu vas voter pour moi, eh, Claude?

PAQUETTE: Fuck you! Tu me poigneras pas une deuxième fois!

JOHNNY comes out and goes down the stairs. When he reaches the bottom of the stairs, he turns around and throws some eggs back at BOLDUC. They miss him and hit PAQUETTE.

PAQUETTE: Hey!

BOLDUC: C'est un joke, ça? Tu vas entendre parler de mes avocats, toi.

BOLDUC comes down the stairs and exits hurriedly. JOHNNY hands the eggs to THIBAULT to make it seem as if he had thrown them. He exits after BOLDUC.

PAQUETTE: Qu'est-ce que c'est ça? Qu'est-ce que c'est ça?

CÉCILE comes out. She looks at PAQUETTE.

CÉCILE: Claude, c'est quoi? Un oiseau?

THIBAULT starts coming up the stairs.

PAQUETTE: *(to THIBAULT)* Thibault, est-ce que t'as qu'que chose sur la toiture?

THIBAULT: La toiture?

PAQUETTE: Oui … la toiture.

THIBAULT: *(looking up at the roof)* Non.

PAQUETTE sees the eggs that JOHNNY has given to THIBAULT.

PAQUETTE: C'est quoi ça?

He takes the eggs from THIBAULT and starts throwing them at him. THIBAULT runs down the stairs.

THIBAULT: Hey! Hey! …

PAQUETTE: Ah, mon petit, tabarnac …

JOHNNY enters and goes up the stairs to his balcony.

THIBAULT: C'est pas moi. C'est pas moi … *(He points to JOHNNY.)* C'est lui. C'est lui.

JOHNNY stands on his balcony laughing.

PAQUETTE: C'est toi ça, eh? Big joke, eh? Big joke.

He throws an egg at JOHNNY.

JOHNNY: You watch yourself … Okay?

JOHNNY crosses to PAQUETTE's balcony.

PAQUETTE: Hey, keep on your own side! Keep on your own side!

JOHNNY: You and Bolduc, eh? Ya suck!

PAQUETTE: Hey, c'est toi qui vote pour les Libérals, eh? Pas moi.

JOHNNY: Yeah, eh?

They start shoving each other. IRENE comes out and she and CÉCILE try to break up the fight.

CÉCILE: Claude …

IRENE: Johnny, stop it …

IRENE starts hitting JOHNNY with a towel.

JOHNNY: What are ya hitting me for?

IRENE exits into the house with JOHNNY in tow. DIANE laughs at PAQUETTE from inside the house.

PAQUETTE: La petite crisse, elle trouve ça drôle? Ça t'fait rire? Ça t'fait rire?

DIANE: *(from inside the house)* Oui, je trouve ça drôle … Lâche ça … Lâche ça …

PAQUETTE goes into the house, takes one of DIANE's records and throws it out the window.

PAQUETTE: Est-ce tu trouves ça drôle?

DIANE: *(from inside the house)* Sors de ma chambre … Va-t-en d'ici …

TOM enters and knocks at MURIEL's door.

MURIEL: *(coming to the door)* Yeah, yeah. *(She opens the door.)* You're back.

TOM: Yeah.

MURIEL: Well, you better wash up … There's some food in the fridge.

TOM: Ma?

MURIEL: Yeah?

TOM: Uh … nothing …

He walks into the house. DIANE comes out of the house and sits in the rocking chair. She is crying. JOHNNY comes out of his house and sits on the balcony. CÉCILE comes out on her balcony.

CÉCILE: J'ai hâte qu'il fasse froid. Ton père peut pas dormir quand il fait trop chaud. Ça le rend de mauvaise humeur. *(She checks her plants.)* C'est vrai. Il y a de la place ici. Je pense que je vais déménager mes plantes sur le balcon d'en avant.

She sees that DIANE is crying.

Diane … Diane, qu'est-ce qu'y a?

DIANE: Y a rien.

CÉCILE: Tu vas voir, ton père va être malheureux de ce qu'il a fait, il va être gentil avec toi.

DIANE: Oui, mais j'suis pas un jouet, moi, maman.

CÉCILE: Diane …

DIANE: Laisse-moi tranquille …

CÉCILE goes back into her house.

JOHNNY: Irene? Hey, Irene? …

IRENE: *(coming to the screen door)* Yeah?

JOHNNY: Lend me a few bucks. I wanna go uptown ... Yeah, yeah, I know ... Look, why don't you just tell me to leave. Ya know, tell me to leave and it's all over.

IRENE: You're so weak.

JOHNNY: Just tell me it's over and I'm gone.

IRENE: I have to be strong for the both of us.

JOHNNY: It's so easy for you. You do this because of that. You do that because of this. It's not that easy for me.

IRENE: (throwing him five dollars, yelling) I hate you ... I hate you ...

She goes back into the house and slams the door.

JOHNNY: One more night, Irene ...

He exits. MURIEL comes out and throws a pair of boots in the garbage can. TOM follows her out. He has nothing on his feet.

TOM: Hey, Ma ... what are you doing?

MURIEL: You're not wearing these. They stink.

TOM: What do ya mean?

MURIEL: They stink and I'm throwing them out.

TOM: Ma, it's the only pair of boots I've got.

MURIEL: You're not wearing them in the house ... and just because your father is a bum, doesn't mean you have to be one too.

She goes back into the house. TOM takes the boots out of the garbage can and puts them back on.

TOM: She's nuts. I mean, she's clinical ...

DIANE: You? ... You're back again?

TOM: Yeah. Did a circle ...

DIANE: Why did you come back here?

TOM: I had no choice ... Same old shit, eh?

DIANE: They drive me crazy, all these people ...

TOM: I know what you mean.

DIANE: They're not happy, so they want everybody else to be the same way.

TOM: Yeah ...

DIANE: Me? I want to get out ... But how? Where do you go?

TOM: Not to Ormstown, I'll tell ya that ... Bunch of farmers ...

DIANE: You don't like New York City?

TOM: Never got there ... Wouldn't let me cross the border ... No money.

DIANE: You need money, eh?

TOM: Yeah.

DIANE: Always the same thing ...

TOM: Yeah. They don't make it easy for ya.

DIANE: They? ... Oui ... they.

TOM: You, uh ... get my letter?

DIANE: Oui.

TOM: So ... what do ya think?

DIANE: Why do you worry about what I think?

TOM: I don't know ...

DIANE: The letter was ... okay.

TOM: Oh, yeah? I meant what I said, ya know? ... in the letter.

DIANE: I'm not beautiful.

TOM: I don't know ... Girls that never blink turn me on.

DIANE: That's too bad for you.

TOM: Hey, uh ... I'm gonna look for work here and when I got some money, maybe I'll try New York again.

DIANE: What for? It's the same thing everywhere.

TOM: Hey, uh ... you're in a good mood, eh?

PAQUETTE comes out carrying some pop bottles down the stairs.

PAQUETTE: Hey, Diane. Je m'en vas au magasin. As-tu besoin de qu'que chose?

DIANE: Je veux rien qui vient de toi.

PAQUETTE: Tu pourrais au moins être polie, câlice, apart de ça. J't'ai pas dit que j'voulais pas que tu t'tiennes avec les têtes carrées.

DIANE: You don't tell me what to do.

PAQUETTE: Crisse, parle-moi en français, par exemple.

DIANE: Fuck you!

PAQUETTE: *(to TOM)* Et toi-là. Keep on your own side.

He exits.

TOM: Good to be home again ...

DIANE: Nobody tells me what to do ... Nobody.

TOM: All those French guys over thirty ... Grease!

DIANE: Et toi, tête carrée. What do you look like, eh?

TOM: Don't know ... Have to wear a box for a hat, I guess.

DIANE: That's right ... Aw, it's so hot!

TOM: You, uh, want to take a walk? ... No, eh?

DIANE: A walk?

TOM: Yeah, a walk.

DIANE: Where?

TOM: I don't know ... the Boardwalk? I always walk there.

DIANE: Okay.

TOM: Uh ... which way?

DIANE: I don't care.

TOM: This way ...

They begin to exit. MURIEL comes out of the house.

MURIEL: Tom?

TOM: Yeah?

MURIEL: Just look at you ... You're a mess!

TOM: We're going for a walk.

MURIEL: Tom, come here ... I want to speak to you ...

TOM: What?

MURIEL: Do you think this is fair to me?

TOM: What?

MURIEL: All of this? ...

TOM: I guess not.

MURIEL: You guess not?

TOM: Look, I had nothing to do with this. I was just born here, that's all.

MURIEL: Listen, don't think you can start in all over, hanging around here daydreaming, 'cause I won't have it. Either you get a job or you get out. It's one or the other ...

TOM: Job! Job! Job! I'm gonna get a job!

MURIEL: I've heard that one before.

TOM: This time I'm gonna look.

MURIEL: Sure ... and then, you'll move out with your first cheque.

TOM: Ma?

MURIEL: Don't you "Ma" me.

TOM: Ma? I don't wanna fight with ya, Ma.

MURIEL: So, don't fight ...

MURIEL exits into her house.

TOM: Home, sweet home ...

He bangs a garbage can and exits down the lane with DIANE.

Blackout.

Scene Three

The sound of sawing is heard offstage. JOHNNY is in the shed working. CLAUDE enters carrying his lunch bucket. He is coming home from work early. CÉCILE is watering her plants on the balcony.

CÉCILE: Claude, t'es de bonne heure. Qu'est-ce qui arrive? Es-tu malade?

PAQUETTE: Non, je ne suis pas malade.

CÉCILE: Qu'est-ce qu'y a qui va pas?

PAQUETTE: J'ai perdu ma job. Je suis revenu à pied.

CÉCILE: Veux-tu une chaise, Claude?

PAQUETTE: Pas une crisse d'avertissement. Je suis allé voir le boss en haut. Il a dit que ça lui faisait ben de la peine, mais il pouvait rien faire. Là, je suis allé voir le gars de l'union. Tu sais ce qu'il m'a dit, le gars de l'union, eh? "There's nothing we can do. The company is stopping their operation in Montreal. They're going to relocate it in Taiwan." ... Taïwan!

CÉCILE: Taïwan? C'est au Vermont, ça?

PAQUETTE: Treize ans de ma vie … Treize ans de ma câlice de vie …

CÉCILE: Quatorze, Claude. Je me souviens. Quand t'as eu ta job, c'était en octobre.

PAQUETTE: J'ai quarante-deux ans, tabarnac. J'peux pas recommencer à zéro. Qu'est-ce que j'vas faire?

CÉCILE: Tu l'aimais pas ta job de toute façon.

PAQUETTE: J'sais que j l'aimais pas, mais y faut ben manger.

CÉCILE: Oui.

PAQUETTE: Les crisses y sont ben toutes pareils. Les tabarnacs. Y s'servent de toi pis quand y'ont pu besoin de toi, y te câlicent dehors comme un vieux torchon sale. Pis, fuck you! Mange d'la merde. Pis si tu meures, c'est encore mieux. Y'ont pu de welfare à payer.

CÉCILE: Welfare? Mais on a jamais été sur le welfare, Claude.

PAQUETTE: Cécile, c'est pas de ma faute. C'est pas de ma faute.

CÉCILE: Je sais que je dis des choses stupides, mais je sais pas quoi dire.

The broadcast VOICE is heard.

VOICE: Don't forget tomorrow. Voting day … Re-elect Gaëtan Bolduc, the man for you … available and dynamic …

The sound fades away. DIANE and TOM enter together.

DIANE: *Apocalypse Now?* C'est quoi, *Apocalypse Now?*

TOM: It's a film about that war there in the States.

DIANE: What war?

TOM: Uh … China … Somewhere over there … Wanna go? Tonight?

DIANE: Okay … Salut … *(She goes up the stairs.)*

TOM: See ya … *(He goes into his house.)*

DIANE: *(at the top of the stairs)* Allô, Maman. Ça va?

PAQUETTE: Diane, tu peux oublier ton école.

DIANE: Qu'est-ce qu'y lui prend lui?

CÉCILE: Ton père a perdu sa job.

DIANE: Sa job?

CÉCILE: Oui, Diane.

DIANE: Bon. Y a pas d'quoi se plaindre.

CÉCILE: Ah, Diane.

DIANE: C'est bien mieux de même. Comme ça, on l'entendra plus chicaner. Cette job-là, nous a toutes rendus fous. C'est vrai.

CÉCILE: Elle est jeune, Claude.

PAQUETTE: Laisse-la faire.

DIANE: Je vais m'en trouver une job, moi. Inquiète-toi pas. C'est facile. Ils ont toujours besoin de waitress cute. Puis moi, je suis cute. Je vais en parler avec Irene, okay?

PAQUETTE: Moi, il faut que je fasse quelque chose.

DIANE: Va quelque part avec Cécile. Vous êtes libres, là. C'est le temps ou jamais. Oubliez ça pour un bout de temps.

PAQUETTE: Oh, non.

CÉCILE: Mais où est-ce qu'on irait?

PAQUETTE: Diane, tu te souviens quand tu étais petite, petite de même, on montait en haut sur la montagne, eh? On regardait les beaux arbres, les beaux oiseaux. C'était beau, hein? Diane, j'ai toujours voulu ce qu'il y avait de mieux pour toi. Je suis fatigué. Je ne sais plus quoi dire.

CÉCILE: Viens t'allonger, Claude. Viens t'allonger.

CÉCILE helps PAQUETTE to the door.

DIANE: Papa.

They exit into the house. DIANE sits on a chair on the balcony. MURIEL and IRENE enter.

IRENE: So what did they say this time?

MURIEL: Ah, you know doctors … They just try to scare ya …

IRENE: Hey, you're going to be okay.

MURIEL: Nope. They said it was serious.

IRENE: Yeah? How serious?

MURIEL: I'm gonna have an operation.

IRENE: Oh no, Muriel.

MURIEL: Yeah ... on the stomach. Ulcers.

IRENE: Oh no.

MURIEL: Aw, now that I know what they're gonna do, I'm not worried about it. It's just thinking about it that drives ya nuts.

IRENE: Ulcers ... Hey, so I was right, eh?

MURIEL: Yeah. Now, I'm gonna have to drink lots of milk ... Yuk!

IRENE: Does Tom know?

MURIEL: Yeah, he seems worried about it.

IRENE: Well, of course.

MURIEL: Ya know what those bastard doctors told me? Told me, I had to stop being so nervous ... Yeah, there's this fat pig making $80,000 a year, living in Côte Saint-Luc, telling me not to be a nervous wreck ... Well, I got so mad, I tell ya ... I got so mad, I couldn't talk.

IRENE: I can't blame ya.

MURIEL: It makes ya wanna kill yourself just out of spite.

IRENE: Ya oughta go to the clinic in the Pointe. The doctors there treat ya like a human being.

MURIEL: I dunno ... I heard they're all Commies or something.

IRENE: So what?

MURIEL: Yeah, well, guess they couldn't be any worse ... Oh, Irene, wait ... I wanna show ya something. *(She takes a small box out of her purse and opens it.)* Look.

IRENE: A brooch ... That's beautiful.

MURIEL: Tom bought it for me with his first pay.

IRENE: It's beautiful.

MURIEL: Yeah ... stupid kid. Now, he doesn't have enough money for car fare.

JOHNNY enters from the shed carrying some lumber and tools. He has built a new step for the stairs.

IRENE: Does he like his new job?

MURIEL: Well, he's lasted a month. That's some kind of record. *(She sees JOHNNY and the step.)* Holy shit! Hey, watch your thumbs!

JOHNNY glares at her.

MURIEL: Just a joke ... *(She goes into her house.)*

JOHNNY: Irene, gimme a hand with this ... Yeah, I know, officially, we ain't talking, but I need a hand ...

IRENE: I don't believe it.

She goes over to help JOHNNY put the new step in place.

JOHNNY: So, what's new? ... How are ya?

IRENE: I don't know ... Haven't been talking to myself lately.

JOHNNY: I've been off the sauce for a week now, right?

IRENE: Yeah.

JOHNNY: Yeah.

IRENE: You want a medal or what?

JOHNNY: Irene ... It's not easy, okay?

IRENE: Try being a woman for a while ...

DIANE: *(from upstairs)* Oui, that's right.

JOHNNY: *(taking IRENE over to one side)* Irene, all that crap about you being strong for the both of us ...

IRENE: It's not crap.

JOHNNY: Yeah, okay ... it's true, but I didn't make up the rules of the game, okay? I mean, it wasn't me.

IRENE: It wasn't me.

JOHNNY: I'm sorry, Irene. You know that? ... I'm sorry.

IRENE: I was worried ...

JOHNNY: About what?

IRENE: I've never seen you that bad before ...

JOHNNY: Hey, I don't melt in the rain ... I don't get diarrhea in the snow. I'm a survivor.

IRENE: Yeah ... *(They embrace.)* So, what are you gonna do?

JOHNNY: Maybe I can get back into music.

IRENE: You've been miserable ever since ya quit playing.

JOHNNY: You're the one who nagged me to quit.

IRENE: All I wanted you to do was stop drinking and screwing around so much ... Music had nothing to do with it.

JOHNNY: What do you know about the nightlife, Irene?

IRENE: Yeah, well ... Anyhow, no matter what happens, we'll always be friends, eh?

JOHNNY: Is that a threat?

TOM comes out with his guitar and starts to play a song.

IRENE: Hi, Tommy.

IRENE goes up the stairs and into the house. JOHNNY comes over to talk to TOM.

JOHNNY: So, how's the new job?

TOM: Aw, Troy Laundry ... What can I say? Some guys been there twenty years and I'm there twenty days and already going nuts.

JOHNNY: Bad news, eh?

TOM: Hey. Can't talk to anybody ... They're all deaf from the noise.

JOHNNY: They probably got nothing to say anyhow.

TOM: Ya don't get a watch when you retire, ya get a hearing aid.

CÉCILE comes out on her balcony to speak to DIANE.

CÉCILE: Tu sais, Diane, j'ai vu ton père pleurer juste une fois. C'est quand t'étais petite puis bien malade.

DIANE: Je ne me souviens pas de ça.

CÉCILE: Ça fait longtemps. On restait sur la rue Joseph.

TOM plays a tune on his guitar.

TOM: *(to DIANE)* Hi, Diane ... You like that? ...

DIANE: No ... Know any disco?

TOM: Disco! ... Disco Duck ... I don't got the right buttons on this thing.

MURIEL: *(from inside the house)* Tommy?

TOM: Yeah?

MURIEL: I'm gonna need a hand in here ... I'm moving out your old man's junk into the shed.

TOM: You're moving it out?

MURIEL: Yeah ... He's never here and we can use the room.

TOM: Okay.

He goes in to help her move the things out to the shed. IRENE comes out of her house and goes down the stairs.

IRENE: All the trouble that step caused us over the last year and look at that, it's fixed.

JOHNNY: Yeah, I'm gonna send Giboux the bill.

DIANE: *(to IRENE)* Irene, is there any jobs at your place?

IRENE: What?

DIANE: I have to find work. My father, he lost his job.

IRENE: He lost his job?

CÉCILE: Yes. The company is going to Taiwan, but they don't want to take Claude.

IRENE: The bastards.

JOHNNY: He got the axe, eh?

IRENE: How is he?

DIANE: Not so good ... Maybe you can talk to him, Irene.

IRENE: Be better if you talk to him, Johnny.

JOHNNY: What the fuck am I gonna say? He don't even want to speak my language.

IRENE: *(shouting)* Hey, Muriel. Paquette lost his job.

MURIEL comes out of her house.

MURIEL: What? Another one for your Unemployment Committee. *(to CÉCILE)* Sorry, madame. I really am.

IRENE: We can get him out on our next demonstration.

JOHNNY: Another one?

IRENE: We're gonna march in front of the U.I.C. building. Let them know we don't like the forty percent unemployment down here.

JOHNNY: Demonstration in the Pointe? That's not news.

MURIEL: We should do it in Westmount. That's where all the money is. Go up there and sit on their goddamn front lawns.

DIANE: Oui. Go right up there and let them know what we look like.

TOM: Yeah.

CÉCILE: It's very nice up in Westmount ... It's very nice.

JOHNNY: Yeah, you can take Thibault and leave him up there ... Boom! Into the woodwork ... Westmount's infested ... Thousands of little Thibaults running around ... Boom! Another Pointe Saint-Charles!

MURIEL: Thibault ... our secret weapon.

TOM: So secret, he don't even know.

IRENE: Johnny, talk to Paquette ...

JOHNNY: You talk to him ...

IRENE: Johnny?

JOHNNY: Look, it's the principle of the thing ...

IRENE: Principle of what?

JOHNNY: Well, he started it, right?

IRENE: Started what?

DIANE: Maudit crisse, Johnny!

JOHNNY: Alright. Ya want me to be the nice guy ... Why do I always got to be the nice guy?

He goes up the stairs and knocks on PAQUETTE's door.

Hey, Porky ... Peace in the valley, okay?

PAQUETTE: *(from inside his house)* Quoi?

JOHNNY: Let's kiss and make up.

PAQUETTE: Quoi?

IRENE: Tell him you're sorry he lost his job.

JOHNNY: Look, I'm sorry you lost your job ...

IRENE: Tell him in French.

JOHNNY: I don't know how.

IRENE: Try ... J'ai de la peine ...

JOHNNY: J'ai de la peine ...

IRENE: J'ai de la peine que tu as perdu ... que tu as perdu ...

JOHNNY: J'ai de la peine que tu as perdu ...

IRENE: Ta job.

JOHNNY: Ta fuckin' job ... He's not talking.

IRENE: He's upset.

JOHNNY: Diane, how do you say, "Together, we can fuck Bolduc"?

DIANE: "Ensemble on peut fourrer Bolduc."

JOHNNY: Hey, Paquette ... "Ensemble ... "

PAQUETTE: *(at his screen door)* Hey, you go away with the bullshit, okay? Take it somewhere else ... It's just another Pepsi who loses his job. T'es content ... Alors, viens pas m'écoeurer avec ça.

He slams the door shut.

JOHNNY: Irene!

He goes into his house and slams the door shut.

IRENE: Oh boy!

She goes up the stairs to PAQUETTE's door and knocks on it. There is no answer.

MURIEL: Talking's easy, Irene, but try to get people together ... Ppphht!

IRENE: What does it take to move you guys? ... We gotta help ourselves. That's easy to understand, isn't it?

DIANE: They don't want to understand ... it's easier to eat shit.

IRENE: I don't know why I bother.

MURIEL: Ah, we can still do the demonstration without them.

CÉCILE: We need the government to help us.

MURIEL: What are you talking about? Bolduc is the government!

IRENE: Well ... I'm tired ...

THIBAULT enters on his bike. He has a case of beer for PAQUETTE.

THIBAULT: Chez Momo's is here.

TOM: Hey, Thibault. How's the girls?

THIBAULT: Oh, boy, don't talk to me about that … Trouble all the time …

He goes up the stairs and discovers the new step.

Hey! *(He dances on the new step.)* Où est Paquette? *(He puts the case of beer down on the balcony.)*

CÉCILE: Claude est pas bien aujourd'hui. Il a perdu sa job.

THIBAULT: Il a perdu sa job? Aw, everybody's got trouble now, eh? Me, last week, I got hit by a Cadillac.

MURIEL: By a what?

THIBAULT: A Cadillac, oui … Big car, eh? … So, I phone the boss and he says, "How's the bike?" "How's the bike?" hostie … Hey, me, I know the boss. Sometimes he talks nice, but he's still the boss, eh?

MURIEL: Aw, bosses … they're all the same, Thibault.

THIBAULT: Sure, I know that … Maybe I'm crazy, but I'm not stupid, eh?

MURIEL: They do what they want, the bastards. They always do what they want.

She starts ripping down Bolduc posters.

THIBAULT: Hey, Bolduc won't like that …

MURIEL: Ppphht on Bolduc.

THIBAULT: Okay … He won't like that, that's all.

DIANE: Irene, do you smell something?

IRENE: Yeah …

TOM: Probably someone burning garbage.

MURIEL: Do you see any smoke?

IRENE: Yeah, but I don't know where it's coming from.

CÉCILE: C'est un feu.

THIBAULT: Un feu? Où ça un feu?

IRENE: *(to JOHNNY, inside the house)* Johnny, go down the lane and take a look.

JOHNNY: *(coming out of his house)* Why do I always have to do everything around here?

He dashes off down the lane, followed by TOM and DIANE. They all yell. "Fire!" JOHNNY comes running back on.

JOHNNY: Irene, call the cops! It's a big one! Just a few houses down …

He runs back down the lane.

CÉCILE: Claude? Claude, y a un feu!

IRENE: I can't get the cops. The lines are busy …

PAQUETTE comes running out of his house.

CÉCILE: Claude, dis à Diane de ne pas aller trop proche …

He exits down the lane.

IRENE: It's a big one.

CÉCILE: Oh, yes … a big one …

MURIEL: Those old houses go up like matchsticks …

PAQUETTE: *(yelling offstage)* Ça s'étend aux sheds d'à côté!

CÉCILE: Mon Dieu!

MURIEL: What did he say?

IRENE: It's spreading …

MURIEL: Where the hell are the firemen?

IRENE: If this were Westmount, there wouldn't be a fire.

MURIEL: Yeah, right …

PAQUETTE comes running back on.

PAQUETTE: Ça continue à s'étendre!

MURIEL: What's he saying?

PAQUETTE: Cécile, on va sortir les meubles!

JOHNNY comes running back on, followed by TOM and DIANE.

JOHNNY: Hey, Irene, start moving our stuff out!

There is general running around and shouting. THIBAULT gets in everyone's way. JOHNNY and PAQUETTE carry down their TV sets and their beer first. CÉCILE carries down her plants.

MURIEL: Tom, move your ass!

TOM: Aw, we're insured anyhow …

MURIEL: Move it!

PAQUETTE: *(to CÉCILE)* C'est pas le temps toi et pis tes hostie de plantes.

MURIEL: Thibault, get your bike out of the way!

THIBAULT: Hey, don't touch my bike!

MURIEL: Then get it out of the way!

THIBAULT: Eh, Madame Paquette, y a un gros feu là-bas! Hey, good thing we fix that step, eh?

JOHNNY: *(to PAQUETTE)* Keep your shit on that side …

PAQUETTE: Va donc chier, câlice!

JOHNNY and PAQUETTE collide at the top of the stairs. They start pushing and shoving each other to see who will go down the stairs first.

PAQUETTE: Ote-toi de là, hostie!

JOHNNY: Get out of my way!

IRENE, CÉCILE and DIANE rush in to break up the fight.

IRENE: Don't be so stupid … Now, get out of the way … both of you. Come, you guys … Hey, Muriel, Tom … we'll do a relay … We'll move them out upstairs, then we'll do you.

MURIEL: Why upstairs first?

IRENE: Muriel, come on!

The relay begins. They all start passing stuff down. It comes at them through the windows and through the doors. PAQUETTE calls JOHNNY over to give him a hand with the sofa.

PAQUETTE: Lève-toi … Lève-le …

JOHNNY: Irene, he's speaking French!

IRENE: Lift it!

PAQUETTE: Tourne-le … Tourne-le …

JOHNNY: Yeah, yeah … tour-ney …

PAQUETTE: À droite …

IRENE: To the right.

PAQUETTE: Laisse-le slyer sur la rampe … la rampe …

JOHNNY: What???

IRENE: Slide it down the banister!

They slide the sofa down the banister. JOHNNY hurts himself when he and PAQUETTE put the sofa down at the foot of the stairs.

PAQUETTE: Okay, allez, Johnny … We go move ton sofa …

He helps JOHNNY up the stairs. When they get halfway up, a huge crashing noise is heard.

TOM: There goes the roof!

CÉCILE: Mon Dieu!

IRENE: Here it comes …

MURIEL: Christ, we're next!

The broadcast VOICE is heard once again.

VOICE: Citizens of Pointe Saint-Charles, we live in a time when we need a strong government, a just government, one that is not afraid to deal harshly with disrupters, sabotage, corruptions and criminals. Remember, a vote for Gaëtan Bolduc is a vote for security, for justice, for law and order … and for the future. Le futur …

JOHNNY, IRENE, MURIEL and TOM: *(turning to the audience)* What are we going to do?

PAQUETTE, CÉCILE, DIANE and THIBAULT: *(turning to the audience)* Qu'est-ce qu'on va faire?

Blackout.

END

SHARON POLLOCK （b. 1936)

In her program notes for the second production of *Doc*, at Toronto Free Theatre in 1984, Sharon Pollock wrote about how she had dealt with historical and broadly sociological material in her early plays rather than confronting her own personal past: "possibly I found my personal history too frightening and confusing to confront directly." The history she dramatizes in *Doc* is based on that of her own family during the years she was growing up in Fredericton, New Brunswick: her father, Ev, devoting himself to his work as a respected physician and pillar of the community while her mother slowly came apart at home, and she herself as a child watching the unfolding of this terrible drama of guilt, recrimination, alcoholism and eventual suicide.

Much of Pollock's stage work would appear to divide along a line between history plays like *Walsh*, *The Komagata Maru Incident*, *One Tiger to a Hill* and *Fair Liberty's Call*, and more personal family plays, beginning with *Blood Relations* and including *Generations*, *Whiskey Six Cadenza* and *Doc* (although her later plays don't easily fall into either category). But in another sense, as Pollock herself has said, she has really been writing the same play over and over, a play about fathers or father figures betraying the trust of those who depend on them, driven to those betrayals by their own adherence to a set of external, systemic values, and usually refusing to acknowledge responsibility for the damage they do. With *Doc* she cuts closest to the autobiographical bone, projecting herself directly into the play in the form of two characters, and creating one of the most powerful and affecting experiences in the Canadian theatre, a play that Ray Conlogue has called "Sharon Pollock's *Long Day's Journey into Night*."

Pollock was born Mary Sharon Chalmers in Fredericton, where she first became involved in the theatre at university. Later, with the Prairie Players she toured B.C. and Alberta in 1966, and was voted Best Actress at the Dominion Drama Festival. She settled in Calgary the next year, and while pregnant with her sixth child she began writing her first play. The absurdist farce *A Compulsory Option* won the 1971 Alberta Playwriting Competition and was produced in 1972 by the New Play Centre in Vancouver, where Pollock and her family were now living. *Walsh* (1973) explored the relationship between the North-West Mounted Police officer of the title and Sitting Bull's Sioux on the Canadian prairies in the 1870s. Its Theatre Calgary premiere and subsequent production at Stratford in 1974 brought Pollock to wide public attention. A productive association with the Vancouver Playhouse between 1973 and 1976 resulted in six plays for children as well as *And Out Goes You?* (1975), a political comedy about urban redevelopment, and *The Komagata Maru Incident* (1976), which powerfully dissects the politics of racism behind the refusal to admit Sikh immigrants into Vancouver in 1914. Pollock herself played the title role of Lizzie Borden in the Douglas College production of her next play, *My Name Is Lisbeth* (1976), which would go on to become her most popular success, *Blood Relations*, first staged professionally in 1980 by Edmonton's Theatre Three. Her volume *Blood Relations and Other Plays* won the inaugural Governor General's Literary Award for Drama in 1981.

Pollock moved to Edmonton in 1976 to teach playwriting at the University of Alberta, but except for a few brief periods since 1977 she has made her home in Calgary. From 1977–79 she ran the summer Playwrights' Colony at Banff and was playwright-in-residence for Alberta Theatre Projects, which produced her fine study of a family of prairie farmers, *Generations*, in 1980. That same year Edmonton's Citadel Theatre mounted *One Tiger to a Hill*, her dramatization of a fatal hostage-taking at the B.C. Penitentiary. She spent 1981–82 as artist-in-residence at the National Arts Centre, returning to Theatre Calgary to present *Whiskey Six Cadenza* (1983) and *Doc*, and serve briefly as artistic director in 1984. The former play is a tale of rum-running, coal mining and sexual abuse in 1920s Alberta.

After a couple of unhappy years as artistic director of Theatre New Brunswick, Pollock returned to performing in 1989, premiering her one-woman play *Getting It Straight* at the International Women's Festival in Winnipeg. A lyrical feminist monologue about male aggression and abuses of power spoken by an apparent madwoman beneath a rodeo grandstand ("I am not mad I am getting it straight"), the play was remounted at Toronto's Factory Theatre in 1990. The Stratford Festival produced *Fair Liberty's Call* (1993), the tale of a Loyalist family's travails in New Brunswick following the American Revolution. Pollock herself directed *Saucy Jack* (1993), a metatheatrical examination of Jack the Ripper, at her own Garry Theatre in Calgary, which she ran from 1992 to 1997. Calgary's Theatre Junction produced the historically based dramas *Moving Pictures* (1999), about Canadian silent-film actress Nell Shipman, and *End Dream* (2000), Pollock's study of a notorious murder case in 1920s Vancouver involving race, class and gender matters. Pollock's ongoing concern with both feminist and Native issues was reflected in *The Making of Warriors* (1990), one in a long line of her radio plays that includes the 1980 ACTRA Best Radio Drama Award winner, *Sweet Land of Liberty*.

Doc was commissioned and first produced by Theatre Calgary in April 1984 with Pollock's own daughter Amanda making her professional stage debut in the role of the young daughter Katie. The play was extensively revised for the Toronto Free Theatre production later that year, and has gone on to a number of regional theatres including Manitoba Theatre Centre and the Vancouver Playhouse, where the title role was taken by Pollock's ex-husband Michael Ball in another interchange between Pollock's art and her family life. In 1986 the play won Pollock her second Governor General's Award, and she herself directed a production for Theatre New Brunswick under the title *Family Trappings*. Her father attended opening night and provided program notes.

Doc takes the form of a memory play, but with three variations on the traditional memory play structure. First, the lens through which the memories are filtered is bifocal. Rather than a single protagonist, two characters share—and shape—the past conjured in the play: Catherine and her father, Ev. What is remembered will not necessarily be less subjective or distorted, but it will have at least two sides. Catherine's accusing memories are met and in effect rebutted by Ev's self-justifying ones. In the memory scenes Ev's wife Bob and his friend Oscar tend to support Catherine's accusations, while Katie, Catherine's younger self, most often sides with Ev. This ability of the characters to talk to each other across the memory frame is the second variation that Pollock plays on the form. Insofar as the play resembles a trial, with Catherine sitting in judgment of Ev, and Bob acting as prosecutor, the fluid form allows an elaborate complex of cross-examinations to be conducted from both sides of the frame.

The third variation is probably the most important: Pollock's decision to split the character of the daughter into an older and younger self, Catherine and Katie, played by two different actors. This results in Catherine's struggling not only with her ambivalent feelings for both her parents, but with her own sense of personal fragmentation and alienation. She hated seeing her father's selfishness and not so benign neglect drive her mother deeper and deeper into alcoholic depression, chipping away at Bob's sense of identity and self-worth, actively conspiring to neutralize her strength and even her sexuality. At the same time she hated her mother's weakness in allowing herself to be so diminished, hated her for the terrible games of hide-the-bottle that Katie was forced to play. And she admired her father's strength and self-sufficiency, the stubborn singlemindedness that made him such a good doctor—and such a terrible husband. The Catherine/Katie split represented by the two actors in such graphic theatrical terms is also the wound that adult Catherine carries within her, a kind of internal hemorrhaging made more acute by her perception of her own guilt in her mother's death. The play moves towards a reconciliation of the two selves: in the vocabulary of contemporary therapeutic literature, Catherine comes to accept and embrace her inner child.

But that self-reconciliation is possible for Catherine only through reconciling with her father. Since she has been accusing herself of essentially the same crime as Doc, she has really only two choices: to convict him or drop the charges. She chooses, in effect, the latter. Not only is the potentially incriminating evidence of Ev's mother's letter not introduced, but it is destroyed—by Catherine herself. At the end she speaks her father's language, lets him have the last word, and smiles at him a smile that smacks of complicity. Throughout the play Catherine and Katie have wondered and worried about which of their parents they most resemble, whose character they are most likely to have inherited. Catherine appears finally to have cast her lot with the charismatic (and living) father. But the cost is heavy: a silencing of the dead victims, mother and perhaps grand-mother, whose cries for justice reach from the grave. They are heard, but in the end rejected, that the living might carry on.

Doc was first produced at Theatre Calgary on April 7, 1984, with the following cast:

EV	Michael Hogan
CATHERINE	Susan Hogan
KATIE	Amanda Pollock
BOB	Kate Trotter
OSCAR	Chuck Shamata

Directed by Guy Sprung
Designed by Terry Gunvordahl
Music and Sound Score by Allan Rae

DOC

CHARACTERS

EV, *an elderly man in his 70s*
CATHERINE, *his daughter, in her mid-30s*
KATIE, *Catherine, as a young girl*
BOB, *Ev's wife, Catherine's mother*
OSCAR, *Ev's best friend*

AUTHOR'S NOTES

Much of the play consists of the sometimes shared, sometimes singular memories of the past, as relived by EV and CATHERINE, interacting with figures from the past. Structurally, shifts in time do not occur in a linear, chronological fashion, but in an unconscious and intuitive patterning of the past by EV and CATHERINE. A stage direction (Shift) marks these pattern changes which are often, but not always, time shifts as well. In production, music has been used to underscore the pattern shifts; however, the characters' shifts from one pattern to another must be immediate. They do not "hold" for the music. The physical blocking must accommodate this immediacy and the stage setting facilitate it.

The "now" of the play takes place in the house in which CATHERINE grew up and in which EV now lives alone. The play is most effective when the set design is not a literal one, and when props and furniture are kept to a minimum. I think of the setting as one which has the potential to explode time and space while simultaneously serving certain naturalistic demands of the play.

A kaleidoscope of memory constitutes the dialogue and action of the opening sequence. It is followed by a scene set more firmly in the "now." EV is "old" during these two segments, as he is at the opening and closing of Act Two. Although EV relives the past as a younger man, we never see CATHERINE any age but in her mid-thirties. She is able to speak across time to her father, to her mother and to her younger self. CATHERINE and KATIE blend, sharing a sense of one entity, particularly in the scenes with her father's best friend, OSCAR. This should not be interpreted to mean that CATHERINE and KATIE share one mind or are always in accord. They are often in conflict.

OSCAR is first seen in the opening sequence wearing a Twenties-era hockey uniform. He is a young man about to enter medical school. OSCAR's scenes with KATIE cover a four year period prior to and ending with BOB's death. In the scenes he shares with BOB and EV there is a longer, more chronological unfolding of time. For the most part, we see him as a man in his mid-thirties.

We see BOB in her mid-twenties to mid-thirties. She wears a dressing gown which has a belt or tie at the waist, and under this she wears a slip. The material of the gown is satin or satin-like; the gown itself has the look of a tailored long dinner gown when appropriately belted. On other occasions, undone and flapping, it has the appearance of a sloppy kimono. Is it necessary to say that her descent into alcoholism, despair and self-disgust must be carefully charted?

EV as an old man wears glasses and a worn cardigan sweater.

There are liquor bottles on stage in Act One; they have been removed from the set in Act Two. A trunk is useful on stage; it holds photos and memorabilia; as well, it provides a storage place in Act One for OSCAR's hockey uniform, and the clothing into which he and EV will change.

In some productions all characters are always on stage with the exception of EV, who is free to exit and enter during the play, and KATIE, BOB and OSCAR, who exit near the end of the play. In other productions there has been a greater freedom of movement re: characters' exits and entrances. The script indicates where a character "may enter" or "may exit." If this is not indicated, the character must remain on stage.

ACT ONE

In the black there is a subtle murmuring of voices, with the odd phrase and word emerging quite clearly. They are repeats of bits and pieces of dialogue heard later in the play. The voices are those of KATIE, OSCAR, BOB and the young EV; they often speak on top of each other.

Light grows on EV, who is seated by the open trunk. He holds an unopened letter. A match flares as BOB lights a cigarette in the background. Light grows on BOB, on OSCAR who is smoothing tape on his hockey stick, and on KATIE who concentrates on moving one foot back and forth slowly and rhythmically. EV slowly closes the trunk, his focus still on the envelope he holds.

CATHERINE enters. She carries an overnight bag as well as her shoulder bag. She puts the overnight bag down. She sees KATIE. She watches KATIE for a moment, and then speaks to KATIE's rhythmic movement.

CATHERINE: Up-on the carpet ... you shall kneel ... while the grass ... grows in the field

KATIE's motion turns into skipping as KATIE turns an imaginary skipping rope and jumps to it.

CATHERINE:
Stand up straight
Upon your feet

The murmuring of voices can still be heard but they are fading.

KATIE: *(speaks with CATHERINE)*
Choose the one you love so sweet
Now they're married wish them well
First a girl, gee that's swell

KATIE's voice is growing louder, taking over from CATHERINE.

KATIE and CATHERINE:
Seven years after,
Seven to come

KATIE: *(alone)*
Fire on the mountain kiss and run
(jumps "pepper" faster and faster)
Tinker, tailor, soldier, sailor,
Rich man, poor man, beggar man, thief

BOB: Doctor

KATIE: Doc-tor!!! *(stops skipping)*

CATHERINE: *(removing her gloves)* Daddy?

EV: *(looks up from the envelope)* Katie? *(stands up)* Is that you, Katie?

KATIE: *(skipping towards EV, singing)* La da da da daah.

KATIE continues her "la dahs," skipping away from EV as OSCAR speaks.

OSCAR: Hey, you and me, Ev. *(EV looks at the letter and sits back down.)* Best friends. Ev and Oscar, Oscar and Ev—and if we weren't—I think I'd hate you.

KATIE: *(stops skipping but continues)* La dada da daah.

BOB: Why don't you open it?

OSCAR: You see, Ev—you're just too good at things.

BOB: Go on, open it.

The murmuring voices have faded out.

OSCAR: It makes people nervous. *(sound of an approaching train whistle)* It makes me nervous.

BOB: Listen.

The train whistle is growing in volume. KATIE stops her "la da da dahs."

BOB: Your Gramma, Katie, his mother. She'd set her clock by that train. Set her clock by the junction train crossing the railway bridge into Devon. Must be what? Three-quarters of a mile of single track spanning the river? And midnight, every night, that train coming down from the junction—half-way across three-quarters of a mile of single track its whistle would split the night ... and that night do you know what she did?

EV: *(his focus on the letter)* No.

BOB: She walked out to meet it.

EV: No.

BOB: You wanna know something, Katie?

KATIE: No.

BOB: Your father's mother, your grandmother, killed herself ... Katie!

KATIE: What!

BOB: She walked across the train bridge at midnight and the train hit her.

KATIE: That's an accident.

BOB: She left a letter, and the letter tells him why she did it.

KATIE: There isn't any letter.

BOB: What's that?

KATIE: Daddy?

BOB: And he won't open it 'cause he's afraid, he's afraid of what she wrote.

KATIE: Is that true, Daddy?

EV: No.

KATIE: Is that the letter?

EV: Your grandmother was walking across the Devon bridge—

KATIE: What for?

EV: Well—it was a kind of short cut.

BOB: Short cut?

EV: And she got caught in the middle of a span and she was hit and killed.

CATHERINE: I stayed with her once when I was little … I can hardly remember.

EV: *(continuing to talk to KATIE)* It was after your mother had Robbie.

KATIE: Why didn't I stay with you and Robbie and Mummy?

EV: Your mother was sick so you stayed with your Gramma.

CATHERINE: Yes … and she made me soft-boiled runny eggs, and she'd feed me them and tell me stories about Moses in the bullrushes, and I … and I … would peel the wallpaper off behind the door, and she'd get angry.

EV: That's right.

CATHERINE: Why didn't she jump?

OSCAR: A hat trick Ev! Everybody screaming— everybody on their feet—what's it feel like, Ev?

BOB: He doesn't care. He doesn't care about anything except his "prac-tice" and his "off-fice" and his "off-fice nurse" and all those stupid, stupid people who think he's God.

EV: *(to KATIE)* Don't listen to her.

BOB: You're not God.

EV: Your mother's sick.

KATIE: No she isn't.

OSCAR: God, you're good. You fly, Ev.

KATIE: Why do you keep saying she's sick?

OSCAR: You don't skate, you fly.

KATIE: She's not sick.

EV: Your mother's—

KATIE: Why do you keep saying that!

EV: Katie—

KATIE: No!

CATHERINE: For a long time I prayed to God. I asked him to make her stop. I prayed and prayed. I thought, I'm just a little girl. Why would God want to do this to a little girl? I thought it was a mistake. I thought maybe he didn't know. I don't know what I thought. I prayed and prayed … Now, I don't believe in God.

KATIE: And if there is a God, then I don't like him.

EV: She isn't well.

BOB slowly opens a drawer, feels inside it and runs her hand along a chair cushion. She continues quietly, unobtrusively looking for something as KATIE and EV speak.

KATIE: Tell Robbie that. He wants to believe that. I want the truth.

EV: I'm telling you the truth.

KATIE: No! Do you know what I did yesterday? She kept going to the bathroom and going to the bathroom and I went in and looked all over and I found it. In the clothes hamper with all the dirty clothes and things. And I took it and I poured it down the sink and I went downstairs and I threw the empty bottle in the garbage so don't tell me she's sick!

BOB: It's gone.

BOB looks at KATIE. In the following sequence, although CATHERINE is the speaker, BOB will act out the scene with KATIE.

CATHERINE: No. No, don't.

BOB: It's gone.

CATHERINE: No.

BOB: You.

CATHERINE: No.

BOB: You took it and I want it back. *(BOB grabs KATIE.)* I want it back!

CATHERINE: It's gone now and you can't have it.

BOB: Where? You tell me where?

CATHERINE: I poured it out.

BOB: No.

CATHERINE: Down the sink.

BOB: No.

CATHERINE: It's gone, forget it.

BOB: It's mine, I want it back!

CATHERINE: Gone.

BOB: No fair!

BOB struggles with KATIE.

CATHERINE: Let me go!

BOB: No right!

CATHERINE: Let me go!

BOB: You had no right!

KATIE strikes BOB, knocking her down.

CATHERINE: Daddy!

EV: Katie?

EV gets up from his chair and moves to look for CATHERINE. OSCAR may follow him. EV does not see CATHERINE, nor she him.

OSCAR: You know my father wishes I were you. He does. He wishes I were you. "Oscar," he says, "Oscar, look at Ev—why can't you be like Ev?"

BOB: Look at what your father did.

KATIE: You lie.

OSCAR: I say nothing. There's nothing to be said. "You got to have that killer instinct on the ice," he says. I play goalie—what the hell's a killer instinct in a goalie? Then he says, "Oscar," he says, "Oscar, you are goin' into medicine."

EV: Katie?

OSCAR: My Dad's a doctor so I gotta be a doctor.

BOB: Your father hit me and I fell.

KATIE: You're always lying.

BOB: See.

KATIE: He didn't hit you.

BOB: See?

KATIE: I hit you!—Get away from me!

OSCAR: What's so funny is you're the one so bloody keen on medicine—you'd kill for medicine. *(laughs)* Hey Ev, kill for medicine, eh. *(laughs)*

BOB: Your father's mother, your Gramma, killed herself and he's afraid to open it.

KATIE: *(covers her ears)*
Now they're married wish them joy
First a girl for a toy
Seven years after, seven to come,
Fire on the mountain, kiss and run

EV returns from his search for CATHERINE. OSCAR follows him. KATIE sees CATHERINE, and moves towards her, speaking the verse to her.

KATIE:
On the mountain berries sweet
Pick as much as you can eat
By the berries bitter bark
Fire on the mountain break your heart

KATIE and CATHERINE: Years to come—kiss and run—bitter bark—

CATHERINE sees EV, who sees her. CATHERINE speaks softly, almost to herself.

CATHERINE: Break your heart ... It's me, Daddy.

EV: Katie?

KATIE: When I was little, Daddy.

CATHERINE: It's Catherine now, call me Catherine ... well ... aren't you going to say anything?

EV: You're home.

CATHERINE: Ah-huh ... a hug, a big hug, Daddy, come on. *(CATHERINE and EV embrace.)* Ooh.

EV: What.

CATHERINE: How long has it been?

EV: Be ah ...

CATHERINE: Four years, right? Medical convention in where? Vancouver, right?

EV: That's right. Vancouver.

CATHERINE: Montreal, Toronto, Calgary, Van, where haven't we met, eh?

EV: Here.

CATHERINE: Yup. Not ... not met here. *(CATHERINE notices the envelope in EV's hand.)* What're you doing with that?

EV: Oh—just goin' through things. Clearin' things out.

CATHERINE, getting out a cigarette, turns away from EV.

BOB: Katie's afraid of what she wrote.

KATIE: *(to CATHERINE)* Is that true?

EV: Are you here for this hoopla tomorrow?

CATHERINE: Not really.

EV: There's gonna be speeches and more speeches. I lay the cornerstone, and dinner I think.

CATHERINE: Ah-huh.

EV: I got it all written down with the times.

CATHERINE: Ah-huh.

EV: I got it downstairs ... You wanna take a look? ... Not here for that, eh.

CATHERINE: No. I came home to see you.

EV: Pretty sad state of affairs when your own daughter's in town and can't attend a sod-turnin' in honour of her father.

CATHERINE: So I'll go, I'll be there.

EV: Coulda sent a telegram, saved the air fare.

CATHERINE: Christ Daddy, don't be so stupid.

EV: Sound like your mother.

CATHERINE: I learnt the four letter words from you.

EV: Bullshit.

CATHERINE: I said I'd go, I said I'd be there. So. *(pause)* I'm proud of you, Daddy.

EV: Did you know it was a write-in campaign.

CATHERINE: Oh?

EV: The niggers from Barker's Point, the mill workers from Marysville, they're the ones got this hospital named after me. Left to the politicians God knows what they'd have called it.

CATHERINE: Well, I'm proud.

EV: Some goddamn French name I suppose—what?

CATHERINE: Proud, you must be proud having the hospital named after you.

EV: The day I first started practice, that day I was proud. Was the day after you were born ... There was a scarlet fever epidemic that year, you remember?

CATHERINE: No Daddy.

EV: Somebody ... some couple came in, they were carryin' their daughter, what was she? Two, maybe three? I took her in my arms ... could see they'd left it too late. I remember that child. I passed her back to her mother. Hold her tight, I said. Hold her tight till she goes ... Do you remember that woman holdin' that child in the hallway?

CATHERINE: No Daddy.

EV: No. That was your mother ... that was your mother.

BOB: Blueberries, Katie.

EV: You were just little then.

BOB: Blueberries along the railway tracks, and every year we'd pick them and sell them. I was the youngest, and Mama was always afraid I'd get lost, but I never got lost. *(CATHERINE looks at BOB.)* Not once.

Pause.

EV: What are you thinkin'?

CATHERINE: *(looks away from BOB)* Nothing ... You've lost weight.

EV: Of course I lost. I damn near died. You didn't know that, did you.

CATHERINE: No. No, nobody told me.

EV: Well it was that goddamn heart man. It was him gave me a heart attack.

CATHERINE: Really?

EV: What the hell's his name?

CATHERINE: Whose?

EV: The heart man's!

CATHERINE: I wouldn't know, Daddy.

EV: Demii—no, Demsky. I go to him, I tell him I been gettin' this pain in my ticker, and he has me walkin' up and down this little set of stairs, and runnin' on treadmills. Jesus Christ, I said to him, I'm not tryin' out for a sports team, I'm here because I keep gettin' this pain in my ticker! For Christ's sake, I said, put a stethoscope to my chest before you kill me with these goddamn stairs!

CATHERINE: So how are you now?

EV: It would've served the bastard right if I'd died right there in his office—do you remember how good Valma was with your mother?

CATHERINE: I remember.

EV: Every statutory holiday your mother's killin' herself or seein' things crawlin' on the walls or some goddamn thing or other, and Valma is like a rock, isn't that right?

CATHERINE: I guess so.

EV: So I come home from Demsky's, and I get the pain in my ticker and I wait all night for it to go away, and long about four or four-thirty, I phone Valma. Valma, I say, I'm havin' a heart attack, Valma—and she drops the phone nearly breakin' my ear drum and I can't phone out and I'm damned if I'm gonna get in that car and die all alone on Charlotte Street like that foolish Hazen Arbeton—If you were livin' in town, I'd have phoned you.

CATHERINE: You couldn't if Valma dropped the phone, Daddy.

EV: I'd have phoned you first!

CATHERINE: Would you?

EV: Well if I'd known she was gonna drop that goddamn phone I would have.

CATHERINE: What about Robbie?

EV: Who?

CATHERINE: Your son—Robbie.

EV: I'm not senile, I know who the hell Robbie is, what about him?

CATHERINE: You could have phoned him.

EV: I couldn't phone anyone! I was connected to Valma and I couldn't get disconnected!

CATHERINE: Would you have phoned him if you could?

EV: He wouldn't be home.

CATHERINE: How do you know?

EV: He's never home.

CATHERINE: Do you see him much?

EV: How the hell could I if he's never home?

CATHERINE: Do you *try* to see him!

EV: Of course I try! Have you seen him, phoned him, been over to visit?

CATHERINE: For Christ's sake Daddy, I just got in.

EV: Do you write?

CATHERINE: Robbie?

EV: Yes to Robbie! You sure as hell don't write to me!

CATHERINE: I don't have the time.

EV: Some people make time.

CATHERINE: Why don't you?

EV: I'm busy.

CATHERINE: So am I.

EV: Mn. *(pause)* Does he ever write to you?

CATHERINE: No.

EV: Do you wonder why?

CATHERINE: He's busy! Everybody's busy!

EV: Bullshit. It's that woman of his.

CATHERINE: It isn't.

EV: Paula.

CATHERINE: Who's Paula?

EV: She thinks we're all crazy.

CATHERINE: Well maybe we are, who in hell's Paula?

EV: His wife!

CATHERINE: You mean Corinne.

EV: What did I say?

CATHERINE: You said Paula.

EV: Well I meant Corinne! *(pause)* Paula. Who the hell's Paula?

Pause.

BOB: Pauline.

EV: Pauline now, that was a friend of your mother's. Died a cancer, died in your room, and where did you sleep?

CATHERINE: In this room

EV: because

CATHERINE: the maid had left

EV: and your mother nursed Pauline right through to the end. Didn't touch a drop for three months.

As CATHERINE turns away, she sees BOB.

BOB: Not a drop for three months, Katie.

Pause.

EV: Best ... best office nurse ... I ... ever had.

CATHERINE: Who, Mummy?

EV: Not Mummy, no. Valma. She ran that office like Hitler rollin' through Poland, and good with your mother—

CATHERINE: *(turns back to EV)* I know, forty years like a rock.

EV: That's right, like a rock, but I call her with that heart attack, and she goes hysterical. I never saw that in her before. It was a surprise. It was a goddamn disappointment. She comes runnin' into the house and up the stairs and huffin' and puffin' and blue in the face and—I'm on the bathroom floor by this time. She sees that, she gets more hysterical. She's got to run next door— my phone not workin' bein' connected to her phone which she dropped breakin' my ear drum—and she phones the hospital. And then we sit—I lie, she sits—and we wait for the goddamn ambulance, her holdin' my hand and bawlin'.

CATHERINE: Poor Valma.

EV: Poor Valma be damned! If I'd had the strength I'd have killed her. I kept tellin' her two things, I said it over and over—one, you keep that Demsky away from me—and you know what she does?

CATHERINE: She is sixty-seven.

EV: I'm seventy-three, you don't see me goin' hysterical! And I'm the one havin' the heart attack!

CATHERINE: Alright.

EV: You know the first thing I lay eyes on when I wake up in that hospital bed? Well, do you!

CATHERINE: No, I don't know, no.

EV: First thing I see is that goddamn Demsky hangin' over me like a vulture. Demsky who gave me the heart attack! ... Next death bed wish I make I sure as hell won't make it to Valma.

CATHERINE: Well ... it wasn't a real death bed wish, Daddy. You're still here.

EV: No thanks to her!

Pause.

CATHERINE: So?

EV: So what?

CATHERINE: Jesus Daddy, so how are you now?

EV: I don't read minds, I'm not a mind-reader!

CATHERINE: How are you!

EV: I'm fine!

CATHERINE: Good.

EV: What?

CATHERINE: I said good. Great. I'm glad that you're fine.

EV: Got the nitro pills ... pop a coupla them. Slow down they say. Don't get excited, don't talk too fast, don't walk too fast, don't, don't, don't, just pop a pill.

CATHERINE: Is it hard?

EV: Is what hard?

CATHERINE: Is it hard to slow down?

EV: ... The nurses could always tell when I'd started my rounds. They could hear my heels hittin' the floor tiles, hear me a wing away. *(OSCAR starts to laugh quietly.)* Did I ever tell you ...

OSCAR: That's what you call a Cuban heel, Ev.

EV: ... 'bout those white woman's shoes I bought on St. Lawrence?

CATHERINE: For the O.R.

EV: That's right. They were on sale, real cheap, but they fit my foot 'cause my foot is so narrow.

OSCAR: Still, a woman's shoe, Ev?

EV: A good shoe for the O.R. was hard to find then!

CATHERINE: So you bought two pair.

EV: And I wore 'em.—How did you know?

CATHERINE: You told me.

EV: I told you.

CATHERINE: Don't you remember? You and Uncle Oscar would act that whole story out … Do you see Uncle Oscar? *(pause)* Daddy? *(pause)* Well … anyway … so, what was the other thing?

EV: Mn?

CATHERINE: The other thing. You kept telling Valma two things, Demsky, and what was the other?

EV: Don't tell Katie. I musta said that a dozen times. I could hear myself. You're not to tell Katie. You're not to tell Katie.

CATHERINE: Why not?

EV: Because I didn't want you to know.

CATHERINE: Why not?

EV: Because I knew, even if you did know, you wouldn't come—and my heart would've burst from that pain. *(CATHERINE and EV look at each other. CATHERINE looks away.)* Look at me—look at me! … *(CATHERINE looks at EV.)* You knew. That goddamn Valma, she told you.

CATHERINE: No—

EV: You think I don't know a lie when I hear it, I see it, right in your goddamn eyes I can see it.

CATHERINE: Alright, alright, Valma did write—

EV: Ignores every goddamn thing I tell her.

CATHERINE: You could have died, Daddy.

EV: If you gave a damn you'd have been here!

CATHERINE: I don't want to fight.

EV: You afraid?

CATHERINE: No.

EV: I'm not afraid.

CATHERINE: God.

EV: Looked death in the face in that goddamn bathroom. It's not easy starin' death down with Valma bawlin' beside you. Every bit a your bein' directed, concentrated on winnin', not lettin' go … *(He gets out nitro pills; unscrews top while talking; takes pill by placing it under his tongue during his speech.)* Hated, hated losin'! Always. Hockey, politics, surgery, never mattered to me, just had to win. Could never let go. Do you know … do you know I saved Billy Barnes' life by hangin' onto his hand? I would not let him go till the sulfa took hold. I hung onto his hand, and I said Billy, goddamn it, you fight! And he did. They said it was the sulfa that saved him, miracle drug in those days, but you could never convince Billy of that. "Goddamn it, Doc, it was you!" … I opened his belly two or three years ago. Opened his belly and closed his belly. Inoperable carcinoma … "Are you tellin' me this thing is gonna kill me, Doc?" I reached out my hand and he took it … Hung … onto my hand …

CATHERINE: I would have come, but you didn't want me to know.

EV: But you did know, didn't you. That goddamn Valma, she told you, and you didn't come.

CATHERINE: I'm here now.

EV: Bit of free time, drop in and see the old man, eh?

CATHERINE: No.

EV: But if his ticker gives out and catches you typin', too bad.

CATHERINE: Don't.

EV: So were you workin' or weren't you workin'?

CATHERINE: I'm always working.

EV: And that's more important than your own father.

CATHERINE: Don't start.

EV: A woman your age should be raisin' a family.

CATHERINE: What family did you ever raise? You were never home from one day to the next so who are you to talk to me about family?

EV: Your father, that's who. The one who damn near died with no one but an office nurse by his side.

CATHERINE: Valma loves you!

EV: That's not what we're talkin' about here. We're talking about you and your work and your father dyin', that's what we're talkin' about!

CATHERINE: Are we?

EV: That's what I'm talking about—I don't know what the hell you're on about—I don't know what the hell you're doin' here!

CATHERINE: I just came home to see you, I wanted to see you ... have you got any idea how hard it was for me to come home, to walk in that door, to, to come home? ... Have you! ... and when I leave here ... my plane ... could fall out of the sky, you could get another pain in your ticker, we could never talk again ... all the things never said, do you ever think about that?

EV: You mean dyin'?

CATHERINE: No, more than that, I mean ... I don't know what I mean.

Pause.

EV: Are you still with that ... whatshisname?

CATHERINE: Sort of.

EV: What's his name?

CATHERINE: What's it matter, you never remember.

EV: What's his name? Dugan? or Dougan?

CATHERINE: That was before, years before, Daddy.

EV: You should get one and hang onto one, Katie. Then I'd remember.

CATHERINE: I ...

EV: What?

CATHERINE: I said it's difficult to keep a relationship goin' when you're busy, right?

EV: Why don't you marry this whosits?

CATHERINE: Yeah, well ... Whosits talks about that.

EV: I'm still waitin' for a grandson you know.

CATHERINE: I'm too old for that.

EV: You're soon gonna be—how old are you anyway?

CATHERINE: Besides I'd only have girls.

EV: Robbie's got girls ... girls are all right ... . You can have girls if you want.

CATHERINE: I said I don't know if I want.

EV: But get married first.

CATHERINE: Actually—I've been thinking ... of ... of maybe calling it quits with whosits.

EV: Quits?

CATHERINE: Ah-huh.

EV: You're callin' it quits.

CATHERINE: The work you know. Makes it hard.

EV: I thought this was the one. What the hell was his name, Sturgeon or Stefan or—

CATHERINE: His name doesn't matter.

EV: Stupid goddamn name—an actor, an actor for Christ's sake.

CATHERINE: We're not goin' to get into whosits and me and marriage and me and kids and me, all right?

EV: You go through men like boxes of kleenex.

CATHERINE: I don't want to talk about it!

EV: Jesus Christ, I can't keep up.

CATHERINE: No you can't! You can't even remember his name!

EV: Burgess Buchanan, that was his name! And you sat in the lounge at the Bayside and you said, "Oh Daddy, you just got to meet him, he's such a nice fella, he's so understanding, and he's so this and he's so that and he's ... " So explain to me what went wrong this time?

CATHERINE: Why do we always end up yelling and screaming, why do we do that?

EV: I care 'bout you! ... I want to see you settled, Katie. Happy. I want you to write letters, not ... I want you close.

CATHERINE: ... I do write somebody you know. I write Uncle Oscar ... every once in a while ... when the spirit moves me.

EV: Not often.

CATHERINE: No. Not often. But I do. Write letters to someone. I do make the time. I know you and he don't keep in touch any more but I like to.

EV: Not lately.

CATHERINE: No, not lately. I … why do you say that?

EV: He was fly-fishin'. He slipped and fell in the Miramichi with his waders on.

CATHERINE: *(upset)* No … Did—did you—see him?

EV: At the morgue when they brought him in.

CATHERINE: I mean before. Did you see him before? Were the two of you talking? *(EV shakes his head.)* Why not?

EV: Too late.

CATHERINE: Now it's too late.

EV: Too late even then. Even before. Too much had been said.

CATHERINE: I wish you'd have told me.

EV: Would you have come home for him?

CATHERINE: … Probably not.

EV: So what difference does it make?

CATHERINE: I like to know these things. Whether I can come or not. I can't help it if I'm in the middle of things.

EV: You make sure you're always in the middle of something. It's an excuse. How old are you now?

CATHERINE: Stop asking me that.

EV: You're gonna end up a silly old woman with nothin' but a cat for company.

CATHERINE: It'll be a live-in cat which is more than you've got with Valma.

EV: If I wanted Valma here, she'd be here.

CATHERINE: So you don't want her here, eh? You like it alone. Sitting up here all alone!

EV: I am not alone!

CATHERINE: You and Robbie, the same city, you never see Robbie!

EV: Go on! Why doncha go on! You got so goddamn much to say, why don't you say it! I am alone and it's you left me alone! My own daughter walkin' out and leavin' her father alone!

CATHERINE: How many years before you noticed my bed wasn't slept in?

EV: Don't go pointin' your finger at me! Look at yourself! What the hell do you do? Work, work, work—at what, for Christ's sake?

CATHERINE: I write! I'm good at it!

EV: Writing, eh Katie?

CATHERINE: Don't call me Katie!

EV: I'll call you by the name we gave you and that name is Katie.

CATHERINE: It's Catherine now.

EV: Oh, it's Catherine now, and you write Literature, don't you? And that means you can ignore your brother and your father and dump this Buchanan jerk and forget kids and family, but your father who gave his life to medicine because he believed in what he was doin' is an asshole!

CATHERINE: I never said that!

EV: My whole family never had a pot to piss in, lived on porridge and molasses when I was a kid.

CATHERINE: Alright!

EV: And fought for every goddamn thing I got!

CATHERINE: And it all comes down to you sitting up here alone with Gramma's letter!

EV: I am goin' through things!

CATHERINE: Why won't you open it?

EV: I know what it says.

CATHERINE: Tell me.

EV: You want it, here, take it.

CATHERINE grabs the letter from EV. She almost rips it open, but stops and turns it in her hand. Pause.

CATHERINE: Did Gramma really walk out to meet it?

EV: It was an accident.

CATHERINE: What was Mummy?

EV: You blame me for that.

CATHERINE: No.

EV: It was all my fault, go on, say it, I know what you think.

CATHERINE: It was my fault.

EV: Oh for Christ's sake!

EV moves away from CATHERINE. He sits, takes off his glasses and rubs the bridge of his nose. He looks at CATHERINE, then back to the glasses which he holds in his hand.

EV: … Your mother …

CATHERINE: Yes?

EV: Your mother and I—

CATHERINE: Tell me. Explain it to me.

BOB: There were eight of us, Katie, eight of us.

OSCAR: *(softly)* Go, go.

BOB: How did my mama manage?

OSCAR stands up, holding two hockey sticks. He is looking at EV, whose back is to him. EV puts his glasses in his pocket.

OSCAR: Go.

BOB: All older than me, all born before he went to war.

OSCAR: Go.

BOB: Him, her husband, my father, your grandfather, Katie.

OSCAR: Go. Go!

BOB: And her with the eight of us and only the pension.

OSCAR: Go!! Go!!

BOB: How did my mama manage?

BOB may exit. Shift.

OSCAR: Go!!! Go!!!

OSCAR throws a hockey stick at EV who stands, turns, plucking it out of the air at the last minute. They are catapulted back in time, rough-housing after a game.

OSCAR: Go!!! The Devon Terror has got the puck, out of his end, across the blue line, they're mixing it up in the corner and he's out in front, he shoots! He scores! Rahhhh!

OSCAR has ended up on the floor with his hockey sweater pulled over his head. EV, who's scored, raises his arms in acknowledgement of the crowd's "Rah!" EV helps OSCAR up.

OSCAR: You know somethin' Ev? This is the truth. Honest to God. Are you listenin'?

EV: Yeah.

EV takes off his "old man" sweater and hangs it on the back of a chair. During the following dialogue, OSCAR changes out of his hockey clothes, putting them in the trunk. He removes a jacket, pants and shoes for EV, and a suit of clothes plus shoes for himself.

OSCAR: When I think of medicine I get sick. Yeah. The thought of medicine makes me ill. Physically ill. Do you think that could be my mother in me?

EV slips out of his slippers and removes his pants. OSCAR will put the pants in the trunk.

EV: Maybe.

OSCAR: My father says it's my mother in me. At least she had the good sense to get out. Leaving me with him. How could she do that?

EV: I dunno. *(puts on suit jacket)*

OSCAR: The old man calls her a bitch. And now nuthin' for it but I got to go into medicine.

EV: So tell him so.

OSCAR: I can't.

EV: Stand up to him.

OSCAR: I can't.

EV: Just tell him.

OSCAR: It'd break his heart.

EV: Shit Oscar, it's your life, you can't think about that.

OSCAR: Yeah.

EV: You just gotta tell him what you really want to do … how does that look?

OSCAR: Great.

EV: Which is?

OSCAR: Which is what? *(OSCAR throws EV a tie.)*

EV: What you really want to do.

OSCAR: Oh.

EV: What do you really want to do?

OSCAR: I dunno.

EV: Come on.

OSCAR: Live someplace where it's hot.

EV: Come onnn ...

OSCAR: New Orleans, I'd like to live in New Orleans.

EV: Oscar—

OSCAR: How hot is New Orleans anyway?

EV: And *do what*—in New Orleans, Oscar?

OSCAR: Do what. I dunno. Something. Anything. Not medicine. *(OSCAR reties EV's tie for him.)*

EV: Look, if you're gonna tell your father you don't want to do what he wants you to do, you can't just say your life's ambition is to live someplace where it's hot.

OSCAR: What if it is?

EV: That is not gonna work, Oscar.

OSCAR: You're a lot like my Dad, Ev. The two of you. You're always ...

EV: What?

OSCAR: Forging *ahead.*

EV: What's wrong with that? *(puts on pants)*

OSCAR: Nothing. Forging is fine. I admire forging, I do, I admire it. It's just—not for me, do you think that could be my mother in me?

EV: Forget your mother. Concentrate on what you're gonna tell your father—and New Orleans is out.

OSCAR: It's honest, don't I get points for honest?

EV: Belt?

OSCAR: No points for honest.

EV: Or suspenders?

OSCAR: What's honest, honest is nothing, nobody wants honest.

EV: Honest is good, New Orleans is bad, belt or suspenders?

OSCAR: Belt. *(OSCAR throws EV a belt.)*

EV: Thanks.

OSCAR: It's not fair.

EV: I don't wanna hear about fair.

OSCAR: Right.

EV: Face it, you're a lazy son of a bitch.

OSCAR: I know.

EV: You've got no drive.

OSCAR: I know.

EV: You've got no push.

OSCAR: I know.

EV: I worked my ass off last summer in construction, what did you do?

OSCAR: I lay in the sun.

EV: That's right.

OSCAR: I'm a loser.

EV: And a whiner.

OSCAR: Right. *(pause)* Why are we friends?

EV: Eh?

OSCAR: I agree with everything you say, it's the truth, what can I say? So why are we friends—I figure it's the car and the clothes.

EV puts on shoes. By the end of the scene he is dressed in suit, tie and shoes.

EV: That's a pretty shitty thing to imply.

OSCAR: I wasn't implying, I was just wondering.

EV: You've got other qualities.

OSCAR: Name one.

EV: We grew up together.

OSCAR: Go on.

EV: So we've known each other for a long time.

OSCAR: Yeah.

EV: Since Grade One.

Pause.

OSCAR: Well I figure it's the car and the clothes and the fact that the old man dotes on you.

EV: Jesus Oscar.

OSCAR: Everybody knows I'm just a—

EV: Don't whine!

OSCAR: I'm not whining. I'm analyzing!

EV: I'm tryin' to help, Oscar. Now you must have some ambition, some desire, something you're at least vaguely interested in, that you could propose to your father as a kinda alternative to medicine, eh?

OSCAR: You mean apart from New Orleans.

EV: That's what I mean.

OSCAR: My mother might have gone to New Orleans.

EV: Forget your mother! Alternative to medicine! Not New Orleans!

OSCAR: Algeria.

EV: Oscar!

OSCAR: I know.

EV: I try to look out for you and it's like pissing on a forest fire.

OSCAR: I'm telling you exactly how I feel. I don't have ambitions and desires and goals in life. I don't need 'em. My old man has my whole life mapped out for me and I know what I'm supposed to do. I'm supposed to read and follow the map. That's it.

EV: *(moves away from OSCAR)* There is no wardrobe and no car and no amount of dotage from your old man that would compensate a person for putting up with you!

Shift.

CATHERINE: Uncle Oscar?

OSCAR looks at KATIE as if it was she who had spoken. KATIE holds her shoe out to him.

CATHERINE: Fix my shoe.

KATIE: It's got about a million knots—but keep talking.

CATHERINE: I want to know something.

OSCAR: Construction work in the summer, hockey in the winter, and when we went to McGill, they'd bring him home on the overnight train to play the big games, the important games—and that's how he paid his way through medical school.

KATIE: Keep talking.

OSCAR: My father was their family doctor—I was there at his house the night his brother George died from the influenza—and that left him, and his sister Millie and his Mum and Dad.

CATHERINE: My Gramma.

KATIE: What was she like?

OSCAR: Proper. United Church. Poor and proper. *(OSCAR gives KATIE back her shoe.)* That's all I remember.

KATIE: *(hits OSCAR with the shoe)* Remember more!

OSCAR: I think your father got his drive from your Gramma and you get yours from him.

KATIE: Are you saying I'm like her?

OSCAR: In some ways perhaps.

KATIE: I would never walk across a train bridge at midnight!

OSCAR: You might.

KATIE: I would not!

OSCAR: Well it was an accident she—

KATIE: What do you mean I might!

OSCAR: It was a short cut.

KATIE: I'm not like her! I would never do that!

OSCAR: It wasn't anything she did.

KATIE: I'm too smart to do that!

OSCAR: It was just something that happened.

KATIE: You don't know! You don't know anything!

OSCAR: Katie—

KATIE: Get away from me!

CATHERINE: Stop.

Shift.

EV: If you want to know about this crazy bastard—if you want to know about him—When I needed a friend at my back, in a fight, in a brawl? This silly son of a bitch in sartorial splendour has saved my ass more than once— and me his—I'm gonna tell you a story. Now listen—we used to drink at this hole in the wall, this waterin' hole for whores and medical students, eh? And we'd sit there and nurse a beer all night and chat it up with the whores who'd come driftin' in well after midnight, towards mornin' really, and this was winter, freeze a Frenchman's balls off—and the whores would come in off the street for a beer and we'd sit there all talkin' and jokin' around. They were nice girls these whores, all come to Montreal from Three Rivers and Chicoutimi and a lotta places I never heard tell of, and couldn't pronounce. Our acquaintance was strictly a pub acquaintance, we students preferin' to spend our money on beer thus avoidin' a medical difficulty which intimacy with these girls would most likely entail. So—this night we're stragglin' home in the cold walkin' and talkin' to a bunch a these whores, and as we pass their house, they drop off there up the steps yellin' "Goo-night goo-night" ... 'Bout a block further on, someone says: "Where the hell's Oscar?" Christ, we all start yellin': "Where the hell's Oscar? Oscar! Oscar!" Searchin' in gutters, snowbanks and alleys, but the bugger's gone, disappeared! Suddenly it comes to me. Surer than hell he's so pissed he's just followed along behind the girls when they peeled off to go home, and he's back there inside the cat house. So back I go. Bang on the door. This giant of a woman, uglier than sin, opens it up. Inside is all this screamin' and cryin' and poundin' and I say: "Did a kinda skinny fella"—and she says: "Get that son of a bitch outa here!" "Where is he?" I say. "Upstairs, he's locked himself in one of the rooms with Janette! He's killin' her for Christ's sake!" She takes me up to the room, door locked, girl inside is screamin' bloody murder and I can hear Oscar makin' a kinda intent diabolical ahhhhhin' and oohhhin' sound. "Oscar! Oscar! For Christ's sake, open up!" The girl's pleadin' with him to stop, beggin' him, chill your blood to the bone to hear her. And still that aaahhhhhin' and ooohhhhh-hin'! Nothin' for it but I got to throw myself at the door till either it gives or my shoulder goes. Finally Boom! I'm in. I can see Oscar is not. He's got Janette tied to the bed, staked right out, naked and nude. He's straddlin' her but he's fully clothed, winter hat, scarf, boots and all, and he's wieldin' his blue anatomy pencil. He's drawin' all of her vital organs, he's outlinin' them on her skin with his blue anatomy pencil. He's got her kidneys and her lungs, her trachea and her liver all traced out. Takes four of us to pull him off— me and three massive brutes who've appeared. Janette is so upset they send her back to Rivière-du-Loup for two weeks to recover, Oscar has to turn pimp till he pays back the price of the door, and everyone swears it's the worst goddamn perversion and misuse of a whore ever witnessed in Montreal ... what in God's name did you think you were doin' that night? (OSCAR shrugs and smiles. EV is taking out a letter and opening it as he speaks.) Jesus Christ ... silly bastard ...

Shift.

EV: It's from Mum ... the old man's been laid off.

OSCAR: She sound worried?

EV: She says go ahead with the Royal Vic.

OSCAR: The General would be closer to home.

EV: What good would that do?

OSCAR: I don't know.

EV: No money to be made in post-graduate work anywhere.

OSCAR: I thought moral support, you know, being close.

EV: The Vic's the best in the country.

OSCAR: I know that.

EV: Mum would probably kill me if I gave up the Royal Vic.

OSCAR: She definitely would ... What about Millie?

EV: Millie?

OSCAR: Yeah.

EV: What about her?

OSCAR: I guess she could probably help out. Get a job.

EV: There's no jobs anywhere. Besides Millie's still in school.

OSCAR: Will she quit?

EV: What the hell do you want me to do?

OSCAR: I don't want you to do anything. I just wondered if Millie would quit school to help out at home, that's all.

EV: What the hell're you tryin' to say to me? Are you sayin' I should quit?

OSCAR: No, I just meant there are hospitals closer to home.

OSCAR may exit. EV calls after him.

EV: You can't be serious. The Vic's the best post-graduate training in the country. I've worked goddamn hard for it and I won't give it up—not for Mum if she asked me! Not for Millie! Not for anyone!

CATHERINE: But you did, Daddy. *(EV looks at CATHERINE.)* You gave it up for her.

EV: If … if you could have seen her.

Shift. BOB may enter. She carries a music box.

BOB: He would step off the elevator—every nurse on the floor, "Yes Doctor"—"No Doctor"—"Is there anything else" dramatic pause, sighhhh, "I can *do* for you, Doctor?" Even Matron. Yes, Matron! And the goo-goo eyes—I remember those eyes.

EV: Do you know what they said?

CATHERINE: What did they say?

EV: Forget her, she is immune to the charms of the predatory male.

BOB: They were right.

EV: No fraternization between doctors and nurses on pain of dismissal.

CATHERINE: So why did you ask her?

EV: I—

BOB: He couldn't resist me—and I—

BOB passes CATHERINE the jewellery box to hold. BOB opens the box. It plays "Smoke Gets In Your Eyes." BOB takes out a pair of earrings and puts them on as she's speaking. The lid of the box remains up and the music box plays during the scene.

BOB: I don't give a fig for regulation or rules, only ones I make myself. And if in the past I chose to observe that regulation, it was only because a suitable occasion to break it hadn't arisen.

EV: Be serious.

BOB: My goodness, here I am without two pennies to rub together, and I rush out and buy a new sweater for a bar date with you, and you don't call that serious?

EV: When our eyes first met over what? … a perforated ulcer, were you serious then?

BOB: Do you know how many floors my mama scrubbed for that sweater?

"Smoke Gets In Your Eyes" played by a big band fades in.

CATHERINE: *(closes jewellery box)* Was she really like that?

EV: If you could have seen her.

OSCAR may enter.

OSCAR: Why risk it?

EV: Wait till you meet her.

EV moves towards BOB, who is swaying to the music.

OSCAR: I don't need to meet her. For Christ's sake, Ev, you're … Ev? … Ev!

EV and BOB dance to a medley of Thirties tunes. OSCAR watches, drawn into that warm atmosphere. EV and OSCAR take turns cutting in on each other, as they ballroom dance with BOB. They're all very good dancers, and OSCAR is as captivated as EV by BOB. OSCAR dances with BOB. She is looking over his shoulder at EV. Shift.

KATIE: *(interrupts, a sudden scream)* Stop that! You stop it! *(The dancers stop: a soft freeze.)* I know things! I can figure things out!

The soft freeze breaks. Shift.

OSCAR: Have you told your mother?

EV: Not yet.

OSCAR: She had her heart set on a specialist.

EV: She'll settle for a grandson.

CATHERINE: But that's not what you got, you got me.

Shift.

KATIE: Why did he marry her?

OSCAR: He loved her.

KATIE: Why didn't you marry her?

OSCAR: She loved him.

KATIE: They didn't want to have me.

OSCAR: That isn't true.

KATIE: Did your mother want to have you?

Shift.

BOB: Your mother, ooohhh, your poor father, Ev.

EV: I know.

BOB: And Millie—you never told me about Millie.

EV: I mentioned her once or twice.

BOB: If you were only Catholic she could be a nun.

EV: Don't judge her by what you've seen tonight.

BOB: And your mother could be Pope.

EV: She liked you.

BOB: She hated me.

EV: When you get to know her, it'll be different.

BOB: I don't want to know her. Look at Millie under her thumb.

EV: Millie isn't under her thumb.

BOB: And your father.

There is a sense of intimacy, rather than irritation, between EV and BOB.

EV: Look, you saw them for the first time for what—four or five hours—you can't make generalizations based on that.

BOB: You were there. You heard her. "Poor Ev. Giving up the Vic." You'd think a general practice was the end of the earth—And why've you fallen so far?

EV: She never said any of those things.

BOB: She implied I'd caught you by the oldest trick in the book.

EV: She didn't.

BOB: "Why does a girl go into nursing?" Why to marry a doctor of course! And Millie nodding away and your father smiling away—I wanted to stand up and scream.

EV: You're tired.

BOB: And you, you're there, way up there, the shining light, can do nothing wrong, except one thing is wrong, we are wrong!

EV: She had certain expectations, I'm not defending her, I'm just trying to explain how things are, or have been—Bob? … Bob!

BOB: For years she's been practising, "I'd like you to meet my son, The Specialist."

EV: Things haven't been easy, you know. You've seen Dad, he's a good man but he's—when Georgie died, the old man wept on her—there was no one for her to weep on. It was hard on her losin' Georgie, and now all of her hopes for me and for Georgie are all pinned on me … You can understand that.

BOB: She'll be counting the months.

EV: Let her. *(EV kisses BOB.)* Again. *(EV kisses BOB.)* Again.

BOB: You.

EV: You smile that smile at my Mum and she'll love you. It's a beautiful smile.

BOB: We aren't wrong, are we?

EV: We'll have a boy and we'll call him George after my brother. She'll like that.

BOB: Or William, after my brother Bill.

EV: And he'll have a beautiful smile.

BOB: And he'll have a nose like yours.

EV: And he'll …

Shift. EV and BOB may exit.

CATHERINE: I notice this thing about having boys first. I mean what is that all about?

KATIE: Who was I named after?

OSCAR: Kate was your grandmother's name.

KATIE: Nobody calls me Kate.

OSCAR: That's your name.

KATIE: It's an ugly name. Why did they call me that? Couldn't they think of anything else?

OSCAR: Kate isn't ugly.

KATIE: Do I look like a Kate to you?

OSCAR: What's a Kate look like?

KATIE: Do you think names are like dogs?

OSCAR: In what way like dogs?

KATIE: I read dogs start to look like their owners or owners start to look like their dogs. Do you think if you get an ugly name you start to look like your name?

CATHERINE: Or be like who you were named after?

Shift. EV and BOB may enter. BOB carries EV's suitcoat. EV carries a doctor's bag. BOB will help EV on with his jacket.

BOB: I want to go back to work.

EV: Where would you work?

BOB: I'm an R.N., I'll apply at the hospital.

EV: No.

CATHERINE: Why not?

EV: I don't want her there.

CATHERINE: Why not?

EV: A matter of policy.

CATHERINE: Whose?

EV: What about Katie?

BOB: What about her?

EV: You should be home with her.

BOB: Why?

EV: You're her mother.

BOB: You're her father, you're not home from one day to the next. What am I supposed to do, rattle around with a four-month-old baby to talk to?

EV: So get somebody in.

BOB: Let me work, Ev.

EV: I don't want you down at the hospital.

BOB: Why not?

EV: Because as a surgeon operating out of that hospital, I don't want my wife on staff. I don't want any surgeon's wife on staff. And I don't know any surgeon who wants his wife on staff.

Shift.

KATIE: They were fighting last night.

OSCAR: Oh?

KATIE: Do you want to know what they were fighting about, if you don't already know.

OSCAR: How would I know?

KATIE: How do you think! Someone would tell you! Behind Daddy's back they would tell you! They would whisper.

OSCAR: That doesn't happen.

CATHERINE: Then why, Uncle Oscar, did you spend so much time talking to me if you didn't want to find out about them?

Shift.

BOB: I could work at the office. *(pours herself a drink)*

EV: No.

BOB: McQuire's wife—

EV: Is a silly bitch who keeps McQuire's office in an uproar from the time she comes in in the morning till she leaves at night.

BOB: I'm not Marg McQuire.

EV: I have an office nurse, she does a good job and she needs the job and I don't intend letting her go.

BOB: I could work for somebody else!

EV: I don't know what doctor would hire another doctor's wife as an office nurse.

BOB: Why not?

EV: Look, you're not just an R.N. anymore.

BOB: No.

EV: You're not Eloise Roberts, you're not Bob any more.

BOB: Who am I?

EV: My wife.

CATHERINE: Daddy.

EV: She's working the O.R., the surgeon hits a bleeder, starts screaming for clamps, she's slow off the mark, and when the whole fuckin' mess is under control, he turns round to give her shit, she takes off her mask and who does he see? Not a nurse, another surgeon's wife. *My* wife. Is he gonna give her shit?

BOB: I'm not slow off the mark in the O.R.

EV: That's not the point, you're my wife, is he gonna give you shit?

BOB: That's his problem, not mine.

EV: I'm in the O.R. I hit a bleeder. I scream for a clamp. I look at the nurse who's too fuckin' slow and who do I see? My wife!

BOB: I'm not slow! I'm good in the O.R.

EV: That's not the point.

CATHERINE: Why don't you just say you don't want her there instead of all this bullshit?

EV: Jesus Christ I said it! I don't want her there!

Shift. KATIE is holding her wrist. She speaks to OSCAR.

KATIE: My father works hard! My father works really hard!

CATHERINE: I know. I know.

KATIE: You don't work as hard as my father. My father is never home. He goes to the hospital before we're up, and when he comes home we're asleep.

CATHERINE: Robbie's asleep.

KATIE: I'm surprised Daddy knows who Robbie is. I'm surprised Robbie knows who Daddy is … I hate Robbie.

OSCAR: How did this happen?

KATIE: I dunno.

OSCAR: Yes you do.

KATIE: I'm accident-prone. Some people are you know. Accident-prone. I do dangerous things. I like doing dangerous things.

OSCAR: How'd you do this?

KATIE: It was just something that happened.

OSCAR: Ah-huh. *(taping KATIE's wrist)*

KATIE: I do lots of things. Last Sunday when we were supposed to be in Sunday School, Robbie and I, do you know what we did?

OSCAR: Might hurt.

KATIE: Won't hurt. We went to the freight yards and played. I crawled under the train cars twice and Robbie crawled over where they're hitched

together. He was too scared to crawl under. I wasn't scared.

OSCAR: You shouldn't do that.

KATIE: We decided together, Robbie and I. I didn't make him. Do you believe that?

OSCAR: What?

KATIE: That Robbie and I decided together to go to the freight yards instead of to Sunday School, do you believe that?

OSCAR: No.

KATIE: Anyway we had these gloves on. You know the ones Mummy made out of kid or leather the last time she was away? She made about a million pair. She probably gave a pair to you.

Shift.

BOB: It's not my fault if other people don't know who I am! It's not my fault if all they can see is your wife!

EV: Aren't you my wife?

BOB: That's not all I am!

EV: Don't yell at me.

BOB: Who do I yell at!

EV: Half the nurses in that goddamn hospital are lookin' for a doctor to marry so they can sit on their ass, and here you are screamin' 'cause you're not on your feet twelve hours a day bein' overworked and underpaid.

BOB: I am on my feet twelve hours a day!

EV: So let me get somebody in.

BOB: I feel funny with somebody in … If I'm here, I feel I should be doing it.

EV: You want to get out more.

BOB: I know I'm a good nurse. I'm as good as anyone. When I'm out … I'm never sure which fork to use.

EV: Who gives a shit which fork you use? Whichever one comes to hand.

BOB: When you "go out" that fork's important.

EV: Get Oscar to teach you how to play bridge. First year of university that's all he did.

BOB: I feel as if I wasted something.

Shift. KATIE is still with OSCAR.

KATIE: I don't know how she's supposed to get better by making gloves and painting pictures. Her pictures are awful. It costs a fortune to send her there and it never works! … Anyway … I got black all over my gloves and it wouldn't come off so I made Robbie give me his 'cause Mummy never gets mad at him and that's one of the reasons I hate him, as soon as we got home do you know what he did?

CATHERINE: Told.

KATIE: He told. He said I *made* him go to the freight yards and then I *made* him change gloves. He's always telling and that's another reason I hate him.

OSCAR: You're the oldest—you should look out for Robbie.

KATIE: I am trying to teach Robbie to look out for *himself!* I am! … She didn't even ask and he told. She's always saying Robbie's just like her side of the family and I'm just like Daddy's—Have you met my Uncle Bill?

OSCAR: I might have.

KATIE: Well I wouldn't want to be like her side of the family. I'd rather be like his!

Shift.

BOB: Nobody else in my family finished high school, did I tell you that?

No one is listening to BOB.

CATHERINE: Was she a good nurse, Daddy?

EV: That's not the point, Katie.

CATHERINE: Was she?

EV: I'm late for my rounds.

BOB: I was the smartest.

EV: You get some sleep now.

EV may exit.

CATHERINE: Daddy?

BOB: And I always won, Katie! Because I played so hard! Played to win! And school—*first*, always first! "Our valedictorian is Eloise Roberts." (*CATHERINE moves away from BOB, who con-*

tinues speaking with the drink in her hand.) Eloise Roberts, and they called me Bob, and I could run faster and play harder and do better than any boy I ever met! And my hair! It was all the way down to there! And when I asked my Mama—Mama?— She said, we have been here since the Seventeen Hundreds, Eloise, and in your blood runs the blood of Red Roberts! Do you know who he is? A pirate, with flamin' red hair and a flamin' red beard who harboured off a cove in P.E.I.! A pirate! And inside of me—just bustin' to get out! To reach out! To grow! … And when I sat on our front porch and I looked out—I always looked *up*, 'cause lookin' up I saw the sky, and the sky went on forever! And I picked and sold berries, and my Mama cleaned house for everyone all around, and my sisters and my one brother Bill everything for *one thing.* For *me.* For Eloise Roberts. For Bob.

Shift. EV enters, carrying his bag. He is speaking to OSCAR.

EV: You know somethin'!? The goddamn health care services in this province are a laugh!

BOB: Katie?

EV: I had a woman come into my office yesterday. I've never seen her before, but she's got a lump in her breast and she's half out of her mind with worry. Surer than hell it's cancer, but there's nothin' I can do till I damn well find out it is cancer. So what do I have to do? I gotta take a section and ship that tissue to Saint John on the bus for Christ's sake! And then what? I got to wait for three days to maybe a week to hear. Do you know how often I get a replay of that scenario? She's a mother or she works for a living or she's at home lookin' after her old man and I can't tell her what's wrong or what we have to do till I get that goddamn report back from Saint John! We need a medical laboratory in this town, and by God, I'm gonna see that we get one!

OSCAR: Have you seen Bob?

EV: When?

OSCAR: Do you know you've a son?

EV: Georgie, we're callin' him Georgie, a brother for Katie. Hell of a goodlookin' boy, have you seen him?

OSCAR: I popped into the nursery.

EV: Looks like his old man.

OSCAR: Where were you?

EV: Had a call in Keswick.

OSCAR: What the hell would take you to Keswick when your wife's in labour?

EV: I hear it went as smooth as silk.

OSCAR: Ev?

EV: ... Frank Johnston's kid fell under a thresher.

OSCAR: Bad?

EV: Bad as it can get.

OSCAR: You ... could have sent someone else.

EV: Frank's been a patient of mine since I started practice. Who the hell else could I send?

OSCAR: What about Bob?

EV: Valma was with her.

OSCAR: She didn't want Valma, she wanted you.

EV: Look, I brought Frank Johnston's kid into the world—and eight hours ago I saw him out, kneelin' in a field, with the kid's blood soakin' my pants ... And afterwards, I sat in the kitchen with his mother, and before I left, I shared a mickey of rum with Frank.

OSCAR: It was important to Bob you be here, she needed you.

OSCAR may exit. EV calls after him.

EV: Well Frank Johnston needed me more! *(EV looks at CATHERINE.)* The last baby I delivered was in a tarpaper shack. They paid me seven eggs, and when the crabapples fall, the mother's bringin' some round. Would you like to talk need to that woman? ... *(CATHERINE looks away.)* She's got the best maternity care this province provides, and the best obstetrician in town. She's got a private nurse, and a baby boy. What the hell else does she want?

EV carries a chair over near BOB.

CATHERINE: She wants you.

EV: She's got me.

EV sits beside BOB. Shift.

BOB: I like Robert.

EV: I thought it was George or William.

BOB: Robbie's better.

EV: What's wrong with George?

BOB: Nothing's wrong with it, I like Robbie best.

EV: George was my brother's name.

BOB: I know.

EV: Robert George?

BOB: Robert Dann.

EV: Where the hell did you get that name?

BOB: Out of my head.

EV: Well, you can stick George in someplace, can't you?

BOB: I'm not calling him George.

EV: It's my goddamn brother's name!

BOB: I know.

EV: It means a lot to my mother.

BOB: I know.

EV: So stick it in some place!

BOB: No.

EV: Jesus Christ do you have to make an issue outa every little thing?

BOB: I don't like George.

EV: What the hell harm does it do to stick George in somewhere. Robert Dann George, George Robert Dann, George Damn Robert.

BOB: He's my son.

EV: He's our son.

BOB: So register him whatever you like.

EV: I will. *(stands up)*

BOB: I'm calling him Robbie.

EV: *(returns chair to original position)* I work my ass off. Why do I do it if it's not for her?

CATHERINE: Why?

EV: For her. Oscar!

Shift. OSCAR may enter.

OSCAR: Ah-huh?

EV: What're your evenings like?

OSCAR: What're your evenings like?

EV: I'm doin' rounds at night and squeezin' in house calls after that—could you drop over to see her till she comes round a bit?

OSCAR: What about my house calls?

EV: You never made a house call in your life.

OSCAR: I made one once.

EV: You lazy son of a bitch. If it weren't for the remnants of your old man's practice, you'd starve to death. What'll you do when the last of his patients die off?

OSCAR: Move some place where it's hot.

EV: Listen, what she needs is someone to talk to, play a little golf, shit, the Medical Ball's comin' up next month, take her to that. I'm too goddamn busy.

OSCAR: When do you sleep?

EV: I don't.

OSCAR: How the hell did she ever get pregnant?

EV: I didn't say I never laid down.

EV may exit with his bag. Shift.

BOB: I want to go to New York next month. Go to New York and see the shows—do you want to do that?

Sound of Forties dance music.

OSCAR: Can Ev get away?

BOB: We'll ask. *(OSCAR lights BOB's cigarette.)* Look around us. Look at all these pursey little lips. Look at all these doctors' wives. Do I look like that? Do I?

OSCAR: Not a bit.

BOB: *(holding glass)* Well thas good. Look at them … D'you know I joined the I.O.D.E.? The I.O.D.E. I joined it. And do you wanna know what's really frightenin? I could prolly, after a bit, I could prolly achully—forget. I could get to like the I.O.D.E. Isn't tha' frightening? … Isn't tha' frightening! … Ah, you're as bad as Everett. Whasa matter with doctors, you're a doctor, you tell me, so busy savin' lives you've forgotten how to talk? Talk!

OSCAR: The I.O.D.E. eh?

BOB: Thas right … next year I might run as Grand Something … The I.O.D.E. does some

very importan' work you know. *(OSCAR smiles and casually takes the glass from her.)* … I don't like anybody here, do you? … *(BOB takes the glass back as casually, takes a drink.)* Do you know my mother … and all my sisters … and my one brother Bill who taught me how to fish—hey! We could go fishing some time if you want.

OSCAR: Bob.

BOB: Everett doesn't fish! Everett doesn't do anything except go … round …

OSCAR: Bob.

BOB: Anyway—so all these people, mother, sisters, Bill, they all worked to put me through nursing, wasn't that wonderful of them? … And now Ev, he lent Bill the money for something Bill thinks he wants to do and it'll all be a disaster 'cause it's about the tenth time he'd done it, but Ev's always giving money to his mother, so I don't care. Why should I care? But you know what I don't like? Do you?

OSCAR: What don't you like?

BOB: I don't like the cleanin' lady. Because every time … the cleanin' lady comes in, I think of my Mama who cleaned all around so I could go into nursing *(music out; silence)* and you want to know what's worse? My Mama's so happy I married a doctor. I'm successful you see. I made something of myself. *(She moves away smiling, lifting her glass in a toast.)* I married a doctor.

Shift. KATIE carries a hairbrush.

KATIE: Why don't you get married?

OSCAR: I'm waiting for you.

KATIE: I'm not related to you.

OSCAR: No.

KATIE: But you're always here, you're always about … . Do you love my mother?

OSCAR: I love you.

KATIE: Do you want to brush my hair?

OSCAR: If you want me to.

KATIE: You can if you want.

KATIE gives OSCAR the brush, and sits at his feet. He brushes her hair. She enjoys it for a moment before speaking.

KATIE: I'm named after my Gramma, but I'm not like my Gramma ... I know when trains are coming ... and when they're coming, I don't go that way then ... Do you like brushing my hair.

OSCAR: It needs it.

KATIE: I don't care if it's messy. It's how you are inside that counts.

OSCAR: That's true.

KATIE: I'm surprised you don't know that.

CATHERINE: Did you love my mother, Uncle Oscar?

OSCAR: When your mother's not well, you should think about that.

KATIE: About what?

OSCAR: How she feels inside.

KATIE: ... I wonder—what my father sees in you. (grabs the hairbrush) You're not a very good doctor. What does he see in you?

OSCAR: Katie—

KATIE: Do you like brushing my hair? Do you like brushing my hair?

OSCAR: Katie—

KATIE: I hate you!

KATIE moves away from OSCAR, who follows her. Shift. BOB moves to the liquor and refills her glass. It is late, and she drinks while she waits.

BOB: Ev! ... is that you, Ev?

EV may enter. He will sit, his bag at his feet, with his head back and his eyes closed.

EV: Yeah.

BOB: What time is it? ... Where were you?

EV: Just left the hospital. They brought in some kid with a ruptured spleen ... car accident ... took out every guard rail on that big turn on River Road ... damn near bled out when we got him.

BOB: How is he?

EV: Mnn?

BOB: I said, how is he?

EV: 'Bout half a million pieces ...

BOB: ... Ev?

EV: What time is it?

BOB: Late.

EV: Takin' out a stomach in the mornin'.

BOB: ... Can we talk?

EV: Talk away ...

BOB: I let the maid go today. It wasn't working out—

EV: Medjuck call?

BOB: What?

EV: Did Sam Medjuck call?

BOB: I said I let the maid go today—

EV: Mn?

BOB: (moves to refill her drink) Valma phoned and said he'd called her.

EV: Christ. (gets up; picks up his bag)

CATHERINE: Why would he phone Valma's looking for you?

EV: He knows her, she kids him along.

CATHERINE: Were you over at Valma's?

EV: I was takin' out a spleen.

CATHERINE: Should I believe that?

EV: I was takin' out a spleen!

BOB: I said I let the maid go today!

EV: How many's that?

BOB: She was a smarmy bitch and I fired her!

EV: I said how many's that? (EV may exit.)

BOB: Where're you going?

EV: (offstage) House call to Medjuck's!

BOB: It's the middle of the night!

EV: (offstage) It's morning!

BOB: Ev! Ev!

CATHERINE: He's gone.

BOB: You'll fall asleep, Ev! You'll fall asleep and run off the road!

KATIE: Shut up Mummy!

BOB: Ev!

KATIE: Why don't you shut up and let people sleep!

BOB: Oscar!

CATHERINE: He isn't here, Mummy!

BOB: Count on Oscar!

KATIE: He's not here, Mummy!

OSCAR: When you need me you call, I'll be there.

CATHERINE: Daddy!

EV may enter, isolated on stage. Music filters in: "Auld Lang Syne."

EV: Buy a Packard I always say! Best goddamn car on the road!

CATHERINE: Do something.

EV: I'd be drivin' along, middle of the night—

BOB: It's seven maids, that's how many!

EV: All of a sudden, swish, swish, swish, tree branches hittin' the car, look around—

BOB: And I'll fire the next seven whenever I damn well feel like it!

CATHERINE: Daddy!

EV: Car's in the middle of a goddamn orchard.

BOB: Oscar!

EV: I've fallen asleep and failed to navigate a turn and here's me and the car travellin' through this goddamn orchard.

BOB is joined by OSCAR. They dance to "Auld Lang Syne," as KATIE watches. CATHERINE's focus slowly switches from her father to BOB and OSCAR.

BOB: Oscar.

EV: And me without a clue in the world as to where I'm headed. Black as pitch, not a light to be seen, and me drivin' over bumps and skirtin' fences and tryin' to remember where in the hell I'm going. Then I catch a glimpse of this little light, almost like a low-lyin' star in the sky.

BOB kisses OSCAR.

EV: ... head for that—what the hell—could end up on Venus! Door opens and someone is standin' there—

BOB sees KATIE watching.

EV: "We been waitin' for you, Doc."

BOB: What do you want?

EV: "Is the coffee hot?"

BOB: What do you want!

EV: "Melt a spoon."

KATIE: *(screams)* Don't! You don't! *(KATIE launches herself at OSCAR and BOB.)*

EV: "We been waitin' for you, Doc."

KATIE hits OSCAR and BOB, and BOB steps away from OSCAR. During all the action she continues to scream.

KATIE: You! You! Get away! Get away! I hate you! I hate you! You don't! Get away!

CATHERINE runs to KATIE and tries to restrain her.

CATHERINE: Stop. Stop. Daddy. Daddy!! *(KATIE collapses against CATHERINE.)* Help me.

ACT TWO

The house is silent. EV and CATHERINE are most prominent on stage. KATIE is not far from CATHERINE. BOB and OSCAR are in the background. CATHERINE looks at EV, who is wearing an old cardigan and glasses. CATHERINE holds Gramma's letter.

CATHERINE: ... Go on.

EV: ... When I was little, Katie ... when I was a kid, I saw my own father get smaller and smaller, physically smaller, 'cause he was nothin', no job, no ... nothin'. I was only a kid but I saw him ... get smaller like that ... Georgie now, he was the one in our family would have gone places.

CATHERINE: Haven't you "gone places"?

EV: Seen half this province from their mother's belly to the grave.

CATHERINE: Was it worth it?

EV: ... When that goddamn Demsky let me up, I'd wander all round the hospital. I'd look in the wards, Intensive Care ... You get to be my age, the only place better than a hospital for meetin' people you know is a mortuary ... Frank Johnston died while I was there in his room. They had him hooked up to all these goddamn monitors. And do you know how they knew he was dead? Straight lines and the sound from the monitors. Nobody looked down at Frank. Just at the monitors … . And that is the kinda hospital they're gonna put my name on? … I wouldn't like to go like Frank.

CATHERINE: You won't go for ages, Daddy.

EV: If I can keep away from that Demsky I got a chance …

CATHERINE: Daddy?

EV: What?

CATHERINE: About Mummy.

EV: … If I could—I'm gonna show you somethin', I want you to see this … you see this, you'll understand. *(opens trunk and begins to sort through it)* Six or seven kids standin' by the car, and the car outsida this Day Clinic … Valma and I, we were doin' these check-ups and physicals and what-have-you … where the hell … we were doin' that one day a week in Minto, families a miners, poor goddamn buggers, most of 'em unemployed at the time. And this bunch a little ragtag snotty-nosed kids, smellin' a wet wool and Javex, were impressed all to hell by the car—and Valma, out with the goddamn camera, and she took this here picture … it's in here, where the hell is it? *(stops looking for the snapshot)* … I don't care about this hospital thing, I don't care about … I cared about those little kids! I looked into their faces, and I saw my own face when I was a kid … was I wrong to do that? So goddamn much misery—should I have tended my own little plot when I looked round and there was so damn much to do—so much I could do—I did do! Goddamn it, I did it! You tell me, was I wrong to do that!

Pause. EV is about to look again for the picture.

CATHERINE: It isn't there, Daddy.

EV: I had to rely on myself 'cause there was fuckin' little else to rely on, I made decisions when decisions had to be made, I chose a road, and I took it, and I never looked back.

CATHERINE: You've always been so sure of things, haven't you.

EV watches CATHERINE as she looks down at the envelope and turns it over in her hands.

EV: … You're like her, Katie.

CATHERINE: Like Gramma?

EV: Like your mother. *(removes his glasses)*

CATHERINE: She always said I was just like you.

EV: Like her.

CATHERINE: Don't say that.

KATIE: Am I like Gramma, Daddy?

EV: You're like yourself, Katie.

KATIE: Why don't you open it, Daddy? *(KATIE is looking at the letter CATHERINE holds.)*

EV: I will.

CATHERINE: When I was little I stayed with her once. *(CATHERINE looks at KATIE.)*

EV: After your mother had Robbie.

KATIE: And I swore, and she said, "You never say those words, Katie, only in church," and when I dropped my prayer book I said, "Jesus Christ, Gramma" and she said, "Kay-Ty!"

CATHERINE: And I said, "But we are in church, Gramma."

KATIE and CATHERINE laugh. EV takes off the old cardigan and hangs it over his chair as he speaks.

EV: She'd write that kinda thing in a letter. That's all that she'd write. That's what's in that letter. *(exits)*

CATHERINE: *(to KATIE)* I don't want to be like her, and I don't want to be like Mummy.

KATIE: *(sings to CATHERINE)*
K-K-K-Katie, my beautiful Katie,
You the only G-G-G-Girl that I adore
When the M-M-M-Moon shines

KATIE looks at a notebook; she has not carried one before.

I'll be waiting …
K-K-K-Katie … Katie …

Shift. OSCAR is watching KATIE.

KATIE: *(to CATHERINE)* Everything's down in here. I write it all down. And when I grow up, I'll have it all here.

CATHERINE: Will it be worth it?

KATIE: I used to pray to God, but I don't anymore. I write it all down in here. I was just little then and now— (*KATIE senses OSCAR is watching her.*) Are you interested in this, Uncle Oscar? 'Cause if you aren't, why do you listen?

OSCAR: For you.

KATIE: I don't like people doing things for me. I can do things for myself ... (*KATIE starts to write in the book, the only time she does so.*) "Now Mummy has a 'medical problem' p-r-ob." Did you know that, Uncle Oscar? Mummy has a *medical problem*—that's apart from her *personal problems*, did you know that?

OSCAR: No.

KATIE: Really?

Shift. EV enters with bag and suit jacket. OSCAR may help him on with it.

EV: I thought you knew.

OSCAR: How the hell would I know?

EV: I'm sending her to the Royal Vic.

OSCAR: Who to?

EV: You remember Bob Greene from McGill?

OSCAR: Bit quick to cut, isn't he?

EV: You never liked him.

OSCAR: Neither did you.

EV: So he's an asshole, was, is, and will be, but he's goddamn good at his job.

OSCAR: He's too quick to cut.

EV: And the best gynecologist in the country.

OSCAR: He'll have her in surgery before the ink on her train ticket dries.

EV: This is your professional opinion, is it, based on your *extensive* practice?

OSCAR: There's gotta be other options.

EV: We could go someplace where it's hot and lie in the sun till she grows a tumor the size of a melon—why don't we do that?

OSCAR: I—

EV: You wanna look at her medical records? Go talk to Barney, tell him I said to pull 'em and show you—fibrous uterus, two opinions.

OSCAR: Greene'll go for radical surgery and—

EV: What the hell do you want me to do?

OSCAR: Does she know?

EV: Of course she knows! What the hell do you mean, does she know?

OSCAR: You gotta take some time with her, she's gonna need that.

EV: I got no time.

OSCAR: What's wrong with just takin' off—the two of you go just as soon as she's able.

EV: I can't.

OSCAR: Look, you lie on the sand in the sun and you relax for Christ's sake.

EV: I got patients been waitin' for a bed for months, I can't just leave 'em to whoever's on call.

OSCAR: I'll take 'em, you go.

EV: They count on me bein' there, Oscar.

OSCAR: The population of this province will not wither and die if you take a three week vacation—I'll handle your patients.

EV: I'd go nuts doin' nothin'.

OSCAR: You're doin' it for her.

EV: I'd go nuts.

OSCAR: You're drivin' her nuts!

EV: Were that to be true, three weeks in the sun wouldn't change it.

OSCAR: Don't think of her as your wife—think of her as a patient who's married to an insensitive son-of-a-bitch.

EV: I was an insensitive son-of-a-bitch when she met me; I haven't changed.

OSCAR: I give up.

EV: O.K. O.K., I'm thinking ... I'm thinking ... I'm thinking you like sand and sun, you could take her.

OSCAR: I didn't marry her.

EV: You like her.

OSCAR: I like her.

EV: She likes you.

OSCAR: Listen to yourself! You're asking me to take your wife on a three week vacation to recover from major surgery, do you realize that?

EV: She needs to get away, I can't take the time, you can.

OSCAR: It's one thing I'm not gonna do for you.

EV: So do it for her.

OSCAR: No.

EV: It makes sense to me.

OSCAR: No.

EV: Why not?

OSCAR: No, I said no.

EV: You're the one suggested it.

OSCAR: I didn't. *(EV looks at his watch.)* We're not leaving it there!

EV: Look. There's an alumnae thing in six or seven months, I can schedule around it and the three of us'll have one hell of a good bash, but right now I cannot get away so I'm askin' you to do me this favour. How often do I ask for a favour? Take her to one of those islands you go to, eat at the clubs, lie in the sun, and—Christ, Oscar, I got to go, so gimme an answer, yes or no? *(pause)* You make the arrangements, I'll pick up the tab.

OSCAR: Half the tab.

EV: Fifty-fifty all the way.

OSCAR: Are you sure you don't want me to check her into the Vic, observe the surgery, hang around the recovery room and generally be there?

EV: I can clear three or four days for that.

OSCAR is silent. As EV is about to leave he notices OSCAR's silence and stops.

EV: Say—how did that burn case go?

OSCAR: That was four months ago, Ev.

EV: Seems like yesterday, so how did it go?

OSCAR: Zip, kaput.

EV: What the hell did you do?

OSCAR: Did it ever occur to you that I might find Bob very attractive?

EV: I know she's attractive, hell, I married her, didn't I?

OSCAR: That she might find me very attractive?

EV: Don't let it go to your head.

OSCAR: You know rumours fly.

EV: I'm too damned busy to listen to rumours.

OSCAR: Your mother isn't. She listens. After that, she phones.

EV: Who?

OSCAR: Me. She phones me. To talk about you. She's a remnant of my old man's practice, remember?

EV: Last time I saw her she didn't—

OSCAR: When was that anyway?

EV: Oh I was over—no—ah—

OSCAR: She can't remember either. I've seen you, you son-of-a-bitch, I've seen you take time with some old biddy, you laugh, you hang onto her hand, and she leaves your office thinking she's Claudette Colbert, and has just stolen a night with you at the Ritz—and I—I get the phone calls from your mother who is reduced to writing you letters and crying to me on the phone. You don't call, you don't visit, you don't ... and now she's got it into her head that ...

EV: What?

OSCAR: Rumours fly.

EV: So you reassure her. I gotta go, Oscar.

EV: What if I can't reassure her?

EV: Then you laugh, hang onto her hand, and make Mum think she's Claudette Colbert at the Ritz.

OSCAR: It's not that simple. *(EV is moving away from OSCAR.)* I do find Bob very attractive!

EV: Total agreement.

OSCAR: You never think for one minute there could be one iota of truth in those rumours?

EV: I just don't believe you'd do that to me.

OSCAR: How can you be so sure?

EV: I know you.

OSCAR: Better than I know myself?

EV: I must. *(speaking as he exits)* Barbados eh, or someplace like that.

Shift.

BOB: I don't plan on having any more children.

CATHERINE: No more children.

BOB: I didn't plan, didn't.

CATHERINE: No children.

BOB: Don't have to plan now. All taken care of. Are you listening to me?

Shift. KATIE and CATHERINE will end up together, a mirror image.

KATIE: I'll tell you what she does. What she does is, she starts doing something. Something big. That's how I can tell. She's all right for awhile—and then she decides she's gonna paint all of the downstairs—or we're gonna put in new cupboards—or knock out a wall! ... We got so many walls knocked out, the house started to fall down in the middle! Can you believe that?—And we had to get a big steel beam put through in the basement! Can you believe that?

CATHERINE: It's true.

KATIE: And before she gets finished one of those big jobs—she starts.

CATHERINE: And she never finishes. Someone else comes in, and they finish.

KATIE: But that's how I can tell when she's gonna start. And I try to figure out—

CATHERINE: I ask myself—

KATIE: Does the big job make her start—or does she start the big job because she knows she's gonna start?

CATHERINE: But that's how I could tell, that's the beginning.

Shift.

BOB: So ... why does it ... why do I feel that it matters? Two were enough, Katie and Robbie, so why do I feel that it matters? I don't want any more ... Oscar!

OSCAR: I'm here.

BOB: Does it matter?

OSCAR: Well ... from the medical—

BOB: Medical, medical, medical, I don't wanna talk about medical.

OSCAR: It affects—

BOB: Me! Me! I'm talkin' about me! Why do I feel like, why do I feel—we didn't want any more children! I can't have any more children! Me, the part of me that's important, here, inside here—Me! That's the same. I'm the same. So ... why do I feel that it matters?

OSCAR: It doesn't matter.

BOB: Why don't you listen? I'm trying to explain. We didn't want any more, I can't have any more, so why does it matter?

OSCAR: It doesn't matter.

BOB: It does matter! ... I'm the same. Inside I'm the same. I'm Eloise Roberts and they called me Bob and I can run faster and do better than any boy I ever met!

OSCAR: It's all right.

BOB: No.

OSCAR: Come here.

BOB: I try to figure it out and I just keep going round.

CATHERINE: It's all right.

BOB: I need to do more, I need to ... I need ...

CATHERINE: Why don't you just do what you want?

BOB: Sometimes I want to scream. I just want to stand there and scream, to hit something, to reach out and smash things—and hit and smash and hit and smash and ... and then ... I would feel very tired and I could lie down and sleep.

OSCAR: Do you want to sleep now?

BOB: No. I'm not tired now. I want to drink now. Want a drink, and then we'll ... what will we do?

CATHERINE: Why couldn't you leave.

BOB: Leave?

CATHERINE: Just leave!

BOB: Katie and Robbie.

CATHERINE: Did you care about them!

BOB: And your father!

Shift. EV enters, carrying a bag. He is isolated on stage.

EV: We had the worst goddamn polio epidemic this province has seen, eleven years ago. We had an outbreak this year. You are lookin' at the attendin' physician at the present Polio Clinic—it is a building that has been condemned by the Provincial Fire Marshall, it has been condemned by the Provincial Health Officer, it has been condemned by the Victoria Public Hospital, it's infested by cockroaches, it's overrun by rats, it's the worst goddamn public building in this province! When is the government gonna stop building liquor stores and give the doctors of this province a chance to save a few fuckin' lives!

BOB: Haven't you got enough?

EV: Enough what?

BOB: Enough! Enough everything!

EV: You're drunk.

BOB: You'll never get enough, will you?

EV: Did Valma phone?

BOB: I don't answer the phone, just let it ring and ring— *(EV starts to exit.)* Where're you going?

EV: Valma's.

BOB: What for?

EV: To pick up the messages that she'd give me by phone if you'd answer the phone.

BOB: Maid could answer it. Does answer it, but she's not good with messages, no.

EV: You run them through the house so goddamn fast they don't have time to pick up a phone. Why don't you get one and keep one?

BOB: Interviewin' them gives me somethin' to do. I enjoy interviewin' them. Purpose and direction to my life! Where're you goin'?

EV: *(exiting)* Valma's.

BOB: Stay.

CATHERINE: Stay. *(EV stops.)* Don't go. Sit for a little while. *(There is a moment of silence.)* Talk.

EV: If I sit down ... my head will start to nod.

CATHERINE: That'd be all right. She wouldn't mind. You'd be here.

EV puts down his bag. He moves to BOB and sits beside her. He takes his hat off and takes her hand. BOB smiles and strokes EV's hand, then holds it against her face.

BOB: Do you remember ... sometimes I ... we had some good times, didn't we?

EV: We can still have good times.

BOB: I don't know.

EV: You've got to get hold of things.

BOB: I try.

EV: I know I'm busy.

BOB: Always busy.

EV: I know.

BOB: If I could do something.

EV: There's the house and the kids. Just tell me what you want and I'll get it.

BOB: I can't do anything.

EV: You can.

BOB: No. There's nothing I can do.

EV: Sure there is. *(BOB slowly shakes her head.)* Come on ... hey, listen, did you know the Hendersons were sellin' their camp on the Miramichi? *(pause)* Well they are. What say we buy it? You'd like that, wouldn't you? You could get away from the kids and the house, do some fishin', you like fishin', don't you? *(BOB nods her head.)* Well, that's what we'll do. *(checks his watch)* Shit. You get to bed. Get some sleep. *(exits)*

BOB: Can't sleep.

There is the sound of a train whistle; BOB listens to it. It fades away. Shift.

BOB: ... Half-way across three-quarters of a mile of single track ... its whistle would split the night, and that night ... do you know what she did?

CATHERINE: No, and neither do you.

BOB: She walked out to meet it.

CATHERINE: And you say I'm like his side of the family, you say I'm like her?

BOB: She did.

CATHERINE: I would never do that!

Shift.

KATIE: Mummy didn't like her. I could have gone to see her with Daddy, but Daddy was always too busy to go, so it was all his fault I didn't see her … I guess that's true.

CATHERINE: She would phone, she would ask for me.

KATIE: But I could never think of anything to say … They're the ones I'm supposed to like, his side of the family, so it would have been nice to see her … was she old? … *(CATHERINE doesn't answer.)* Is that what she died of? … *(CATHERINE doesn't answer.)* What did she die of, Uncle Oscar?

OSCAR: It was an accident.

CATHERINE: We know "accidents," don't we.

KATIE: I never saw anybody dead before. I don't know if I wanted to see her dead … it didn't matter because they didn't take us anyway—I was a bit happy not to go because I don't like to go anywhere with Mummy when she's like that. She said Gramma was a bitch who went around saying bad things about her and Mummy was glad she was dead—and Daddy just kept getting dressed and pretended Mummy wasn't talking— You can only pretend for so long.

CATHERINE: And when they came home he went out.

KATIE: And Mummy phoned all over but he wasn't any place she could find, and …

CATHERINE: … then she tripped at the top of the stairs and she fell. I went to my bedroom as soon as that happened …

KATIE: … and Robbie screamed and cried and screamed and cried and …

CATHERINE: … the maid got up and put her to bed—she'll be leaving soon and we'll get a new one …

KATIE: … you'd think if a person kept falling down stairs it would hurt them!

CATHERINE: It never did a thing to her.

Shift.

BOB: Katie! … Katie! You wanna know somethin'?

KATIE: No.

BOB: Your father's mother killed herself! … *(Pause. KATIE stares at BOB.)* You look at me … you look at me and what are you thinking?

KATIE: Nothing.

BOB: This isn't me you know. This isn't really me. This is someone else … What are you thinking?

KATIE: I don't think anything.

BOB: Katie!

CATHERINE: Leave her alone.

BOB: You know what your father's mother said?

CATHERINE: Leave her alone!

BOB: Do you know?

KATIE: No!

BOB: Why would a nurse—to catch a doctor, that's why. Why would he marry me, eh? Why would a brilliant young man, whole life ahead of him, why would he marry me? Eh? Do you know why? Do you know!

KATIE: No.

BOB: Why would he do that?!

KATIE: I don't know.

BOB: Answer me!

KATIE: I don't know!

BOB: No! You don't know! Nobody knows!

KATIE: I know. Inside I know. He had to.

CATHERINE: Don't.

KATIE: Inside I do know. Because of me—and that's what went wrong.

CATHERINE: He loved her and she loved him, Uncle Oscar says.

KATIE: No.

CATHERINE: That's true, Katie!

KATIE: Do you believe that? *(EV enters in his shirt sleeves.)* Daddy!

KATIE runs to EV and he puts his arms around her.

EV: Your mother sometimes says things that she doesn't mean. She's sick and she—

KATIE: She isn't sick!

EV: She loves you.

KATIE: I don't love her.

KATIE quickly moves away. EV starts after her.

EV: Yes you do.

Shift.

BOB: Valma, Valma, Valma, Valma, Valma, Valma I am so sick of that woman's name. What're you and her doing, that's what I'd like to know!

EV: Nothing. *(sits)*

BOB: Oooh, you don't tell me that! I know better than that! She's like your right arm, your left arm, part of your leg!

EV: Leave Valma out of it.

BOB: I don't wanna leave Valma out of it! She'd do anything for you—put your wife to bed, get her up—why does she do that, eh? Tell me why?

EV: She's the best office nurse in the city and I couldn't run that office without her. Why the Christ don't you go to bed?

BOB: Why the Christ don't you go to bed?

EV: Go to bed.

BOB: Gonna go over to Valma's and go to bed? You don't love me, you never loved me! You never loved me.

EV: Go to bed.

BOB: You don't even see me. You look at me and there's nobody there. You don't see anybody but those stupid stupid people who think you're God. You're not God! *(CATHERINE and KATIE are together and BOB moves towards them. BOB grabs CATHERINE's hand.)* And it's so funny … do you know what he's done, do you know? … If I … If I go into the liquor store, do you know what happens? They say … sorry, but the Doc says *no.* He says … they're not to … and they don't. They don't. He tells them don't sell it to her

the Doc says don't do that and they don't. But what's so funny is … every drunk in the city goes into that office on Saturday and they say … "Jeez Chris Doc, spent the whole cheque on booze, the old lady's gonna kill me," and he gives them money … Gives *them* money. *(KATIE moves away.)* And Valma says he says maybe one of them takes it home instead of just buyin' more, can you believe that? … And when I go in, they say, "The Doc says no" … but I don't have to worry. *(moves to refill her glass)* So long as I keep interviewin' the maids … I don't have to worry about a thing.

Shift.

KATIE: You don't have any family.

OSCAR: You're my family.

KATIE: I'm not related to you, and you're not related to me, you can't be my family, Uncle Oscar.

Shift.

BOB: *(leaves her glass)* Hey! Do you want to know what a bastard he is? *(CATHERINE turns her head away as BOB advances on EV.)* Well I don't care if you want to know or not—I'm gonna tell you. I put the clothes out, put the suit out for the cleaners and I went through his pockets, and do you know what I found, do you know? It was something he didn't need for me, something he wouldn't use with me, because I can't have any more, no, I've been fixed like the goddamn cat or the dog so what the hell did you have it for?

EV: If you found it, that means I didn't use it, so what the hell's your problem?

BOB: *(runs at EV)* You bastard! *(BOB strikes at EV's chest. He grabs her wrists.)* You bastard you.

BOB attempts to strike EV several times before collapsing against EV's chest. He picks her up, carries her to a chair and puts her in it. He looks down at her for a moment, then moves away, to sit isolated on the stage. OSCAR joins him. Shift.

OSCAR: She tells me you're bangin' Valma.

EV: If I wanted to bang someone, it sure as hell wouldn't be Valma.

OSCAR: So who are you bangin'?

EV: Has she posted that condom story in the staff room, or is it just you she's told?

OSCAR: I asked you a question.

EV: I'm not bangin' anyone! Who the hell are you bangin'! ... I ... I lost Jack Robinson the other night ... I felt so goddamn bad. I thought he was gonna make it and then everything started shuttin' down. He gets pneumonia, we get that under control, then his heart starts givin' us problems, we get that solved, then his goddamn kidneys go—I don't know why, just one thing after another. Someone was callin' his name and I couldn't do a damn thing about it ... and I felt so bad, I thought ... I don't want to go home, you can see what she's like so ... you know what I did? I bought a mickey of rum and that goddamn condom and I ... I drove around for a coupla hours. And that was it ... That was it.

OSCAR: Things can't go on.

EV: Don't start on that give her more time shit. Her problem's got nothin' to do with time nor work nor any other goddamn thing.

OSCAR: Her problem is the crazy son-of-a-bitch she's married to.

EV: Who the hell is crazy here? I'm the one can't keep a bottle of booze in the house, I'm the one's gotta put the fear of God in the help so they're too damn scared to buy it for her—and now she's into the vanilla or any other goddamn thing she can pour down her throat! I can't keep pills in the bag and she'd let the kids starve to death if it weren't for the maid! I'm the one goin' eighteen hours a day tryin' to hold the fuckin' fort so I can hear you say what!? That I'm crazy! I'm not a goddamn machine!!! I thought if anyone would understand, it would be you ... and you ... *(exits)*

OSCAR: Ev. Ev!

OSCAR may exit after him. Shift.

BOB runs her hand along the cushion in the chair. She gets on her knees, lifts the cushion up. CATHERINE watches her search. KATIE too observes, from a distance. BOB continues her search.

BOB: Everyone has something hidden in this house. I hide it and he hides it and you hide it.

CATHERINE: Do something.

BOB: Do something. Just like your father. Do, do, do.

CATHERINE: Just stop!

BOB: Just stop. *(She finds a bottle of pills.)* Stop doing. *(She unscrews the bottle; pours pills in hand; looks at CATHERINE.)* Stop. *(She swallows the pills; settles back in the chair; shuts her eyes.)*

Shift. KATIE slowly approaches BOB. She and CATHERINE stand, looking at BOB. Pause.

KATIE: She was blue ... I'd never seen anybody blue before. Robbie went in the kitchen and cried. I stood at the bottom of the stairs and watched them bring her down on the stretcher. I didn't cry ... I don't know what she took—was it the pills that make her sleep?

CATHERINE: Uncle Oscar said.

KATIE: She was asleep all right. And really blue. I thought ... I thought ...

CATHERINE: Go on, you can say it.

KATIE: I thought maybe she was dead. *(moves away)* ... and now she's going to Connecticut? Will she be better then?

CATHERINE: *(joins KATIE)* Uncle Oscar said.

KATIE: All better? *(CATHERINE doesn't answer.)* I wonder ... do you know what I wonder? I wonder, did she take the pills to sleep like she sometimes does, or did she ...

CATHERINE: It was

KATIE: An accident? ... Sometimes I look ...

CATHERINE: ... in the mirror, I look in the mirror ...

KATIE: ... and I see Mummy and I see ...

CATHERINE: ... Gramma, and Mummy and me ...

KATIE: ... I don't want to be like them.

Shift. OSCAR may enter. BOB is sitting. She will get up and very carefully tie her gown. There is a certain formality, seriousness, alienation and deliberation about her. She moves and speaks somewhat slowly. OSCAR stands a distance from her, still watching.

BOB: You have to get hold of things. Routine's important. Get out. Get around. Do things. The I.O.D.E., bridge ... . The doctors' wives have this sort of club and it meets on a regular basis, I ...

OSCAR: Tired?

BOB: No. Feeling fine. How do I look?

OSCAR: Good.

BOB moves to another chair and sits. OSCAR remains in the same position, watching her. BOB doesn't speak till seated. She does not look at OSCAR.

BOB: Leisure activity is big. Structured leisure activity. Very big. *(pause)* Painting. I paint now. You know. *(pause)* Pictures. *(pause; speaks softly)* What else? *(pause)* Gorgeous place. If you'd been there, it would have been perfect. *(pause; speaks softly)* What else. *(pause)* Psychiatrists, psychiatrists. They ask you obvious things and you give them obvious answers. It's all very obvious ... Obvious ... *(softly)* What else. *(long pause; softly)* Nothing ... nothing else ... I can't think of ... anything else.

BOB sits very still. OSCAR stands watching her. BOB begins to rock back and forth very slightly and sings very softly to herself. She is not singing words, but merely making sounds. OSCAR moves to her. He stands behind her looking down for a moment. He slowly places a hand on her shoulder. She reaches up and holds his hand, pressing it to her shoulder. She continues to rock slightly but the words of the song can be heard. She is singing "Auld Lang Syne." OSCAR moves around her without letting go of her hand and draws her up to dance, which they do rather formally.

BOB: *(sings)*
Should auld acquaintance be forgot
And never brought to mind
Should auld acquaintance
Be forgot—and auld lang syne
an auld lang syne m'dear
an auld lang syne

BOB begins to cry but continues singing and dancing.

Let's drink a cup of kindness up
For auld lang syne.

Shift. EV enters. He is isolated on stage. He carries his bag, and his hat is pushed back on his head. There is an air of powerful relaxation and poise about him. He might almost be standing in a glow of golden sunshine. When he speaks BOB and OSCAR stop dancing, They turn to stare at

him and OSCAR will step away from BOB. BOB is drawn towards EV, who does not acknowledge her.

EV: I say three or four of us go in together. I mean look at the situation now. A patient comes in from Durham Bridge, and has to run all over this Christless city, G.P. here, lab tests there, pediatrician someplace else. I've got my eye on a place on the hill. We renovate it—

BOB: Bar date with him.

EV: And we open a Medical Clinic, lab, X-ray, everything in that one building—

BOB: And you don't call that—

EV: We solicit the best specialists we can to take office space there. We give the people of this goddamn province the medical care they deserve, without havin' to run all over hell and hackety to get it!

BOB: And I laughed—and he said—and it was so funny—such a long time ago ...

Shift.

KATIE: You lied to me.

OSCAR: When?

KATIE: People lie to me quite a bit. They think I don't know it, but I do.

OSCAR: I didn't mean to lie.

KATIE: You didn't tell the truth.

OSCAR: What did I lie about?

KATIE: Guess—one guess.

BOB: S'funny thing.

KATIE: You promised me she'd get better, Uncle Oscar! You promised and you lied!

Shift. BOB lights a cigarette during her speech. By the end of her speech it is apparent she's been drinking.

BOB: The more you do of certain things, the less it seems you do. You fill your time up, my time's filled up. I sit at these tea luncheons, s'always ... sherry. I hate sherry. I never have any sherry. I know what they think, but that's not the reason. I just don't like sherry. No. No sherry. *(pause)* Children are important. *(pause)* And the I.O.D.E. ... I go to—and bridshe, play a lot of bridshe, I'm good at that. Win, always win ... I like bridshe. And ahh *(pause)* I don't really like them but— everything's working for them and everything can work for me too. I can be them. It isn't hard, I can do it. I can. If I ... if I want to.

BOB moves to drawer, opens it and feels inside. She is looking for a bottle, slowly and methodically. She becomes aware of KATIE watching her.

BOB: What do you want?

KATIE: I don't want anything.

BOB: What're you doing?

KATIE: I'm watching you.

BOB: Your father tell you to do that?

KATIE: No.

BOB: Then why are you watchin'?

KATIE: I want to remember.

BOB: Remember what?

KATIE: Remember you.

BOB: I know what you're thinking. It's all right. You can say it ... do you want me to say it?

KATIE: No.

BOB: I'm not afraid. I can say it.

KATIE: If I were you—I wouldn't let Robbie see me like that. It makes him feel bad. He has to pretend that you're sick.

BOB: What do you pretend, Katie?

KATIE: I don't have to pretend anymore.

CATHERINE: Katie.

BOB: *(stops her search, turns to KATIE)* Did you take something of mine?

KATIE: Did I?

BOB: You took something of mine and I want it back.

KATIE: It's gone.

BOB: No.

KATIE: I poured it out, let go!

BOB: Give it back!

CATHERINE: Don't.

BOB and KATIE struggle.

BOB: You had no right you ...

KATIE: Let go!

BOB: No.

CATHERINE: Let her go.

BOB: Give it to me.

KATIE: Let go, let go!

BOB: You had no right!

KATIE: Go! *(She strikes at BOB, knocking her down.)* I'm not gonna cry. I'm not gonna cry!

BOB: I tried. I really did try.

CATHERINE: I'm not gonna cry.

BOB: Listen. *(BOB grabs CATHERINE's hand.)* Listen Katie. I want ... I want to tell you—when— when I was little, do you know, do you know I would sit on our front porch, and I would look up, look up at the sky, the sky went on forever. And I just looked up. That was me, Katie. That was me.

CATHERINE: I'm holding my breath and my teeth are together and my tongue, I can feel my tongue, it presses hard on the back of my teeth and the roof of my mouth ...

KATIE: ... and I hang on really tight. Really tight, and then ... I don't cry.

CATHERINE: I never cried ... *(to BOB)* but I couldn't listen like that.

BOB releases CATHERINE's hands, and moves away from her. CATHERINE runs after her as she speaks.

CATHERINE: It's one of the things you can't do like that!

KATIE: It's better not to cry than to listen.

CATHERINE: Is it?

KATIE: It's how you keep on. It's one of the ways. I'm surprised you don't know that.

KATIE moves away from CATHERINE, who then follows her. Shift.

EV: Close this time.

OSCAR: How close?

EV: Too damn close. We pumped her stomach and prayed. The kids spent Christmas Day at

Valma's ... I think ... I think the psychiatrist she sees is nuttier than she is ... I'm alright ... *(EV sits in the same chair he sat in as "Old Ev" at the start of the play. Pause.)* Did you know ... what the hell is their name ... live over on King Street, married someone or other, moved to Toronto ... I'm alright. *(pause)* Some silly son of a whore didn't look close enough, she kept tellin' him she had this lump in her breast ... I'm alright ... She's got a three-month-old kid and she's come home to die ... Thing is no one's got around to tellin' her that's how it is. They asked me to come over and tell her ... patients of mine ... come home to die ...

OSCAR may exit. Pause. EV takes Gramma's letter out of his pocket and looks at it.

EV: I'm alright ...

Shift.

BOB: Open it! Go on, open it!

EV: You're drunk.

BOB: I'm drunk. So I'm drunk. What the hell are you, what's your excuse? What's his excuse, Katie?

EV: Leave her alone.

BOB: Why don't you open it!

EV: What for?

BOB: To see what it says.

EV: Says nothing.

BOB: Your father's mother killed herself, Katie. She walked across the train bridge at midnight and—

KATIE: That's an accident!

BOB: She left a letter and the letter tells him why she did it.

KATIE: What's in the letter, Daddy?

EV: Your Gramma—

OSCAR may unobtrusively enter, and stand silently in the background.

BOB: She killed herself because of him!

KATIE: Because of you!

EV: Your Gramma loved us.

KATIE: Why don't you open it?

EV: She didn't see us so she'd write.

BOB: So open it!

EV: That's all it is.

BOB: Pretending! He's pretending!

KATIE: He is not!

BOB: He pretends a lot!

KATIE: You do!

BOB: Valma! Valma! Valma!

KATIE: I hate you!

BOB: Not afraid to say it!

KATIE: I hate you and I wish that you were dead.

CATHERINE: No.

KATIE: It's true!

CATHERINE: No.

KATIE: I wish and wish and

CATHERINE: No.

KATIE: someday you will be dead and I'll be happy!

OSCAR: It's all right, Katie!

KATIE: *(to EV)* You all say she's sick, she isn't sick.

BOB: *(to KATIE)* Katie!

KATIE: She's a drunk and that's what we should say!

BOB: *(to CATHERINE)* Katie!?

CATHERINE: Stop.

KATIE: And if I find her next time, I won't call for Daddy!

CATHERINE: No.

KATIE: I won't call for anyone!

CATHERINE: Stop Katie please.

KATIE: *(sits)* I'll go back downstairs and I'll sit in the kitchen and I'll pretend that I don't know, I'll pretend that everything's all right, I'll shut my eyes, and I'll pretend!

BOB: Katie! *(retreats)*

KATIE: *(chants)* Now they're married wish them joy

BOB: Katie. *(exits)*

KATIE: *(puts hands over ears; chants louder)*
First a girl for a toy
Seven years after seven to come

BOB: *(voice-over on mike, offstage)* Katie!

KATIE: *(chants louder)*
Fire on the mountain, kiss and run
On the mountains berries sweet

BOB: *(on mike, offstage)* Katie!

KATIE: *(chants)*
Pick as much as you can eat
By the berries' bitter bark

BOB: *(on mike, offstage)* Katie!

KATIE: *(chants louder)*
Fire on the mountain break your heart
Years to come—kiss and run
Bitter bark—break your heart

KATIE slowly takes her hands from her ears. There is silence. Pause.

KATIE: I don't hear you! *(pause)* I don't hear you! *(pause)* I don't! *(KATIE jumps up and whirls around, to look over at where she last saw BOB. Pause. Softly.)* I don't hear you at all.

CATHERINE: You can cry, Katie … it's all right to cry …

KATIE: Would you want to have me?

CATHERINE: Yes, yes I would.

Shift.

EV: All over now.

EV gets up from the chair and moves to the table where CATHERINE left the jewellery box in Act One. He stands, looking down at it.

CATHERINE: No, Daddy.

OSCAR: When was it we played scrub hockey on the river ice … Ev and Oscar, Oscar, Ev … "We're rough, we're tough, we're from Devon, that's enough" … *(EV lifts the lid of the music box. It plays "Smoke Gets In Your Eyes.")* … driving my old man's car, watering his whisky, Ev and Oscar …

EV: Ever since Grade One.

OSCAR: I knew you then, and I knew you after that, and then I got to know you less and less—

and here we are … I said why risk it? And I saw her and I knew why … well, she's gone now … What the hell does that mean to you, Ev. That's something I want to know. What's it mean? … For Christ's sake, say something, say something.

EV: There's nothing to say.

OSCAR: It shouldn't have happened.

EV: It did. *(closes the music box)*

OSCAR: She asked for goddamn little and you couldn't even give her that.

EV: You got no more idea of what she wanted than I have.

OSCAR: You never knew her and you don't know me.

EV: How can you say that? I carried you on my back since Grade One 'cause I liked you, I loved you, like a brother.

OSCAR: I could see it in my father, I can see it in you. You got your eye fixed on some goddamn horizon, and while you're striding towards that, you trample on every goddamn thing around you!

EV: The biggest dream you ever had, what the hell was it? What was it, Oscar? New Orleans! New Orleans.

OSCAR: She understood what that meant.

EV: Bullshit. You been a pseudo-doctor for your old man, a pseudo-husband to my wife, and a pseudo-father to my kids! I gave you that, Oscar, like I gave you everything else 'cause I knew you'd never have the goddamn gumption to get it for yourself!

OSCAR: I should have taken your wife.

EV: My wife wouldn't have you! *(OSCAR starts to leave. EV calls after him.)* She knew you! She knew what you were! And because of that you say I killed her! It was all my fault? *(OSCAR stops. EV moves to him.)* Supposin' it were, her death my fault, put a figure on it, eh? Her death my fault on one side—and the other any old figure, thousand lives the figure—say that worth it? *(OSCAR exits.)* Was it? I'm askin' you a question! Was that worth it!

Silence. Shift. KATIE approaches EV. As he removes his suitcoat, he speaks to her.

EV: What the hell do you mean?

KATIE: I don't know what I mean.

EV: Where the hell would you go?

KATIE: I don't know. Away. Away to some school.

EV: I don't want you to go.

KATIE: Send me anyway. For me, Daddy. Do it for me.

EV: What if I said no.

KATIE: You won't say no.

EV: You wanna hear me say no!

KATIE: I'm like you, Daddy. I just gotta win—and you just gotta win—and if you say no—you'll have lost. *(exiting as she speaks)* I'll come back … every once in a while … I'll come back …

EV: Katie? *(screams)* Katie!

CATHERINE: I'm here.

Shift. CATHERINE and EV are alone onstage, As CATHERINE speaks, EV puts on his old cardigan, which was hanging on the back of his chair. He puts on his glasses. CATHERINE has Gramma's letter.

CATHERINE: Do you remember when she gathered together all the photographs and snapshots, all the pictures of her, and she sat in the living room, and she ripped them all up? So … after she died, we had no pictures of her … And Oscar, remember Oscar came over with one … it was taken at a nightclub somewhere, and she was feeding this little pig—a stupid little pig standing on the table and she—she was feeding it with a little bottle like a baby's bottle …

EV: Her with …

CATHERINE: … a baby bottle feeding the pig with the bottle …

EV: *(small chuckle)* Her and Oscar at some goddamn Caribbean nightclub feedin' a pig …

CATHERINE: Like a baby. She was looking up at the camera. She was smiling a bit. You could see her teeth. She didn't look happy, or unhappy. She looked as if she was waiting. Just waiting.

EV: For what?

CATHERINE: I don't know. But whatever it was, she couldn't grab it.

EV: Do you know what you want?

CATHERINE: … Yes … Yes, I do.

EV: Then you grab it.

Pause. CATHERINE looks at Gramma's letter, which she is holding in her hand.

CATHERINE: What are you gonna do with this?

EV: Do you wanna open it?

CATHERINE: I can. Do you want me to?

EV: I know what's in it.

Pause. CATHERINE strikes a match. She looks at EV.

CATHERINE: Should I? … should I? …

CATHERINE blows the match out and gives the letter to EV. He sits looking at it for a moment.

EV: Burn the damn thing.

EV holds the letter out. CATHERINE sets it on fire and it flares up as EV holds it.

CATHERINE: Be careful!

EV: I am bein' careful. *(EV drops the burning envelope into an ashtray. Lights are fading.)* Two minutes home you're as bad as Valma.

CATHERINE: Bullshit, Daddy.

EV: Jesus Christ I hate to hear a woman talk like that.

As lights fade to black, CATHERINE looks at EV and smiles. Black except for the dying flame from the letter.

END

SKY GILBERT

(b. 1952)

Sky Gilbert says he wrote *Drag Queens on Trial* when he "began to realize that the drag queen was the most potent and eloquent symbol of the 'otherness' which is, I think, the gay man's most enduring wound, and his prize, also." On opening night of the play in 1985, he recalls, "I strode into the theatre dressed in hopeless drag"—he had never worn drag publically before—"and plopped myself down right next to the critics. I truly thought my career might be over ... " Instead, the critics from even Toronto's straight press were delighted. In retrospect Gilbert concluded that "they missed the political point, but loved the traditional characterization of gay men as campy queens. The gay community got the point, but was not so certain about its response."

Over the course of his controversial career as playwright and actor, director and artistic director, radical queer activist and drag queen, Gilbert has elicited uncertain responses from both ends of the political and sexual spectrums. He has been celebrated and vilified. R.M. Vaughan writes: "Critics on the left denounce his work as exploitative and hyper-sexual, liberals simply find it confusing, and right-wingers believe Gilbert is satanic, and possibly poisoning their children." Outspoken and outrageous, he has been a central character in his own drama onstage and off, a prolific and underrated playwright, a key figure in Canadian new play development, and altogether one of the most dynamic individuals in the contemporary Canadian theatre.

Schuyler Lee Gilbert, Jr. was born in Norwich, Connecticut, his father an insurance company manager, his mother the scion of a family with deeply conservative American roots. (Gilbert travesties family life in 1950s Norwich in his drag comedy *Lola Starr Builds Her Dream Home*. See *Canadian Theatre Review* 59 [Summer 1989].) When Gilbert was twelve, he moved to Toronto with his mother and sister following his parents' divorce. He completed an Arts degree at York and two years of graduate work in theatre at University of Toronto before dropping out to co-found Buddies in Bad Times Theatre in 1979. That same year he co-founded the Rhubarb! Festival of new plays (its philosophy, "opportunity without interference"), and served as artistic director of both the theatre and the festival until 1997. Soon after their inception both Buddies and Rhubarb! became identified primarily, though not exclusively, with gay and lesbian work, Buddies especially after 1985 when Gilbert instituted its 4-Play Festival which commissioned four new plays by gay and lesbian writers each year.

Gilbert himself came out as a gay writer in 1979 with a play called *Lana Turner Has Collapsed*. It was one of dozens he wrote, directed and/or performed at Buddies and Rhubarb! while moving himself and his theatre in increasingly radical directions over the next two decades. At the same time as the quality of his work was being acknowledged by Dora and Chalmers nominations, the Pauline McGibbon Award for Directing (1985) and invitations to direct at the Shaw Festival, Gilbert was pushing the envelope hard; drag, pedophilia, sado-masochism and explicit gay sex came to mark his plays. He often appeared as his drag queen alter ego, Jane, for highly publicized political protests in shopping malls, traffic court and city council meetings. He attacked with equal vigour the homophobia of straights and what Marjorie Garber has called the transvestophobia of main-stream gays and lesbians who feel their status threatened by high-profile deviance. Soon he was calling his work "queer theatre." "If I was a sweeter nicer guy," Gilbert wrote in 1993, "I'd call Buddies in Bad Times Theatre a 'gay and lesbian theatre for all people.' But I'm not that nice. I'm an orgiastic poet and a drag queen, and I feel compelled to call something queer what it is." Nevertheless, his successes were practical as well as ideological. In 1992 he managed to leverage over two million dollars from various levels of government to move Buddies into a larger space, the defunct Toronto Workshop Productions' former theatre.

Of the more than thirty plays of his own that Gilbert has had produced, some of the most notable remain unpublished, including *The Postman Rings Once* (1987); *The Whore's Revenge* (1989); *Ban*

This Show (1990), a response to the Robert Mapplethorpe controversies; and *Ten Ruminations on an Elegy Attributed to William Shakespeare*, which toured the UK in the late '90s. More than a dozen of his plays are in print, the majority in two collections, *This Unknown Flesh* (1995) and *Painted, Tainted, Sainted* (1996). The latter includes *Drag Queens on Trial*; its less successful sequel *Drag Queens in Outer Space* (1986), which featured Gilbert himself as Lana Lust in its 1990 San Francisco production; and the Austin Powers-ish drag musical *Suzie Goo: Private Secretary* (1991), which climaxes, so to speak, in the anthemic Gilbertian line, "Let the liquids spurt." These plays celebrate transgressive sexuality and critique the fears and hypocrisies of mainstream society through the parodic, self-conscious comedy of camp.

Another large group of Gilbert's plays focuses more seriously on the power of illicit desire acting on and through the gay artist/intellectual. *Pasolini/Pelosi, or The God in Unknown Flesh* (1983), a sequel *In Which Pier Paolo Pasolini Sees His Own Death in the Face of a Boy* (1991), and *More Divine* (1994), about Roland Barthes and Michel Foucault, are among the best of them. Others concern David Hockney, Truman Capote, Frank O'Hara, Tennessee Williams, Cavafy, Mapplethorpe and Shakespeare. Related in theme, *Theatrelife* (1987) and *Play Murder* (1995) explore the metatheatrical underpinnings of all Gilbert's work: the performative elements of gender and sexuality. Sex, drag and theatricality also comprise the themes of a poetry collection, *Digressions of a Naked Party Girl* (1998), and two novels about a character called Jack Sprat— *Guilty* (1998) and *St. Stephen's* (1999). In addition Gilbert has made three short films which have played the North American gay festival circuit, and has written essays on theatre and queer culture for *Canadian Theatre Review*, *This Magazine* (on the left) and *The National Post* (on the right).

In *Drag Queens on Trial* Gilbert puts his own spin on material that has precedent and resonance in the Canadian theatre. Queenie in Herbert's *Fortune and Men's Eyes* and Tremblay's *Hosanna* are Gilbert's queens' older sisters in drag, both tried and found guilty as well—the latter of living inauthentically as a gay man by pretending to be a woman. But as heroic as they might have been in their embrace of drag's radical otherness in the 1960s and '70s, Queenie and Hosanna were also sad and defeated. Later, in the 1980s, Michel Marc Bouchard's baroque romantic crossdressers would appear noble but melancholy and somewhat otherworldly. But there's nothing sad or otherworldly about Gilbert's three queens. They are triumphant and unapologetic, streetwise and foul-mouthed. Their explicit, aggressive sexual language, still pretty shocking even today when *Sex and the City* can be seen on prime time TV, would have seemed a lot more raw in 1985 before the mainstream theatrical success a few years later of plays such as Brad Fraser's similarly overt *Unidentified Human Remains* and *Poor Super Man*.

The structure of *Drag Queens* is highly schematic, not unlike the B-movie melodramas starring Joan Crawford or Lana Turner which it shamelessly parodies. In each of the three sections Judy, Lana and Marlene sit in front of their mirrors bitching and arguing while they make up and dress up for the three courtroom scenes. Each has her day in court where she is accused of the crime of being a drag queen while the other two play the prosecutor, the surprise witness and the judge. (In the original production a male judge spoke from a video screen.) The fourth actor is a taped Voice, "male and authoritative," which sometimes sounds like the preview of a bad movie or prime-time soap ("they lived by the skin of their spike heels"), sometimes like a stage manager calling the actors in a play to their places, and sometimes like Charlie commanding his Angels, who in this case respond with hilarious, unangelic obscenity.

The style of the play, like the queens' own style, is hyper-consciously theatrical: "Another day, another performance," says Lana as they take off their makeup at the end. Art, as Oscar Wilde knew, is a lie, but a beautiful one, and ultimately truer than the so-called truth. (In my favorite of many Wildean moments in the play the prosecutor challenges the accused. Lana: "How do you explain the fact that you sit before us, wearing breasts which are obviously not your own?" Marlene: "I hope that you do not wish to imply that I stole these breasts. They are mine. I bought them.") So too, Marlene admits at her trial, is the lie the essence of a drag queen's life. But it is "somehow the lie that tells the truth," the obvious artifice that aspires to something different and better than the ordinary, unglamorous "reality" which it rejects. Marlene and Judy both offer improved, fictionalized versions of their pasts and impassioned confessions of guilt for being true to themselves rather than to the straight Canadian norm. (Marlene's diatribe against "cold puritanical sad grey" Canada recalls similar complaints in Robertson Davies' comedies of the late 1940s!). But any moment that threatens to become maudlin is instantly deflated, if not by the queens themselves (e.g., Judy's tragedy-queenish mock suicide), then by the Voice declaiming: "DRAG QUEENS ON TRIAL!" or "they batted their eyes until they bruised their lids."

In an essay called "Closet Plays" Gilbert has written that "in the language of camp, humour is terribly serious." This becomes evident in Act Two at Lana's trial. She has taken great pride in her drag queen's lifestyle. (Prosecutor: "Do you have sleazy sex with men in back alleys, toilets, steam baths ... ?" Lana: "As often as humanly possible.") But when the surprise witness, her doctor, reveals that Lana is dying of AIDS and blames it on her homosexual promiscuity, Lana has a moment of self-doubt. This is the play's Big Scene, Lana's aria in which she faces down her doubt and embraces her truth. The rhetoric of her speech is both genuinely stirring in its unrepentant forth-rightness and hopelessly campy in its melodramatic excess—music from *Tristan and Isolde*, a spotlight and "spontaneous, taped, thunderous applause."

Suddenly turning *Drag Queens on Trial* into a play "about" AIDS is one of Gilbert's more audacious moves, but he makes it work wonderfully. Staring into the apocalypse, the play ends with a chorus from drag queendom's favourite diva, Judy Garland. The last lines resonate with both the joy and terror of being alive and queer in the mid-1980s: "Sing hallelujah come on get happy / Get ready for the judgment day."

Drag Queens on Trial premiered on October 17, 1985 at the Metro Cinema in Toronto, produced by Buddies in Bad Times Theatre, with the following cast:

JUDY GOOSE	Leonard Chow
LANA LUST	Kent Staines
MARLENE DELORME	Doug Millar
JUDGE (in video)	Bill Zaget

Directed by Sky Gilbert
Set Design by Tanuj Kohli
Costume Design by Laura Divilio
Lighting Design by Patsy Lang
Video by Christopher Gerrard-Pinker

DRAG QUEENS ON TRIAL
A COURTROOM MELODRAMA

[A]s truth is nonexistent it can never be anything but illusion—but illusion, the by-product of revealing artifice, can reach the summits nearer the unobtainable peak of Perfect Truth. For example, female impersonators. The impersonator is in fact a man (truth) until he re-creates himself as a woman (illusion) and, of the two, the illusion is truer.

Truman Capote, *Answered Prayers*

CHARACTERS

MARLENE DELORME, *a tall, dignified blonde; also plays Dr. Dimchick*

JUDY GOOSE, *a short, undignified blonde, also plays Anita Hrupki*

LANA LUST, *a romantic redhead; also plays Hermoine Rosemount*

Clerks, judges, prosecuting attorneys: all played by the three drag queens

NOTES ON LOCALE & GLOSSARY

Although both *Drag Queens on Trial* and *Drag Queens in Space* were originally performed in Toronto during the 1980s, they have since been performed throughout the USA. It's a small gay world, and every city has its own landmark gay pubs and institutions. I give the director total freedom in changing local Canadian and Toronto references to specific places and institutions in your own town or city. Here is a glossary of some of these Toronto terms, from the 1980s, that will help the creative director to transpose the local terms:

Church and Wellesley—The core of the gay community. Church Street is Toronto's "Castro" or "Christopher Street."

The Body Politic—Toronto's gay and lesbian newspaper.

Rites—Toronto's politically correct lesbian and gay newspaper.

Wellesley Fitness—The local gym where *all* the fags hang out.

Queen's Dairy—Greasy spoon where drag queen hookers have breakfast and fags bring their tricks the morning after.

Cornelius—Premiere drag club in the city.

Chaps—Premiere butch/preppie bar in the city.

ACT ONE

In the black we hear a musical chord, then a taped VOICE speaks in the dark. The voice is very deep, male and authoritative.

VOICE: Scorned by home, church, family, and their best friends, they lived by the skin of their spike heels, they were—

Lights up on the drag queens in poses.

ALL: DRAG QUEENS ON TRIAL!

Blackout.

VOICE: Chosen outcasts by fate or by design, they fed on scraps of discarded desire. Unwanted, lonely, and more dangerous than you might imagine, they were—

Lights up, they pose.

ALL: DRAG QUEENS ON TRIAL!

Blackout.

VOICE: Poised on the precipice between immortality and irrelevance, they filed their nails until their fingers fell off. They were—

Lights up, they pose.

ALL: DRAG QUEENS ON TRIAL!

Blackout, pose again.

MARLENE: Painted.

JUDY: Tainted.

LANA: And, some say, nearly sainted.

MARLENE: Flaunted.

JUDY: Haunted.

LANA: And quite unnecessarily taunted.

MARLENE: Hated.

JUDY: Fated.

LANA: And rarely, rarely mated.

MARLENE: Sick.

JUDY: Chic.

LANA: And much too fond of dick.

ALL: They were—DRAG QUEENS ON TRIAL!

The three take various poses of pain and suffering and then groan one by one.

MARLENE: Ughghghghgh!

JUDY: Arghghghghgh!

LANA: Ahhhhhhhhhh!

Blackout.

VOICE: See ... maudlin denials of almost certain guilt.

MARLENE: *(on the stand)* I didn't do it. I promise you, I didn't do it. If I'm guilty please please let the good Lord above put a run in my stocking! *(looking down at her stocking she screams in pain)* AHHHHH!

Blackout.

VOICE: See ... careless confessions of brazen behaviour.

JUDY: *(on the stand)* Alright ... so I did let him buy me a Coke. What of it? That doesn't mean anything does it? A girl has a right to let a boy buy her a coke doesn't she? It doesn't make her a tramp does it? Well, does it? *(She looks around, paranoid.)* Well?

Blackout.

VOICE: See ... unexpected breakdowns in which the truth is finally told.

LANA: Alright yes, I did it, I killed him. But I didn't mean to. Besides, he treated me like a human turd. Everything I did was inadequate, wrong, double plus ungood. The lovemaking, the cooking, yes even the cocktail parties. It seemed I could do nothing right, and finally it all got too much for me and ... the doors did it ... it wasn't me *(She goes crazy.)* it was the doors, they killed him not me—the doors! *(She screams.)* The electric seeing eye doors! *(She breaks down.)* ARGGGHGHGHGHGH!

ALL: DRAG QUEENS ON TRIAL!

Blackout. Voice in the dark.

VOICE: In the tenuous existence, the tortured life-term of a drag queen, there are many trials. But perhaps the most arduous trial of all, and indeed the most important, is the premiere trial of the day, that is, getting out of bed and facing the morning ahead. Many a drag queen has faltered, nay died, while enduring this strenuous ordeal, fraught with dangers. And here, for the first time, live on stage, we allow you to witness this heroic act. Ladies and gentlemen, three drag queens, getting up in the morning and confronting their own faces in the dreaded bathroom mirror.

The sound of three alarm clocks ringing. Lights up on the three drag queens, each in their own beds. They are all wearing sleeping masks. They reach out to find the clocks and turn off the alarm. The overture to Tannhauser *begins. They spend the beginning of the overture—the horn section—sitting up in bed, taking off their sleeping masks, and pulling on robes. When the strings begin, they start crawling along the floor towards their mirrors. Then the strings and horns join triumphantly, and they are finally at their mirrors. When they face their own images, they turn away with cries of horror. They spend most of the triumphal march brushing teeth and wiping faces, mouthwash, etc. The music fades. They are ready for makeup and costumes. But first all three get up and sing.*

ALL: Forget your troubles come on get happy
You've got to chase all your cares away
Sing hallelujah come on get happy
Get ready for the judgement day

They tap dance, taps having been glued to their spike heels. Their high heels are permanently attached to their feet and are skin colour, thus looking like extensions of their legs. After this song, quite an ordeal, they collapse, tired, annoyed and bored, into their chairs and begin putting on their makeup and costumes for the first trial scene. It's just three girls here, "shooting the shit."

MARLENE: So, do you girls want to hear about last night or what?

LANA/JUDY: Yes!

MARLENE: Well I was mortified, I almost wet my pants I was so pissed off—

JUDY: What what what what what.

MARLENE: Well it was Chaps, right?

JUDY: I told you not to go to Chaps. They're prejudiced.

MARLENE: But that's just the point, I don't care.

LANA: What happened.

MARLENE: Well he wouldn't let me in.

JUDY: Oh my God!

LANA: Which one was this.

MARLENE: The little beefy one with the tattoos for days.

JUDY: Oh you mean Frank.

MARLENE: I don't know what his fucking name is.

LANA: Yes, Frank.

JUDY: Oh God, he is so cute.

LANA: He is not cute.

JUDY: I would die to make it with him.

LANA: He is a pig, Judy, and if I ever see you go anywhere near him in a sexual way I will cut your balls off and use them for earrings.

JUDY: I've seen you flirt with him.

LANA: Only in my tragic past. So what happened?

MARLENE: Well, first of all, I was wearing the white sweater, with the tight black skirt—I mean I looked positively business-like and I had spent about two hours on my makeup and hair—well I looked fantastic—

LANA: We'll take your word for it—

MARLENE: Lana.

LANA: What?

MARLENE: What do you mean by that?

LANA: I mean, we'll take your word for it you looked like Jessica Lange, darling, so get on with the story.

MARLENE: Well, whether or not my outfit was perfect has a direct bearing on the outcome of my little moral tale if you don't mind.

LANA: I don't. (turning) Do you have any real red, Judy?

JUDY: Red what?

LANA: Lipstick.

JUDY: I have jungle red.

LANA: Sounds great.

JUDY: I think maybe it's fluorescent.

LANA: Are you kidding?

JUDY: No.

LANA: Let me see.

MARLENE: Is anybody listening, does anybody care?

JUDY: I'm listening. I care.

LANA: (looking at the lipstick) Where did you get this lipstick?

JUDY: At a second-hand store on Queen Street.

MARLENE: You guys. I am like talking about the most important thing to happen to me since I decided not to have a sex change practically and all you guys can talk about is jungle red—

LANA: This stuff is lethal.

JUDY: What?

LANA: This lipstick is filled with radiation.

MARLENE: Oh come on, what are you—

LANA: No honey, really look, come here ... (as they gather round) It says on the label that this lipstick contains radium. Judy, if you're putting this gunk on your mouth it's equivalent to eating nuclear waste.

JUDY: The guy told me it was like antique lipstick. And that it was made in the Fifties. And it cost me twenty dollars.

LANA: Are you serious?

JUDY: Yes.

MARLENE: Let me see that. (pause) Oh my God, she's right.

LANA: (grabbing it) Of course I'm right. Judy, you don't need this. (raising her arm to throw it)

JUDY: (screaming) WAIT! WHAT ARE YOU DOING!

LANA: I'm saving your fucking life, darling, I'm getting rid of this lipstick for once and for all—

JUDY: But—WAIT!

LANA: What is it?

JUDY: That's jungle red, that's the reddest lipstick I've ever had!

LANA: You don't understand.

MARLENE: Here bitch. Let me explain. Judy, honey, you know—well you've heard of the Second World War, haven't you?

LANA: Oh God this is going to take hours.

MARLENE: Shut up, will you, I can communicate with her, if anybody can. Now you've heard of World War Two.

JUDY: Yea, but I don't—

MARLENE: Now you just shush yourself and listen. You know the big mushroom cloud that happens when they drop one of those atomic bombs?

JUDY: Yeah, I know.

MARLENE: Well the stuff that they put in those atomic bombs is the same stuff they put in this lipstick.

JUDY: Oh wow. (pause) It must be fantastic lipstick, eh?

LANA: (to MARLENE) Wonderful. You should work for the U.N. Give it to me. (grabbing it) Listen Judy, I'm throwing this fucking lipstick in the garbage because it will rot your mouth.

LANA throws it.

JUDY: Ahhh. (Pause; she stares out sadly.) I'll never get lipstick that red again.

LANA: People are starving in Africa and you're crying over shades of red.

MARLENE: Oh, leave her alone. You, who invented the word superficial, should talk.

LANA: You, who blows old men in alleys, should talk.

MARLENE: I only blew one old man and I was desperate and very drunk. And it wasn't in an alley. It was at the Club Baths.

LANA: I never cruise public thoroughfares. Never after one A.M.

MARLENE: Yeah, but you live in the toilets.

LANA: (suddenly turning into Joan Crawford in Mildred Pierce) Veda. I feel as if I'm seeing you for the first time, and you're cheap, and horrible!

MARLENE: (turning into Veda, horrified) You think just because you get a little bit of money, you can get a fancy hairdo and buy some expensive clothes and turn yourself into a lady, well you can't—you'll never be anything but a common frump …

LANA: (as if slapped) Ahh!

MARLENE: … whose father lived above a shop, and whose mother took in the washing—

LANA: Veda! Get out before I throw you out! Get out—before I kill you.

They hiss at each other.

JUDY: Are you guys going to stop arguing or not?

They look at each other.

LANA: She sure told us.

JUDY: Well I get tired of it, that's all. Marlene, finish your story.

MARLENE: Well, as I was saying before I was so rudely interrupted by this overly glamorous refugee from the peace movement—

LANA: Oh, fuck off, cunt—

MARLENE: I was refused admission to Chaps.

LANA: Listen bitch, haven't you figured out yet why you keep getting thrown out of bars?

MARLENE: I wasn't thrown out, I was refused admission.

LANA: La même chose. It has nothing to do with being in drag. I go to Chaps all the time in drag. It's because you're a rude bitchy cunt.

MARLENE: Fuck off, toilet queen.

LANA: Well, the truth hurts. I've heard you ordering your drinks. Marlene, at the bar (imitating MARLENE, putting on a truck driver voice): Could I have a gin and Sprite please—you call that a slice of lemon—I'm sorry dear, but that's not a full shot. (resuming her own voice) If I was a bartender I'd throw your drink in your face.

MARLENE: Lana, just because you're pushing forty and well hung doesn't mean you're talented. *(JUDY giggles.)* And Judy, you've been in more hotel rooms than the Bible. *(JUDY stops giggling.)*

VOICE: DRAG QUEENS ON TRIAL. Scene One.

LANA: Oh my God, I haven't got my hair combed.

JUDY: What am I going to use for lipstick?

MARLENE: Use blood, it's not nuclear.

LANA: Speak for yourself, I'm constantly aglow.

JUDY: Oh I look so awful, I hate this costume.

VOICE: I repeat. DRAG QUEENS ON TRIAL. Scene One.

MARLENE: Alright already, keep your nuts on.

LANA: Oh God, I can't find my beauty mark.

MARLENE: A beauty mark does not an Alexis Carrington Colby Dexter make.

LANA: Fuck off, Crystal, or else I'll induce another miscarriage.

MARLENE: *(as they find their places)* Let's go girls.

JUDY: Alright. I look ucky.

LANA: We all do, but that's our zany wacky charm. Go, girl.

They are set. The lights come up full on the court-room. It is a vast chamber of marble. The judge's podium is huge—twice normal size—as is the vast witness box. The courtroom should dwarf these pitiful specimens of humanity, the drag queens. The opening of Wagner's Tristan and Isolde—"Love Death." LANA plays the prosecuting attorney. JUDY plays the judge, and sits on the podium with the huge gavel. JUDY will play the surprise witness Anita Hrupki later in the scene. She also plays the clerk. MARLENE is on trial and stands, stoic, silent and arrogant, with her back to the audience.

Note: each drag queen playing the surprise witness later in each of the three trials should exit after she is finished playing the clerk or judge.

JUDY: *(as judge)* Toronto District Court #345 now in session. *(bangs gavel)* The court will now come to order.

LANA: The prosecution calls Marlene Delorme to the stand.

JUDY: *(as clerk)* Marlene Delorme. Marlene Delorme.

MARLENE turns. There is a look of defiance on her face. She is proud, and radiantly beautiful. She takes her place on the stand.

Marlene Delorme, do you swear to tell the whole truth and nothing but the truth, so help you God.

MARLENE: I do.

JUDY: *(as clerk)* Please be seated.

MARLENE: Thank you.

The clerk looks at her oddly. She looks at him oddly.

LANA: Marlene Delorme, you are accused of being a drag queen. How do you plead?

MARLENE: *(after a pause)* Not guilty.

There is a taped sound effect of reaction in the courtroom. MARLENE smiles perceptibly.

JUDY: *(as judge)* Silence in the courtroom. *(She bangs her gavel.)* You may proceed.

Pause.

LANA: Miss Delorme, may I call you miss?

MARLENE: Certainly.

LANA: Miss Delorme. You were born in 1960 in Winnipeg, Manitoba of natural parents?

MARLENE: That is true.

LANA: A simple yes or no will be sufficient. Now, Miss Delorme, can you tell me something about your childhood?

MARLENE: I had a depraved childhood.

LANA: Pardon me, but don't you mean deprived?

MARLENE: I mean … depraved.

LANA: Now Miss Delorme, in your own words, tell us something about your childhood in Winnipeg, Manitoba.

MARLENE: Well, at first, my childhood was much like that of any blonde-headed little boy. I played volleyball by the river near our thatched cottage with my chums, Mary, Ellen, and Louise.

I had a pink Harley motor scooter, and a pet frog named Desirée. Life was carefree then—there was school and the usual after-school circle jerks, evenings being consumed by my overwhelming, almost embarrassing passion for my long, red train. In the afternoons there were pot parties on the lawn, and my father would serve us schnapps and tell us dirty stories. He was French and German in extraction.

LANA: I see. A life not unlike that of many other immigrant Winnipeg children.

MARLENE: You could say that, yes.

LANA: I find your story almost too idyllic to believe.

MARLENE: Well that's your problem, isn't it?

LANA: I have no problems, Miss Delorme. It is you who have the "problems." That is why you are here today, on trial.

MARLENE: I don't agree.

LANA: That is irrelevant. *(pause)* Now, although your childhood was idyllic and, to quote you, much like that of any blonde-headed little boy, you made some fatal, ultimately tragic decisions in Winnipeg, did you not?

MARLENE: Why, I do not know to what you refer.

LANA: *(lashing out)* Perhaps I am referring to your decision to move to Toronto and become the rudest, most obnoxious drag queen in Eastern Canada?

MARLENE: I made no such conscious decision.

LANA: Well, if you made no such conscious decision, how do you explain the fact that you sit before us wearing breasts which are obviously not your own?

MARLENE: I hope you do not wish to imply that I stole these breasts. They are mine. I bought them.

LANA: *(leaning in for the kill)* Don't toy with me, Miss Delorme. If you made no such fatal decision how did you turn into this monster that we see before us?

MARLENE: *(clearing her throat)* I became the horrible monster, to which you refer, not because of any fatal decision of my own, but due to tragic

circumstances—in fact my own lethally accurate colour sense.

LANA: Colour sense?

MARLENE: Yes, you see, as a child, my mother would dress me up in, for instance, mauve shorts with a pink shirt and purple dicky, with perhaps blue accents in the socks and the usual white and black Oxfords and, of course, I would be forced to point out to her that her colour schemata was quite simply not going anywhere. Yes, perhaps pink with the mauve—though this is a trifle obvious, but the blue accents in the socks lead the eye to expect the wrong things and with the addition of the purple dickey, we have what must be quite simply termed a riot of colour. I refused to wear the outfit.

LANA: Was your mother outraged, then?

MARLENE: Outraged, no. Confused perhaps. But I base my not-guilty plea on what I consider to be my God-given traits—my colour sense and, of course, my passion for accessorizing, which was inherited from my grandmother who, not unlike Isadora Duncan, died when her scarf was caught in a pick-up truck door. But I am a drag queen, and proud of my inherited traits. Indeed, to die because a purse or a scarf were caught in the doorway of any vehicle, particularly one driven by a handsome and masculine sort of man, would be a suitable death, a death I would treasure.

LANA: I don't think I understand the term "suitable death."

MARLENE: But then again, you aren't a drag queen are you? Unless of course, you are hiding something from us!

Laughter in the courtroom.

LANA: *(caught off guard)* I do not know to what you refer.

From the back of the theatre JUDY suddenly enters. She is now Anita, MARLENE'S hairdresser from Winnipeg.

JUDY: Marlene Delorme!

MARLENE: *(reflex action)* What—I—

JUDY: Marlene Delorme—

MARLENE: Anita what are you— *(She stops, covers her mouth.)*

LANA: Marlene Delorme, do you know this woman?

MARLENE: No, I've never seen her before in my life.

JUDY: Don't try and lie, Bobby.

MARLENE: (going crazy) Bobby, she called me Bobby—

LANA: Miss Delorme, I think you are lying, I think you do, in fact, know this woman.

JUDY: You know me, admit it, you know me—

MARLENE: No, you are a complete stranger to me—

JUDY: You're lying, Bobby. At one time I was … I was little Bobby Fitch's hairdresser. And Marlene Delorme is really Bobby Fitch—

MARLENE: No, it's not true, I was never Bobby Fitch … it's not true, it's all vicious, pernicious lies.

LANA: Marlene Delorme (archly), if that is, in fact, your name, will you leave the stand?

MARLENE: (head held high) Yes.

LANA: Anita, will you take the stand?

JUDY: Yes, your prosecutor.

She sits, crosses legs, smiles at nonexistent judge.

LANA: Will you tell us your name please, and what has caused you to interrupt these proceedings?

JUDY: My name is Anita Hrupki. I interrupted these proceedings because I had an important truth to tell.

JUDY smiles at the nonexistent judge.

LANA: And what might that truth be?

JUDY: Well, you see, this silly Bobby Fitch is making up these lies about his background just so that he can get off scot free. But he is guilty of being a drag queen. (She smiles at the nonexistent judge again; this is all memorized.) The reason I say this is because this so-called Marlene Delorme was never the blonde-headed little boy she, sorry—he claims to be. In fact, he once had brown hair, and I was the first one to dye it. (to the judge) And I am sure there has been many a dye job since, your honour.

MARLENE: (rising suddenly) You vicious bitch! Who paid you? How much did they pay you? You can't even get your story straight.

LANA: Miss Delorme, please control yourself. It is only too obvious to the courtroom that the truth hurts. Continue, Miss Hrupki.

JUDY: Well, that is it, your honour. And Marlene Delorme is guilty of being a drag queen. Totally and completely guilty. Because she had her hair dyed blonde when she was thirteen. Through her own choice. And I did it.

LANA: And you have not been coached or paid any money to make this unexpected surprise confession.

JUDY: (very memorized) No your prosecutor. I have not been coached. (She looks at judge, smiles.) Not to my knowledge.

LANA: Thank you, Miss Hrupki. You may leave the stand.

JUDY: You're welcome.

She steps down and then stops to talk to the prosecutor. She slips her some money. She smiles at the judge and moves on. Pause. MARLENE is weeping. LANA looks at her.

LANA: Marlene Delorme, will you take the stand?

MARLENE: (wiping away the tears, dragging herself up) Yes.

As MARLENE walks to the stand, Wagner music and a VOICEOVER come up.

MARLENE: (voiceover) As I approached the stand, every nerve in my body quivering, I reviewed the accusations. They said I had lied, and I began to think about the lies, the years of lies, of living like a non-person in Winnipeg, of gazing up at the vast blue sky and feeling small, ever so small. Yes, my life had been lies, nothing but lies, but wasn't that the essence of being a drag queen? And wasn't the life of a drag queen somehow the lie that tells the truth? The words of Picasso and Norman Mailer swirled around in my head and then I finally decided, yes, I had to take the stand and finally tell the truth, the truth in all its bitterness, its violence, its sordid detail. I had entered that courtroom a proud Marlene Delorme, and whatever the outcome, I refused to leave it a cringing Bobby Fitch.

LANA: Now Miss Delorme, I am going to ask you again if that is your name, and I will remind you that you are under oath.

MARLENE: Yes, my name is Marlene Delorme, but I was born Bobby Fitch.

LANA: So your name is really Bobby Fitch.

MARLENE: No, it is really Marlene Delorme—

LANA: So you continue to lie—

MARLENE: *(passionately)* How can I make you understand? When a drag queen lies, she tells the truth. That is what defines a drag queen. Yes I was a boring little boy named Bobby Fitch, yes I lived in a horrid little house, not a thatched cottage, yes I had a pet frog, and his name wasn't Desirée—it was Fred, and my motor scooter wasn't pink, it was green like the motor scooters of other children. Yes, I made up those lies about my past, but only because my past could never be my past, because I am too fascinating and romantic a human being to have ever had a normal upbringing in Winnipeg.

LANA: I'm sorry, but in a court of law there is only truth and lies, and it seems obvious to me—

MARLENE: Don't talk to me about what is obvious. This may be a court of law but what about the court of the human heart. *(a murmur in the courtroom)* Let me tell you something. Yes, I admit I … *(pause)* I was born a brunette. But to quote Norman Mailer: "Any lady who chooses to be a blonde is truly a blonde."

LANA: I'm sorry, the testimony of Norman Mailer is not admissible in a court of law.

MARLENE: What is admissible? Just think for a minute. What was admissible for me, a little boy with dusty brown hair, for I had light-coloured roots, who was a blonde in his heart? Don't let anyone tell you anything else, blondes do have more fun, and I made a pact with myself as a child that I would live my life as a blonde, no matter how much money I had to spend on conditioner. Before you condemn me, before you condemn the other little drag queens in the world, I want you to think about me—to the world outside, a brunette yes, but born blonde, sitting in the living room of our two bedroom house in Winnipeg in the middle of a bitter Winnipeg winter, and it's two o'clock in the morning and I'm sitting in front of the TV with the sound turned down to nothing watching the signoff signal. And do you know why?

LANA: Well, I don't really feel it's relevant—

MARLENE: No, it isn't relevant to anyone, but it is to me, and all the other little drag queens in the world, because the last thing to appear on that screen was the Canadian national anthem and a collage about Canada, with pictures of The Royal Family, and The Prairies and The Rockies and finally what I had been waiting for, two ballet dancers. A woman, blonde, who I imagined myself to be, and a man with his buttocks almost naked, holding her. Imagine me, at seven years old waiting for the station to sign off, terrified that my father would find me, for this was the image that kept me alive, the image of those ballet dancers during the "O Canada" signoff, during those lonely, bitter Winnipeg years. Find me guilty if you wish, guilty of being true to myself, guilty of being true to my innermost instincts instead of repressing everything honest, alive and real that is inside of me, like the rest of the population of this cold puritanical sad grey country where people have forgotten how to experience real joy, where bars close at one o'clock and marijuana is illegal, where people feel guilty for touching one another, where the only real happiness seems to be getting together on Saturday night and watching a bunch of idiots get their heads bashed in, in a stupid and savage sport they call hockey!

Taped applause.

LANA: Well, Marlene, or Bobby, or whatever your name is, the fact remains that you have lied on this witness stand, and in a court of law. That is perjury. I cannot see how any jury, however impassioned your plea, could acquit a liar.

MARLENE: Unless of course, I have a jury of drag queens.

LANA: I rest the case for the moment. I call the second drag queen to the stand. Judy Goose.

The three drag queens break out of their characters and walk to their mirrors to start changing for the next courtroom drama.

MARLENE: So, anyway, when this guy told me he was not going to let me into Chaps I told him I was going to let him have it.

LANA: Marlene—how butch!

JUDY: So did you?

MARLENE: No, I chickened out. He has such big arms. So, anyway, I decided to lodge this formal letter of protest with *The Body Politic* and—

LANA: Marlene, darling, dearest.

MARLENE: Yes, Lana, lovelorn, lonely.

LANA: Are we to spend the whole evening being treated to boring stories of your tawdry melodramatic encounters with burly doormen?

MARLENE: Why, I suppose we don't really *have* to.

LANA: No?

MARLENE: No, I mean I suppose we could sit around and listen to your maudlin self-indulgent stories about the last man to beat you up in bed.

LANA: Oh Marlene, you're a card.

MARLENE: Oh Lana, you're a toilet queen.

LANA: I can't believe what a bitch you are. I tell you in confidence that I did, as a confused and effeminate young man, on occasion, cruise the toilets and you insist on torturing me about it for the rest of my life.

MARLENE: I guess what bothers me is every time I stand on the corner of Jarvis and Wellesley you insist on screeching at me at the top of your lungs—did you make any good tricks honey? One thing I have never been is a prostitute.

LANA: Well, my philosophy is men are going to abuse you anyway, so you might as well make them pay cold hard cash for doing it.

JUDY: I had this guy really abuse me last night.

MARLENE: *(suddenly interested)* You did?

LANA: Who was it.

JUDY: His name was Dirk.

MARLENE: Oh God. Dirk. I've never met a Dirk I didn't hate.

LANA: Not that waiter at Buddies.

JUDY: Yup.

LANA: Judy, he's luscious.

JUDY: I know. And he has the dick of death too.

LANA: Stomach muscles?

JUDY: For days.

MARLENE: Lana please. I cannot believe the superficiality of your remarks. The tone of this conversation is reaching gutter level. *(pause, to JUDY)* Did he fuck you?

JUDY: I wouldn't let him. You know. AIDS.

MARLENE: I know. I always make them wait until the second date before I let them fuck me. And then they have to use a condom—ribbed.

JUDY: Ohhhhhh. Condoms, I hate them.

MARLENE: But it is the only thing that saves you from AIDS, besides not fucking, and you can forget that.

LANA: Yes darling. It's one thing being fashionably self-destructive, but actually killing yourself and other people, well I draw the line there—

JUDY: But don't you have trouble getting them on?

MARLENE: No, and you can accessorize, see? *(pulling out a pack of Fiesta condoms)* They come in lovely different vibrant colours to go with your bracelets and lingerie. I am particularly fond of a black bra with black condoms. I think the accents go quite nicely with my new dark lashes—

LANA: So get to the punch line, dear. Did he hit you?

JUDY: No, nothing like that. But this guy, Dirk, he was really rude.

LANA: Hmmm. I don't know if really rude actually counts as abuse.

MARLENE: Well, if you haven't been abused for days, it kind of makes you feel warm and cuddly and alive inside again. So what did he say, dear.

JUDY: Well. When we were all done and, it took a while, it takes him a long time to come, and when he finally did and he was lying in bed, and I asked him if he wanted a drink or a coffee and he said, yes a drink.

MARLENE: How like a Dirk.

JUDY: So I went up to get him one but I was like naked, so I went to my closet to get a robe and I opened it up and there was all my stuff—

MARLENE: He saw the dresses—

LANA: The primal moment of a drag queen's existence. *(pause)* Was he shocked?

JUDY: Well, like at first he didn't get it, right, and he asked me if I had a roommate—

LANA: *(scoldingly)* Judy.

JUDY: What.

LANA: You didn't tell him you had a roommate.

JUDY: No. I was like really proud of myself, Lana, because I said no I don't have a roommate—those dresses are mine, and then, just like that, I said, "I am a drag queen," because you said it's better to say it yourself than have them say it, right? So I did.

LANA: I'm proud of you, dear. If there's one thing a drag queen should be honest about, it's that she's a liar. So what did he do.

JUDY: He started yelling at me.

LANA: What did he say.

JUDY: He started saying drag queens were the lowest of lows and that he'd never go out with a drag queen and wasn't I a man or what.

LANA: So you told him off, right?

JUDY: Well—

LANA: I told you—

MARLENE: Lana darling, give it a rest.

LANA: I will not give it a rest. She should have told him off. He maligned our race.

MARLENE: Lana, look, it's hopeless, drag queens will always be thought of as the lowest scum on the face of the earth and the best thing to do is just accept that salient fact. It's called going with the flow. It's very Zen.

LANA: We may have a lot of bad press. But that doesn't mean we have to take it lying down.

MARLENE: Your favorite position—

LANA: Judy listen to me—

MARLENE: Stop lecturing her. She doesn't have to confront everybody with the facts all the time—

LANA: Marlene, after what you said on the witness stand. I'm surprised at you.

MARLENE: I have my principles, but that doesn't mean I go around making a fool of myself in daily life.

LANA: Well I have my principles and I live them every day of my life—

MARLENE: Please Lana, don't start, I mean—

LANA: Don't …

She breaks into her own powerful rendition of "Don't Rain on My Parade" from Hello, Dolly.

MARLENE: *(interrupting her)* Oh God, Saint Babs again.

LANA: And you just wait Marlene Delorme, when it comes time for my trial, there will be no surprise witnesses.

MARLENE: You wanna bet?

VOICE: DRAG QUEENS ON TRIAL. Scene Two. Drag Queens on Trial.

JUDY: Oh shit.

MARLENE: It's all your fault, bitch.

LANA: What, cunt—

MARLENE: I've been so busy talking I haven't got my makeup straight.

JUDY: I'm really helpless without my jungle red.

LANA: *(to MARLENE)* Have you been using my cold cream?

MARLENE: No.

LANA: Then why is it all greasy?

MARLENE: Don't talk to me. You're the one with all the pores, darling.

VOICE: DRAG QUEENS ON TRIAL. Scene Two.

MARLENE: Alright already. Hold onto your tits. God, I hate that voice.

LANA: It sounds like Orson Welles. I always loved him, fat or no fat. It's talent that really counts in this world, thank God.

MARLENE: Let's go girls.

They enter the trial area again. This time JUDY is on trial, LANA is the judge, clerk and surprise witness, and MARLENE is prosecuting attorney.

LANA: *(as judge)* Toronto District Court #878 now in session. *(She bangs the gavel.)* The court will now come to order.

MARLENE: The prosecution calls Judy Goose to the stand.

LANA: *(as clerk)* Judy Goose. Judy Goose.

JUDY stands up and fixes her stockings. She is still the dumb, guileless, sweet and flirtatious girl she always is, only in this scene she has a Brooklyn accent and sounds a lot like Judy Holiday. She walks up to the witness stand.

LANA: Judy Goose, do you swear to tell the whole truth and nothing but the truth, so help you God.

JUDY: You bet.

LANA: *(as clerk)* Please be seated.

JUDY: Yeah.

LANA looks at JUDY oddly. She looks at LANA oddly.

MARLENE: Judy Goose you are accused of being a drag queen. How do you plead?

JUDY: Not guilty. With extenuating circumstances.

A murmur in the courtroom. JUDY looks around, confused.

JUDY: What's that?

LANA: *(as judge)* A murmur in the courtroom.

JUDY: Oh. I thought it was the pipes or something.

MARLENE: Now Miss Goose, I may call you miss?

JUDY: *(nonplussed)* Yeah.

MARLENE: Miss Goose, you said you are pleading guilty with extenuating circumstances.

JUDY: That's right.

MARLENE: And what might those extenuating circumstances be?

JUDY: *(as if by rote)* My tortured existence.

MARLENE: What?

JUDY: Are you deaf?

MARLENE: Pardon me, and what might that tortured existence be?

JUDY: *(starting off)* Well, in the sad and sorry tale of my bizarre hurly burly life story, I hardly know where to start. *(clearing her throat)* I was born many many years ago, 25 to be exact, on a remote sled in the Yukon.

MARLENE: Excuse me, you were born on a sled?

JUDY: *(looking at him as if he's crazy)* Yeah.

MARLENE: Somehow I find that hard to believe.

JUDY: *(a small laugh)* Ha ha. *(pause)* So?

MARLENE: *(annoyed)* Please continue.

JUDY: My father was a cruel and heartless monster who beat me. Repeatedly. Hince, there was little choice—

MARLENE: I'm sorry, what was that you said?

JUDY: Where?

MARLENE: Before "there was little choice".

JUDY: Hince?

MARLENE: Ah. You mean *hence.*

JUDY: Hence. Hence. Jeeze. Hence there was little choice but for me to escape. Thus I ran away to Switzerland. At the age of 17. At that tender age I was an innocent virgin unschooled in the ways of men. I found myself drinking alone on trains. A lot. And soon, unbeknownst to my own conscious mind, I had plunged myself into a snowdrift. I thought there was little hope then, lo and behold, someone found me. The next thing I knew, I woke up in a lovely bed with coopids—

MARLENE: With what?

JUDY: Coopids—you know, those little fat babies—coopids around my head. My benefactor was none other than Hans Von Friedenbatch, composer of "The Swedish Rhapsody." With care and love, he brought me back to life. Though he had many years seniority over me, he wanted to marry me. However, I could not do this, due to my past. Then—

MARLENE: Excuse me, Miss Goose.

JUDY: Yeah?

MARLENE: I'm afraid you have neglected to tell us very much about the tragic details of your past.

JUDY: What do you think I've been doing for the past ten minutes?

MARLENE: That's all well and good, but the only really vaguely tragic detail you have revealed is that you were born in the Yukon, on a sled.

JUDY: Well isn't that tragic enough for ya?

MARLENE: Well, really.

JUDY: Well, how would you like to be born on a sled?

MARLENE: I have to admit—

JUDY: Can I go on now?

MARLENE: Well, I'm just concerned that—

JUDY: Alright already. Jeeze. *(She straightens her skirt and smiles at the nonexistent judge.)* I will continue my story, your honour. So anyway, where was I—

MARLENE: You could not marry the composer of "The Swedish Rhapsody" due to your tragic past on a sled.

JUDY: Yeah, well something like that. So, I could not marry him, though in my heart I wanted to, therefore the only thing to do was run away to Switz— *(realizing she means)* Mexico. There I stayed for many years, dissipating. Until finally, in a drunken stupor I met a man who wanted to put me into a show. He was a big producer so I said, "Okay!" But in order to be in this show I'd have to wear a dress. Thus I became a sad and tragic drag queen due to the intenuating circumcisions of my existence. *(pause, then looking at the prosecuting attorney)* There. How's that?

She begins flirting with the nonexistent judge.

MARLENE: Miss Goose, ahh … Miss Goose, could I please have your attention?

JUDY: Yeah?

MARLENE: May I ask you—

JUDY: Sure.

MARLENE: How you can expect an intelligent adult person in possession of his or her sanity to believe your story.

JUDY: I don't know. That's your problem.

MARLENE: Well, first of all, that is not my problem Miss Goose, in fact it is very definitely your problem. It is patently obvious from your badly memorized little performance that your testimony is nothing but a bald-faced lie.

JUDY: Hey! *(to judge)* Can he say that? *(to MARLENE, noticing judge is gone)* Where's the judge? I was getting along real swell with him.

Suddenly the back door of the theatre is flung open.

LANA: *(from off, as Hermoine)* Judy Goose.

JUDY: What?

LANA: Judy Goose. Do you remember me?

JUDY: Hey what's that voice? Where's it coming from?

A woman appears at the back of the courtroom. She is Hermoine Rosemount, an ugly middle-aged woman, soberly dressed and wearing a parka.

LANA: It was my voice. I'm sorry to interrupt. My name is Hermoine Rosemount. I knew Miss Goose many years ago, before she was Miss Goose. I would like to say a few words.

MARLENE: Judy Goose, do you know this woman?

JUDY: Well I … I don't know, I might …

MARLENE: Hermoine Rosemount, will you take the stand.

JUDY: What about me?

MARLENE: We'll get back to you. But it does sound as if this testimony might be very relevant to your case.

JUDY: Well alright. But I don't understand.

MARLENE: Now, Miss Rosemount, please tell the court how long you have known Miss Goose.

LANA: I have known Miss Goose since she was five years old, and her name was Billy Bunt.

MARLENE: I see. Now was this Billy Bunt that you know, like Miss Goose, born on a sled in the Yukon?

LANA: Well as strange and fantastical as it may sound, he was. In fact being born on a sled is, oddly enough, the one detail of Billy's story that is actually true.

JUDY: What's she talking about, the tight-assed bitch, I've never seen her before in my life.

MARLENE: Miss Goose, you will shut up or kindly leave the courtroom.

JUDY: Fuck you. *(She sits down.)*

MARLENE: How did you come to know Billy Bunt?

LANA: Well, Billy's tale is a complex one, and quite tragic in its own way. During his formative years, his elementary school days, I was Billy's guidance counsellor. It's not easy being a guidance counsellor in Whitehorse. Children are children everywhere, of course, but these children always had special problems, and well, Billy's problems were the most special of all.

MARLENE: Is it true that Billy's father beat him?

LANA: No. I'm sorry. That is not true at all. Billy's father was a nice quiet kindly man, he used to manufacture sleds, and many a sunny day in Whitehorse would see little Billy pulled along gaily, as it were, by his father's gentle hand.

MARLENE: When did you first perceive that Billy was a problem child?

LANA: Well, his grade three teacher came to me quite concerned because she noticed, first of all, Billy refused to take off his clothes to undress for gym class. We were concerned of course that he thought he had some sort of physical deformity. We insisted to little Billy that he needn't worry about taking off his clothes with all the other little boys, because, after all, all little boys looked the same naked. Billy replied, I remember his intent little eyes gazing at us with almost righteous indignation, "All little boys," he solemnly scolded us, "do not look alike naked." *(pause)* It was then that we first knew that something was wrong.

MARLENE: So what did you do then?

LANA: Well, we put little Billy in a special class for exceptional children we call them, those that don't quite fit in with the others but are unique in their own way. Unfortunately, Billy didn't fit into that class either. In fact little Billy didn't fit into any class anywhere. It was then that Billy's descent into madness began.

MARLENE: What exactly do you mean by madness?

LANA: Well, in case you haven't noticed—Billy is mad. Not only is Billy a drag queen, living a lie, pretending to be a woman, but somewhere around grade three he went totally bonkers, and I do not use this term lightly.

JUDY: What's she talking about?

MARLENE: Please, Miss Goose.

JUDY: But I don't understand.

MARLENE: Please remain seated.

JUDY sits, obviously worried.

Please continue.

LANA: In grade three, Billy began watching Hercules cartoons. He began to identify dangerously with Newton, Hercules' weak and witty sidekick, so much so that he would go up to boys in class, usually the most handsome and strapping among them, and say "How's it going, Herc?"

MARLENE: I see, and did these delusions continue?

LANA: Most certainly. Now if you analyze closely Billy's little speech today, you will see that most of what he claims has happened to him, except the birth in the sled, all occurred to Lana Turner in the movie *Madame X*.

MARLENE: I see.

LANA: Yes, Billy, like many modern homosexuals, finds his life so depressing that he must find solace in trashy melodrama. Of course this is unhealthy, but for Billy it has become a fatal obsession. Billy believes, in fact, that he is Madame X. He believes that he was rescued from a snowdrift by the composer of "The Swedish Rhapsody," etc. What we have here, in fact, is the tragic end for the child who refused to adjust to normal life, and hides in fantasy. Billy is a misfit, and he has finally gone insane.

MARLENE: Is there any hope left for little Billy Bunt?

LANA: None whatsoever. He has descended into the maelstrom of schizophrenia and there is no turning back.

JUDY has started to cry softly in the corner.

MARLENE: Thank you, Miss Rosemount. It must have been difficult for you to come here and tell this sorry tale.

LANA: Yes, well it was. We guidance counsellors have our trials too, you know. But just so that one little child out there can be pulled from turning to drugs, excessive sex, or punk rock music, and become a useful, normal, productive member of society, for the sake of that misguided child for whom there is still some hope, unlike Billy, it is for he/she that I speak.

MARLENE: Thank you again, Miss Rosemount.

LANA: You're welcome.

LANA gets down and walks away, with her usual "martyr" stance. Pause. The prosecutor calls out.

MARLENE: Judy Goose, will you take the stand.

JUDY: *(strangely)* Yea?

MARLENE: I said, Judy Goose will you take the stand?

JUDY: *(weirdly)* Sure.

She gets up. Music. Voiceover, as she walks.

VOICEOVER: I was real screwed up. This stuck-up old lady said I was crazy. Could it be true? I didn't know for sure, that is, sometimes I sure didn't know what the hell I was thinking. For some reason, I felt real weak and I almost couldn't walk. When I did open my mouth, I didn't know what words were going to come out.

JUDY: Um I ummm ...

MARLENE: Miss Goose?

JUDY: *(a shadow of her former self)* Yeah?

MARLENE: What do you have to say now, in the light of the testimony of Miss Rosemount?

JUDY: Well I ... *(turning to the audience)* Gee, I don't know what to say. This lady says I'm crazy but *(starting to cry)* I'm not crazy, am I? I mean ever since I was a kid I've been different, not like the other kids but does that mean I'm crazy? I know I like old movies, but I didn't know that was a sickness and I know I like to dress up like a girl but it's really hard being like this, having these feelings ever since you're little and they're not the feelings everybody else has, but they're still your feelings and if you tell people you're afraid they'll just laugh at you and then you feel so alone, you just want to kill yourself and well if it's true that I'm crazy because I like old movies and I like to dress up as a girl well then maybe the best thing for me to do is kill myself, so I'll do it right now. *(taking out a gun)* Here—

MARLENE: Miss Goose—

JUDY: Here goes ...

She lifts up the gun. There is a struggle between the three for the gun, then the voice on tape interrupts just in time.

VOICE: DRAG QUEENS ON TRIAL.

Blackout. Music.

They lived so close to the edge they thought they might fall off.

ALL: *(in a pose)* DRAG QUEENS ON TRIAL.

Blackout.

VOICE: They batted their eyes until they bruised their lids, always praying for that special man to marry them and give them kids—

ALL: DRAG QUEENS ON TRIAL.

Blackout.

VOICE: What will happen? Will Judy Goose kill herself? Will Hermoine Rosemount ever have an orgasm? What do you drag queens think?

Lights up.

MARLENE: I think we need a break, darling.

LANA: Oh fuck yes.

MARLENE: Doing the prosecuting attorney is an absolutely thankless role, especially in that scene.

JUDY: And my mascara is running.

LANA: And trying to make myself ugly for that Hermoine role is a real trial since I have to squash my natural beauty and sexual *je ne sais quoi.*

MARLENE: I think we should have an intermission.

VOICE: Okay. INTERMISSION. DRAG QUEENS ON TRIAL.

Lights up, the drag queens are caught trying to get offstage.

MARLENE: Honey, put a lid on it, will ya?

LANA: Yeah, yeah, right. *(to audience)* Why don't you go out into the lobby for a Coke or a coffee and please don't come back for at least fifteen minutes, I have this incredible costume change which—

MARLENE: Yeah, someday she's going to suffocate in her own size D cups.

LANA: If I need any shit from you, Marlene, I'll squeeze your head.

VOICE: DRAG QUEENS ON TRIAL.

ALL: AGHGHGHGHGHGHGHGHGHGGH!

They scream, then sing cheerily.

Let's go out to the lobby
Let's go out to the lobby
Let's go out to the lobby

And have a cigarette, or a Coke, or a beer, or a joint!

ACT TWO

Lights come up on a forlorn LANA, who mouths the words to a tawdry rendition of "Black Coffee" sung by Peggy Lee, or some other suitably tacky number about a woman being abused by a man. When this is over, the lights come up on all three. The queens are at their mirrors again, chatting, getting ready for the final trial scene—LANA's.

MARLENE: Well, all I can say, Miss Lust, is that you are acting incredibly immature for a girl who's always carrying on like she's Miss Together.

LANA: Look who's talking.

MARLENE: *(to JUDY)* Have you got a cigarette?

JUDY: Yeah.

LANA: Well if I don't want to phone the doctor back it's my business, slut, not yours.

MARLENE: It's my business because I love you as only one slut can love another, even though I never take money as you do. We're at the bottom of this garbage heap and we have to stick together. Phone him.

JUDY: It's probably only herpes or something.

MARLENE: Only herpes. Herpes is like a major disease, Judy.

JUDY: It's just like warts, isn't it?

LANA: It's not like warts and for your information I already have herpes. *(pause)* Yes, don't look so shocked.

MARLENE: And you never told your sister? After all these years I've been sharing your lipstick?

LANA: You can only get it from licking open sores.

MARLENE: True, I only lick your open sores once a week or so, so I should be fine. Well, now that we know you're herpetic, I'd like my mouthwash back.

LANA: Oh stop being such a witch. So anyway, the reason I refuse to phone my doctor is because I already have every major disease. The only one left is death.

MARLENE: Pity, they haven't found a cure for that yet.

JUDY: Do we have to talk about this? I'm getting depressed.

MARLENE: That's just it, you dizzy doll, diseases are depressing, but that doesn't mean you shouldn't phone your doctor. Phone him back, or else.

LANA: I won't. The way I look at it is, if I'm going to die, I'm going to die.

MARLENE: Oh, that's a tremendously healthy attitude. You know what? I think you're suicidal.

LANA: Oh, not your psychological analysis please. Somebody gave me that *I'm Okay, You're Okay* book and I said, "Honey look, I think we'd get along a lot better if we both agreed we're two lousy hopeless fucked-up shits."

JUDY: What happened?

LANA: I guess the truth hurts. He never phoned back.

JUDY: Are there men who phone back?

LANA: Yes. They're called heterosexuals.

MARLENE: That also happens to be a pile of fresh smelly bullshit. I know a lot of straight women who—

LANA: Here she goes again—next thing you'll tell us is they don't know you're a man.

MARLENE: Some of them don't, anyway, and they all have as much trouble as we do with men.

LANA: Listen, bitch, the difference between straight men and gay men is this. Straight men make you pay for a movie and a dinner and then don't call you back, right?

JUDY: Yea, right.

LANA: But gay men make you pay for a movie and a dinner and then fuck you in the ass badly, spill poppers all over your finest gown, rip your nipples off with rusty tit clamps and then don't phone you back.

MARLENE: Straight women don't have it easier than us. It's men that are the problem.

LANA: It's men that gave me this disease. It's men that killed me.

MARLENE: You're really giving me a pain in the hemorrhoid, darling, You obviously want to die. Or else you'd go to the doctor and find out what's wrong.

JUDY: Why would Lana want to die?

MARLENE: Because she's a sad, not-too-great-looking, rapidly-aging drag queen who can't even get into her old dresses anymore.

LANA: At least my back isn't so mashed up with acne scars that I can't wear my low cut lamé.

MARLENE: You leave my acne scars out of this or I'll tell every bartender in town you're herpetic, and you won't be able to suck them off anymore to get a free drink.

LANA: Frigid bitch!

MARLENE: Cavernous cunt!

LANA: Size queen!

MARLENE: Dinge queen!

LANA: Rice Queen!

MARLENE: (à la Bette Davis in Whatever Happened to Baby Jane) The bird got out, here's your lunch.

LANA: Oh Jane, you wouldn't say these awful things to me if I wasn't in a wheelchair.

MARLENE: Butchya are Blanche! Ya are! (pause) And you are nothing but a ten-dollar-a-blowjob whore.

LANA: That is bullshit. I have never gotten less than twenty dollars for a blowjob in my life.

JUDY: (holding them back) Wait a minute—for two girls who are supposed to love each other so much, how come I always have to keep you from killing each other.

MARLENE: We have an open relationship. There's always room for hate.

LANA: Just give up and let me die.

MARLENE: I refuse to get involved anymore in this immature melodramatic discussion. Judy is right.

JUDY: Thanks.

MARLENE: If you don't want to call your doctor, fine. It's literally your funeral. And I won't be there.

VOICE: DRAG QUEENS ON TRIAL.

MARLENE: Fuck off.

LANA: Oh dry up.

JUDY: My eyelashes are not sticking. My nail polish isn't dry.

MARLENE: That asshole seems to scream at us earlier and earlier each time.

VOICE: I'm just following the script. I'm pre-recorded.

LANA: It's not his fault.

JUDY: Oh, I'm never going to remember all these lines. I hate this scene.

LANA: Well, if you get tongue-tied, I'll just ask myself a question.

VOICE: DRAG QUEENS ON TRIAL. Hurry up!

They go out.

ALL: Alright already, we're going—jeeze, give it a rest.

They take their places. LANA is on trial. JUDY is the prosecuting attorney. MARLENE is the judge, clerk and surprise witness, Dr. Dimchick.

MARLENE: (as judge) Toronto District Court number 5,768 now in session.

MARLENE bangs the gavel. LANA looks at the judge, annoyed.

The court will now come to order.

JUDY: The prosecution calls Lana Lust to the stand.

MARLENE: *(as clerk)* Lana Lust Lana Lust Lana Lust—

LANA: *(turning suddenly)* I heard you. *(She does a melodramatic toss of her head.)* Yes.

MARLENE: *(as clerk)* Lana Lust, do you swear to tell the whole truth and nothing but the truth, so help you God, or are you going to lie as usual.

LANA: I promise to tell the whole truth to the best of my knowledge for my simple yet passionate heart can allow me to do no less in the face of—

MARLENE: *(as clerk)* Please be seated.

LANA glares at clerk and sits. Pause.

JUDY: Lana Lust.

LANA: She is I.

JUDY: Lana Lust, you have been accused of being a drag queen. How do you plead.

LANA: I plead ... *(pause, for effect)* guilty.

A woman screams somewhere in the courtroom.

MARLENE: *(as judge)* Silence in the courtroom. Someone get that woman to a doctor.

The woman is dragged out. The judge bangs his gavel.

You may proceed.

JUDY: Miss Lust. I may call you miss?

LANA: It doesn't much matter what you call me now.

JUDY: A simple yes or no will be ... proficient.

LANA: Sufficient.

JUDY: That's what I said. Now, Miss Lust I want to ask you a few questions.

LANA: Whatever you wish.

JUDY: First of all *(consulting notes)*: You say ... that you are ... guilty of being a drag queen. Is that true?

LANA: I cannot say otherwise.

JUDY: And why are you guilty?

LANA: Being a drag queen is my life.

JUDY: And why is that?

LANA: Because ... I love to dress as a woman. I always have. It makes life thrilling for me, somehow. Who knows why? But for me, male clothing is boring, restrictive, impractical, it's a contradiction, isn't it—

JUDY: *(interrupting)* I see. *(pause)* Do you have sleazy sex with men in back alleys, toilets, steam baths and other dark and disgusting and dangerous places?

LANA: As often as humanly possible.

JUDY: I see. *(shuffling through papers)* You admit this?

LANA: Yes, I must. I am Lana Lust and ... I must.

JUDY: I see. *(pause)* Well ... *(finds paper)* Do you have sex for money, that is, are you a prostitute?

LANA: Yes.

JUDY: How often.

LANA: Whenever I run out of money.

JUDY: I see. And when is that?

LANA: Well I ... always seem to be running out of money.

JUDY: Well, Miss Lust, if you admit to these accusations, and you admit to being a drag queen, then it seems that you must be guilty, and there is no choice but for the jury to find you so—

LANA: Wait, I— *(She gets up, stops.)*

JUDY: What is it?

LANA: I want to say something, that is I ... *(sits)*

JUDY: Yes.

LANA: Well, it suddenly occurred to me, something about belonging, and well, I always think of Joan Crawford's words at the end of *A Woman's Face*. I want to have a home and children, she says, and I want to go to market and cheat the grocer and fight with the landlord. I want to belong to the human race. Ironically, I have always identified with—

MARLENE: Lana Lust.

LANA: *(gets up, crazed)* What's that—

JUDY: I think it's … the surprise witness, I can't remember her name.

LANA: Oh my God—

MARLENE: Lana Lust.

MARLENE enters as Dr. Dimchick. She resembles Margaret Hamilton, the Wicked Witch of the West in The Wizard of Oz, *and she wears a lab coat.*

Lana Lust, at last I have found you.

LANA: I don't know what she's talking about.

JUDY: Lana Lust, do you know this surprise witness?

LANA: No … no I've never seen her before in my life, that is, wait a minute, I think she might be my long lost sister, who often used to dress up as a doctor, but of course she's out of her mind.

MARLENE: Don't try and be funny, Miss Lust. I am not Miss Lust's crazed sister, though she would prefer you to believe that. No, we had her sister put in a home years ago. Now, thank God, we will be able to have Miss Lust herself put away forever, when my true and factual testimony is finally heard.

JUDY: Miss Lust, will you leave the stand?

LANA: No … I refuse, this woman is an imposter, a lying, cheating, deceiving imposter. She thinks that just by putting on a lab coat and a stethoscope she can become a doctor but it takes years of medical school … *(as MARLENE approaches)* No … no, stay away from me or I'll … *(taking out a gun)* I'll shoot!

A reaction in the courtroom.

JUDY: Miss Lust.

MARLENE: Don't worry. *(calmly walking up to LANA)* No weapon is dangerous enough to protect you from the brutal truth. Sit down right now, you depressing, self-defeating, unfortunately dressed, promiscuous slut.

LANA starts to cry and stumbles to her seat in tears. Pause. MARLENE deposits the gun in her pocket and sits down.

JUDY: Dr. Dimchick, how long have you known the defendant?

MARLENE: I have been Miss Lust's personal family physician since she was a tiny, effeminate child. Her name was Davey Dollop then.

JUDY: And what have you come to tell us today?

MARLENE: The simple facts. Miss Lust has been avoiding me, refusing to answer my calls. Well, I have finally caught up with her. The simple facts are these. Miss Lust has contracted the deadly disease, AIDS.

LANA: *(a strangled cry)* Ughggh.

MARLENE: I would give her only a few months to live. A few days, if she continues on in her present lifestyle. Her years of loose living, of flaunting authority, have finally caught up with her.

LANA: Ahhh!

MARLENE: Yes Miss Lust, there's no turning back now. You see, Miss Lust has always favoured promiscuous sex, in which she has been the passive partner. She has swallowed busloads of male sperm, as well as drugging herself into a semi-conscious state every evening in order to loosen her so-called inhibitions, though I firmly doubt that she ever had any in the first place. These activities, combined with the fact that she has been almost constantly under medication for some venereal disease or other, have caused her to contract this fatal illness. There is, in fact, no need to convict Miss Lust, for this human dogshit is going to perish anyway, and for all intents and purposes by her own hand. Like many modern homosexuals, Miss Lust has committed a form of suicide due to her promiscuous habits, and now she must pay the price.

JUDY: What you are saying is that Miss Lust is already just about dead.

MARLENE: That's the long and the short of it. I choose this phrase because it is a pun that Miss Lust, an infamous size queen, would easily understand.

JUDY: Thank you, Dr. Dimchick, your testimony has made many things clear.

MARLENE: You're welcome.

JUDY: You may leave the stand.

MARLENE: I will. I will leave Miss Lust's medical file as Exhibit A. *(She pulls out a chart which has an obviously plunging arrow on it with "DEATH" scrawled all over it.)* And your little dog too!

Pause. Only LANA's tears can be heard. Then the duet from Wagner's Tristan and Isolde *is heard, with LANA's voice on tape as she moves to the stand.*

LANA: *(voiceover)* So it was true. What I had suspected all along, that my filthy sexual habits had caused my downfall. It was a nightmare, almost too horrible to be real. For a moment, I was so lost and sad and alone that I felt I would collapse there in the courtroom and never recover my senses. I felt like ripping off my wig, my dress, all the symbols of my otherness, and giving myself up to what the doctor had predicted would soon be my almost certain death. Surely every drag queen, nay, every homosexual dreams this nightmare. The sadistic doctor with the facts, the brutal facts, the balance sheet where it says in cold, hard, computer printout—I was a passive partner in sex, as if all my passivity, all my femininity, all my womanliness which I always treasured was the essence of my disease, my heartbreak, my tragedy. I stood up, and looked around the courtroom, and then the strangest thing happened.

A spotlight picks out an attractive young man in the audience.

As I stood up, my eye happened to fall on an attractive boy in the audience. He couldn't have been more than twenty years old and there was something lovely and gentle about his fragile beauty. I sensed that he was confused in his sexual identity, that he was at that turning point in his life when he had to choose between becoming a normal, productive member of society or being a drag queen. Suddenly all my shame, all my terror shattered like glass. Yes, I was promiscuous. Yes, I was even a prostitute. Yes, I had swallowed busloads of sperm in my brief and eventful life span. Yes, I was condemned to death but for that boy, for that lovely confused gentle child, for his sake, I could not succumb to despair. I looked around me at the faces of the people who waited so eagerly for my response. And then slowly, tentatively, for I was sickly now, the physical pain seemed quite real, I began the torturous trek to the witness stand. I knew that all eyes were upon me and I held my head high. And then, somehow, thinking

of that lovely confused boy, there was a lightness to my feet, because I had a mission; after all, people would have to believe me now, for why would a drag queen, condemned to certain death, lie? What, after all, would I have to gain? Finally, I reached the witness stand and sat down proudly, defiantly, almost exultantly. I awaited the prosecutor's question. I would tell everyone. I would tell the world. I would be a saviour. I would triumph even over my own death.

JUDY: Now Miss Lust, I am going to ask you again, now that you have heard this damaging testimony from Dr. Dimchick, are you still proud of the deed which you in fact admit being guilty of, or have you repented.

LANA: *(weakly)* No.

JUDY: Pardon me?

LANA: I say … *(louder)* No.

JUDY: *(incredulous)* But how can you—

LANA: I say no, because that is the word I was born with on my lips, the word *no.* Since I was a tiny, yes effeminate, child, I have always known I was different. So have many others. Unlike those many others I did not choose the path of conformity, I chose to think for myself and live my own particular lifestyle according to my own particular lights. And if that is wrong, then I will pay for it.

JUDY: Miss Lust, how can you say that, when you have heard positive proof that your habits will lead to your own death?

LANA: Yes, it's strange, isn't it? I suppose I should be repentant, but I'm not. That is what we are like, those who do not live as others do—the different ones, those who do not surrender their minds and souls, their originality and spirituality to the multitude.

JUDY: Don't you think this is a trifle pretentious? Perhaps you forget that you have admitted that you are a common prostitute.

LANA: And who are you, who is anyone to judge? Yes I am a drag queen and yes I am dying of AIDS. Perhaps I have made choices many would not agree with but I followed my heart and did the best I could with my life. For, after all, I have vowed to live dangerously and it has not been an easy vow to take. The life of a homosexual is by nature dangerous. We have always been laughed at, derided, persecuted, hounded, arrested, beaten, maimed, killed— and why? Because we dared to be ourselves. Because we dared to live on the edge, to do those things that other people might be frightened to do, and so often secretly wish to do. Why do you think so many homosexuals have become famous writers, artists, crusaders— because a passion to dare to be different, to live dangerously is the most enthralling disease in the world. And it's catching. Because when you have the disease you experience no pain. Because the real pain, the real disease is not being true to what's inside, it's in being afraid to be afraid. I have not been afraid to look inside myself, to live on the edge of morality, society, of the world itself and if I must die for it, so be it. And to all the little boys out there who don't want to wear their little blue booties but pick out the pink ones, to all the little girls who would rather wear army boots than spike heels, to anyone who has ever challenged authority because they lived by their own lights I say don't turn back. Don't give up. It was worth it.

The courtroom bursts into spontaneous, taped, thunderous applause. LANA smiles humbly. Then the voice on tape.

VOICE: DRAG QUEENS ON TRIAL.

Blackout.

The address to you, the jury. First, the prosecuting attorney's speech.

Lights up. All three drag queens play prosecuting attorneys and address the audience.

JUDY: I ask you to

MARLENE: Think carefully.

LANA: Ladies and gentlemen of the jury.

JUDY: These pitiful scum

MARLENE: Who have arrived in court

LANA: Their skirts above their heads

JUDY: Their lecherous, disgusting,

MARLENE: Anti-morality

LANA: A shock to any decent

JUDY: God-fearing

MARLENE: Law-abiding

LANA: *Humane* being.

JUDY: All have admitted

MARLENE: Their crimes

LANA: In one way or another.

JUDY: There is nothing to do but

ALL: Convict them.

LANA: You have been asked here

JUDY: To decide

MARLENE: If these men are guilty

LANA: Of being drag queens.

JUDY: Undoubtedly

ALL: They are.

LANA: This leaves no recourse

JUDY: Than for you to call

MARLENE: For the stiffest sentence.

LANA: The gas chamber

MARLENE: Or dismemberment

JUDY: Might be appropriate.

LANA: Or perhaps the ancient method

MARLENE: From which the word *faggot* comes

ALL: Frying over burning wood

LANA: This too might be effective.

MARLENE: To protect your children, your families

JUDY: Your two-car garage

LANA: Your upwardly mobile lifestyle

MARLENE: And to protect you from your own

JUDY: Secrets

LANA: And unconfessed desires

MARLENE: We urge

ALL: THAT THEY BE BURNED AT THE STAKE!

Blackout.

VOICE: DRAG QUEENS ON TRIAL. The defense attorney's address.

JUDY: These young men are not

MARLENE: On trial

LANA: For being drag queens

JUDY: But rather for being themselves.

MARLENE: If they have erred in

LANA: Any way

JUDY: Perhaps it is society's fault

MARLENE: For making it so difficult

LANA: For the misfit

JUDY: To live.

MARLENE: Think

LANA: What would you do

JUDY: If your son

MARLENE: Or daughter

LANA: Turned out to be

ALL: A DRAG QUEEN!

Expressions of horror.

ALL: Ughghgh. Arghghgh. AHHHH!

JUDY: Remember

MARLENE: It is perhaps not a matter

LANA: Of choosing pink booties

JUDY: Over blue ones

MARLENE: For a drag queen is born

LANA: With pink booties in her heart.

JUDY: There was a long speech

MARLENE: I was going to make

LANA: But I can't now

JUDY: I have been too moved

MARLENE: By the final drag queen's

LANA: Simple words.

JUDY: Indeed

MARLENE: To condemn these men

LANA: Is to condemn everything

JUDY: Brave

MARLENE: Alive

LANA: And dangerous

ALL: IN OURSELVES.

Blackout. Lights up on the drag queens taking off their makeup.

MARLENE: I'm glad that's over.

JUDY: That final scene gives me the creeps.

LANA: How do you think I feel? I'm the one with the AIDS nightmares.

MARLENE: Well, it's all over now girls.

JUDY: Yeah.

LANA: Another day, another performance.

JUDY: Hey, I just thought of something.

LANA: What, girl—are you missing your jungle red, or what.

JUDY: We forgot about them.

MARLENE: Who, doll?

JUDY: The audience

They all look out.

ALL: Oh yeah.

MARLENE: Well, they're not our problem. They should be able to leave the theatre by themselves.

LANA: I'd like to help that one home, the cute boy that I spotlighted during my big moment.

MARLENE: *Très* tacky, bitch—

LANA: You should talk.

JUDY: Well, you know what I think?

LANA & MARLENE: No, girl.

JUDY: I think we should sing them a song.

MARLENE: What a great idea.

LANA: I like it. Listen, *(as they get up)* the point is, a drag queen always leaves you humming. You may get a lousy blowjob, or a bitchy dinner date, but a drag queen always leaves you tits up, humming a tune.

JUDY: What should we sing.

LANA & MARLENE: The only song we know.

ALL:
Forget your troubles come on get happy
You got to shake all your cares away
Sing hallelujah come on get happy
Get ready for the judgement day

END

WENDY LILL

(b. 1950)

In the mid-1970s Wendy Lill moved north from Toronto to work as a consultant for the Canadian Mental Health Association. Her job was to determine whether they should set up operation in Northern Ontario. She quit after six months. As she told interviewer Judith Rudakoff in *Fair Play*, "I concluded that there were already forty-four associations in Kenora trying to work with alcoholics and violence, none of them making much of a dent or doing much good in terms of the basic socio-economic problems. I didn't leave the organization in much glory." But she did leave with a profound sense of the harshness of northern Native life, and with an outline for a short story about a group of white outsiders whose work in the North brings them face to face with what seems to them its alien and intransigent problems. The story eventually became *The Occupation of Heather Rose*, a play about one young woman's harrowing journey into the heart of a darkness she reluctantly comes to acknowledge is her own.

Born in Vancouver, Lill grew up in London, Ontario, graduating from York University in 1972 with a B.A. in political science. After spending most of the decade working and occasionally writing in Toronto, she moved to Winnipeg in 1979 and began writing full-time for CBC radio, winning ACTRA awards for both the documentary *Who Is George Forest?* and the radio drama *Shorthanded* in 1981. Her first stage play, *On the Line* (1982), was produced by Winnipeg's Agassiz Theatre. Though more heavily rhetorical and politically one-sided than her subsequent plays, this sympathetic account of a strike by immigrant women garment workers in Winnipeg established the essential subject matter of Lill's dramatic world: the lives of women in crisis, isolated from mainstream society and its values.

With *The Fighting Days* (1983), Lill began a productive association with Winnipeg's Prairie Theatre Exchange and its artistic director, Kim McCaw. Another treatment of Manitoba history, the play deals with the women's suffrage movement in the early part of the century. But instead of the well-known Nellie McClung, its focus is the more obscure, more radical Francis Beynon, who opposed McClung's support of the Great War and her failure to champion the rights of foreign-born women. *The Fighting Days* has twice been revived in Winnipeg and had productions across Ontario and the prairies.

The Occupation of Heather Rose premiered at Prairie Theatre Exchange in 1986, directed by Kim McCaw. By that time Lill had moved to Dartmouth, Nova Scotia, where she still lives with her husband and two sons, although she remained for awhile, as Doug Smith wrote in 1989, "Winnipeg's most popular writer in non-residence." Her next play, *Memories of You* (1988), also opened at PTE. It examines Canadian writer Elizabeth Smart's life-long obsession with her lover, British poet George Barker, in a memory play in which the elderly Elizabeth conjures up her past in response to accusations of neglect by her adult daughter. Strongly influenced by Sharon Pollock's *Doc*, the play was directed by Pollock at Theatre New Brunswick, and performed in Ottawa, Halifax, Victoria and Toronto, where it received a Chalmers Award nomination, and in French translation in Montreal (as *Les Traverses du coeur*).

Sisters (1989) had its second production at PTE, but premiered in Parrsboro, Nova Scotia, commissioned by Ship's Company director Mary Vingoe, another important collaborator in Lill's theatrical career. A study of the Catholic nuns who ran a Native residential school, this memory play exposes the horrors of that system while at the same time attempting to understand the forces that (mis)shaped the white women charged with administering it. Like *The Occupation of Heather Rose*, *Sisters* does not bring any Native characters onstage nor attempt to tell the Natives' story. Lill did, however, dramatize Native experience directly in her screenplay *Ikwe*, part of the National Film Board series *Daughters of the Country*, about Métis women. *Ikwe* won a Golden Sheaf Award in 1986, and Lill's television adaptation of *Sisters* received a Gemini nomination as Best Performing

Arts Program in 1991. In 1993 *All Fall Down* premiered at Alberta Theatre Projects, earning a Governor General's Award nomination for its powerful portrayal of hysteria in a community where a female daycare worker is accused of sexual abuse.

Since moving to Nova Scotia, Lill has been writer-in-residence at Mulgrave Road Co-op (1984) and Neptune Theatre (1991), and co-founded the Eastern Front Theatre Company in Dartmouth in 1993. It produced *The Glace Bay Miners' Museum* (1995), Lill's dramatization of Sheldon Currie's story and novel best known in its film version, *Margaret's Museum*. Lill's memory-play treatment of love and loss in Cape Breton's hardscrabble coal mining community earned her a third Governor General's nomination and has proven one of her most popular plays. In 1997 Lill was elected NDP Member of Parliament for Dartmouth, and while sitting as an MP she wrote *Corker* (1998). Halifax's Neptune Theatre premiered this study of a neo-conservative provincial politician whose life is invaded by a mentally handicapped man.

The very first production of the Eastern Front Theatre Company was *The Occupation of Heather Rose* in the revised version printed here. This is a slightly expanded revision of the script originally published in the collection *NeWest Plays by Women*, and nominated for the Governor General's Award in 1987. The play has been produced across Canada, from Vancouver Island to the Yukon to Newfoundland, as well as in Copenhagen, Edinburgh and Düsseldorf.

Lill's two epigraphs capture the flavor of Heather's experience on the remote northern reserve: its *Alice in Wonderland* surreality and *Heart of Darkness* nightmarishness. But the historical source of those two texts, late-imperial Britain, also tells us something about the nature of Heather's confrontation with the North. Not only is she young, naive, and ill-trained to cope with the exigencies of northern/Native life, but she comes bearing all the characteristic attitudes of the imperial centre towards the alien, colonial margins. Her norms she presumes to be those of sanity and light—Canada Food Guides and fitness classes; their world is madness and darkness. Unable to impose her facile solutions on their complex problems, she opts for blame, guilt, and the temporary expediency of alcohol. But Heather resolves nothing and understands only a little. In the end her occupation has become a preoccupation, an obsession. Like Marlowe in *Heart of Darkness*, she feels compelled upon returning to "civilization" to tell others her story. (In the version of the script produced in Toronto in 1988, less effective, in my opinion, than this version, Heather tells her tale while still on the reserve, in the form of letters home to her sister.)

Heather's monologue is a confession, a warning, a lesson (complete with blackboard illustrations), an attempt to comprehend what she can't, and a plea for our understanding and forgiveness. She appeals to us in the audience to understand her, presumably, because she is one of us. And thus she implicates us in her guilt, ignorance and responsibility. The urgency of her narrative is reinforced by the directness of the monologue form, as is the poignancy of its message by her aloneness. She felt absolutely isolated by the physical environment of the North, and estranged from both the white and Native communities. On her return she feels equally alone. Her professional lifeline, the inept Miss Jackson, never does show up. And Heather has been through too much to go back to where or who she was. She's been bushed, been through "break up" (and breakdown), and in nine months away has experienced something akin to giving birth, though her offspring may be nothing more than monstrous disillusion.

Partly out of desperation, and partly to give material form and clarity to the jumble of memories and images she has carried away with her, Heather "occupies" other characters in her tale, giving them distinctive voices and, on stage, physical shape and gesture. We see how these people have literally gotten under her skin, and how she must exorcize them. But we also see the humour of that world on the other side of the looking glass, its caricatures and its absurdities. Like Billy Bishop, Heather wins us over by her ability to conjure these characters before our eyes. The comic and dramatic range demanded in the solo role, along with the virtuoso character work, makes Heather Rose one of the juiciest parts for an actress in the Canadian theatrical repertoire. Performers like

Laurel Paetz in Winnipeg and Tamsin Kelsey in Vancouver have created unforgettable Heathers, as well as the Lorraines and Ramsays who live inside her.

But in some ways the most vivid characters in the play are the ones whose presences Heather does not physically or vocally recreate because they so adamantly represent her failure. Camilla Loon and Naomi the Raven, her first patient and her last, haunt Heather. Naomi won't play either role in which Heather casts her: little sister or resurrection myth. Camilla's song of protest as she occupies Heather's nursing station—the only sound effect in the script—carries on under the horrific final scene. Initially wanting "to engulf them," Heather is in the end engulfed by them, consumed by her inability to bear the white woman's burden in the alien dark.

The Occupation of Heather Rose was first performed at Prairie Theatre Exchange in Winnipeg on February 27, 1986.

HEATHER ROSE   Laurel Paetz

Directed by Kim McCaw
Lighting Design by Larry Isacoff
Original Music by John McCulloch

THE OCCUPATION OF HEATHER ROSE

"What sort of people live about here?"

"In that direction," the cat said, "lives a Hatter and in that direction lives a March Hare. Visit either one you like. They're both mad."

Alice in Wonderland

"I went a little farther ... then still a little farther—till I had gone so far that I don't know how I'll ever get back."

Heart of Darkness

CHARACTERS

HEATHER ROSE, *who also plays*
  RAMSAY
  LORRAINE McCAIN
  MARY KWANDIBENS

SCENE

The mid-1980s. A classroom or training area in a government building, in a southern Canadian city.

HEATHER ROSE enters the room wearing a light jacket over a nurse's uniform, carrying a brown paper bag. There is a table and chair in the room, a blackboard, promotional posters for Northern Medical Services, Indian Affairs, Ministry of Natural Resources, Northern Affairs, etc. on the walls. HEATHER looks around at the posters, puts down her paper bag, and looks at her watch.

HEATHER ROSE: *(to herself)* I wonder if I still look the same. I asked her to meet me at nine o'clock. But I'm always early.

Oh, I'm not ready for this.

She turns toward the audience.

I have always been an optimistic cheery type of person. I take after ... both my parents on this score. On Saturday mornings, the three of us competed to see who could be the most bubbly, the most cheerful at the breakfast table.

That's probably why my sister left home so young. She just couldn't stand the pressure.

It began nine months ago. No, of course it didn't. It began long before that.

My mother had been a nurse in the slums of London. And my dad was a high school principal, the kind everyone visits years after with things like plastic ice cubes with bugs inside. Every Christmas, we had refugees from the International Centre sent over for turkey dinner.

So when I told my parents I was going to work on an Indian reserve, they were positively bubbly. I guess they thought I was ... following in their footsteps.

I remember that first day barrelling through space in that hollow hairspray can of a plane, the sound of a thousand mosquitoes approaching my pillow in the dark, the hard cold metal wing vibrating against my thigh, long pink and purple tubes of land forming then breaking off into water, then land, more water, more wing ... and in front of me, Ray, the pilot, lighting one Player's after another, blowing lazy circles of smoke back towards my waiting nostrils.

Did he know how sexy I thought he was?

"What's it like being king of the skies, Ray?" Carrying the Royal Mail and life-giving medicines, on the lookout for red handkerchiefs and downed planes and forest fires and horny ... living out one's dreams?

"You must really love your work, Ray. No speed limits, no parking tickets, no Sunday drivers." What a flirt.

"Who me? What brings me here? Oh, I've always been attracted to the North ... like a firefly to light. No ... never this far before. Mainly the Barrie area, but it's a lot like this. One-sided trees, fiery sunsets, loons ... You've heard of Camp Cocano?"

The bugger didn't answer me. Just laughed. And turned the nose of the plane down. Suddenly I was on the Salt and Pepper Shaker at the CNE, giggling and holding onto my pockets so my money wouldn't fall out!

I was going down, down, downward into another place, another time, falling through a rabbit hole into a green and silver world below. I was Alice in Wonderland. Shall I fall right through the earth? Splashing into a shower of diamonds and purple morning mist and water ... bobbing up and down in a plane which had miraculously become a boat.

"No Ray, I didn't mind. Rough? Was that rough? Hey! I love *rough*. Excitement, danger. Makes me feel like I've really arrived! Really alive!"

And I had.

Arrived.

Nurse Rose had arrived. The metal door swung open and the sun blasted in. And there below me, on the dock, was a sea of brown faces all looking up at me, in my slingback pumps and my seer-sucker dress. What made me suddenly feel that my heart would fall out, that I would die on the spot? And also, that I was ... the Queen?

HEATHER gives a regal smile, even a wave.

But not for long.

"Holy Jesus Mary ... what the hell have we got here?"

He stood there inspecting me like a catfish just hauled in off the bottom. Then he laughed ... no, he snorted at me.

"Name's Ramsay, Miss Rose. The local freetrader, skirtchaser, swindler, philosopher and long-term survivor. Welcome to Snake Lake."

Suddenly back in the present, HEATHER looks at her watch, then towards the door. She seems agitated, uncomfortable, then retreats back into her recollections.

The nursing station. It had such a nice ring to it, I thought. The nursing station. Where the nurse was stationed. Where she was present and waiting for people in distress. In need of help. The first thing I did was unpack Mother and Grandmother. I mean their pictures! I set them up on the arborite desk with their nursing caps and serene smiles to guide me in my work at Snake Lake. Then I began to plow through Nurse Bunny's eight months of medical records. I've brought back a couple of entries to show Miss Jackson.

She takes some rumpled papers from the bag and reads.

"March 10. Jobit Loon died of a shaking fit. Out on his trapline with a beaver in his mitt. And no toque on. The day was dark when they brought him in, his skin grey, his wife watching. Her eyes a long way away."

That's quite poetic I think.

She holds up the paper. Then a sketch of a broken snowshoe.

Bunny did a lot of things like that. Sketches, cartoons. And cigarette burns. Bunny was a chain smoker. And this. *(reads another)*

"March 15. Moonias Turtle died of exposure. Frozen stiff like a chicken you take out of the freezer." Imagine someone even thinking a thing like that? But Bunny did. Then this one.

"May 15. Entire bottom end of reserve has diarrhea. Toilet backed up. Closed early." *(laughs)* That one always killed me! Entire bottom end ... toilet backed up ...

Then a series of "closed earlys." Translation: "Hung over." But I only learned that later. Once Miss Jackson gets a better picture of the place ...

HEATHER turns and sticks the pages up on the bulletin board. Then she turns back to the audience, looking nervous.

I don't really drink. *(not completely convincing)* But Nurse Bunny did.

Lorraine McCain, one of the Snake Lake teachers, came by ten minutes after I arrived at my trailer with a bottle of scotch and a bag of chocolate chip cookies ... "just to welcome the latest lamb to the slaughter." Immediately started telling tales out of school about Bunny—about what a *good head* she was, and about how they'd had to take two cartons of Jack Daniels empties out of our trailer after she left. I'd been told that Snake Lake was a *dry* reserve and I thought that meant *dry*. No alcohol. When I mentioned that to Lorraine, she just gave me sort of a fishy look, said I could be as dry as I wanted, or as wet.

(friendly) "Would you like some herbal tea? I've got Spicy Apple, Morning Thunder, and Sleepy Time somewhere in my suitcases, if I can find it ... " I really said that. Yeah, I did.

"Never touch the stuff," she said. Tugged down her bra, hauled herself up off the chesterfield. Said she'd better let me get some sleepy time myself. And then was out the door ... with the bottle of scotch.

Rough and tough Lorraine. What a character. But I felt sort of rough and tough myself. Gutsy. Ready for anything. I unpacked, got my posters up on the wall, toothbrush in the little holder in the bathroom, shoes lined up in the closet. Uniform pressed and ready for the morning. My Indian Affairs parka was waiting for me in the closet—all downfilled, the hood trimmed with animal fur. When I put it on I felt like I was inside the stomach of a wolf or a bear. I remember I wandered from room to room, touching everything, and when I caught sight of myself in the bedroom mirror, I couldn't help smiling. No ... grinning! It was like "Hey, look at me. I've really done it! I'm *here*! In the middle of an adventure."

And then it was night. Black night. There were no street lights. No big blue neon "H" from the hospital bathing my room with light 'til I closed it out with sleep. No strains of Tina Turner coming through the flimsy residence walls. A gentle autumn breeze stirring the pines outside ... sh-h-h-h-h ... the drip drop drip drop of the nylons I'd hung to dry in the shower stall. Were there animals out there in the darkness? Bears, wolves, moose? Were there Indians out there? My patients? Was there a world outside in the shadows waiting for me? Of course there was. But what was more important right then was what was going on *inside* me! I've heard women describe a feeling that comes over them right after giving birth. Sort of a humming. That's how I felt that first night lying in the dark. Kind of a humming.

Big sigh. She looks at her watch and paces, clearly agitated.

I think it's really shitty to keep people waiting. I flew eight hundred miles to be here this morning and I'm ten minutes early. Miss Jackson just lives a couple of blocks away. And she's already ten minutes late. I guess she wants to keep me waiting. Well, I'm used to it. I probably won't be able to really talk to her anyway. I tried on the phone one time but she wasn't "amused." Might as well have been talking to a brick wall, or a wooden ...

HEATHER goes over to the blackboard and writes the word INDIANS.

Indians.

One night in the middle of winter I wrote that word four hundred times on my dining room tablecloth.

My first patient was Camilla Loon. She arrived with Mary Kwandibens, the nurse's aide. Mary and her beautiful daughter Naomi. Camilla and Naomi. My first patient and my last.

Camilla's face was like a worn old leather purse without the coins. And when she opened her mouth, soft little noises came out, like coos from a dove. Her wooden leg was hurting her.

"Well no wonder Mrs. Loon. I've never seen such an old prosthesis! We'll have to get you fitted for a new one, and while we're at it, how about a new set of false teeth."

HEATHER looks pleased with herself, competent. Then she looks behind her.

"What is she looking at, Mary? Does she understand what I'm saying?"

At orientation, Miss Jackson told us Indians don't look you in the eye. And it's true. She was at least right about that. Camilla Loon looked at the top button of my uniform as if it had some mysterious power over her. And Mary K. looked at my feet when I tried to shake hands with her. But that didn't bother me 'cause it gave me a chance to study them.

Mary and Naomi Kwandibens for God's sake. Loon. Moonias. Atlookan. Quill. Makoop. Names that hold laughter one bubble below the surface. Names out of the blue, out of the any old where ... soft, velvety names like their eyes. Which don't look into yours.

Indians.

Mary Kwandibens is very fat. Her skin is very brown and there is so much of it. And when she laughs, her whole body jiggles and she was laughing a lot that day. So was Naomi. So was Camilla. She probably felt great about ordering up a new set of legs and teeth. They were eating their lunch at the diagnostic table while I kept on with old Bun's medical records. But really I was studying them.

All my life I'd wanted to have hair like Naomi's. Black and silky like a raven's. Not this dirty old mop. And other things too. I'd wanted to be dark, not fair. Straight, not curly. Enigmatic, mysterious, not an open book. It wasn't that I wanted to be an Indian, but I sure wouldn't have minded being a bit more complex.

As I watched Mary and Naomi and Camilla sitting there, I had this overwhelming urge to hug each one of them. To engulf them. As if some of the good things might rub off them onto me. And vice versa. I'd learn their customs and they'd learn mine. About my Scottish grandmother, my highland dancing lessons and Robbie Burns' poetry. And we'd all get on like a house afire. And when I caught Naomi's eye and she smiled, I remember thinking she was going to be just like my little sister.

"Move over, Naomi. How 'bout letting me try some of that bannock!"

I went to see the chief.

"This is a real honour, sir. Chief Red Sky. I've never met an Indian chief before. I guess I was expecting you to be … older. Kind of like Dan George.

"Where did you get those topaz rings? God, they're so beautiful! I love it here. It's … beautiful! The air smells so fresh, and the birds, and the wildflowers … "

(to the audience) He'd already heard about my order for artificial limbs and false teeth.

"Oh heavens, they'll show up. I ordered them through Northern Medical Services. They promised them within four to six weeks!"

Unlike most Indians, the chief had eyes that looked into yours, sort of drew you in then pushed you away again. Maybe that's why he got to be chief. Told me it was getting harder and harder to eat well and stay healthy at Snake Lake. That the fish were full of chemicals from the paper plant up the river, that the wild rice didn't grow since the government put in the hydro dam. And that it was hard to keep your kids clean when there wasn't enough money for proper sewage. And that …

HEATHER holds up her hand to interrupt.

"Hey! Excuse me, Chief! But I know all about the problems. (I learned it all at my orientation week.) I want to talk about solutions. I've been thinking about an exercise club for women to improve their self-image … women always need to improve their self-image. And a good food club to work on our eating habits now that fish and wild rice have been kind of blown out of the water. Ha ha. We'll draw up a list and get Mr. Ramsay to start stocking more nutritional foods … I mean I've taken a look at his store and … (gesture of dismissal) Cling peaches and red hots are all right, but a little goes a long way …

"And at orientation, I heard your alcohol and drug abuse committee has kind of lost direction. So I want to join that and add some life to it. *(big confident smile)*

"And as for the teenagers, well, they just don't have anything to do! When I was that age, I'd have gone crazy without camp. If we could get a drop-in centre happening at the high school—do some arts and crafts, show movies … *(listens)*

"I'm twenty-one, sir. I guess you're thinking that I'm kind of young and inexperienced. But I like to think I've got a fresh new outlook.

"Mr. Chief Red Sky, I know there are some really terrible problems here but … look at me! I managed to scrape through nursing school and I'm no Einstein! And I've been dieting for ten years so I wouldn't look like an elephant leaping about in my kilt at dancing competitions.

"Things can get better, can't they? Well, can't they?"

HEATHER walks around the room, musing over the experience in her mind. She goes to the blackboard and writes the word WHITES.

Whites.

That's a funny expression, isn't it?

Whites. 'Cause we're not really white, are we? We're sort of pink and beige. The whites at Snake Lake dress in Saturday-at-the-laundromat clothes seven days a week, and they march purposefully about, from store to community hall, to church, to canteen, to dock, to teacherage …

"Hiya Janie, how's by you!"

"How's she goin' Ray?"

"Takin' her easy are ya?"

Pushing the Indians off the roads as they barrel from place to place. And always visiting … no … checking on one another.

Lorraine lived in the teacherage, a pink town-house complex built, she said, to lure teachers to the North. Wall-to-wall carpets, central heating, glass doors on the shower, wrought iron bannisters, cathedral ceilings, but according to Lorraine, the units were cold in the winter and not bright enough. They needed skylights and more cupboard space, more this, more that ...

I would have sold my soul to the devil to live in one of those units. I'd hang spider plants and wandering jews from the ceiling, swish up and down the broadloomed staircase in my velour robe ... who needs skylights?

"You're gonna kill yourself and then what'll they do for a nurse?"

Lorraine was visiting with her cannister of gin gimlets, watching me puff my way through my Jane Fonda workout. Filling me in on the Snake Lake gossip. About the legendary teacher Annadora.

Apparently Annadora "did it" with anything that wore pants. Every Friday night, she'd make a batch of butter tarts, then bellow over to Ramsay to come help her eat them. By ten o'clock, they'd be riproaring drunk, full of tarts and chasing the cat up and down the redwood staircase.

Annadora laughed backwards like a donkey. And as the evening wore on, the sound of her laughter rose higher and higher so that it kept the whole reserve awake. You'd think that would have been enough of a reason to fire old Annadora, but in fact, what finally did her in was something else.

Annadora began inviting Indian boys over after school. That's when Joe Red Sky told Education Services that they didn't want Annadora teaching their children anymore. In fact, the Indians actually carried her down to the dock and shoved her on the plane. Goodbye Annadora.

Lorraine said she got "hooked" on brown meat, that Indian men were different than white men. That they smelled different, and that they had warm skin and that they were better in bed. I could tell she was trying to shock me, so I just kept doing my exercises all the harder, my face to the wall.

"Got a boyfriend, honey?" She actually called me honey!

"No, but I'm keeping myself in shape in the event that someone might come along."

(as LORRAINE) "You have to take what you can get here. I have a little thing going with a Mountie stationed at Sioux Falls. 'Bout Thursday I start praying for hunting accidents or drownings, so he'll fly in for the weekend to investigate. Rest of the time, I make do with Ray, the bootlegger. Keeps me in gin."

(as HEATHER) "Do you mean Ray, the pilot Ray?" None other. He was probably carrying booze that day I arrived, not antiseptic and the Royal Mail. So much for living out one's dreams.

Lorraine and her Mountie, Annadora and Ray, and then Ramsay. Ramsay! When I went to see Ramsay about stocking brown rice and fresh vegetables ...

(as RAMSAY) "Nice to see a new tail wagging around my humble emporium. I hear you're stuffing hygiene down their throats like there's no tomorrow."

"There's nothing wrong with good hygiene, Mr. Ramsay." You should try it yourself sometime, I wanted to say, but I didn't.

(as RAMSAY) "Guess not, but it's kind of hard to stay clean when there's shit floating up your water intake pipe."

Hold on, Heather. "I don't like talk like that, Mr. Ramsay. It sets a bad example. Surely even you know what to do when you have water with impurities. (Beat. HEATHER smiles.) You boil it."

(as RAMSAY) "You go fucking boil it!"

And then he came up really close to me. "Why don't we be ... friends? Hmmm? It's hard living on an Indian reserve. Your friends in the South forget you, your magazines never come. People hear every word you're saying on the radio tele-phone so you can't be intimate with someone a long way away. Everyone will talk about you, even laugh at you. It'll get to the point that you even think the ravens are laughing at you, and when that happens, come and see me. Old Ramse will give you a shot of stamina."

Thanks but no thanks. What were all those people doing at Snake Lake? Not exactly the type you'd invite home for Sunday dinner. Not exactly sparkling representatives of our culture. They were there because they didn't fit anywhere else. But they'd be the last to admit it.

Lorraine told me she didn't much like Indians 'cause they were a "broken people" but not to worry 'cause they didn't like us much either.

Well what's to like, I wanted to say. If all you're getting is leftovers, how do you know whether you'd enjoy the meal. I was determined not to be like them.

HEATHER writes the word CULTURE *on the blackboard.*

Culture.

At orientation, we spent a whole afternoon on culture. Miss Jackson told us that going from white to Indian culture was like going from your rumpus room into your fruit cellar.

She said that cultures were all about imagining. For example, she told us when Indians looked out on a lake, they imagined shaking tents and spirit visions and powwows and canoes filled with braves moving silently across the water, thunderbirds circling overhead …

Whereas when we look out on a lake, we see something different. When I looked out on Snake Lake, I imagined hundreds of bodies lying elbow to elbow on little sandy towels, sailboats and air mattresses bobbing, tiny voices emerging from sandy radios …

Culture.

Norma Redbird lived with her new baby, her parents, her brother, her wrinkled grandmother, and five assorted others in a white frame shack no bigger than my kitchen nook and living room combined.

Part of my culture was to feel uncomfortable about barging into other peoples' homes uninvited, but that was my job, so I swallowed hard and …

(cheery) "Hi, Norma! How's the new mom! I'm here to check you and the baby! What are you doing inside on a beautiful day like this? This is Indian summer. *(laughs)* I've heard about your winters that last from October to May. You and little Dolores should be outside getting some fresh air, some exercise while you still can!"

Watching *Let's Make A Deal* reruns is what they were doing, all of them, including the five-day-old infant.

HEATHER looks uncomfortable, smiles, shifts about.

"The baby looks good. Good colour. Alert. Curious. That's a cute top she's wearing. I think she could use some eyedrops. Why don't you bring her in this week and I'll give her a thorough checkup."

A huge piece of frozen meat thawing out in front of the TV; Monty Hall making jokes with two women from South Dakota dressed up as chickens; me in my nurse's uniform yacking away about cute tops and eye drops.

How did I feel? Like a spaceship which had landed in the middle of their living room, sending out little beeps.

"Spaceship Rose to earth … I've located the Indians … What am I supposed to do now?"

Focus on food. Highlight hygiene. Win them over. Make connections.

"Oh-h-h-h … it's so *dark* in here. I saw some calico at the store for two-fifty a yard … it would make nice curtains for those windows, and if you had some leftovers, you could make a tablecloth to cover up that oilcloth. Really brighten up the place. *(smiles nervously, fidgets)*

HEATHER pulls out some filecards from her brown bag.

"What are you having for dinner tonight? Oh … I'm not inviting myself. I just saw that piece of meat thawing on the floor. I've never *seen* such a large roast. It looks so *fresh*! Wild! But I'm trying to cut down on meat. Have you ever heard of cholesterol? It's very bad for us. Very. These are some suggestions to help us all be a little less meat-dependent. I'll just leave them here to help you with your meal planning."

HEATHER shudders, rips up her meal plans, tacks up the pieces on the bulletin board.

That day, at Norma Redbird's, was the first time I really began wondering about … a lot of things.

Someone was lying and I wasn't sure who.

Miss Jackson told us that part of Indian culture was close family ties, and that was why they lived in such cramped quarters. Bullshit. They were poor. They had no jobs. And nothing to do all day but watch reruns. And nothing to do tomorrow either. No prospects. I had never seen or tasted or smelled poverty before, and it scared me.

What did she know about Indians or family ties, or poverty or culture? All that shit about rumpus rooms and fruit cellars. And imagining. What were the Redbirds imagining—me standing there with my *Canada Food Guide* and sunburned nose, trying to out-shout two women dressed in chicken suits, telling them their house was dirty and their food disgusting. Who the hell did I think I was?

Saying someone has a different culture is just a polite way of saying they're *weird*. Not special, not privileged. Not exotic. Not mysterious at all. They're inferior. And therefore need to be helped. Translation: Altered. So much for culture! *(rips up* Canada Food Guides)

Distraught, pacing.

An Indian reserve is not a nine-to-five place. Nor a September-to-June place. It's a hanging-around place. I watched Naomi the Raven and her silent stalking friends in their bright satin jackets that said DEF LEPPARD and METALLICA, sauntering around the reserve in their Nikes and blue jeans, quiet; making long-legged circular treks along the dusty roads that went nowhere. They went in and out of school like casual visitors. They never carried books or pencil cases. Even though Naomi was in Grade 10, she could hardly read. Mary said she was getting into trouble. That she was a bad girl. "Oh Mary, who isn't *bad* at that age? Everyone wants to be bad!"

So bad! I did. But I wasn't. In fact, I was still trying to be bad six years later, but without success! Instead, I settled for gourmet dinners on Friday nights with Nancy Anderson, the gym teacher. My only *real* friend at Snake Lake. The first time I met her, she was jogging along the beach in sweatpants and a t-shirt that said HAVE AN INDIAN AFFAIR!

Nancy and I were kindred spirits. She was helping me with the women's fitness program, which after eight weeks of promotion still just brought out two women—Nancy and me. We were both on the alcohol and drug committee. Trying to get some action on the reserve's bootlegging problem. Apparently Ray flew the booze in and Ramsay sold it at any hour, and at any price. Both of us had written off the "white trash" at Snake Lake; and both of us were saving for trips to Europe. We talked for hours about Eurail-passes and adapters for hairdryers, and the Orient Express and running into Jean Paul Belmondo on the Champs Elysée. It passed the time. Summer was gone and the nights were getting longer and longer …

There was a cold mist on the lake in the mornings when I opened the station.

I felt kind of lonely, adrift …

She mimes picking up a phone.

"Hi Mom! Hi. I sound far away? Well I guess that's because I am! Ha ha. I sound *funny*? It must be the line. No. There is nothing wrong. No, I just called … to talk. To talk! *Talk.* You know … *talk.* I'm fine. Great. Oh yeah … lots of fun. Lots of buddies. Lots of fun. Tons. I said *tons*! No, it's just the line. It's a radio phone. That's why it's so fuzzy. Gloomy? No, I'm *not* gloomy! Great. Put him on. Hi Dad! No … it's just the line. Oh yeah. Cold … brrr … Frost in the air! How's Skippy?"

She hangs up the phone and begins pacing.

There was more than frost in the air.

Naomi the Raven and her friends stopped frequenting school altogether. There was a rash of vandalism on the reserve. Nancy Anderson had her tumbling mats slashed. She cried one whole evening in my trailer. Lorraine was happy. Her Mountie flew in two weekends in a row.

One night, there were gunshots outside my trailer. I lay in the dark waiting for the end. Hoping that it was a nightmare and I was going to wake up. But it wasn't a nightmare. It was the real thing. Someone shot out the windows of the Catholic church. It sat there like a scared, hapless, toothless face against the cold autumn sky. What kind of people shoot the windows out of churches? I was getting discouraged about our Indians. Things weren't working out. They still seemed so far away … yet their problems were so close! The drinking, the fights. I dreaded the weekends. The nights. The nightmares. I dreaded what I was going to see in the morning. I dreaded it all …

Except when the plane arrived. That little silver sliver of wing cutting through the clouds and it was magic every time. It became a day blessed with … possibility.

November 2nd. I remember because it was my birthday and I was at the dock waiting to get a present from my parents, waiting for my medical supplies, my order of teeth and legs … my *Chatelaine* magazine, maybe for the results from the water samples.

And there was a man framed in the doorway of Ray's plane. A white man. But he was really brown. I mean *tanned*. And he had the clearest robin's-egg blue eyes in the northern hemisphere.

I closed the nursing station an hour early so I could rush home and have a leisurely bubble bath. Wash my hair. The works. Put on my tweed slacks, my most clingy sweater. Then fashionably late, wandered over to the community hall where Mr. Blue Eyes was giving a talk about land claims. Why not? I was a member of the community. Sort of. Wasn't I? I was trying to make connections.

(flirtatious) "Hi! I'm Heather Rose. The resident Florence Nightingale! I had no idea that aboriginal rights and treaties could be so stimulating … so pressing … so … " *(sexy)* "Like I really feel the need now to probe even deeper. Why don't you come home with me and we can … "

No such luck. He was tied up all night with the Indians. Velvet-eyed Camilla in her red beret, tapping her cane on the floor, and dozens more weathered old souls, one after another talking about the good old days before the white man.

(growing realization) I'll be as honest as I can about this. All I wanted to do at that moment was to take that particular white man back to my trailer. Take off his clothes … and mine … and forget about Indians and land claims and hideous social conditions. But the hours ticked away. And my hair went limp. I felt embarrassed about my silly fantasies. That's all they were. Fantasies. There was no connection between the Romance of the North and my tired lonely existence as a Northern Nurse. I'd been tricked somehow. So like old Bun probably did a hundred times before me, I went home alone.

I've tried not to even think about Greek Night. Let alone talk about it.

Nancy and I cooked up *dolmathes* with cabbage instead of grape leaves, and pork *souvlaki*, and Greek salad without the *feta* cheese and black olives; wearing the Greekest things we owned; listening to Nana Mouskouri, planning our four hundredth trip to Europe. The candlelight glowed softly around the table, the music blocked out the endless wind outside. Suddenly, the door flew open and there was Lorraine's big shiny face leering at us through the candlelight. Bulgy, lurid Lorraine and gin-running Ray just come for a visit, just come to see how we were enjoying our *petite soirée*.

(as LORRAINE) "Got anything to drink besides this horse piss?" Meaning the fruit punch. "What kind of a nurse are you if you don't have any medication? You must have something! I mean, what do you do here every night if you're not drinking? The two of you. That's the sixty-four dollar question here at Snake. Play scrabble? Play with each other?"

Now why did they say that? Why did they even think that? Why did they have to destroy the only real comfort we had?

HEATHER is silent, reliving this painful memory, almost grieving.

Nancy left a week after that. Went back to Thunder Bay to work in a junior high school. Said she didn't like being away from her home and family. Said she missed her boyfriend. She left me all of her books including a cookbook called *Two Hundred Ways to Make Hamburger Sing.* Isn't that a funny title?

HEATHER looks vulnerable, almost in tears, suddenly trapped.

Oh, it's sweltering in here!

HEATHER starts to exit—stops. Pause.

I realize that I still haven't been very honest about this. It's all still a bit romanticized, polished up. I haven't got to the heart of this. And if I don't, you'll never understand …

Snow. Snow white.

Sometimes, during the winter, my fantasies weren't much different than my reality. I'd see a raven or I'd dream a raven … and each evoked the same aloneness, the same gaping separateness.

I'd see an Indian boy a mile out on the lake, walking towards me, a boy with a red toque and a fur parka, perfectly placed in the light between the sky and the world. Walking across the lake, across a bright white desert. His legs would move but he never seemed to get any closer ... or further away.

Mary Kwandibens told me—that was before she stopped talking to me—that winter was a time of holding on, that the soul went underground to lie like a woman long and straight upon a bed of ice, to sleep and be restored, to rise up new and refreshed in the spring like a young girl.

But that makes winter seem like a time of peace and it wasn't. It was a horrible onslaught.

One-thirty on a dark afternoon and Ramsay is down on his hands and knees working on his snowmobile.

(as RAMSAY) "Well, if it isn't Miss Nightingale. Relax, I won't eat you."

He got up and lurched towards me. The smell of scotch nearly knocked me out.

"Mr. Ramsay, your dog just bit Louis Loon as he was leaving your store."

He laughed. He seemed ... almost pleased to hear it.

(as RAMSAY) "Well, he must have been trying to steal something. Come here and let me have a look at you. What are you so nervous about, you're twitching like a little rabbit. Jesus, you've got a lousy bedside manner! How come? You're from the city, aren't ya? You're a sweet city woman ... like Annadora. She had a real gut on her from eating all those tarts ... It's hard to tell what you got under that parka."

"That's none of your business."

(as RAMSAY) "No? How come it isn't? How come you find it so easy to resist my offers? You've been here for three goddamned months ... What are you afraid of? That one of my dirty thoughts might seep into your lilywhite head? Hmmm? Or that one of them Indians is gonna sneak into your trailer and scalp you ... or even worse ... ?"

"Shut up! Shut up!" A strange hysterical voice echoing in my brain and I realize it is me screaming and crying. And then a door slams in the wind and he's gone, then a familiar voice.

Mary Kwandibens standing beside me with her big warm arm around me. It smells like soap.

(as MARY) "What's this ... you're a funny little mouse. You should cry! It's good to cry. You let everything build up inside you till you explode!"

Rocking me, soothing me ... Naomi watching me. Always watching.

(as MARY) "Here, let's cheer her up, eh. I'll read your cards. That'll cheer you up. (MARY turns the invisible cards.) Is Heather Rose the mouse ever going to get married?" Turn the card. "Hmmm ... maybe.
Who on earth will she marry?
Is she going to marry a soldier? No, not a soldier.
A sailor? No.
A tinker? No. What's a tinker?
A tailor? A lawyer? Definitely not!
An Indian chief? Maybe."

I close my eyes and I'm bouncing my rubber ball against the brick wall at school.

(as MARY) "Is Mary going to lose 80 pounds before breakup?" Turn the card. "Yes!"

Laughing like a big tongue licking me.

(as MARY) "Is there a storm gathering on the lake?"

Yes, and the wind never stops, and then the big warm arm, the smell of soap going away, taking her laughter away and a handful of chocolate bars.

(as MARY) "I'll take these over to Louis Loon to cheer him up. We'll charge them to Ramsay, eh? He won't miss them, he's already got too many, maybe that's his problem, maybe he's got chocolate bars in his pants instead of you know what." Naomi giggles. "Don't worry little mouse. We'll get someone to take care of the dog."

Then just as they leave, Naomi comes over and places an O'Henry bar in my hand. That's all she did. And then they were gone. But not the wind, the wind never stops.

HEATHER writes the word ALCOHOL on the board.

I do know something about alcohol. On New Year's Day, I joined with two of the teachers in a rum toddy, to welcome in a brand new year. If only I could describe how *good* it tasted. Hot, fiery, sensual, merry, hospitable. For the first time in my life I felt … witty!

"A little rum? Why not? To warm our cockles, wherever the hell they are!" *(laughs)*

Leslie Walters, the new gym teacher, arrived at the end of February. I beat Lorraine over to her trailer with my bottle of Bluenose. I desperately needed an audience.

"Oh, it's not a bad place, if you don't mind scraping ice from your bedroom window in the morning just to see out. *(laughs)*

"What d'you want to know? Heather Rose tells all. The church? The natives got restless and there was a big shootup one night. It really does look like hell, doesn't it? I guess everyone prays in private now … I'm not exactly a practising anything. The last thing I practised was the flute in grade ten. *(laughs)*

"Run into Ramsay yet? He's part of the landscape here like the garbage around his store. He's harmless unless you've got a heart and soul. What else do you want to know?

"The Indians? Hard to know what they're thinking. Blow hot and cold like the frigging winds. Pardon my French. They're a broken people. It is really sad, given how beautiful the land is up here and all but … like it's not an *ideal* reserve, eh, otherwise none of us would even be here, I guess that's how you gotta look at it. Hey! Don't look so glum! Lighten up! Want another drink? Don't mind if I do. Don't mind if I do. Don't mind if I do."

With difficulty, an admission.

After being witty, with Leslie Walters, or just with myself—I thought I was the best audience of all—I put a towel over the bathroom mirror. It made the mornings easier.

Indians.

I remember when I was small, Mom told us not to talk to any of the men who changed buses at the corner of our school. They were Indians. From Munsey Reserve who worked at the mill. I wonder if I'm prejudiced towards Indians because of that?

Our next door neighbours had a daughter named Donna who studied archaeology at UBC and married an Indian. I remember Donna's father

sitting in the back yard with my dad. I was under the picnic table. He was drinking a lot and he was crying. I remember him saying that digging bones with Donna was one thing, but he sure as hell didn't want one of them plugging her.

HEATHER smashes the table. Very agitated.

Where is Miss Jackson? This is just like it was up there. No one to tell things to. To help straighten things out. I needed help. I did! Heather Rose! I planned on talking to the fly-in shrink when he came to see the Snake Lake crazies, tell him about the drinking, how I was losing my temper in front of the patients, the missed days at work.

"Doctor Allen," I rehearsed this, "I'm finding the isolation here sort of … getting to me."

But after Mabel Turtle told him about her husband appearing in a vision and Albert Loon describing the animals running around inside his head, and all of us sitting on orange plastic chairs around the great white doctor, and the wind howling and the windows like teeth rattling and the room spinning, all I could do was excuse myself and run out of the room—just in time to get to the bathroom.

What did he know about those people? About spirits on Snake Lake, about visions, and animals running around inside your head and long nights and dark days and crying jags and ravens that laugh at you and freezeup and no mail and … what the hell did he know?

All those fucking high-paid whites coming through to help the Indians—not little me! Flying in and out, in and out, in and out, consulting on this, consulting on that, flashing their million dollar smiles, stalking about the reserve from plane to community hall, to band office, to plane, with their Indian friends, being helpful and advisory, then back in the air. Once a month old Blue Eyes came and went, his tan always the same. Perfect. Probably used a sun lamp. Hope he gets skin cancer. Probably played squash, told women in satin shorts about his latest junket to desolate Indian reserves … about what losers we all were … There was no help for me, except my rum toddies. Want another one? Don't mind if I do.

HEATHER sits down heavily.

Sometimes when I'd lie in bed at night, I'd think the wind was trying to crack the backbone of my trailer. I'd think it was trying to pull off the roof and I'd be sucked out across the lake dressed only in my nightgown, sucked into a whirl of wind and ice and laughter ... Annadora's laughter and the wind ...

I felt like a wild animal was running around inside my head. Or maybe a wild bird flying against ... Bang! Bang! ... bang ... *(slamming her hand against her forehead)* Trying to get out into the light ...

HEATHER seems to be reliving something painful. She is hearing Camilla's singing and rocking back and forth.

Oh this is hard.

The occupation of Heather Rose.

"Mary? Mary? What is Camilla doing here, Mary? Why is she singing like that? Mary?"

Something registered in Mary's big dark face but I didn't know what. She used to make me bannock in the mornings, but not anymore. Not after I yelled at her for leaving the station unlocked. It was only for half an hour, but I yelled at her, in front of her daughter Naomi, and called her a stupid ... Oh God!

"Mary! Answer me! I'm the nurse here. You're supposed to be helping me!"

Camilla Loon was holding a sit-in. An occupation. She was going to occupy the nursing station 'til her new leg and teeth arrived. She'd waited eight months and was tired of waiting. She was going to stay right there on that orange chair as a reminder. That she had been depending on me.

Jesus Christ, I was angry. That's right. Angry. Was it my fault that her new leg had gone to a bush camp by mistake and by the time it was shipped back, it wasn't fit for a moose to strap on? Or that the second leg got waterlogged sitting in a leaky warehouse. Or that the Department's policy was that they were only allowed new dentures every four years, so that they wouldn't be filling orders every time an Indian got drunk and dropped ... Hey! I didn't make the rules!

Was it my fault that the goddamned plane took the leg to the wrong place. That half the time, the plane couldn't land because of the wind ... that things got lost in snowstorms or landing strips or alcoholic blackouts; that pilots forgot shifts or their windshield wipers wouldn't work or they couldn't take off or didn't care enough to.

"So! You think you're going to *occupy* the nursing station. Well it is *my* nursing station. My orange chairs that you stick your Bazooka gum on. My tile floors that you spill your ice cream sandwiches on. I change the toilet paper in the washroom, scrub the waiting room at the end of the day after dozens of you sit with your big snowmobile boots and silent dark eyes waiting ... for service."

Well if I was going to service them they would have to take what I had to dish out.

"You know what really bothers me about you people? You expect me to stitch you up, give you pills, send you out to the hospitals, wipe your bloody noses and I have never once heard anyone say what you're supposed to say when someone does something *nice* for you.

"What do you say? You say 'Thank you!' To just once hear 'Thank you Miss Rose' would be music to my ears! But instead I get silence. Dark eyes. Secrets. Why is that?

"I never know what you're thinking. Never know what you really want from me. Should I stand on my hands, tell jokes, disappear? Are you glad, sad, mad when you see me? Do you like me, hate me, laugh at me, pity me, blame me?

"ANSWER ME!

"You know what I think you are? I think you're all snobs. Yes, SNOBS.

"You think you're the only ones with a goddamned history. Whenever I've tried to talk about my family ... about being Scottish ... things my grannie told me, little stories, or some beliefs ... whenever I've tried to share my life ... nobody shows any interest. Nobody gives a good goddamn about me!

"And you never bloody LOOK at me! Look at me! I know you watch me, but you won't look at me. And you talk about me, don't you? Don't you?

"You've been talking to your chief. He came to see me, said he'd heard about problems with the new nurse. NEW! That's a laugh! I feel about as

NEW as the frozen dog shit all around this place. You don't come right out and SAY things. You never let things really pour out like we do! We whites! You don't do that, do you? It's all indirect with you. Well, I'm tired of it. Tired of this goldfish bowl ... big brother, sister, aunt, uncle watching me ... judging me, as if I've done something wrong, as if I'm responsible for the pitiful states of your lives ... Jesus! When in fact I've had the charity and decency to try and help you. And I told your chief that. And I told him that I didn't want to see the next sad-eyed dark-skinned Indian coming through the door. That I wanted to see a smiling, bouncing, blonde-haired, lacy, pregnant white woman ... who would yack away about how her baby was kicking inside, and the little clothes she was buying.

"And you know what else I told him? I told him that if he didn't like the quality of my nursing care, he could kiss my ass! And that goes for the rest of you!"

HEATHER looks mad, then slowly changes to look shaken, sickened by what she's said.

I became attached to a particular label on a bottle of white rum, A perfect picture of a perfect ship on a perfect horizon.

What I especially liked was the way the sky kind of lit up the background. That's one of the redeeming graces about Snake Lake. In winter. The sky. And the ravens.

I spent two weeks drawing ravens. Ta hell with nursing.

HEATHER digs through the paper bag, brings out sketches of ravens and holds them up for people to see.

Black ink on thick white Medical Services paper ... white like the whiteness all around me.

Ramsay came by. Like a mongrel dog that's caught wind of a scent. Just for a visit, he said. Looked at me, at my bottle, then he laughed ... no, he snorted.

"That's not a fucking ship," he said, "that's an eye. The iris of a blue-eyed woman."

Took off his snowmobile suit. Then he asked me to sit on his lap. And he kissed me. Said he

brought me some stamina. And we ... partied. For two weeks.

I didn't go near the nursing station. For two weeks. Sick leave.

The onslaught.

Expansively, drunkenly.

The North has always fascinated me. Ever since I was very very young. Its wilderness. Its mystery.

She begins singing a camp song.

Land of the silver birch,
Home of the beaver,
Where still the mighty moose,
Wanders at will ...

She laughs.

"Who the hell is Will?" Ramsay'd say, and I'd laugh every time.

Blue lakes and rocky shores,
I will return once more,
Boom did ee ah ah ... boom did ee ah ah
Boom did ee ah ah ... boom!

And so it would go ... me telling him about our house on Highland Crescent with the grey shutters and the Queen Anne's lace on the trellis and the dance competitions at the Tam-o'-shanter and him telling me about eating lard sandwiches in Timmins. And then we'd flip on the *Edge of Night* and watch Mrs. Turner get leukemia and her husband get caught in a homosexual roundup of a subway men's room.

She gets to her feet.

"Wanna see me dance, Ramse?"

HEATHER attempts to dance the Highland Fling, but loses her balance, trips, and perhaps falls to the floor.

(to RAMSAY) "Don't laugh you ignorant pig. Colleen Stewart and I won the Junior Girls for that dance when we were fifteen. And my parents took us out for dinner after, too ... I can't remember the name of the place! How could I forget? That was the nicest restaurant I ever went to."

She phones Mom and Dad.

"Hi Mom? Hi. Yeah hi. Yeah it's me. Hi. Sure, get him on the extension. Why not? The more the merrier. Listen, the reason I called is 'cause I can't remember the name of the restaurant we went to after I won the Junior Girls. *(shouts)* Oh God! Of course! It was the Latin Quarter. *(to RAMSAY)* It was the Latin Quarter. *(to parents)* Yeah, I've got someone with me. Yeah … for dinner. *(to RAMSAY)* What time is it? *(laughs)* Is he male or female? I guess you could call him male! So what else? I got your postcard from Malaga and the castanets. Yeah, real cute. I said CUTE. Why the hell did you go to Malaga anyway? Why don't you stay where you belong. Right here in Canada. If you want to see colourful culture, you could come North for a weekend, see the Indians. They're poor, sick, unhappy, uneducated, fucked over … oops … sorry about that! Good photo opportunities. And I'm sure the storekeeper would honour all major credit cards. I sound like I've been drinking? *(laughs)* Yeah well I have. I've been drunk for two weeks. Because it's too insane here to stay sober. God you sound far away. I don't know when it started happening … but I've fallen apart. Completely apart. *(She listens; her face changes; her voice becomes more vulnerable.)* Well I'll try to. I know you do. I know. I love you too."

HEATHER turns to RAMSAY.

"Get out."

I had to get my ducks in a row. People have difficulties and then they rally. They get back on track. People think they'll never recover and then six months later, they can't even remember what they were upset about. They pull themselves together.

"Hold on Heather, get your ducks in a row." That's what Dad always said. I was bushed. That happens in the North in the winter. And six months later, I'd laugh about it.

I cleaned the trailer. I cleaned the walls. Cleaned the shower curtain. The kitchen drawers. Sewed the hems and all the lost buttons.

People throw themselves into work. Work is supposed to get people through the rough spots. It was all still there waiting for me. Camilla was still there, her eyes a long way away. And Mother and Grandmother. Still smiling at me. *(to photos)* I had such a steady diet of nurses. Clean, competent, responsible, healthy women. How did you manage? Who cared for you? Bandaged

you? Hold on Heather. And the wind still howling and ripping around outside the nursing station. And Annadora's laughter still inside my head. Hold on Heather. And the big cheese poster still on the wall and the t-bone steak, the wet lettuce … and a dozen messages from Miss Jackson like little pink petals all over the desk.

HEATHER *steels herself, then picks up the phone.*

"Hello, Miss Jackson? Hi. Heather Rose. Just fine. 110 percent! Just catching up on my paper work. I see you've been calling, but I've had the flu. A bug. Some kind of a bug. I'm all right now though, really. The chief called you? No, I'm all right really. I've got my ducks in a row. I was derailed temporarily but I'm back on track. *(shouts)* Jesus Christ! I said BACK ON TRACK! Why the hell can't they get decent telephones in the North.

"You what? You want me to come out? No. I'm not coming out. I'm staying right here. I have a job to do here and I'm going to do it. There is no question that these people need medical attention. No question at all. I have five vaccinations to do this week and there's always lots of business on the weekends. I don't care who you talked to. I won't. I can't. Go back to what? There's nothing for me to go back to. It's all distorted now, twisted … *(listens)* Who do you think you are? God? Parachuting little people hither and yon, then scooping them out again whenever you please. It makes them crazy.

"Fuck you, Miss Jackson. There's an old woman here with a wooden leg and I've got to make hot meals for her. There's an ancient Indian with a wooden leg occupying the nursing station and Nurse Rose is going to join her."

Crossfade. The sound of CAMILLA LOON singing.

Break up. The breaking up of winter—that winter that I thought would never end.

Break up.

That's what they call it when winter finally ends. Because the ice on the lake begins to break up like a hundred million ice cubes.

Outside, the sound of drums coming from the community hall. There was a powwow going on. A coming-through-winter festival.

HEATHER remembers the pulse of the music, tries to reproduce it. She listens to the music.

It wraps them up, their music. It puts a spell on them. But it drummed me out. It felt sad to be an outsider. So sad. I remembered lying in bed at home on Highland Crescent and hearing the garbage trucks grinding their garbage as they moved along the streets in the darkness. *(pause)*

Darkness everywhere. Dark except for the flashlights going back and forth, back and forth in the darkness … and the glow from the community hall.

When I looked out into that darkness there was a glare from the window and I looked … different. Looked like a photograph of me … only as an old woman.

HEATHER sighs and takes a plastic bag from her paper bag. She holds it up for the audience to see.

This is how they do it. Like this.

She demonstrates gasoline sniffing to the audience.

They brought Naomi in. Found her in the corner of the washroom at the community hall, stinking of gasoline. Yellow fluid all over her face. Her beautiful face. Wearing her red satin jacket, her mother behind, carrying her navy blue mitts.

CAMILLA's song continues under. HEATHER's face is transfixed as she remembers NAOMI's body being brought into the nursing station.

"Oh Naomi, what have you done? What have you gone and done?"

At orientation I'd learned all about this … but not the horror.

"Naomi, wake up! Say something if you can hear me. Talk! Look, your mother and Camilla are here! Talk!"

And I was shouting her name over and over and slapping her face.

"Naomi! Hey! *(claps hands)* Hey! it's good to talk. I always talk when I'm having troubles. That's what I do. Talk! Talk. Please, Naomi. Tell me what you did today before you … Hey!"

But she was floating in another world.

"Hey, what do you want to do when you grow up? When you finish school?"

She was drowning.

"Hey! You're in love, aren't you Naomi? With Clarence Loon. I know because I've seen you holding hands with him. Think of him. Live for him. For Clarence. Live for me. Please Naomi!"

But her eyes were closing.

"No! I demand you open your eyes. Damn it! Open them! Naomi. Hey! It's spring. Rise up! You're supposed to RISE UP! It's your legend. You're not allowed to die, Naomi. To give up. You can't do that. You've got to survive. We've got to survive. That's all that matters … "

Naomi's heart stopped.

HEATHER puts her head down and cries. She looks up at the audience, wearily.

Miss Jackson's not coming. But what did I think would happen here? That I would somehow be able to unload this. I can't. It's inside me now.

Camilla's artificial leg arrived on the same plane that I left on. But not her false teeth. And that's about it, I guess. The occupation of Heather Rose.

Lights go down on HEATHER.

END

A SELECTIVE BIBLIOGRAPHY OF SOURCE MATERIAL

I. Selected Websites

The CanDrama Home Page provides an index of all the most useful links and sites: www.unb.ca/web/english/candrama

John Ball and Richard Plant's *Bibliography of Theatre History in Canada: The Beginnings Through 1984*:
www.lib.unb.ca/Texts/Theatre/ Bib/Search

The Canadian Theatre Encyclopedia:
www. canadiantheatre.com

For recent reviews of Canadian plays in production: www.canoe.ca/TheatreReviews

II. Backgrounds, Surveys and General Studies

Anthony, Geraldine, ed. *Stage Voices: Twelve Canadian Playwrights Talk about Their Lives and Work*. Toronto: Doubleday, 1978.

Benson, Eugene, and L.W. Conolly. *English Canadian Theatre*. Toronto: Oxford Univ. Press, 1987.

———, eds. *The Oxford Companion to Canadian Theatre*. Toronto: Oxford Univ. Press, 1989.

Bessai, Diane. *Playwrights of Collective Creation*. Toronto: Simon & Pierre, 1992.

Boni, Franco, ed. *Rhubarb-o-rama! Plays and Playwrights from the Rhubarb! Festival*. Winnipeg: Blizzard, 1998.

Brask, Per, ed. *Contemporary Issues in Canadian Drama*. Winnipeg: Blizzard, 1995.

Brisset, Annie. *A Sociocritique of Translation: Theatre and Alterity in Quebec, 1968–1988*. Trans. Rosalind Gill and Roger Gannon. Toronto: Univ. of Toronto Press, 1996.

Brookes, Chris. *A Public Nuisance: A History of the Mummers Troupe*. St. John's: Institute of Social and Economic Research, Memorial Univ. of Newfoundland, 1988.

Canada on Stage: Canadian Theatre Review Yearbook. Ed. Don Rubin. Toronto: CTR Publications, 1974-88.

"Canadian Theatre Before the 60s." Special Issue. *Canadian Theatre Review* 5 (Winter 1975).

Canadian Writers Since 1960, 1st and 2nd ser. In *Dictionary of Literary Biography*. Ed. W.H.

New. Vols. 53 and 60. Detroit: Gale Research, 1986–87.

Carson, Neil. *Harlequin in Hogtown: George Luscombe and Toronto Workshop Productions*. Toronto: Univ. of Toronto Press, 1995.

Conolly, L.W., ed. *Canadian Drama and the Critics*. Rev. ed. Vancouver: Talonbooks, 1995.

"Contemporary Drama." Special Issue of *Canadian Literature* 118 (Autumn 1988).

Donohoe, Joseph I., Jr. and Jonathan M. Weiss, eds. *Essays on Modern Quebec Theatre*. East Lansing: Michigan State UP, 1995.

Drainie, Bronwyn. *Living the Part: John Drainie and the Dilemma of Canadian Stardom*. Toronto: Macmillan, 1988.

Filewod, Alan. *Collective Encounters: Documentary Theatre in English Canada*. Toronto: Univ. of Toronto Press, 1987.

Fink, Howard, and John Jackson, eds. *All the Bright Company: Radio Drama Produced by Andrew Allan*. Kingston and Toronto: Quarry/ CBC Enterprises, 1987.

Frick, Alice. *Image in the Mind: CBC Radio Drama, 1944-1954*. Toronto: Canadian Stage and Arts Publications, 1987.

Garebian, Keith. *A Well-Bred Muse: Selected Theatre Writings, 1978–1988*. Oakville, Ont.: Mosaic Press, 1991.

———, ed. *William Hutt: Masks and Faces*. Oakville: Mosaic, 1995.

Gilbert, Helen and Joanne Tompkins. *Post-Colonial Drama: Theory, Practice, Politics*. London: Routledge, 1996.

Glaap, Albert-Reiner with Rolf Althorp, ed. *On-Stage and Off-Stage: English Canadian Drama in Discourse*. St. John's: Breakwater, 1996.

Goldie, Terry. *Fear and Temptation: The Image of the Indigene in Canadian, Australian, and New Zealand Literatures*, Chap. 9. Kingston and Montreal: McGill-Queen's Univ. Press, 1989.

Grace, Sherrill, Eve D'Aeth and Lisa Chalykoff, eds. *Staging the North: Twelve Canadian Plays*. Toronto: Playwrights Canada Press, 1999.

Green, Lynda Mason and Tedde Moore, eds. *Standing Naked in the Wings: Anecdotes from Canadian Actors.* Toronto: Oxford Univ. Press, 1997.

Henighan, Tom. "Theatre: From Kitchen-Sink to Mega-Musical." In *Ideas of North: A Guide to Canadian Arts and Culture*, 41-74. Vancouver: Raincoast, 1997.

Hochbruck, Wolfgang and James O. Taylor, eds. *Down East: Critical Essays on Contemporary Maritime Canadian Literature.* Trier: Wissenschaftlicher Verlag Trier, 1996.

Hodkinson, Yvonne. *Female Parts: The Art and Politics of Female Playwrights.* Montreal: Black Rose, 1991.

Johnston, Denis. *Up the Mainstream: The Rise of Toronto's Alternative Theatres.* Toronto: Univ. of Toronto Press, 1991.

King, Bruce, ed. *Post-Colonial English Drama: Commonwealth Drama since 1960.* NY: St. Martin's, 1992.

Knowles, Richard Paul. *The Theatre of Form and the Production of Meaning: Contemporary Canadian Dramaturgies.* Toronto: ECW, 1999.

Lecker, Robert, ed. *Canadian Canons: Essays in Literary Value.* Toronto: Univ. of Toronto Press, 1991.

Miller, Mary Jane. *Turn Up the Contrast: CBC Television Drama Since 1952.* Vancouver: UBC Press, 1987.

Moore, Mavor. *4 Canadian Playwrights.* Toronto: Holt, Rinehart, 1973.

———. *Reinventing Myself: Memoirs.* Toronto: Stoddart, 1994.

Much, Rita, ed. *Women on the Canadian Stage: The Legacy of Hrotsvit.* Winnipeg: Blizzard, 1992.

Nardocchio, Elaine. *Theatre and Politics in Modern Quebec.* Edmonton: Univ. of Alberta Press, 1986.

New, William H., ed. *Dramatists in Canada: Selected Essays.* Vancouver: UBC Press, 1972.

Parker, Brian. "Is There a Canadian Drama?" In *The Canadian Imagination: Dimensions of a Literary Culture.* Ed. David Staines, 152-87. Cambridge, Mass.: Harvard Univ. Press, 1977.

———, and Cynthia Zimmerman. "Theatre and Drama [1972–84]." In *Literary History of Canada: Canadian Literature in English.* Ed. W.H. New. 2nd ed. Vol. 4, 186-216. Toronto: Univ. of Toronto Press, 1990.

Patterson, Tom, and Allan Gould. *First Stage: The Making of the Stratford Festival.* Toronto: McClelland and Stewart, 1987.

Perkyns, Richard, ed. *Major Plays of the Canadian Theatre, 1934–1984.* Toronto: Irwin, 1984.

———. *The Neptune Story: Twenty-Five Years in the Life of a Leading Canadian Theatre.* Hantsport, N.S.: Lancelot, 1989.

Pettigrew, John, and Jamie Portman. *Stratford: The First Thirty Years.* 2 vols. Toronto: Macmillan, 1985.

Podbrey, Maurice. *Half Man, Half Beast: Making a Life in Canadian Theatre.* Montreal: Véhicule, 1997.

Profiles in Canadian Literature, ser. 4-8. Ed. Jeffrey M. Heath. Toronto: Dundurn Press, 1982–91.

Ripley, John. "Drama and Theatre, 1960-73." In *Literary History of Canada.* Ed. Carl F. Klinck. 2nd ed. Vol. 4, 212-32. Toronto: Univ. of Toronto Press, 1976.

Rubin, Don, ed. *Canadian Theatre History: Selected Readings.* Toronto: Copp Clark, 1996.

———. "Creeping Toward a Culture: The Theatre in English Canada since 1945." *Canadian Theatre Review* 1 (Winter 1974): 6-21.

———, and Alison Cranmer-Byng, eds. *Canada's Playwrights: A Biographical Guide.* Toronto: CTR Publications, 1980.

Rudakoff, Judith, ed. *Dangerous Traditions: A Passe Muraille Anthology.* Winnipeg: Blizzard, 1992.

———, ed. *Questionable Activities: Canadian Theatre Artists Interviewed by Canadian Theatre Students.* 2 vols. Toronto: Playwrights Union of Canada, 1997.

———, and Rita Much. *Fair Play: 12 Women Speak: Conversations with Canadian Playwrights.* Toronto: Simon & Pierre, 1990.

Ryan, Toby Gordon. *Stage Left: Canadian Theatre in the Thirties.* Toronto: CTR Publications, 1981.

Saddlemyer, Ann and Richard Plant, eds. *Later Stages: Essays in Ontario Theatre from the First World War to the 1970s.* Toronto: Univ. of Toronto Press, 1997.

Stuart, E. Ross. *The History of the Prairie Theatre.* Toronto: Simon & Pierre, 1984.

Tait, Michael. "Drama and Theatre, 1920–1960." In *Literary History of Canada.* Ed. Carl F. Klinck. 2nd ed. Vol. 2, 143-67. Toronto: Univ. of Toronto Press, 1976.

Theatre Memoirs: On the Occasion of the Canadian Theatre Conference. Toronto: Playwrights Union of Canada, 1998.

Tompkins, Joanne, ed. *Theatre and the Canadian Imaginary.* Special Issue of *Australasian Drama Studies* 29 (October 1996).

Usmiani, Renate. *Second Stage: The Alternative Theatre Movement in Canada.* Vancouver: UBC Press, 1983.

Vogt, Gordon. *Critical Stages: Canadian Theatre in Crisis.* Ottawa: Oberon, 1998.

Wagner, Anton, ed. *Contemporary Canadian Theatre: New World Visions.* Toronto: Simon & Pierre, 1985.

———. "The Developing Mosaic: English-Canadian Drama to Mid-Century," In *Canada's Lost Plays.* Vol. 3, 4-39. Toronto: CTR Publications, 1980.

———, ed. *Establishing Our Boundaries: English-Canadian Theatre Criticism.* Toronto: Univ. of Toronto Press, 1999.

Wallace, Robert. *Producing Marginality: Theatre and Criticism in Canada.* Saskatoon: Fifth House, 1990.

———, ed. *Making, Out: Plays by Gay Men.* Toronto: Coach House, 1992.

———, and Cynthia Zimmerman, eds. *The Work: Conversations with English-Canadian Playwrights.* Toronto: Coach House, 1982.

Wasserman, Jerry, ed. *Twenty Years at Play: A New Play Centre Anthology.* Vancouver: Talonbooks, 1990.

Weiss, Jonathan M. *French-Canadian Theater.* Boston: Twayne, 1986.

Whittaker, Herbert. *Whittaker's Theatre: A Critic Looks at Stages in Canada and Thereabouts, 1944–1975.* Ed. Ronald Bryden with Boyd Neil. Greenbank, Ont.: The Whittaker Project, 1985.

Zimmerman, Cynthia. *Playwriting Women: Female Voices in English Canada.* Toronto: Simon & Pierre, 1994.

III. Individual Plays and Playwrights

Note: Wherever a book in this section has already appeared as an entry in Part II (Backgrounds, Surveys and General Studies), I have used the short form here. *Canadian Theatre Review* is indicated by *CTR*; *Dictionary of Literary Biography* is *DLB*; *English-Canadian Theatre* is *ECT*.

DAVID FENNARIO

A. BIOGRAPHY AND CRITICISM

Bagnall, Janet. "At Home in Verdun with David Fennario." *Montreal Gazette*, 23 February 1997, D5-6.

Benazon, Michael. "From Griffintown to Verdun: A Study of Place in the Work of David Fennario." *Matrix* 19 (1984): 25-34.

Byrnes, Terence. "The Matrix Interview: David Fennario." *Matrix* 48 (1996): 11-17.

Collet, Paulette. "Fennario's *Balconville* and Tremblay's *En Pièces détachées*: A Universe of Backyards and Despair." *Canadian Drama* 10 (Spring 1984): 35-43.

Conlogue, Ray. "Tough-Guy Playwright from the Point." *Globe and Mail*, 4 October 1980, E1.

Conolly, L.W., ed. *Canadian Drama and the Critics*, 227-37.

Desson, Jim and Bruce K. Filson. "Where is David Fennario Now?" *CTR* 46 (Spring 1986): 36-41.

Fennario, David. *Banana Boots.* Vancouver: Talonbooks, 1998.

———. *Without a Parachute.* Toronto: McClelland and Stewart, 1974.

Gilman, Marvin. "Fennario and Ryga: Canadian Political Playwrights." *Australasian Drama Studies* 29 (October 1996): 180-87.

Goldie, Terry. "*On the Job* and *Nothing to Lose.*" *Theatre History in Canada* 2 (Spring 1981): 63-67.

Gonick, Cy. "David Fennario: A Revolutionary Playwright." *Canadian Dimension* 21 (April 1987): 22-27.

Grigsby, Wayne. "The Bard from Balconville." *The Canadian Magazine*, 20 January 1979, 16-18.

Horenblas, Richard. "David Fennario: Burning Houses Down." *Scene Changes* 8 (March 1980): 26-29.

King, Dierdre. "The Drama of David Fennario." *Canadian Forum* 60 (February 1981): 14-17.

Milliken, Paul. "Portrait of the Artist as a Working-Class Hero: An Interview with David Fennario." *Performing Arts in Canada* 17 (Summer 1980): 22-25.

Nunn, Robert C. "The Interplay of Action and Set in the Plays of David Fennario." *Theatre History in Canada* 9 (Spring 1988): 3-18.

Page, Malcolm. "David Fennario's Balconville: Document and Message." *On-Stage and Off-Stage: English Canadian Drama in Discourse.* Ed. Albert-Reiner Glaap, 138-47.

Podbrey, Maurice. *Half Man, Half Beast: Making a Life in Canadian Theatre*, Chap. 5.

Ravel, Aviva. "David Fennario." In *Canadian Writers Since 1960*. 2nd ser. DLB 60: 60-64.

Salter, Denis. "Six Characters in Search of a Hero." *CTR* 69 (Winter 1991): 87-91.

Thalenburg, Eileen and David McCaughna. "Shaping the Word: Guy Sprung and Bill Glassco." *CTR* 26 (Spring 1980): 30-43.

Wallace, Robert and Cynthia Zimmerman, eds. *The Work*, 293-303.

B. **BALCONVILLE**: SELECTED REVIEWS

Abley, Mark. "The Shabby Intimacy of Daily Life." *Maclean's* 94 (13 April 1981): 66.

Ashley, Audrey M. "Play Provides Biting Humour, Raw Language." *Ottawa Citizen*, 6 November 1979, 59.

Blazer, Fred. "Bilingual Drama is Universal." *Globe and Mail*, 10 February 1979, 37.

Burke, Tim. "Art in *Balconville* Mirrors Chunk of Life at Its Grittiest." *Montreal Gazette*, 16 February 1980, 93.

Conlogue, Ray. "*Balconville* Maintains Status Quo." *Globe and Mail*, 11 January 1992, C4.

———. Masterful Acting Abounds in Fennario's *Balconville*." *Globe and Mail*, 10 February 1979, 13.

Donnelly, Pat. "Fennario's *Balconville* Has Changed, But Stands the Test of Time." *Montreal Gazette*, 11 January 1992, C3.

Dykk, Lloyd. "Forceful Play Hits Balance of Comedy and Seriousness." *Vancouver Sun*, 16 June 1987, E6.

Garebian, Keith. "*Balconville*." *Scene Changes* 7 (March/April 1979): 33-34.

Knelman, Martin. "Bilingualism Among the Hopeless." *Saturday Night* 94 (November 1979): 101-04.

Mallet, Gina. "Montreal Play Brings Slum to Life." *Toronto Star*, 4 October 1979, B1.

Peterson, Maureen. "Fennario's *Balconville* a Loveable Play." *Montreal Gazette*, 6 January 1979, 68.

Porter, Mackenzie. "Symbolic Promise of a Union." *Toronto Sun*, 5 October 1979, 88.

Wardle, Irving. "Nationalist Tension and Physical Congestion." *The Times* (London), 3 April 1981, 11.

DAVID FRENCH

A. BIOGRAPHY AND CRITICISM

Adams, John Coldwell. "From Coley's Point to Broadway." *Atlantic Advocate* 70 (July 1980): 59-61.

Anthony, Geraldine, ed. *Stage Voices*, 234-50.

Bemrose, John. "Romancing the Rock." *Maclean's* 101 (31 October 1988): 58-59.

Benson, Eugene, and L.W. Conolly. *ECT*, 93-95.

Bruhier, Catherine. "Darkness Visible: A Multiracial *Salt-Water Moon*." *Theatrum* 20 (Sept.-Oct. 1990): 13-15.

Carson, Neil. "Towards a Popular Theatre in English Canada." *Canadian Literature* 85 (Summer 1980): 62-69.

Conolly, L.W., ed. *Canadian Drama and the Critics*, 87-98, 128-34, 238-45.

French, David. "David French Looks at His 17-Year Love Affair with the Mercer Family." *Toronto Star*, 15 October 1988, F3.

Glaap, Albert-Reiner. "Family Plays, Romances and Comedies: Aspects of David French's Work as a Dramatist." In *On-Stage and Off-Stage: English Canadian Drama in Discourse.* Ed. Albert-Reiner Glaap, 161-74.

———. "*Noises Off* and *Jitters*: Two Comedies of Backstage Life." *Canadian Drama* 13.2 (1987): 210-15.

Gross, Konrad. "Looking to the Far East? Newfoundland in David French's Mercer

Tetralogy." In *Down East: Critical Essays on Contemporary Maritime Canadian Literature*. Ed. Wolfgang Hochbruck and James O. Taylor, 247-63.

Horenblas, Richard. "*One Crack Out*: Made in His Image." *Canadian Drama* 2 (Spring 1976): 67-72.

Jewinski, Ed. "Jacob Mercer's Lust for Victimization." *Canadian Drama* 2 (Spring 1976): 58-66.

Johnson, Chris. "David French." In *Canadian Writers Since 1960*. 1st ser. *DLB* 53: 191-94.

———. "Is That Us? Ray Lawler's *Summer of the Seventeenth Doll* and David French's *Leaving Home*." *Canadian Drama* 6 (Spring 1980): 30-42.

Kareda, Urjo. "introduction." In *Leaving Home* by David French, v-ix. Toronto: new press, 1972.

Mullaly, Edward. "Canadian Drama: David French and the Great Awakening." *The Fiddlehead* 100 (Winter 1974): 61-66.

Neary, Peter. "Of Many-Coloured Glass: Peter Neary Interviews David French." *Canadian Forum* 53 (March 1974): 26-27.

Noonan, James. "The Comedy of David French and the Rocky Road to Broadway." *Thalia* 3 (Fall/Winter 1980–81): 9-16.

Nothof, Anne. "David French and the Theatre of Speech." *Canadian Drama* 13.2 (1987): 216-23.

Nunn, Robert. "The Subjects of *Salt-Water Moon*." *Theatre History in Canada* 12 (Spring 1991): 3-21.

Perkyns, Richard. "*Of the Fields, Lately*: An Introduction." In *Major Plays of the Canadian Theatre, 1934–1984*, 479-83.

Rusted, Brian. "The Plays of David French." *Newfoundland Quarterly* 82 (Fall 1986): 42-43.

Thalenburg, Eileen, and David McCaughna. "Shaping the Word: Guy Sprung and Bill Glassco." *CTR* 26 (Spring 1980): 30-43.

Tyson, Bryan F. "'Swallowed Up in Darkness: Vision and Division in *Of the Fields, Lately*." *Canadian Drama* 16.1 (1990): 23-31.

Wallace, Robert, and Cynthia Zimmerman, eds. *The Work*, 304-16.

Zimmerman, Cynthia. "David French." In *Profiles in Canadian Literature*. 4th ser., 117-23.

B. **LEAVING HOME**: SELECTED REVIEWS

Bevis, R.W. "Sins of the Fathers." *Canadian Literature* 59 (Winter 1974): 106-08.

Coe, Richard. "Toronto's Theatre Scene." *Washington Post*, 28 June 1972, E5.

Dafoe, Christopher. "*Leaving Home* Will Strike Home." *Vancouver Sun*, 13 November 1973, 35.

Doolittle, Joyce. "Leaving Home." *NeWest Review* 14 (Dec.-Jan. 1989): 51-52.

Dykk, Lloyd. "Tale of a Family Broken by Father's Heavy Hand." *Vancouver Sun*, 10 July 1985, B11.

Heller, Zelda. "Newfoundland Life Observed." *Montreal Star*, 12 October 1972, C16.

Kareda, Urjo. "Tarragon Theatre's Dynamic Play: Quite Exceptional." *Toronto Star*, 17 May 1972.

MacCulloch, Clare. "Neither Out Far Nor in Deep." *Canadian Drama* 2 (Spring 1976): 115-18.

McKendrick, Coral. "*Leaving Home* a Hit." *Winnipeg Free Press*, 19 March 1980, 42.

Mezei, Stephen. "Toronto Scene." *Performing Arts in Canada* 9 (Summer 1972): 17.

Pederson, Stephen. "Actors Overcome Flawed Script." *Halifax Chronicle Herald*, 5 November 1990, A11.

Siskind, Jacob. "Leaving Home the Right Way." *Montreal Gazette*, 14 October 1972.

Whittaker, Herbert. "Some Fine Domestic Brawling." *Globe and Mail*, 17 May 1972, 18.

———. "Kate Reid as Mother Dominates *Leaving Home*." *Globe and Mail*, 15 November 1973, 14.

SKY GILBERT

A. BIOGRAPHY AND CRITICISM

Boni, Franco. "An Interview with Sky Gilbert." *Rhubarb-o-Rama!* 16-20.

Gilbert, Sky. "Closet Plays: An Exclusive Dramaturgy at Work." *CTR* 59 (Summer 1989): 55-58.

———. "Diary of a (Reluctant) Radical." *This Magazine* 30 (May-June 1997): 34-37.

———. "Drag and Popular Culture." *CTR* 58 (Spring 1989): 42-44.

————. "Playwright's Foreword." *Painted, Tainted, Sainted: Four Plays* by Sky Gilbert. Toronto: Playwrights Canada, 1996. 15-17.

Kastner, Susan. "Sky Queen." *Toronto Star*, 9 October 1994, C1, 11.

Vaughan, R.M. "Arguments in Motion." *Books in Canada* 23 (April 1994): 16-19.

————. "Bullet-Proof Heels, 3 A.M. ... and Other Problems: An Introduction." *Painted, Tainted, Sainted: Four Plays* by Sky Gilbert, 11-13.

Wallace, Robert. "Making Out Positions: An Introduction." *Making, Out: Plays by Gay Men*, 11-40.

————. "No Turning Back: An Introduction." *This Unknown Flesh: A Selection of Plays by Sky Gilbert*, 11-26. Toronto: Coach House, 1995.

————. "Theorizing a Queer Theatre: Buddies in Bad Times." *Contemporary Issues in Canadian Drama*. Ed. Per Brask, 136-59.

————. ""To Become: The Ideological Function of Gay Theatre." *CTR* 59 (Summer 1989): 5-10.

Webb, Margaret. "What's Eating Sky Gilbert?" *Toronto Life* 31 (March 1997): 45-48.

B. DRAG QUEENS ON TRIAL:
SELECTED REVIEWS

Braun, Liz. "Sky's the Limit for Gilbert." *Toronto Sun*, 16 October 1985.

Burrows, Malcolm. "On Society's Fringe." *The Varsity*, 18 November 1985.

Kaplan, Jon. "Female Ethos and Drag Queen Life." *Now* 5.8 (October 1985): 21.

Kierans, Genevieve. "*Drag Queens on Trial* ... A Plea for Understanding." *Toronto Tonight* 3.22 (October 1985).

Mietkiewicz, Henry. "*Drag Queens on Trial* Is Not for the Faint-Hearted." *Toronto Star*, 20 October 1985, G4.

Scott, Jay. "Drag Queens Tackle Stereotypes." *Globe and Mail*, 21 October 1985, C12.

JOHN GRAY with ERIC PETERSON

A. BIOGRAPHY AND CRITICISM

Anderson, Ian. "Coming Home from Billy Bishop's War." *Maclean's* 94 (16 March 1981): 17, 20.

Bemrose, John. "Billy Soars Again." *Maclean's* 111 (28 September 1998): 69-70.

Bessai, Diane. "Discovering the Popular Audience." *Canadian Literature* 118 (Autumn 1988): 7-28.

————. *Playwrights of Collective Creation*, 179-214.

Bolin, John S. "The Very Best of Company: Perceptions of a Canadian Attitude towards War and Nationalism in Three Contemporary Plays." *American Review of Canadian Studies* 23.3 (1987): 309-22.

Conolly, L.W., ed. *Canadian Drama and the Critics*, 217-26.

Cruise, David. "John Gray, Writer." *Atlantic Insight* 5 (August 1983): 22-27.

Galloway, Myron. "Life Is a One-Man Show [Eric Peterson]." *Montreal Star*, 24 February 1979, D8.

Gray, John. *Local Boy Makes Good: Three Musicals by John Gray*. Vancouver: Talonbooks, 1987.

Knelman, Martin. "Roots." *Saturday Night* 100 (December 1985): 69-71.

MacIntyre, Jean. "Language and Structure in *Billy Bishop Goes to War*." *Canadian Drama* 13.1 (1987): 50-59.

————. "The Male-Bond World of John Gray's Musicals." *Canadian Drama* 16.1 (1990): 123-28.

Miller, Mary Jane. "*Billy Bishop Goes to War* and *Maggie and Pierre*: A Matched Set." *Theatre History in Canada* 10.2 (1989): 188-98.

Richler, Noah. "Billy Bishop Goes to Kenya." *Saturday Night* 102 (August 1987): 52.

Steed, Judy. "John Gray's Progress." *Toronto Life*, 15 (May 1981): 66, 97-103.

————. "Mike and Eric and Chris and John: The Night Mike Nichols Met Billy Bishop." *The Canadian Magazine* (26 May 1979): 2-6.

Twigg, Alan. "John Gray: Filius." In *For Openers: Conversations with 24 Canadian Writers*, 97-106. Vancouver: Harbour, 1981.

Usmiani, Renate. *Second Stage*, 67-71.

Wallace, Robert and Cynthia Zimmerman, eds. *The Work*, 44-59.

Wasserman, Jerry. "Flying Low into Another Tour of Duty: Jerry Wasserman Speaks With John Gray." *Books in Canada* 28 (February 1999): 25.

Wyman, Max. "The Billy Bishop Story Soars to Great Theatrical Heights." *Performing Arts in Canada* 16 (Spring 1979): 18-21.

———. "From the Wild, Blue Yonder to the Great, White Way." *Vancouver Magazine* 12 (July 1979): 65-71.

B. **BILLY BISHOP GOES TO WAR**: SELECTED REVIEWS

Ashwell, Keith. "Peterson is a Stupendous Billy Bishop." *Edmonton Journal*, 24 January 1980, D9.

Birnie, Peter. "Billy's Back at War." *Vancouver Sun*, 21 November 1998, D1.

Beaufort, John, "Canada Visits Broadway with Biography and Song." *Christian Science Monitor*, 4 June 1980, 18.

Corbeil, Carole. "*Billy Bishop* Lands Safely." *Globe and Mail*, 13 January 1982, 17.

Donnelly, Pat. "Geordie Productions' *Billy Bishop* Is Fringe Festival's Ace in the Hole." *Montreal Gazette*, 20 June 1991, D11.

Dykk, Lloyd. "*Billy Bishop* Worth Another Flypast." *Vancouver Sun*, 19 April 1991, C5.

Galloway, Myron. "Canadian Musical Celebrates Flying Ace." *Montreal Star*, 16 February 1979, B4.

Gussow, Mel. "Capital Sees *Billy Bishop Goes to War*." *New York Times*, 13 March 1980, III, 20.

Hopkins, Thomas. "Can You Bake a Cherry Bomb, Billy Boy, Billy Boy?" *Maclean's* 91 (4 December 1978): 70.

Johnson, Bryan. "*Billy Bishop Goes to War*: Flying Ace a Soaring Success." *Globe and Mail*, 14 February 1979, 13.

Kerr, Walter. "*Billy Bishop* Flies In." *New York Times*, 30 May 1980, III, 3.

Knelman, Martin. "Dancing in the Sky with Billy Bishop." *Saturday Night* 94 (June 1979): 50-51.

Lardner, James. "Lighter Than Air." *Washington Post*, 6 March 1980, D1.

Mallett, Gina. "*Billy Bishop* Deserves Some Medals." *Toronto Star*, 14 February 1979, C3.

Morrow, Martin. "Canada's Billy Bishop Still Flying High," *Calgary Herald*, 24 October 1992, D1.

Porter, Mackenzie. "Gray's Believable Bishop Stirring Salute to Heroism." *Toronto Sun*, 15 February 1979, 92.

Sullivan, Dan. "*Billy Bishop Goes to War* and Likes It." *Los Angeles Times*, 17 October 1980, VI, 1.

Taylor, Kate. "Billy Bishop Still Flying High." *Globe and Mail*, 26 September 1998, C9.

Wagner, Vit. "Billy Bishop Hasn't Lost His Old Charm." *Toronto Star*, 25 September 1998, D13.

Wardle, Irving. "*Billy Bishop Goes to War*." *The Times* (London), 21 August 1980, 9.

Wasserman, Jerry. "Giving Up the Toy Plane for the Cane." *Books in Canada* 28 (February 1999): 23-24.

Wyman, Max. "Give *Billy Bishop* Show a Victory Roll." *Vancouver Sun*, 12 July 1979, B5.

JOHN HERBERT

A. BIOGRAPHY AND CRITICISM

Anthony, Geraldine. "John Herbert's *Fortune and Men's Eyes* and Other Plays." In *On-Stage and Off-Stage: English Canadian Drama in Discourse*. Ed. Albert-Reiner Glaap, 175-88.

———, ed. *Stage Voices*, 165-206.

Benson, Eugene, and L.W. Conolly. *ECT*, 73-75.

Boire, Gary. "Theatres of Law: Canadian Legal Drama." *Canadian Literature* 152/153 (Spring/Summer 1997): 124-44.

Carson, Neil. "Sexuality and Identity in *Fortune and Men's Eyes*." *Twentieth Century Literature* 18 (July 1972): 207-18

Conolly, L.W., ed. *Canadian Drama and the Critics*, 45-54.

Fulford, Robert. "A Canadian Play Makes Its Way Around The World." *Saturday Night* 90 (October 1975): 8, 12.

Gilbert, Reid. "'My Mother Wants Me to Play Romeo Before It's Too Late': Framing Gender on Stage." *Theatre Research in Canada* 14 (Fall 1993): 123-43.

Herbert, John. "My Life and Hard Times in Cold, Bitter, Suspicious Toronto." *Saturday Night* 86 (December 1971): 21-24.

Hofsess, John. "*Fortune and Men's Eyes*—A Report from the Set in a Quebec City Prison." *Maclean's* 83 (December 1970): 81-83.

Johnson, Chris. "John Herbert." In *Canadian Writers since 1960*. 1st ser. *DLB* 53: 222-25.

Lister, Rota. "Interview with John Herbert." *Canadian Drama* 4 (Winter 1973): 173-76.

McLarty, James. "The World According to John Herbert." *Motion* 1 (March-April 1973): 16-21.

Messenger, Ann P. "Damnation at Christmas: John Herbert's *Fortune and Men's Eyes*." In *Dramatists in Canada*. Ed. W.H. New, 173-78.

Perkyns, Richard. "*Fortune and Men's Eyes*: An Introduction." In *Major Plays of the Canadian Theatre, 1934–1984*, 276-81.

Teague, Francis. "Prisons and Imprisonment in Canadian Drama." *Journal of Canadian Fiction* 19 (1977): 112-21.

Tyson, Brian F. "'This Man's Art and That Man's Scope': Language and the Critics in *Fortune and Men's Eyes*." *Canadian Drama* 4 (Spring 1978): 34-39.

B. **FORTUNE AND MEN'S EYES**:
SELECTED REVIEWS

Barnes, Clive. "Question Marks at Stage 73." *New York Times*, 23 October 1969, 55.

Bryden, Ronald. "Theatre." *The Observer* (London), 14 July 1968.

Cohen, Nathan. "When *Fortune and Men's Eyes* Opened." *Toronto Star*, 7 September 1967.

Devin, Susan. "*Fortune and Men's Eyes* Showed a Lot of Foresight." *Toronto Star*, 3 May 1985, D15.

Dykk, Lloyd. "Prison Drama Held Captive by Contrived Archetypes." *Vancouver Sun*, October 1992, C5.

Fraser, John. "*Fortune and Men's Eyes* Stands the Test of Time." *Globe and Mail*, 20 November 1975, 18.

French, Philip. "Serving Time." *New Statesman*, 19 July 1968, 88-89.

Oliver, Edith. "Theater." *The New Yorker* 43 (4 March 1967): 134.

Pedwell, Susan. "Gripping Plays Offers Slice of Life Behind Bars." *Calgary Herald*, 19 March 1980, B14.

Pritchett, Oliver. "The Power Politics of Homosexual Life." *The Guardian* (London), 21 July 1968.

Sullivan, Dan. "A Distressing *Fortune and Men's Eyes*." *New York Times*, 24 February 1967, 29.

Whittaker, Herbert. "Toronto's Jack Brundage Has a Winner." *Globe and Mail*, 4 March 1967, 18.

WENDY LILL

A. BIOGRAPHY AND CRITICISM.

Anderson, J., Sherrill Grace, and A. Eisenberg. "Women Speaking: *The Occupation of Heather Rose* and the Culture of Health Care." *Northern Parallels*. Ed. Shauna McLarnon and Douglas Nord, 84-101. Prince George: UNBC Press, 1997.

Bennett, Susan. "The Occupation of Wendy Lill: Canadian Women's Voices." In *Women on the Canadian Stage*. Ed. Rita Much, 69-80.

———. "Who Speaks? Representations of Native Women in Some Canadian Plays." *Canadian Journal of Drama and Theatre* 1.2 (1991): 13-25.

Bergman, Brian. "Enter Stage Left." *Maclean's* 111 (16 February 1998): 61.

Bessai, Diane. "Introduction." In *NeWest Plays by Women*, vii-xvii. Ed. Diane Bessai and Don Kerr. Edmonton: NeWest Press, 1987.

Enright, Robert. "The Explorer of Human Emotions: An Interview with Wendy Lill." *Border Crossings* 10 (January 1991): 12-17.

Everett-Green, Robert. "Political Playwright Turns Theatrical Politico." *Globe and Mail*, 14 February 1998, C7.

Grace, Sherrill. "Gendering Northern Narrative." *Echoing Silence: Essays on Northern Narrative*. Ed. John Moss, 163-81. Ottawa: Univ. of Ottawa Press, 1997.

Heald, Susan. "Wendy Lill and the Politics of Memory." *Canadian Dimension* 29 (April-May 1995): 54-56.

Lill, Wendy. "The Playwrighting Politician." *Theatre Memoirs*, 66-68.

Metcalfe, Robin. "Profile: Letters Out." *Books in Canada* 19 (March 1990): 21-24.

Mitchell, Nick. "A Feeling for Our History: An Interview with Wendy Lill." *Prairie Fire* (Winter 1985): 16-19.

Perkins, Don. "Necessary Adjustments: The Problem of Community Solidarity in *Paper Wheat*, *The Fighting Days* and *The Shipbuilder*." *Prairie Forum* 21 (Spring 1996): 43-53.

Rudakoff, Judith and Rita Much, eds. *Fair Play*, 37-48.

Smith, Doug. "Writer in Non-Residence." *NeWest Review* 14 (April/May 1989): 52-54.

Walton, Glenn. "Lill Women, Lill Men: Glenn Walton Interviews Playwright/MP Wendy Lill." *ArtsAtlantic* 16 (Fall 1998/Winter 1999): 41-43.

B. **THE OCCUPATION OF HEATHER ROSE**: SELECTED REVIEWS

Barnard, Elissa. "*The Occupation of Heather Rose* Full of Wit, Vivid Imagery, Poignancy." *Halifax Mail-Star*, 5 May 1993, A14.

Conlogue, Ray. "*Heather Rose* Built on Shaky Premise." *Globe and Mail*, 20 January 1988, C5.

Dykk, Lloyd. "Heather Rose's Tale Masterfully Told in Fringe Reprise." *Vancouver Sun*, 12 April 1990, D12.

Flynn, J. "Fascination of the Abomination." *NeWest Review* 11 (April 1986): 19.

Matheson, Sue. "Heather's Tale." *Western Report* 1 (24 March 1986): 49.

Mietkiewicz, Henry. "Author's Wry Humor Fends Off Melodrama." *Toronto Star*, 20 January 1988, D4.

Pedersen, Stephen. "Lill's 'Heather Rose' a Real Education." *Halifax Chronicle-Herald*, 27 September 1994, C7.

Skene, Reg. "Nurse's Journey Related with Dramatic Effect." *Winnipeg Free Press*, 28 February 1986, 34.

Wyman, Max. "Magnificence Preserved in *Heather Rose*." *Vancouver Province*, 19 April 1990, 59.

SHARON POLLOCK

A. BIOGRAPHY AND CRITICISM

Bessai, Diane. "Introduction." In Sharon Pollock, *Blood Relations and Other Plays*, 7-9. Edmonton: NeWest Press, 1981.

———. "Sharon Pollock's Women: A Study in Dramatic Process." In *Amazing Space: Writing Canadian Women Writing*. Ed. Shirley Neuman and Smaro Kamboureli, 126-36. Edmonton: Longspoon/NeWest, 1986.

———. "Women Dramatists: Sharon Pollock and Judith Thompson." In *Post-Colonial English Drama*. Ed. Bruce King, 97-117. NY: St. Martin's, 1992.

Clement, Susan and Esther Beth Sullivan. "The Split Subject of *Blood Relations*." In *Upstaging Big Daddy: Directing Theater as if Gender and Race Matter*. Ed. Ellen Donkin and Susan Clement, 53-66. Ann Arbor: Univ. of Michigan Press, 1993.

Conolly, L.W., ed. *Canadian Drama and the Critics*, 135-44, 259-76, 317-23.

Dunn, Margo. "Sharon Pollock: In the Centre Ring." *Makara* 1 (August-September 1976): 2-6.

Fraser, Matthew. "*Doc* May Be Tough Pill for New Brunswick." *Globe and Mail*, 7 March 1986, A12.

Grace, Sherrill and Gabrielle Helms. "Documenting the Komagata Maru Incident." In *Painting the Maple: Essays on Race, Gender and the Construction of Canada*. Ed. Victoria Strong-Boag and Sherrill Grace, 85-99. Vancouver: UBC Press, 1998.

Gilbert, Reid. "Sharon Pollock." In *Profiles in Canadian Literature* 6. Ed. Jeffrey M. Heath, 113-20. Toronto: Dundurn, 1986.

Hall, Sharon K., ed. "Sharon Pollock: *Doc*." In *Contemporary Literary Criticism: Yearbook 1987*. Vol. 50, 222-27. Detroit: Gale Research, 1988.

Hofsess, John. "Families." *Homemaker's*, 15 (March 1980): 41-60.

———. "Sharon Pollock Off-Broadway: Success as a Subtle Form of Failure." *Books in Canada* 12 (April 1983): 3-4.

Holder, Heidi J. "Broken Toys: The Destruction of the National Hero in the Early History Plays of Sharon Pollock." *Essays in Theatre* 14 (May 1996): 131-45.

Kerr, Rosalind. "Borderline Crossings in Sharon Pollock's Out-Law Genres: *Blood Relations* and *Doc*." *Theatre Research in Canada* 17 (Fall 1996): 200-215.

Knowles, Richard Paul. "Replaying History: Canadian Historiographic Metadrama." *Dalhousie Review* 67 (1987): 228-43.

Loiselle, André. "Paradigms of 1980s Québécois and Canadian Drama: Normand Chaurette's *Provincetown Playhouse, juillet 1919, j'avais 19 ans* and Sharon Pollock's *Blood Relations*." *Quebec Studies* 14 (1992): 93-104.

Metcalfe, Robin. "Interview with Sharon Pollock." *Books in Canada* 16 (March 1987): 39-40.

Miner, Madonna. "'Lizzie Borden Took an Ax': Enacting *Blood Relations*." *Literature in Performance* 6 (April 1986): 10-21.

Much, Rita. "Theatre by Default: Sharon Pollock's Garry Theatre." *CTR* 82 (Spring 1995): 19-22.

Nothof, Anne. "Crossing Borders: Sharon Pollock's Revisitation of Canadian Frontiers." *Modern Drama* 38 (Winter 1995): 475-87.

———, ed. *Sharon Pollock: Essays on Her Works*. Toronto: Guernica, 2000.

Nunn, Robert C. "Sharon Pollock's Plays: A Review Article." *Theatre History in Canada* 5 (Spring 1984): 72-83.

Page, Malcolm. "Sharon Pollock: Committed Playwright." *Canadian Drama* 5 (Autumn 1979): 104-11.

Perkyns, Richard. "*Generations*: An Introduction." In *Major Plays of the Canadian Theatre, 1934–1984*, 605-08.

Pollock, Sharon. "Dead or Alive? Feeling the Pulse of Canadian Theatre." *Theatrum* 23 (April/May 1991): 12-13.

———. "Many Brave Spirits." *Theatre Memoirs*, 13-17.

———. "Reflections of a Female Artistic Director." In *Women on the Canadian Stage*. Ed. Rita Much, 109-14.

Rudakoff, Judith, and Rita Much, eds. *Fair Play*, 208-20.

Saddlemyer, Ann. "Crime in Literature: Canadian Drama." In *Rough Justice: Essays on Crime in Literature*. Ed. Martin L. Friedman, 214-30. Toronto: Univ. of Toronto Press, 1991.

Salter, Denis. "(Im)possible Worlds: The Plays of Sharon Pollock." In *The Sharon Pollock Papers: First Accession*. Ed. Apollonia Steele and Jean F. Tener, xi-xxxv. Calgary: Univ. of Calgary Press, 1989.

St. Pierre, Paul Matthew. "Sharon Pollock." In *Canadian Writers Since 1960*. 2nd ser. *DLB* 60: 300-06.

Stone-Blackburn, Susan. "Feminism and Metadrama: Role-Playing in *Blood Relations*." *Canadian Drama* 15 (1989): 169-78.

Wallace, Robert, and Cynthia Zimmerman, eds. *The Work*, 115-26.

Wasserman, Jerry. "Daddy's Girls: Father-Daughter Incest and Canadian Plays by Women." *Essays in Theatre* 14 (November 1995): 25-36.

Wylie, Herb. "'Painting the Background': Metadrama and the Fabric of History in Sharon Pollock's *Blood Relations*." *Essays in Theatre* 15 (May 1997): 191-205.

Zichy, Francis. "Justifying the Ways of Lizzie Borden to Men: The Play Within the Play in *Blood Relations*." *Theatre Annual* 42 (1987): 61-81.

Zimmerman, Cynthia. *Playwriting Women: Female Voices in English Canada*, 60-98. Toronto: Simon & Pierre, 1994.

———. "Towards a Better, Fairer World: An Interview with Sharon Pollock." *CTR* 69 (Winter 1991): 34-38.

B. **DOC**: SELECTED REVIEWS

Aird, Elizabeth. "*Doc* Sits Us Head Down in Mud." *Vancouver Sun*, 24 March 1990, D7.

Brennan, Brian. "Pollock Offers Best Work Yet." *Calgary Herald*, 8 April 1984, F2.

Conlogue, Ray. "A Highly Personal Drama." *Globe and Mail*, 10 April 1984, M7.

Côté, Marc. "Remembrances of Things Past." *Books in Canada* 16 (March 1987): 17-18.

Cowan, Cindy. "*Doc*." *CTR* 52 (Fall 1987): 95-96.

Crew, Robert. "*Doc* Examines a Shattered Family." *Toronto Star*, 4 October 1984, F2.

Czarnecki, Mark. "Ghosts in a Family Attic." *Maclean's* 97 (23 April 1984): 52.

Finlayson, Judith. "*Doc* Explores Social Ailment." *Globe and Mail*, 26 October 1984, 11.

Godfrey, Stephen. "*Doc* a Superb Family Drama." *Globe and Mail*, 4 October 1984, E5.

Kennedy, Janice. "*Doc* a Powerful Look Behind Family Masks." *Ottawa Citizen*, 28 November 1997, E3.

Knelman, Martin. "Daddy Dearest." *Saturday Night* 99 (October 1984): 73-74.

Knowles, Richard Paul. "Sharon Pollock: Personal Frictions." *Atlantic Provinces Book Review* 14 (February-March 1987): 19.

Skene, Reg. "MTC Shows Ability with *Doc* Production." *Winnipeg Free Press*, 6 February 1987, 29.

Smith, Patricia Keeney. "Looking Back." *Canadian Forum* 64 (January 1984): 39-40.

Stewart, Alan. "A Look at Family Affairs." *Globe and Mail*, 26 October 1984, 11.

Wasserman, Jerry. "Drama." *University of Toronto Quarterly* 57 (Fall 1987): 67-69.

JAMES REANEY

A. BIOGRAPHY AND CRITICISM

Anthony, Geraldine, ed. *Stage Voices*, 139-64.

Campbell, Wanda. "To Flow Like You: An Interview with James Reaney." *Windsor Review* 29 (Spring 1996): 9-21.

Conolly, L.W., ed. *Canadian Drama and the Critics*, 145-55, 167-86, 302-07.

Day, Moira. "James Reaney," In *Canadian Writers, 1920–1959*. 1st ser. *DLB* 68: 282-90.

Dragland, Stan, ed. *Approaches to the Work of James Reaney*. Downsview, Ont.: ECW Press, 1983; rpt. of James Reaney Special Issue, *Essays on Canadian Writing* 24-25 (1982–83).

———. "James Reaney's 'Pulsating Dance In and Out of Forms.'" In *The Human Elements*. Ed. David Helwig, 112-33. Ottawa: Oberon, 1978.

Grandy, Karen. "Playing with Time: James Reaney's *The Donnellys* as Spatial Form Drama." *Modern Drama* 38 (Winter 1995): 462-74.

Huebert, Ronald. "James Reaney: Poet and Dramatist." *CTR* 13 (Winter 1977): 125-28.

Johnston, Denis. *Up the Mainstream*, 237-49.

Jones, Manina. "'The Collage in Motion': Staging the Documentary in Reaney's *Sticks and Stones*." *Canadian Drama* 16.1 (1990): 1-22.

Kenney, Patricia. "James Reaney: Playmaker." In *On-Stage and Off-Stage: English Canadian Drama in Discourse*. Ed. Albert-Reiner Glaap, 214-23.

Knowles, Richard Paul. "Replaying History: Canadian Historiographic Metadrama." *Dalhousie Review* 67 (1987): 228-43.

Lee, Alvin. *James Reaney*. New York: Twayne, 1969.

———. and Eleanor R. Goldhar. "James Reaney." In *Profiles in Canadian Literature*. 4th ser., 17-28.

Mayo, John. "Expectations and Compacts in the Beckwith-Reaney Operas: A Case Study." *University of Toronto Quarterly* 60 (Winter 1990–91): 305-18.

McNamara, Tim. "*Three Desks*: A Turning Point in James Reaney's Drama." *Queen's Quarterly* 94 (Spring 1987): 15-31.

Meyer, Bruce and Brian O'Riordan. "James Reaney: Horses, Buggies and Cadillacs." In *In Their Words: Interviews with Fourteen Canadian Writers*, 56-70. Toronto: Anansi, 1984.

Miller, Mary Jane. "The Use of Stage Metaphor in *The Donnellys*." *Canadian Drama* 8.1 (1982): 34-41.

New, W.H., ed. *Dramatists in Canada*, 114-44.

Noonan, James. "The Critics Criticized: An Analysis of Reviews of James Reaney's *The Donnellys* on National Tour." *Canadian Drama* 3 (Fall 1977): 174-82.

———. "Foreword" and "Concluding Essay." In *The Donnellys*. James Reaney, 1-8, 275-88. Victoria: Press Porcépic, 1983.

Nothof, Anne. "Variant Tellings: The Reconstruction of Social Mythology in James Reaney's *The Donnellys*." *International Journal of Canadian Studies* 10 (Fall 1994): 1-15.

Parker, Gerald. "History, Story and Story-Style: James Reaney's *The Donnellys*. *Canadian Drama* 4 (Spring 1978): 150-59.

———. *How to Play: The Theatre of James Reaney*. Toronto: ECW Press, 1991.

———. "'The Key word … is "listen"': James Reaney's 'Sonic Enviroment.'" *Mosaic* 14 (Fall 1981): 1-14.

Perkyns, Richard. "The Innocence of the Donnellys: James Reaney's Three-Ring Circus." *Canadian Drama* 3 (Spring 1977): 162-73.

Reaney, James. *Fourteen Barrels from Sea to Sea*. Erin, Ont.: Press Porcépic, 1977.

———. "James Reaney Looks Towards a National Repertory." *Theatre History in Canada* 6 (Fall 1985): 218-26.

———. "A Letter from James Reaney: Halloween." *Black Moss* 2.1 (Spring 1976): 2-10.

———. "Ten Years at Play." *Canadian Literature* 41 (Summer 1969): 53-61; rpt. in *Dramatists in Canada*. Ed. W.H. New, 70-78.

———. "'They are Treating Us Like Mad Dogs': A Donnelly Biographer's Problem." *Biography* and Autobiography: Essays on Irish and Canadian History and Literature. Ed. James Noonan, 247-52. Ottawa: Carleton UP, 1993.

———. "Your Plays Are Like Movies—Cinemascope Ones." Canadian Drama 5 (Spring 1979): 32-40.

Reaney, J. Stewart. James Reaney. Toronto: Gage, 1977.

Ricou, Laurie. Everyday Magic: Child Languages in Canadian Literature, Chap. 8. Vancouver: UBC Press, 1987.

Roberts, Eric. "Sticks and Stones: History, Play, and Myth." Canadian Drama 4 (Fall 1978): 160-72.

Stingle, Richard. "James Reaney and his Works." In Canadian Writers and Their Works. Poetry Series, Vol. 7. Ed. Robert Lecker, et al, 191-246. Toronto: ECW Press, 1990.

Walker, Craig Stewart. "James Reaney's The Donnellys and the Recovery of 'the Ceremony of Innocence.'" Australasian Drama Studies 29 (October 1996): 188-96.

Woodman, Ross. James Reaney. Toronto: McClelland and Stewart, 1972.

B. **THE ST NICHOLAS HOTEL**:
SELECTED REVIEWS

Carroll, Michael. "The Donnellys: A Canadian Phenomenon in Print and on the Stage." The Canadian Review 3 (September 1976): 34-36.

Donnelly, Pat. "The Black Donnellys Live Again." Montreal Gazette, 26 October 1996, E14.

Kareda, Urjo. "New James Reaney Play Filled with Delights." Toronto Star, 18 November 1974, D6.

Leggatt, Alexander. "Letters in Canada 1976: Theatre." University of Toronto Quarterly 46 (Summer 1977): 383-85.

Morrow, Martin. "The Donnellys: Second Part of Trilogy … Proves Exciting Theatre." Calgary Herald, 11 August 1997, B7.

Salter, Denis. "The Donnellys: Part II. The St. Nicholas Hotel, Wm. Donnelly, Prop." Canadian Drama 5 (Spring 1979): 66-68.

Souchotte, Sandra. "Assessing The Donnellys." CTR 7 (Summer 1975): 131-35.

Whittaker, Herbert. "More About Those Legendary Donnellys." Globe and Mail, 18 November 1974, 14.

In addition James Reaney has reprinted twenty reviews of The Donnellys in Fourteen Barrels from Sea to Sea, his account of the Trilogy's national tour in the fall of 1975. The reviews cover performances in London (Ont.), Winnipeg, Vancouver, Edmonton, Calgary, Ottawa, Halifax, Hamilton and Toronto. The following are the most informative:

Beaven, Scott. "The Donnellys Production Extraordinary." The Albertan (Calgary), 30 October 1975.

Dawson, Eric. "The Donnellys: St. Nicholas Hotel." The Charlatan (Ottawa), 14 November 1975.

Fraser, John. "NDWT's Weighty Donnelly Saga Makes a Sterling Return." Globe and Mail, 12 December 1975.

Galloway, Myron. "The Donnellys' Death." Montreal Star, 1 December 1975.

Kucherawy, Dennis. "Donnellys: Weep for One … Not for Four," The Gazette (London, Ont.), 10 October 1975.

GEORGE RYGA

A. BIOGRAPHY AND CRITICISM

Bennett, Susan. "Who Speaks? Representations of Native Women in Some Canadian Plays." Canadian Journal of Drama and Theatre 1.2 (1991): 13-25.

Benson, Eugene and L.W. Conolly. ECT, 80-83.

Boire, Gary. "Theatres of Law: Canadian Legal Drama." Canadian Literature 152/153 (Spring/Summer 1997): 124-44.

———. "Tribunalations: George Ryga's Postcolonial Trial 'Play.'" ARIEL 22 (April 1991): 5-20.

———. "Wheels on Fire: The Train of Thought in George Ryga's The Ecstasy of Rita Joe." Canadian Literature 113-14 (Summer-Fall 1987): 62-74.

Carson, Neil. "George Ryga and the Lost Country." Canadian Literature 45 (Summer 1970): 33-40; rpt. in Dramatists in Canada, ed. W.H. New, 155-62.

Chevrefils, Marlys and Appolonia Steele, eds. The George Ryga Papers. Calgary: University of Calgary Press, 1995.

Conolly, L.W., ed. *Canadian Drama and the Critics*, 41-44, 55-68.

Gilman, Marvin. "Fennario and Ryga: Canadian Political Playwrights." *Australasian Drama Studies* 29 (October 1996): 180-87.

Grace, Sherrill. "The Expressionist Legacy in the Canadian Theatre: George Ryga and Robert Gurik." *Canadian Literature* 118 (Autumn 1988): 47-58.

Grant, Agnes. "Canadian Native Literature: The Drama of George Ryga and Tomson Highway." *Australian-Canadian Studies* 10.2 (1992): 37-56.

Hay, Peter. "George Ryga: Beginnings of a Biography." *CTR* 23 (Summer 1979): 36-44.

———. "The Psychology of Distortion: A Rebuttal of Christopher Innes." *Theatre History in Canada* 7.1 (Spring 1986): 119-24.

Hoffman, James. *The Ecstasy of Resistance: A Biography of George Ryga*. Toronto: ECW Press, 1995.

Innes, Christopher. *Politics and the Playwright: George Ryga*. Toronto: Simon & Pierre, 1985.

Johnson, Chris. "Amerindians and Aborigines in English Canadian and Australian Drama, 1606–1975." *Canadian Drama* 10.2 (1984): 167-87.

Maracle, Lee. "A Question of Voice." *Vancouver Sun*, 6 June 1992, D9.

Martinez, Jill. "An Interview with George Ryga." *Journal of Canadian Fiction* 35/36 (1986): 106-21.

Moore, Mavor. *4 Canadian Playwrights*, 68-75.

———. "Introduction," In *Two Plays by George Ryga*, 1-7. Winnipeg: Turnstone Press, 1982.

Parker, Brian. "The Ballad-Plays of George Ryga." In *The Ecstasy of Rita Joe and Other Plays*, vii-xx. Toronto: new press, 1971.

———. "Is There a Canadian Drama?" In *The Canadian Imagination*. Ed. David Staines, 152-87.

Parker, Dorothy. "George Ryga." In *Profiles in Canadian Literature* 4th ser.: 61-68.

Rubin, Don. "George Ryga: The Poetics of Engagement." *On-Stage and Off-Stage: English Canadian Drama in Discourse*. Ed. Albert-Reiner Glaap, 224-39.

Ryga, George. *The Athabasca Ryga*. Ed. E. David Gregory. Vancouver: Talonbooks, 1990.

———. *Summerland*. Ed. Ann Kujundzic Vancouver: Talonbooks, 1992.

Saddlemyer, Ann. "Crime in Literature: Canadian Drama." In *Rough Justice: Essays on Crime in Literature*. Ed. Martin L. Friedland, 214-30. Toronto: Univ. of Toronto Press, 1991.

Teague, Francis. "Prisons and Imprisonment in Canadian Drama." *Journal of Canadian Fiction* 19 (1977): 112-21.

Wasserman, Jerry. "George Ryga." In *Canadian Writers Since 1960*. 2nd ser. *DLB* 60: 320-24.

Watson, David, and Christopher Innes. "Political Mythologies: An Interview with George Ryga." *Canadian Drama* 8.2 (1982): 160-72.

Wilson, Peter. "*Rita Joe* Still Leads to More Anger than Ecstasy." *Vancouver Sun*, 19 March 1992, C1, 5.

Worthington, Bonnie. "Ryga's Women." *Canadian Drama* 5 (Fall 1979): 139-43.

Zichy, Francis. "*Rita Joe* in New York: An Interview with Gordon McCall." *NeWest Review* 10 (Summer 1985): 15-17.

B. **THE ECSTASY OF RITA JOE**:
SELECTED REVIEWS

Barber, James. "Rita—An Exhausting Emotional Experience." *Vancouver Province*, 25 November 1967, 38.

Cohen, Nathan. "A Non-Production of a Non-Play." *Toronto Star*, 25 November 1967, 30.

Conlogue, Ray. "Long Awaited *Rita Joe* Misses the Mark." *Globe and Mail*, 11 November 1989, C10.

Crew, Robert. "More Agony Than Ecstasy in *Rita Joe*." *Toronto Star*, 12 November 1989, C10.

Donnelly, Pat. "High Energy Approach in *Rita Joe*." *Montreal Gazette*, 10 March 1989, C6.

Donnelly, Tom. "Theater Journal: Two Views." *Washington Post*, 9 May 1973, F4.

Dykk, Lloyd. "Odd Poetic Touch Fails to Fill Emotional Void." *Vancouver Sun*, 20 March 1992, C5.

Howard, Irene. "Vancouver Theatre Diary: Two Companies and Their Audience." *Canadian Forum* 47 (February 1968): 252-54.

Kucherawy, Dennis. "Play Stirs New Controversy." *Vancouver Province*, 30 November 1981, B6.

McCracken, Rosemary. "Young Cast Electrifies Play." *Calgary Herald*, 5 April 1984, D1.

Popkin, Henry. " *The Ecstasy of Rita Joe*: A Drama of American Indian Life." *Christian Science Monitor*, 11 June 1973, 12.

Portman, Jamie. "*Ecstasy of Rita Joe* Still Manages to Shock and Scourge." *Vancouver Province*, 12 April 1976, 10.

Richards, Jack. "World Premiere Lays Bare Tragedy of Canadian Society." *Vancouver Sun*, 24 November 1967, 6.

Shales, Tom. "*Ecstasy of Rita Joe*." *Washington Post*, 3 May 1973, B1, 8.

Skene, Reg. "*Ecstasy of Rita Joe* a Powerful Piece of Theatre." *Winnipeg Free Press*, 26 November 1981, 55.

Wardle, Irving. "A Pogrom in Canada." *The Times* (London), 23 September 1975, 12.

RICK SALUTIN and THEATRE PASSE MURAILLE

A. BIOGRAPHY AND CRITICISM

Arnott, Brian. "The Passe Muraille Alternative." In *The Human Elements*. Ed. David Helwig, 97-111. Ottawa: Oberon, 1978.

Bessai, Diane. *Playwrights of Collective Creation*. Toronto: Simon & Pierre, 1992.

Conolly, L.W., ed. *Canadian Drama and the Critics*, 156-66.

Copeman, Peter. "Rick Salutin and the Popular Dramatic Tradition: Towards a Dialectical Theatre in Canada." *Canadian Drama* 10 (Spring 1984): 25-34.

————. "Rick Salutin: The Meaning of It All," *CTR* 34 (Spring 1982): 190-97.

Düsterhaus, Gerhard. "Rick Salutin's Dramatic Revisions of History." In *Crisis and Creativity in the New Literatures in English*. Ed. Geoffrey V. Davis and Hena Maes-Jelinek, 111-22. Amsterdam: Rodopi, 1990.

Filewod, Alan. *Collective Encounters*, Chap. 1-2.

Johns, Ted. "An Interview with Paul Thompson." *Performing Arts in Canada* 10 (Winter 1973): 30-32.

Johnston, Denis. *Up the Mainstream*, Chap. 2, 4.

Knowles, Richard Paul. "Replaying History: Canadian Historiographic Metadrama." *Dalhousie Review* 67 (1987): 228-43.

Miller, Mary Jane. "The Documentary Drama of Paul Thompson." *Saturday Night* 89 (July 1974): 35-37.

————. "Two Versions of Rick Salutin's *Les Canadiens*." *Theatre History in Canada* 1 (Spring 1980): 57-69.

Noonan, James. "Rick Salutin." In *Profiles in Canadian Literature*. 8th ser., 61-68.

Nunn, Robert C. "Performing Fact: Canadian Documentary Theatre." *Canadian Literature* 103 (Winter 1984): 51-62.

Rudakoff, Judith, ed. *Dangerous Traditions: A Passe Muraille Anthology*. Winnipeg: Blizzard, 1992.

Posesorski, Sherie. "Interview: Rick Salutin." *Books in Canada* 14 (April 1985): 40-41.

Salutin, Rick. *Living in a Dark Age*. Toronto: HarperCollins, 1991.

————. *Marginal Notes: Challenges to the Mainstream*. Toronto: Lester & Orpen Dennys, 1984.

————. *1837: William Lyon Mackenzie and the Canadian Revolution*. Toronto: Lorimer, 1976.

Thompson, Paul. "Facing the Landscape." In *Theatre Memoirs*, 26-29.

Usmiani, Renate. *Second Stage*, 43-65.

Wallace, Bob. "Paul Thompson at Theatre Passe Muraille: Bits and Pieces." *Open Letter* 2.7 (Winter 1974): 49-71.

————. and Cynthia Zimmerman, eds. *The Work*, 237-63.

Wilson, Paul. "Blyth Spirit [Paul Thompson]." *Books in Canada* 12 (April 1983): 10-13.

B. 1837: THE FARMERS' REVOLT:
SELECTED REVIEWS

Ashley, Audrey M. "Skimpy Sketches Illustrate Drama." *Ottawa Citizen*, 9 November 1976, 71.

Boru, Brian. "The Spirit of '37: History as Hypothesis." *That's Show Business*, 14 August 1974, 5.

Buttle, Jeff. "*Farmers' Revolt* Disproves Claim Canadian History Dull." *Vancouver Sun*, 20 July 1989, 10.

Chapman, Geoff. "Rebels without a Pause Lack Humanity." *Toronto Star*, 28 September 1997, B6.

Conlogue, Ray. "Farmers' Rebellion Stands Test of Time." *Globe and Mail*, 8 December 1987, D7.

Kareda, Urjo. "History Comes to Life." *Toronto Star*, 18 January 1973.

Moore, Christopher. "The Return of the Firebrand." *Books in Canada* 17 (March 1988): 3.

O'Toole, Lawrence. "*1837*: Dull History Played as Fiercely Involving Anarchy." *Globe and Mail*, 13 September 1974, 13.

Pappert-Martinello, Margaret. "Revolutionary Parallels." *Essays on Canadian Writing* 7/8 (Fall 1977): 196-99.

Skene, Reg. "*Farmers' Revolt* Slowed by Stretches of Theatrical Tedium." *Winnipeg Free Press*, 2 April 1981, 27.

Taylor, Kate. "Rebellion with a Cause and No Effect." *Globe and Mail*, 29 September 1997, C2.

Whittaker, Herbert. " *1837* Engrossing Handling of History." *Globe and Mail*, 19 January 1973, 15.

———. "Passe Muraille Becoming Top Touring Company." *Globe and Mail*, 29 May 1974, 14.

Wood, Susan. "Found History." *Canadian Literature* 81 (Summer 1979): 111-12.

Wyman, Max. "An Indisputable Star in a Troupe Not Meant to Have any Stars." *Vancouver Sun*, 29 March 1976, 43.

MICHEL TREMBLAY

Note: Only English-language books, articles and reviews are listed below; a much more substantial body of commentary on Tremblay is available in French. For an annotated bibliography (in French) of both English and French criticism and reviews of Tremblay's work through 1982, see *Voix & Images* 7.2 (Winter 1982): 225-306. For an excellent collection of critical essays, see Gilbert David and Pierre Lavoie, *Le Monde de Michel Tremblay*. Montreal: Cahiers de théâtre Jeu, 1993.

A. BIOGRAPHY AND CRITICISM

Ackerman, Marianne. "Sweet Jesus! Who's That, Ma?" *Saturday Night* 103 (June 1988): 40-47.

Anthony, Geraldine, ed. *Stage Voices*, 275-90.

Antosh, Ruth B. "The Hermaphrodite as Cultural Hero in Michel Tremblay's Theatre." *Essays on Modern Quebec Theatre*. Eds. Joseph I. Donohoe, Jr. and Jonathan M. Weiss, 207-22.

Babington, Doug. "The Shared Voice of Michel Tremblay." *Queen's Quarterly* 99 (Winter 1992): 1074-81.

Cardy, Michael. "Varieties of Anger in Some Early Plays of Michel Tremblay." *Romance Studies* 31 (Spring 1998): 5-17.

Chadbourne, Richard. "Michel Tremblay's 'Adult Fairy Tales': The Theatre as Realistic Fantasy." *Québec Studies* 10 (Spring/Summer 1990): 61-68.

Collet, Paulette. "Fennario's *Balconville* and Tremblay's *En Pièces détachées*: A Universe of Backyards and Despair." *Canadian Drama* 10 (Spring 1984): 35-43.

Conolly, L.W. ed. *Canadian Drama and the Critics*, 308-16.

Dorsinville, Max. "The Changing Landscape of Drama in Quebec." In *Dramatists in Canada*. Ed. W.H. New, 179-95.

Findlay, Bill. "Translating Tremblay into Scots." *Theatre Research International* 17.2 (Summer 1992): 138-45.

Gobin, Pierre. "Michel Tremblay: An Interweave of Prose and Drama." *Yale French Studies* 65 (1983): 106-23.

Harvie, Jennifer. "The Real Nation? Michel Tremblay, Scotland, and Cultural Translatability." *Theatre Research in Canada* 16 (Spring/Fall 1995): 5-25.

Hulan, Renée. "Surviving Translation: *Forever Yours, Marie-Lou* at Tarragon Theatre." *Theatre Research in Canada* 15 (Spring 1994): 48-57.

Kapica, Jack. "The Incredible Saga of Les Belles-Soeurs, or ... How a Writer Found Fame Could Be a Costly Gain." *Montreal Gazette*, 27 October 1973, 25.

Knelman, Martin. "The Outlandish *joual* World of Michel Tremblay." *Saturday Night* 90 (May 1975): 79-83.

Koustas, Jane. "From Gélinas to Carrier: Critical Response to Translated Quebec Theatre in Toronto." *Studies in Canadian Literature* 17.2 (1992): 109-28.

Loiselle, André. "Film-Mediated Drama: André Brassard's Film *Il était une fois dans l'Est* as a Pivot in Michel Tremblay's Dramaturgy." *Essays in Theatre* 10.2 (May 1992): 165-80.

McQuaid, Catherine. "Michel Tremblay's Seduction of the 'Other Solitude.'" *Canadian Drama* 2 (Fall 1976): 219-23.

"Michel Tremblay Casebook." *CTR* 24 (Fall 1979): 11-51.

Nunn, Robert C. "Tremblay's *Hosanna* and Pirandello's '*teatro dello specio.*'" *Canadian Drama* 6 (Fall 1980): 201-12.

Parker, Brian. "Is There a Canadian Drama?" In *The Canadian Imagination*. Ed. David Staines, 152-87.

Quig, James. "The Joual Revolution: Playwright Michel Tremblay." *The Canadian Magazine*, 14 May 1977, 16-19.

Rabillard, Sheila. "The Seductions of Theatricality: Mamet, Tremblay, and Political Drama." *Australasian Drama Studies* 29 (October 1996): 33-42.

Rae, Lisbie. "Tremblay at P'tit Bonheur, 1982–1985." *Canadian Drama* 13.1 (1987): 1-26.

Ripley, John. "From Alienation to Transcendence: The Quest for Selfhood in Michel Tremblay's Plays." *Canadian Literature* 85 (Summer 1980): 44-59.

Rudakoff, Judith. "Michel Tremblay." In *Profiles in Canadian Literature*. 6th ser., 65-72.

"*Sainte-Carmen of the Main* and the Plays of Michel Tremblay: A Panel Discussion." *Canadian Drama* 14.2 (1988): 206-23.

Salter, Denis. "Who's Speaking Here? Tremblay's Scots Voice." *CTR* 74 (Spring 1993): 40-45.

Schwartzwald, Robert. "From Authenticity to Ambivalence: Michel Tremblay's *Hosanna*." *American Review of Canadian Studies* 22 (Winter 1992): 499-510.

Smith, Donald. *Voices of Deliverance: Interviews with Quebec and Acadian Writers*. Trans. Larry Shouldice, 205-41. Toronto: Anansi, 1986.

Twigg, Alan. *For Openers: Conversations with 24 Canadian Writers*, 151-61. Madeira Park, B.C.: Harbour, 1981.

Usmiani, Renate. "The Bingocentric Worlds of Michel Tremblay and Tomson Highway: *Les Belles-Soeurs* vs. *The Rez Sisters*." *Canadian Literature* 144 (Spring 1995): 126-40.

———. *Michel Tremblay*. Vancouver: Douglas & McIntyre, 1982.

———. "Michel Tremblay." In *Canadian Writers Since 1960*, 2nd ser. 60: 342-52.

———. "Michel Tremblay's *Sainte-Carmen*: Synthesis and Orchestration." *Canadian Drama* 2.2 (1976): 206-17.

———. "The Musical Comedies of Michel Tremblay: A Lighter Side of Alienation and Identity Crisis." *Canadian Drama* 6 (Fall 1980): 192-200.

———. *The Theatre of Frustration: Super Realism in the Dramatic Work of F.X. Kroetz and Michel Tremblay*. N.Y.: Garland, 1990.

Weiss, Jonathan M. *French-Canadian Theatre*. 27-48.

B. **LES BELLES-SOEURS**: SELECTED REVIEWS

Abrams, Tevia. "Théâtre du Rideau-Vert Opens New Season with *Les Belles-Soeurs*." *Montreal Gazette*, 29 August 1968, 24.

Ackerman, Marianne. "*Belles-Soeurs* Stands Test of Time." *Montreal Gazette*, 31 March 1984, C9.

Bolster, Charles. "*Les Belles-Soeurs* a Microcosm of Quebecois Society." *Edmonton Journal*, 17 May 1980, B16.

Chapman, Geoff. "*Soeurs* Cast Lights Up Social Comment." *Toronto Star*, 3 June 1991, B3.

Conlogue, Ray. "A Celebration of Woman's Progress." *Globe and Mail*, 2 March 1993, A11.

———. "Keeping Tremblay's Masterpiece Relevant." *Globe and Mail*, 6 April 1999, C3.

———. "Working-Class Heroines." *Globe and Mail*, 4 June 1991, A10.

Corbeil, Carole. "The Aging of Tremblay's *Les Belles-Soeurs*." *Globe and Mail*, 28 June 1984, E2.

Cushman, Robert. "Staging a Slice of Quebec Life—30 Years Later." *National Post*, 9 April 1999, B12.

Heller, Zelda. "Tremblay's *Belles-Soeurs* Landmark in Quebec Theatre." *Montreal Star*, 25 May 1971, 64.

Kapica, Jack. "*Les Belles-Soeurs* a Triumph." *Montreal Gazette*, 11 October 1973, 36.

Kareda, Urjo. "*Les Belles-Soeurs* a Breath of Life." *Toronto Star*, 4 April 1973.

Kelly, Brendan. "A Gem in Any Language," *Financial Post*, 5 October 1992, S7.

Malina, Marten. "Rideau Vert Opens New Season with Play by André Brassard." *Montreal Star*, 29 August 1968, 38.

Mezei, Stephen. "Tremblay's Toronto Success." *Performing Arts in Canada* 10 (Summer 1973): 26.

Monahan, Iona. "Dynamic Quebecers Triumph: Parisians Bow to *Les Belles Soeurs*." *Montreal Star*, 23 November 1973, B8.

Portman, Jamie. "London's *Belles Soeurs* Bubbles." *Montreal Gazette*, 8 March 1977, 42.

Rivers, Bryan. "Production Effective." *Winnipeg Free Press*, 24 January 1993, B7.

Sabbath, Lawrence. "*Belles-Soeurs*: Canadian Masterpiece." *Montreal Star*, 11 October 1973, C10.

———. "New Run Proves Greatness of *Les Belles-Soeurs*." *Montreal Star*, 20 June 1974, B15.

Siskind, Jacob. "At the Rideau Vert Tremblay Comedy Revived Brilliantly." *Montreal Gazette*, 31 May 1971, 26.

Wagner, Vit. "Tremblay's Stamp Resonates." *Toronto Star*, 2 April 1999, D6.

Whittaker, Herbert. "*Les Belles-Soeurs* Milestone Play." *Globe and Mail*, 4 April 1973, 13.

———. "*Belles Soeurs* Bright Light for St. Lawrence." *Globe and Mail*, 7 May 1973, 14.

Wyman, Max. "*Les Belles Soeurs*: A Gem of Comic Commentary." *Vancouver Sun*, 4 March 1976, 37.

GEORGE F. WALKER

A. BIOGRAPHY AND CRITICISM

Borkowski, Andrew. "Theatre of the Improbable: George F. Walker." *Canadian Forum* 70 (September 1991): 16-19.

Bortolotti, Dan. "Dramatic Intensity." *Books in Canada* 24 (April 1995): 24-27.

Conolly, L.W., ed. *Canadian Drama and the Critics*, 207-16, 297-301.

Corbeil, Carol. "A Conversation with George Walker." *Brick* 58 (Winter 1998): 59-67.

De Raey, Daniel. "Introduction." *Suburban Motel* by George F. Walker. Rev. ed., 4-6. Vancouver: Talonbooks, 1999.

Gass, Ken. "Introduction." In *Three Plays by George Walker*, 9-15. Toronto: Coach House, 1978.

"George F. Walker." In *Contemporary Literary Criticism: Yearbook 1989*. Vol. 61. Ed. Roger Matuz, 422-34. Detroit: Gale Research, 1990.

Hadfield, Dorothy. "The Role Power Plays in George F. Walker's Detective Trilogy." *Essays in Theatre* 16 (November 1997): 67-84.

Haff, Stephen. "The Brave Comedy of Big Emotions: An Introduction." *Shared Anxiety: Selected Plays by George F. Walker*, xi-xvii. Toronto: Coach House, 1994.

———. "Slashing the Pleasantly Vague: George F. Walker and the Word." *Essays in Theatre* 10 (November 1991): 59-69.

Hallgren, Chris. "George Walker: The Serious and the Comic." *Scene Changes* 7 (March-April 1979): 23-25.

Johnson, Chris. *Essays on George F. Walker: Playing with Anxiety*. Winnipeg: Blizzard, 1999.

———. "George F. Walker: B-Movies Beyond the Absurd." *Canadian Literature* 85 (Summer 1980): 87-103.

———. "George F. Walker Directs George F. Walker." *Theatre History in Canada* 9 (Fall 1988): 157-72.

———. "George F. Walker." *Post-Colonial English Drama: Commonwealth Drama since 1960*. Ed. Bruce King, 82-96. NY: St. Martin's, 1992.

———. "'I Put It in Terms Which Cover the Spectrum': Mixed Convention and Dramatic Strategies in George F. Walker's *Criminals in Love*." *On-Stage and Off-Stage: English Canadian Drama in Discourse*. Ed. Albert-Reiner Glaap, 257-69.

Johnston, Denis W. "George F. Walker: Liberal Idealism and the Power Plays." *Canadian Drama* 10.2 (1984): 195-206.

Knowles, Richard Paul. "The Dramaturgy of the Perverse." *Theatre Research International* 17 (Autumn 1992): 226-35.

Lane, William. "Introduction." In George F. Walker, *The Power Plays*, 9-14. Toronto: Coach House, 1984.

———. "Introduction." In *Zastrozzi: The Master of Discipline*, 3-6. Toronto: Playwrights Co-op, 1979.

Nyman, Ed. "Out with the Queers: Moral Triage and George F. Walker's *Theatre of the Film Noir.*" *Australasian Drama Studies* 29 (October 1996): 57-66.

Sinclair, Gregory J. "Live from Off-Stage." *Canadian Forum* 65 (August/September 1986): 6-11.

Usmiani, Renate. *Second Stage*, 35-38.

Walker, Craig. "Three Tutorial Plays: *The Lesson, The Prince of Naples* and *Oleanna.*" *Modern Drama* 40 (Spring 1997): 149-62.

Wallace, Robert. "George F. Walker." In *Profiles in Canadian Literature.* 6th ser., 105-12.

————. "Looking for the Light: A Conversation with George F. Walker." *Canadian Drama* 14.1 (1988): 22-33.

————, and Cynthia Zimmerman, eds. *The Work*, 212-25.

Wasserman, Jerry. "Introduction." *Somewhere Else: Four Plays by George F. Walker*, 5-6. Vancouver: Talonbooks, 1999.

————. "'Making Things Clear': The *film noir* Plays of George F. Walker." *Canadian Drama* 8.1 (1982): 99-101.

Wynne-Jones, Tim. "Acts of Darkness," *Books in Canada* 14 (April 1985): 11-14.

B. **ZASTROZZI**: SELECTED REVIEWS

Bernrose, John. "Satan with a Sword." *Maclean's* 100 (25 May 1987): 55.

Conlogue, Ray. "A Triumph of Gothic Comedy." *Globe and Mail*, 14 May 1987, C3.

Crew, Robert. "*Zastrozzi* Returns in Splendid Form." *Toronto Star*, 14 May 1987, F3.

Galloway, Myron. "*Zastrozzi* Cast Superb." *Montreal Star*, 28 November 1978, A12.

Huebert, Ronald. "Letters in Canada 1978: Drama." *University of Toronto Quarterly* 48 (Summer 1979): 362-70.

Johnson, Bryan. "*Zastrozzi* Wields a Satanic Rapier." *Globe and Mail*, 3 November 1977, 17.

Mallet, Gina. "Theatre Finds Strength with Style." *Toronto Star*, 3 November 1977, F1.

McLean, Colin. "Great Look at Good and Evil." *Edmonton Express*, 8 December 1999.

Messenger, Ann. "Canajun, Eh?" *Canadian Literature* 86 (Fall 1980): 89-93.

Moore, Kerry. "Good Old Evil." *Vancouver Province*, 8 October 1986, G5.

Morrow, Martin. "*Master of Discipline* a Young Person's Play." *Calgary Herald*, 31 October 1992, C5.

Read, Nicholas. "*Zastrozzi*: It's Interesting and Funny in a Black Sort of Way." *Vancouver Sun*, 7 October 1986, C6.

Rich, Frank. "Serban Directs *Zastrozzi* at the Public." *New York Times*, 18 January 1982, C14.